Survey of

Contemporary Literature

Survey of
Contemporary Literature

Revised Edition

UPDATED REPRINTS OF 2,300 ESSAY-REVIEWS
FROM MASTERPLOTS ANNUALS, 1954-1976, AND
SURVEY OF CONTEMPORARY LITERATURE SUPPLEMENT

WITH 3,300 BIBLIOGRAPHICAL REFERENCE SOURCES

Edited by
FRANK N. MAGILL

Volume Seven
Let - Mid
4283 - 4970

SALEM PRESS
Englewood Cliffs, New Jersey 07632

R
809.04
M194s
v. 7

LIBRARY OF CONGRESS CATALOG CARD NUMBER: 77-79874

Complete Set: ISBN   0-89356-050-2
Volume 7:   ISBN   0-89356-057-X

REVISED EDITION
First Printing

Some of the material in this work also appears in *Masterplots Annuals* (1954-1976)
and *Survey of Contemporary Literature Supplement* (1972)

PRINTED IN THE UNITED STATES OF AMERICA

LIST OF TITLES

(*Indicates that the article is accompanied by a "Sources for Further Study" section.)

lxxiii

49396

LIST OF TITLES

Survey of

Contemporary Literature

LETTING GO

Author: Philip Roth (1933-   )
Publisher: Random House (New York). 630 pp. $5.95
Type of work: Novel
Time: The 1950's
Locale: Chicago, New York, Iowa City, Gary, Indiana

A novel about neurotic and involved intellectuals, one of whom takes too seriously for too long his responsibility to the others

Principal characters:

GABE WALLACH, a well-meaning, prudent young college teacher of English
DR. MORDECAI WALLACH, his father
PAUL HERZ, a friend and associate of Gabe
LIBBY HERZ, his wife
JOHN SPIGLIANO, the head of Gabe's department
MARTHA REGANHART, Gabe's paramour
MAURY and
DORIS HORVITZ, old friends of Paul Herz
SIDNEY JAFFE, a lawyer
THERESA HAUG, a fellow worker of Martha's
HARRY BIGONESS, Theresa's husband
MRS. FAY SILBERMAN, a widow, Dr. Wallach's mistress and fiancée

The many enthusiastic readers of Philip Roth's *Goodbye, Columbus,* which was published in 1959 and won the National Book Award in 1960, will find no letting up of talent or letting go of skill in this new book. But they may wish that Roth had found for his ambitious theme a vehicle somewhat less prodigious than this particular construction of subject. The more than six hundred pages are filled with full-bodied narrative, composed in a solid, mature, and evocative style. There is little doubt that Roth is one of the most proficient young masters of the novel writing in America today. But there is a corpulence of form here which could be healthily reduced by a more selective diet of "objective correlatives" and a greater exercise of deletion. The scope of the theme simply does not warrant a handling on this scale.

The title states the theme of the book. "Letting go" suggests both the passive function of letting go the apron strings and the active function of letting go the reins. The protagonist, Gabe Wallach, has all but fulfilled the first of these functions. The mother to whom he has been deeply devoted, who has influenced him radically, is dead. The father, in all his crassness and would-be possessiveness, is held successfully at bay. Therefore, it is the second or active function, letting go the reins, which in the course of this novel constitutes Gabe Wallach's problem.

What he does is get intricately involved with people, his friends, his illusory paramours, and many of their associates. All his resources of mind, imagination, and money are at their disposal. Gabe has a superior intellect, a deep human sympathy, and an enviable independence of means. He does not get any particularly egotistical satisfaction from making his benefactions of advice, kindness, or money, but volunteers them, nonetheless, almost compulsively. It becomes a kind of duty to share with others his personal security. The responsibility to see his self-imposed obligations through to completion becomes his very *raison d'être*, and the price of his control of life.

Despite this kind of motivation, however, Gabe Wallach's involvements are not altogether of a vicarious nature. He is the sort of man who is confident of his attractiveness to women, who assumes that he is desirable if not indeed necessary to them, and who frequently acts with impetuosity—and impunity —toward them, and yet who is most likely to romanticize or idealize his role. For all his willingness to take temporary responsibility for others, he holds back from a commitment to a very personal or very binding responsibility on his own part. To this extent his involvements are vicarious. On the other hand, in at least two instances he gets involved in affairs which are actual in a sexual way, *not* vicarious; one of these is committal to the extent of mere adventurousness, bravura, or expedience; the other is committal to the extent of sentimentality and domesticity, but is undermined by defeatism and preoccupation. As one commentator has put it, Gabe makes "desperate attempts to find a proper relationship between his own worldly good fortune and the misfortune of others. [His behavior is] a frenetic contest between his sympathies and his instinct for self-protection—an instinct to which we all are prey, but of which Gabe becomes a victim."

The events of the novel cover a span of about six years, from days in graduate school at Iowa City, where Gabe forms his friendship with Paul and Libby Herz and conducts his adventurous affair, to the period of his in-structorship in the English Department of the University of Chicago, where he is joined by the Herzes and conducts his sentimental affair. Gabe Wallach is Jewish, the son of a prosperous New York dentist. Being Jewish is for him no problem at all, but he is surrounded by people whose Jewishness makes them self-conscious, xenophobic, defensive, or, for external reasons, miserable. The major instance of the dilemma is the marriage of Paul and Libby, a marriage which neither of the families—his Jewish, hers Gentile— has ever forgiven. They exist in a state of marital dyspepsia, loving each other but persistently bickering, feeling cursed and suffering from poverty, doggedly vowing happiness and getting psychosomatic illnesses. The relationship with Gabe begins with his lending Libby a copy of Henry James's *The Portrait of a Lady,* goes through a series of illusions, trials, misunderstandings, and periods of kindness and friendship, and ends with his engineering the adoption of a child for the hapless couple and bringing an overdue rapprochement with Paul's now widowed mother.

Gabe's efforts to ease the situation of the Herzes is his major and most significant undertaking. Helping them, after all, is the root and the flower of what ought to be a lasting friendship. So it is, then, that when at the end of the novel we find Gabe fleeing to Turkey or Greece to gain respite from this and other relationships, we know how crucial it is for him to break the pattern of standing in and begin the struggle of letting go. It is too easy to give, and so aimless: easy to give in the sense of having resources and wanting to give; difficult and painful in the sense of not knowing what and how and to whom. He cannot give more than a token love to his father, who wants more but exists in the vulgar world of Fay Silberman, Grossinger's, and friends who wonder what a poet named E. E. Cunningham is up to. Because Gabe is sensitive, he cannot give much more than his presence to his colleagues, particularly John Spigliano, who is not even quite one of the worst, "filled with passionate intensity," but one of the mediocre, driven by a paltry success at cool image-making.

Earlier, in Iowa City, Gabe gives his body to Marjorie Howells, a graduate student, because she wants him, needs him, but he is forced by his boredom and her intrusiveness to retreat. While trying to intercede with Paul's family during a visit to New York, Gabe encounters old friends of Paul's named Maury and Doris Horvitz, the latter of whom advises: "You ought to read *Marjorie Morningstar*. . . . It's about a girl who one of her problems is, I don't think she wants to be Jewish. I think maybe Paul ought to read it." Gabe's involvement as advocate enmeshes him even here; finding the occasion to kiss Doris, he is responsible for sending out ripples of complication upon the placid surface of her matronly life.

Gabe's relationship with Martha Reganhart is the nearest he ever comes to marriage. They are not only compatible but friendly, not only friendly but complementary to each other. But she is the abandoned wife of a painter, the mother of two fairly sophisticated young children, and soon Gabe finds himself caught up again in the whirlpool of almost unbelievable involvement, which amounts to concern with problematic situations about which he can probably do little but about which something seems to need

doing in order to set the world to rights. There is Martha's sister who comes to live with her for a while, creating a difficulty even though she refrains from having men, including her Negro lover, in the house. There is Martha's old suitor Jaffe. There are the children, and the children's friends, and the scandal of the children's friends' parents. There is the reclaiming of the children by their father and the violent death of the young son. Preëminently there is Martha's co-worker at a restaurant, Theresa Haug, whose illegitimate child Gabe arranges to have adopted privately by his desperate friends the Herzes. When Theresa proves to be the stray wife of Harry Bigoness of Gary, Indiana, Gabe finds himself involved in one of the most absurdly complex and painfully compulsive efforts to please everybody, in the annals of fiction. He drives himself nearly to distraction. He no longer knows quite who he is, what he is doing, or why he does it. In the huggermugger of it all he concludes that contrary to all intent, he is really an irresponsible person creating more consternation than he can cure. He loses Martha and knows that he must run. He is not the fisher of men he took himself to be; as he says at the end of the novel, he is on a larger hook than he knew anyone could be.

The kind of self-knowledge which distinguishes between helpfulness and responsibility constitutes a major theme for fiction. And it is delineated clearly here by Philip Roth. But the monumentality of his presentation almost obscures the essence. The impact of meaning would be more intense, and perhaps more profound, in a novel stripped of excessive scenes involving minor characters whose stories contribute little or nothing, of excessive details about minor characters in major scenes, of excessive and prolix dialogue between principals, and of excessive development of relationships and situations the point and purpose of which have been already well established.

Sources for Further Study

Criticism:

Donaldson, Scott. "Philip Roth: The Meaning of *Letting Go*," in *Contemporary Literature*. XI (1970), pp. 21-35. Donaldson delves into the very complex psychological aspects of the novel.

Hyman, Stanley Edgar. "A Novelist of Great Promise," in *On Contemporary Literature*. Edited by Richard Kostelanitz. New York: Avon Books, 1964, pp. 532-536. A discussion of the literary merits of Philip Roth as displayed in the novel *Letting Go*.

White, Robert L. "The English Instructor as Hero: Two Novels by Roth and Malamud," in *Forum*. IV (Winter, 1963), pp. 16-22. A comparison of the main characters in the works of Roth and Malamud in their roles as English teachers.

Reviews:

Atlantic. CCXI, July, 1962, p. 111. 490 words.

New Statesman. LXIV, November 30, 1962, p. 784. 1,500 words.

New York Herald Tribune Books. June 17, 1962, p. 4. 1,050 words.

New York Times Book Review. June 17, 1962, p. 1. 1,700 words.

Saturday Review. XLV, June 16, 1962, p. 16. 850 words.

Times Literary Supplement. November 23, 1962, p. 885. 550 words.

LEYTE: JUNE 1944-JANUARY 1945
History of United States Naval Operations in World War II: Vol. XII

Author: Samuel Eliot Morison (1887-1976)
Publisher: Atlantic-Little, Brown and Company (Boston). Illustrated. 445 pp. $6.50
Type of work: Military history
Time: June, 1944-May, 1945
Locale: The Pacific Ocean Area

The most recent and definitive study of the most controversial sea battle in World War II

Principal personages:
American Forces:
GENERAL DOUGLAS MACARTHUR, Supreme Commander, Allied Forces, South-West Pacific Area
VICE ADMIRAL THOMAS C. KINKAID, Commander, Seventh Fleet and Central Philippines Attack Force
REAR ADMIRAL DANIEL E. BARBEY, TF 78 Northern Attack Force
VICE ADMIRAL T. S. WILKINSON, TF 79 Southern Attack Force
REAR ADMIRAL THOMAS L. SPRAGUE, TG 77.4 Escort Carrier Group
ADMIRAL WILLIAM F. HALSEY, Commander, Third Fleet
VICE ADMIRAL CHARLES A. LOCKWOOD, TF 17 Supporting Submarines, Pacific Fleet
REAR ADMIRAL RALPH W. CHRISTIE, TG 71.1 Supporting Submarines, Seventh Fleet
Japanese Forces:
ADMIRAL SOEMU TOYODA, Commander Combined Fleet
VICE ADMIRAL JISABURO OZAWA, Commander, Main Body (Northern Force)
VICE ADMIRAL TAKEO KURITA, Commander, First Striking Force
VICE ADMIRAL SHOJI NISHIMURA, Commander, Force "C" (van of Southern Force)
VICE ADMIRAL GUINICHI MIKAWA, Commander, Southwest Area Force

Leyte is Volume XII of a planned fourteen-volume *History of United States Naval Operations in World War II*, written by the distinguished historian, Rear Admiral Samuel Eliot Morison. This might well become the most popular volume of the series, surpassing such outstanding earlier volumes as those covering the action at Pearl Harbor, Midway, and the battle of the Philippine Sea. It is written in the same readable and flowing style, and the reader feels as though the contest for Leyte is taking place before his eyes. The work at hand involved a tremendous job of research on the greatest sea fight of all history, and the account given seems to have exhausted both official and unofficial sources. In the opinion of many, Morison is writing in this series the outstanding military history of World War II.

During the earlier part of the war, in such battles as those of the Coral

Sea and at Midway, the engagements were fought by air force against air force, with the big carriers commanding complete attention and surface ships seldom participating in the action. At Leyte, as Morison points out, the carrier fulfilled an important role but was not the major element it had been in earlier battles, for the stage was shared with battleships, cruisers, destroyers, submarines and even small motor torpedo boats, all of which participated in the victory.

The series of battles, as outlined by Morison, was fought in three major phases spread over a great area and involving unusually large numbers of men and ships. The United States, according to the author, had a total of two hundred and eighteen ships and the Japanese had committed sixty-four ships in this battle. The United States Navy had 143,668 officers and enlisted men, a greater number than the entire strength of the U.S. Navy and Marine Corps in 1938.

The major factor in the defeat of the Japanese, in Morison's opinion, was the lack of air power: without this weapon the Japanese were helpless to capitalize upon American mistakes. Greater success might have been achieved had the Japanese had better communications and coördination. As events have proved, the overwhelming victory was not as decisive as at Midway, but it did give the American Navy control of the Pacific for the remainder of the war.

Morison begins his study with the strategy and war planning following the capture of the Marianas. General Marshall and Admiral King favored Formosa and China as the next targets, while General MacArthur strongly recommended the Philippines.

The decision to invade the Philippines is supposed to have been reached in Honolulu on July 26, 1944, during a meeting between President Roosevelt and General MacArthur aboard the cruiser *Baltimore;* the author concludes that the Japanese were not duped as to the selection of the Philippines as the next objective but were forced to delay positive action until it became apparent where the main invasion would occur. At first they refused to believe that Leyte was more than a probe to maneuver them out of position. As it became apparent that the landing at Leyte was the primary objective, the Japanese began to move by invoking plan "Sho-Go," which means "Victory Operation."

Having made plans for a decisive battle, the Japanese were determined to commit their entire navy to hold the Philippines, but the intention to bring the American fleet under aerial bombardment of land-based planes was a failure because most of the planes were destroyed on the ground and there were too few qualified mechanics to service those remaining. The plan, as it is brilliantly described by Admiral Morison, had two major objectives: to destroy the fleet, then to force the invaders out of the Philippines. To carry out the plan of destroying the fleet, the Japanese Navy was divided into four forces. The northern Ozawa force was to lure Admiral Halsey and the Third Fleet out of Leyte Gulf, while the Nishimura force "C" and the Shima second striking force entered Leyte Gulf by way of Surigao Strait. At the same time the Kurita first striking force was sent through San Bernardino Strait to form the other half of a giant pincer to crush the American forces.

To prevent the Japanese from carrying out their plans, the American forces were disposed in the following manner: The task of guarding Surigao Strait was in the hands of Admiral Kinkaid and the Seventh Fleet, while San Bernardino Strait was guarded by the Third Fleet of Admiral Halsey. In this engagement one of the great controversies of the war developed, stemming from the decision of Admiral Halsey to leave San Bernardino Strait in an effort to crush a decoy fleet in the north. After dealing the Kurita force a supposedly killing blow, Halsey felt that he was free to take the entire Third Fleet north to engage the Ozawa force which had just been located. This decision was reached without informing Admiral Kinkaid of his plan or leaving a single ship to give the alarm should the Japanese attempt to pass through San Bernardino Strait.

Admiral Morison, in reconstructing the evidence, concludes that Kinkaid and the Seventh Fleet were well aware that the Shima and Nishimura forces were heading for Surigao Strait. These forces sailed into a well-prepared trap which cost them every ship in the two forces except one destroyer. But as dawn arrived, the central force of Admiral Kurita sailed undetected and unopposed through the San Bernardino Strait. Morison places the blame squarely on Admiral Halsey for this error because, he argues, the Third Fleet could have been divided and still have remained strong enough to defeat both the central and northern forces of the Japanese.

As soon as the undetected Japanese force entered Leyte Gulf the battle of Samar developed. The scene, as described by the author, indicates that the American forces were caught by complete surprise. The only thing that saved the Escort Carrier Groups was their great determination to fight; he cites this action as the most gallant in naval history. The engagement could have been a great victory for the Japanese because of their preponderance of fire power, but they failed to take advantage of their opportunity and broke off the action when events looked darkest for the American forces. This encounter was the last forceful opposition of the Japanese Navy in World War II.

THE LIBERATION OF LORD BYRON JONES

Author: Jesse Hill Ford (1928-   )
Publisher: Little, Brown and Company (Boston). 364 pp. $5.95
Type of work: Novel
Time: 1963
Locale: Somerton, a small town in western Tennessee

A narrative of the liberation, through personal courage and at the cost of an obscene death, of a single Negro in a small Southern town, and of the enslavement to a distorted view of the past by the town's whites, who administer a partial justice

Principal characters:
GEORGE GORDON LORD BYRON JONES, a Negro undertaker
EMMA JONES, his wife, whom he seeks to divorce
OMAN HEDGEPATH, a white attorney
STEVE MUNDINE, his nephew and law partner
NELLA MUNDINE, his wife
WILLIE JOE WORTH, a white policeman, Emma Jones's lover
SONNY BOY MOSBY, a young Negro man
MAMA LAVORN, his foster mother
LUTHER X, a spokesman for the Nation of Islam

Perhaps only a "blood-and-bone Southerner for generations back" is qualified to write about real life in the modern South. The story urgently needs telling, for despite the glare of publicity which has bathed that region during the 1960's, individual human motives have often remained dark to observers who view the civil rights struggle chiefly in sociological or political terms.

In *The Liberation of Lord Byron Jones*, Alabama-born Jesse Hill Ford, now a Tennessean, has produced a powerful novel of racial crisis. The narrative centers on the divorce action of George Gordon Lord Byron Jones, a Negro undertaker who is the richest man in Somerton, Tennessee. Hurt and humiliated by the brazenly lewd behavior of his wife Emma, Jones seeks to divorce her in the courts of white men.

Oman Hedgepath, the town's leading attorney, reluctantly takes the Negro's divorce suit at the insistence of his nephew and law partner, Steve Mundine. Hedgepath is a memorable character, a man who perceives the tangled relationships and the motives of violence better than anyone in town, but who deludes himself tragically about his own role in the drama. Symbolizing the Southerner whose unique insight alone might bring both peace and justice into his deeply disturbed region, Hedgepath refuses to admit responsibility. This gifted, charming segregationist comes to life more fully than any of the characters around him. A complex personality, he admits that he once loved a Negro woman: "I laid her upstairs and downstairs all summer long, morning, noon and night. . . . After that first time I couldn't stop. Steve, where I made my mistake, was *when I stopped seeing Cassie as a nigger and saw her as a woman—a person."*

Steve declares pride that his uncle has seen at least one Negro "as a human being," but Oman implies that his kinsman has missed the point. When Steve asks how he is expected to take this confession, Oman oberves, "Under the right circumstances nearly anybody can get tangled up with some nigger bitch. When he does it's no sign you have to ruin him—take his job, shame his family. Is it?"

For Willie Joe Worth, the pathetically wanton policeman who has been Emma Jones's lover, Oman wants a break, some measure of consideration. He feels obliged to protect "Not just him, not merely the man for his own sake, Steve, but for Somerton—our town, our community. This whole region of the civilized world." In other words, the South.

Emma's decision to contest the divorce will mean naming Willie Joe in open court, a possibility that Oman fears may involve "innocent" townspeople. Appealing to Steve, he asks, ". . . would you want the shame of Willie Worth's innocent children on your conscience? . . . So it takes a little extra effort to do the right thing. I could say to hell with it—let the chips fall like they will. What's the reputation of a daddy of little girls mean to me anyhow? No, Steve, I'm going to look Willie Joe up. I must try to talk sense to him." Yet Oman feels no such compulsion to protect his client Jones from Willie Joe, who proceeds to murder the Negro a few days later.

To develop this explosive situation, Ford uses a multiple viewpoint technique. Either his concept of the uses of first and third persons is extremely subtle and does not succeed, or his grasp of the technique is awkward. Why one character gets first-person treatment and another third-person is unclear. Hedgepath's sections are related in first person, and very effectively, while Steve's sections are told in third person. Is Ford's motive here to humanize the segregationist and to show the young Southern moderate's opacity? This theory seems untenable when it is

noted that Nella, Steve's wife, is also presented in first-person narrative passages; yet Nella, the beautiful San Francisco liberal, fails to come alive at all, in spite of the author's dogged efforts. Her passages are distressingly literary:

> . . . when the moon stood like a pale flower blooming above the Pacific sea, love was let down between us, love came down between and upon and out of him and into me, this man of mine built so to carry burdens, to turn wheels, and fell forests and generally lay every God-damned thing in sight to waste; to burn stumps and whip slaves while he disputed his land's sovereignty in his ancestral memory even while it is between us and on us—God, God help the memory of that and hear my moans and love cries. . . .

Nella's interior monologue embarrasses the impatient reader, who knows that her Steve is only an earnest small-town lawyer. The distance of third-person narrative would have improved her chapters.

Seemingly careless shifts from first to third person mar the point of view in the sections titled "Mosby" and "Lavorn." Sonny Boy Mosby, a young Negro who had fled the town years earlier after a brutal beating by a Somerton policeman, returns determined to kill his sadistic attacker. The author's handling of Mosby's uncomplicated outlook is easy and adept whether presented in first or third person; it is the apparently pointless change from one to the other that weakens Mosby's role in a well-constructed subplot. Similarly, the novelist wavers in chapters devoted to the viewpoint of Mama Lavorn, who raises Mosby and who has agreed to serve as a witness for Jones against Emma. The dying proprietress of a Negro hotel and brothel, Lavorn is a vivid and credible character; yet the awkward shift from "I" to "she" in these chapters detracts from her dramatic effectiveness.

Curiously, Lord Byron Jones gets rather distant and deferential treatment at the author's hands. The central character, around whom the action focuses, Jones is invariably referred to as "the undertaker" in those chapters where the reader is invited to see what he has seen. The smell of pressed funeral flowers and embalming fluid hovers over the novel's hero, even when Willie Joe Worth and a fellow policeman pull up in the police cruiser next to Jones's limousine and he must finally decide whether to stand up or run. "Run? The undertaker smiled. The hushed wind from the dark street fluttered at the window beside him. No, the nigger wouldn't; wouldn't run. *I won't.*" Later the policemen ruthlessly beat the undertaker in a junkyard across from Lavorn's hotel, as Mosby watches silently. Suddenly ashamed of his own passivity, Mosby asks the Negro junk dealer. "Who was he?" although he knows the victim had to be Jones. The blind man assures him: "It was. I smelled him. . . . They shot the dog and I smelled that and he come up then and they put the steel bracelets on him. Flowers and that other; death the way you smell dead peoples at a funeral. I knew it *was* him."

Somerton's racial crisis attracts a sinister outsider, Luther X, who appears at Lord Byron Jones's funeral to capitalize on the failure of justice. By denying the simple and just demands of a Negro individual, and by allowing Willie Joe Worth to get away with murder, the town's whites must now face the Nation of Islam. Luther X

tells Emma: "Important work is to be done here in Somerton," as she hands him a down payment of two thousand dollars. "Justice, Freedom, Equality, Islam, and me," muses the Negro, as he contemplates weekly visits to Emma "to fluff her . . . to keep her in condition. . . . Play it cool and keep it snappy. Play it non-violent. Keep her happy."

A simmering, covert sexuality underlies the racial fears of many of Ford's Southerners. Integration is already a fact, he implies, at least under cover of darkness. The white man's dread of open miscegenation is exceeded only by his concealed, prurient behavior toward Negro women. The rabid harangue of a White Citizens Council speaker—"*nigger syphilis,* the one great scientific contribution the nigger has given to Western civilization"—excites the crowd eager to believe that sexual attraction between the two races is a Negro plot to destroy "white brains." Secretly ashamed of their sex relations with Negro women, Hedgepath and Willie Joe Worth respond with apparent relief to the speaker's tale of "The poor Canadian white girl lured into marriage to the rich, lascivious nigger; her degradation as she submits to the filthy caresses of this nigger who bought her body. He befouls her at every opportunity." Unacknowledged guilt for deeds and desires is thus transferred to a blind and obscene hatred for the Negro race.

Emma appears at her husband's funeral dressed all in white and wearing a maternity dress. Her baby will be white, fathered by Willie Joe. She will name the baby Victor. Thus, Ford asks, what manner of child will this "victor" be, this new son of the new South.

Another new son of the South is

born to Steve and Nella, after they have moved from Somerton in despair. Steve joins a demonstration in Georgia, where he is jailed. In a letter, Steve blames his uncle for the murder of Jones and holds him responsible for the assassination of President Kennedy a few months later. Characteristically, he gives no return address; he is positive Oman has nothing important to say to him.

Jesse Hill Ford has constructed a vital and absorbing novel about Negroes and whites in a small Tennessee town. Yet he reveals a larger intention. Confronting Oman with the murder, Steve asks, " 'Is Somerton typical?' "

"Yes," I said. For a moment hope flared in me. Might he have survived his baptism of truth? I thought: If only he can accept it.

He shook his head sadly. He turned and walked slowly out of my office. I called after him. He didn't answer.

Roberta Madden

Sources for Further Study

Reviews:

Atlantic. CCXVI, August, 1965, p. 92. 1,450 words.

Book Week. June 27, 1965, p. 4. 950 words.

New York Times Book Review. July 11, 1965, p. 4. 850 words.

THE LIBERATOR
William Lloyd Garrison

Author: John L. Thomas (1924-   )
Publisher: Little, Brown and Company (Boston). Illustrated. 502 pp. $8.50
Type of work: Social history
Time: 1798-1873
Locale: The United States

The definitive biography of William Lloyd Garrison and of his struggle to obliterate the social and moral evils in nineteenth century America

Principal personages:
  WILLIAM LLOYD GARRISON, editor of the *Liberator*
  HELLEN BENSON GARRISON, his wife
  WENDELL PHILLIPS,
  THEODORE WELD, and
  BENJAMIN LUNDY, Abolitionist leaders

The most recent study of William Lloyd Garrison, one of the most controversial figures in the reform movements of the nineteenth century, is a brilliant and penetrating analysis of the thoughts and actions of this great protagonist in his struggle for human rights. Professor Thomas evaluates his subject fairly and objectively in the setting of Garrison's life-span rather than by the ethical standards of today.

Early childhood weighed heavily in the formation of the personality and attitudes of the earliest spokesman of the reform movement in New England. William Lloyd Garrison was the son of an alcoholic father and a domineering mother who bordered upon religious fanaticism. The father made little or no positive impact upon Garrison, for he deserted his rather large family before the boy could scarcely walk. All Garrison could learn of his father was through his mother, and she constantly instructed him to guard against his father's weaknesses for demon rum and tobacco. As a result of the influence of his mother, he was more comfortable in the company of strong-willed women than in the company of men.

The future editor of the *Liberator* was almost completely self-educated, and he was able to become an editor only because he struggled diligently, while serving as a printer's apprentice, to overcome his lack of formal education. As soon as he had completed his apprenticeship, Garrison became an editorial writer in Newburyport, Massachusetts. Because he was a conservative Federalist, his political views were in complete agreement with those held by the people of the community. However, the young journalist was not satisfied to remain an editorial assistant; more than anything else he wanted a newspaper of his own. Using borrowed money, Garrison bought the Newburyport *Free Press.* As editor and printer of the paper he began to attack such evils as Sabbath-breaking, free thought, dueling, prostitution, theatergoing, and drinking. The newspaper failed six months after Garrison became editor, and he left for Boston immediately thereafter.

In Boston, although he was not too well received, he became active in the Abolitionist crusade. He met Benjamin Lundy and other leaders of the movement who aided him in solidifying his own views on slavery. From Boston he went to Baltimore to serve as an editorial assistant on Lundy's periodical, *The Genius of Universal Emancipation*. After the two encountered trouble in Baltimore, Garrison returned to Boston, where he again became associated with the leading Abolitionists of the city. Shortly after his return, with the aid of friends and borrowed equipment, he began a newspaper which would ultimately bring fame and success. The *Liberator* was dedicated to the immediate abolition of Negro slavery by every possible means. A perfect example of the aims, attitude, and crusading spirit of the editor is the statement printed on January 1, 1831:

I will be as harsh as truth, and as uncompromising as justice. On this subject, I do not wish to think, or speak, or write, with moderation. No! No! Tell a man whose house is on fire to give a moderate alarm; tell him to moderately rescue his wife from the hands of the ravisher; tell the mother to gradually extricate the child from the fire into which it has fallen;—but urge me not to use moderation in a cause like the present. I am in earnest—I will not equivocate—I will not excuse—I will not retreat a single inch—and I will be heard.

The circulation of the *Liberator* was quite limited, as only four hundred copies of this edition were published. However, Garrison received much publicity, and before long the *Liberator* was known in every section of the country, even though most of the people in Boston and New England disapproved of his editorials and refused to buy the paper. In time he came to be one of the men most hated and feared by the planter class in the South. But the *Liberator* received far more credit than was actually due it. Garrison was blamed for supplying the catalyst

which started the Nat Turner slave revolt in South Hampton County, Virginia, at a time when not a single issue of the *Liberator* was circulated in the South.

Garrison admitted that the *Liberator* was primarily a Negro journal because Negroes were his main financial supporters. In addition to Negro subscribers, there was a small group of white supporters. Most of these belonged to Quaker or other religious groups which condemned slavery, but there was a small group of wealthy supporters as well. Garrison depended upon placing the *Liberator* in strategic locations rather than on large-scale circulation. Before the end of his first year he was utilizing more than a hundred exchanges which insured wide-spread publicity. Southern editors found the organ highly offensive, and it was outlawed in many Southern states.

Garrison began to achieve notoriety. The Georgia Legislature offered a reward of five thousand dollars to anyone who would cause the arrest and trial of Garrison in Georgia. Numerous persons wrote him letters which included threats on his life. Senator Robert Y. Hayne wrote to the mayor of Boston asking that the *Liberator* be suppressed immediately. This act aided the cause greatly, for many people who had shown little inclination toward the anti-slavery cause came to believe that it was a struggle to prevent the loss of the basic freedoms.

Although Garrison had gained popularity, he still had to supplement the meager contributions if his journal was to survive. He began an attempt to raise funds by accepting engagements to speak in public. In addition, on November 13, 1831, the New England Anti-Slavery Society was formed in the hope that funds could be procured from its members. Even though both ideas achieved some success, the *Liberator* was plagued with financial problems until shortly before the Civil War.

The year 1833 was a turning point with Garrison. He journeyed to England, where he was accepted by Bishop Wilberforce and the English Abolitionists as the leading American Abolitionist. Upon his return to the United States he became associated with such leaders of the American movement as Arthur Tappan, Theodore Weld, the Grimpke sisters, Benjamin Lundy, Theodore Parker, and Elizur Wright. It was with this group that Garrison helped to found the American Anti-Slavery Society.

Although Garrison continued to work with this group, he was disliked by most. One cause of controversy between the reformers was Garrison's demand that women be permitted to enjoy the same political and social rights that were extended to the male population. Additional strife was created because Garrison refused to support candidates or political parties, such as the Liberty Party or Free Soil Party, in an effort to achieve the aims set forth by the various Abolitionist societies. His refusal to permit his followers to utilize the ballot to achieve his goals was based upon his belief that politicians were corrupt and that all political parties, fighting sham battles for votes, had no real interest in seeing any reforms accomplished. He maintained this attitude until Abraham Lincoln issued the Emancipation Proclamation in 1863, at which time Garrison instructed his followers to support the Republican Party.

Living in a nation which permitted the institution of slavery to exist so embittered Garrison that he eventually destroyed a copy of the Declaration of Independence and a copy of the Constitution. In this ceremony he declared himself no longer a citizen of a republic which would not abolish slavery. However, after the Civil War many people began to honor him as the first great leader of the Abolitionist movement. As a result, before he died, he achieved mass popularity.

The Liberator offers deep insight to the tensions and stresses of a decisive period of American history.

J. Perry Cochran

THE LIE

Author: Alberto Moravia (Alberto Pincherle, 1907-   )
Translated from the Italian by Angus Davidson
Publisher: Farrar, Straus and Giroux (New York). 334 pp. $5.95
Type of work: Novel
Time: October, 1962,–January, 1963
Locale: Rome, Italy

The diary of a journalist who is determined to extract a realistic novel from the undramatic and irrelevant incidents of daily existence

Principal characters:
FRANCESCO MERIGHI, a would-be novelist
CORA, his wife
BABA, her daughter by a German soldier during the war

"The fact of dreaming" is without doubt real, and this shred of logic is possibly the one conclusion which emerges in Alberto Moravia's *The Lie.* The novel, as a whole, is a desperate jaunt through the labyrinth of a journalist's diary which reveals an obsession for objective reality and for "genuineness" in the act of reporting. Unreality achieves an almost allegorical significance in its recurrences and tangible qualities which, in turn, lend it a reality in itself. This presumption is vital to Moravia's theme.

The plot has been subjugated to an analysis of ideas, but the particulars of the story have been carefully selected and screened to fit the author's purpose. Francesco Merighi, the narrator, has married a woman beneath his class in a search for the genuine, has tired of her, and has taken a position as a foreign correspondent to escape the meaninglessness of a marriage without love. For ten years he has immersed himself in "nothingness," even reveling in its absurdity, but has continued to share an apartment with his wife during his infrequent visits to Rome. Suddenly, he decides to fulfill an earlier desire to write a novel, basically autobiographical, and concludes that a diary will be the most logical starting point.

Immediately, a problem presents itself. He is determined to present the facts accurately regardless of the results and even has a preconceived notion of his novel as a sort of exposè of "nothingness" and hypocrisy. The immediate problem is the fact, revealed to him through an anonymous letter, that his wife has been practicing the profession of a procuress for the past ten years and has even tried to introduce her daughter Baba into the trade as one of her girls. Ironically, this knowledge and its effect on him, in regard to possible confrontations or violent scenes, is intensely dramatic and thus unreal to him. In other words, the initial result of involvement, even for objective research, is drama, a concept totally alien in his "nothing" world—the world of little lies comprising the all-pervading life. Compounding the problem are his vague but deeply-rooted guilt feelings and his persistent incestuous thoughts concerning his stepdaughter.

Moreover, Moravia the purist has imbued his would-be novelist with an idealistic tendency to overcompensate. Francesco begins to doubt which plan of existence is valid. For example, he writes:

One of the unforeseen consequences of my undertaking to keep a diary and planning to extract a novel from it afterwards is that my behavior is beginning to come indirectly under the influence of this plan. In other words, when I am on the point of doing something or other, it occurs to me more and more often to ask myself: "What if this thing which I am about to do, and which, of course, I shall note in my diary, should in a negative yet irreparable way, alter the novel I am proposing to write later?"

Thus Francesco's diary becomes a "touchstone" and a "way of understanding [his] relationship with reality," rather than a mere chronological sequence of events. He adds, "Incapable of acting in a genuine manner, I rediscover genuineness as if by enchantment as soon as I make the novel a go-between reality and myself." In like manner he burdens the diary with the additional role of a conscience to stifle his increasing desire for Baba.

If Francesco had remained static at this point, he might have achieved his original aim, that of writing a chronicle of the "big lie," but Moravia begins to play with irony on a double plane. In short, Francesco discovers that not only is he purging his life of any action which might prove detrimental to the novel, but he is also expanding, completing, and actually distorting events in the diary to suit his literary purposes or his suppressed desires. This fact is not a cause for any great concern as long as he can distinguish the truth from his personal comments or the editorial treatment of an event. However, he begins to fabricate alternate episodes and conclusions, then denies these alternatives, and at times denies the denials. The result is the loss of an objective basis for truth, but the motive, that of reality, remains pure. Francesco comments:

> The difference between the thing imagined and the thing that really happened, at least as far as my diary is concerned, is the difference which exists between the inherent reality of falsehood and the inherent reality of truth. The latter stands firmly in place, immediate and direct, it is the fact itself while it is happening; the former, on the other hand, comes through an intermediary, indirectly, and lies, not in the fact itself as it occurs and presents itself, but in the significance of the fact.

At the end of the diary Francesco includes two possible conclusions, both of which he claims are valid in different ways. In the first, he denies the existence of the diary's final confessional scene with Baba, in which he informs her that he knew of Cora's secret profession and even allowed her to offer Baba to him. In the second, he admits the validity of the confession and denies the first conclusion. He then observes blandly, "With the first face of the conclusion, I should have a dramatic novel: with the second, the drama of a novel." He states that, after all, his problem is not so much to accuse or to justify himself as to write a novel. With this comment, Moravia has succeeded in turning a vicious literary circle into a parody of the novel form, that is, a search for the novel itself. Predictably, the diary, with a prologue and an epilogue, is the finished product.

Moravia's justification for the book's point of view can be found in his collection of essays, *Man As an End*. In "Notes on the Novel," he states:

> The nineteenth-century novelist had believed in the existence of a language

and a reality that were common and universal; now the novelist suddenly found himself confronted with the relativism of language and reality. It is from this time that we must date the impossibility of writing novels in the third person except by disguising the autobiographical "I" in a way false to science and objectivity; and from that time, too, that the novel has become "fragmentary," if by that we understand the non-existence of a common language and the impossibility of an unchanging relationship between the author and reality.

In this light, *The Lie* can be compared with Joyce's *Ulysses* or Proust's *Remembrance of Things Past* in its lack of any one basis for reality, but it is more of a unit, not only in subject matter, but also in thematic repetition. Undoubtedly, translation from the Italian has seriously affected the smooth flow of narrative of which any Romance language is capable. The style, at times, becomes heavy and even pretentious, to the point of obscuring the easy flow of ideas with difficult grammatical constructions.

The tone of the novel borders on a conscious parody of Greek tragedy. Elements of ancient drama are probably the most frequently recurring theme symbols in *The Lie*. The parallels are tenuous, however, because they are made part of "the lie" itself. For example, early in the novel Francesco compares his situation with that of Oedipus in *Oedipus Rex* in respect to general concepts of guilt, escape from responsibility, and divine retribution. However, he actually includes a passage from the drama in his diary, claiming that he had picked up *Oedipus Rex* at random late at night and had noted certain relevancies. In reality, he has dramatized the incident for the effect it will produce in his novel. Apart from this episode, Francesco

predicts the death of his wife and anticipates it as a rather satisfying form of "deus ex machina." The dialogue consists essentially of stichomythia, in its finest, choppiest tradition. In fact, the principle of cartharsis is made a part of the novel in Francesco's purgation of his emotions and desires through his diary. However, since most of these allusions to Greek tragedy are obviously planted and repeated, they lose any serious significance, apart from an ironic contrast with tragedy in an epic sense, as the Greeks understood it. Francesco does not attain the stature of a tragic hero, nor does the diary have a definite tragic flow. Instead, he is the contemporary distortion of Oedipus, unable to become a secular Christ-figure and assume the responsibility of atonement. Oedipus blinds himself; Francesco gives up his novel and accepts the diary as reality.

On the surface, *The Lie* is sensual, but to call the entire work a novel of sensuality is misleading. The incident of projected incest and prostitution serve only as a pale façade to Moravia's essential message, a humanistic rejection of the unreal. His characters appear cold and flat at times, but they are presented with a sympathetic eye for frailty, which pierces the bubble of non-involvement and plunges each individual into the common trap of existence. The specter of fatalism can not be overlooked in *The Lie*, simply because nothing is changed or improved, or even justified, despite any self-knowledge or objective perception in any character. Reality, as a concept, evolves from a highly definitive ideal to the most indiscriminate of abstracts. Hence, Francesco concludes:

In other words, if it was true—as I

was convinced it was—that a novel cannot but be realistic, my diary demonstrated that there were no limits to realism, that nothing could be excluded from reality, not even dreams, not even lies, not even the vital illusion which had once made me ashamed of having lived.

Thus the irony of the search is complete. There is no existential joy in acceptance, only an aftertaste of disappointment. "The lie" is not only real, but a form of the truth by its very fact of being.

Malcolm H. McGregor

LIES

Author: C. K. Williams (1936–   )
Publisher: Houghton Mifflin Company (Boston). 62 pp. $4.00
Type of work: Poetry
  A first book of poems

The title of this first collection indicates the poet's concern with the failure of truth as a bond between people in a world of bestial cruelty. It may also apply to the sharp and startling metaphors that are fundamental to Mr. Willams' art.

For me, the latter meaning is more important in evaluating the strength of this book. For when a poet creates "lies" as metaphors for ineffable suffering (the poet is "an empty bottle with no message" in one of these pieces), he must make the falsehoods end by becoming real. And C. K. Williams' metaphors are the "lies" of his poetry, devices that are central to the truth of his work.

Mr. Williams' metaphors are dangerous enterprises. Often he uses difficult conceits remarkably well. For example, "Giving it Up" begins:

It is an age
of such bestial death
that even before we die
our ghosts go.
I have felt mine while I slept
send shoots over my face,
probing some future char
there, tasting the flesh
and the sweat
as though for the last time. . . .

In many of the poems an extended image such as this, based on an adage (as here), or on a commonplace, is rescued from banality by the poet's resolute tonality and precision. Also, his use of the extended metaphor is most successful when he is writing about a personal, fiercely ambivalent search for love. For example, he writes in "The World's Greatest Tricycle Rider":

The world's greatest tricycle-rider
is in my heart, riding like a wildman,
no hands, almost upside down along
the walls and over the high curbs
and stoops, his bell rapid firing,
the sun spinning in his spokes like a
    flame.

But he is growing older. His feet
overshoot the pedals. His teeth set
too hard against the jolts, and I am
    afraid
that what I've kept from him is what
tightens his fingers on the rubber grips
and drives him again and again on the
    same block.

This poem is quoted in its entirety because it is an example of Mr. Williams' poetry at its best. In this, in "On the Roof," and in a few other poems in this book, he writes in a kind of lyric voice. Love's force, that seems to extend the boundaries of what can be given or received in the corrupt world of the poet's vision, is embodied by the extended metaphor. Here, the energetic rhythm, the use of the four-stress line and the lengthened concluding lines, are the devices, those "lies" that reinforce the poem's truth.

However, many of the poems are almost entirely devoid of poetic devices. Further, love is hardly his true theme: his poems focus on the deflated realities of modern existence, on death, dying, and corruption. His imagery, outrageously fresh though it is, is employed to evoke horror: "Those dead already roll over / and rub their retinas into the pebbles"; "he sees the intricate geography / of ruined backs"; "the sewer people and the junk people"; Nazi officers "cutting babies in half on bets"; an alley containing "the usual filth spilling from cans"; people "sick with the stench of mash." These and fouler images are landmarks of the poet's demonic world.

Unlike Robert Lowell, Sylvia Plath, and Anne Sexton, Mr. Williams does not use these images to describe an interior landscape, nor does he explore a private hell that illuminates our own. His poetry is not "confessional," nor even profoundly personal. If the poems are nightmares, they are externalized. Frequently he deals with the victimizer and with a kind of abstract suffering; less frequently, with its internal effect on the victim. Or, he presents images of decay in the world around us. "Downwards," for example, is a vision of life's end:

This is the last day of the world. On
  the river docks
I watch for the last time the tide get
  higher
and chop in under the stinking pilings.
  How the small creatures
who drift dreaming of hands and lungs
  must sting,
rotting alive in the waste spill, coming
  up dead
with puffy stomachs paler than the
  sky or faces. . . .

In "Dimensions," the poet adumbrates his vision of the modern predicament. Each of the three stanzas contains a different aspect of life's suffering. In the first stanza, he delineates a world in which natural forces provide intolerable pain, and whose inhabitants "are like boats bleating wearily in fog." In the second, he depicts the ordinary world in which "we know where we stand"; in this, love or dreams are sources of agony. In the third stanza, he presents the cruelty in human beings as the greatest dimension of suffering:

There is a world that uses its soldiers
    and widows
for flour, its orphans for building stone,
    its legs for pens.
In that place, eyes are softened and
    harmless like God's
and all blend in the traffic of their
    tragedy and pass by
like people. And sometimes one of us,
    losing the way,
will drift over the border and see them
    there, dying,
laughing; being revived. When we
    come home, we are half way.
Our screams heal the torn silence. We
    are like scars.

This is the vision that informs most of the poems in this book. The poet is an innocent exposed to brutality and repelled by it; yet his fascination with horror is betrayed by this preoccupation with it and by his use of extended metaphors as embodiments of cruelty: "It Is This Way with Men" is typical:

They are pounded into the earth
like nails; move an inch,
they are driven down again.
The earth is sore with them.
It is a spiny fruit
that has lost hope
of being raised and eaten.
It can only ripen and ripen. . . .

Because of his focus on public suffering, rather than on private pain, the question of whether his "lies" ring true is essential. The scope of his vision, the frequent use of "we" and "they" rather than "I," somehow demand an imaginative rightness of rhythm and precision of imagery.

The rightness of his effects varies a good deal. I find the weaker poems to be those that are unpunctuated and have few poetic devices, such as "Three Seasons and a Gorilla." In this, for example, the unsparing hatred and pain seem to require more control. Occasionally, as in "The Man Who Owns Sleep," unabashed hatred is unhappily combined with obscurity.

In "A Day For Anne Frank," a long sequence that ends this book, there are nine visions of putrescent death and, in the final section, an address to the young victim:

> Come with me Anne. . . .
> Come sit with me here
> kiss me; my heart too is wounded
> with forgiveness.
>
> There is an end now.
> Stay.
> Your foot hooked through mine
> your hand against my hand
> your hip touching me lightly . . .

Despite its length and centrality to the book, the poem is not one of the stronger pieces. The poet's involvement with Anne is really for an abstract state of innocence rather than with a person, and his hatred of the victimizers dominates his compassion for the victims. The impact of the poem is of unalleviated universal horror—but the horror is impersonal, and there are too few of the contrivances of art, paradoxically, to make it come alive as truth.

The majority of poems, though, do have these contrivances, and that is why "truth" is the predominant effect of Mr. Williams' "lies." In general, he achieves mastery of metaphor, precision, and natural rhythmic effects. Reading a good poem by C. K. Williams is like hearing a fresh, new voice:

> The trouble with me is that whether I
>   get love or not
> I suffer from it. My heart always seems
>   to be prowling
> a mile ahead of me, and by the time
>   I get there to surround it,
> it's chewing fences in the next country,
>   clawing
> the bank-vault wall down or smashing
>   in the window
> I'd just started etching my name on
>   with my diamond.
>
> And that's how come I end up on the
>   roof. Because even if I talk
> into my fist everyone still hears my
>   voice like the ocean
> in theirs, and so they solace me and I
>   have to keep
> breaking toes with my gun-boots and
>   coming up here
> to live—by myself, like an aerial, with
>   a hand on the ledge,
> one eye glued to the tin door and one
>   to the skylight

Grace Schulman

4304

A LIFE

Author: Wright Morris (1910-   )
Publisher: Harper & Row Publishers (New York). 152 pp. $5.95
Type of work: Novel
Time: The present
Locale: From Chapman, Nebraska, to the vicinity of Roswell, New Mexico

A moving account of the last day in the life of Floyd Warner, during which his life comes as sharply into focus as a saint's life

Principal characters:
> FLOYD WARNER, an eighty-one-year-old man wandering through the land of his past
> VIOLA WARNER, his late sister
> MURIEL DOSEY WARNER, his late wife who was part Indian
> KERMIT OELSLIGLE, his twelve-year-old nephew
> GEORGE BLACKBIRD, an American Indian veteran, Warner's executioner
> EFFIE MAE HOLTORFER, a feeble-minded old lady who warns Warner of the danger of Indians

The novel as a literary form was created in the eighteenth century and achieved its fullest development in the nineteenth century as a direct aesthetic parallel to Newtonian physics, to an understanding of the world as a vast machine in which all of the parts fitted together to form the whole. In other words, the whole, whether it be the cosmos or a well-made novel, was precisely the sum of its parts. The art of writing and the craft of writing were seen as essentially the same thing, and the meaning of a novel could be arrived at by a careful examination of how its parts fit together to form the whole. There could be no loose ends in a well-made novel and no inner contradictions. It must function exactly like a steam engine or an egg beater. Therefore, a Thackeray was more highly prized than a Sterne, for stability and completeness were the earmarks of artistic value.

Today, thanks to the scientific developments of Einstein's relativity physics and the quantum physics of men like Schrödinger and Heisenberg, the mechanistic view of life has collapsed and been replaced by a much more open and subjective understanding. Life is, to use a term coined by Arthur Koestler in *The Ghost in the Machine,* holonic. There is no such thing as an absolute part or an absolute whole; the basic units of materiality are at once themselves and parts of the whole, at once free and independent and also subservient to and dependent upon the whole. Subatomic particles obey no laws (not even the laws of chance), but they are involved fully in structure and movement of the cosmos which obeys the laws of relativity physics. The simple, objective world of Newtonian physics no longer exists, and its aesthetic partner, the traditional novel, is no longer a completely vital art form in harmony with life as we know it.

Heisenberg's principle of indeterminacy tells us that, in science, absolutely objective truth can no longer be arrived at and, further, that it does not even exist. In other words, in science, the whole story cannot be told, because it does not exist. The telling of the story itself is part of the whole. Our reality has become much closer to Zeno's paradox than it is quite comfortable to believe.

In human and artistic terms, the whole story also can no longer be told. Even the multiple point of view of *Rashomon,* Ford's *The Good Soldier,* or Faulkner's *The Sound and the Fury* does not tell the entire story. This realization has led to the rediscovery of Sterne and of Poe's "unfinished" *The Narrative of Arthur Gordon Pym,* and to the creation of a new fiction of indeterminacy in, say, Durrell's *The Alexandria Quartet* with its appended "Workpoints" or Barth's *Chimera* with its stories contained within each other. The reader, the writer, and the characters all experience the story, but none of them knows or can know the whole thing.

Only in parable is the novelist able to approach the whole story, to suggest in the form of his tale the form of the whole. But even in parable, the artist is never able, as Borges reminds us, to express the whole, but only to allude to it. Nevertheless, those allusive parables of Borges and novels like David Lindsay's *A Voyage to Arcturus* or the later novels of John Cowper Powys come much closer to a satisfactory artistic rendering of the truth of things than all of the careful mechanistic ("realistic") novels of the Bellows and Roths and their imitators that are published every day.

Wright Morris, with his roots firmly planted in the soil of the American Middle West, would no doubt feel very uncomfortable to find himself placed in the company of Durrell and Barth, or Borges and Powys. But he has never been a mechanist, and his fiction, for all its carefully rendered "realistic" detail, has always defied categorization. It has always been concerned with ordinary people in an ordinary and familiar locale, but it has never treated them in an ordinary way. Morris' novels have always pressed the traditional forms of the novel forward, harnessing them to his own consciousness, his sense of reality which is truly holonic in the fullest sense. Characters and events appear and reappear in his novels; he uses multiple point of view fully and effectively; he speaks directly to the reader and invites his full participation in the story. (The first sentence of *A Life* is typical: "From the highway to the east, where his car is parked to the left of a mailbox propped in a milk can, we can see him standing in the knee-high grass at the edge of a field of grain stubble.") The world in Morris' fiction is that of the vital present, one in which past and future are both real and alive, one in which each moment is filled with multiform potentiality. And never has his fiction been richer, more alive and more truly holonic than in the paired novels, *Fire Sermon* (1971) and *A Life.*

The two books tell the story (and stories) of two people who share the same present, although one of them is moving into the future while the other slips away into the past. *Fire Sermon* tells how Kermit Oelsligle and his great-uncle Floyd Warner travel from California to Chapman, Nebraska, in search of a real home for the boy with Warner's sister Viola. They find Viola dead and buried, and even her house goes up in flames at the novel's end. Kermit discovers another home more appropriate to himself and the world he inhabits with two wandering "hippies," for his world is one of continuing change and renewal, one purified by the destructive fires of change.

That story, the story of a youth's break with the past and his discovery of the burden and promise of the future, seems a particularly accurate parable of American life. As one critic writes, "It is the story of us as Americans—in a nation which more drastically, more dramatically, lives and dies, changes and is renewed every second, every ticking life."

But, of course, there is more to the story. *A Life* picks up where *Fire Sermon* ends, but it does not follow Kermit into his future. It follows instead another life to its end, an end which lies in that world of continual change, but one in which freedom has been translated into fate by the long life before it. The wheel of life turns as it does in *Fire Sermon,* but in *A Life* it turns back on itself, or rather, it turns on to come full circle.

Floyd Warner realizes, long before the shock of his sister's death and the fire, that he and Kermit are going two different ways:

> Leaving California, the morning sun in his eyes, he had sensed that he was traveling backward, but that the boy, in the seat at his side, at the same moment was hurrying forward, free as the wind. The same direction in space proved to be the opposite direction in time.

And he realizes later that not only is he traveling into the land of his past, but literally into the past itself, inner and outer journeys for once in harmony:

> The wheel of his life having come full circle, the past was now coming toward him as the present mysteriously receded. What had happened last night fell away, slipped away, like the road visible in the rear-view mirror, but what had happened in the distant past flowed toward him like objects approaching on the highway.

Once the boy has gone away with his new companions, Floyd Warner begins to lose touch with the present that moves into the future and instead slips into another present that exists only as a fulfillment of the past. He begins to see his life whole, a full and finished event which has such form and unity that it seems truly to have been designed by fate (although his previous philosophy had always been that "one goddam thing always led to another"). At the same time, he begins to discover the life within himself that gives that other, outer, apparently random life its form and meaning.

A rebel, a loner, a follower of Ralph Ingersoll, Warner sees himself as a man who has lived solely by the force of his own will, free of belief and dependence, in a windy world without sense or value. But on this last day of his life, he discovers that not will but feeling has sustained him, that he has never really been alone, and that his free choices were never selfish but were always made for the good of others. Most importantly, he discovers that he has never been aware of the true shape of his life: "That his own life had passed without his knowing about the life within him pleasantly dazed him."

Warner picks up a hitchhiker, his own death in the person of George Blackbird, and fulfills his destiny to be the last man from his county to be killed by Indians. But his real destiny is to see himself as he really is at long last. *"I have been walking in my sleep,"* he thinks, *"and now I am awake."*

A Life is the summing up of a life which is a great deal more (and perhaps less) than the sum of its parts. Warner, surely no saint, as surely is a saint; the paradox is at the book's heart. His goodness lay in his being unaware of it. "He wanted no more than he had found," and what he finds, in his death, is all any of us could want, for he "had lived in the manner he believed he had chosen, not knowing that he had been one of those chosen not merely to grow old, but to grow ripe."

Fire Sermon celebrates freedom and change. *A Life* celebrates with equal intensity fate and the end of change. Freedom and fate, youth and age, selfishness and love, inner life and outer life, life and death—all are holonic equivalences. We are free as the wind, and we are gone with the wind.

These two small novels may not express the whole of life, but they do give us an aesthetic awareness of its shape and of its reality and value. They are masterpieces by an American master, one of our finest who has not told anywhere near his whole story yet.

R. H. W. Dillard

Sources for Further Study

Criticism:

Weeks, Edward. "A Life" in *Atlantic*. CCXXXII (September, 1973), pp. 116-117. Morris' gradual delineation of Floyd's character is explored.

Reviews:

Library Journal. XCVIII, September 15, 1973, p. 2572. 180 words.

New York Times Book Review. August 26, 1973, p. 6. 750 words.

Saturday Review/World. I, October 9, 1973, p. 28. 250 words.

Time. CVII, September 24, 1973, p. 126. 390 words.

THE LIFE AND TIMES OF LUCREZIA BORGIA

Author: Maria Bellonci
Translated from the Italian by Bernard Wall
Publisher: Harcourt, Brace and Company (New York). 325 pp. $5.00
Type of work: Biography of a family
Time: 1480-1519
Locale: Italy

The recognized standard history of the Borgias, translated into English for the first time

Principal personages:

LUCREZIA BORGIA
CESARE, her brother
POPE ALEXANDER VI, her father
VANNOZZA CATTANEI, her mother
DON CHERUBINO JUAN DE CENTELLES, Lord of Val d'Azora in
    Valencia, Spain
GIOVANNI SFORZA, Lucrezia's first husband
ALFONSO, of the House of Aragon, Lucrezia's second husband
ALFONSO D'ESTE, Lucrezia's third husband
PETER BEMBO, Italian poet
FRANCESCO GONZAGA, Lucrezia's brother-in-law
THE DUKE OF GANDIA, Pope Alexander's favorite son

Originally appearing in Italian in 1939, this definitive biography of Lucrezia Borgia has been translated into English by Bernard Wall. Winner of the Viareggio Literary Award and the Galante Prize in Italy, it has been published in nine different countries. Even those who are ignorant of the dark history of the Borgia family will find *The Life and Times of Lucrezia Borgia* a rewarding book. Even to the reader who is already familiar with the names and main events of the Borgia chronicle, Signora Bellonci's biography is a fascinating study. The portrait of Lucrezia Borgia is intended to dispel the myth which has grown up about her, and it does this most definitely. Lucrezia emerges, not as a figure of evil, but as a warm human being who sacrificed her life to her family's interests.

Perhaps the most striking feature of the Lucrezia here presented is her unhappiness. Except for a few brief periods of romance, her life ran a hectic course of tragedy perpetrated largely by the machinations of her power-seeking family. She never rebelled against them, however, and tried to the last to save from ruin her evil brother Cesare.

One of the four children of Pope Alexander VI and Vannozza Cattanei, Lucrezia was born at Subiaco in April, 1480. Attended with respect like a legitimate princess, she probably had a very happy childhood. Although little is known of her early education, it is supposed that she attended a convent because, until the end of her life, she was a highly religious woman. She resembled her father physically and inherited the slightly receding chin which was his distinguishing feature. Much of her personality and her characteristics may be attributed to the Spanish roots of her ancestry.

When she was eleven, a marriage was contracted for her with Don Cherubino Juan de Centelles, Lord of Val d'Azora in Valencia, Spain. Later this was changed in favoi of a more influential Spanish nobleman. Neither of these two marriages ever took place because the fortunes and desires of the Borgia family had altered by the time Lucrezia was thirteen. Her first husband was Giovanni Sforza, Lord of Pesaro, a rather insignificant fellow. He was young and a widower, however, and since a tie was needed to strengthen the relationship between the Pope and the powerful Sforza family, Giovanni was chosen. They were betrothed by proxy.

This was the first of a long succession of episodes in which Lucrezia was used as a tool by the Borgias. In this case she was probably quite submissive, for the lavish preparations for the wedding were compensation enough for marrying a stranger. The married life of Giovanni and Lucrezia was not much different from that of most state marriages. He was allowed his mistresses as long as she became pregnant.

By 1498 the political situation in Italy had changed. The French had marched through much of Italy, conquering sections here and there, and the Sforza family had made a political alliance with them. Since their power in Rome was definitely waning, the Pope was anxious to dissolve Lucrezia's marriage. On Good Friday, the Count of Pesaro fled to his home state in terror of his life. There is substantial evidence to support the rumor that the Pope planned to have him killed. Lucrezia, according to the most careful research, was entirely innocent in the affair and even gave her husband the warning to flee. Finally, through devious maneuverings, the Pope succeeded in having the marriage annulled.

He gave Lucrezia's hand next to Alfonso, of the House of Aragon. This marriage was part of a plot by Alexander VI and his son Cesare to play both sides of the French-Neapolitan dispute over the kingdom of Naples. Since Alfonso was the natural son of the King of Naples, Lucrezia would become the first link between Naples and the Pope. She would become Duchess of Bisceglie and receive a large allowance from the King of Naples.

This second marriage was very happy. The two young people loved each other and they lived in Rome at the Castle of Santa Maria in Portico. Lucrezia soon had a son. Trouble arose once more when the Pope and Cesare finally cast their lot with the French and decided to dissolve their tie with the weaker Neapolitans. Cesare had Alfonso murdered in 1500. This time, however, Lucrezia was not nearly so submissive. In fact, her mourning and despair were so great that she began to irritate her father greatly. At the end of August she left Rome for her castle at Nepi, where she continued to mourn. Nevertheless, plans were already on in Rome to marry her off once more.

The third marriage was to Alfonso d'Este, son of the Duke of Ferrara. One of the oldest families in Italy, the ducal house of Ferrara was certainly stooping beneath itself in seeking Lucrezia, in view of her shady past. However, there was the growing power of Cesare Borgia to be reckoned with, and the d'Estes wanted to consolidate themselves with the Borgias. In 1501 Lucrezia married Alfonso d'Este, who soon afterwards succeeded his father as Duke of Ferrara. Lucrezia went to live in Ferrara and never returned to Rome again.

From then on she is known best as a patron of literature. In particular, she sponsored Bembo, the great Italian Renaissance poet, and their personal passion is celebrated in a number of his sonnets. Besides the affair with Bembo, she had one other great romance with her brother-in-law, Francesco Gonzaga. The Duke of Ferrara was a selfish, cold husband, and though he may have known of these escapades of Lucrezia's, he paid so little attention to her that they hardly seemed to matter. He did keep her pregnant most of the time, and she died bearing his seventh child in 1519. She was thirty-nine.

This, then, is the general outline of Lucrezia's life and the three marriages made by her for the advancement of the Borgia family. In only one was she happy, and this ended with tragedy and murder. She managed to produce a total of ten children in her life, and was a devoted and responsible parent. She found her solace chiefly in religion and seemed happiest in the atmosphere of the convent to which she occasionally fled in periods of great tension.

Signora Bellonci, in *The Life and Times of Lucrezia Borgia,* gives us a very sympathetic picture of her heroine. The strongest stories about Lucrezia are denied. For instance, there is almost nothing to support the myth that Lucrezia had a child by her father. Nor is Signora Bellonci willing to admit that there was much possibility for anything but a platonic love affair between Bembo and Lucrezia. Signora Bellonci is so anxious to set the record straight about Lucrezia Borgia, that at times we get a very watered-down version of the "most fascinating woman of the High Renaissance." Only occasionally does the writer admit that Lucrezia was anything but lily-white.

The Pope and Cesare are much more real, one feels. Signora Bellonci includes enough derogatory material to justify the origin of the myths about them. Her Pope Alexander VI is a fiercely devoted father whose reign was rank with nepotism and perilous schemes to place his children in the choicest positions in Italy. His favorite son, the Duke of Gandia, is a worthless rogue who well deserves the hatred of Cesare, the more talented son. The portrait of Cesare shows us a sinister, cat-like man whose ambition knows no limits. The minor women in the book, Vannozza, Guilia Farnese, Isabella d'Este, are especially well done.

Perhaps the highest achievement of the book is that, despite its historical accuracy and attendant necessity for documentation, *The Life and Times of Lucrezia Borgia* remains a very readable piece of literature. Part of its effect is due to the subject matter, certainly, but much credit should go to Signora Bellonci, who, even in translation, reads exceptionally well.

Sources for Further Study

Criticism:

Gilbert, William. *"The Life and Times of Lucrezia Borgia,"* in *American Historical Review.* LIX (July, 1954), p. 981. This commentary evaluates Bellonci's work from the author's own point of view—the importance of women in history—and comments on her use of source material in developing her thesis.

Reviews:

Commonweal. LX, April 9, 1954, p. 21. 490 words.

New Statesman. XLVII, January 9, 1954, p. 46. 650 words.

New York Herald Tribune Book Review. January 24, 1954, p. 6. 950 words.

Times Literary Supplement. January 15, 1954, p. 35. 1,150 words.

THE LIFE AND WORK OF SIGMUND FREUD
Vol. III: The Last Phase, 1919-1939

Author: Ernest Jones, M.D. (1879-1958)
Publisher: Basic Books (New York). Illustrated. 537 pp. $7.50
Type of work: Biography
Time: 1919–1939
Locale: Vienna and London

The concluding volume of Dr. Jones' highly individual attempt to present a near-definitive personal and critical biography of the originator of psychoanalysis

> *Principal personages:*
> SIGMUND FREUD, the founder of psychoanalysis
> ERNEST JONES, a friend, the author of this biography
> AMALIE FREUD, Freud's mother
> MARTHA FREUD, his wife
> ANNA,
> SOPHIE, and
> MATHILDE FREUD, his daughters
> ERNST,
> MARTIN, and
> OLIVER FREUD, his sons
> ALEXANDER FREUD, his brother
> KARL ABRAHAM,
> MAX EITINGON,
> OTTO RANK, and
> SANDOR FERENCZI, Freud's friends

Ernest Jones, M.D., long a friend and admirer of Sigmund Freud, has at last finished his detailed personal and critical biography of the distinguished scientist. This volume deals with the "Last Phase, 1919–1939," while the first two volumes dealt with, respectively, "The Formative Years and the Great Discoveries, 1856–1900" and the "Years of Maturity, 1901–1919." As with the other volumes, this third section of the biography is enlivened by numerous reports of conversations, quotations from letters, and illustrations of Freud, his family, his friends.

Jones set out initially to write a biography, but not a popular one. His aim, he said in the preface to the first volume, was to "record the main facts of Freud's life while they are still acces-

sible, and . . . to try to relate his personality and the experiences of his life to the development of his ideas." But Jones has never been reluctant to take issue with Freud, and he has been at considerable pains to make the exposition of Freud's ideas as clear as possible within biographical limits. The result has been a study in depth which does as much justice to Freud as he is likely to get from any man.

The years after the World War I were difficult ones economically for Freud. Living in Vienna, he managed to make ends meet by taking visiting patients and students of his methods, some of them sent his way by his good friend Ernest Jones. His days were enlivened by visits from friends and colleagues such as Otto Rank, Max Eitingon, Karl Abraham, Sandor Ferenczi, Hanns Sachs, and Jones. He was further encouraged by the establishment of *Internationaler Psychoanalytischer Verlag*, a private publishing house which proved to be important as an outlet for much of the advanced work in psychoanalysis.

Freud's *Beyond the Pleasure Principle*, begun in 1919, was completed the following year. Although this period was pleasant on the whole, it was marred by the death of his friend, Toni von Freund, in January, 1920, and by the death of his daughter Sophie a few days later.

The period 1921–1926 is labelled "Disunion" by Jones, primarily because of the quarrel about theory and technique which separated Otto Rank from the "Committee" of psychoanalysts centered about Freud. This dissension was another in a series of fallings out referred to in earlier volumes, disagreements involving Adler, Stekel, and Jung.

Freud's *Ego and Id* was published in April, 1923, and his collected works in the summer of 1924. The following year was distinguished by the publication of *Inhibition, Symptom and Anxiety* and the latest of his autobiographies. Freud's reputation was strengthened by these works, but his personal satisfaction was spoiled by the news that an ulcer of his hard palate was malignant. This was the beginning of a sixteen-year bout with the encroaching cancer.

The next blow was the death of his friend and colleague, Karl Abraham, in December, 1925, but the following year saw various celebrations of his seventieth birthday, and acknowledgments of his preëminence in psychoanalysis were made in various publications and at professional conferences.

Sandor Ferenczi was the next member of the "Committee" to find himself at odds with Freud, and the dispute ended only with Ferenczi's death after a period of insanity. Since Ferenczi had been one of Freud's closest friends for a quarter of a century, this disastrous close to a professional difference of opinion upset Freud considerably.

Freud's last years in Vienna were spent in physical suffering from his cancer and in growing apprehension of the activities of the Nazi government in Germany. In May, 1933, Freud's books were burned in Berlin, and in March, 1938, he decided to leave Vienna and take up residence in London. In September of that year he had his last operation, and a year later, on September 23, 1939, he died after being unconscious for twenty-four hours.

The most important work of this last period of Freud's life was his *Moses and Monotheism* (1938). In this interesting speculative work of historical reconstruction and philosophical reflection Freud contended that Moses was an Egyptian who acquired a belief in monotheism in Egypt and converted the Jews to his views. Freud also claimed that Moses was murdered, and that his murder was regarded (unconsciously) as a parricide. In Freud's words, commenting on the death of Jesus, "It had to be a Son, since the sin had been the murder of the Father. . . . The Mosaic religion had been a Father religion; Christianity became a son religion. The old God, the Father, took second place; Christ, the Son, stood in his place, just as in those dark times every son had longed to do. . . ."

The character of this last important book has implications, it might be argued, for an evaluation of Freud's work as a thinker. Despite the empirical confirmation of much of what he had to say about psychoanalysis—if success in treatment can be taken as confirmation of a theory concerned with the ground of a disturbance—Freud was much more than a mere analyst or inventor of analysis. He was a speculative psychologist and a speculative philosopher (as well as a speculative historian) rolled into one. His theories might reasonably be regarded as wish projections of a peculiarly valuable sort, related as they are to what most, if not all men, wish to believe.

For those who enjoy reflecting critically about Freud's ideas and influence there is an entertaining section, taking up a good part of the last half of the book, in which Jones considers Freud's clinical contributions, his metapsychology, and his influence on biology, anthropology, sociology, religion, occultism, art, and literature. Finally, in a chapter entitled "Retrospect," written at the publisher's request, Jones makes a series of provocative comments on Freud's influence.

Dr. Jones credits Freud with "the vast extension of the field of psychiatry" and with bringing about a wider recognition of the nature of neurosis. The result has been an increased willingness, even in those mentally affected, to consider insanity something that can be treated.

Freud's work has influenced the field of education, Jones argues, by making educators aware of the importance of the early years in the development of the child. What used to be regarded as "naughtiness" is now considered the symptoms of a problem.

Jones also makes the interesting point that Freud's work on psychology was based on a study of psychopathology, and that this suggests the most fruitful way of dealing with the study of psychological factors in human character and conduct.

By his theory of the unconscious Freud was able to resolve two of the most troublesome problems of philosophy—the problem of free will and the problem relating to the relativity of ethics. A decision which seems to be free may actually be motivated by unrecognized motives, and an ethics which seems absolute to the conscience may turn out to have its thoroughly naturalistic base.

In criminology the emphasis has gone from punishment to treatment; in social life there is greater freedom and less tension in the discussion of sexual problems; and there is an increasing awareness of the importance of dreams and of such daily mistakes as "forgettings, mislaying, slips of the tongue and pen," and so on.

Jones concludes by suggesting that there is one proposition about modern life which commands nearly universal assent: "The control man has secured over nature has far outrun his control over himself," and Jones goes on to write that "Man's chief enemy and danger is his own unruly nature and the dark forces pent up within him." He says:

> If our race is lucky enough to survive for another thousand years the name of Sigmund Freud will be remembered as that of the man who first ascertained the origin and the nature of those forces, and pointed the way to achieving some measure of control over them.

Sources for Further Study

Reviews:

New Republic. CXXXVII, December 9, 1957, p. 29. 1,050 words.
New York Herald Tribune Book Review. October 13, 1957, p. 3. 1,250 words.
New York Times. October 13, 1957, p. 7. 1,800 words.
Saturday Review. XL, November 2, 1957, p. 18. 1,250 words.
Spectator. October 18, 1957, p. 518. 1,400 words.

LIFE AT THE TOP

Author: John Braine (1922-   )
Publisher: Houghton Mifflin Company (Boston). 308 pp. $4.50
Type of work: Novel
Time: The present
Locale: Yorkshire and London

A narrative of retribution, maturing, and acceptance in the life of a man who came up the hard way

> *Principal characters:*
> JOE LAMPTON, a tough Yorkshire accountant turned junior executive
> SUSAN, his willful, passionate wife
> BARBARA, his adored daughter
> HARRY, his independent son
> ABE BROWN, his overbearing father-in-law
> MRS. BROWN, his haughty mother-in-law
> NORAH HAUXLEY, a widow, briefly his mistress
> SYLVIA, Susan's cousin
> MARK, her husband
> TIFFIELD, an important customer of Brown

John Braine gained wide public attention with a first novel which was a transatlantic best seller. *Room at the Top* told the story of Joe Lampton, a tough young Yorkshireman who pulled himself by his bootstraps from the meanness of his Dufton origins, rising as a municipal clerk to the point at which he could move on the fringes of the moneyed managerial class. At the book's end he had gained entry into that class by seducing and then marrying Susan Brown, the daughter of a tough, self-made steel manufacturer, Abe Brown, of Warley. Joe had found room at the top.

Life at the Top reveals what Joe Lampton's new life, ten years of it, is like. Although this sequel can be read without one's having read its predecessor, there is a constant reference to earlier events, now viewed in retrospect. Joe's rise from Dufton's squalor, his affair with Alice Aisgill which culminated in her suicide when he rejected her for Susan Brown and the life to which she was his entree—these events are put in perspective, examined in the first-person narrative of the determined, lusty opportunist who had just begun to come into a measure of self-knowledge at the end of *Room at the Top.*

It had been a hard and bitterly won success, and it left him with the realization that it was a mixed blessing that he had gotten everything he had wanted and never been wholly blamed for the cost in grief and misfortune to others. In *Life at the Top* nearly all of the fruits of his victory have turned to dust and ashes in his mouth. A kind of retributive justice overtakes Joe Lampton which ultimately, however, brings with it some measure of understanding, compassion, and acceptance.

The troublesome situations which soon become potentially disastrous confront him in both his personal and his professional life. Although he tries to retain some measure of independence and self-respect, his father-in-law gives him only limited responsibility in his job and sends him on debasing if important errands. An index of his position is his yielding to Abe Brown's pressure and allowing himself to be elected to the Warley Council, of which Brown is Chairman. The young rebel has become Conservative Councillor Lampton. This post, in which he cynically goes through the motions of conscientiously attending to local government, is also costly to him in his relations with his wife. Sexually compatible though they are, Susan is jealous of Joe's interest in other women and the business pressures which increasingly absent him from home. The councillorship is to her simply one more such incursion. Although Joe finds his marriage palling after ten years, he has not quite allowed his most promising flirtation to become adultery. This reserve is in part because he finds romantic intrigue somehow incongruous now that he is thirty-five, overweight, and softened by all his possessions, the clothes and car, the house and income. And the role of lover sits less well on him now, father of an independent nine-year-old son and an adored four-year-old daughter.

The crisis that completely turns his life upside down is the revelation, in a battle of recriminations following his discovery of Susan *flagrante delicto* with her dowdy cousin's worthless husband Mark, that it is Mark who is the father of the Lamptons' daughter Barbara. In a characteristic response, Joe strikes out at the loving wife who has cuckolded him (out of anger and loneliness) and the domineering father-in-law who has by-passed him. He leaves her and his life in Warley to go to London with Norah Hauxley, the attractive widow he has taken as his mistress. His response to an appeal to return to Warley, for the sake of the small son who seems for the first time to need him, is doubly significant: it begins the reversal of the downward path into drifting and dissipation which his life has taken and it is the first phase of what may be an enlargement of his understanding and his spirit. Another such phase is completed when he returns to his wife and to a kind of happiness resulting, paradoxically, from their survival of the storms they have endured.

Judged by one of the oldest and simplest criteria of the novelist's art, narrative drive, *Life at the Top* is clearly successful. The pace is skillfully varied, and the reader, neither sated nor wearied, keeps on wanting to know what will happen next. On other counts, the result is not so unequivocally clear. Joe Lampton's character and personality come through as fully and convincingly as they did in the first novel, and old Brown is skillfully sketched in. But Susan never wholly materializes as a complete character for all her importance to the novel, and even less so does Norah Hauxley. Also, Braine rests much of Joe's motivation on his deep love for his daughter, and though some of the reflective passages bearing on this relationship are touching, the dialogue between father and four-year-old—an admittedly tricky challenge—fails to come off.

Room at the Top was a *bildungsroman* of a type familiar in the English novel. And the story of the cheeky young upstart who fights his way beyond his original station is familiar enough so that it has rather wide relevance. The same width of relevance cannot be attributed to *Life at the Top*, though corollaries of the experience it portrays are surely not uncommon in twentieth century British and American life. The reader may also be inclined to feel that some of the insights which Joe's tribulations bring him are somewhat mechanical, seeming workings-out of the plot. He learns, for instance, that the manufacturer who tries to lure him away from Brown had been an unsuccessful suitor for the hand of his haughty mother-in-law, who then and later experienced, apparently, something like the heartscald Joe endures. Earlier he has encountered an early, unsuccessful suitor for Susan's hand. And the brief dialogue and exposition which explain Joe's son's seeming disdain, and accomplish his rapprochement with his fa-

ther, have a rather contrived air.

There is no subtle texture of symbolic reference, no pattern of motifs enriching this novel in the tradition of which James Joyce and Thomas Mann are a part. Nor, to draw close to home, is there the kind of passion or exhortation that marked D. H. Lawrence's novels of varieties of love. But there are in this highly readable, though often intensely melancholy, novel narrative gifts not possessed by some of the subtler practitioners among Braine's contemporaries in this taxing art.

LIFE HISTORY AND THE HISTORICAL MOMENT

Author: Erik H. Erikson (1902-   )
Publisher: W. W. Norton and Company (New York) 283 pp. $9.95
Type of work: Essays

A collection of essays, book reviews, and lectures in which the author discusses his understanding of the nature of psychiatry and the place of his work within it

Erik Erikson is perhaps the most well-known and influential of American students of Freud. In a long and distinguished career of analysis, teaching, and writing, he has brought his understanding of Freudian analysis to the attention of vast numbers of patients, students, and readers in both the professional and general publics. Best known for his books on the mental histories of Martin Luther and Gandhi, Erikson's most important contribution to the theory and practice of psychoanalysis has been in his development of a growth model for the progress of the human psyche. Moving beyond the Freudian model, with its emphasis on childhood traumas, Erikson, in his *Childhood and Society,* posits that everyone moves through a series of mental and emotional crises which must be resolved if the individual is to grow toward maturity. The advantages of this model are manifold; it enables an individual to see his emotional difficulties as opportunities for growth, while it makes possible the understanding of life as a long process of growth, divided into discrete stages with specific issues to be dealt with at each stage. Erikson is the father (perhaps unwillingly in some cases) of many of the American adaptations of Freudian theory and practice.

His best-known contributions to the popular understanding of psychoanalytic theory, however, have come with his studies of historical figures. His study of Luther's adolescence (*Young Man Luther*) and Gandhi's maturity (*Gandhi's Truth*) have brought him a wide readership, as well as public acclaim and numerous awards. The praise has not been total, however; both books have been criticized for their use of the tools of analysis on historical figures unavailable for interview, and for their applications of psychiatric insight to the actions and teachings of such important figures in the history of ideas. Freudian theory is always open to the charge of reductionism; many have felt that Erikson reduces the beliefs of such figures to the level of infantile crises. In so doing, critics argue, the independent truth or falsehood of those ideas is belittled. But such argument is itself the result of misunderstanding Freudian, and Eriksonian, thinking; Erikson's work stands on its own as a valid means of understanding the events of the past and the motivations of the important figures of history. If our purpose in the study of the past is to understand not just what happened, but how and why it happened when and in the way it did, then we are indebted to Erikson for providing us with another means of getting at the truth which the past holds for the modern student.

For these reasons, the volume *Life History and the Historical Moment* is a valuable addition to the shelf of

Erikson's works. A collection of book reviews, essays, and lectures, some printed earlier but here given wider and well-deserved readership, this work presents us with a more informal Erikson reflecting on the history of Freudian analysis, the development of his techniques for investigating the past, and some aspects of the contemporary scene, from student rebellion to women's liberation. The style here is relaxed, often conversational; we see Erikson the man reflecting on himself and on his lifelong involvement in what is perhaps the most important intellectual movement of the twentieth century.

It is appropriate that such a work begin with a backward look. The work is divided into three sections. The first, entitled "Backgrounds and Origins," consists of a long essay and two book reviews. The essay is a lengthy autobiography; written originally for a symposium on important ideas in twentieth century science, it presents a warm portrait of the man himself, while it traces his early years, his involvement with the circle around Freud, his journey to America, and the progress of his work in a variety of clinical and academic settings. Even more important, perhaps, is the fact that the essay is written as an attempt to clarify Erikson's definition of the "identity crisis," a key concept in his thinking which has entered the vocabulary of all Americans, especially those with adolescent children. What comes across is the honesty of the man—his ability to see himself clearly and to talk about himself without illusion. Freud began his work with self-analysis; Erikson exemplifies the fact that Freud's disciples have continued in this tradition.

The second part of this first section consists of two book reviews which also take Erikson back to the founding days of Freudian theory. The first review is of a collection of letters written by Freud to Wilhelm Fliess, a close friend and confessor to Freud in the days during which Freud began to develop his theories of human personality. A fascinating review of a significant work, this essay is a small example of the use of Erikson's psychohistorical method. Through a careful reading of Freud's letters, Erikson is able to reconstruct for us the psychological dynamics of Freud's relationship with his friend, and to suggest its importance for the development of Freudian theory. The second review is of the psychobiography of Woodrow Wilson, written jointly by Freud and the American diplomat William C. Bullitt. Erikson's review of this work is highly critical; if the first review reveals his ability to be objective as well as loving about the founder of his profession, the second demonstrates that to Erikson, Freud was easily capable of error and of bad judgment. Erikson demonstrates the questionable history of this book; mostly the work of Bullitt, it also reveals many of Freud's prejudices and blind spots. To Erikson, a student deeply indebted to Freud, this work is an embarrassment, but one he finally turns to an advantage. As a practitioner of the psychohistorical method of approach to the past, Erikson sees this work as a reminder of the difficulties which such an approach to history entails for the investigator.

The second section of the book, entitled "In Search of Gandhi," is made up of two essays which grew out of Erikson's studies leading up to the publication of *Gandhi's Truth*. The first, "On the Nature of 'Psycho-Historical Evidence' " is an account of the beginnings of Erikson's interest in Gandhi. It is, as well, an essay descriptive of the method of historical research practiced by Erikson in this book and in the earlier *Young Man Luther*. The author describes his search for evidence, his methods of evaluating that evidence, and the development of his models for understanding what he has learned from his research. The second of the two essays in this section is entitled "Freedom and Nonviolence," and was originally given as the T. B. Davie Memorial Lecture at the University of Cape Town in South Africa. Growing out of his studies into the nature of Gandhi's devotion to nonviolence as a force for political change, Erikson's lecture is given special force by Gandhi's own close links with South Africa and by the fact that students at the University were soon to resort to nonviolent protest of the racial policies of the South African government.

The third and final section of the book, entitled "Protest and Liberation," is, perhaps, the section of the book of most interest to the general reader. It consists of three essays, each of which treats a major aspect of the social changes wrought in American life by the events of the 1960's. The first, entitled "Reflections on the Revolt of Humanist Youth," is perhaps the most dated piece in the whole volume. Erikson attempts to discover the roots of adolescent rebellion in the 1960's and to make some predictions about the nature of future society based on his analysis. While his view of the future may yet

be right, it is clouded by the fact that the rebellion on which it is based has, at least outwardly, subsided. The second essay is more relevant; entitled "Once More the Inner Space," it surveys the traditional Freudian concept of woman in light of the movement for women's liberation. Perhaps its most interesting point is that the concept of penis envy, with which many leaders in the woman's movement take issue, has its male counterpart in what might be called womb envy. Men, angry that they are unable to bear children, may attempt to crush their feminine natures and thus distort their personalities in response. Erikson maintains that biology must have some role to play in the development of personality and destiny, even as history and social circumstance have theirs. The final piece in this section, and in the volume, is entitled "Psychoanalysis: Adjustment or Freedom?" This essay is a response to the criticism of Freudian analysis which claims that it attempts to make all people the same by adjusting them to fit an artificial norm; it defends the usefulness of Freudian theory and its developments for the freeing of men and women to do what they want to with their lives.

Erikson's work has always been a testimony to the importance of psychoanalysis for the modern world. This book is, finally, an affirmation of faith in that proposition, as well as effective proof of it. In the hands of men like Erikson, the essential concepts and methods of Freudian analysis continue to reveal their value in illuminating our world and freeing us for creative participation in it. *Life History and the Historical Moment* is a valuable guide to the history of the psychoanalytical movement, as well as an important commentary on the moment in which we now live. More importantly, it is a significant testimony to the value of Erik Erikson as a man who has given us the tools for understanding both our lives and our unique time in the history of man.

John N. Wall, Jr.

THE LIFE OF CAPTAIN JAMES COOK

Author: John C. Beaglehole (1901-1971)
Publisher: Stanford University Press (Stanford). Illustrated. 760 pp. $18.50
Type of work: Biography
Time: 1728-1779
Locale: Great Britain, New Zealand and the South Seas, Alaska and the North Pacific

The story of one of the greatest of eighteenth century discoverers, a sea captain who visited and charted a quarter of the globe

Principal personages:
CAPTAIN JAMES COOK
ELIZABETH BATTS, whom Cook married in 1762
JOSEPH BANKS, a rival and admirer
"DR."DANIEL C. SOLANDER, Swedish botanist on the first voyage
SAMUEL HOLLAND, who taught Cook to use a plane table
CAPTAIN CHARLES CLERKE, commander of the *Discovery* who succeeded Cook
GEORGE VANCOUVER, a seaman on Cook's voyages
PEDRO FERNANDES DE QUIROS, Portuguese explorer of the Pacific, discoverer of New Hebrides
ABEL JANSZOON TASMAN, Dutch discoverer of New Zealand

Captain James Cook, according to his biographer, had no sea connection either through heritage or environment. Chance took his family from his birthplace in the Yorkshire village of Marton-in-Cleveland to the port of Whitby. Luck brought to his attention a South Sea shilling in the till of the coal company where he worked, and roused his interest. His employer was a Quaker, and aboard one of his colliers James got his first taste of sea life. Liking it, but ambitious for more rapid advancement, he enlisted in the royal navy in June, 1735, and soon became master's mate aboard the *Eagle,* a commerce raider during the French and Indian War. His carefully kept journal records his advancement, as he passed an examination to qualify as master on any of His Majesty's ships, and was assigned the *Pembroke,* a troop carrier used in Wolfe's attack on Quebec.

Afterward, when it was learned he had put in a dull winter learning from a Dutch sea captain how to chart a coast from a vessel, Cook was sent to chart the coastline of Newfoundland, and his perfection of a system to work from a ship in motion won him membership in the Royal Society. Later, when the Society wanted to put a party of scientists ashore in Tahiti to make observations, it turned to Cook.

He hardly had time to marry Elizabeth Batts before he found himself en route to the South Seas aboard the *Endeavor,* bought and outfitted for him. Among his passengers was the wealthy naturalist Joseph Banks, who brought along a staff of seven, including two Negro servants, and his friend, "Dr." Solander, a pupil of Linnaeus, toward whose expenses Banks had contributed ten thousand pounds. Cook's first voyage had three

4324 The Life of Captain James Cook/BEAGLEHOLE

objectives: to get the observers to Tahiti before June 3, 1769, to look for the *Swallow*, last sighted fighting to pass the Straits of Magellan in 1767, and to keep his eyes open for uncharted land reported by earlier explorers, including a mysterious large Southern Continent. One stop at Rio de Janeiro for supplies and one at Tierra del Fuego for repairs were the only interruptions encountered before he reached Matavai Bay, Tahiti, in ample time to set up observation stations.

He had also been requested to learn what he could about the natives, and his education began at once, according to Beaglehole. The scientists put their equipment ashore, including a quadrant and heavy stand, both of which had disappeared by morning. Though they quickly identified the thief, who could have had no possible use for the instrument, it took a long time to recover it. No floggings or threats of hanging could stop pilfering of metal objects; this native characteristic, about which he frequently complains in the journal, would eventually bring about Cook's death.

While waiting to carry his passengers home, Cook's ship cruised among the neighboring islands, on one of which he found the natives so cooperative that he named the place the Friendly Islands. One of the inhabitants, Tapia, was taken aboard as a pilot, and shortly afterward the ship set sail "in search of whatever chance and Tapia might direct us." Their search very soon discovered New Zealand, first sighted in 1642 by Admiral Tasman, who had made an error in recording its position. After charting this lovely island, the expedition took leave of it at a place appropriately called Cape Farewell. Two weeks later Cook began another assignment; the ship sighted a part of Australia that he named New South Wales, and he set about "reducing to marks on paper 2,000 miles of coast line."

In the process, the *Endeavor* went aground on June 11, 1777, an accident for which the biographer suggests a logical explanation: no earlier voyager had warned against the Great Barrier Reef. The crew spent six weeks plugging holes and making needed repairs, while other sailors explored for an opening in the coral. Finally, with two boats preceding and testing the depths ahead, the captain navigated the *Endeavor* through Providential Channel to open water, a feat at which subsequent navigators marvel. Yet Cook's journal only expresses the hope that his eagerness to get away from this dangerous situation would not bring charges that cowardice prevented completion of the charting. He does comment that the charts he completed contain as few errors as most charts, though he warns sailors of the future against trusting them too completely. He devotes several more pages to lyrical descriptions of New Holland (Australia) "whose inhabitants are bound to be happy because of the beauties of Nature." Then, being a good hydrographer, he concludes with five hundred words about currents and tides.

Free again, Cook headed for Djakarta (Batavia) for more thorough repairs. There he got news of the arrival of the *Swallow* and its four-month struggle through the Straits of Magellan. Then, his jobs completed, he headed back for England. His biographer sums up the results of his first voyage: "The *Endeavor* had called at 40 previously unknown islands, while Mr. Banks and Dr. Solander brought back 1,000 plants unknown to Europe and 7,000 more never before seen in Europe." Upon their return, Banks got the celebrity treatment, including an interview with King George, who proposed a colonizing trip to St. George in the South Seas.

Capt. Cook next undertook a voyage in search of a Northeast Passage connecting the north Pacific and the Atlantic Ocean across the top of North America through some vague ice-free Arctic river. Two shallow draft colliers were bought and fitted out; one was named the *Resolution,* the other the *Adventure.* Banks asked for a third ship to carry his gear and associates, but since he had so greedily claimed the glory from the first voyage, the antagonized Society refused. When he threatened to back out, they gladly accepted his resignation, and he and Solander sailed for Iceland on July 13, 1772, while Cook and his vessels headed again for Cape Horn.

The second voyage was more or less a repetition of the first, with special attention to be given to the Northeast Passage; however, Cook had a special project of his own to pursue. Scurvy had always been the scourge of long sea voyages. Since consumption of citrus fruit had helped some ships, Cook asked for a supply of thickened orange and lemon juice combined with sugar or honey, and determined to force his sailors to swallow their daily dose. It proved to be a new medical discovery. His *Resolution* reached the Horn a few days behind a Dutch Indiaman which had lost half of its four hundred passengers. The *Adventure,* too, since no one aboard insisted on the daily medication, had many passengers ill, but aboard the *Resolution* there was only one sick sailor.

After rounding the Horn, which he had found speedier than the Straits, and continuing south to cruise dangerously among the ice floes in a vain search for the mysterious southern continent, he picked up Clerke and the *Adventure* at their rendezvous for another sweep of the area. As he wrote, "Having been absent from England for three years and 18 days during which time I lost four men, only one through sickness," he returned to England on July 27, 1775.

His earlier journal had been enthusiastically received, and upon this return Cook was welcomed and promoted by the Admiralty to command the seventy-four-gun *Kent*; Cook chose instead, however, to accept the Royal Society's proposal that he man his old vessels to search once again for the elusive Passage. Leaving the manuscript of his journal with a shipmate, John Forster, to edit, Cook and the *Resolution* again sailed southward around the Horn to the northern Pacific. Fog and head winds delayed them, but eventually they sighted an Alaskan village where Russian fur traders lived among the Eskimos. The Russians who looked at and corrected his charts could suggest no ice-free rivers leading toward the Atlantic Ocean, nor could Cook's exploring parties find any. Their disappointment is indicated by such entries as "Seduction River." The captain decided he had arrived too late; the ice had closed in. They decided to return the following year, after spending several months in the pleasant climate of the Sandwich (Hawaiian) Islands. Thus Cook began a leisurely voyage toward the tragedy awaiting him in Kealakekua Bay, which Beaglehole chronicles in Chapter XXV.

Borrowing from many accounts and letters, the author tells how, on the afternoon of February 13, 1779, a village chief, Palea, previously friendly to the whites, came aboard the *Discovery* for a chat with Captain Clerke. A native paddled alongside, climbed aboard and, seizing an armorer's tong from the deck, leaped overboard, where he was hauled into a canoe and hustled ashore. Palea was then rowed ashore, promising to recover the tongs. Once on land, a stone-throwing scuffle ensued between sailors and natives, during which one sailor struck Palea with his oar. The chief, anxious to maintain friendship with Cook, appeased everybody and sent a report to the incensed Cook.

Unfortunately, during the night someone stole the *Discovery*'s largest cutter. Furious now, Cook went ashore at daybreak with a double-barreled shotgun, Lieutenant Phillips, and nine Marines, to call the tribal chief to account, first sending other boats to patrol the shore to prevent any escape of the natives.

The sleeping chief was awakened, obviously innocent, and invited aboard to talk things over. But the sight of their leader among the whites angered the natives. The shooting, at that moment, of a native trying to put out in a canoe provided the final spark. One villager came at Cook with a knife. Protected by his heavy war mat, he was unharmed by the discharge of small shot, while other natives stabbed Phillips, who had been felled by a stone; shots from four pounders aboard the ships put the attackers to flight, but by the time the overloaded boat returned slowly to the *Resolution,* it left Cook and four soldiers dead on the shore.

Beaglehole, quoting Captain King, reports that next morning, under a flag of truce, a boatload of sailors went ashore for the bodies. The villagers, glad of forgiveness, received them peacefully and their head priest met them to explain that the bodies had been carried inland and would take a little time to collect. Two days later he reappeared with some charred flesh and a pile of bones. Twenty years later, according to the biographer, a missionary reported that the captain's bones were still being carried by inland Indians in their religious rituals. It was a cannibal tradition, he explained, that the bodies of brave men transferred their qualities to those who ate their flesh or preserved their bones.

Willis Knapp Jones

THE LIFE OF DYLAN THOMAS

Author: Constantine FitzGibbon (1919-   )
Publisher: Little, Brown and Company (Boston). Illustrated. 370 pp. $7.95
Type of work: Biography
Time: 1914-1953
Locale: South Wales, Swansea, London, and the United States

A perceptive biography of Dylan Thomas as man and poet, with attention, paid to the formative forces in his life, to his personality, values and habits, and to the nature and significance of his art

> *Principal personages:*
> DYLAN THOMAS
> CAITLIN THOMAS, his wife
> D. J. THOMAS, his father
> FLORENCE THOMAS, his mother
> PAMELA HANSFORD JOHNSON, another writer and friend
> DONALD and MARGARET TAYLOR, friends who helped Thomas financially
> JOHN MALCOLM BRINNIN, a friend in America

Here Constantine FitzGibbon accomplishes with thoroughness and perceptiveness the two major responsibilities of a biographer, the responsibilities to present faithfully the truth of his subject and to determine the natural and logical patterns implicit in a life that, during its course, must seem anything but patterned. To support the mere facts of his subject's life he presents illuminating anecdotes, numerous letters from various sources, reports of conversations, and rich personal information gained from his own close acquaintance with Dylan Thomas. Mr. FitzGibbon's selectivity of details, emphases, and insights clearly identifies the patterns— natural and logical relationships and repetitive behavior—essential to a comprehension of the poet as man and artist. He pauses along the way in his chronological study of Thomas to consider carefully the nature and significance of all facets of the writer's world: his environment, human relationships, principles, habits, and literary works. In his examination of each he is concerned with formative forces, as well as with identifying characteristics.

Dylan Thomas' grandparents on both sides were small farmers, living off the lonely hillsides of the Welsh-speaking part of South Wales and relying for their inner sustenance upon the Bible, volumes of sermons, Welsh classics, and chapel on Sundays. In this heritage Constantine FitzGibbon finds the roots of Thomas' taste for rare Welsh imagery, his democratic attitudes, his fundamental strain of Puritanism, and his respect for poetry and poets.

These are some of the quiet, restful forces beneath the surface of a life that was anything but serene. There are many of these forces, and most receive expression in Thomas' poetry. In the poet's father one can see the overt characteristics which were to mark his son's personality and to identify the real fire of his character. D. J. Thomas, his own literary ambitions thwarted, consoled himself by teaching English in the Grammar School of English-speaking

Swansea. Early in his life the elder Thomas, as the son was later to do, escaped from himself through heavy drinking. In fact, although while at Swansea his sense of social obligation empowered his will against shameful excess, the father drank heavily all his life. Furthermore, Thomas' father, partly influenced by his move to Swansea and partly by the naturalistic thinking of the time, was in the painful, lonely position of a radical caught between two worlds, that of his fathers and that of his own discovery. Nevertheless, between his worlds was the broad, fertile field of a scholar who loved literature and whose rich mind was a joy to others.

If Thomas inherited from his father traits which contributed both to his literary talents and to his unconventional behavior, from his mother he inherited the gentler graces of the spirit and received the protective indulgence that perhaps contributed to his inability to cope with normal obligations.

According to Mr. FitzGibbon, Swansea was a formative force in Thomas' literary life in that a young man of this provincial area was protected from the bad influences of London and yet had a pure accessibility to elements that encouraged and guided literary genius. In FitzGibbon's words, "In Swansea the young men had time to formulate their own artistic values, create their own techniques, and find their own modes of expression unpressurized by fashion." Furthermore, Thomas' childhood home in Swansea, with the distant sea and nearby park, provides the environment reflected in much of his poetry and stories.

Thomas' Tom-Sawyer-like boyhood reflects both the enviable attractiveness and the forgivable inadequacies of his personality. Thomas was perennially a bad little boy at heart, often more childish than childlike. But he was the kind of boy who saves humanity from dullness and stagnancy.

As a child his education was haphazard, its effectiveness limited by his own interests. Where his interest lay, however, he was strong. He was almost always a competent writer, composing some very promising poems while he was in his early teens. His poetry at this time, Mr. FitzGibbon informs us, was either comic or derivative. His ability with words was remarkable but, as his biographer notes, "the feel, taste colour, above all the sound of a word were infinitely more important to him than its sense." Mr. FitzGibbon also finds in Thomas at this time a feeling for and an interest in the theater that account to some extent for his later success as a script-writer.

Thomas did not attend a university. He entered the working world as a journalist, first on a paper and then as a freelance writer. During this period, while he was still at home but out of school, he wrote all the poems of his first volume, *18 Poems*, most of those of his second volume, *Twenty-five Poems*, many poems to appear in print later, and twenty to twenty-five short stories. According to Mr. FitzGibbon, all poems written after this, his most productive period, mark a new direction in style and concept. He experimented at this time with the sound and meaning of words, though the forms and rhythms of his poetry were rigidly traditional. An early theme, of which he soon tired, was the diabolic, such as madness and witchcraft. A theme that persists throughout his poetry, however, is that of death. Mr. FitzGibbon recognizes in this poetry what he calls a

Freudian synthesis between the death-wish and the urge to procreate which achieves a reconciliation that is, according to this biographer, Thomas' principal contribution to English poetry.

Thomas was not a conscientious reporter and his Swansea days were restless and undisciplined, made more so, perhaps, because he had some success on the stage. He began to make excursions into London, where he soon became part of a literary coterie which brought him in contact with people eager to assist young writers. These associations resulted in the publication of his poetry in periodicals and, by 1936, the publication of his first two books of poetry by leading publishers.

In his discussion of this period, Mr. FitzGibbon focuses attention upon Thomas' habits, especially his drinking and sexual indulgences; his relationships with the artists and intellectuals who helped shape his developing sensibilities and intellectual horizon, especially his relationship with Pamela Hansford Johnson; and his attitudes toward himself and the world.

His relation with Miss Johnson tended to curb his excessive drinking and smoking, thereby improving his health, which was never good. Perhaps more importantly, the relation provided an intellectual and artistic rapport constructive to the creative talents of both. Nevertheless, his drinking, as Mr. Fitz-Gibbon seeks to show, resulted from character forces which sincere resolutions could not check. Thomas frequented the pubs of Soho where the young aspirant artists met. There he drank because of his love of companionship, driven chiefly by his own self-persecuting timidity and, if Mr. Fitz-Gibbon is correct, his inferiority complex. His relation with the sympathetic but uncompromisingly proper Miss Johnson was doomed from the start.

On July 11, 1937, Thomas married Caitlin Macnamara, a high-tempered, spirited girl perfectly suited to her husband's improvident and unpredictable behavior, who loved him untiringly and literally fought for the preservation of his unadulterated role as a poet of genius. The tension that existed between them, that developed uneven and growing complexity as the years went on, that reached explosive tenseness near the end, could be used fairly accurately to gauge Thomas' spiritual life from the time of his marriage to his death. Caitlin Thomas, in her own way, was always stretching her husband toward what she thought was his better self; pulling in the opposite direction, from within, was Thomas' own unmanageable will. Mr. FitzGibbon's perception and appraisal of this tension are highly illuminating.

In 1940, Thomas disposed of his notebooks in which all of his early poetry was written. To Mr. FitzGibbon this act signifies a turning point in the poet's career. According to Mr. Fitz-Gibbon, the ten poems of 1944 and 1945 are among the best of Thomas' poetry because these later poems, more highly polished and complex than the earlier poetry, reflect his mature abilities. These poems make up a large part of his fourth book of poetry, *Deaths and Entrances,* and established him finally as a poet of real significance.

During these years, the years of the war and afterwards, Thomas spent much of his time in activities which, despite Caitlin's objections, diverted his energies from poetry. He was a scriptwriter during the 1940's and made numerous broadcasts and public appearances until his death in 1953. He sought in these activities release from financial burden. This he was never to enjoy, however, for he died in New York just before he realized his expected successes there.

The facts of this biography are presented with scholarly objectivity and thoroughness. Constantine FitzGibbon is critical, even suspicious, of all evidence which seems inconsistent or lacks authority. He substantiates his own judgments and weighs those of others. He distinguishes mere opinion from factual evidence. He is not satisfied, however, with mere history or simply with a surface interpretation of the inner man. He is concerned that his reader understand Thomas as he himself understands him. To the extent that Mr. FitzGibbon's understanding is sound, this biography is important beyond the significance of the recorded facts. That Mr. FitzGibbon

knew Thomas intimately and admired him greatly is apparent in these pages. Admiration, of course, can mislead a biographer by putting him too strongly on the defensive. An example of Mr. FitzGibbon's most questionable defenses is his contention that despite Thomas' frequent acts of infidelity he was always emotionally true to his wife. Even this defense, however, which seems on the surface to be an outrageous rationalization, in the context of Mr. FitzGibbon's understanding seems quite permissible. At the same time, as biographer and critic, he does not pretend to understand the significance of every act and expression of the poet. Though he seems to have an easy grasp of his subject, he frequently and wisely allows for that inviolable mystery of humanity which presents itself only to close acquaintances and which defies identification.

Charles Workman

Sources for Further Study

Criticism:

Gersh, G. "The Life of Dylan Thomas," in *Prairie Schooner*. XL (Spring, 1966), p. 82. In-depth analysis of the book in relation to Thomas' works.

Vendler, H. H. "The Life of Dylan Thomas," in *Yale Review*. LV (March, 1966), p. 439. 1250 words. The reviewer criticizes Fitzgibbon for writing an analysis of Thomas' major works rather than a biography, as the title implies. The book is a good introduction to the poet, however.

Reviews:

Commentary. XLI, April, 1966, p. 89. 3,550 words.

New Statesman. LXX, October 29, 1965, p. 1. 1,700 words.

New York Times Book Review. October 31, 1965, p. 1. 1,850 words.

THE LIFE OF EMILY DICKINSON

Author: Richard B. Sewall
Publisher: Farrar, Straus and Giroux (New York). Illustrated. 2 vols. 821 pp. $30.00
Type of work: Biography
Time: Nineteenth century, especially 1830-1886
Locale: Amherst, Massachusetts

A scholarly, well documented, and highly readable account of the life and poetry of Emily Dickinson

Principal personages:
EMILY ELIZABETH DICKINSON
SAMUEL FOWLER DICKINSON, her grandfather
EDWARD DICKINSON, her father
LAVINIA DICKINSON, her sister
WILLIAM AUSTIN DICKINSON, her brother
SUSAN GILBERT DICKINSON, his wife
MABEL LOOMIS TODD, his confidante and lover
OTIS PHILLIPS LORD, Emily's intimate friend

Of all the lives of literary figures chronicled in biographies, Emily Dickinson's is one of the most veiled in mystery. Both her life and her art conspired to secrecy: a voluntary recluse for nearly thirty years, her poetry reflected her love of the cryptic phrase, the elliptical line, the circuitous proof. Her enjoyment of riddles was symptomatic of the larger, lifelong commitment to intellectual probing so central to her nature; she believed, as she wrote in a letter to her cousins, that "the unknown is the largest need of the intellect." Emily Dickinson's method of exploring the unknown was always metaphoric, and her manner of living as well as of writing carried out her famous injunction to "Tell all the Truth but tell it slant—/Success in Circuit lies."

Given a life of such complete privacy and retirement and a poetic canon of such passionate intensity and bewildering complexity as Emily Dickinson's, it is hardly surprising that endless myths and legends have arisen to take the place of factual evidence. Richard Sewall, therefore, faced two formidable—at times insurmountable—obstacles at the outset of his story of the elusive poetess of Amherst. The first was the problem of laying to rest the myths which have become so entrenched; the second, the task of producing a thorough, objective, and realistic biography from records which are often scanty, biased, or mysterious. Sewall succeeded admirably. *The Life of Emily Dickinson* is a remarkable blend of exhaustive scholarly research with thoughtful and sensitive organization and editing, of thorough and painstaking documentation with a lucid, graceful, and highly readable prose style. Particular attention should be given to the final chapter of Volume 1, "The Dickinson Rhetoric and the Structure of a Life," and the final chapter of the book, "The Poet"; both are excellent, and deserve to be read with the same care and thoughfulness with which they were obviously composed. In addition, Sewall has buttressed his work with a comprehensive chronology, a substantial bibliography, and extensive appendices which often make as fascinating reading as the main text.

Sewall's approach is based upon his conviction that an artist must be understood in terms not only of his daily environment, but also of his cultural and moral or religious antecedents; he believes, in Goethe's words, that "nothing achieves meaning apart from that which neighbors it." The author's aim is thus twofold: to re-create in rich detail and realism Emily Dickinson's background and surroundings, and to illustrate how her peculiar genius was affected by them. The entire first volume is devoted to establishing the poet within a social tradition and a family framework; the lives and personalities of grandparents and parents are described, and the crucial relationships between members of Emily's generation are examined extensively.

The section "Forebears and Family" opens with a key chapter entitled "The New England Dickinsons and the Puritan Heritage" which gives thematic continuity to the entire work. Sewall identifies a cluster of traits central to the nineteenth century New England character, such as stamina, industry, ambition, thriftiness, and reticence, and shows how these traits were passed on from Samuel Fowler Dickinson's day into Emily's own. He also examines the strength of the Puritan influence—with its values of simplicity, austerity, and hard work; its view of life as a continual struggle between the embattled soul and worldly temptations; its tendency toward introspection and

constant use of interior monologue—on the Dickinson line. Peculiarly Dickinson traits were first apparent in Emily's grandfather Samuel Fowler, and were later to manifest themselves most strongly in his son Edward and his grandchildren Austin and Emily. One of these—also symptomatic of late Puritanism and responsible for the common accusation of hypocrisy—was a reluctance to be open about his personal life; Samuel Fowler and his descendants kept their own counsel, and shrank from exposing their emotional lives to outsiders.

In 1813 Samuel Fowler built the brick mansion that came to be known as the Homestead; it was here that Emily Dickinson was born, and here that she would spend the last thirty years of her life. Emily's grandfather was one of the most prominent figures in the Amherst, Massachusetts, community, and he founded Amherst Academy and Amherst College. In his total dedication and incredible capacity for work on the latter project, he exhibited another Dickinson trait—one which, in this case, led to his ruin. His ambition to complete his mission grew to such fanatical proportions that he neglected a profitable law practice to devote more energy to his project, and when public funds ran dry, he preferred to donate his own money rather than halt construction. Such zeal eventually brought Grandfather Dickinson to bankruptcy. In 1833 he was forced to sell his half of the Homestead (his son Edward had purchased the other half in 1830) and move to Ohio, where he died in 1838, "disillusioned, neglected, and forgotten."

The circumstances surrounding his

decline and death dramatize two more crucial Dickinson characteristics which shed light on Emily's life and personality. One is the propensity, shown in three generations of Dickinsons, for experiencing intense extremes of anguish and joy; the other is an unusually powerful attachment to home—in Sewall's phrase, "home-centeredness." There is no Dickinson on record who enjoyed extensive travel. There are several hints that Samuel's relatives felt some sense of responsibility and guilt for his death, probably realizing that, like a native plant, he withered when forcibly transplanted from his natural clime; but by the time of Emily's adulthood, the Homestead had become, psychologically and literally, an inviolable fortress.

After a fifteen-year stay in a house on North Pleasant St., Edward Dickinson moved his family back into the Homestead, where he, his wife, his two daughters, and to a great extent his son, were to spend the rest of their lives. Within the few years following the move, Emily's withdrawal from society became almost complete; the period also saw such significant changes in family patterns as those occasioned by the onset of the long illness of her mother, Emily Norcross Dickinson, and William Austin Dickinson's marriage to Susan Gilbert.

One of the most deeply rooted myths obscuring our understanding of Emily Dickinson's life is that which pictures the poet's father, Edward, as a domestic tyrant whose presence loomed large and formidable in the Homestead, creating a stifling atmosphere and preventing his daughter's healthy emotional growth. In dismantling this long-established fallacy,

Sewall—through a rich profusion of detail based on numerous and varied sources—shows us a very different man from the ogre of legend. Outwardly, Edward Dickinson was a typical, ambitious nineteenth century American, hard-working, success-oriented, and active in public affairs. But privately he was a lonely and melancholy individual; reserved and private to a fault, he was never understood, even by his family and friends. Emily came closest. She had some revealing insights into his character, as when she wrote that he lacked "the low, enjoying power" and that "he never played"; yet even she, in a moment of bewilderment, admitted, "I am not very well acquainted with father."

Edward was a good father, if aloof. He was strict, undemonstrative by nature, and never outwardly affectionate, but his care and constant concern for his children's welfare is evident from the personal records. As in any household peopled with bright children and a wide variety of personalities, there were clashes, but the children were far from cowed or fear-ridden. They sneaked books, considered too racy or radical for tender young minds, past Edward's watchful Puritan eye; and, far from being awestruck by their father's impressive position in the Amherst community, Emily and Austin loved to make mischievous jokes about his public image. Emily's tone as she grew older was most often one of fond playfulness—certainly not the sign of an oppressed spirit. However, after her father's death, which was a devastating blow to Emily, her attitude changed; the affection and whimsical joking was replaced by a mood of bleakness and regret. One probable explanation is that she suffered, in retrospect, from the thought that she might have brightened his life much more had she devoted more selfless and concentrated energy to the effort.

Most of the myths which do not blame an oppressive father for what is considered the "tragedy" of Emily Dickinson's life, attribute her withdrawal from society to any number of ill-fated love affairs. Various lovers have been claimed, the most common being Charles Wadsworth and Judge Otis Phillips Lord, described by a contemporary as "one of the very ablest men in this State." That Emily admired Rev. Wadsworth there is no question; but theirs was a friendship conducted almost solely through letters, and based upon shared religious feelings. In the light of later evidence, it seems highly possible that the rumor of a love relationship between the two was deliberately circulated by Susan in order to draw attention from the real affair with Judge Lord. Concerning the latter, very little is known, as might be expected given Emily's life of privacy and seclusion. There are hints that after Mrs. Lord died in 1877, Emily and Judge Lord considered the possibility of marriage, but such a union never came about. Following several years punctuated by periods of illness, Lord, eighteen years Emily's senior, died in 1884—only two years before the poet herself.

Of much more serious and far-reaching consequences than either her relationship with her father or her friendships with men was the unpleasant and often tense family situation examined at great length in the section entitled "War Between the

Houses." The situation was one that had tremendous impact on all those caught up in it, and the space Sewall devotes to its study is proportional to its importance in understanding Emily Dickinson's character and poetry.

Austin and Emily had been extremely close since childhood. They shared a sharp wit; a love of spirited discussion; a sense of humor sometimes sharply satirical, sometimes whimsical; and a confidential manner of communicating that amounted to a private language. Brother and sister held many intellectual concerns in common, among them being their lifelong preoccupation with cosmic questions and their overwhelming sense of the magnitude of death. When Austin married Susan Gilbert in 1856 and moved into the Evergreens, the house neighboring the Homestead, it seemed an ideal arrangement. Emily had been extremely fond of Susan, and held her in an esteem that amounted to infatuation; she approved of the match in spite of the gap in social standing involved, and encouraged Austin in his engagement.

Emily soon found that she had been totally mistaken in her judgment. Her own original intimacy with Susan all but vanished; signs of strain in the marriage appeared almost immediately. Austin had ardently hoped for a large family; as it turned out, he had three children. The pride of his life, his son Gilbert, died of a fever at age eight; he was never close to his eldest son Ned; and in the split that eventually developed, his daughter Martha was her mother's faithful and outspoken ally. Later testimony, albeit unproven as yet, claimed rather convincingly that Susan had a "morbid fear" of childbirth, and made repeated attempts—including four successful ones—at abortion. It soon became clear that Austin's and Susan's interests were incompatible. Promptly after the marriage, Susan set about establishing the Evergreens as the social center of Amherst, the closest thing to a salon in the Massachusetts community, and building a reputation as hostess to local and visiting dignitaries. Austin, ill-adapted by temperament for such a role, simply retreated from his wife's growing circle of guests, friends, and protégés.

Although Emily and her sister-in-law kept up a reasonably steady and friendly correspondence during their thirty years as neighbors, it is reported that at the time of young Gilbert's death in 1883, Emily visited the Evergreens for the first time in fifteen years; on the other hand, Austin spent nearly all of his leisure hours at the Homestead. Thus, family relations were in a dismal state at best when Mabel Loomis Todd entered the Dickinsons' lives in 1881. Austin and Mrs. Todd (twenty-seven years his junior) fell in love and embarked on a relationship of total confidence and intimacy that lasted until Austin's death thirteen years later. Their association was eventually the gossip of Amherst, and the town, in imitation of the Dickinson family, divided itself into two camps over the question of who was the villain of the drama—Susan or Mabel. Within the family, lines of loyalty were sharply drawn as the feud took on the dimensions of a war. The main antagonists were Susan, her daughter Martha, and sometimes her son Ned, against Austin, Mabel, Emily, and Lavinia Dickinson (Vinnie), who acted as go-between and director of correspondence for the lovers. The love relationship, while it meant everything to both parties, almost proved too great a strain toward the end for Mabel, and was probably at least partially responsible for Austin's unexpected death in 1895.

Whatever its emotional toll on the participants, the Todd/Dickinson affair had two results of crucial significance to the student of Emily Dickinson's poetry. First, we owe the very survival of the poetry to the tremendous talent and devotion of Mabel Loomis Todd, who, inspired by both her love of Austin and by her perceptive appreciation of his sister's genius, accomplished the almost impossible task of collecting, deciphering, sorting, editing, and publishing the poems. Second, in Mrs. Todd's voluminous and meticulous journal entries we have a source of information and insight into a situation which probably exerted a stronger, more constant pressure in the poet's life than any other—and which, owing to the Dickinson reticence, would otherwise have gone virtually unrecorded.

Nancy G. Ballard

THE LIFE OF EZRA POUND

Author: Noel Stock
Publisher: Pantheon Books (New York). 472 pp. $10.00
Type of work: Biography
Time: 1885–1969
Locale: United States, England, France, Italy

A full-length biography of America's octogenarian expatriate polemicist, propagandist, political prisoner, and internationally honored poet and critic

His friend and fellow poet William Carlos Williams once wrote of young Ezra Pound: ". . . not one person in a thousand likes him, and a great many people detest him . . . he is . . . full of conceits and affectation. . . . It is too bad, for he loves to be liked, but there is some quality in him which makes him too proud to try to please people." William Butler Yeats at first found him a "queer creature" and "a solitary volcano." Yeats's father reported that among young literary Americans whom he knew, Pound was thought "surly, supercilious and grumpy," though J. B. Yeats added, "I liked him myself very much. . . ." Richard Aldington once contrasted Pound the man as he knew him and Pound the author as he revealed himself in some of his early satiric writing: "Mr. Pound is one of the gentlest, most modest, bashful, kind creatures who ever walked the earth; so I cannot help thinking that all this enormous arrogance and petulance and fierceness are a pose." Wyndham Lewis in 1927 called Pound "a sort of revolutionary simpleton." A dozen years later Pound reminded the retired teacher-philosopher George Santayana of "several old friends (young, when I knew them) who were spasmodic rebels, . . . emulators of Thoreau, full of scraps of culture but lost, lost, lost in the intellectual world." Such impressions as these give a hint as to the vari-

ety of reactions that Pound has aroused in the many people who have known him.

A large part of Pound's long life has been marked by controversy ranging from personal disagreements and quarrels to violent opposition to the governments of the United States and England. The public expression of his strong political opinions over the Italian radio during World War II led to an imprisonment of nearly thirteen years, first in a military prison and then in a mental institution. A man of enthusiasms and obsessions, of quick affections and set prejudices, of wide-ranging intellect and many abilities, Pound is ranked among America's leading poets of the twentieth century and he seems sure of a continuing reputation based on the best of his work published in a writing career of sixty years. Pound has never achieved the great public recognition accorded Robert Frost or T. S. Eliot, but critics have long regarded him as one of the best of our modern poets and as a literary critic of considerable importance.

Pound was quick to recognize the capabilities or genius of such contemporaries as Yeats, Joyce, Williams, Frost, and Eliot. All of these except Eliot were older than Pound, but he did not hesitate to give them advice about their writing in conversation, through letters, or sometimes in print. When he might have been trying more diligently to promote his own career, he spent generously of his boundless energy in editing or suggesting improvements in manuscripts, discussing emendations or excisions, placing work with editors or publishers, and reviewing published work. Yeats, Williams, and Eliot were grateful for Pound's aid and Eliot dedicated *The Waste Land* to him. Joyce appreciated Pound's praise of his *Portrait of the Artist* and *Ulysses* but thought him not much of a critic when Pound disparaged *Finnegans Wake*. Frost was pleased when Pound favorably reviewed *A Boy's Will* in Harriet Monroe's magazine *Poetry*, but when Pound began to talk and act as if Frost were his discovery and protégé, Frost resisted and had nothing more to do with him. Frost did, however, join the group of famous writers who, in 1958, urged that the United States government release Pound from his long imprisonment in St. Elizabeth's Hospital in Washington, D.C.

Noel Stock, an Australian now living in England, has written two earlier books on Pound: *Poet in Exile: Ezra Pound* (1964) and *Reading the 'Cantos'* (1967). His *The Life of Ezra Pound* is packed with factual information drawn from a great variety of sources mentioned in Stock's preface. In addition to a number of books on Pound's life and work, Stock has had access to many unpublished materials, and he frequently refers to conversations with Pound, Mrs. Pound, and others. The arrangement of the biography is generally chronological, with inclusive dates given in the chapter titles, though there is occasionally a shifting back and forth in time as in the chapter on "The Cantos, 1930/1934," where it is necessary to go as far back as 1917 when the first cantos were pub-

lished, in order to relate them to the cantos of the 1930's.

Though Stock thinks highly of Pound and his accomplishments, he is no hero worshipper. He is appreciative of the beauty and artistry of Pound's best writing, particularly his poetry, but he does not hesitate to point out Pound's faults, sometimes citing Pound's own recognition of aesthetic errors, confusion of intent, and slipshod workmanship. ("Afraid," wrote Pound to his father about his *Cantos* in 1927, "the whole damn poem is rather obscure, especially in fragments.") Stock calls attention to Pound's "cool flute tone, issuing in matter-of-fact yet formal language, which I believe will be acknowledged eventually as the distinctive feature of Pound's main achievement as a poet." He quotes passages from many poems to illustrate Pound's skill in phrasing or the simple beauty of particular images or scenes. But of Pound's intended masterwork, the *Cantos*, published in parts from 1917 to 1960, Stock says:

At no stage was he clear about what he was trying to do and further confusion was added when in the wake of Joyce and Eliot he decided that his "epic" would have to be modern and up to date. Although he had no intellectual grasp of the work to be made he was determined nevertheless to write it. Thus persisting against the virtue of his art he lost any chance he may have had to pause and rethink the whole project and went on piecing together an endless row of fragments. Some cantos and some fragments contain high poetry and there is much that is humorous or otherwise interesting; but in so far as the work asks to be taken as a whole it verges on bluff.

Stock devotes a good deal of space to

Pound's critical writings printed in newspapers, magazines, pamphlets, and books in England, the United States, Italy, and even Australia (in a magazine edited by Stock). Much of the early criticism is literary, aesthetic, or cultural, and it is for such criticism that Pound is ranked as a critic. But a very different kind of criticism began to issue from Pound in the 1930's, and it was to become an obsession with him. He had become interested in economics and monetary history and theory. Especially fascinated by a monetary system based on "social credit," he began to advocate and expound the system, at the same time condemning what he called "usurocracy" which he saw as the basis of ill-gotten wealth in such capitalistic countries as the United States and England. The obsession with usury appeared in miscellaneous prose writings, in Pound's radio talks in wartime Italy, and even in his poetry, as in Canto XLV.

Stock holds no high opinion of Pound as an economic theorist. He pictures Pound in the mid-1930's as a man intellectually

> at the mercy of the pseudo-system of thought, which, with his rare zeal, he had manufactured out of . . . bits and pieces of information and learning. He had convinced himself that he possessed a method which enabled him to recognize the meaning of things without having to submit to any discipline or go through any process of abstract thought. . . . With a mind as brilliant as Pound's at work it was inevitable that some of the results should turn out to be stimulating and worthwhile. . . .

But, says Stock, Pound's method was not new. He did sometimes clarify or coordinate pre-existent information or ideas, but more often than not he suffered from "the ignorance of a man now imprisoned inside his own dreams of a better world."

Though one learns in the *Life* a great deal about Pound the man and his relationships with many people, he may be struck by the sudden, cryptic mention in Chapter XV of an attraction between Pound and a concert violinist, Olga Rudge, who bore a daughter Maria (later called Mary) in July, 1925, and left the baby to be cared for by an Italian peasant woman who had lost a child. Less than two pages later Stock mentions just as suddenly and as briefly the birth of Pound's son Omar to his wife Dorothy in Paris in September, 1926. Shortly afterward Omar was turned over to Dorothy's mother to be reared in England. Stock says nothing about Dorothy's reaction to the Pound-Rudge liaison that resulted in Mary's birth, nor does he comment on the seeming indifference of Pound and Dorothy toward the infant Omar. One gathers from later references to Miss Rudge that Dorothy was friendly toward her. As for the two children, they seem, so far as one can learn from Stock's later passages about them as they grew older, not to have resented the lack of interest their parents showed toward them when they were young. Pound did take an interest in Mary's education when she was a teenager living with her mother near the Pound home at Rapallo. He set Mary to translating a Hardy novel and some of his own poetry into Italian. He did not see Omar from 1926 to 1938, when he went to England to help settle the estate of his widowed mother-in-law, who had died in October. Stock leaves the impression that Pound was far less interested in seeing the boy than in giving dinner parties and in seeing a Noh play performed in a theater. Omar did not see his father again until 1945.

Apparently Stock has purposely left to future biographers the treatment of intimate family matters which might be embarrassing at present to those involved and still alive. It does seem paradoxical, though, that Pound, who busied himself condemning so many faults in others, should have cared so little for the two children he had fathered.

The Life of Ezra Pound is an important addition to the studies of Pound. Though it naturally covers much of the same ground as Charles Norman's *Ezra Pound* (1960), it gives a good deal of additional information. Stock's emphasis is primarily biographical rather than critical, but his views and evaluations of Pound's art and thought are sensible and stimulating. So far as the facts of "old Ez's" public life are concerned, it seems that not much of major importance remains for future biographers.

Henderson Kincheloe

Sources for Further Study

Reviews:

Nation. CCII, August 17, 1970, p. 122. 1,450 words.

National Review. XXII, September 8, 1970, p. 956. 1,500 words.

New Republic. CLXIII, October 17, 1970, p. 30. 1,700 words.

New Statesman. LXXX, August 7, 1970, p. 156. 1,700 words.

Saturday Review. LIII, July 18, 1970, p. 27. 3,150 words.

THE LIFE OF IVY COMPTON-BURNETT

Author: Elizabeth Sprigge (1900-   )
Publisher: George Braziller (New York). 191 pp. $7.95
Type of work: Biography
Time: 1884-1969
Locale: England

A brief biography of one of England's foremost novelists

Principal personages:
IVY COMPTON-BURNETT, British novelist
JAMES COMPTON BURNETT, her father
KATHERINE COMPTON-BURNETT, her mother
GUY AND NOEL, her brothers
MARGARET JOURDAIN, a close friend and companion
GRAHAM GREENE,
PAMELA HANSFORD JOHNSON,
ROSE MACAULAY,
VITA SACKVILLE-WEST,
HERMAN SCHRIJVER, and
ARTHUR WALEY, friends of the author
ROBERT LIDDEL and
RAYMOND MORTIMER, critics

Between 1911 and 1969 Ivy Compton-Burnett wrote twenty novels (one of which was published posthumously), and from the first, reviewers in such journals as the *New Statesman* and *The Times Literary Supplement* commented on her originality, wit, and truthfulness. In time she was accorded a place among England's greatest novelists, and prizes and honors were showered upon her. This biography by one of her close friends is an extremely summary introduction to the full and complicated life of this unusual writer. During her own life Ivy Compton-Burnett was considered enigmatic and her novels complicated and demanding. Elizabeth Sprigge has borrowed these traits and in some respects added complications. A vast amount is left unsaid, and the reader must strain to catch hints and allusions. Practically every chapter needs further develop-

ment. Major events, such as the double suicide of Ivy's two sisters, receive a half page of cryptic description and no discussion at all. The notorious experience of Margaret Jourdain's sister at Versailles receives a similar brief treatment. Suggestions are made about her literary antecedents, but there is no full discussion of the subject. Following the tradition of Ivy Compton-Burnett's own works, which were better received by reviewers and a small circle of admirers than the reading public at large, this biography will best be understood and welcomed by those who have already claimed her as their own.

Ivy's parents both came from the comfortable classes of English society. Her father's family, the unhyphenated Compton Burnetts, were an old landed southern English family with Scottish antecedents. Her mother's family, of Welsh ancestry, was also well-to-do. James Compton Burnett was educated in England and on the Continent and received medical degrees from Vienna and Glasgow. He set up a successful medical practice and married twice, Ivy being the eldest child of his second wife. It was her mother, the tyrannical Katherine, who added the hyphen to the family name in order to make it sound more impressive. The large, double family—James had five children by his first wife and seven by his second—was amply provided with butlers, cooks, nurses, and assorted lower orders of servants, but did not get on well together. Katherine considered the children of the first marriage inferior, since their mother was from a lower social level than herself, and they removed themselves from the household as quickly as they could. After their departure there is no further mention of them by Sprigge, though relations with Ivy's true brothers and sisters continued throughout their lives. In fact, Ivy's closest relations were with her brothers Guy and Noel and with their friends, rather than with other girls, and she was proud of the fact that she received a man's education, being tutored first at home and then eventually attending a branch of the University of London where she studied the classics.

Despite the comfort and security of her economic and social environment, disaster struck repeatedly in Ivy's early life. Her father died when she was seventeen and her beloved brother Guy only three years later. In 1911, when she was twenty-seven, her mother died, and Ivy was left in charge of the huge household which she so tyrannically handled that in 1914 all the remaining children packed up and moved elsewhere. Her other brother, Noel, to whom she was greatly attached, was killed in action in 1916. In the same year, the two younger sisters, one aged nineteen and the other in her early twenties, committed suicide, and their bodies were not discovered for several days. The shock of all these events is not discussed by the author, but the effect they had on Ivy must have been enormous, perhaps accounting for some of the anxiety she so frequently felt for her financial security, despite her successful publishing career and more than adequate private sources of income.

Unwilling to live alone, Ivy first set up home with Dorothy Beresford, her brother Noel's sister-in-law; and when Dorothy left to marry in 1919, the author had the good fortune to meet Margaret Jourdain through yet another friend of her brother's, Elliott Felkin. The two became close friends and lived together until Margaret's death in 1951. Margaret was from a gifted family and had already something of a literary reputation before the two met. She translated, wrote poetry and articles for various magazines, and eventually developed a specialty in furniture and decoration which brought her a steady income and which she willed to Ivy on her death. Both women were tyrannical, Ivy being once described by her brother as contemptuous of the human race, but they got along well with each other. Together they were a formidable pair as they presided stiffly (Ivy always in black) at their famous four o'clock teas where the *cognoscenti* of London literary and cultural life gathered. Starched and formal housekeepers announced the guests at the drawing room door and lateness was not tolerated. Newcomers were sometimes unnerved by Ivy and Margaret, though usually they recovered themselves quickly upon closer acquaintance. The novelist Olivia Manning describes her first encounter with them at a restaurant dinner:

> . . . The place was packed to the doors. I was very young, nervous and unimportant. Everyone else seemed a celebrity. Ivy was there with Margaret — they stood together, observing and, it seemed to me, talking to no one. They looked severe and unapproachable. As a pair they gave me the impression of close self-sufficiency.

Manners mattered profoundly to Ivy and she did not mind letting her disapproval become known. She went to extreme lengths to organize her busy life into predictable patterns and demanded that the rest of the world follow suit, which of course, it did not. She recoiled, with good reason, from wars, and had little interest in international affairs or foreign countries; she deplored people going to live abroad. She surrounded herself with her treasured possessions, her good furniture and ornaments, and loved making expeditions into the well-stocked shops of her comfortable Kensington neighborhood.

It was remarked by one critic that her books were full of "power, money and death," and certainly her interest in economic matters was significant throughout her life. Sprigge remarks in her introduction that "[m]oney was one of her favorite subjects" of conversation. She was disappointed by the poor sales of her many books and once wrote to her publisher, Victor Gollancz, to encourage him to push sales. Gollancz replied that pushing her books would not help in the least:

> In the case of a book like yours, "splash" advertising is not only useless (in the sense that it would not sell a single extra copy), but actually — in my experience — damaging, at the stage when there cannot be a single person who reads books at all who doesn't know that *Mother and Son* has been published, or what its quality is — it has had enormous splash reviewing, that one could not possible miss, in the *Sunday Times,* the *Observer* and *The Times Literary Supplement.* . . .

She worried about her income in her declining years and at one stage asked the Royal Literary Fund for assistance. Upon investigation it was discovered that her funds were more than adequate and in the end she was able to leave a large sum to her publishers for a new collected edition of her works.

Despite Sprigge's attempt to put down the belief that "Ivy is admired by a clique of self-satisfied intellectuals," she makes no real effort and offers no evidence to dispel this impression. Critically acclaimed from the time of the publishing of her first novel, she always remained a "writer's writer." Her early admirer, Raymond Mortimer, wrote:

> I can boast that I was one of Miss Compton-Burnett's earliest admirers. Though almost all my friends who are writers came quickly to share my enthusiasm, her reputation has taken a long while to expand. . . . She is in the first place "a writer's writer," be-

cause she is fascinated by words and phrases as such, juggling with them like a logician; and because no novelist has been less concerned to seem plausible. What we usually look for in novels, and what the great novelists have usually given us, is a picture of human beings talking and acting in a way we recognize as "like life." We are ready to accept fantasy and caricature, but Miss Compton-Burnett challenges us with creatures that might inhabit another, colder and more intellectual planet. . . . Indeed, the writers of whom she most reminds me are not novelists: they are Sophocles and Plato.

Such phrases as "[W]ell known to connoisseurs" or "For years the *cognoscenti* have considered Compton-Burnett one of the finest of living novelists" seem to have come naturally to her reviewers, and Sprigge does not discuss why the general reading public was never as enthusiastic about Ivy's novels as Ivy herself expected it to be.

The question of literary influences and antecedents is raised in a number of places. Sprigge suggests Henry James as one possibility although Ivy herself did not care for James. Jane Austen, Emily Brontë, and George Eliot were mentioned by the critics, and Ivy was inclined to allow some influence from the first, but considered Emily Brontë (along with E. M. Forster) overrated. The author's own choice is hard to determine, though the number of times she quotes reviewers who detected classical Greek influences might indicate a preference in this direction. On one occasion Ivy declared "The Greek dramatists I read as a girl, as I was classically educated, and read them with the attention to each line necessitated by the state of my scholarship; and it is difficult to say how much soaked in, but I should think very likely something." Her great themes of murder, incest, secrets, and power also suggested this as a likely source to many others. In an obituary printed in the *Spectator* one of her admirers wrote of her that

[s]he saw life in the relentless terms of Greek tragedy, its cruelties, ironies — above all its passions— played against a background of triviality and ennui. . . . [Death was a subject] never very far away in her books or, one may guess, in her imagination too. Nevertheless death, like everything else, is treated by her with a sense of proportion, an awareness that its threat is only for those who fear it. . . .

D. Brendan Nagle

THE LIFE OF LADY MARY WORTLEY MONTAGU

Author: Robert Halsband (1914–   )
Publisher: The Oxford University Press (New York). 313 pp. Illustrated. $7.00
Type of work: Biography
Time: 1689–1762
Locale: England, Turkey, Italy

A new and informing biography of the most famous blue-stocking of her day

Principal personages:
LADY MARY WORTLEY MONTAGU, nee Pierrepont
EDWARD WORTLEY MONTAGU, her husband
EDWARD MONTAGU, her dilettante son
COUNTESS OF BUTE, her daughter
ALEXANDER POPE
JOHN GAY
WILLIAM CONGREVE
HORACE WALPOLE
LORD HERVEY
FRANCESCO ALGAROTTI, an Italian adventurer
COUNT UGOLINO PALAZZI, an Italian adventurer and swindler

Perhaps the crowning irony of a long life not particularly marked by felicitous circumstance was that Lady Mary Wortley Montagu's seeming good fortune to have among her associates many of the leading social, political, and literary figures of her day proved to be her misfortune in the end. This is not to say that she is a personage whom biographers and literary historians have neglected; the brilliant wit and almost masculine vigor of her *Letters* would have dictated otherwise, as well as her secure place in the gallery of great English eccentrics. The truth of the matter is, however, that she has too seldom appeared as a personality in her own right and too often as a kind of appendage to the career of one of the greats and near-greats whom she encountered in her erratic orbit between the world of fashion into which she had been born, the diplomatic world of foreign travel into which she married, the turbulent world of letters to which her poems and satires were the password, and the lonely world of exile into which she retreated after twenty-seven years of married life.

A woman of genius overshadowed by her public legend, she is often remembered, not for what she did or said, but for what someone else said about her. Alexander Pope and Horace Walpole, two of the most malicious men of the time, are the true villains in the piece. After his flattering admiration had turned to sour hatred Pope reviled her constantly in his verse, sometimes openly, sometimes thinly disguised as Flavia, Lesbia, or the Sappho who left her suitors no choice but to be "pox'd by her Love, or libel'd by her Hate." Horace Walpole, who met her while traveling on the Continent, painted a portrait equally unflattering: "Her dress, her avarice and her impudence must amaze anyone that never heard her name. She wears a foul mob, that does not cover her greasy black locks, that hang loose, never combed or curled; an old maza-rine blue wrapper, that gapes open and discloses a canvas petticoat. . . ." Joseph Spence's estimate is more extravagant but more just: "Lady Mary is one of the most extraordinary shining characters in the world, but she shines like a comet; she is all irregular and always wandering. She is the most wise, most imprudent; loveliest, disagreeablest; best natured, cruellest woman in the world." Interestingly enough, the game of making fun of Lady Mary, the cruel sport of the great satirists and the mediocre hacks of her own time, has continued into the present; Edith Sitwell has described her as a "dilapidated macaw."

Robert Halsband's fascinating biography should do much to restore a proper balance in the contemporary estimate of a remarkable and probably misunderstood woman. His book is the result of long and scrupulous research, a scholarly work in every sense of the word, its material drawn chiefly from original sources and many not previously available, the whole presented without that display of professorial authority which makes so many books of this type a bore. The footnotes are there, the lists of references, and the indexes for those who wish them, but the material is presented in such lively and lucid fashion that the book still has its appeal for those who must read as they run. Best of all, Mr. Halsband's study is free from cant or slant. He allows his facts, carefully gathered, expertly arranged, to speak for themselves. He writes in his introduction:

If the reader feels that I have not sufficiently "interpreted" Lady Mary's character and personality, I can only plead that in the past she has so often been interpreted on insufficient, biased, or superficial grounds that it seemed to me most important to set down what facts I could discover; from these the reader can draw his own conclusion.

What of the facts? Born in 1669, the oldest daughter of Evelyn Pierrepont, later the Duke of Kingston, she grew into a lively, handsome, talented girl who seemed likely to make a brilliant match within her own circle. Instead, when she was twenty-three, after a stormy three-year courtship filled with sly nagging and false suspicions on the part of her future husband, she made a runaway marriage with Edward Wortley Montagu, a solemn, priggish man many years her senior, of whom her family could not approve. Wortley Montagu's ambition was for a career in politics, but when money and influence finally secured for him a post as ambassador to Turkey, he failed miserably in his diplomatic duties. Nevertheless, his two years in the British embassy at Constantinople gave his wife the material for some of the most vivid and entertaining of her letters. It was there that she took the precaution of having her young son innoculated against smallpox. Her marriage to Wortley Montagu seems to have bred indifference rather than infidelity or dislike, and she bore him a son who became an eccentric dilettante of a later generation and a daughter who became the wife of Lord Bute.

As the leading bluestocking of her day, Lady Mary gave her patronage to Henry Fielding, the country cousin who eclipsed her in literary fame, and associated on terms of equality with William Congreve, John Gay, Pope, and other literary lights of the time. To her contemporaries she was best known as a poet, mistress of a pen almost as acid-sharp as that of Pope himself. Mr. Halsband throws no new light on her famous quarrel with the waspish satirist of Twickenham. In one of his letters to her Pope had written: "It is not without vexation that I roam on the Thames in a fair evening or walk by moonlight in St. James's Park: I can scarce allow that any thing should be calm, or any thing sweet without you." But suddenly his mood changed, and in "To a Lady who father'd her Lampoons upon her Acquaintance" he began the series of brutal vilifications which he directed at her for the rest of his life. The cause may have been trifling, the parodying of his own poems that he himself described somewhat ambiguously as the borrowing of some of his sheets and returning them unwashed. Or it may be that he had made advances which Lady Mary could not accept with honor or which she had rejected with hearty humor. This may be the circumstance she had in mind when she wrote, "Too near he has approached who is denied."

The important new material in Mr. Halsband's book does much to clear up the mystery of Lady Mary's sojourn abroad between 1739 and 1762. It now appears that she became infatuated with a twenty-four-year-old Italian scientist and adventurer named Francesco Algarotti, described by Mr. Halsband as "a handsome young man of great charm and androgynous tastes." Infatuated, she wrote to him with the passionate entreaties of a lovesick, foolish girl, and for a short time London society was entertained by the spectacle of Lady Mary and her friend Lord Hervey, the noted politician and wit, contending for the affections of the same heartless young man. When Algarotti finally returned to the Continent, Lady Mary decided at last to follow him. This romantic gesture, like so many others in her unsettled life, came to nothing. She settled in Italy in expectation that he would join her, but Algarotti, in St. Petersburg at the time, met Frederick of Prussia on his return journey and remained a number of years at the German court. They met once in Turin and quarreled bitterly; her letter of reproach still survives. In Brescia she became the victim of another drawing-room adventurer, the sinister Count Ugolino Palazzi, who with his mother preyed on the eccentric Englishwoman and made her life miserable with their greedy demands, their quarrels and reconciliations. In 1761 Wortley Montagu died, and in the following year Lady Mary, as she said, "dragged my ragged remnant of life to England." Her return might have been a triumph of sorts for this indominatable old woman who had for years been a legend of the coffee houses and the tea tables, but she was already ill and died a few months later.

"General notions are generally wrong," said Lady Mary on one occasion. Mr. Halsband's lively and informing biography proves the truth of her statement, for his research into the particulars of this tempestuous life puts his subject into a completely new light. His book may well be the definitive biography. Unless new and significant material should come to light there will be little need for anyone else to repeat the story he has told so well.

THE LIFE OF LENIN

Author: Louis Fischer (1896-   )
Publisher: Harper and Row (New York). Illustrated. 703 pp. $10.00
Type of work: Biography
Time: 1870-1924
Locale: Tsarist and Soviet Russia

The biography of one of the most controversial and significant men of modern times by a writer who was personally acquainted with Lenin and many of his associates as well as the conditions and events that produced the opportunity for Lenin's emergence into greatness

> *Principal personages:*
> VLADIMIR I. LENIN, organizer of the second Russian Revolution and head of the Soviet state until his death in 1924
> LEON TROTSKY, Lenin's protégé on the revolutionary magazine *Iskra*, who deserted him for the Mensheviks
> GEORGI V. CHICHERIN, Commissar for Foreign Affairs, 1918-1930
> NIKOLAI BUKHARIN, Marxist theorist, revolutionary, and editor of *Pravda*, 1917-1928
> GENERAL ANTON I. DENIKIN and
> ADMIRAL ALEXANDER V. KOLCHAK, former tsarist officers who led counterrevolutionary forces against the Bolsheviks
> MAXIM GORKY, novelist and short story writer, a leading figure in Soviet cultural life
> LEO B. KAMENEV, Bolshevik revolutionary, trade expert, and commissar, 1918-1924
> ALEXANDER KERENSKY, Prime Minister of the Provisional Government from July to November, 1917
> NADEZHDA K. KRUPSKAYA, social worker, schoolteacher, Marxist revolutionary, and wife of Lenin
> KARL RADEK, the Polish-born Bolshevik who directed Communist efforts in Germany
> JOSEPH STALIN, a Bolshevik from Russian Georgia, Commissar for Nationalities, 1917-1922, and Secretary General of the Communist Party, 1922-1953
> GREGORY ZINOVIEV, Lenin's collaborator, and head of the Third International, 1919-1926
> ANATOLI LUNACHARSKY, a Machist opposed to Lenin's philosophy, later the Commissar of Education
> FELIX DJERZHINSKY, chief of the Cheka under Lenin
> GREGORY SOKOLNIKOV, an old-line Bolshevik purged in the Moscow Trials of the 1930's

After his several adquate analyses of Soviet affairs in *The Soviets in World Affairs* (1930) and *Russia, America, and the World* (1961), Louis Fischer, eminent journalist and historian, has now presented the life and times of the controversial and enigmatic Vladimir I. Lenin. Although Fischer's is the best of the three Lenin biographies to appear this year, including those of Stefan T. Possony and Robert Payne, it is still not the long-awaited, definitive life study of the founder of the Soviet republic. Fluent in spoken and written Russian before he traveled as an American journalist to Soviet Russia in the 1920's, Fischer became personally acquainted with Lenin, Trotsky, and Stalin. Even more than Fischer's firsthand knowledge, however, his thorough and open-minded research makes his work authoritative.

Most of the fifty-two roughly equal chapters tell the story of Lenin's last five years, when he organized the second Russian Revolution of 1917 and became the head of the Soviet state. It is no coincidence that Fischer's Russian experiences also were concentrated in that period.

In all too cursory fashion Fischer disposes of the essential influences exerted on Lenin in early life. Born Vladimir Ilyich Ulyanov in April, 1870, the son of a school administrator of Russo-Kalmuk background, Vladimir Ilyich received the social and educational advantages common to the child of a petty bureaucrat. Family environment instilled in him diligence and austerity, his most significant character traits. The death of Vladimir Ilyich's father in 1886 and the hanging of his older brother in 1887 for implication in a plot to assassinate the tsar left a lasting imprint on the youth.

Vladimir Ilyich's expulsion from the University of Kazan in 1887 because of his role in a mild student demonstration (contrary to Soviet historians, the demonstration was non-Marxist) resulted in exile to his grandfather's estate in Kazan province. After reading law and Marx voraciously, the young

man passed the law examinations in St. Petersburg, where in 1892 he was admitted to the bar and became an active Marxist revolutionary. His illegal political activities resulted in arrest and exile to Siberia in 1895. A prolific writer during his Siberian exile, Vladimir Ilyich also found time to import and marry Nadezhda Konstantinovna Krupskaya, a schoolteacher and fellow Marxist, whom he previously had met in St. Petersburg.

After his exile he traveled in Western Europe, where he was welcomed by colonies of Russian revolutionary exiles. In 1900 he and several high-ranking Russian Marxists founded *Iskra* (*The Spark*), a Russian-language magazine smuggled into Russia. Using many pseudonyms, he contributed numerous articles to the journal until in 1901 he selected Lenin, a name chosen, indicates Fischer, in remembrance of a high-school classmate named Lena.

Fischer's account of the Bolshevik-Menshevik rupture at the International Social Democratic Party Congress of 1903 is inadequate. There Lenin, with the aid of Georgii Plekhanov, the founder of Russian Marxism, gained for the Bolsheviks a momentary majority with which they secured adoption of their more violent program and the consequent removal of Mensheviks from the editorial board of *Iskra*. When Plekhanov later realized that he was being used by Lenin, he reinstated the Mensheviks. Resigning from *Iskra*, Lenin founded a new Bolshevik weekly, *Vperyod* (*Forward*).

In the Russian Revolution of 1905, the important role was played by Leon Trotsky, Lenin's former protégé on *Iskra*, who had deserted him for the Mensheviks. Events of 1905 threw into sharp contrast Trotsky, the man of appeal to the masses, and Lenin, the organization man. The moment was Trotsky's; Lenin's was yet to come.

The period between 1907 and 1917 was for Lenin one of theoretical development and prolific writing. His *Materialism and Empiro-Criticism* (1909) assailed bourgeois idealism and reaffirmed Marxist materialism; his *Imperialism, the Highest Stage of Capitalism* (1916) predicted the coincident demise of imperialism and capitalism.

Lenin's ten-year period of European exile ended in 1917. Hoping to weaken Russia's role in World War I, Germany allowed him and some Bolshevik colleagues to cross from Switzerland to the Baltic in a sealed railway car. Better than the Germans had hoped, Lenin crystallized Russian discontent against Kerensky's bourgeois-democratic Provisional Government, which had succeeded that of the Tsar Nicholas.

Fischer clearly demonstrates the close relationship between the war and the Russian Revolution: the anger of the army at the rotten tsarist regime and the indecisive Provisional Government; the success of Leninist propaganda to create anarchy among the soldiers and workers; the unrealistic pressure exerted by Britain, France, and the United States on Russia to remain at war; the Provisional Government's fruitless efforts to restore discipline to the army; and general war-fatigue and peace-hunger affecting military forces and civilians alike.

Lenin, the successful revolutionary and master of the Soviet state after the overthrow of the Provisional Government, "groped as everyone does in politics, cutting theory to match reality." In his *State and Revolution* (1917), Lenin declared that Russia was proving the truth of the theory that government would inevitably wither away once the workers had dethroned the class enemy and set up a national state. But under Lenin what began to wither away in Russia "was the idea of withering away." At first Lenin advocated obedience to the majority will expressed through a Constituent Assembly. When the Constituent Assembly majority went against him, however, he did not hesitate to seize power by force, without proof of majority support, and to disband the Assembly. Although the Bolshevik ideal of world revolution demanded prosecution of the class war in Europe, Lenin made at Brest-Litovsk a humiliating peace with Germany, whose military forces were dangerously pressing the young regime.

Fischer carefully and painstakingly traces the seismic pressure of events which conditioned the Bolshevik government during the critical years following the treaty of Brest-Litovsk. The terror carried out by the radical Left Social Revolutionaries, culminating in the attempt on Lenin's life, was ruthlessly suppressed. In the civil war, Western-supported forces opposing the Soviets at first seemed overwhelming, but the White Russian leaders were responsible for such cruel treatment of the peasants and other citizens and for such reactionary ideas as restoring lands to former landlords and reëstablishing control over subject nationals that the counterrevolutionary movement lost vital popular support. Mr. Fischer articulately contends that "when battles are fought in suburbs and wheatfields rather than on a fixed front, and when citizens can therefore choose sides, the real battlefield is in the minds of man, and that is where the tsarist generals lost the war and Lenin won it. They stood for the past. He handed out promissory notes on the future." Lenin built support for himself and for the Soviet state not only with "rifle, trowel, and whip," but also with his pen.

Lenin suffered many disappointing setbacks. His peace overtures to the Allies failed to prevent their intervention in Russia. Aid to German Communists failed to generate a successful revolution because, according to Fischer, "the workers and intellectuals did not believe in it, the farmers did not need it, and the army, middle class, and temperate politicians opposed it." Nor did the hoped-for Communist revolutions occur elsewhere in Europe, except for the short-lived Bela Kun regime in Hungary. Closer to Mother Russia than these was the disastrous "miscalculation" of the Polish campaign, which weighed heavily on Lenin's last years.

As the Soviet regime emerged victorious from the civil war and established a somewhat disadvantageous border with its neighbors, it could then face the monumental problem of reconstruction. Economic rapprochement with the West was necessary for Russia's recovery from the ruin of world war, revolution, and civil war. Internal reforms were likewise essential. The New Economic Policy expressed to the West the Soviets' peace-and-trade program; it was at home Lenin's two steps back toward capitalism from absolute state control. The program was intended to stimulate industrialization through state capitalism and to permit private farming and private retail trade to expand, as long as they did not pose a political hazard to the regime. Although subversive acts abroad by the

Third International, or Comintern, occasionally embarrassed the Soviets, both their foreign and domestic efforts during the era of the NEP generally were crowned with success.

The writer too often plays the "If" game, such as when speculating on whether Hitler's rise to power and the outbreak of World War II would have occurred if the Germans had not permitted Lenin to go to Russia in 1917. He also tries to oversentimentalize Lenin by recounting instances of his "private tenderness." Although Lenin may have had a velvet hand, the fact remains that he often "put on an iron glove" to cover it. Lenin denounced the growth of Russian bureaucratic tyranny and nationalism in the 1920's, but it was he who provided the opportunity for their development with his "scientific emancipation from ethics and morals, centralization, and total dictatorship." Fischer devotes more than justifiable attention to lesser figures such as Chicherin, apparently for the simple reason that he was close to them.

Fischer paints his portrait of Lenin with the hand of a skilled artist. Through accounts of interviews with Lenin and with many who knew the Soviet leader intimately, and through the effective utilization of the numerous memoirs of Lenin's associates, the author presents a clear view of the inner man. Lenin was dogmatic and irritated by opposition. His was the either/or-ism of an extremist behind an opaque nationalism. That he saw the world through "distorting Russian spectacles" accounts for many of his errors and false prophecies. Always willing to sacrifice ideology to political expediency, he enjoyed many successes. Lenin, austere by nature, hated waste and luxury. Although he "loved children—and cats," his capacity for friendship never overcame his propensity to use people too much. Yet many admired and loved him, as this biographical study clearly reveals.

The Life of Lenin received the 1965 National Book Award for history and biography.

John P. Posey

THE LIFE OF MAYAKOVSKY

Author: Wiktor Woroszylski (1927-   )
Translated from the Polish by Boleslaw Taborski
Publisher: Grossman Publishers, The Orion Press (New York: 1970). 600 pp. $15.00
Type of work: Biography
Time: 1893-1930
Locale: Moscow and St. Petersburg

A biography of Soviet Russia's major poet of the 1920's, told through selections from his contemporaries' memories, public documents, and articles from the press

Principal personages:
VLADIMIR VLADIMIROVITCH MAYAKOVSKY
LILA BRIK, Mayakovsky's great love
DAVID BURLIUK, painter, poet, leading futurist
MAXIM GORKI,
BORIS PASTERNAK,
VICTOR SCHLOVSKY, and
ILYA EHRENBURG, of the Soviet artistic world

Wictor Woroszylski's *Life of Mayakovsky* is an immense collection of materials relating to the composition of a biography of the major Soviet poet of the first half of this century. It is composed in the form now so fashionable for "biographies"—where relevant documents from the public press and state files, paragraphs from the memoirs of the subject's contemporaries, passages of autobiography and the subject's literary works, and letters of the subject to his friends or from them to him, are all edited by the biographer and pasted together into a scrapbook whose organization and "subtleties" of choice and editing are supposed to reveal the true lineaments of the central moments in the subject's life. The model, of course, is the *collage* in visual art and the eclectic-allusive verse of the early part of the century, best known to English readers in the *Cantos* of Pound and *The Waste Land* of Eliot. The form has a singular advantage for the author, it matches the evanescence of the historical moment and the similitude of a mind in the act of intuitive perception of the shape of events. A further advantage, though a dubious one, is that the *collage* of "found" objects, in this case the biographical material, relieves the biographer of the necessity of organized exposition, and, concurrently, of any commitment to an interpretation of the shape of events beyond what may or may not be implied by the possibly fortuitous selection and organization of the material.

That Woroszylski is clearly an admirer of Mayakovsky, including a preponderance of "defenders" of the poet over "attackers" in the chapters devoted to the attack on Mayakovsky's "bohemian individualism" made by the official literary organs of the State from 1927 to 1930, may be to his credit as instancing his reluctance to give in to the temptation of quasi-impartiality the form allows. But somehow the reader desires more interpretative discussion of the complicated issues at stake in these literary quarrels than the summary remarks from the biographer that precede each chapter. Such skeletal commentary as the one opening Chapter

33 gives little help to the reader. Woroszylski laconically says:

> In the period that Mayakovsky writes and stages *The Bedbug*, the literary group he is the leader of declines and dies. Mayakovsky breaks with New LEF and "grants amnesty to Rembrandt." Old enemies and those who shortly before were friends attack the poet.

Vladimir Vladimirovitch Mayakovsky was an artistic force in modern Russian literature too great to be easily assimilated into the "Proletarian Establishment" of the Soviet Revolution. His lyric intensity, the compelling rhetoric of his verse that combined Russian apocalyptic hope as embodied in Leninist Communism with his own denunciation of all natural limitations on human desire, that made the Bolshevik revolution, in his own words, *"my* revolution," and wrote his violent symbols and metaphors into the imagination of crowds of admirers in all classes of the new classless State, was too great an emotional and intuitive leap for the less daring of his literary contemporaries. And the attack on him in the years preceding his death was as violent as his own embrace of the revolutionary hope.

Mayakovsky was born July 7, 1893, to a family of impoverished lower gentry. His father and uncle were both foresters in the national service. At that time they were living at Bagdadi in Georgia. He was the only son of the family and was given every opportunity their provincial situation could afford. Schooling was poor and not easily available, but the family arranged for some private instruction. His mother's account of it, included in this book, does not make it sound very impressive. We may gather from the scanty information given here that Mayakovsky's lack of formal education was in some way a factor in his later literary direction.

In 1906 his father died and the mother took her two daughters and son to Moscow, where they lived poorly on a meager pension from the State. Before he was twenty, Mayakovsky had become involved with revolutionaries, the Social Democrats; he had been arrested three times, as documents from the files of the Tsarist police given in the book testify; and he had entered the school of Painting, Sculpture, and Architecture, with the intention of becoming a painter. In 1911 he met David Burliuk, his friend and mentor for the next ten years, who opened up for him the possibility of his true genius in poetry. Burliuk, well-to-do, painter and symbolist poet, well known in Moscow art circles, took the impoverished revolutionary under his protection and gave him the praise and the literary connections he needed.

Woroszylski quotes from Mayakovsky's autobiography:

> Today I wrote a poem. Or to be exact: fragments of one. Not good. Unprintable. "Night." Sretenski Boulevard. I read the poem to Burliuk. I added: written by a friend. David stopped and looked at me. "You wrote it yourself!" he exclaimed. "You're a genius!" I was happy at this marvelous and undeserved praise. And so I steeped myself in poetry. That evening, quite unexpectedly, I became a poet.

With Burliuk and his friends, Mayakovsky formed the first of his literary-artistic "movements," the Futurists (*Budyetlan* in Russian). Their manifesto, "A Slap to the Public's Taste," declared "Pushkin, Dostoyevsky, Tolstoy, etc., etc., must be thrown overboard from the steamer of the Present Time."

In 1913 Mayakovsky published his first volume, *I!* with illustrations by Tchekhrygin and Zhegin, and shortly thereafter purchased the yellow tunic which he made his personal emblem during the next years, wearing it even beneath his frock coat at public functions. His "tragedy," the monologue *Vladimir Mayakovsky* was produced December 2 of that year, creating quite a stir in St. Petersburg. The reminiscences of Lyvshits, Shklovsky, and Matyushin on the occasion all remark the poet's command of the evening and the audience as principal actor. "One heard only Mayakovsky's voice," Matyushin says. Pasternak, who also was present that night, says: "We all remember that close, mysterious, hot text . . . There was in it that impenetrable spirituality without which there is no originality, the infinity, opening from any point of life in any direction, without which poetry is only a momentarily unexplained misunderstanding."

It is precisely that "spirituality," that "infinity," that is found in Mayakovsky that this biography fails to communicate or include. We find it only in the poet's works themselves, available in several recent translations, the best of which is Haywood and Reavey's *The Bedbug and Selected Poems*. The translations in Woroszylski's *Life* would leave us wondering what besides his reading voice captured the Russian ear. But perhaps these translations have undergone a double change, from Russian to Polish, and then to English.

But why did the poet throw himself so totally into the revolution in 1917?

The materials included in the relevant chapters tell us nothing of the depths of the poet's mind, the attraction of the political not only on Mayakovsky, but the Russian artistic mind itself. The revolution was clearly a religious experience for Mayakovsky, an apocalypse that fulfilled Messianic hopes burning in Russian hearts for three centuries, since the spiritist *raskolniki* movements of the late seventeenth century. Why do Christs, icons, churches, domes, resurrection in the body, recur throughout Mayakovsky's art? On what did his mind brood, and what was the inner progression that motivated the outer manifestations of his life, the events of his career? This biography tells us nothing of those central things.

Of the outer events, there is a wealth of related materials offered us. The organizing of Mayakovsky's second art movement, LEF (Left Art Front) including several of the former Futurists, and the backers of a magazine by that name, occupies a chapter. Mayakovsky's trips abroad to France and the United States occupy a chapter each. But the ode on the death of Lenin, "Vladimir Ilyich Lenin," is given only one chapter, consisting of contemporary commentary on its reception, pro or con; while the ode, treating Lenin as a messiah-figure and meditating on a physical resurrection, much like the thought of Fedorov, marks a major turn in Mayakovsky's real life, his poetic life.

In December of 1925, Sergei Yesenin, Mayakovsky's fellow poet and rival for the public's affection, hanged himself. Mayakovsky wrote to his memory an impassioned lyric, "Sergeyu Yeseninu" in which he finds Yesenin's suicide a moral failure. Woroszylski quotes the conclusion of which this is the last word:

We must discover
> joy
>> in future days.

To die—
> in life
>> is not so hard.

To make life—
> harder by far.

During the next four years, Mayakovsky found it increasingly harder "to make life" or "to discover joy." He found the friendship of several women necesary to his hold on his art. He produced a large quantity of good work, including the ode on the twenty-fifth anniversary of the revolution, "Good!," the plays, *The Bedbug*, and *The Bathhouse*. But his hold on the official literary establishment evaporated.

Attacks on him began in *Izvestya* and other state publications. His literary group, LEF, dissolved, was reformed, and dissolved again. Mayakovsky then joined the official writers' organization, RAPP, the Russian Association of Proletarian Writers. He began to suffer from a throat illness that grew increasingly worse. And then in 1930, he celebrated his twenty-year jubilee with a retrospective show of his art. Many old friends had turned against him, and he felt deeply his loneliness. He published "At the Top of My Voice" as an address to posterity, and wrote a scenario, *Moscow in Flames,* for the anniversary of the 1905 revolution.

On April 14, 1930, the poet was in deep depression. He was unable to persuade Veronica Polonskaya to remain with him in their apartment as she had a rehearsal at the Moscow Arts Theater. She writes:

> I went out, walked a few steps to the front door. I heard a shot. My legs gave way under me, I began to shout and rave about the corridor; I should not make myself open the door to the room.

Boris Pasternak remembered the last sight of him:

> He was lying on his side, face to the wall, stern, big, under the sheet reaching up to his chin, with his mouth half-open, as if asleep. Proudly turned away from everyone, even lying here, even asleep thus, he was stubbornly tearing himself away and going somewhere.

Rollin A. Lasseter

THE LIFE OF SAMUEL JOHNSON, LL.D.

Author: Sir John Hawkins, Knt. (1719-1789)
Edited by Bertram H. Davis
Publisher: The Macmillan Company (New York). 341 pp. $5.95
Type of work: Biography
Time: 1709-1784
Locale: England

A useful and interesting biography of Johnson, which has been for too long eclipsed by Boswell's greater work

Principal personages:
> SAMUEL JOHNSON, author, critic, lexicographer, and table-talker
> MICHAEL JOHNSON, his father
> SARAH FORD JOHNSON, his mother
> GILBERT WALMESLEY, a cultured older friend in Lichfield
> ELIZABETH JERVIS JOHNSON ("TETTY"), the widow, Mrs. Porter, whom Johnson married in 1735
> EDWARD CAVE, a London bookseller and publisher
> DAVID GARRICK,
> JAMES BOSWELL,
> SIR JOSHUA REYNOLDS,
> DAVID HUME, and
> OLIVER GOLDSMITH, members of the "Johnson Circle"
> HENRY THRALE, a Southwark brewer, and
> HESTER LYNCH THRALE, his wife, close friends of Samuel Johnson for almost twenty years

Sir John Hawkins has been one of the most unfortunate of literary men. In 1787 he published what was probably the best and most comprehensive biography of a man which had ever been produced up to that date, only to have his work put into a nearly total and permanent eclipse by another, and far better, biography of the same man which appeared four years later. After Boswell's *Life of Johnson* appeared, almost no one has wanted to read Hawkins. Since the second edition of 1787 his book has remained out of print until Professor Bertram Davis rescued it this year.

Mr. Davis, previously author of a study of Hawkins' *Life* called *Johnson Before Boswell*, has reprinted this very useful and interesting book, made it more useful by correcting certain minor errors of fact and supplying information in places where Hawkins had been reticent (though reticence is by no means a characteristic of the book), and by editing out Hawkins' various irrelevant and self-aggrandizing asides on subjects of particular interest to himself. The editing is skillful, scrupulous, and unobtrusive. Hawkins, at last, has received not merely justice but something better. His book was not so good as it is now. The question which remains is exactly how good a book it is.

In its historical context it is a very good book, indeed. Biography as a scientific art could hardly be said to have begun when he wrote. Such works of biographical interest as Plutarch's *Lives,* Walton's *Lives,* and even Johnson's *Lives of the Poets* were far from exact, factual biographies. The usual form of biography was the short, interpretive "Life," not the fully detailed study which we associate with the word "biography." Thus, in giving us a book-length view of Johnson, Hawkins was something of a pioneer. As Johnson's executor, he had access to diaries and other private papers which gave him an unusually intimate view of his subject, and as a long-standing friend he could add personal reminiscence and direct observation to his written sources. He was not, however, a genius. Boswell had as much material in letters and additional sources as Hawkins did, and he also had personal observations of Johnson to work into his text. His genius for recording and re-creating scenes, for bringing moments and characters to life, made his work inevitably superior to Hawkins'.

The main value of Hawkins' book, then, may be said to lie in his treatment of those parts and aspects of Johnson's life which Boswell did not have personal knowledge of, and a secondary value may be found in the difference between his attitude and Boswell's. Hawkins is a good deal further "this side idolatry" than Boswell. In fact, he seems at times deliberately attempting to redress a balance and cut Johnson down to size. This attitude, more in keeping with the spirit of our age than with the Age of Johnson, should endear him to the twentieth century if anything could.

The parts of Johnson's life which Hawkins knew better than Boswell are the early days and the last moments. Hawkins met Johnson before Boswell did and his documentary sources for Johnson's early days as a journalistic hack in Grub Street were excellent. (For Johnson's youth and schooling, however, there is no substitute for Pro-fessor James Clifford's *Young Sam Johnson,* published a few years ago.) His presentation of Johnson's relationship with the printer, bookseller, and editor of the *Gentleman's Magazine,* Edward Cave, is one of the best things in the book—accurate, informative, and lively.

After covering Johnson's youth and his career as Cave's man, Hawkins proceeds to follow the life of Johnson chronologically, centering his chapters on the major works produced in the years covered. Thus we find grouped material on his essays—the *Rambler, Idler,* and *Adventurer*—a chapter centering on the *Dictionary,* one on the *Shakespeare,* one on the *Lives of the Poets.* (The chapter divisions are actually Mr. Davis', but they merely emphasize Hawkins' own plan.) In these chapters one of Hawkins' real weaknesses as a biographer emerges. He was incapable of appreciating Johnson's literary work. He consistently underrates Johnson's performance as an editor and critic. He dismisses the *Shakespeare* in a few lines as an inadequate job which Johnson tried to recoup in the "Preface." This attitude persists in Hawkins' criticism of the *Lives of the Poets,* in which he accuses Johnson of being too harsh a critic, deliberately trying to spoil flourishing reputations.

Where Hawkins comes to life and gives us material which is absolutely invaluable is in the last days of Johnson. These he chronicles minutely, in the fashion of a diary, and even occasionally preserves the exact words of conversations in a Boswellian way. In his last terrible illness Johnson fought with enormous vigor against death. No pain involved in the rude medical treatments of the time was too much for him to bear if it held any hope for extending his life. At the same time he refused narcotics, not wanting to meet his Maker in a drugged state. Hawkins records some of his last words, during a painful scarification for dropsy: "Deeper, deeper;—I will abide the consequence: you are afraid of your reputation, but that is nothing to me." To those about him, he said, "You all pretend to love me, but you do not love me so well as I myself do." In moments like these the sense of overpowering reality is truly vivid and moving. But these moments are all too few in this biography. It will never be anything but a supplement to Boswell, but for those who do want to go beyond Boswell it will be indispensable.

THE LIFE OF THE MIND IN AMERICA

Author: Perry Miller (1905–1963)
Publisher: Harcourt, Brace and World (New York). 338 pp. $7.50
Type of work: American intellectual history
Time: 1776–1860
Locale: United States

A study of the intellectual life in America between the Revolutionary and Civil Wars

Perry Miller died before he could finish *The Life of the Mind in America,* and the present work is only a fragment of the projected nine books he had planned. Miller completed two and one half books in this volume: one on "The Evangelical Basis," a second on "The Legal Mentality," and an unfinished third book on "Science—Theoretical and Applied." According to the published outline, in the unwritten books he intended to discuss education, political economy and associations, philosophy, theology, nature, and the self.

In some respects Miller's magnificent project resembles Vernon L. Parrington's *Main Currents in American Thought,* which was also interrupted by the untimely death of the author. But where Parrington concentrated only on literature and politics, Miller dealt with a whole range of topics; and where the former imposed upon American thought a simple categorical scheme of liberalism versus conservatism, the latter avoids projecting a central ideological theme upon the multivarious contours of American intellectual history. Earlier, when Miller devoted much of his life to the study of American Puritanism, he rightly focused upon theology as the organizing principle of his investigations into seventeenth century American thought. In the nineteenth century, however, no clear, articulated system of thought had emerged to replace theology. To lesser historians, American thought in the nineteenth century is an organizational nightmare. To Perry Miller it was a challenge that had to be met, a challenge only he could master.

The first book of *The Life of the Mind,* a penetrating study of the religious history of the early nineteenth century, offers the provocative thesis that American revivalism cannot be understood solely as a response to Enlightenment rationalism. The anxiety that unsettled American thought was not simply the threat of European social radicalism and spiritual infidelity. Rather, the "Second Great Awakening" of the 1830's was as much a product of the changing structure of American society and the latent quest for community. Miller also sees parallels between the revivalism of the Jacksonian era and the period of Jonathan Edwards in the previous century. Both stressed the need for releasing the "affections" and making the heart a higher realm of value and knowledge than the mind. But aside from the epistemological similarity, Miller notes that Puritan revivalism fed on the thirst for individual salvation, whereas the later revivalism had distinct communal overtones. This "mystery of communion" would later make the nineteenth century religious impulse sympathetic to utopian socialism. Miller is intrigued by the comparisons between the popular revivalist, Charles Grandison Finney and the unpopular theologian, Jonathan Edwards. Like Edwards in the eighteenth century, and, incidentally, like some counter-culture missionaries of the twentieth century, Finney called upon his followers not to reason their way to salvation but simply to act: "Don't wait for feeling, DO IT." Although Finney's camp meetings did not become orgies of sheer emotion, his defense of feeling over reasoning and imagination over demonstration caused an uproar among such staid, fundamental schools as Princeton and Yale. The essence of Finney's argument, one that appealed to tens of thousands of believers who turned out at gatherings up and down the Ohio valley, held that "excitement qua excitement was justification enough." Yet the phenomenon of Finneyite revivalism, which directly or indirectly influenced a wide array of reform movements, including abolitionism, was not a species of Jacksonian anti-intellectualism. Finney may not have grasped Edwards' delicate balance of mind and emotion, but he strongly believed, according to Miller, that he was "preserving the intellect— 'consciousness'—from corruptions that had been foisted upon it. . . ." No other American historian has been as concerned about the problem of consciousness as Perry Miller. Small wonder, then, that Finney takes his place besides Edwards and Emerson as one of Miller's intellectual heroes.

In a chapter titled "Unity Through Diversity," Miller displays again, as he did in so many other works, his subtle feeling for irony. In the context of European history, the achievement of religious liberty in America could be regarded as a radical triumph. Yet, Miller observes, religion in America became a conservative force. For the church in America, unlike that of Protestant or Catholic Europe, believed that a greater unity could be achieved through a diversity of creeds, that dissent could nourish truth, that community could be made compatible with individuality, and that nationalism, a secular faith, was an expression of America's sense of mission. With an even greater perception of irony, Miller describes how the religious impulse toward public benevolence externalized religion, leading to "the idea that the action of mind upon objects outside itself is the sole stimulant of vital religion." The emphasis on the practical side of religion tended to transform religion "from an excitement into a job," so that the original spiritual vision of "sublimity" became "transmuted into mere efficiency." The Revival, Miller wryly notes, "was confronted with a metaphysical antinomy it had no equipment for resolving." Revivalists not only confused the realm of thought with the realm of action; they also confused the role of the church with the role of the state. Somehow the experience of religion became identified with the destiny of America, and revivalists called upon Americans to purify their hearts in order to preserve the Republic. Once again it was Miller's sense of irony and paradox that enabled him to perceive how a radical impulse yielded a conservative instinct.

Book Two on the legal mind begins with a learned discussion of James Fenimore Cooper's *The Pioneers,* which depicts the heroic man of nature coming into conflict with the laws of civilization. The drama of Natty Bumppo pitted against Judge Temple serves to introduce the whole subject of law in the nineteenth century. But after discussing the rise of the legal profession, Miller's subsequent chapters on common law, equity, legal rhetoric, church versus state, inductive versus deductive jurisprudence, and the concept of law as science all tend to focus on the most minute detail and the most obscure cases. Miller's insistence on specificity and his intricacy of argument is nowhere better revealed than in these chapters, but the larger significance of each chapter had not yet crystallized in this posthumuous work. Far more illuminating is Miller's discussion of law and morality, the concept of property, and the ideas and values of Justices John Marshall, Joseph Story, and Roger Taney. Miller explains how American theorists, originally defenders of a neutral, rationalist scholarship of law, lose their grip and become defenders of a law that finds its justification in Americanism and Christianity. The quest for the law's purpose had not been pursued in American legal thought, notes Miller. Thus law became a "definition by negation," an instrument used only to confine the area of freedom against the encroachments of the state. Instead of using law as a positive instrument, American legal thinkers became so fearful of abolitionist excesses that they condoned anti-abolitionist mobs and thus lost the ability to preserve the Union through the legal institutions to which they are so dedicated.

In the final and unfinished section on science, Miller discusses the gradual impact of technology upon American life and thought. From the beginning of the Republic, America had been committed to science, which was part of the Newtonian climate of opinion. In the minds of Franklin and Rittenhouse,

the method of science was regarded as synonymous with the method of thought itself, and as a result speculative as well as inventive science flourished in early America. Particularly influential was astronomy, which seemed to require no exertion of the mind other than passive contemplation. The craze for cataloguing also became part of America's scientific temper. Refuting De Tocqueville, Miller holds that democracy did not make America "inherently suspicious of science," partly because Americans could take pride in the cosmopolitan culture which science promoted. The concept of "benevolence," which runs through Miller's treatment of religion and law, also emerges in the area of science. To the dismay of Thoreau and other Transcendentalists, the American public accepted labor-saving machinery not merely as profit-making instruments but as devices of human and moral progress. Americans believed the machine was compatible with piety and that the factory "was a victory for pure science and not a degradation of the mind."

Perhaps it is fitting that Miller's unfinished work ends on this note. For Miller had been deeply troubled by the conflict of intellect and technology, and in his later years he had called for a reassertion of the individual mind in the face of a numbing civilization of machines. In contrast to the machine, the mind offers ethics, beauty, purpose, and freedom—values which Miller wanted to see preserved. Had Perry Miller finished this beautiful skeleton of a book, he may have been able to resolve one of the greatest dilemmas facing modern man.

John Diggins

LIFE STUDIES

Author: Robert Lowell (1917-   )
Publisher: Farrar, Straus and Cudahy (New York). 90 pp. $3.50
Type of work: Poetry

In a volume that is an autobiography in poetic episodes, Robert Lowell presents his friends, his relatives, and himself

Robert Lowell's *Life Studies* might be described as sprightly and intense, adjectives intended to be highly complimentary in these days when the E. E. Cummingses are few and far between and most poets are as gloomy as the dark doom they foresee for mankind. Lowell is not only sprightly but also understandable, a virtue lacking in many modern poets. If the reader is looking for a complicated philosophy and great depth of feeling, he will not find it in Lowell's short volume; but if he wants to be entertained by a sharp and playful mind, then Lowell is the poet.

Life Studies is aptly named, for this is a book filled with people ranging all the way from writers like George Santayana and Hart Crane to Lowell's fascinating relatives and friends like Uncle Devereux Winslow and Commander "Bilgewater" Harkness. The chief character, however, is Robert Lowell himself: *Life Studies* is really an episodic autobiography which employs both prose and poetry to reveal the personal life and poetic career of a young man who has undoubtedly undergone great emotional crises but who never whimpers in self-pity. And as a craftsman, Robert Lowell, in *Life Studies,* comes forth as a poet with a keen eye, a painter's flair for portraiture, a witty outlook, and a tender (if somewhat restrained) compassion for his companions in this jittery twentieth century.

As a background for more personal matters to come, Lowell devotes Part One of his volume to what might be called historical events. In "Beyond the Alps" he describes with great verve the confusion in modern Italy, a country which has, against its fabulous historical backdrop, recently produced a Mussolini and a Pope who, after making "Mary's Assumption dogma," listened to the cheers of the crowd gathered outside the Vatican, meanwhile calmly shaving himself with an electric razor. "The Banker's Daughter" is Marie de Medici, who speaks from the tomb concerning the assassination of her husband, Henry IV. Lowell next turns to Inauguration Day in 1953, which in New York (where the narrator had viewed Grant's Tomb) was cold and snowy. The poem ends with these lines:

> Look, the fixed stars, all just alike
> as lack-land atoms, split apart,
> and the Republic summons Ike,
> a mausoleum in her heart.

The last poem in Part One is presented as the words of "A Mad Negro Soldier Confined at Munich"; the reader enters a confused mind which rebels against the sterile routine forced on a mental patient and which remembers most pleasantly the "electric shock" the soldier had experienced while making love to his German girl friend.

In Part Two, when Lowell moves into poetic prose in order to sketch his childhood and young manhood, the result is less successful than his compact and evocative poetry. Lowell writes narration well enough, but the reader has already come to expect something far better. His prose, when compared with the same sort of writing by Dylan Thomas, for instance, finishes far down the track, a poor second or third. The reader does, however, meet some sharply drawn characters: Lowell's father, a frustrated man who gave up his naval career for a series of business failures; his mother, who constantly engaged in verbal tiffs with her husband, tiffs which the young Lowell overheard, seemed to expect, and actually came to enjoy; and other folk like Commander "Bilgewater" Harkness, whose weird social graces were almost as embarrassing to this proper Bostonian family as the antics of Amy, another Lowell with leanings toward poetry. One of the things Robert does best in this prose part is to reproduce the excruciating naval jargon that his father and his cronies worked into their conversation. A sample from this same Billy "Bilgewater" Harkness while in the presence of Father and Robert will serve as an example:

"So this is the range-finder you are raising for future wars!" They would make me salute, stand at attention, stand at ease. "Angel-face," Billy would say to me, "you'll skipper a flivver."

"Angel-face," without actually saying so, makes the reader feel that such verbal gaucherie sounded like the screeching and grating of an anchor chain to the ears of a young boy already developing a feeling for words.

But all in all, Part Two, which is called "91 Revere Street," seems an unnecessary inclusion, particularly so when the reader finds many of the same characters and incidents re-created in later poems.

In the next section Lowell pays trib-

ute to four literary men he has known. They are Ford Madox Ford, who was the unorthodox sort of man who "used a niblick on the green"; George Santayana, that great unbeliever who was bedeviled in his declining years "by those geese-girl sisters" praying for his soul (Lowell has Santayana come up with the line: "There is no God and Mary is His Mother."); Delmore Schwartz, with whom Lowell had literary discussions and drinking bouts at Cambridge in 1946; and Hart Crane, the tragic homosexual genius whom Lowell seems to feel was the Shelley of his age. Lowell is extremely effective in these poems, for they are not blunt "character sketches" but subtle, oblique glimpses into the lives of four fellow writers.

Lowell winds up *Life Studies* with Part Four, which again presents, and in more memorable fashion, Uncle Devereux, his grandparents, and his parents. The longest and best of these poems is "My Last Afternoon with Uncle Devereux Winslow"; this favorite uncle died at twenty-nine and Lowell ends his moving poem about a little boy at play and a dying man with these lines:

He was animated, hierarchical,
like a ginger snap man in a clothes-
    press.
He was dying of the incurable Hodg-
    kin's disease. . . .
My hands were warm, then cool, on the
    piles
of earth and lime,
a black pile and a white pile. . . .
Come winter,
Uncle Devereux would blend to one
    color.

Toward the end of *Life Studies* the reader discovers that Lowell was evidently a conscientious objector during

World War II (a biographical check reveals that he spent five months in a federal prison), later became a teacher, and then spent some time in what he calls "the house for the mentally ill." At this point the reader may start speculating on the origins of this book. Could it be that it was written (especially the prose part about his childhood) because a doctor suggested that he get the whole business out of his system? No portion of the book is in any way clinical (and the last poem is a charming irrelevancy called "Skunk Hour"), but the "get-it-out-of-your-system" idea may persist in the reader's mind. If this theory is true, then *Life Studies* is probably the finest, the most delightful book ever written on the advice of a physician.

The book received the National Book Award for poetry in 1960.

Sources for Further Study

Criticism:

Hollander, John. "Life Studies," in *Poetry*. XCV (October, 1959), pp. 41-43. Hollander finds *Life Studies* less spectacular than its predecessors but just as moving.

Rosenthal, M. L. "Life Studies," in *Nation*. CLXXXIX (September, 1959), pp. 154-156. *Life Studies* is not merely a collection of small victories over hysteria and self-concealment, says Rosenthal, but also a beautifully articulated poetic sequence.

Reviews:

Atlantic. CCIV, July, 1959, p. 76. 550 words.

Commonweal. LXX, July 3, 1959, p. 356. 700 words.

New Republic. CXL, June 8, 1959, p. 17. 850 words.

New Statesman. LVII, May 2, 1959, p. 614. 750 words.

Yale Review. XLIX, December, 1959, p. 303. 600 words.

THE LIGHT AROUND THE BODY

Author: Robert Bly (1926–   )
Publisher: Harper and Row (New York). 62 pp. $2.25
Type of work: Poetry

A second book of poems and winner of the 1967 National Book Award by a highly controversial figure

The relatively short but hectic career of this young Minnesotan began quietly enough with modest praise of his first book of poems, *Silence in the Snowy Fields,* in 1962. Prior to this time, however, we had encountered—rather, been bumped into—by Bly's rambunctious magazine, *The Fifties* (since become *The Sixties*) in which he published several deserving North American poets and undertook a program of exposing our public to the leading poets of Spanish-speaking countries. But what began to emerge centrally in Bly's career was his *personality,* which compelled this man of immense energy and ambition to spend years in literary politicking, so that by arrogant, half-baked, and high-handed attacks on the poetic practices of Eliot, Pound, Tate, and the literary Establishment in general, he had achieved a notorious prominence all out of proportion to his talent, which until the past four years showed very small hope.

An instance of his brand of snobbery are these lines from the jacket of his book: "He lives on a farm. . . . He does not farm his land and by choice has stayed away from teaching, believing that a poet is best off outside the university." One might ask what kind of farmer is it that does not farm, and what kind of writer is it who depends upon university audiences but scorns the academies? Himself a Harvard man and a darling of the Establishment, Bly has decided to bite all the hands that feed. In September of 1967 he refused a grant offered by the Foundation of Humanities and Arts in Washington, wrote an attack on the recent work of James Dickey, who was at the time consultant at the Library of Congress, and in March of 1967 threw the National Book Awards meeting into a dramatic uproar by an act of defiance against the United States' role in Vietnam. He declared that we had no reason to be proud of our own culture when at the same time we were "murdering" one at least as fine as ours.

Against this dark sky of our contemporary storm the cultural and political poetry of Robert Bly may be seen most clearly, in flashes of protest which are often vivid as lightning. At their best, Bly's political attacks are both imaginatively and morally on target. The poem "Johnson's Cabinet Watched by Ants" is both politically brave and poetically sound. It is a powerful indictment and a very solid reason for the poet's much deserved prominence at this moment, in contrast with his earlier bombastic and reckless attempts to come into the public light:

1

It is a clearing deep in a forest: over-
    hanging boughs
Make a low place. Here the citizens we
    know during the day,
The ministers, the department heads,
Appear changed: the stockholders of
    large steel companies
In small wooden shoes: here are the gen-
    erals dressed as gamboling lambs.

2

Tonight they burn the rice-supplies; to-

morrow
They lecture on Thoreau; tonight they
move around the trees,
Tomorrow they pick the twigs from
their clothes;
Tonight they throw the fire-bombs, tomorrow
They read the Declaration of Independence; tomorrow they are in church.

3

Ants are gathered around an old tree.
In a choir they sing, in harsh and
gravelly voices,
Old Etruscan songs on tyranny.
Toads nearby clap their small hands,
and join
The fiery songs, their five long toes
trembling in the soaked earth.

Stanza 2 is brilliant in its passionate
ironic juxtapositions.

A few titles will serve to underline
Bly's compulsive emphasis: "Listening
to President Kennedy Lie about the
Cuban Invasion," "The Great Society," "Three Presidents," "The Current Administration."

It is not often that a "protest" poem
can be wrought of such adamantly
durable stuff as the furiously grotesque
"Counting Small-Boned Bodies," which
deserves to be printed in full:

Let's count the bodies over again.

If we could only make the bodies
smaller,
The size of skulls,
We could make a whole plain white
with skulls in the moonlight!

If we could only make the bodies
smaller,
Maybe we could get
A whole year's kill in front of us on
a desk!

If we could only make the bodies
smaller,
We could fit

A body into a finger-ring, for a keep-
sake forever.

This poem is even more simple and
terrifying in its moral implications
than Henry Reed's famous and fine
poem "Naming of Parts." The horror,
skillfully understated, arises from the
same impulse that led earlier Americans to bind the Holy Bible in the skin
of a dead Indian. One may suggest that
Bly's poem has the chance to live
longer than Reed's.

Bly's sharp-eyed satire, as in "The
Executive's Death," is a telling footnote to the large texts of psycho-
sociological comment on urban stultifi-
cation, paralysis, decay, loss of dream:

Commuters arrive in Hartford at dusk
like moles
Or hares flying from a fire behind
them,
And the dusk in Hartford is full of
their sighs;
Their trains come through the air like
a dark music . . .
Meanwhile, high in the air,
executives
Walk on cool floors, and suddenly fall:
Dying, they dream they are lost in a
snowstorm in mountains,
On which they crashed, carried at night
by great machines . . .

Such a passage is strong enough to
be a legitimate heir to Hart Crane's description of the young accountant on
Wall Street who dreams of ships sail-
ing across the pages of his figures to be
filed away "Till elevators drop us from
our day." And the common elements
Crane and Bly share are not merely in
imaginative accuracy but in the basic
sympathy and regret for the city
dweller.

Less successful, yet still pertinent is
the satiric device in "The Busy Man

Speaks" of letting the truly busy American have enough literary rope to hang himself. The busy American denies solitude, love, conversation, art, sorrow, and declares he is a man of steel, "the steel of money." One recalls Roethke's "I run to the whistle of money." Another fine poem, "Watching Television," underscores deftly all the recent journalistic controversy over our national saturation with the incredibly immediate violence of filmed "news."

But after praising Bly for what he does most strongly, even truly sympathetic critics have found many crows to pick with him.

Certainly Bly is guilty of fabricating *easy* images, but worst of all, preposterous images. For example:

> There is a joyful night in which we
>   love
> Everything, and drift
> Like a radish
> Rising and falling . . .

This image of the radish, so totally out of place, results from the influence on Bly of the Spanish surrealists, some of whom he has translated. Those Spaniards can create flying cabbages and lizards with wings in their beautifully crazed mysticism, but their kind of irrationality is certainly not suitable to imitation by a Minnesota Spaniard.

Bly's failures of sensibility and taste come as naturally to him as his precise brilliances. Here is an example of incredible lapse:

> Come with me into those things that
>   have felt this despair for so long—
> Those removed Chevrolet wheels that

> howl with a terrible loneliness,
> Lying on their backs in the cindery
>   dirt, like men drunk, and naked.

Obviously those Chevy wheels could not howl when *removed*, only while turning. Later in this weak poem Bly compares abandoned innertubes to human bodies, a device so ridiculously sentimental as to put off any sensible reader.

It is ironic that Bly is at his worst with the subject he knows best, the rural earth, its creatures, sights, sounds. He begins a rural poem vividly

> The blind horse among the cherry
>   trees—
> And bones, sticking from cool earth . . .

but then gives up the poem in favor of a pale, outmoded cry

> The heart leaps
> Almost up to the sky!

In the poem "Those Being Eaten by America" we need only quote in passing the preposterous lines

> Ministers who dive headfirst into the
>   earth
> The pale flesh
> Spreading guiltily into new literatures

to discover an illness, a religio-sexual content which is so embarrassingly symptomatic that we wonder if the poet took the trouble to understand what he had written.

Still and all, one does not expect uniform quality from impassioned poets nor hold their bad writing against them, provided they have at times written powerfully and well.

Robert Hazel

Sources for Further Study

Reviews:

Atlantic. CCXXI, February, 1968, p. 141. 300 words.

Nation. CCVI, March 25, 1968, p. 418. 1,400 words.

New York Review of Books. XX, June 20, 1968, p. 22. 2,550 words.

New York Times Book Review. February 18, 1968, p. 10. 800 words.

Poetry. CXVII, September, 1968, p. 423. 160 words.

THE LIGHT IN THE PIAZZA

Author: Elizabeth Spencer (1921-   )
Publisher: The McGraw-Hill Book Company (New York). 110 pp. $3.00
Type of work: Novel
Time: The present
Locale: Florence, Italy

A sensitive and beautiful novel in which a mother examines her sense of values and makes a difficult choice that may guarantee her daughter's happiness

Principal characters:

MARGARET JOHNSON, an American tourist in Florence
CLARA JOHNSON, her daughter
FABRIZIO NACCARELLI, Clara's Italian suitor
SIGNOR NACCARELLI and
SIGNORA NACCARELLI, Fabrizio's parents

Henry James found his dominant theme in the situation of moral ambiguity created when the innocent American came into contact with the complexities of European society. This is Elizabeth Spencer's theme, too, in *The Light in the Piazza*, winner of the first McGraw-Hill Fiction Award. A novel deceptive in its brevity and fairly uncomplicated line of narrative, it deals within its brief scope with far more important matters than do many novels whose values can be measured by bulk as well as by literary merit. In the space of 110 pages Miss Spencer develops a Jamesian theme of considerable moral weight and implication, brings to life a small complex of characters, tells a story filled with suspense, and deals expertly with problems of belief and conduct that arise when two cultural streams join.

More important, it is all effortlessly done, the kind of performance we have come to expect from this writer of excellent short stories and novels like *The Crooked Way* and *The Voice at the Back Door*. Consider, for instance, the cadence and luminous clarity of the opening paragraphs, the attention to detail, the unobtrusive handling of images, so that in this carefully ordered, almost old-fashioned beginning the way is prepared for the symbolism of the ending:

On a June afternoon at sunset, an American woman and her daughter fended their way along a crowded street in Florence and entered with relief the spacious Piazza della Signoria. They were tired from a day of tramping about with a guidebook, often in the sun. The café that faced the Palazzo Vecchio was a favorite spot for them; without discussion they sank down at an empty table. The Florentines seemed to favor other gathering places at this hour. No cars were allowed here, though an occasional bicycle skimmed through; and a few people, passing, met in little knots of conversation, then dispersed. A couple of tired German tourists, all but harnessed in fine camera equipment sat at the foot of Cellini's triumphant Perseus. . . .

Margaret Johnson, lighting a cigarette, relaxed over her apéritif and regarded the scene which she preferred before any other, anywhere. She never got enough of it, and now in the clear evening light that all the shadows had gone from—the sun being blocked away by the tight bulk of the city—she looked at the splendid old palace and forgot that her feet hurt. More than that: here she could almost lose the sorrow that for so many years had been a constant of her life. Above the crenellated tower where the bells hung, a few swallows darted.

We are not long in learning the cause of Margaret Johnson's secret grief. Her daughter Clara is vivacious, virginal looking, incredibly lovely. But she is mentally retarded. As a child, she was kicked in the head by her pony, with the result that her mentality became fixed at the time of the accident. Her beauty and radiance are a cruel mask. At twenty-six, Clara Johnson has the mind of a ten-year-old child.

This is the tragic circumstance to which Mrs. Johnson, "a busy American housewife, mother, hostess, cook and civic leader, who paid attention to her looks," has learned to adapt herself. Her life has not been easy. Clara, although she has a child's mind, lives with a woman's emotions; the trip to Italy, in fact, was a desperate solution to an embarrassing situation created by Clara's amorous assault on a delivery boy. Then Mrs. Johnson realizes that she has merely traveled from one limbo to another. Clara meets Fabrizio Naccarelli, a young Italian shopkeeper, and falls radiantly, completely, in love. Seeing her daughter and the gallant young Italian together, she is tempted to consider a possibility which she knows is socially and morally wrong. "It was as if a curtain had lifted before her eyes. The life she had thought forever closed to her daughter spread out its great pastoral vista. After all, she thought, why not?" This is the light in the piazza suffusing Miss Spencer's novella: the possibility of happiness for a loved daughter after all hope of such happiness had apparently been denied.

Before she realizes, Mrs. Johnson finds herself involved in the family intricacies of an Italian courtship. There is Fabrizio's family to be considered, his shrewd, practical father, his gentle, adoring mother. There is the barrier of language, difficult enough under the most commonplace circumstances, an impossible bar when she considers telling Fabrizio's parents the truth about Clara's condition. There are other matters of great importance to the Naccarellis: the question of Clara's purity, the amount of her dowry. Mrs. Johnson is compelled to act on her own in these matters, for her husband, Noel Johnson, is back home in Winston-Salem, North Carolina. She knows what his reaction would be. She knows what her moral obligation is, but she finds herself unable to speak up. On the one occasion when she does try to tell Signor Naccarelli the truth, the explosion of a cannon in the square creates a diversion and the moment of truth is lost.

After a Presbyterian minister and a brisk official at the American consulate fail to give Mrs. Johnson the help she needs, she takes Clara to Rome. There the sight of her daughter's misery is more than she can bear, and they return to Florence. By this time she feels that perhaps her dream for Clara, the hope that some day her daughter would be perfectly well, might come true. In the sheltered place a wife holds in Italian society, she thinks, there will be no great demands on Clara. Once she herself accepts the idea of the marriage, however, the situation is still unresolved. Signor Naccarelli, his masculine vanity offended by Mrs. Johnson's American efficiency, raises difficulties on the day the wedding forms are to be filled out. Clara is twenty-six; Fabrizio, he says, is twenty; the young man is actually twenty-three. If the signor is prepared to use his power to put an American matron in her place, Mrs. Johnson is equally ready to use her own power to secure her daughter's happiness—American money. In a scene that is both touching and funny, Mrs. Johnson and Signor Naccarelli gamble with their children's future and Mrs. Johnson wins when she raises Clara's dowry to fifteen thousand American dollars. So the bargain is struck and the wedding takes place, but not before Italian deviousness and practical desire for gain and American materialism and moral innocence have met and bent but remain unbroken.

The novel ends with a beautifully achieved effect of symbolism. After the ceremony Mrs. Johnson watches some tourists trying to take a picture in the piazza. Suddenly she remembers the accident on the day the cannon exploded and she was unable to tell Signor Naccarelli the truth about Clara. She recalls the hurt man struggling to get to his feet "while near him, silent in bronze, Cellini's Perseus, in the calm repose of triumph, held aloft the Medusa's head." That image of triumph ties the elements of the novel together in one meaningful whole.

The Light in the Piazza is the story of a woman who possesses courage and the strength that comes of moral testing. Perhaps she has wisdom, too. Miss Spencer does not say. She is too honest and sensitive a writer to make her novel any less ambiguous than life itself or the moral problems it presents for human choice.

THE LIGHT INFANTRY BALL

Author: Hamilton Basso (1904-1964)
Publisher: Doubleday and Company (Garden City, N. Y.). 476 pp. $4.50
Type of work: Novel
Time: 1861-1865
Locale: Pompey's Head, South Carolina, and Richmond

A novel of the Civil War in which the collapse of the plantation class is set against the background of Pompey's Head, an imaginary South Carolina city

Principal characters:

JOHN BOTTOMLEY, a young South Carolina planter
CORWIN BOTTOMLEY, his father, ex-governor of the state
VIRGINIA BOTTOMLEY, his mother
CAMERON BOTTOMLEY, his scapegrace younger brother
MISSY, his sister
ULES MONCKTON, a newspaper publisher and fanatic secessionist
LYDIA STANHOPE, John's secret love
SENATOR STANHOPE, her husband, a secretary in the Confederate government
ARABELLA STANHOPE, the senator's daughter by his first marriage, later John's wife
ALLBRIGHT, a free mulatto barber
CLAY VINCENT, a fire-eating young Southerner

The View from Pompey's Head was a novel in which Hamilton Basso took a long, steady look at the social structure of the modern South—its ideas of caste, the inner tensions and fears of its mixed society, the threat of disintegration and violence beneath the smooth formalism of its manners, the whole steeped in an atmosphere of reverence for the past. It was an excellent and perceptive work dealing with two important themes: the first a Chekhovian revelation of truth about the tradition of the region, the second the story of one man's discovery that no man ever really leaves home, that some essential part of himself remains irretrievably rooted in the life of the homeplace.

The novel owed no small part of its effectiveness to the solid construction of its setting. Like William Faulkner in his Yoknapatawpha stories, Mr. Basso was creating his own Southern enclave and giving it the reality of his imagination. Pompey's Head—"Old Pompey," as it is called locally—will not be found on any map of South Carolina, a circumstance which does not make it any less believable as a place. Geographically, it seems to be located near the city of Beaufort, but it borrows also from Charleston and Savannah. In *The View from Pompey's Head* it presented several aspects of reality. Its physical geography was carefully charted and landmarked. Its social classes were as carefully described—the old families, the "new" residents from the North, clerks, tradesmen, white millworkers, and Negroes—in every detail of ancestral background, class, occupation, and color. More than that, the writer made his imaginary city the center of a limited but authentic moral universe, for the situations in which Anson Page found himself involved when he returned to Pompey's Head were those that had grown out of concepts of conduct and value embodied in the regional tradition. This was one reason why the reader's understanding of that novel depended in part on the fact that Anson Page had once written a book called *The Shinto Tradition in the American South.*

Now, in *The Light Infantry Ball,* Mr. Basso takes another look at the same scene from the same point of vantage. He has moved a century back in time, however, for his purpose here is to show how the world of Anson Page came into being and the origin of the tradition its society perpetuates. In the process he has created a Civil War novel with almost none of the familiar romantic trappings. True, the Pompey's Head Light Infantry seizes Fort Signal and its twenty-nine-man garrison at the mouth of the Cassava River and the guns fired on Fort Sumter rumble in the distance, but not a single great battle is described and no historic figure walks across the stage. Mr. Basso fixes his attention on more serious business. In this novel he is not only trying to explain the Southern present in terms of its past but also attempting to show the issues by which the South felt compelled to stand and the elements of disunity within the Confederate cause.

For his purpose he presents two figures who stand at the opposite poles of Southern life and character. Young John Bottomley belongs to the planter aristocracy; his father had been a governor of the state and his ancestors had been among the original settlers on the rice coast. He himself had been educated at the College of New Jersey in Princeton, where, a man of moderation and reason, he had formed the conviction that slavery was morally wrong. After leaving college he had taken over the management of Deerskin, one

of the Bottomley plantations. In January, 1861, he has just turned thirty, a pleasant, friendly man who spent most of his time at Deerskin, felt the hurt of a disastrous love for Lydia Chadwick, who had married a pompous senator for his position and money, and had private doubts that the South could ever win out over the North in a sectional war. When we see him for the first time he is on his way to fight a duel with Ules Monckton.

Ules Monckton is John Bottomley's opposite in every respect. A man of no particular background, he has risen to a position of social acceptability and considerable political influence through his law practice and the ownership of a newspaper which first clamors for secession and then civil war. A fanatic and a jingoistic orator, he is motivated by a wild dream of conquest and power. His belief is that the South has an empire within her grasp if she is bold enough to act. The vision is as dazzling as it is foolish. First Mexico would be seized by a filibustering expedition like that of William Walker in Sonora, then the countries of Central America and after them the islands of the Caribbean, all to be made prosperous by reopening the slave trade—"a golden circle of slave countries which would be under Southern control: truly an empire: a dazzlement of power and riches that would make the Confederacy one of the mightiest nations in the world." But Ules Monckton's dream does not stop at this vision of the future. The institution of slavery is divinely sanctioned. The North, which opposes slavery, must be crushed, and that example will prove to all the world that the Southern cause is right. This character is Mr. Basso's own creation, a fantastic and sinister figure partly invented and partly reconstructed, one imagines, from the speeches and activities of Robert Rhett, Edmund Ruffin, General P. G. T. Beauregard, and William Walker. His slur on John Bottomley's loyalty on the night of the Light Infantry Ball leads to the duel. John fires into the air and Monckton, shooting to kill, wounds his opponent in the elbow.

At the time of the duel John has both a public problem and a private one. The private problem involves the strange disappearance of his younger brother Cameron, who has vanished shortly before the announcement of his engagement to a local belle. John's investigations lead him into the Channel where the Irish workingmen live and to a barbershop owned by Allbright, a free mulatto. Time passes, however, before he learns that Cameron has fled after killing the brother of an Irish girl and that Allbright is in reality one of his Bottomley kin.

The public problem is one common to many Southerners of the time. John belongs to a class that has always thought of the Union as one nation, divided by sectional differences at times in the past but only now brought face to face with the reality of secession and the threat of war. His hesitation to commit himself while in a group of fire-eating young bloods on the night of the ball brings about his quarrel with Ules Monckton. He is unhappy, too, in the knowledge that loyalty to the South means support of the slave system, which he accepts but does not believe in. And he shares somewhat the distrust the rice aristocracy of the coastal area holds for the inland cotton growers. To them Jefferson Davis is "that Mississippi fellow . . . hand and glove with the cotton crowd." As one character puts it:

"What they ought to call this new government is the Cotton Confederacy. And another thing, why didn't they hold the convention here? Or in Charleston? Why did they pick Montgomery? Fifty years ago there was no Montgomery. There was no Alabama either, for that matter, or any Mississippi, Louisiana, Florida or Texas. Not as states, that is. But if you listen to this cotton crowd you'd think they're the ones who provided the statesmanship from the very beginning, not us and Virginia. I don't like that gang."

When the war comes, John takes a post under Senator Stanton, now one of the secretaries in the new government in Richmond. There he fights a paper war, his duties relating chiefly to the export of cotton. Through the activities of a junior clerk, he comes on evidence which seems to prove that the senator is engaged in the illegal smuggling of cotton. The unexpected appearance of Cameron, now on his way to California and oblivion, helps to clear the senator, but by the time his wife, John's former love, has been revealed as the brains of the smuggling ring, Senator Stanhope has committed suicide. Cured of his infatuation and hurt, John marries Arabella, the senator's daughter.

The novel closes with a scene which symbolizes the public and private violence revealed in the plot. In the closing days of the war John, who has become a field officer after Senator Stanhope's death, is in the neighborhood of Pompey's Head. When he hears that General Ules Monckton is calling for a force of irregulars to continue the resistance and that volunteers have been ordered to report to the Bottomley plantation, he goes there at once. He arrives in time to see Allbright, his father's mulatto half brother, confront

Ules Monckton, who is now attempting to burn or destroy everything in the path of invading Union troops. Allbright is killed and Ules Monckton burns to death after firing the house. If the house is intended to stand for the plantation society of its owners, it has been destroyed from within by reckless and despairing fanaticism. While John, his wife, and his sister Missy watch the house burning, the ragged volunteers, their leader lost, wait and look on.

The Light Infantry Ball tells a somber and yet gallant story. There are no faked scenes of heroism or glory in the novel, no false emotions or regional nostalgia. This, as Mr. Basso seems to say, is the way things happened then, along with everything else that has happened since.

LIKE A BULWARK

Author: Marianne Moore (1887-1972)
Publisher: The Viking Press (New York). 32 pp. $2.50
Type of work: Poetry

Eleven new poems by an American writer capable of compressing the larger issues of life and art into narrow perspectives

Long before the year's end it had already become apparent that 1956 was to be a lean year for poetry. The young poets seemed active enough, but most of them had little to say, and the older poets, who might have spoken out with authority and insight for our common understanding, for the most part said nothing. This is one reason why Marianne Moore's modest offering goes a long way toward redeeming an otherwise undistinguished season.

Like a Bulwark is Miss Moore's first book of verse since her *Collected Poems* was awarded the Bollingen Prize, the National Book Award, and the Pulitzer Prize for 1951. These honors have caused our expectations to run high ever since, so that at first glance this collection of eleven poems may appear a slim showing for the intervening period. Let it be said at the beginning, therefore, that Miss Moore has never been a writer whose work can be measured by bulk.

Whatever else may be unclear about the poetry of Marianne Moore, one thing is plain: the originality of her mind and vision. Here is a poet widely praised nowadays, after years of critical neglect, and an honored figure in the anthologies, but she wears her bright reputation with becoming modesty and without allowing time or circumstance to dull her habit of looking at the world about her as if she were seeing it for the first time on the morning of Creation. It is safe to say that she has never used a trite image or written a banal line. This quality of her poetry is the most difficult to define; even her stanchest and most perceptive admirers are hard put to it at times to explain how she manages to reshape the materials of this familiar, commonplace world into fresh and significant forms in which structure and meaning become one and the typographical arrangement of the lines on the page creates a new ordering of experience. This effect is partly the result of her ability to see the strange or portentous in the most trivial objects, partly the working of a discriminating mind capable of imposing her own particular order on the chaos of thought and feeling that plagues the human animal, and partly her power to absorb into her writing the oddities and varied details gathered from the wide range of her reading.

Miss Moore's poems sometimes convey the impression that she has read everyone and everything that has ever appeared in print: poets, scientists, philosophers, critics, newspapers, text books, advertisements, comic strips, histories, medical journals, diaries, letters. Her borrowings from the most unlikely sources might be expected to give her poetry an air of mannered quaintness or erudite pretense. But Miss Moore is not writing literary pastiche. Her method, the most direct "accessibility to experience," as she sees it, results in poems which are lively, learned, and colloquial at the same time. Years ago this poet took her stand among the "literalists of the imagination" in art, and the impact of her verse lies in its indelible pictorial sense, a mastery of precise metrics, and her shrewd, sensitive observations of the human and natural worlds. To her, as she has said elsewhere, poetry is a landscape of "imaginary gardens with real toads in them."

The poems in *Like a Bulwark* reveal once more her ability to combine the fanciful and the literal in new and arresting patterns in which details are presented with imagistic precision in a context of symbolic reference. Reading them is somewhat like looking at a Japanese flower arrangement in which every blossom and twig has been carefully chosen and as carefully placed for deliberate esthetic effect. Her subjects are the simplest—man's armament against disaster in "Bulwarked against Fate," a porcupine in "Apparition of Splendor," the ermine in "Then the Ermine," a champion race horse's performance in "Tom Fool at Jamaica," "The Staff of Aesculapius," "The Sycamore," esthetic ideals in "Style" and "Blessed is the Man." All are refractions of an intelligence as evocative as it is angular and precise, and all extend beyond the zoölogical, botanical, or human present into the realms of wit or moral speculation.

The dominant criticism of our time is a serious affair, and it insists that poetry be grimly serious as well. But Miss Moore breaks the rules of the critical game. Her poems are enlivened with a quality of playful wit which takes delight in the fanciful and the incongruous. "Apparition of Splendor" begins:

> Partaking of the miraculous
> since never known literally,
> Dürer's rhinoceros
> might have startled us equally

> if black-and-white-spined elaborately.

It ends:

> Maine should be pleased that its animal
> is not a waverer, and rather
> than fight, lets the primed quill fall.
> Shallow oppressor, intruder,
> insister, you have found a resister.

This is the true spirit of play in poetry, not as bucolic or sage-like as Robert Frost's, but still the real thing and just as effective.

Of the poems in *Like a Bulwark*, Miss Moore's firm control of structure and theme is perhaps best illustrated in "Tom Fool at Jamaica." The subject of the poem is complex: the idea of moral excellence underlying achievement and the problem of behavior. The first stanza presents a picture of opposites, the determination of Jonah, whom nothing short of being swallowed by a whale could turn aside from his purpose, and a schoolboy's amusing drawing of a mule halted in mid-stride by the appearance of an insignificant snail in his path:

> Look at Jonah embarking from Joppa,
> deterred by
> the whale; hard going for a statesman
> whom nothing could detain,
> although one would not rather die
> than repent.
> Be infallible at your peril, for
> your system will fail,
> and select as a model the schoolboy in
> Spain
> who at the age of six, portrayed a
> mule and jockey
> who had pulled up for a snail.

In the next three stanzas the poem expands to suggest Victor Hugo's idea of "submerged magnificence" in Tom

4378   *Like a Bulwark*/MOORE

Fool, a race horse that always "makes an effort and makes it oftener than the rest," to present an ideal of championship in several fields. The fifth stanza, conversational in tone, brings together various examples of achievement and makes them relevant to the central theme of the poem:

> Of course, speaking of champions,
>   there was Fats Waller
>   with the feather touch, giraffe eyes, and
>   that hand alighting in
>   Ain't Misbehavin'! Ozzie Smith
>   and Eubie Blake
>   ennoble the atmosphere; you
>   recall the Lippizan school;
> the time Ted Atkinson charged by on
>   Tiger Skin—
>   no pursuers in sight—cat-loping
>   along. And you may
>   have seen a monkey
>   on a greyhound. "But Tom
>   Fool . . .

The suggestion of the final ellipsis is that qualities which make a champion, whether animal or human, defy analysis, and the imaginative and moral qualities determining the value of character or performance have now been contrasted in implication with the abstract inflexibility of Jonah ironically presented in the opening stanza. In this poem sensation and intelligence sustain reflection; details trivial in themselves combine to express a theme of esthetic subtlety and moral significance.

As the notes to these poems show, Marianne Moore's verse is often little more than a rearrangement, compressed with shrewdness of insight and expert imaginative control, of materials drawn from various sources such as the bestiary, the garden, art galleries, museums, the opera, sport, and the daily papers. She plays fair with her readers, however, and carefully annotates her borrowings. Sometimes these notes are as interesting as the poems for the revelation given of the creative mind at work and for the way in which they extend the meanings of her verse. The poet's facts may be the simplest to begin with, but the finished poem is never trite or trivial. Her poems—and again it is best to let the poet speak for herself—represent a

>   . . . flowering
> in more than talent for spectacle.
> Because the heart is in it as well.

Sources for Further Study

Criticism:

Koch, Kenneth. "Like a Bulwark," in *Poetry*. XC (April, 1957), p. 47. Koch explores "some of the graces of Miss Moore's style" but finds some of the poems lacking her customary intensity.

Scott, W. T. "Marianne Moore," in *Saturday Review*. XL (February 2, 1957), pp. 17-18. 950 words. The moral statements and didacticism of the *Like a Bulwark* poetry are analyzed.

Reviews:

Nation. CLXXXIV, March 16, 1957, p. 240. 600 words.

New York Herald Tribune Book Review. January 27, 1957, p. 5. 280 words.

Spectator. October 11, 1957, p. 488. 300 words.

Times Literary Supplement. November 22, 1957, p. 704. 2,650 words.

THE LIME TWIG

Author: John Hawkes (1925-   )
With an Introduction by Leslie A. Fiedler
Publisher: New Directions (New York). 175 pp. Clothbound, $3.50; paperbound,
    $1.35
Type of work: Novel
Time: The present
Locale: Somewhere in England

An experimental novel about the painfulness and absurdity of so much experience in the modern world, fraught with violence, frustration, and lovelessness

Principal characters:
SIDNEY SLYTER, a columnist
WILLIAM HENCHER, a Londoner
MICHAEL BANKS, his friend
MARGARET BANKS, Michael's wife
COWLES,
LARRY, and
SPARROW, crooks
ROCK CASTLE, a horse
JIMMY NEEDLES, a jockey
LOVELY, a stableboy
THICK, a thug
LITTLE DORA, his wife
SYBILLINE, a moll
ANNIE, the Bankses' neighbor

Although the name of John Hawkes is probably unknown to a great many readers of current American literature, *The Lime Twig* is his sixth novel. The others are *Charivari* (1949), *The Cannibal* (1950), *The Beetle Leg* (1951), and *The Owl* and *The Goose on the Grave* (published together in one volume, 1954). It is hard to say why they have not caught on, why they have not received a critical accolade in those journals or those circles which would assure them greater circulation, but they simply have not. They are, of course, all experimental in technique, and it may be a tribute to their originality that they have not yet found a wide public.

Experiment as it was manifested in the 1920's has been tempered into the conventions of good craftsmanship, and no complaint against this healthy level of art and intelligence on which many of our younger novelists work should be registered; the whole point of literary revolution is to create a new and consistent order. But at any time, a young novelist may appear who forces us, almost against our will, to revise our mode of apprehending experience. Such a novelist is John Hawkes, who is certainly not without a full share of art and intelligence, but who exercises these faculties to create a special mirror of life which startles us by the absolute clarity with which it reflects the distortions of dignity and decency in the life of man. Hawkes does not attempt to resolve or explain these distortions; he renders them truly. They convey that sense of unreality which is one of the realities of modern life.

Hawkes is of course not without his

kinships and predecessors. He is in direct descent from the Gothic visions of Poe, whose imp of the perverse sits also upon the shoulder of Hawkes's contemporary, Flannery O'Connor. Among English writers, we might look back to William Beckford or, updating the comparison, to some of the earlier works of Graham Greene, particularly *Brighton Rock.* Hawkes goes beyond any of these, however, in his coolly composed delineation of mundane terror. His perception of psychological experience grows organically from the clinical documentation provided by modern psychiatry; much of his imagery derives clearly from the painting and poetry of the Surrealists; the atmosphere in which his story takes place is a compounding of the elements of Gothic atmosphere and Wasteland terrain; and the motivation of his characters is rooted in the despair and absurdity which are so much a part of the modern temper. In Hawkes's work the traditional and the experimental, the typical and the unique, the natural and the monstrously grotesque are all fused in a vision of verifiable mid-century experience.

Developing a technique suitable for his purpose has been Hawkes's creative problem. Some of the earlier books projected complexity in such a way as only to cause difficulty for his readers. *The Lime Twig,* though still full of pitfalls for the unwary, is remarkable for the clarity of its outline and the accessibility of its substance. One device is a kind of choric newspaper column which appears at the beginning of each chapter. Written by a gaily inquisitive reporter by the name of Sidney Slyter, the column serves to provide narrative continuity, to establish a distance wherefrom to observe the events in the tortured lives of the characters, to suggest a moral norm, to offset with levity the horror felt at the center of things, and to disjoint the element of time in the manner that we are normally made aware of things—by piecing together fragments of cause and effect.

The rest of the book is developed in scenes which range in mood from the tenderly pathetic to the sardonic, from the merely confused to the phantasmagorical, from the depressing to the overwhelmingly outrageous. Many of the episodes have the weird and memorable quality of frightful dreams from which you awake to find you have been awake all the time. Others leave the reader bemused with his recognition of the inevitably absurd complexion on the face of serious situation. All the episodes are informed with sympathy, but are projected with a feeling of utter helplessness.

The central character of the first part of the book is William Hencher, a denizen of London's East End who returns sometime after the war to the tenement flat in Violet Lane near Dreary Station where he had lovingly endured the blitz with his slatternly mother, now to find as occupants Michael Banks and his wife Margaret. Hencher takes up his abode with these people, and quickly transfers to them a love so intense as to be a kind of fetishism. Together, partly in exploitation of this love, they hatch a plot to steal a famous race horse which under a new name will win their fortune. The theft is successfully executed, though Hencher is promptly trampled to death within the first moments of illicit stabling.

His confederate Banks proceeds with indifference, but like John Donne's Death soon becomes "slave to fate, chance, kings, and desperate men,/ And [does] with poison, war, and sickness dwell." That is to say, he is surrounded by a gang of professional crooks who stop at nothing to achieve their ends or satisfy their egos. There follows one fantastically lurid and terrifying scene after the other. Banks temporarily deserts his wife, eventually is seduced to play the stud to a disdainful but strong-willed arch-moll Sybilline, seeks solace from Annie, who is an old neighbor from Violet Lane, is subjected to cruel threatenings from the gang, and at the end, when he sees into the heart of darkness, makes a desperate bid for redemption which is answered by the deadly thunder of racing hooves upon his skull.

Meanwhile his wife Margaret suffers in her desolation of love, then pursues him to the Aldington track, but on the train is kidnaped by a traveling companion named Little Dora, who with Thick, her husband, keeps Margaret a hostage—even after she is beaten to death.

Apocalyptic visions of clothed assassins dripping at their grisly work in a Turkish bath, of the agony of a dope addict receiving his fix in the presence of curious but cold-blooded observers, or of a silver horse being hoisted ashore by a winch while the barge is scuttled in the oily murk—such visions complete the fabric of the book. It must be emphasized that such material is not presented for the sake of sensation, but that such sensations are effected for the sake of meaning. The novel is moving precisely because the reader does not look on the horror objectively, but is made to identify with those characters who, frustrated in their need and desire for love, suffer horror at the hands of others who are dehumanized by their indifference to love.

Hawkes succeeds admirably in sustaining the tone of this book. Its rhythm is the ebb and flow of well-paced action; its harmony is the accumulation of gradually meaningful perceptions; and its melody is the terrible cry of poor wingless man caught, snared on the lime twig which is the world.

No one else writes novels quite like Hawkes's. To find their equivalent in theme and mood, it is necessary to turn to what is now called the theatre of the absurd—the works of Beckett, Ionesco, and others. There are real echoes of Brecht's *Dreigroschenoper*. Like some of these writers, Hawkes has also found his meaning in a focusing upon the meaningless, in a comic resignation to the terrible, and in the sympathetic response inevitably to be evoked from the beholder of suffering and stupidity.

Criticism:

Edenbaum, Robert J. "John Hawkes: *The Lime Twig* and Other Tenuous Horrors," in *Massachusetts Review*. VII (Summer, 1966), pp. 462-475. This article looks at the treatment of fantasy in *The Lime Twig* and at certain aspects of Hawkes's comic style.

Reviews:

Library Journal. LXXXVI, May 1, 1961, p. 1,794. 280 words.

Nation. CXCIII, September 3, 1961, p. 122. 2,500 words.

New York Herald Tribune Lively Arts. June 25, 1961, p. 32. 650 words.

New York Times Book Review. May 14, 1961, p. 31. 400 words.

New Yorker. XXXVII, April 29, 1961, p. 149. 150 words.

LINCOLN FINDS A GENERAL
Vol. V: Prelude to Chattanooga

Author: Kenneth P. Williams (1887-1958)
Publisher: The Macmillan Company (New York). Illustrated. 395 pp. $7.50
Type of work: History
Time: January to October, 1863
Locale: The Western Theater of the Civil War

A detailed account of the battles of the Western Theater from Helena to Chickamauga in an unfinished volume, unfortunately the last, of what was to have been a
complete military history of the Civil War

Principal personages:
ABRAHAM LINCOLN
CHARLES A. DANA, Assistant Secretary of State
HENRY W. HALLECK, Union General-in-Chief
ULYSSES S. GRANT,
BENJAMIN M. PRENTISS,
NATHANIEL P. BANKS,
WILLIAM S. ROSECRANS,
AMBROSE E. BURNSIDE,
FREDERICK STEELE,
JOHN M. SCHOFIELD, and
WILLIAM T. SHERMAN, Union generals commanding in the West
JEFFERSON DAVIS
JOSEPH E. JOHNSTON,
BRAXTON BRAGG,
KIRBY SMITH,
JOHN C. PEMBERTON,
STERLING PRICE,
FRANK GARDNER, and
JAMES LONGSTREET, Confederate generals commanding in the West

When Kenneth Powers Williams first began his military history of the Civil War, his purpose was, apparently, to trace the rise of Ulysses S. Grant to its triumphant culmination in his appointment as General-in-Chief of the Union Armies and to show how destiny solved what, in the preface to his first volume, Williams announced as Lincoln's primary problem, the need "to find a general equal to the hard task the North faced in the Civil War."

To trace such a rise, to demonstrate such a solution, would certainly have been accomplishment enough. But Williams' passion for detail could not be confined even within limitations that he himself had set up. As the work progressed, its scope widened; a broader form emerged until, finally, his intention was to cover the entire war and to fill seven volumes. For a decade Williams labored to realize this intention. Then, on September 25, 1958, death ended his labors, two volumes and two chapters short of completion.

Ironically, those two chapters were the ones needed to fulfill his original purpose. Volume V contains nine of the eleven chapters it was planned to have. It ends with the Federal defeat at Chickamauga and the resultant reorganization of the West that put Grant in command of the newly established Military Division of the Mississippi. As supreme commander of the Western Theater, Grant was to come to Chattanooga, where he·would plan the Union victories of Lookout Mountain and Missionary Ridge in November of 1863. On the strength of these triumphs, which would virtually end the war in the West, he would be called to Washington where, in March of the following year, he would assume command of all the Union forces. The final two chapters were to have covered these events so that, at the end of Volume V, Lincoln would have found the general he was looking for and Williams would have reached his original goal. That he fell short is a loss to all who are interested in the Civil War or in military history. Still, the value of what has been done is not diminished by what is missing, and as far as this volume is concerned the nine chapters that are presented are worth while, even though the larger pattern remains incomplete.

What the complete pattern was to have been can be determined by what is present and by what Williams had done in the preceding volumes. Moreover, the pattern of the entire work can be projected; it was to have been the same, on a larger scale, as that of each individual volume. Volume V, incomplete as it is, reflects in miniature the truncated design of the whole.

The pattern was the natural result of Williams' method—one that might be described as the thunderstorm method. Just as, on a hot day in summer, thunderheads will begin to pile up slowly on the horizon, so Williams begins a volume by the slow and leisurely piling up of fact upon fact, detail upon de-

tail. Then, as gradually the oppressive clouds will fill the sky and distant lightning will flash, followed by the roll of approaching thunder, so Williams gradually (and, to the impatient reader, oppressively) fills in completely the given period of time he has selected, goes over and over the same chronological area until it is completely covered, lightening it with occasional flashes of battle, punctuating it with the boom of opposing cannon. Finally, as the calm is broken and the shattering storm breaks loose, so Williams turns loose his creative energy in the deluge of the battles for which all the filling in and all the piling up of detail have been a preparation. The culminating battles are, of course, in each case decisive ones: Gettysburg in Volumes I and II, Shiloh and Corinth in Volume III, Vicksburg in Volume IV, Chickamauga and (had he been spared) Lookout Mountain and Missionary Ridge in the present volume.

The pattern of the whole would have been produced by the working of the same method on a larger scale. The first four volumes and the first part of this book constitute the building up process for the climactic battles of the entire war. The first two volumes cover the events in the East to July 3, 1863. The second two go over the same period of time, dealing with the activities in the West and terminating but one day later, July 4, 1863. This volume begins with the preparations for a battle which will take place on that same Independence Day. Before we are taken to Rosecrans' headquarters in Murfreesboro, Tennessee, however, we get no farther chronologically (except for two brief glances ahead) than August of that same year. When we finally meet Rosecrans, we are taken back in time again, and, when we move with him after his six-month idleness, it is still only June. It is not until we reach Chattanooga that the time thrust begins. But the deluge it produces is not the deluge of Volume V alone. The piling up of the entire summer of 1863—a piling up that lasted for over four volumes—is now being turned loose in a torrent that will inundate the South. Chickamauga is its beginning. From Chickamauga we can project the remainder of the pattern. With it we can discern the master plan that Williams' method produced.

The advantage of his method is twofold: rational and aesthetic. The thorough presentation of detail produced by the piling-up process forces on the reader a complete knowledge of the conditions that give rise to a significant battle; he must, if he attends to the detail, see the battle against a fully drawn background, as a part of the totality of the war. Moreover, the battle, when it finally comes, is a contrast to and a psychological relief from all that has been built up so slowly before. The effect is dramatic. As a result, an understanding of the significance is attained on another level; it is appreciated emotionally as well as rationally, and thus comprehension is complete.

Of course, there are obvious disadvantages to the method, too. For the reader who lacks understanding or background the mass of detail will not gradually achieve coherence. And to the reader who lacks patience, all of the first part will move too slowly; he will lose the effect in his desire for the excitement of major battles. To such a reader Williams has this to say:

. . . unless one knows about the minor campaigns and operations that were a necessary basis for the great campaigns, or a consequence of them, and about the marches, the railroad and river movements, and about the way in which all-important problems of supply were handled, and knows something about the information of the enemy on which decisions were based, one's knowledge of war is pitifully circumscribed.

This statement constitutes a defense of his own method. He might have said that one who lacks patience has no business with history.

But for one with adequate background and sufficient patience, the values of Williams' method may be fully realized here in Volume V. The subtitle is apt. The totality of the volume provides the background for those twin battles that were to bring Grant into prominence.

The image of Grant dominates the book from the beginning. The volume opens with the Confederate attack on Helena, which occurred on the same day that Grant took Vicksburg in an attempt, against the better judgment of many of the Southern commanders, to relieve Pemberton, the defender of Grant's objective. Led by Sterling Price, the Confederates were repulsed by the Federals under Prentiss, thanks to the shells of the gunboat *Tyler*, which was lying off shore. The Confederate failure here, coupled with Grant's concurrent victory farther south, meant that Port Hudson remained the only obstacle to complete Northern control of the river. Williams then turns his attention south to that Louisiana town.

In dealing with Port Hudson, Williams, as always, doubles back in time, filling in the background completely. The coördination of the plans of Banks, the Union commander at New Orleans, with those of Grant prior to Vicksburg is shown, and the three-cornered correspondence of Grant, Banks, and Halleck in Washington is cited; the disposition of Confederate troops in the area is thoroughly dealt with, and the skirmishes and minor battles leading up to the siege are portrayed; moreover, the all-important river activity of the Union Navy is fully considered. Then the focus is narrowed to Port Hudson, itself. Actually, the siege lasted two weeks. Finally, on July 9, General Frank Gardner, the Southern commander, agreed to give up his defense of the city if the rumors he had heard about Vicksburg were true. Upon receiving Banks' word that Vicksburg had fallen, Gardner promptly surrendered, Banks accepting the surrender but graciously returning his adversary's sword.

Delighted with this sign of honor among warriors, Williams next turns his attention directly to Grant in his new location. There we learn in detail of Johnston's evacuation of Jackson, Mississippi, of the destruction of a group of Confederate gunboats on the Yazoo, and of Ransom's peaceful capture of Natchez. There also we are shown more correspondence among Halleck, Banks, and Grant to decide whether the next Union objective, now that the river was safe, would be the strategic Gulf port of Mobile or the formidable state of Texas. Texas (for political reasons, we are informed) was the choice, but because of the subsequent action in Tennessee, the invasion of the Lone Star State was abandoned and attention was turned eastward.

Our attention is to be turned that way, too, but not until the full story of the West is told. Rosecrans is ready to move, but one more section of the background he is to move against must be filled in. Williams concentrates now on Major General John M. Schofield in St. Louis and on the problems in the area under his command in Missouri, Arkansas, and Kansas. The highlights here are a consideration of the political unrest and the guerrilla warfare that Schofield had to contend with in this section and an account of Frederick Steele's brilliant capture of Little Rock, Arkansas. The climax is a description of the notorious William C. Quantrill's barbaric raid on Lawrence, Kansas, and of Thomas Ewing's futile attempt to track the Missouri soldier-raider to his lair.

Finally we see that, despite the unrest in Schofield's department, the work in the West is complete. Finally we join Rosecrans in Tennessee. But we are not yet ready for the deluge. True to his method to the last, Williams must fill in the chronological area immediately behind Rosecrans. Stones River, the battle for Murfreesboro, began on the last day of 1862 and ended on January 2, 1863. It was a Union victory by only a slight margin. Bragg withdrew to Shelbyville and waited. Rosecrans occupied Murfreesboro and waited until June 23. In accounting for the details of this long period of delay Williams is at his data-presenting best. The main interest here is the correspondence between Murfreesboro and Washington. Halleck urges. Rosecrans pleads a lack of cavalry support. Halleck becomes insistent. Rosecrans demands horses, support from Grant, support from Burnside. Halleck orders. Rosecrans becomes petulant. The commander-in-chief himself takes a hand.

Rosecrans moves out. The deluge begins as he pursues Bragg across Tennessee, through Chattanooga, and down into northern Georgia, only to be beaten back, thanks to Longstreet's arrival, by Bragg's return thrust at Chickamauga. Here the stage is set for Grant, and here, except for an appendix that stanchly defends the much-maligned Halleck, the volume abruptly ends. So ends the whole work—with the torrent raging. For those who had the patience to wait for it, the only regret is that its ending in the two additional projected volumes will never appear.

LINCOLN THE PRESIDENT
Last Full Measure

Authors: James G. Randall (1881-1953) and Richard N. Current (1915-   )
Publisher: Dodd, Mead and Company (New York). 421 pp. $7.50
Type of work: Biography
Time: 1863-1865
Locale: Washington, D. C.

The troubled life of Abraham Lincoln, 1863-1865, in the last volume of a scholarly work

Principal personages:
ABRAHAM LINCOLN
WILLIAM H. SEWARD, Secretary of State
HORACE GREELEY, editor of the New York *Tribune*
GENERAL ULYSSES S. GRANT
GENERAL GEORGE G. MEADE, commander of the Army of the
   Potomac
ADMIRAL DAVID G. FARRAGUT, hero of the battle of Mobile Bay
GENERAL GEORGE B. McCLELLAN, Democratic presidential candi-
   date in 1864
GENERAL WILLIAM T. SHERMAN, leader of the march to the sea
GENERAL GEORGE H. THOMAS, commander of the Army of the
   Cumberland
GENERAL JUBAL A. EARLY, Confederate general unsuccessful in his
   attempt to capture Washington.

When Professor Randall began the publication of his life of Lincoln, in 1945, his purpose was to carry the study only to the time of assassination. As he said: "This biography knows only the living Lincoln." At his death, in 1953, three volumes had been printed. For Volume IV, he had completed eight chapters, with the other half outlined. Realizing his serious illness, he selected Dr. Current as the scholar best able to carry on his work and express his own point of view. Thus, while half of this, the final volume, is "pure Randall," the last eight chapters represent the work of another pen, but one guided by Randall's research and interpretations. The book is really a remarkable welding of minds.

The present volume barely covers two whole years in Lincoln's life, the chapters on politics alternating with those concerning war problems. They are reinforced by many footnotes for the scholar and skeptic; these may be skipped by the general reader.

The early pages deal with Lincoln's ideas about Reconstruction, crystallized in his December, 1863, message to Congress, but already foreshadowed by his Congressional message of the year before and, in fact, as early as his Cooper Union speech of February, 1860. The President's conciliatory attitude is stressed. In the proclamation and the message to Congress of 1863 he offered pardon to almost everybody and restoration of all rights except to hold slaves. Qualification could be met by a simple oath to support the Constitution of the United States and "the union of the states themselves." He planned to welcome back the seceding states as soon as not less than ten percent of the citizens who had voted in 1860 should reestablish a republican government. Dr.

Randall remarks in a footnote on the lack of a capital letter in *republican;* by it Lincoln meant non-monarchical and non-dictatorial.

Some Conferedate states were already regretting their participation in the Civil War. Tennessee had been an enemy state only ten months, between May, 1861, and March, 1862. Florida's soil had been battleground only once, and Floridians were anticipating sending delegates to the political convention the next year. Arkansas, too, was proof of the workability of Lincoln's plan. For the rest, he believed the Unionists were in the majority, and while he was unwilling to impose a government, even though benevolent, upon an unwilling state, he thought the chances he was taking were worth the risk. Even as early as November, 1863, a captured Union general had sent from Libby Prison an assurance to Lincoln that "the masses were heartily anxious for the war's close on any terms."

In Chapter III, Randall considers the power of the press. Though irresponsible reporters with the armies had hampered the conduct of the war, publishing reports that conveyed information to the enemy and at times even acting as spies, the President had not restricted their privileges. He was one of the few who stood firm against censorship. Yet most of the influential newspapers were hostile to him, and he found it difficult to disseminate his views. He held no White House conferences, and his two inaugural speeches, his Gettysburg Address, and the Reconstruction speech, his final public utterance on April 11, 1865, were about the extent of his direct communication with the people.

He did, however, write letters, especially the open letter. Dr. Randall scrutinizes the famous and often counterfeited Bixby letter of November 21, 1864. Written to a mother who had supposedly lost five sons in battle, he shows that only two had been killed. One was a prisoner, and the other two were probably deserters. As to the charge, sometimes made, that Lincoln did not write the letter, while not able to deny it categorically, he shows that the chance that his secretary composed it was slight.

Dr. Randall traces the President's developing ability in matters of diplomacy, though Lincoln was wise enough to appoint the suave Seward as Secretary of State and trust him to handle the complicated foreign situation. The situation was delicate. While pressing for the removal from Mexico of French soldiers who were bolstering the unpopular Emperor Maximilian, Seward had to maintain cordial relations with France and at the same time maneuver the French into a position where they removed friction between the United States and Mexico by disavowing intentions of remaining permanently on New World soil.

Behind the scenes, however, it was Lincoln who laid down the American policy of forbearance and friendly relations abroad. It was he who stressed avoidance of war and patient attention to foreign points of view. Though he knew nothing of foreign history, he made all who worked with him respect his strong common sense that did ease foreign problems. It may be news to some readers that the Italian Garibaldi was offered by Seward a generalship in the Union forces, some say post of commander-in-chief, following the disastrous Battle of Bull Run. Garibaldi had lived in America and with more good will than accuracy often referred to himself as an "adoptive citizen of the United States." Here was one occasion where Lincoln overrode the ideas of his Secretary of State.

Then came the gloomy spring of 1864. Union forces were being beaten back. No results were apparent from the encircling movement on all fronts worked out by what was a miraculous coöperation between Meade, the actual commander of the Army of the Potomac, and Grant, whose title was only that of a leader in the field. The only outcome seemed to be increased ill will toward Lincoln because of mounting battle casualties. One stock market manipulator even managed to get newspapers to print a bogus pessimistic proclamation over Lincoln's signature, lamenting conditions and calling for a new draft of soldiers.

Efforts were being made to capitalize on the desires for peace. Horace Greeley, of the New York *Tribune*, met with Confederate representatives at Niagara Falls to discuss terms laid down by the President in granting safe conducts: restoration of a peaceful Union and abolishment of slavery. But it was quickly discovered that the Confederate envoys were more interested in discrediting the Lincoln administration and damaging the Union cause than in ending the war.

Things grew no better with the arrival of summer. Bickering in Congress continued as lawmakers sought substitutes for Lincoln's ten percent plan. Wade and Davis wanted a majority of the voters to have a share in revamping any state government and wished to restrict civil rights to those who had never taken arms against the United States or been office holders in the Confederacy. Only by a pocket veto was Lincoln able to defeat that project.

Militarily, the announcement that Early was trying to raise the siege of Richmond and Petersburg by marching against Washington filled the capital with terror. Lincoln was uncertain of his fate at the nominating convention, since many felt he would have no chance against General McClellan, the Democratic contender.

Suddenly the picture changed. Late in July, the *Kearsarge* captured the Confederate commerce raider, the *Alabama*, which had sunk sixty-two United States merchant ships and sent others scurrying to protection under foreign registry. Admiral Farragut fought the battle of Mobile Bay and sealed off another Confederate port. Atlanta fell to the Union army and Sheridan made his dramatic ride. In the face of such victories, opposition to Lincoln faded and he was renominated and reëlected.

Reëlection brought still more problems—political office seekers, Cabinet changes, and a Supreme Court appointment posed by the death of Taney. Nor was the war over. Sherman marched to the sea, and Thomas, for whose retention Lincoln had to struggle, won the victory of Nashville, the only battle of the Civil War that resulted in the wiping out of a complete army.

At the end of the volume several important questions are posed. Did Grant's peace offer exceed his authority? Did Lincoln break faith with Virginia? How much of a Christian was Lincoln? (The author declares: "Lincoln was a man of more intense religiosity than any other president the United States has ever had.") Tired after the strenuous war years, Lincoln found the theater relaxing. On the evening of April 14, 1865, he decided, in spite of Mrs. Lincoln's headache, to attend Ford's Theater. "And so they went." With those four words this fascinating volume ends.

4392   *Lincoln the President*/RANDALL AND CURRENT

There have been many books and articles written about Lincoln. The bibliography of this volume contains 375 items, in addition to the large number at the end of Vol. II. What are the advantages of this work, the differences between it, for example and Carl Sandburg's monumental study, condensed in 1954 to one of 762 pages? The four volumes of Randall's study combine scholarship and art, set down by an ob-jective, analytical, dispassionate mind. It does not displace the literary production of Sandburg, but it does say something fresh about Lincoln and shows him as a sorely tried and confused human being, earnestly seeking the right answers to the perplexing problems of state. This book, like the earlier volumes, will appeal to readers who want to know what Lincoln did and why.

LINDMANN

Author: Frederic Raphael (1931-   )
Publisher: Holt, Rinehart and Winston (New York). 335 pp. $4.95
Type of work: Novel
Time: The present
Locale: London

A moving, biting commentary on modern manners and morals focusing on one of
the horrors of World War II

Principal characters:
JACOB LINDMANN, a Jewish philosopher, an alienated man
MILSTEIN, a TV idea-man
GLADSTONE,
FINE, and
LOOMIS, Lindmann's bridge-playing friends
BLOTSKY, captain of the ship *Broda*
FRITZ GERSTENBERGER, a German expatriate
ISOLDE, his daughter-in-law
LINCOLN EDWARDS, a Negro painter
RACHAEL ASCH, Lindmann's fellow passenger aboard the *Broda*

Frederic Raphael is not an unknown author. In 1960 his *Limits of Love* won the Lippincott Award, and in 1962 his *A Wild Surmise* received general praise from critics. It would be fair to say, however, that neither of his previous efforts compare with *Lindmann*.

In *Lindmann*, Raphael takes an unexplained incident during World War II, an incident so terrible in its implications that it has never been thoroughly researched, and builds his story around it. The incident occurred when a group of Jewish immigrants were permitted to leave Germany (accompanied by the kicks and jeers of Nazi soldiers) for a trip to Palestine in a ship that was practically sinking when it reached Istanbul. At that port, Blotsky, the ship's captain, attempted to get from the Turkish government a permit allowing his passengers to go ashore while the ship was put in drydock for repairs. Turkish authorities refused on the grounds that the passengers had no visas to enter Palestine and thus were considered to be illegal immigrants. Blotsky then tried to get the British to

issue any type of visa that would suffice to permit his ship to get its desperately needed repairs. The British, worried over antagonizing the Arabs, refused to issue any visas at all.

The ship *Broda* was towed out of Istanbul by Turkish tugs and, upon being cut loose just outside Turkish territorial waters, sank with the loss of over six hundred souls; Jacob Lindmann and Rachael Asch, the only survivors among all the passengers, managed to escape drowning.

The official British version of the sinking of an immigrant ship off the Turkish coast was to the effect that the vessel had probably struck a mine. Raphael, in a flyleaf inscription, notes that he has used the incident as a basis for a piece of fiction without in any way implying that his fiction is fact. Yet one wonders and knows that government intransigence and bureaucratic love of regulations could well have caused the type of tragedy here described.

Be that as it may be, Lindmann managed to swim ashore and ulti-

mately ended up in London. His life in
that city forms the basis of at least one
half of this novel. Lindmann devotes
his time to engaging in dialogue with
anyone who will allow himself to be so
engaged.

> He devoted himself without profes-
> sorial self-regard to talking, talking all
> the time with those who, sunk in the
> mud of the world's discourses, toiled to
> see the sun of reality. He dived in the
> mud with them, to clean it from their
> eyes.

In his search for reality, for clarity,
Lindmann is often guilty of a certain
unkindness in language. Talking with
an itinerant preacher, he says: "You
are the dictionary which leaves out all
the words." Again, to the same man, he
describes "The speech of one who can
learn nothing in this world."

In his commentary on the new Germany, Raphael—through Lindmann—
speaks with great bitterness. "They
have, for instance, exceptional safety-
making arrangements for the crossing
of highways so that one may never be
killed by accident. Against such deaths
they make eminent precautions."
Speaking of Germany's compensation
of those persecuted by the Nazis, he
declares: "The Germans are perhaps
the first people to pay compensation for
nationalizing people to death." And he
comments, referring to the fact that the
new Germany is not held responsible
for the atrocities of the Nazis:

> The more modern the state, . . . the
> more unpleasing to the authorities is
> any attempt to raise issues from the
> past. . . . The new company has a
> separate identity and is not responsible
> for the debts of the old, even if it has
> directors in common with it.

When one of Lindmann's bridge-

playing friends writes the story of the
S.S. *Broda* and attempts to sell it to a
movie producer, the latter rejects it
with a stinging indictment of the level
of audience appeal in the Western
world:

> "I'll tell you straight but straight what
> it lacks, Mr. Milstein my old friend, it
> lacks S*E*X. I don't see one scene of
> woman suckling child, with nipple or
> without, keeping the one and niners
> from their goggle boxes of a Saturday
> night.

When Lindmann finds that the one
woman he admires is having an affair
with a Negro painter, and that the
London Jewish community is interested only in things material, he retreats to the safety of the past by lapsing into a deep coma, broken only by
the fact that he continually moves his
arms in a swimming motion. The sense
of futility, of a meaningless existence,
of an inability to understand or to be
understood, is best summed up by
these words that could well have appeared on the flyleaf.

> You are a senseless verbiage. . . . You
> are dead as the drowned are dead but
> you are not drowned, you are alive as
> the man dropping on his long rope is
> alive, though death is waiting with him.
> Alive you are dead, dead you are alive.
> You are between life and death, you are
> about to be born into death, you are dy-
> ing in life. . . . This is where you are,
> between life and death, between the liv-
> ing and the dead.

Lindmann can be read on two levels: it is a stirring novel of the tragedy
of the Jew, a tragedy that needs constant retelling; but in a deeper sense it
is a sad, relevant, and moving commentary on the lack of societal values, on
the relative meaningless of life in a materialistic and mechanistic world.

Frank K. Gibson

THE LION AND THE THRONE
The Life and Times of Sir Edward Coke (1552-1634)

Author: Catherine Drinker Bowen (1897-1973)
Publisher: Atlantic-Little, Brown and Company (Boston). 652 pp. $6.00
Type of work: Biography
Time: 1552–1634
Locale: England

A study of the life and times of Sir Edward Coke, famed English legal writer, Attorney-General under Elizabeth I, and Chief Justice of the King's Bench

Principal personages:
> SIR EDWARD COKE
> SIR FRANCIS BACON, James I's Attorney-General and Coke's rival
> QUEEN ELIZABETH I
> KING JAMES I, successor to Elizabeth I
> SIR WALTER RALEGH, favorite of Elizabeth and victim of James
> ROBERT, Earl of Essex, traitorous favorite of Elizabeth
> KING CHARLES I, successor to James I
> DUKE OF BUCKINGHAM, favorite courtier of James and Charles

Several classes of readers are able to enjoy Catherine Drinker Bowen's prize-winning *The Lion and the Throne* and to profit by it. Those interested in the life and times of Elizabethan and Jacobean England will discover hours of pleasure. Persons in search of information about an important chapter in the development of English and American law will find a storehouse of information. Lovers of biographical writing will be pleased at this volume written by one of the century's ablest practitioners of the biographer's art. Students of Renaissance England will find an exceptionally well-written narrative packed with an organized body of information and followed by an exceptional bibliography which includes, among others, sections on Sir Edward Coke himself, Queen Elizabeth I, James I, the powerful Cecil family, the obscure Father John Gerard, London, the city of Norfolk, the Inns of Court, Elizabethan education, and gossip writers of the time.

The Lion and the Throne is the third in a series of biographies written by Catherine Drinker Bowen to tell the story of the development of free government; earlier studies have dealt with Justice Oliver Wendell Holmes of the United States Supreme Court and John Adams, second President of the United States. In this book Coke stands as a pioneer, almost a prophet, in the development of constitutional and representative government. During the reigns of James I and Charles I, from 1603 to his death in 1634, Coke fought to establish, on the basis of common law and statutes, the rights of Parliamentary representatives over the royal prerogative. As a justice of the Court of Common Pleas, as a justice of the King's Bench, as a member of the House of Commons, and as a writer, Coke worked on behalf of the laws he revered. Sometimes he was successful; sometimes he was not. He rejoiced that Charles I accepted the joint petition of Parliament for rights in 1628, with the king giving the royal formula of acceptance, "Soit droit comme il est desire." Coke had also, even as a judge, to prostrate himself before James I for daring to uphold his principles against the king.

Coke lived in what is for many students the most interesting era of English history, and in that era Coke became an important, key figure. As Catherine Drinker Bowen says, "Coke's life covered a long span, a wide arc of time; with him the Middle Ages ended and today began. Coke was English law personified. The volumes that he wrote—*Reports* and *Institutes, Commentary upon Littleton*—remained for nearly three centuries the backlog of legal studies in England and America. Such a career is looked on as quiet, philosophic. Coke's life was no more retired than a buccaneer's." The author's subtitle for this volume is "The Life and Times of Sir Edward Coke." That subtitle is important, too, for it indicates what the author saw as her task: to narrate the life of Sir Edward Coke and to put it into a cultural setting amid the historical events which retrieve Coke and his life from the dimness of old records and place them vividly before the mind's eye of the reader.

Through the book pass figures important in Coke's life and his times: Queen Elizabeth, the greatest of the Tudors; Sir Francis Bacon, Coke's rival for royal favor and office; Sir Walter Ralegh, Elizabeth's sometime favorite and James I's victim; the Cecils, valiant upholders of both Elizabeth and James; the Earl of Essex, Elizabeth's favorite who, according to Coke, sought to become Robert I of England and actually became the traitorous Robert the Last. In the narrative, too, are figures less well known but important in Coke's life: Bridget Coke, his pleasant first wife; Lady Hatton, Coke's egocentric second wife; Clem Coke, Sir Edward's bellicose, even unruly, son and fellow Parliamentarian; Frances Coke, Sir Edward's favorite daughter; and Justice Doddridge, "the sleeping judge" who sat with Coke on the bench. In addition to these people, the author has given life to the background, the situations, and the events of England in Sir Edward Coke's time—events, situations, and background against which Coke loomed as an important figure through his service as a member of the House of Commons, as Attorney-General, as Justice of the Court of Common Pleas, as Chief Justice of the King's Bench, as High Steward of Cambridge University, as High Sheriff of Buckinghamshire, and as the author of legal studies recognized in his own times as influential and important. The career of Coke took him to the heart of such events as the trials of Sir Walter Ralegh and the Earl of Essex, the Gunpowder Plot, the Lopez conspiracy to assassinate Queen Elizabeth, the intrigues of Father Gerard and other Jesuits to return England to Roman Catholicism, and the battles between Parliament and the Stuart kings.

In addition to the people and the events, there are the great issues of Elizabethan and Stuart England. Sir Edward Coke's career took him into such problems as the authority of the ecclesiastical courts, the question of whether the crown could tax subjects without the consent of the House of Commons, the prerogatives of the crown in jailing persons suspected of crime without benefit of hearing or trial, and the right of the crown to dictate to Parliament. Once raised to the bench, Coke was always on the side of the common law, its precedents, and Parliament. As the outstanding legal authority of the time, he was the center of the fight against royal prerogative, while his lifelong rival and more familiar Elizabethan, Sir Francis Bacon, acted on behalf of the crown.

Throughout her biography of Sir Edward Coke, the author keeps before the reader the thesis that her subject was fighting an early battle for constitutional, as opposed to monarchical, government, the same thesis that ties this volume to her biographies of President John Adams and Justice Oliver Wendell Holmes. But neither her thesis nor the weight of the carefully recounted legal procedures bears too heavily upon the reader, and for this Catherine Drinker Bowen deserves commendation. In a biography of this kind many chapters are of necessity concerned with law cases and their presentation before the courts. By writing in narrative, rather than expository fashion, the biographer has made these cases invite careful reading, even when the actual cases, like those of the Five Knights and Commendams, lack the dramatic quality intrinsic to such trials as those of the Earl of Essex and Sir Walter Ralegh. Wishing to document her work and yet minimize interruptions in reading, the author has put her source references in a separate section of the book, listing them chapter by chapter and citing the pages and lines in the text to which they refer. The result is a decided help to the general reader and probably no hindrance to scholarly use of the volume. The explanatory notes have been gathered into a separate section for the reader's convenience. One other organizational aspect of the book deserves notice, the almost copious index provided to give the reader easy reference to materials he has read.

Although most educated Englishmen and Americans know of, if not about, Sir Edward Coke, very few biographies have been written about him in the three centuries since his death. Only three were published prior to *The Lion and the Throne*. One reason for so little apparent interest on the part of biographers has probably been the fact that the usual documents used in biography—letters, diaries, and domestic records—are, as Catherine Drinker Bowen points out in her statement of "Sources and Method," lacking in the case of Sir Edward Coke. The biographer must look for the personality of the subject in more scattered places, especially in comments Coke made, almost in passing, in his *Reports* and *Institutes*. To bring together these relics of a personality gone for more than three centuries was a formidable task; to set that personality into a meaningful background increased the difficulty greatly. Catherine Drinker Bowen accomplished both purposes and did it well. She even makes law Latin and law French, often a stumbling block in legal biographies, no obstacle for her reader.

Subject, treatment, and style marked this biography for literary honors. It has received the Phillips Award of the American Philosophical Society, the Philadelphia Award established by the late Edward W. Bok, and the National Book Award for an outstanding work of non-fiction.

LION IN THE GARDEN
Interviews with William Faulkner, 1926–1962

Editors: James B. Meriwether (1928–   ) and Michael Millgate (1929–   )
Publisher: Random House (New York). 299 pp. $6.95
Type of work: An anthology of interviews

A meticulously edited anthology assembling interviews from the early days when Faulkner's reputation was at best obscure, through the days when the word "Faulkner" was a term of notoriety if not of opprobrium, and into the times when William Faulkner became established as a modern-day sage whose every word should be greeted with unquestioning reverence

A collection of interviews, dating over some thirty-six years, with a man who described himself as "a writer not a talker" and who was notoriously hostile and incommunicative with interviewers, may threaten to be tedious or unrewarding reading. It is neither. *Lion in the Garden* provides an illuminating and often amusing gauge of critical judgment and a revealing portrait of the great lion of modern literature, William Faulkner.

The interviews, chronologically arranged, illustrate how fickle public opinion may be. Early reviewers seemed often to equate Faulkner's writing with "putting nasty people on paper," while *The New Yorker*, in 1931, in condescendingly reproducing his Southern accent, managed to establish William Faulkner as merely a sort of L'il Abner in tweeds: "Ah write when the spirit moves me," he says, "and the spirit moves me every day." Often the early interviewers were oblivious to Faulkner's sense of ironic humor and to the "put-on." They recorded, with complete credulity, how he had written best when a power plant's huge dynamo was humming away beside his bunk or how he preferred a return to slavery because there were no lynchings in the slave days. Not all of the early interviewers were, of course, so credulous. Marshall J. Smith, though largely taken in, could nevertheless understand that Faulkner's humorous evasions were his "barrier, the hazard he places around the sensitive part of him that can create such novels as *Soldier's Pay, Mosquitoes, Sartoris,* and *As I Lay Dying.*" But Faulkner was approached by few interviewers so perceptive. All too often they were obnoxiously audacious interlopers who felt a press card gave them the perogative to plunder through the personal affairs of William Faulkner; all too often they came with contempt for, misunderstanding of, or ignorance about the writings themselves. What the interviewers needed to understand was that Faulkner believed, as he wrote in 1953, ". . . that, until a writer committed a crime or ran for public office, his private life was his own"; that as Madeleine Chapsal put it in 1955, "There is no use looking at Faulkner. You must read him."

After the awarding of the Nobel Prize in 1950 more people did, apparently, read Faulkner. Interviews with him are more frequent, more expansive, and more illuminating. The editors of *Lion in the Garden* explain that "the public appearances he made, the public responsibilities he accepted in his last years, do not represent a weakening, as some have supposed, but only a change in Faulkner's conception of his duty as an artist." Furthermore, Faulkner's later loquaciousness may be attributed to a change not so much in the novelist as in the interviewers. Faulkner could still be scathingly hostile to the patronizing and superficial approach (as, apparently, he was at a Paris garden party in 1955 to a woman who, putting down her cocktail, approached him saying, " 'And now I am going out to put a few questions to our dear, our great Faulkner' "); but interviewers who were, after 1950, generally more sensitive, more intelligent, and more interested in and knowledgeable about Faulkner's work itself found the writer amiable and even eager to talk with them.

Throughout *Lion in the Garden,* however, what one principally senses is not so much the sensitivity or insensitivity of the interviewers, but the grandeur of the man William Faulkner. His humor never wanes; he is always capable of statements such as "You can't drink eight hours a day. Or make love. Work's about the only thing a fellow has to do to keep from being bored." But in the later comments there is care lest his flippancy be misinterpreted. The man is beautifully humble. When asked for his reaction to André Gide's remark that "there is not one of Faulkner's characters who properly speaking has a soul," Faulkner merely replies: "Well, I would say that the trouble with that is not my characters but with me, that the fault is in me, that I could not describe the soul. To me they had souls . . ." and, without rancor, he can say of Gide, "Yes— good talent, very intelligent talent." In Japan when asked if he were "giving a lecture or something in Nagano?" he simply states, "I attend the seminar in American literature." During the Japanese interviews, which are reprinted complete from *Faulkner at Nagano,* Faulkner displays immense good will

and patience. He endures the repetitive and certainly irksome standard questions about his style, his influences, and his estimate of Hemingway with amazing tolerance. Only once does he become exasperated enough to say, "I just answered that."

Faulkner seems determined in the later years to continue the rhetoric of the Nobel Prize address. It is as if he has taken the responsibility on himself of countering and setting straight the years of criticism which had assumed that his style, his characters, and, indeed, the author himself were all debased and degenerate. Faulkner talks repeatedly of the necessarily "absolute" integrity of the writer and of his responsibility to deal with truth and "set it on fire so that people will remember it." Truth, to Faulkner, is roughly equivalent to natural law: ". . . it's what man knows is right and that when he violates it, it troubles him"; but he does not talk of truth or value as being objective or suprahuman, but rather as being highly subjective and humanistic. He considers Christianity to be "every individual's individual code of behavior by means of which he makes himself a better human being than his nature wants to be, if he followed his nature only." Although he insists that "neither God nor morality can be destroyed," Faulkner's concept of God is secularized and, in fact, humanized; it involves "a God who is the most complete expression of mankind. . . ." Faulkner's faith, then, rests ultimately with man. He says: "I believe in man in spite of everything," and he believes because man is capable of accepting the agony of his situation, of confronting the atrocities in his own nature, and of, nevertheless, prevailing. Faulkner explains: ". . . man's immortality is that he is faced with a tragedy which he can't beat and he still tries to do something with it"; he is "indestructible because of his simple will to freedom."

James B. Meriwether and Michael Millgate have edited and indexed *Lion in the Garden* with scrupulous attention to detail. They have consulted with each of the interviewers or their original editors. Evidencing total familiarity with the Faulkner canon, they correct, in footnotes, the interviewers' often flagrant mistakes, while they insist that they make notations only of those errors which might "mislead the reader about significant matters of fact." They invite comparisons of Faulkner's positions on different occasions as well as comparisons of the interviews themselves (noting, for instance, the consistency of style in the two *New Yorker* pieces). In the footnotes they pass no judgment on (though they do correct) such errors as one reviewer's placing an incident in *The Sound and the Fury* rather than in *Absalom, Absalom!* or another's speaking of the capital of Mississippi as "Jacksonville," but in the editorial remarks preliminary to each interview they do allow themselves considerable subjectivity. Of the 1931 *New Yorker* article they write that "it contains, considering its brevity, more than its share of biographical errors." They call attention to Faulkner's "interesting and appealing" recollection of his early days in New Orleans when he was "a free man." Meriwether and Millgate explain the success of Loïc Bouvard's interview, in which Faulkner talked of

Bergson and the fluidity of time, of the myth of Sisyphus, of Flaubert, Balzac, Proust, and Malraux, of the South, of morality, and of God, by commenting that "perhaps no other interviewer brought to a meeting with Faulkner quite the same personal and intellectual resources." Of Madeleine Chapsal's account of Faulkner at a French garden party, they say that "it is perhaps the best account of Faulkner interviewed that has ever been written." And of *The Paris Review* treatment, Meriwether and Millgate do not hesitate to say: "This is in many ways the most important and most influential of all Faulkner's interviews."

Every interview with William Faulkner ever printed is not, of course, included in *Lion in the Garden*. These interviews have been chosen on the basis of their being "significant" and, presumably, relatively inaccessible. (A fairly significant interview with Robert Cantwell, for instance, is not included, perhaps because it is anthologized elsewhere.) Although further explanation of the editors' standards for inclusion and an exhaustive bibliography of interviews not included would have been helpful, *Lion in the Garden* is otherwise flawless. A meticulously edited compilation of interviews which are indeed significant, the book's real strength lies in the person of William Faulkner who reveals himself, in comments the editors never presume to condense or to bowdlerize in any way, as a man of immense sensitivity, genius, stature, and vision.

Panthea Reid Broughton

LITTLE BIG MAN

Author: Thomas Berger (1924-   )
Publisher: The Dial Press (New York). 440 pp. $5.95
Type of work: Novel
Time: 1852-1876
Locale: The West

A wildly picaresque novel combining history and myth in the story of the American West from the end of the gold rush to Custer's Last Stand

Principal characters:

JACK CRABB, called Little Big Man by the Indians, a plainsman, buffalo hunter, Indian scout, gambler, mule skinner, and adopted brother of the Cheyenne
CAROLINE, his Amazonian sister
OLGA, his white wife
SUNSHINE, his Indian wife
AMELIA, his adopted niece
THE REVEREND SILAS PENDRAKE and
MRS. PENDRAKE, his white foster parents
OLD LODGE SKINS, a Cheyenne chief, his Indian foster father
YOUNGER BEAR, a Cheyenne brave
LITTLE HORSE, a womanish Cheyenne
GENERAL GEORGE ARMSTRONG CUSTER
WILD BILL HICKOK
WYATT EARP
CALAMITY JANE
LAVENDER, an ex-slave
RALPH FIELDING SNELL, a dilettantish student of Western history and the editor of Jack Crabb's memoirs

Henry David Thoreau, walker and watcher in a tamed countryside of pastures and woodlots, found that his excursions out of Concord invariably drew him toward the West. In his essay "Walking" he wrote: "Eastward I go only by force; but westward I go free. . . . Let me live where I will, on this side is the city, on that the wilderness, and ever more I am leaving the city more and more and withdrawing into the wilderness. I should not lay so much stress on this fact if I did not believe that something like this is the prevailing tendency of my countrymen. I must walk toward Oregon, and not toward Europe. . . . We go eastward to realise history and study the works of art and literature, retrac-ing the steps of the race; we go westward into the future, with a spirit of enterprise and adventure."

These sentences more or less sum up the mood and movement of the frontier experience in America, the westward tug of history deeply grained in the national character and consciousness. For the frontier is still our most enduring image of our passions and energies as a people, and this is one reason why Thomas Berger's *Little Big Man* raises certain problems in connection with the treatment of the West in fiction, matters that put the book's vigor and persuasiveness as a novel within a larger frame of reference.

Mr. Berger writes about the West and the past—two areas in which, as

Bernard DeVoto pointed out years back, there is no clear boundary line between fact and fable. History is the record of what really happened and the story of what other men have thought really happened; it is the hard core of truth and the residue of legend and romance left behind by the flow of history into other places and later times. Certainly to many Americans the West is more a landscape of the imagination than a geographical region. The story of westward expansion was a historical reality, but it was also myth, a summons to freedom and adventure, the promise of the bright, fair land under the sunset. In outline the myth goes back beyond the cowtown, the mother lode, and the covered-wagon trails to Daniel Boone in the Kentucky canebrakes and Natty Bumppo in the forest beside Lake Glimmerglass; in effect it gives shape and drama to our history and confirms our unity and progress as a nation. Because the frontier is the most deeply imagined and possessed experience within the collective memory, we have grown accustomed to seeing it only in a broad and romantic perspective, an account of individual enterprise and heroic achievement, with little regard for the cost in economic waste, hardship, and eroded human values. Too often our image of the West ignores the contrast between illusion and reality, the tensions of history defined in terms of human necessity and moral conflict.

What is true of the history of the West holds also for the literature it produced. Everything that happened occurred too rapidly for assimilation and assay as the cavalryman, the cowboy, and the settler followed the long rifle, the mountain man, and the forty-niner into westward fantasy. Quick to seize upon whatever was colorful and violent in the story of the West, the dime novelists created a literature of melodrama and sentimentality, and out of these crude beginnings the sagebrush romance and the cowpoke classic were born. The Old West became the Wild West too soon. Without a proper distance to give the past depth and meaning, the novelist had little opportunity to evaluate the frontier experience in the West in its social and moral aspects as well as in its historical perspectives. The task confronting the serious writer in the West today is the job of reclaiming the realities of the westward movement from the stereotypes and clichés of the popular "Western." In this connection the work of reassessment now engaging an active group of regional historians may prove as relevant to art as it is to scholarship.

The true story of the West, as history now instructs us, was different from anything we read in the older romances. In one sense the westward advance was a triumphant march of conquest and settlement, but every halt along the way was marked by lost hopes and ruined lives, like the litter left behind the wagon train after an overnight stop. At the same time the darker, wilder side of the pioneer effort was creating new tensions and terrors in the American soul. Often the silence and loneliness of space—mountains, plains, sky—ate into the consciousness of the frontiersman until his struggle to subdue the land became psychic, an urge to lay waste and destroy; the ravages of the machine age did little more than complete a process that the wilderness hunter and the settler began. The physical frontier reached its dead end more than three-quarters of a century ago, but its influence is still apparent in the social and moral structures of our present society. To it we owe in part the dreams on which materialism feeds, the restlessness, the violence, the buried fears and guilt, and the mood of alienation noted by observers from abroad, a sense of lostness and seeking that runs like a melancholy refrain through much of our literature.

The unrest and rootlessness at the bottom of the American experience has always puzzled the perceptive European. D. H. Lawrence, pondering these matters, found their source in the spirit of a place violated by exploitation and the bloody Indian wars; and he wrote a book on the subject, a flawed but imaginatively conceived work offering occasional illuminating insights into our national psyche: "At present the demon of the place and the unappeased ghosts of the dead Indians act within the unconscious or under-conscious soul of the white American, causing the great American grouch, the Orestes-like frenzy of restlessness in the Yankee soul, the inner malaise which amounts almost to madness, sometimes. . . . America is tense with latent violence and resistance. The very common sense of white Americans has a tinge of helplessness in it, and deep fear of what might be if they were not common-sensical." He added prophetically: "The deliberate consciousness of Americans so fair and smooth-spoken, and the under consciousness so devilish. *Destroy! destroy! destroy!* hums the under consciousness. *Love and produce! love and produce!* cackles the upper consciousness. And the world hears only the Love-and-produce cackle. Refuses to hear the hum of destruction underneath. Until such time as it will *have* to hear." Lawrence's theories are relevant to a discussion of *Little Big Man* because the novel is, in general outline, a story of the white man and

the Indian in tragic confrontation on the Western plains: two races, two colors, two cultures, and one doomed.

All of this is an extended preamble to saying that Thomas Berger has brought together such a variety of themes from American life and history, so many aspects of vision, and such skillful adaptation of tall-story humor and techniques that his book stands out as a genuine product of the creative imagination, a new and different kind of novel about the West. As spacious in design as the broad landscape it encloses, it is violent, rambunctious, grotesque, funny, and at times deeply moving. Even if it is read carelessly or naïvely as a boisterous satire on all the Western yarns ever told, it still registers a considerable impact. But under the frontier-bred comedy of exaggerated detail and improbable circumstance Mr. Berger is dealing with deeper, darker matters. Like most of our serious writers, past or present, he is concerned with the problem of being an American, a complicated business in the best of times but one now made even more difficult by the conditions of life within a society grown increasingly aware of its divided existence. The themes of modern fiction have become general: the barren stretches of loneliness and failed communication between the past and the present, between the individual and community thought and feeling, between appearances and reality.

Reading the works of our younger novelists, we sometimes get the impression that their books have been shaped to strange forms between the pressures of a wholly personal vision of experience on the one hand and an almost ungraspable reality on the other. What sets Mr. Berger apart in this case is the way he goes about the business of being a writer. Faced by the complexities and ambiguities of the world around them, most of his contemporaries retreat into some private area of sensibility from which their novels emerge to tell us of absurd or violent happenings in our land. This was also Mr. Berger's way in his two previous novels, *Crazy in Berlin* and *Reinhart in Love*, which juxtaposed the serious and the comic against present-day settings; but in *Little Big Man* he follows a different course. Here he simply moves backward to a time and a place that allow his imagination to deal in free and often irreverent fashion with the history, the myths, the folk clichés of the Western experience. In this novel the rigors and dangers of the frontier do not enlarge upon life for pictorial or dramatic effect; they are its actual substance. The result is a lively chronicle which simplifies much that other men have told us about the West yet manages, by strategic handling of detail, to contain a great deal of historical, social, and moral truth within its catch-all flow.

Presented as the reminiscences of Jack Crabb, a former frontiersman, mule skinner, buffalo hunter, gun fighter, gambler, Indian scout, and adopted Cheyenne who claims, among other things, that he is the only white survivor of Custer's Last Stand, *Little Big Man* is a novel between two notes. The first of these, "Foreword by a Man of Letters," is slyly imitative of the prefaces written by eighteenth century novelists. In it Ralph Fielding Snell, a dillettantish antiquarian and amateur student of the Old West, tells how he first heard of Jack Crabb, how he located him at last in a home for the aged, and how the old man, then 111, dictated into a tape recorder his recollections of life on the plains between 1852 and 1876. A brief epilogue tells of Crabb's death—he was buried, incidentally, on the seventy-seventh anniversary of the Custer massacre—and offers some speculations on the veracity of his story. The editor's conclusion is that "Jack Crabb was either the most neglected hero in the history of this country or a liar of insane proportions." In either case this unsung hero of the West packed into his narrative enough experiences, exciting, ribald, or downright preposterous, to create his own legend and a new version of Western history.

The opening sentence sets the picaresque tone and suggests the episodic pattern of the action to follow: "I am a white man and never forgot it, but I was brought up by the Cheyenne Indians from the age of ten." As he tells it, Jack Crabb was the son of a backwoods evangelist who did his preaching in a saloon to a congregation of river boatmen, gamblers, frontier bullies, and prostitutes. In 1852, when Jack was ten, his father decided to go to Utah and become a Mormon. Somewhere west of Laramie the wagon train with which the Crabbs were traveling encountered a small band of Cheyenne warriors and made the mistake of giving the Indians whiskey. The drunken braves then proceeded to kill the men of the train and rape the women—all except Jack's mother and his Amazonian sister Caroline, who threatened their attackers with her bull-whip. The next day the Indians reappeared bringing some horses in payment for their depredations. This time Caroline decided that the Indians had come for her, and to their bewilderment she insisted on returning with them to their camp, taking Jack along for company. But when she realized that the Indians were not interested in her mannish person, she went off in a huff. Left behind, Jack grew up in the Cheyenne camp. Old Lodge Skins, the chief, became his foster father and mentor. By the time he was fifteen the boy had mastered the arts of the hunt and the war trail and had been given an Indian name, Little Big Man. But when the Cheyenne prepared to engage a troop of U.S. cavalry, Jack decided that he wanted to be a white man after all. Rubbing off his warpaint and yelling in English, he allowed himself to be "rescued" and claimed that the Indians had kept him a prisoner after killing his family five years before.

For a time he stayed with the Army at Leavenworth. Then he was sent to live with the Reverend Silas Pendrake in a town in western Missouri. There he went to school until Mrs. Pendrake, a lovely woman whom he slyly adored, turned out to be another lost lady. Disillusioned, he ran away to St. Louis, almost starved to death, signed up with a wagon train headed west, was captured by Comanches, escaped, and made his way to Santa Fe, where he took up with a Mexican woman. While prospecting for gold in Colorado, he joined a trading partnership in Denver. After another short stay with the Cheyenne he married a Swedish girl, Olga, and fathered a son. He lost his wife and child in an Indian attack on a stagecoach, became a drunk, was rescued from saloon rowdies by his sister Caroline, and for the next two years helped to build the Union Pacific. Work on the railroad took him into Cheyenne country once more. During a raid he acquired an Indian wife and a foster son. With them he returned to the band led by Old Lodge Skins.

That was how he happened to be living with the Indians when their camp was destroyed in a surprise attack by George Armstrong Custer and his troops at the Battle of the Washita in 1868. After helping Old Lodge Skins to safety, Jack escaped by putting on the uniform of a dead cavalryman. His Indian wife and newborn son had disappeared during the fighting. Blaming Custer for their death, he swore that he would kill the general in revenge. His mind filled with visions of Custer dying on the ground, Jack wandered into the Indian Territory, almost perished of exhaustion and cold, was saved by a family of Creeks, met a band of border outlaws, traveled as far as San Francisco looking for his sister, and then returned to Kansas City. There he met Wild Bill Hickok, who taught him to shoot. In a Kansas City sporting house he found Amelia, a girl who reminded him of his sister Sue Ann. Convinced that she was his niece, he placed her in a fashionable school and turned buffalo hunter to earn enough money to make her into a lady. His plan succeeded; she married the son of a state senator.

By that time Jack was no longer pursuing Custer. "I guess most of us have got a sort of statute of limitations within our hearts," the old man explained; "unless a man is a lunatic, violent feelings taper off after a while." So he was moved to a kind of grudging admiration when he and Custer met at last in the Dakota territory in 1876. By that time Jack had attached himself unofficially to Custer's command. "Anyhow, that's why no roster of the men present at the Battle of the Little Bighorn ever contained my name. Custer thought I was a herder; and the herders and teamsters themselves figured I was an interpreter or guide." He was both by the time the Seventh Cavalry encountered the Sioux and the Cheyenne and the battle began. Jack Crabb's story of Custer's Last Stand is masterly in detail and dramatic vigor. According to his account, after Custer's fall he was carried from the field by a Cheyenne whose life he had saved years before. "But I alone was there and lived it and have told the God's honest truth so far as recollection serves. . . . Why have I kept silent till now? . . . I guess my reasons for mainly keeping quiet boil down to this: Who would ever have believed me? But I am now too old to care."

On this framework, like an old squaw tanning hides, Mr. Berger manages to stretch a variety of effects. On one level *Little Big Man* is a work of comic exaggeration, an exercise in our tall-story humor of dry understatement, improbable situation, and masculine vigor. On another it is beguiling melodrama, the Old West of wagon trains, Indian fighting, violence, sudden death. On still a third it is a novel of atmosphere, its pages filled with a sense of wide lands and empty skies, or border towns and Indian camps. But the true meaning of the novel comes through, not in landscape pictures or frontier adventure, but in the patterning of images and ideas that bring the whole into proper focus.

First of all, there is the manner of its telling. When the novel appeared, most reviewers were disturbed by Mr. Berger's method of introducing his story. The intrusion of a supposed editor, they said, was as labored as it was unnecessary. It must be admitted that the device is awkward, but if we examine the novel closely we see that the prologue and epilogue are neither a structural flaw nor a self-conscious way of accounting for Jack Crabb's narrative. The comments of Ralph Fielding Snell serve their purpose because they create an ironic contrast between the younger man, to whom the story of the West is only material read in books or relics, such as Crazy Horse's purported war bonnet, bought from dealers, and the old man who still possesses the West in memory, out of time but not out of mind. What Jack Crabb saw or did will never happen again, but the life of that place and those days still tugs at the common imagination as they recede from us into a past of history and legend.

Then there is the skill with which Mr. Berger presents the archetypal figures of the West in new dimensions of reality and myth. All the familiar characters are here—the hunter, the badman, the trader, the frontier marshal, the madam, the Amazon who was as profane as any man and fast on the draw, the Indian, the soldier. The last two are the most meaningful. Custer and Old Lodge Skins are obviously set in contrast—the cavalryman a creature of vanity, arrogance, and courage, ruthless in his wish to destroy, whose bravery at the end was as foolish as it was heroic; the Indian cruel, reserved, wise in the ways of nature, doomed. Jack Crabb finds him a man to respect. "You might have noticed that Old Lodge Skins started out as a buffoon in this narrative," he comments. "Let me say that was true only around white men. Among the Cheyenne he was a sort of genius. It was him who taught me everything I learned as a boy that wasn't physical like riding or shooting." In the confrontation of the white man and the red in the West, Mr. Berger gives Old Lodge Skins the final word on the true meaning of the white victory: "There is no permanent winning or losing when things move, as they should, in a circle. . . . The buffalo eats grass, I eat him, and when I die, the earth eats me and sprouts more grass. Therefore nothing is ever lost. . . . But white men, who live in straight lines and squares, do not believe as I do. With them it is everything or nothing. . . . They will even fight at night or in bad weather. But they hate the fighting itself. Winning is all they care about, and if they can do that by scratching a pen across paper or saying something into the wind, they are much happier. . . . For killing is a part of living, and they hate life."

Lastly, there is the matter of the style. It is colloquial speech, simple, direct, often ungrammatical, sometimes surprising in its literate turns, but rich in elemental feeling and precise in narrative effect. It is the mixture of the unlearned and the literary that we often find in old letters or the records that the pioneers left behind them in the books they wrote. The language belongs to the country and the time, remote enough from our own speech to be convincing but never archaic or lapsing into dialect.

This is a big book, perhaps a truly important one, for it shows what can still be done with the story of the West when time and change have made it manageable, with the stereotyped and the mechanical drained away. Quite simply, Mr. Berger has repossessed the West—its landscape, its history, its society—given it new dimensions of the imaginative and the fabulous, and presented it as a renewed part of our usable past. That he has done so without solemnity is all to his credit.

Dayton Kohler

Sources for Further Study

Criticism:

Dippie, Brian W. "Jack Crabb and the Sole Survivors of Custer's Last Stand," in *Western American Literature*. IV (Fall, 1969), pp. 189-202. An interesting examination of Berger's blending of the West of history and the West of myth.

Gurian, Jay. "Style and the Literary Desert: *Little Big Man*," in *Western American Literature*. III (Winter, 1964), pp. 285-296. Gurian demonstrates the means by which Berger applied his imagination to realism and widened the possibilities of the Western novel.

Wylder, Delbert E. "Thomas Berger's *Little Big Man* as Literature," in *Western American Literature*. III (Winter, 1969), pp. 273-284. Meaning is achieved in the novel, according to this article, by absurdity being added to absurdity, with a sprinkling of the Western spirit.

Reviews:

Best Sellers. XXIV, November 1, 1964, p. 309. 900 words.

Book Week. October 11, 1964, p. 24. 1,050 words.

Commonweal. LXXXI, November 20, 1964, p. 294. 1,100 words.

New York Review of Books. III, December 17, 1964, p. 21. 500 words.

Saturday Review. XLVII, October 10, 1964, p. 39. 1,050 words.

THE LITTLE GIRLS

Author: Elizabeth Bowen (1899-1973)
Publisher: Alfred A. Knopf (New York). 307 pp. $4.95
Type of work: Novel
Time: The present
Locale: England

The ironic comedy of an elderly widow's search for lost time

Principal characters:
    DINAH DELACROIX ("DICEY"), a poetically whimsical widow
    SHEILA ARTWORTH ("SHEIKIE"), Dinah's former schoolmate
    CLARE BURKIN-JONES ("MUMBO"), a fashion entrepreneur, the
        third of the schoolmate friends
    MAJOR FRANK WILKINS, Dinah's elderly devotee
    MAJOR BURKIN-JONES, Clare's father
    MRS. CORAL, Dinah's hospitable neighbor
    FRANCIS, a curious servant
    WILLIAM and
    ROLAND DELACROIX, the sons of Mrs. Delacroix

It is customary to assert that Elizabeth Bowen is possibly the greatest living English woman novelist in the tradition of Henry James and Virginia Woolf, and in several respects the comparison is a just one. Like Henry James and Mrs. Woolf, Miss Bowen teaches us a very genuine respect for the idea of tradition, for a social order which is a source of individual tribulation and frustration often, but which is nevertheless the custodian of important values still cherished by the person of discriminating sensibility. Throughout her career as a writer, Miss Bowen has been the leading exponent in modern British fiction of the intuitions of the feminine mind and of the sensibilities of the heart, and she has given her readers such wonderfully vivid and understanding portraits of feminine character as Karen Michaelis in *The House in Paris* and Stella Rodney in *The Heat of the Day,* composed in that fluent, subtle, poetic style which to some readers seems so admirable and to others so artificial, convolute, needlessly oblique in its syntax. In this novel the style is less mannered, more direct and colloquial, although not wholly without the characteristic double negatives and odd placement of the adverb: ". . . he sickened with love at the sight of his little daughter duly. . . ."

Her style, nevertheless, is one of the important means by which Miss Bowen gives her distinctive poetic perceptions "shape," by which she transforms social reality to a personal vision of some significant moral and imaginative pattern. She has defined the novel as a "non-poetic statement of a poetic truth," and often in her work this poetic truth resides in the revelation to her romantic heroines of the grave disparity between their absolute ideals and the living if corrupting reality of social experience. In the present work Miss Bowen has seemingly moved away from the persistent theme of the earlier novels, the trauma of innocent adolescence committed to a dream of love which leaves the heroine terribly vulnerable to the incursions of a tawdry milieu, but the attentive reader will nevertheless perceive a not unfamiliar pattern emerging in the plot: a protagonist widowed and unfulfilled in marriage pursuing an impossible romantic desire, not this time for ideal love, but for a meaningful relationship to the past, in E. M. Forster's sense of "only connect." After Dinah Delacroix, the protagonist, a widow living in Sussex, in a flash of recollection recalls a schoolgirl prank in which she and two friends were accomplices, she attempts to rediscover her friends and achieve the restoration of those tenuous links of adolescent affection and devotion with the companions from whom she has been separated for nearly fifty years.

The inspiration for this search for lost time comes from Dinah Delacroix's idiosyncratic undertaking (with her attentive bachelor friend, Major Frank Wilkins) to seal up in a neighboring cave a number of favorite objects expressive of the individual peculiarities of her friends, to be discovered by some far future race with "shattering" inferences as to the nature of these individual personalities which will survive the rigors of archeological research. Dinah has the sudden realization that she has somehow done all this before, a *déjà vu* experience. During the summer when she was eleven, in 1914, she and her two friends Sheila Beaker ("Sheikie") and Clare Birkin-Jones ("Mumbo"), fellow students at St. Agatha's in Southstone, had buried a coffer in the garden containing "secret" precious things and a ritualistic warning against disturbance, written in an "Unknown Language." Dinah undertakes to find her friends again by sending intimate and embarrassing notices to all the metropolitan papers. Sheila has been for years Mrs. Trevor Artworth, wife of the chief real estate broker of Southstone, and Clare, married and divorced, is again Birkin-Jones and owner of a chain of smart "Mopsie-

Pye" shops. The three friends are once more united at Dinah's Sussex home, but Dinah finds her old schoolmates morose, aggrieved, and uncomprehending of her motives. Dig up that coffer again? Absurd. Besides, St. Agatha had "copped" it during a German raid in 1940, and it was no more. Nothing, that is, remained of that past; as Clare remarks, quoting *The Tempest*, "Into thin air."

In Part II the narrative shifts to the distant past of 1914; this section is most entertainingly written, and if the novel is to be regarded as comedy, much of that aspect is here in the depiction of the vibrant, tempestuous relationships of the girls, in their remorseless scrutiny of each other which still survives during the Sussex reunion, and in the adventurous and hilarious plotting to secure and bury the coffer. Here Miss Bowen is at her best in catching the subtle overtones of the relationships of the parents and their children, the unspoken love of Major Birkin-Jones (killed at Mons, August 23, 1914) for Dicey's mother, Mrs. Piggott, the suggestion that Mrs. Piggott was perhaps being "kept" by her mother's cousin in Feverel Cottage, so redolent of English tradition and prewar security. The beach picnic in honor of Olive Pocock, turned twelve on 23 July, 1914, closes the section with an elegiac and nostalgic note— Dicey's parting from Mumbo and Sheikie for nearly fifty years.

The chief incident in Part III is the return of the three "revenants" to the garden at Southstone, now on a private estate, and their discovery that the coffer contains nothing of the past. When Clare refuses to yield to Dinah's pleas to stay with her in Sussex, the climax is reached in Dinah's attempted suicide (so we interpret the reference to

Macbeth and Dinah's remark that she was "her father's child"; he had committed suicide).

It is part of the understanding of this book to see that to Miss Bowen Dinah Delacroix is an introverted romanticist characterized by a cloistered nostalgia for the past, in futile pursuit of its venerable security. "Life works to dispossess the dead," the author remarks in *A World of Love,* and this is evidently the interpretation of the book jacket of *The Little Girls,* where the novel is described as "anti-nostalgic," "a cautionary tale." Nevertheless, to accept without careful qualification this reading of the novel is to overlook the subtlety of Miss Bowen's ironic and compassionate sympathy for a character's search for self-fulfillment and personal identity. There are evidences of Dinah's gradual disillusionment throughout this part of the novel. Her contemplation in Sheila's home of the watercolor of the long vanished picturesque High Street of Southstone concludes with the remark, "It might be better to have no picture of places which are gone. Let them go completely." That she has reached this resolution of her yearning for identity with the past seems evident in the last lines of the novel:

Turning to go, she thought of her last sight of the sands, from the sea wall: the wide sands and the running figure.
"Goodbye, Dicey," she said—for now and for then.
The sleeper stirred. She sighed. She raised herself on an elbow, saying, "Who's there?"
"Mumbo."

"Not Mumbo, Clare. Clare, where have you been?"

The last lines are comparable to the much disputed ending of *The World of Love,* wherein Jane, like Dinah, emerges from her commitment to the past; the parting on the sands at the picnic many years ago becomes symbolic of the separations and disjunctions that life sets up for human frustration.

In a very real sense, there is the artist in Miss Bowen sympathizing, nevertheless, with the artist in Dinah, who refuses to accept the possibility that the life of the individual is unmeaning, without connection, aimless lived through inconsequential fortuities and "prefabricated feelings" of the social environment. However mistaken the individual may be in his illusion, however tragic the consequences, it must be embraced; otherwise, as Dinah mumbles at the discovery of her attempted suicide, "It's all gone, was it ever there? . . . Nothing, No, no, no." In such a context, the despairing allusions to *Macbeth* (a less obtrusive device here than in Virginia Woolf's fiction) become symbolic: " 'All is the fear, and nothing is the love'—that's *Macbeth.*" Miss Bowen makes in her correspondence with Graham Greene a comment very pertinent here: "Even stories . . . which comment on or are pointers to futility, imply that men and women are too big or good for the futility. . . ." It is difficult to find such preoccupations with the tension and irony created by the mysterious incompatibility of ideals with reality either trivial, or snobbish, or sentimental.

John P. Kirby

THE LITTLE HOTEL

Author: Christina Stead (1902-   )
Publisher: Holt, Rinehart and Winston (New York). 191 pp. $6.95
Type of work: Novel
Time: Shortly after World War II
Locale: Montreux, Switzerland

A novel of interactions among eccentric characters residing at a small hotel in Switzerland

Principal characters:

> MME. BONNARD, the proprietor of the Swiss-Touring, a tourist
> hotel
> ROGER BONNARD, her husband and co-proprietor
> MRS. TROLLOPE, a middle-aged Englishwoman who has lived
> mainly in the East
> MR. WILKINS, her "cousin"; actually her lover
> PRINCESS BILI, an American, and the rich widow of an Italian
> nobleman
> MME. BLAISE, a Swiss housewife and drug addict
> DR. BLAISE, her husband
> THE MAYOR OF B., a half-mad Belgian
> MRS. POWELL, a patriotic American expatriate
> MISS ABBEY-CHILLARD, an Englishwoman and a permanent
> invalid

The Little Hotel begins with the voice of Mme. Bonnard, the voice of a preoccupied, lonely, somewhat callous woman who finds it is part of her job as proprietor of the Swiss-Touring to become privy to the inner lives of the guests at her small fourth-class establishment in a resort town on the shore of Lake Leman. Dealing with the confidences of the guests is one of her challenging problems, like dealing with the servants, or with her husband Roger, or with the police when irregularities occur.

Everything interests her, everything gives variety and color to her life, but nothing interests her unduly. "If you knew what happens in the hotel every day! Not a day passes but something happens," she begins, but it is hard to feel enthusiasm in her vague clichés. Yesterday, she says, a former guest, who has frequently called to pour out her joy and sorrow over her son and daughter-in-law, telephoned to tell her something tragic. The daughter-in-law was dead (a suicide? murdered?), the son had left home or was dead, too—but because of a language difficulty, Mme. Bonnard never quite got the straight of the story. Madame is busy; her head often aches; and although she is amused and even sympathetic, she is not really touched. She doesn't quite understand the human language. Her voice ranges from flat and impersonal to sharply satirical. Often she is impatient or even dictatorial.

Mme. Bonnard is lonely but never self-pitying. She has a five-year-old son, but he is always in the background, and her affection for him remains concealed. Some time ago she had a girl friend with whom she shared secrets; then she was happy. But once you marry, she says, you can't expect to be happy anymore.

Her husband Roger is practical and serious; he worries about the behavior of the guests and about the police and about being cheated. Often he spies on the guests while pretending to move furniture or fix a radiator. He chain smokes and has nervous fits and gets blue. Mme. Bonnard's best friend Julie is trying to attract Roger, who goes out quite a bit alone at night. All these details emerge from Mme. Bonnard's accounts, but Roger's real self remains hidden. His wife finds it interesting to be married and to try to keep a husband. She seems to look on him as a project.

Madame is just twenty-six, but seems much older; occasionally she has a good laugh with the servants or a fit of temper with Roger, but usually she seems settled and serious. To her, the elderly guests at the hotel are as irresponsible and disorderly as schoolchildren, and she runs the place like a schoolroom with plenty of rules and an insistence on order.

Mme. Bonnard has a fondness for the hotel servants, but she sees them as difficult and jealous and unreliable. If they dislike a guest, as they dislike the "Admiral," a commanding Englishwoman who is old and poor and does not tip, they spill food and give careless service. Francis, the French chef, insults the German and Italian servants. Charlie, the charming, broken-down handyman, seduces schoolgirls.

But it is the semi-permanent guests at the Swiss-Touring who are most troublesome and receive the most attention in Mme. Bonnard's narrative. The Mayor of B., for example, thoroughly delighted Mme. Bonnard at first. He was an expansive Belgian who bought champagne for the servants. He had come, it seems, for shock treatments at a local mental hospital. Soon he began to complain about Germans whom he imagined to be all over the hotel and poisoning his food. Finally, after running around town naked one night, he had to be locked up and then put on a train for Belgium; but he stole away from the train in France. Despite his fears and his peculiar habits, Mme. Bonnard sees him as a sympathetic, fun-loving man. But her objective view of this sample of the human comedy distances the reader and prevents him from perceiving the Mayor as a real human being.

The Mayor's lunatic fear of the Germans is counterpointed by other guests' fears of the Russians, fears which they discuss at length, especially when Mrs. Powell is in residence. Since inheriting her husband's fortune thirty-nine years ago, Mrs. Powell has traveled abroad to avoid United States income taxes. Though she never sees the United States, she is intent on aiding it in a last-ditch stand against the communists.

Gradually from Madame's interlaced stories and character sketches, a view of the principal guests emerges. Though not all expatriates, most are; all tend to be long-term residents at the Swiss-Touring because of problems with governmental money controls. Mme. Blaise, who is Swiss, is trying to lay claim to the property of enemy aliens which was entrusted to her and which has been sequestered in the United States. Miss Abbey-Chillard is unable to get money out from England, despite medical certificates that her chronic invalidism requires residence abroad.

Mrs. Trollope is gradually transferring funds from England, which she turns over to her "cousin" Mr. Wilkins to transfer from one currency to another. Some of the guests are poor, but most are not; they simply have money problems. Aging, dislocated, nervous, they stay on at the Swiss-Touring because it is cheap. They fuss at the servants and get on one another's nerves. Their lives are drab and pathetic, enlivened at first by little complaints of ill health or stolen property and small quarrels. But gradually it appears that for some, love and its difficulties are still of paramount importance.

In presenting life at the little hotel through the eyes of Mme. Bonnard, Stead has not been able to avoid a certain flatness, which pervades the book. Even though she changes point of view before the middle, the tone cannot change much, and the characters, who are riddled with faults and inadequacies, never become sufficiently vivid to grip the reader.

Less than halfway through the novel, Mme. Bonnard's voice fades away, and the narrative becomes third-person. Now the guests become more themselves, and the satire bites deeper and is mixed with more authentic emotion. The long central scene of the novel is a dinner party in a hotel, given by Mrs. Trollope and Mr. Wilkins. Guests are the Princess Bili, an American widow of an Italian nobleman, and owner of a dreadfully irritating little dog, Angel; Dr. and Mme. Blaise; and an English couple. A dispute over the women's dress, an orgy of ordering food and wines, a great deal of small talk are the surface under which raw tensions reveal themselves. Mme. Blaise,

whose husband brings her drugs when he visits her from Basel, is convinced her husband is having an affair with their housekeeper. Mrs. Trollope, while living in the East, took Mr. Wilkins as a lover; finally she became divorced from her husband only to find that Mr. Wilkins would not marry her. Now she has become deeply unhappy because of Mr. Wilkins' indifference. Her children are alienated from her; other guests condescend to her, thinking she is Eurasian. Mr. Wilkins, a selfish bachelor much attached to a mother and sisters he never sees, has promised his mother never to marry. More and more he makes Mrs. Trollope feel pathetically lonely, neglected, and hopeless. She finds a friend in the domineering Princess Bili, who intends to whip Mr. Wilkins into line before she goes off to South America with a much younger man. Like Dr. and Mme. Blaise, Mr. Wilkins and Mrs. Trollope are separated by years of emotional discord, but are held together by long-term ties as well as resentment of the other couple's behavior.

In this section, Stead's surgical knife peels away outer coverings to show nerves and hearts. The sharp satire and the collisions of lives are a good deal reminiscent of those in Katherine Anne Porter's *Ship of Fools,* as is the technique (long familiar, however) of bringing together various characters and having them play out their interwoven stories. The anguish and selfish cruelty of the characters are quite powerfully displayed, yet even after reading the book, one is not inclined to call the characters by their first names. Christina Stead, an expatriate herself for many years, living in England though born in Australia, never succeeds in making her personages truly sympathetic, despite a fine style and excellent ear for dialogue. Their Chekhovian discourses lack the poignancy and humor of Chekhov. Characters struggle and complain but remain ineffectual and dull. Nor does their eccentricity render them really entertaining. Of Miss Stead's eleven previous novels, *The Man Who Loved Children* is best known and most praised. *The Little Hotel,* however, is artistically superior to the earlier work.

Mary C. Williams

THE LITTLE HUT

Author: André Roussin (1911-   )
Adapted from the French by Nancy Mitford
Publisher: Random House (New York). 178 pp. $2.75
Type of work: Drama
Time: The present
Locale: A desert island

A translation of a French farce on a variation of the eternal triangle

Principal characters:
PHILIP, Henry's best friend
SUSAN, Philip's wife
HENRY, Susan's lover for the last six years

André Roussin has become France's most popular playwright. His play, *La Petite Hutte,* was a success in Paris, as have been many others of his plays. It is said that, since World War II, he has had more performances in more theaters than any of his countrymen.

His play gained momentum when it was carried across the English Channel. In London it ran for three years and was then toured extensively. In the British cast Robert Morley played the husband, Philip, until the part became associated only with his name. Some critics blame that association for the cool reception *The Little Hut* had when it played in New York, since Robert Morley was not in the American cast. Others lay the blame on "the strange sea change" that comes over plays when they are transported from Europe to the United States or vice versa. In any event, *The Little Hut* was a critical success, but not a popular one. Producers, still confident that the play could find an admiring public, took it on the summer circuit. There public reaction was more favorable.

The Little Hut, presented by John C. Wilson and H. M. Tennent, Ltd., opened in New York on October 7, 1953, at the Coronet Theatre. It is a farce, based on a variation of the eternal triangle. Two men and a woman have been stranded in evening clothes on a deserted island. When the play opens, they have been there long enough to have fashioned hammocks and huts from palm leaves, to have set up a mast with gramophone attached to attract prospective rescuers, and to have found coconuts, eggs, fish, and fruit to be their main diet.

The three are Philip and Susan, husband and wife, and Susan's lover for the last six years, Henry. Henry is also Philip's best friend. Their stay on the island has been quite pleasant, but Henry has begun to complain of loneliness. He has exercised himself only in locating truffles on the island while Philip has enjoyed his daily and necessary fishing and his daily but unnecessary hunting for butterflies. Philip has an inquiring mind and an inventive bent so that he has kept busy figuring out uses for products of the island—a coconut paste for blisters, another variation as a substitute for gunpowder, smashed oysters for shaving cream, and the like.

Philip and Susan have occupied a big hut while Henry has used the small one. Henry tells Susan that he has found the answer to his loneliness if she will only agree to let him speak to Philip. He thinks it is time to stop deceiving Philip, and the only way to do that would be to admit they have been lovers. Then he intends to ask Philip to share Susan with him. Susan thinks the idea of being shared an exciting one.

Philip is taken by surprise at Henry's suggestion, but is won over to trying the idea as a logical solution under the circumstances. After all, Henry is his best friend, and as far as he can see Susan has always treated them alike anyway. They plan to share Susan on alternate weeks.

About ten days later Henry is again unhappy, though Susan and Philip are as happy as they can be. This happens to be Philip's week with Susan, and they are sporting like newly-weds. Their happiness offends Henry because during his week on he had felt too guilty to enjoy himself and during this week off he feels too jealous. He tries to explain his feelings to Philip, but Philip feels them to be illogical. Philip himself thoroughly enjoyed Henry's week with Susan and is more thoroughly enjoying his own. He thinks a third person makes a marriage more vital and interesting, and he plans to spread the idea when he gets back home. Henry is horrified. He had failed to get Susan to agree that they should now all live like brothers and sister until a ship could rescue them, and he fails to put over the same idea to Philip. Philip and Susan are happy.

Henry tries to shame Philip by saying that Philip would agree to share Susan with any man who might come along. As the men go to dress for dinner, a splendid-looking stranger appears, dressed in a lei and a loin cloth from which hangs a wicked-looking knife. The men are startled and worried by the stranger, but when Susan sees him she curtsies and speaks of him as a crown prince. Since he can apparently understand no English, they carry on a sign-language conversation. He induces Henry and Philip into a dance during which he leads them into a huge net with which he ties them to the mast. While they are tied he has only to beckon to have Susan follow him into the hut. Henry is again horrified because Philip takes the situation philosophically when Susan says she will have them released before long.

The next day the stranger presents them with a fish cooked in a delicious sauce. Still snorting over Susan's apparent interest in the stranger and Philip's condoning of her method of having them freed from the net, Henry refuses to touch the fish. He will not deal with an enemy even if his whole tribe backs up the stranger. Philip praises Susan's thoughtfulness and self-sacrifice in getting them freed. Henry objects to the impropriety of the stranger's behaviour, but Philip points out that rules of etiquette change in different localities. Here, on a primitive island, they should expect the stranger to act in a primitive fashion.

When the stranger brings in fruit for dessert, Susan sighs that she would like to know how to make the fish sauce. The stranger, breaking his silence, promises to tell her. Then he admits being the Danish cook on the ship on which they all had been wrecked. His change in station from crown prince to cook makes Susan furious. She begs Philip and Henry to beat him up for treating her so shabbily. Henry is delighted to point out that Susan's pride has been hurt, but that basically she is a promiscuous woman. However, he promises to help Philip chastise the Dane. They set a trap for him but are caught themselves. Susan catches the cook unawares and trusses him up to the mast by the time the other men free themselves. Then they decide to let him live with them as long as he acts as their cook and valet. Henry decides to give up Susan, but Philip will not allow him to ruin their threesome. By the time a ship is sighted, Henry has decided their affair will have all the old charm only if he pretends to give up Susan. Then he will feel as though he were deceiving Philip once more.

The Little Hut, though clever and amusing, is little more than a frothy farce about two men and a girl. Its effectiveness on the stage would have to depend on its casting because three dull or slow people could easily kill the sly and subtle wit with which the play abounds. Even the logical Philip has to be played with a light touch. And the complaining Henry is really a ditherer. Susan, of course, is just Susan. All three of them, the husband, the lover, and the willing woman, are a rollicking trio.

THE LITTLE KAROO

Author: Pauline Smith (?-1959)
With an Introduction by Arnold Bennett and a Preface by William Plomer
Publisher: The Vanguard Press (New York). 189 pp. $3.50
Type of work: Short stories
Time: Early twentieth century
Locale: The Little Karoo, in Cape Colony

A reprint edition of a collection of short stories dealing with life among the Boers in South Africa fifty or more years ago—a minor classic of depth insights and great beauty of style

There are generations of critics and readers as well as generations of writers, often with wider gaps than we suppose between them. When *The Little Karoo* was published, for example, some of the reviews commented on the fact that this collection of short stories, originally published in England in the 1920's, was appearing in this country for the first time. But this reviewer, at least, remembers the 1925 American edition in exact detail—both the yellow-and-russet design of its binding and the eight stories it contained, each as clearly incised and as indelible as if copperplate and not print had put them on the page. In that rather distant time, before the present flood of books dealing with the tensions, violence, and squalor of South African life, and before apartheid had become a slogan and a challenge, Pauline Smith's unpretentious stories gave the impression of lasting value because of her fidelity to the facts of external reality and inner truth. A rereading of the book, to which two later tales have been added, merely confirms that memory of literary excellence contained in the simplicity and power of her writing.

At the time of her death, early in 1959, Pauline Smith was regarded as a pioneer among South African writers, a position made all the more apparent by her long silence. She wrote only three books in all: two collections of short stories, *The Little Karoo* and *Platkops Children,* and a novel, *The Beadle.* All appeared in the 1920's, and she apparently wrote nothing after that time. In them, however, her picture of a time and a vanished way of life is complete.

The daughter of an English father and a Scottish mother, Pauline Smith was born—the date remained a well-kept secret—in the Little Karoo, a desolate, mountain-rimmed region of veld and thorny scrubland dotted with small farms and widely separated hamlets set like green oases in that bleak stretch of plain. The neighbors of the Smiths were Afrikaners, descendants of the original Boer settlers, a sturdy, patriarchal people stubbornly resistant to change. In the introduction to the original edition, here reprinted, Arnold Bennett wrote:

They are simple, astute, stern, tenacious, obstinate, unsubduable, strongly prejudiced, with the most rigid standards of conduct—from which standards the human nature in them is continually falling away, with fantastic, terrific, tragic, or quaintly comic consequences. They are very religious and very dogmatically so. They make money and save it. Lastly, they enjoy a magnificent climate, which of course intensifies their passionate love of the Karoo.

Pauline Smith carried memories of

these people with her when, at the age of twelve, she went to school in England. Her first stories were attempts to explain the hardships, meager joys, and deep passions of their lives. This was in the years when she was learning to write, perfecting the Biblical cadences of her style and sharpening her insights to tell the stories of her Afrikaner farmers, millers, schoolmasters, sinners, fools, and saints. Out of these efforts came the tales in *The Little Karoo*.

"The Pain" sets the substance and tone for the collection. For almost half a century Juriaan van Royen and his wife Deltje had lived their childless married life in the remote Aangenaam valley. The rented land was poor, and hard-working Juriaan had never got ahead in the world. Circumstances which would have driven many couples apart had only brought Juriaan and Deltje closer together. But all the tenderness between them could not ease the pain that had begun to clutch at Deltje's side. Seeing her round, plump face twisted in agony when the pain struck, Juriaan felt that he could not stand the sight of her suffering. So when they heard of the new hospital in Platkops dorp, he decided to take her there to see if she could be cured. The journey by ox-cart took three nights and almost four days, and as the cart jolted along Deltje lay "like some gentle dumb animal . . . in the sweat and agony of her pain." At the hospital they were separated for the first night in almost fifty years. Juriaan and Deltje were both unhappy, the old man because his wife was in the care of strangers, Deltje because there was nothing she could do but lie in the hospital bed and remember the empty three-room mud house that Juriaan had built for her when she

was a bride. At last, when they could stand their misery no longer, Juriaan crept into the hospital at night, helped Deltje to dress, and started with her back to their farm, Deltje lying back against the pillows in quiet content. And Juriaan?

> Seated on the waggon-box before her Juriaan drove steadily across the veld, through the drift, and out on to the Platkops-Princestown road. Slowly his numbed heart regained its warmth. Slowly he came to feel that his God was no longer withdrawn. Here, in the ox-cart with his little love, was his God. Had He not eased her pain? If she was weak had He not given His servant Juriaan arms that were strong to carry her? Against his breast like a little child he would carry her, and so should she rest. . . .

The same theme of misery for those caught between the ties of home and the indifference of the outside world is sounded again in "Desolation," in which an old woman and her small grandson wander across the empty veld: "What would one have of life? If the wind blew cold then one was cold. If the wind blew hot then one was hot. One could not heat the wind nor cool it. One could not call forth the wind nor still it. One could but endure it as, by the will of the Lord, it blew across the earth."

Not all of Pauline Smith's stories, however, are tales of longing and love. Her people are equally moved by rage, hatred, greed, and lust. In "The Sinner" a poor farmer has deserted "his wife and his children, his lands and his tobacco, his conscience and his God," and goes to live with another woman. When his madness has passed he returns to his old wife, who in her understanding had sent him a bundle of clothing and a note reading: "God forgive me, Niklaas, if I should judge you, for there is not one of us who has not sinned." "The Schoolmaster" tells of a man who in rage blinds two mules and becomes a peddler drawing a cart to which he harnesses himself. But the reader will look in vain for the tensions of race in these stories. The black man is there but only dimly in the background. Perhaps the isolation of the Little Karoo in the early years of the century accounts for his absence on the immediate scene. When he does appear it is in a situation of trust and love, as in "Ludovitje," in which Maqwasi, a Kaffir laborer, is converted by a dying boy's singing of the 114th Psalm. He digs the boy's grave in the hard ground and before he returns to carry his new faith to his own people he digs two more graves in which the father and the mother will someday rest beside their son.

Pauline Smith was not one to blink squeamishly before all that was ugly and sordid in the lives of her people. But she saw the strong and the good as well, and what she saw she set down in her austere yet moving style which transforms much that is ordinary and harsh into something rich and strange. It is the same with her characters. They are people of a recognizable world and at the same time images of moral force—cruelty and kindness, love and hate, fortitude and weakness, humility and pride, self-sacrifice and greed—as elemental in their simplicity and significance as the primitive landscape they inhabit and the stern, just God they worship. These matters she recorded with a depth of feeling that never lapses into sentimentality and a passionate insight that is far removed from what reviewers call compassion when they find its vulgarized counterpart in today's fiction.

A LITTLE LEARNING

Author: Evelyn Waugh (1903-1966)
Publisher: Little, Brown and Company (Boston). Illustrated. 230 pp. $5.00
Type of work: Autobiography
Time: 1903-1926
Locale: England

Evelyn Waugh's account of his early years and the forces that shaped them

Principal personages:
EVELYN WAUGH
CATHERINE CHARLOTTE RABAN WAUGH, his mother
ARTHUR WAUGH, his father
FRANCIS CREASE, one of his two "mentors"
J. F. ROXBURGH, his other "mentor"
TERENCE GREENIDGE, an Oxford friend
JOHN SUTRO, another Oxford friend
HAROLD ACTON, an Oxford friend and the critic of Waugh's first
unpublished novel

Although *A Little Learning* is but the first of three volumes of Evelyn Waugh's autobiography, and as such must serve as a backdrop against which the drama of the later years will be played, it represents a complete picture in itself. It is the picture, if not drama, of Waugh's early years before he became a writer. The book ends with Waugh's half-hearted suicide attempt. How Evelyn Waugh describes this event gives a key to how he looks at his youth in general. At the time of this incident he had just burned the chapters of what was to be his first novel, had just been turned down as personal secretary to Scott Moncrieff, and had just given notice at an unnamed school on the coast of Flintshire, where he had gone after leaving Oxford and London. The background to the suicide has thus all the aspects of tragedy, but Waugh's description of this most personal of human actions remains half-cynical, half-comical and almost wholly detached. Describing his past, he has refined himself out of it.

One night, soon after I got the news from Pisa, I went down alone to the beach with my thoughts full of death. I took off my clothes and began swimming out to sea. Did I really intend to drown myself? That certainly was in my mind and I left a note with my clothes, the quotation from Euripides about the sea which washes away all human ills. I went to the trouble of verifying it, accents and all, from the school text. . . .
It was a beautiful night of a gibbous moon. I swam slowly out but, long before I reached the point of no return, the Shropshire Lad was disturbed by a smart on the shoulder. I had run into a jelly-fish. A few more strokes, a second more painful sting. The placid waters were full of the creatures. . . . I turned about, swam back through the track of the moon to the sands which that morning had swarmed under Grime's discerning eye with naked urchins. . . . Then I climbed the sharp hill that led to all the years ahead.

Evelyn Waugh is always on top of that sharp hill, looking down on his past, both literally and metaphorically.

If the ending of the book seems to be the description of some Paul Pennyfeather or Tony Last and not that of a real person, the effect is, one believes, intentional. For those who read autobiographies to find out the real man behind the author's mask, this book is bound to be disappointing. For those who read autobiographies to seek the seeds of an author's fictional interests, that is, the events and persons that appear in his novels, this book will offer a fairly fertile field, especially with respect to *Decline and Fall* and *Vile Bodies*. But *A Little Learning* demands to be read in quite a different way. Neither the exploration of the inner man nor a sourcebook for the later fiction, this book is rather the re-creation of the fiction itself. As illustrated above, Evelyn Waugh as a young man is, in the author's eyes, merely a character from the past. The reader is shocked by the photographs that appear in the text because the fiction is suddenly given form and a form that does not seem to have much connection with the fiction. This fiction is surrounded by a cast of other fictions, brilliantly sketched out for us in a style reminiscent of Waugh's early, pre-Brideshead days.

For example, Waugh repeatedly states that his family was the most important influence upon him, an influence separating him from other boys his age who had been shipped off to boarding schools:

> It was a world of privacy and love very unlike the bleak dormitories to which most boys of my age and kind were condemned.

Yet we really don't see his family at all. His mother is only a feeling; his father appears first a caricature to which Waugh becomes more and more attached as he grows older; and his brother Alec, five years older, is but a name, so far removed from contact with Evelyn that Evelyn has had to resort to Alec's memoirs to find out that he had been expelled from school.

The majority of Waugh's friends are likewise without real substance as presented to us: There is no blood in them. What is constantly being stressed is either their sexless or their homosexual natures. There is Francis Crease, one of the author's "mentors":

> He spoke, I found, in soft tones which in moments of amusement rose shrilly. Today he would be identified as an obvious homosexual. I believe he was entirely without sexual interests.

Or J. F. Roxburgh, his other "mentor":

> Mr. Crease, as I have said, was effeminate in appearance and manner; J. F. was markedly virile, but it was he who was the homosexual. Most good schoolmasters—and, I suppose, schoolmistresses also—are homosexual by inclination—how else could they endure their work? —but their interest is diffused and unacknowledged.

Fictional names are mixed with real ones, but the final impression left by all of them is that of a fictional world.

There are many things that could account for this comic and distant stance. As was implied in the suicide passage, Waugh seems to feel that he has changed considerably from his younger days, that there is, in fact, a cliff separating him from the past. In many ways the break must have occurred at the point of Waugh's conversion to Catholicism. The postconversion Waugh feels he is on much safer and more solid ground than the young and rootless Waugh who could not even trace his personal characteristics back to certain ancestral traits.

Indeed, the rather strange beginning of the book, where Waugh peruses his family's genealogy, represents his comment on tradition and the past. When he became a Catholic, he joined a tradition more meaningful and complete for him than his own rather eclectic family background. One of the things that strikes the reader immediately is the trace of anxiety with which Waugh looks back on his family for some antecedents for his conversion. He finds one Catholic, Theodosia Mahon, and one Catholic sympathizer, "my grandfather, Henry Biddulph Cotton, the lonely little boy with the rosary. . . ." Though he does not find the tradition of Catholicism, he finds the love of tradition.

> If there is one characteristic common to all my father's family, it is the habit of setting up house and staying there. I have inherited this propensity.

The older Waugh is at times impatient because his younger self did not feel this pull of tradition more strongly, even cynical about his former doubts, as in his description of the scene when he declared he couldn't be a sacristan because he was an atheist. This moralizing tone in describing his love of the past further removes him from his younger self and increases the fictional aspect of the work.

> More than once already in the preceding pages mention has been made of the obliteration of English villages. The process is notorious and inevitable. Expostulation is futile, lament tedious. . . . To have been born into a world of beauty, to die amid ugliness, is the common fate of all us exiles.

The change from past to present is very well illustrated in the following passage:

> Ivy House, as I have said, stood opposite with its grounds for a time unravaged. Once when the fence was being repaired I wrote my initials in the wet mortar of the low supporting wall and there I found them fifty years later under a mat of moss, somewhat eroded, so that they read "F.W.", but still an infinitesimal private landmark where all else was changed.

In fact, it is abundantly clear that Waugh feels he is writing in a tradition, not that of Augustine, Rousseau, or even Joyce; that is, not in the tradition of the confession, not even in the tradition of autobiography, but rather in the tradition of the memoir. He constantly refers to the fact that his remembrances will find parallels in other memoirs that have preceded his own. Often when he begins to relate an incident, his knowledge of its description in some one else's memoir will bring him up short.

> The Oxford Railway Club, which he originated, has been rhapsodically described by Mr. Harold Acton in his *Memoirs of an Aesthete*. As a sexagenarian I come late to autobiography. Many of my contemporaries have anticipated me. I would be otiose to recount in slightly different form anecdotes already so vividly told.

Memoir is probably a good generic category for this book, because what is related is the memory, not of oneself, but of events, friends, and Waugh's reaction to them.

But if the suicide scene and others like it are more fiction than fact, more representative of a memoir than a confession, they are still very much Evelyn

Waugh. That is, what the reader comes to discover is that this book is not so much a portrait of the artist as a young man, but a portrait of the artist as an old accomplished writer of prose. Once the reader realizes that he is not going to find out too much about Evelyn Waugh as a young man, he can find perpetual delight in his discovery of Evelyn Waugh the writer. In other words, the book's abiding interest will be in the way in which it is written. Here are some examples of this vintage Waugh. Speaking of his great-grandfather, he quotes the old man's injunction about his funeral:

> I desire my funeral to be as plain and simply conducted as is consistent with my Station as Rector of Corsley, and that the most worthy of the communicants carry me to my pillow beside her whom I loved in life and in death.

Waugh comments:

> This, it is scarcely necessary to say, referred to my great-grandmother who had died the year before he issued this direction. He mourned her sincerely, if luxuriantly. Her modest jewellery he had broken up and set in a chalice and flagon which, together with a patten, he gave to the church.

Speaking of a childhood friend, he writes:

> There was another boy, a particular friend of mine, who came early to grief, falling to his death in a Paris street from the window of a notorious pederast and drug-taker. He was richer and more sophisticated than I.

Again, speaking of his tutor at Oxford, C. R. M. F. Cruttwell:

> He was tall, almost loutish, with the face of a petulant baby. He smoked a pipe which was usually attached to his blubber-lips by a thread of slime. As he removed the stem, waving it to emphasize his indistinct speech, this glittering connection extended until finally it broke leaving a dribble on his chin. When he spoke to me I found myself so distracted by the speculation of how far this line could be attenuated that I was often inattentive to his words.

The descriptions of the Oxford days and the characters that peopled them reveal Waugh at his best. In these days of the "bright young people" there was a club created for every occasion and an occasion created for every club. Among the clubs Waugh joined were the Railway Club, the Hypocrites, the Vanoxists, OUDS, the New Reform Club, the Union, and the "Hertford underworld." Clubbing, drinking, and eating took up most of his time. Often Waugh's memory cuts through the alcoholic haze of those days and presents us with such real and imaginary figures as Terence Greenidge—"although wildly unkempt in his person he was a stickler for tidiness and stuffed his pockets with wastepaper from the gutters"—or Robert Byron, who was "short, fleshy and ugly in a painfully ignominious way. His complexion was yellow. He had a marked resemblance, which he often exploited at fancy-dress parties, to Queen Victoria at the time of her jubilee."

Surrounded as he was by such friends as Harold Acton, "Hamish Lennox," Christopher Hollis, Douglas Woodruff, and John Sutro, it is surprising that Waugh took even a Third in History. All he learned from History was its value. What his education or lack of it prepared him for is very clear to him in the present and clear to readers of his descriptions of the past. These early fictional objects on which his prose talent operates seem at first to be peripheral to his education, but then appear at its center, as when he says: "My education, it seems to me, was the preparation for one trade only; that of an English prose writer."

Waugh the traditionalist and moralist sees little to connect him with the young man who happened to have his name. Looking back, he regards the young man's last editorial for his school paper as a "preposterous manifesto of disillusionment" in its assertion that his generation would not be a happy one. It seems preposterous from the point of view of one, who, having found faith, has re-identified himself with tradition and the past, but not preposterous from the point of view of the brilliant young writer of *Vile Bodies, Decline and Fall,* and *A Handful of Dust,* nor, ironically enough, preposterous to the prose stylist of *A Little Learning.* The older Waugh finds the Catholic in his past, but the younger has not forgotten the Morgan side of his family with the family motto, *haeg fy mywall,* "sharpen my axe." The middle-aged Waugh may find that youth revisited is for him not always a pleasant or meaningful experience, but the trip back has rekindled those old prose fires that seem to burn but dimly in some of his more recent works.

Anthony G. Bing

LIVE OR DIE

Author: Anne Sexton (1928–   )
Publisher: Houghton Mifflin (Boston). 90 pp. $4.00
Type of work: Poetry

A Pulitzer Prize-winning collection of poems by one of the best of the "confessional" poets

Anne Sexton's two previous collections of poems, *To Bedlam and Part Way Back* and *All My Pretty Ones*, established her as one of the finest woman poets of the post-war period and as a significant member of the school of "confessional" poetry headed by Robert Lowell and Theodore Roethke. Only two years separated those first two books, but a period of four years elapsed before she collected enough poems—thirty-four—for this third collection, a period during which she has evidently refined and intensified her already considerable talents. She has already begun to be included in significant anthologies and to be discussed in critical studies such as M. L. Rosenthal's *The New Poets: American and British Poetry since World War II.* The present winner of the 1967 Pulitzer Prize for poetry collection, should serve to enhance her reputation.

These poems stand in the first rank of "confessional" poems because they rise above the many limitations of that genre; they do not fall into private symbols of despair nor do they exhibit such tasteless soul-bearing that they embarrass the reader. In the first place, Anne Sexton's poems do not relate only to the speaker's present situation and condition, but reach outside the tortured psyche in an attempt to relate to the whole context in which anyone lives. There are poems which try to establish relationships with others like the poems in memory of John Holmes and Sylvia Plath and like the poignant "Man and Wife." There are poems which try to establish relationships in terms of the religious experience and poems which establish relationships in terms of the speaker's past. Finally, there are poems which try to establish the relationship of the self to its environment.

These poems represent, as perhaps all poems do, the unique search for the identity of self, but that unique search is turned into a universal search and therein lies the power of the poetry. The poems forego the construction of a private symbology and a private mythology for the evocation of precise sensory experiences which become immediate and important to the reader. The situations of the poems are revealed in full so that there is no confusion about the nature of the experience being described. When coupled with Anne Sexton's accomplished technique and control, this clarity of sensory detail makes these poems at once interesting and profound.

That the poet is an accomplished technician is proved by the fact that her more or less "formal" poems are as unstrained as her free verse and her free verse is as controlled as her formal verse. There are five poems which have conventionalized forms. Two of these, "And One for My Dame" and "Two Sons," use an accentual line in a three-line stanza that is rhymed abb, as in these lines from "Two Sons":

On the unique occasion
of your two sudden wedding days
I open some cheap wine, a tin of lob-

ster and mayonnaise.

I sit in an old lady's room
where families used to feast
where the wind blows in like soot from
   north-northeast.

Here the first two three-accent lines are
a preparation for the important or telling detail in the third five-accent line,
and the lines each maintain an integrity which belies any merely arbitrary
adaptation to form. Another poem,
"Wanting to Die," is written in three-
line stanzas with four-accent unrhymed
lines. Two poems are written in
quatrains rhymed *abcb* but these poems
have quite different tones. "Somewhere in Africa" in a mediative tribute
to the poet John Holmes while "Cripples and Other Stories" is a swinging
ballad in which the speaker approaches
the past in the manner of the black
humorists.

Anne Sexton's free verse is ordered
and accomplished, for the most part,
refraining from the excesses of rhetoric
and tone found in too much free verse.
Five lines from "KE 6–8018" show this
free verse at its best:

I will not wait at the rail
looking upon death,
that single stone.
I will call for the boy-child I never had.
I will call for the Jew at the gate.

The first line-break works against the
syntax and sets up the striking second
line, in which in turn sets up the even
more striking image in appositive in
the third line. Then the positive parallel statements in the fourth and fifth
lines parallel the syntax of the negative
statement of the first line to round out
a singularly exciting passage. Not all of
her free verse is so well conceived,
however; in "Imitations of Drowning"

she descends in several places into an
uncontrolled, pedestrian outpouring:

This August I began to dream of
   drowning. The dying
went on and on in water as white and
   clear
as the gin I drink each day at half-past
   five.
Going down for the last time, the last
   breath lying,
I grapple with eels like ropes—it's ether,
   it's queer
and then, at last, it's done. Now the
   scavengers arrive,
the hard crawlers who come to clean
   up the ocean floor.
And death, that old butcher, will bother
   me no more.

The cliché in the last line is particularly cloying. Fortunately, however,
this is the only poem in the collection
in which the technique fails so completely.

There is one long poem in the collection, "Flee on Your Donkey" (239
lines). Often the problem with long
poems is that there are passages of
great intensity and beauty followed by
pedestrian expository passages, but that
is not the case here. There are momentary lapses for a line or two, as in

Six years of such small preoccupations!
Six years of shuttling in and out of this
   place!

The poem concerns the speaker's being
readmitted to a mental institution and
the sheer emotional weight of the material sustains, for the most part, the
tension of the poem. Never is the technique allowed to slip, and such control
produces passages of undoubted effectiveness and power:

Hornets have been sent.
They cluster like floral arrangements on

the screen.
Hornets, dragging their thin stingers,
hover outside, all knowing,
hissing: *the hornet knows.*
I heard it as a child
but what was it that he meant?
The hornet knows!
What happened to Jack and Doc and
    Reggy?
Who remembers what lurks in the heart
    of man?
What did The Green Hornet mean, *he*
    knows?
Or have I got it wrong?
Is it The Shadow who had seen
me from my bedside radio?

The hornets literally and figuratively
weave in and out of the speaker's torture until the past has merged with the
present in the memory of old radio
programs. This is the concrete revelation of isolation and alienation from reality.

The poems encompass many elements of the speaker's environment,
but each poem is, ultimately, a search
for and a revelation of the speaker's essential self. Even the two occasional
poems on the deaths of two poets
finally center on the nature of the
speaker as revealed in her relationship
to these two. "Somewhere in Africa" is
a eulogy to John Holmes which never
grows maudlin or cloying. Instead,
there is the celebration of death as an
experience which enriches the existence and the obviously female speaker
wishes for Holmes a peculiarly sensuous life after death:

Let there be this God who is a woman
    who will place you
upon her shallow boat, who is a woman
    naked to the waist,
moist with palm oil and sweat, a woman
    of some virtue
and wild breasts, her limbs excellent,
    unbruised and chaste.

"Sylvia's Death" is an entirely different
approach to death in which precise images from life are woven into memories
placed in a frame of mourner's wails.

(Sylvia, Sylvia,
where did you go
after you wrote me
from Devonshire
about raising potatoes
and keeping bees?)

The effect is one of strong emotion, as
well as one of reality. For the pitch of
mourning could not be sustained without becoming either trite, overbearing,
or embarrassing, but when the mourning is dampened by rivulets of memory
empathy is created.

Other poems take the search for
identity into the church and into the
religious experience. What is unique
about these poems is that the search
does not fall into a surrender to the
church; the poems reveal a constant
battle which strengthens the suppli-
cant as it strengthens the church's hold
on her. One of the best poems of this
sort is "Consorting with Angels," in
which the speaker consciously takes
hold of a visionary experience to find
her place in the God-universe, but the
mystic experience results in her identification with the spiritual rather than
her absorption into it.

O daughters of Jerusalem,
the king has brought me into his cham-
    ber.
I am black and I am beautiful.
I've been opened and undressed.
I have no arms or legs.
I'm all one skin like a fish.
I'm no more a woman
than Christ was a man.

The speaker may not have gained any
more strength or peace than the aver-

age orthodox Christian, but she has, at least, come to terms with divinity and has maintained her own self in the face of it.

Still other poems look into the past for a clue to the speaker's selfhood, sometimes poignantly and sometimes with a grim humor. The past comes into focus most clearly and is relegated to its proper place most effectively in "Cripples and Other Stories." In this poem disgusting details are juxtaposed to tender ones and the effect is balance:

> Disgusted, mother put me
> on the potty. She was good at this.
> My father was fat on scotch.
> It leaked from every orifice.
>
> Oh the enemas of childhood,
> reeking of outhouses and shame!
> Yet you rock me in your arms
> and whisper my nickname.

The throbbing three-beat line and the strong rhymes enforce the ironies and the contrasts and the reality of frustration and love is created.

Finally there are those poems which focus on the speaker's present, looking out at the world to see if it is hospitable or not and looking into the self to see how willing it is to come to terms with the world. In "Three Green Windows" there is a kind of "Sunday Morning" in the first person instead of the third, with the speaker half-dreaming and half-intellectualizing to find out if she can believe, not in Christ and the supernatural as in Stevens' poem, but in the natural world itself. The conclusion is a kind of uneasy compromise:

> I have misplaced the Van Allen belt,
> the sewers and the drainage,
> the urban renewal and the suburban
> centers.

> I have forgotten the names of the literary critics.
> I know what I know.
> I am the child I was,
> living the life that was mine.
> I am young and half asleep.
> It is a time of water, a time of trees.

The final acceptance without surrender is, perhaps, the theme of all of the poems in this collection. This is not a letter to the world but a truce with the world.

The most completely realized poem in this volume is "Wanting to Die." The first stanza speaks of uncertainty and aimless wandering, but also of desire and passion.

> Since you ask, most days I cannot remember.
> I walk in my clothing, unmarked by that voyage.
> Then the almost unnameable lust returns.

The poem then details the characteristics of the voyage and of the lust, all of which point to aimlessness if not to futility. But the purpose and the possibility are revealed in the last two stanzas.

> Balanced there, suicides sometimes meet,
> raging at the fruit, a pumped-up moon,
> leaving the bread they mistook for a kiss,
> leaving the page of the book careless open,
> something unsaid, the phone off the hook
> and the look, whatever it was, an infection.

The possibility of ending the voyage makes continuing the voyage worthwhile, and the things left undone and unseen are worth going on for. The poem is about the death wish but it is not an expression of it. What the poem says, finally, is that the answer is no answer.

Anne Sexton says in her short "Author's Note" that these poems "read like a fever chart for a bad case of melancholy," but the fever chart records more than that. It records a case of selflessness searching for selfhoodness and the search becomes more and more immediate and more and more important to the reader as the specific details of that effort parallel his own search. To read these poems is to look into Anne Sexton as one looks into a mirror, and if now and then the glass darkens it is because hidden within each of us is a selfhood unlike any other. Nevertheless, the moments of clear vision are many, for this poet has a major talent.

Vincent Stewart

Sources for Further Study

Criticism:

Marx, Patricia. "An Interview with Anne Sexton," in *Hudson Review.* Winter, 1965, pp. 560-570. Author's own discussion of her themes and techniques.

Mills, Ralph J., Jr. "Anne Sexton," in *Contemporary Poets.* New York: St. Martin's Press, 1957, pp. 1373-1375. Mills discusses Anne Sexton's penchant for testing "the raw edges of her personal feelings in her poetry."

Reviews:

Book Week. September 25, 1966, p. 13. 850 words.

Library Journal. XCI, September 15, 1966, p. 4126. 250 words.

Saturday Review. XLIX, December 31, 1966, p. 25. 250 words.

THE LIVES OF A CELL

Notes of a Biology Watcher

Author: Lewis Thomas (1913-   )
· *Publisher:* The Viking Press (New York). 153 pp. $6.95
Type of work: Scientific essays

Perceptive brief essays on recent investigations in biology, written by a distinguished scientist who is also a master of prose style

When a scientific book becomes a best seller, that's news. Lewis Thomas' *The Lives of a Cell,* winner of the National Book Award, has been acclaimed not only by specialists in biology but also by a large general audience of readers. A collection of twenty-nine brief (usually fewer than six pages) but cogent essays, all of which first appeared in the *New England Journal of Medicine,* the volume is both authoritative and readable. Such a combination of virtues is rare. To be sure, articulate scientists such as George Gamow in geo- and astrophysics, James A. Coleman in theoretical physics, George Gaylord Simpson in paleontology, and others have written lucidly for a layman public about recent speculation in their fields. Also, humanists without a specialized scientific background, such as Lincoln Barnett, have occasionally explained technical theory in words that most people can understand. Still rarer are scientist-humanists who attempt not only to popularize scientific thought but also to provide a philosophical framework for their own ideas. Among these writers are J. W. N. Sullivan, whose skeptical *The Limitation of Science* (1933) opposed the exuberant scientific optimism of his time; Julian Huxley, author of many humanistic studies on biology, chiefly the volume of essays *Man in the Modern World* (revised,

1944); and Lecomte du Noüy, whose scientifically flawed *Human Destiny* (1947) argued that conventional religious beliefs have not been fundamentally damaged by modern scientific research. Like these books, but vastly more accurate as an account of recent investigations, Lewis Thomas' brief study is a book that at once makes accessible to the common reader the most exciting thinking of biologists; establishes a philosophical viewpoint that unites, in C. P. Snow's language, the "two cultures" of the humanities and sciences; and provokes religious speculation concerning the great issue of whether a system of intelligence, order, and unity directs the material universe.

Subtitled modestly "Notes of a Biology Watcher," the volume treats some of the vital problems of contemporary science: Is life merely mechanical, or is it purposeful? Is the individual complete, a self-sufficient entity, or is he simply part of a plasm of life, interrelated with other life forms? Is the "destiny" of mankind ascendant, biologically evolving toward greater mastery of the earth; or destructive and degenerative, fated to go the way of nature's genetic mistakes? Thomas' thesis—a popular one for our time—is that all life has a unity, springing from a common chemical-organic source symbolized by the cell; that forms of life are equal, none "higher" or more valuable than others; and that life is interdependent, a giant ecological-sustaining system in which the parts must cohere and contribute to the whole, or the whole will be damaged, possibly beyond repair. It is not surprising that such a thesis is popular. At a time when the notion of a heroic ego—an individual self—has been largely abandoned by behavioral psychologists, it is comforting to believe that we are not alone, not quivering egos dependent upon our own resources for happiness or salvation, but that we are connected parts of a whole society. Moreover, we tend to accept Thomas' premise that the earth support-systems by which life maintains itself—the very air we breathe, water we drink, food we eat—have been contaminated, mostly by selfish human beings in highly developed technical societies such as our own. If this idea leaves us with feelings of guilt and fear, the author's argument is a consolation: In a hostile universe we are not alone, but part of a continuum of life; our responsibility, therefore, is not to serve our selfish ends, but to sustain life wherever we find it.

To support this philosophy of biological determinism, Thomas cites the evidence of advanced research in most of the fields that used to be called the "life sciences." From this base his interests range beyond biology, strictly speaking, to organic chemistry, physics, anthropology, sociology, and even linguistics. He is concerned with the process of death as well as life; with man seen from a microscope as an agglomeration of cells, but also with man seen as a social mass, a community organism.

To Thomas, the distinction between life and death is not absolute. We die by degrees, he says, as our cells fail to function together as a whole body. Thus death is only change, the cells restructuring their chemical constituents. Man's cells are immortal, even though he returns, in conventional religious language, to dust. Just as Thomas refuses to exalt life over death, so he is unconvinced about man's claims for social supremacy. Compared to the supremely fine organization of the cells in his own body, man's social institutions are organized chaotically. Man's genes are intelligent; man himself is sometimes a dunce.

In several brilliant analogies comparing the social organization of ants and termites with that of humans, Thomas elaborates upon this argument. Individual ants stumble, fumble, appear to be erratic in their behavior. But acting together, they resemble a coherent machine; all the parts function as a unit. The single member of the organization is nothing, but in unity he is more than a single ant—the whole colony is his organization. Far from drawing hostile political conclusions from this analogy—that is, treating the ant colony as a totalitarian army—Thomas is sympathetic toward the shared responsibilities of the ant community. Human beings, he believes, are also related members of a complex social organization; by functioning together, they share responsibilities instead of competing for dominance.

Indeed, running through Thomas' argument is the implied threat of man's dangerous *hubris,* his individualism. The individual ego tries to dominate others. Yet in nature, Thomas insists, symbiosis—biological cooperation—is as pervasive as hostility. Animals send out signals ("vibes," as he calls them colloquially in one essay) to their own kind; similarly, humans respond to signals so subtle that we rarely understand them. These signals remind us of our unity, not our diversity. On a basic biological level, Thomas says, life is one instead of many, friendly instead of hostile. Even germs, the oft-publicized enemy of our race, have been much maligned. Most so-called germs, he says, are quite innocent of wrongdoing. The healthy body's system of immunity is quite adequate to ward off most diseases; often physicians, to satisfy their patient's need for attention, prescribe excessive medication, thus breaking down the sick body's ability to fight off its natural microscopic enemies. From Thomas' point of view, the individual should learn how to live in this world and not isolate himself, either by medical technology or social engineering, from the sources of life.

And what *are* the sources of life? A materialist, Thomas believes that life springs from the complex organization of chemical matter. But he is also a religious scientist, who treats with wonder and reverence the nearly miraculous combination of forces that make life possible. The cell, the basic unit of life, is the fragile element of creation that man must understand if he is to survive. As a religious thinker, Thomas does not discount the possibility that all life came from a single cell; that, so long as some cells are alive, life itself is immortal; or that the extinction of the ecology systems that support cell life will destroy life itself, at least on this planet. Thus with religious zeal he insists that the floating "membrane" of the earth's atmosphere must be protected from chemical destruction, lest we all be doomed. Also, like a prophet he urges the reader to cherish the life quality in all things, from the simplest cellular organisms to the complex genius of organization that created Bach's *St. Matthew Passion*.

Pursuing this idea, Thomas compares the marvelous organization of life with that of language. Philology fascinates him. He devotes a brilliant essay, "On Various Words," to showing how languages change, develop, grow, yet never wholly lose their relationship to the original roots of speech, whether Indo-European or some other linguistic source. Similarly, life changes, develops, grows in an evolutionary cycle, yet remains related to its mysterious origins in the cell. More than a "biology watcher," Lewis Thomas is a literary artist, possibly the finest master of English prose style in scientific essays since the psychologist Havelock Ellis or the naturalist W. H. Hudson, and one who perceives that life, in all its exquisite vibrations, is a unity.

Leslie B. Mittleman

THE LIVING ROOM

Author: Graham Greene (1904-　　)
Publisher: The Viking Press (New York). 126 pp. $2.50
Type of work: Drama
Time: The present
Locale: England

A play in which a master of suspense considers in a restrained and intelligent manner the value of accepting pain and death

Principal characters:
　　FATHER JAMES BROWNE, a priest
　　TERESA and
　　HELEN, his sisters
　　ROSE PEMBERTON, their niece
　　MICHAEL DENNIS, Rose's lover
　　MRS. DENNIS, Michael's wife

Graham Greene is best known for his novels, among them *The Third Man, The Heart of the Matter,* and *The End of the Affair.* He has always been an interesting writer because of his curious ability to make tales of fear and tension express a concern for God, love, and compassion. He is a Catholic who speaks in effective dramatic terms to men of any faith, and in this present play, *The Living Room,* he shows how an illicit love affair which ends in suicide for the young girl involved enables the other characters to overcome resentment of pain and fear of death. We may say, then, that this play is Graham Greene's contribution to the literature devoted to the problem of evil. Perhaps not all readers will accept his answer, but few will fail to submit to the power of his play.

Much of the curious and forbidding tone of the play is achieved because the house in which the play takes place has a great many closed rooms. The living room is a third-floor room cluttered with the furniture of many rooms no longer used. When Michael Dennis comes to the house to return Rose Pemberton from her mother's funeral, he feels that there is something strange about the living room; but he cannot decide what it is. When he asks the girl's aunt, Miss Helen Browne, whether the rooms of the house are closed because of war damage, the elderly woman replies, "For one reason or another," and then diverts his attention. Only later, in a scene involving Rose and Father James Browne, Helen's brother, is the reason for this reticence revealed. The priest explains to her that it has become a custom in that house to close any room in which a person has died. Since the house is an old house, few rooms remain as living rooms—as rooms in which to live.

Father James, having been injured in an automobile accident over twenty years before the opening of the play, is confined to a wheelchair. He is intended to be a figure of strength, however, despite his physical handicap and his failure to resolve the problem created by the illicit affair between Michael and Rose.

Michael Dennis is a married man, forty-five years old, charged with the responsibility of executor of the estate left by Rose's mother. A sudden love rising in both of them leads them to spend the night together following the mother's funeral. When they speak to each other in the living room the following morning, in the scene with which the play begins, their words of love, despair, and guilt are overheard by Miss Teresa Browne, sister of Helen and Father James. Thus the conflict between Michael, the Protestant, and Helen, the morally outraged Catholic, begins while Father James tries desperately both to advise against the affair and to curb his sister's almost frenzied attack.

When Helen says, "It's—it's revolting. Seducing a child at her mother's funeral," the priest replies, "There's no point in anger. We only get angry because we are hurt. And our hurt is not of importance in this case. We are dealing with more important people." Helen objects to his calling Michael more important than the Brownes, but Father James replies, "Of course he's more important than we are. You and I are only capable of *self*-importance, Helen. He's still in the middle of life. He's capable of suffering."

As the play develops, the reader comes to realize that the conflict is not primarily between the Protestant sinner and the Catholic family of the "wronged" girl; it is a conflict between Father James and those who fail to realize that life entails suffering and the acceptance of death.

Michael's wife, we learn indirectly, is a neurotic woman who has been only a companion to her husband for a long while. She phones the Browne house, inquiring about Michael, and precipitates the revelation of the affair between Michael and Rose. When Michael attempts to justify himself by telling Father James that he loves Rose and that they intend to be married, the priest advises him to go away and to break the relationship abruptly. The

marriage, were it to occur, would not be a marriage to Rose, however much she might try to rationalize it, for it would not be approved by the Church. In any case, the priest understands something of the power of a marriage, and his remarks about companionship and suffering turn out to be prophetic.

Mrs. Dennis, unwilling to give her husband a divorce, appears at the house and first threatens Rose, then begs. Finally, she breaks down and weeps. When Rose leaves to get her some water, Mrs. Dennis arranges herself with tablets in her hand as if she had been about to take poison. Michael, entering, reveals that the pretended suicide is an old trick and says to his wife, "You promised you wouldn't do that again. It does no good, dear." Rose is surprised when in reply to Mrs. Dennis's objection, "Don't call me 'dear,'" Michael says, "You are dear. I call you what you are." Mr. Greene writes as stage directions: "Rose watches. She is distressed, puzzled. She hasn't yet grown up enough to realize that there are many ways of love."

Rose not only learns that there are many ways of love, but also finds to her dismay that marriage has created a kind of understanding between Michael and his wife which no romance can destroy. As Michael and his wife argue about his desire for a divorce, Rose feels that the argument reveals them as unmistakably man and wife. Subtly, the discussion begins to include references to suffering, and it becomes clear that each person suffers, and that each person uses suffering in his own way; some hide it, some use it as a weapon, and some revolt against it. Rose knows from Michael's hesitation when she tells him that she is free to go away with him that he is so deeply concerned about his wife's pain, despite her using it as a weapon, that Rose cannot hope to offset that concern. She cries out to her uncle, Father James:

"... They are *married,* Uncle. I never knew they were married. Oh, he'd told me they were, but I hadn't seen them, had I? ... I've seen him touch her arm."

When her uncle suggests that she leave Michael, she replies that she could not bear the pain; and when he suggests then that she go with him, she replies that she could not bear Mrs. Dennis's pain. The priest then tells her: "In a case like yours we always have to choose between suffering our own pain or suffering other people's. We can't *not* suffer." Rose tells him that she cannot go on living with her aunts "in a room where nobody has died." The priest is unable to help her, and when he leaves she makes a final appeal to her Aunt Teresa, whose fuddled brain does not respond. Then Rose says a childish prayer in desperation, and takes the tablets left by Mrs. Dennis.

The point of the play is expressed in a conversation between Michael and Father James after Rose's death. Michael asks whether everything is going to be the same as before, and Father James replies that three old people have lost a living room. When Michael says bitterly that he cannot believe in a God who allows such pain, Father James replies, "Suffering is a problem to us, but it doesn't seem a big problem to the woman when she has borne her child. Death is our child, we have to go through pain to bear our death. I'm crying out with the pain like you. But Rose—she's free, she's borne her child." Thus, when Teresa determines to sleep in the room where Rose died, the former living room, she underscores the author's conviction that through pain one comes to a kind of acceptance of death and a freedom from fear.

The Living Room belongs to the new literature of faith which seems likely to supplant the literature of ideas with which an older generation of writers was concerned. Reading the play, one feels, however, that Mr. Greene would have achieved his purpose better if he had cast his story in the form of fiction. The play has dignity and force, but it lacks at times the deeper reality which the analytical processes of the novel might possibly have supplied.

THE LIVING SEA

Author: Jacques-Yves Cousteau (1910-   ), with James Dugan
Publisher: Harper and Row (New York). Illustrated. 325 pp. $6.50
Type of work: Natural-science narrative

A poetically written account of exploration of the sea and its bottom by the author, his crew members, and fellow scientists, operating first from the ship Calypso *and later in the "Diving Saucer"*

Captain Jacques-Yves Cousteau is not a meticulous scientist. For instance, he throws out the old theory that sharks lack maneuverability because one swam straight at him while he was skin-diving, swerved at the last instant, and took off in another direction; such inductive reasoning from only one example will make a plodding researcher grind his teeth. Neither is M. Cousteau (with James Dugan) a dramatic, climactic writer. While the development of the Diving Saucer may seem a great climax to oceanographers, it is no peak of excitement for the reader. And so eager is the author to be always slightly beyond the frontier in ocean science that he sometimes presents his material unfairly; when he writes about experiments in bioluminescence, he makes the reader feel that this, too, is a field never probed before, whereas chemists and others have been working intently on what the layman incorrectly calls phosphorescence for at least thirty years. It is also evident that Cousteau has never, flashlight in hand, been on an old-fashioned American bullfrog hunt: he is startled that a bright light can hypnotize a fish. But when all these trivial grievances are cast into the sea (where they belong), Cousteau —wearing, of course, the Aqua-Lung that he invented—pops up from the waves as a Poseidon among scientific writers. *The Living Sea* is a marvelous book.

Dryly stated, this handsome volume is an account of Captain Cousteau's adventures, assignments, discoveries, and just plain old jobs aboard the oceanographic vessel *Calypso* from 1951 to 1960. Most of the narrative takes place on or in the Earth's Last Frontier, the bottom of the sea, and some readers may find the prospect seems drear; but this prospect is brightened considerably by some twenty-four pages of magnificent color photographs, sixty-four pages of black-and-white photos, a map, and several attractive line drawings. These might be the accouterments of any good travel and adventure book, however, and the real thing that sets *The Living Sea* apart from similar works is its style, its colorful and sometimes lyrical use of words. Here is a sample:

> The coral took unexpected shapes and hues. There were skulls of dwarfs and giants; tufts of ohre and magenta mingled with petrified mauve bushes and red tubiporae fabricated like honeycombs. Superb parasols of acropora spread over idling fish that were painted with electric pigments of red and gold. Through this splendid tilted forest humpbacked sea snails traveled their winding ways. In reef recesses there were enough tridacna clams to furnish fonts for the churches of Christendom. Their shells were ajar, displaying swollen mantles painted like the lips of harlots.

Such descriptions send you scurrying not only to the unabridged dictionary but also to your sporting-goods store for the latest in Aqua-Lungs. Cousteau chooses words delightfully and wittily: note those harlots lounging so close to the fonts of Christendom.

The Living Sea contains plenty of excitement. One of the best episodes comes early in the narrative. The divers on the *Calypso* (they are all skin divers, of course; Cousteau is somewhat rough on what he calls hard-hat divers) decide to bring to the sea's surface the wreck of a Greek merchant vessel of the third century B.C. They have located the wreck in the Mediterranean at a depth of 130 feet, about ten miles from Marseilles. Cousteau skillfully presents the difficulties and the thrills of the operation. The freighter's cargo was chiefly amphorae (wine jars), both Grecian and Roman. Costeau resists the temptation to heighten the archaeological excitement when he almost casually mentions taking a sip or two from an undamaged amphora; not many writers would make so little of a draft of what must be some of the world's most patiently aged wine.

Aside from what is revealed about Cousteau's own intriguing, ambivalent personality (proud, yet modest; poetic, yet scientific; brave, yet prudent), *The Living Sea* is short on human characterization, but the sea itself is, of course, the main character, and although its surface has been magnificently handled by many great writers, we are lucky that one of the earliest and best probers of its coral reefs, its wrecks, its bottoms, its weird and fascinating inhabitants is the free-swimming, keen-eyed Cousteau. Almost every book has a clown in it somewhere. There is one in *The Living Sea* also, and he (or she) turns out to be Cousteau's most charmingly developed character, Ulysses the grouper. The grouper is not a rare fish, but Ulysses is a rare grouper. He makes friends with the divers from the *Calypso* when they are on an expedition to the Seychelles, the Isles of Return, in the Indian Ocean north of Madagascar. While the divers are feeding and studying other fish, Ulysses gets so much in the way that he has to be caged. He is obviously petulant, then furious. The story of the grouper covers two stops of the *Calypso* in the Seychelles; the second part is a tale of grief and suspense, but ends happily, as should all stories about friendly, if bumbling, creatures.

The development of the Diving Saucer, told about with enthusiasm near the end of the book, is also filled with trouble and suspense. The Saucer can go deeper than free divers with lights; and apparently the deeper one goes the more beautiful the sea becomes. "Now the Diving Saucer," says Cousteau, "had placed us among the most elegant chromatics of them all. About us the living forms were tinted suave pink, mauve, and white, with touches of lemon yellow." There is battery trouble, however, on an early dive of this new "ship"; but this story, like Ulysses', ends happily with the use of more conventional batteries and the improvement of electrical circuits. Cousteau leaves us with the feeling he has just begun to explore the ocean depths.

The Living Sea is filled with many unforgettable episodes: the tremendous leaps of dolphins in the Arabian Sea; the sounding of sperm whales as seen from under water (not even Captain Ahab ever saw that amazing spectacle); the accidental mangling of a baby whale by the propellers of the *Calypso*. Captain Cousteau is so stimulated by the unknown challenges of the ocean that his enthusiasm spills like salt water on the layman and the landlubber. One feat that he is very proud of is the firm anchoring of the *Calypso* above the Romanche Trench in the Atlantic. This record anchoring took five and one-half miles of braided nylon cable to hold his ship to the ocean floor some 24,600 feet below.

Readers of *The Living Sea* may find it difficult to resist using a phrase of Cousteau's that describes a dangerous emotional ailment of divers, for the term applies equally well to the pleasurable effect of this book: the rapture of the deep.

Preston Newman

Sources for Further Study

Reviews:

Best Sellers. XXIII, May 15, 1963, p. 65. 650 words.

Christian Science Monitor. April 25, 1963, p. 11. 700 words.

New York Herald Tribune Books. April 28, 1963, p. 7. 750 words.

New York Times Book Review. April 28, 1963, p. 1. 1,550 words.

Times Literary Supplement. August 9, 1963, p. 611. 420 words.

LIVINGSTON'S COMPANIONS

Author: Nadine Gordimer (1923-   )
Publisher: The Viking Press (New York). 248 pp. $6.95
Type of work: Short stories

Sixteen stories which focus on human relationships, the author's fifth collection

Nadine Gordimer has established herself a secure place in twentieth century literature; in twenty years she has published ten volumes, five of them novels and five of them collections of her short stories. A native of South Africa who lives in Johannesburg, she writes mostly, but not exclusively, of Africa. In this collection, thirteen of the stories utilize characters and settings of her native continent. Like many collections of short stories, this one is made up of "twice-told" tales, for the stories have appeared (some under different titles) in various magazines, such as *The Atlantic, The Southern Review, Encounter,* and *London Magazine.* Four of the stories appeared in *The New Yorker.*

The title of this volume is more than just the title of the first story in the collection. As the author has commented, everyone who lives or travels in Africa is, in a sense, a companion of the famous nineteenth-century explorer of the continent. Modern-day residents and travelers are the doctor's companions because Dr. Livingston was, more than anyone else, responsible for bringing Africa and European culture face to face in a confrontation, the problems of which are still being solved, as Nadine Gordimer puts it, "in reality and in irony." The title story, then, sets the tone, the motif, of the entire volume, even though three of the stories do not take place in an African setting. As is common in Nadine Gordimer's fiction, these stories focus on character, rather than events; her stories revolve about

human relationships, the ways in which people see one another and see themselves. The stories frequently involve chance encounters which bring persons together in new, unforeseen ways. Some of the stories utilize relationships among members of a family, showing how we, as human beings, reveal ourselves to one another in times of domestic crisis, whether these crises are, on the surface, trivial or important.

The title story, by the operation of coincidence, brings Carl Church, a British journalist; Mrs. Palmer, owner of an African resort hotel; Mrs. Palmer's grown son, a musician named Dickie; and Zelide, a British girl newly come to work at the resort hotel, together for a few days. Against the background of a great African lake, which almost becomes itself a character in the story, a complex, if temporary web of circumstances brings these people into a circle of interest which takes place only a few yards from where several of Dr. Livingston's nineteenth century companions were buried—and where Mrs. Palmer's dead husband has been buried, too. Hard and brittle on the surface, Mrs. Palmer proves to be terribly concerned about her son, fearful that he may, like his father, commit suicide. On his side the son faces two problems. One is that he needs to escape from his mother to return to his career as a jazz musician; the other is that local scandalmongers have caused a rift between himself and his fiancée by gossiping about an apparently nonexistent emotional tie between him and the girl named Zelide. Against his will, Carl Church becomes both a spectator and a participant in the problems of these people, realizing as he leaves the resort and finally finds the graves he is seeking, that he—like the lake, like African history—is inextricably entwined in the fates of many people, whether he wishes it or not.

Very much like Carl Church is the metallurgist, Crispin Douglas (known as Duggie) of "Why Haven't You Written?" Sent by his company to many parts of the world, he several times makes trips to America, where he has a love affair with Kim Malcolm, wife of a professor at a Midwestern college, whom he meets quite by chance. Drawn to her, and hating the motel-and-bar existence he leads in America, the metallurgist writes a letter to his wife in London, trying to end his marriage. Upon his return home Crispin Douglas discovers that his letter has not been received, thanks to a postal strike. Six weeks later, when he thinks the letter irretrievably lost, it is delivered. His wife, contrary to his expectations, opens the letter and reads it: the confrontation via the letter comes and immediately goes, for Douglas' wife tears up the letter and drops the pieces into a wastepaper receptacle nearby, along with other "used tickets."

Sensitive to minority groups and their problems, Nadine Gordimer has included in this collection stories about Jews, black Africans, and (at least tangentially) Asiatics living in Africa. One such story, probably reflecting the author's years at the convent school at Springs, South Africa, is "The Bride of Christ." Lyndall Berger, a sixteen-year-old Jewish girl who attends a Catholic school, decides to become a Catholic. Her parents, who have deserted their own faith, permit the girl to do so,

after voicing a number of "typical liberal" objections. A crisis arises on the first Good Friday after the girl's confirmation, when she fails to attend Mass but wants to attend a dance. The crisis of doubt arises in which the girl, her brother Peter, and both her parents participate, although none is sure of his role in the crisis or its outcome.

Also about a Jewish girl is "A Third Presence," a story about Rose and Naomi Rasovsky. Naomi, a pretty girl, marries as her parents wish and settles into an existence centered about her husband, her home and her children. Rose, ugly and obviously Jewish in appearance, goes out into the world to earn her own living and to find that she is capable of success in both employment and love. At the age of forty, having become a well-known and successful person, Rose undergoes plastic surgery to change her Jewish nose. Her sister fails to understand, thinking only that the addition of contact lenses might make the sisters' lives the same.

Several of the stories in this collection of sixteen deal with the problems of black-white existence in contemporary Africa, especially in Nadine Gordimer's own South Africa. With the vision of the native-born, who represents in this case the liberal point of view, despite the official views and practices, she tries to portray, within the range open to her as a white person, the meaning of existence for the black as well as for the white. One such story is "Open House," in which Frances Taver, a white woman opposed to apartheid, brings a group of blacks together to visit with Robert Greenman Ceretti, an American journalist, who wishes to meet, as he cannot officially, some black leaders. Mrs. Taver invites Edgar Xixo, a black attorney; Jason Madela, a black businessman; and

Spuds Butelezi, a black journalist. After the luncheon is over Mrs. Taver finds an unsigned note from a black friend who is in hiding from the police. That note, as well as her luncheon party, leaves her wondering just what story there is for an American journalist to see, or to tell: she cannot be sure that the American visitor found what he wanted or what she and her apartheid-enduring friends tried to communicate to him.

Similar to the last is "Inkalamu's Palace," in which a middle-aged white woman, a native of South Africa who narrates the story, stops to visit the crumbling remains of Inkalamu (The Lion) Williamson's home, which she had visited numerous times as a child. After walking and clambering about the ruins the narrator stops at a nearby native store, whose owner is the mulatto daughter of Inkalamu Williamson by one of his several black wives. Nonny Williamson, who now has fatherless children of her own, has little in common with the white visitor; to her both past and present have little meaning. All the visitor can think is that it is good that the daughter is free of her white father and what his generation had done to Africa.

Some of the stories in this collection are simply about family problems, problems in how human beings understand one another and how we try to reach behind the facade of appearances. Nadine Gordimer often uses the perspective available to her as a woman, even her perspective as a liberal woman.

For example, in "The Credibility Gap" Mrs. Doris Aucamp tries to find something to say to her daughter Pattie when a girl friend of Pattie dies in a mountain-climbing mishap. But all Mrs. Aucamp can say seems meaningless, despite her own past, despite her own sufferings as a worker for political liberties. Even the freedom she has taken for herself, and given to her children, seems to no avail.

In "A Satisfactory Settlement" an unnamed white woman who has left her husband, taking her young son with her, finds out something about herself, something not entirely clear, when a black prostitute yells night after night in the yard of the house next door; so does her child learn something when he finds that his bicycle has been stolen from the enclosed yard. One thing they learn, mother and child, is that whatever financial settlement the husband-father may make, life's problems will still persist.

In two stories of this collection Nadine Gordimer specifically uses sex and its problems. In "An Intruder" a young South African white woman discovers her husband's sexual aberration. In "The Rain Queen" a nineteen-year-old white South African girl learns the realities of sex by having a clandestine affair that ends when her lover's wife becomes pregnant.

The stories in the collection are varied, and they are sometimes ambiguous. They are always in the best vein of contemporary fiction.

Gordon W. Clarke

LIZZIE BORDEN
The Untold Story

Author: Edward D. Radin (1909–   )
Publisher: Simon and Schuster (New York). Illustrated. 271 pp. $4.50
Type of work: Crime reportage
Time: 1892-1927
Locale: Fall River, Massachusetts

A reconstruction and reinterpretation of a celebrated murder case

Principal personages:
ANDREW J. BORDEN, a prosperous Massachusetts businessman
MRS. ABBY D. BORDEN, his second wife
EMMA BORDEN, the older daughter of Andrew Borden
LIZZIE BORDEN, his younger daughter
BRIDGET SULLIVAN, the Borden maid
JOHN V. MORSE, brother of Andrew Borden's first wife
ANDREW JENNINGS, the Borden family lawyer
HOSEA M. KNOWLTON, the District Attorney
GEORGE ROBINSON, defense attorney

About 9:30 on the morning of Thursday, August 4, 1892, in the industrial city of Fall River, Massachusetts, a bloody murder occurred in the home of Andrew J. Borden, one of the wealthiest men in the community. In the second-floor guest room someone cleft the skull of Mrs. Abby Borden, Andrew's second wife, with a hatchet or small ax, added eighteen savage blows which scattered a great deal of blood about the room, and left the body lying prone on the floor.

About eleven that same morning, in the same home, the murderer of Mrs. Borden entered the first-floor parlor where Andrew Borden was taking a nap on a horsehair sofa; rained ten blows on his skull, spattering blood on sofa, wall, carpet, and ceiling, and left Borden lying face up with his head on a pillow and his feet on the floor.

The murder weapon was never discovered; neither was the murderer. John V. Morse, a visitor in the Borden home, was at first suspected, but he was quickly cleared. Suspicion shifted quickly to Lizzie, the thirty-two-year-

old younger daughter of Andrew Borden, and one week later, following an inquest, she was formally accused of the murders. On June 5, 1893, ten months afterward, the thirteen-day trial of Lizzie began. On the afternoon of June 20, after deliberating a little over an hour, the jury brought in its verdict: Not Guilty. Spectators in the courtroom applauded so noisily that attendants had to quiet them.

Emma and Lizzie Borden continued living in Fall River, but sometime afterward they moved into a much larger home. Still later, after differences arose between the sisters, Emma moved out. On June 1, 1927, Lizzie died just short of her sixty-seventh birthday. Ten days later Emma died.

Beginning with Lizzie Borden's acquittal, a legend developed about her. According to the tale, in a burst of fury she murdered her stepmother, whom she did not like; a short time afterward she killed her father with whom she had quarreled. Afterward she quickly regained her habitual composure so that, though she pretended to find her father's body, she showed no grief over his death, nor did she become upset when her stepmother's body was found a few minutes later. Not disconcerted by the accusation that she was the murderess, she wisely turned her court defense over to clever lawyers who protected her from cross-examination and testifying except for a brief statement of innocence, and who so confused the testimony of others that they succeeded in legally freeing a guilty woman; she shared with her sister the large fortune they inherited from Andrew Borden; and she enjoyed for thirty-five years her ill-gotten gains, dying unrepentant a wealthier woman than she was when she obtained her inheritance.

Edward Radin, an experienced trial reporter and writer on crime, attempts, in *Lizzie Borden: The Untold Story*, to correct the legend by revealing the many important facts it ignores and by showing how the legend was developed in the beginning largely through sensational journalism and later principally through the several biased and consciously distorted accounts of the Lizzie Borden case published by Edmund Pearson, whom many other writers about the Fall River tragedy have consulted as *the* authority on the crime. Pearson thought Lizzie guilty and he so used the information he gathered about her and the other people involved in the story, that he has probably convinced nearly all of his many readers since 1924, when his first account was published in his well-known *Studies in Murder*. In fact, Mr. Radin admits to having been convinced himself that Lizzie had gotten away with murder.

But, he says, he was disturbed by two errors Pearson made in connection with two dresses belonging to Lizzie. One, of bengaline silk (a fabric of cot-

ton or wool with a few threads of silk added to improve the sheen), was given to the police by Lizzie when they asked for the dress she had worn at the time of the murders. The other, of Bedford cord, Lizzie burned in the kitchen stove the Sunday after the murders because, she said, it was paint-stained and not worth keeping. Pearson remarked upon the absurdity of a New England woman doing morning chores in a silk dress, even though Lizzie's inquest testimony a few days after the murders made it clear that the dress was *not* silk. By withholding or ignoring some of the later trial testimony concerning the cord dress, Pearson made it seem that Lizzie burned it because it was bloodstained, whereas in reality she had not worn it on the day of the murders and she had burned it unthinkingly rather than by design.

Still, says Radin, Lizzie seemed guilty according to Pearson's account, because shortly before the murders she had reportedly attempted in vain to buy prussic acid at a drugstore; the husband of Andrew Borden's sister told of bitter family disputes; a note Lizzie said had come for her stepmother the morning of the murders was never found and therefore might easily have been a fabrication; a policeman testified that there were no footprints on the second floor of the Borden barn, though Lizzie said she had gone there to get some lead for sinkers; another policeman reported finding in the kitchen stove a cylindrical roll of burned paper that could have contained a missing hatchet handle; and Lizzie said she did not see her stepmother's body on the guest room floor as Lizzie went upstairs and later down again, even though she supposedly would have been able easily to see it from the stairs.

Doing research for a possible magazine article on the Borden murders, Radin soon discovered many omissions and distortions by Pearson and, his curiosity increasingly stirred, he decided to investigate the whole case from the beginning. Through the study of the records of the preliminary inquest and of the trial and through a number of interviews with Fall River residents, he reached several conclusions. One was that Pearson had "presented such a biased version of the case that it might be considered a literary hoax." Another was that, though there were some baffling details about the case, Lizzie was actually innocent. A third was that Bridget Sullivan, the Borden maid, was probably the real murderess, though she was not suspected and she was questioned only in connection with Lizzie's possible guilt. This last conclusion Radin does not press unduly, but he argues briefly and rather convincingly as to its probability.

Lizzie Borden: The Untold Story is an absorbing book. Mr. Radin's careful and thorough researches are evident throughout, for he provides background information about Fall River and its people, frequent citations of passages from the records of the inquest and of the long trial ten months later, quotations from various newspapers which reported the case and editorialized about it, remarks by elderly Fall River residents specially interviewed regarding the Bordens and the trial, and references to the various treatments of the case by the many authors who have used it for factual books and articles, for novels, and for plays.

There are many illustrations. These include two gory photographs of the murdered Bordens and also photographs of all the principals. A selective bibliography has been provided for those readers who may wish to compare Mr. Radin's account with those of his many predecessors. It seems unlikely that there will ever be a need for any other author to make a detailed study of the Borden case. Edward Radin has left him almost nothing to work on—except the proved identity of the murderer.

LLOYD GEORGE: A DIARY BY FRANCES STEVENSON

Author: Frances (Stevenson) Lloyd George (Lady Lloyd George) (1888-1972)
Edited by A. J. P. Taylor
Publisher: Harper & Row Publishers (New York). 338 pp. $10.00
Type of work: Diary
Time: 1914-1917; 1919-1922; 1926-1927; 1934-1937; 1944
Locale: London, Walton Heath, Criccieth (North Wales), Cobham, Churt (Surrey)

The revealing account of a famous British Prime Minister and his times, as recorded by the person closest to him

Principal personages:
> DAVID LLOYD GEORGE, successively Chancellor of the Exchequer (1908-1915), Minister of Munitions (1915-1916), Secretary of State for War (1916), and Prime Minister of Great Britain (1916-1922)
> MARGARET OWEN GEORGE, his wife
> FRANCES STEVENSON, his confidential secretary and mistress
> HENRY HERBERT ASQUITH, Prime Minister supplanted by Lloyd George in 1916
> GEORGE V, King of Great Britain
> ARTHUR JAMES BALFOUR,
> WILLIAM MAXWELL AITKEN (LORD BEAVERBROOK),
> AUSTEN CHAMBERLAIN,
> WINSTON CHURCHILL, and
> ANDREW BONAR LAW, political and governmental associates of Lloyd George
> HORATIO HERBERT KITCHENER and
> SIR WILLIAM ROBERTSON, leaders of British military forces
> GEORGES CLEMENCEAU, Premier of France and Chairman of the peace conference
> WOODROW WILSON, President of the United States

It is seldom that we are granted a very close look at any of the world's outstanding political figures. In most cases our nearest approaches derive from colleagues or relatives, often envious, who seek to ensure their own place in history by capitalizing upon an association. The more intimate impressions provided by members of an immediate family are often equally unreliable. In many cases this type of account is a general gloss intended to minimize or conceal human frailty; even more frequently it becomes a personal recital of sacrifices endured through living with someone of politi-cal eminence. In either form it usually has little to do, in any real sense, with its ostensible subject.

Frances Stevenson's diary is particularly welcome in that it embodies a refreshing departure from the norm. As Lloyd George's personal secretary and closest confidante, she heard and transcribed much that he may not have expressed in public; as his mistress and the person he seems to have loved above all others, she knew and recorded the man's more endearing personal attributes in ways that are often touching. Finally, she is more self-effacing than most diarists and makes no attempt to shine by reflected light.

As might be expected, the diary is in no sense an objective account. Miss Stevenson idolized Lloyd George, who encouraged her to write it, and her regard for him is evident throughout. Her approach to the information he supplied is nearly always uncritical, and it seems probable that much of the portrait drawn up is one that he drew intentionally. Nonetheless it is in many ways revealing and it does serve to round out our knowledge of an unusually complex personality.

Lloyd George has always been something of an enigma and it has often been remarked that he was a mass of contradictions. Essentially a nonconformist, he saw himself as a liberal reformer and liked to undercut the social mores of his time; he was strongly sympathetic to labor and many basic premises of the welfare state can be traced to him. At the same time, he cared little for most of his fellow Liberals and appears to have had more in common with Tories. This is not altogether surprising. Regardless of the cause he espouses, any successful politician must be a pragmatist: idealism must always be subordinate to practicality, and idealists—most of whom gravitate to liberal movements—can be something of a nuisance to him. Lloyd George simply found more practical men in the conservative ranks. This would not have seemed an inconsistency to him; he was neither a follower nor a good party man, but considered parties and individuals to be proper subjects for manipulation.

The ability to manipulate others was one of Lloyd George's most striking characteristics. He had great personal charm, was a remarkably persuasive speaker, and never for an instant lost sight of his goal. Obstacles merely strengthened his tenacity, and his thoroughness was such that no possible avenue of approach to his objective was disregarded. These qualities do much to explain his successes in private as well as in public life.

Miss Stevenson had good reason to be impressed by them. She was twenty-three—and twenty-five years younger than Lloyd George—when she met him in 1911. She had grown up in a proper Victorian home and, planning to become a teacher, had attended Royal Holloway College. While in school she had known Lloyd George's older daughter Mair, who recommended her as a holiday tutor for the younger daughter Megan. After interviewing Miss Stevenson, Lloyd George hired her. By 1913 he had persuaded her to abandon her previous standards and cast her lot with him as his mistress and secretary. The relationship endured until they were finally married in 1943, two years after his first wife's death and two years before his own. Miss Stevenson never seriously regretted her decision and always considered theirs "a love that comes to very few people."

For all that their love was genuine and lasting, and in spite of the fact that she idolized him, Miss Stevenson was not always happy. Men like Lloyd George are intensely dynamic forces: they require at least one adoring disciple from whom they can draw spiritual or psychic energy, and those close to them are often kept emotionally drained. It has been said of Lloyd George that he turned those around him into nervous wrecks, and in her diary Miss Stevenson noted (March 1, 1917) that he "needs so much someone who will not hesitate to give him everything, & if necessary to give up everything, & whose sole thought & occupation is for him. Without that it is hopeless to try and serve him." Undoubtedly there were times when Miss Stevenson found herself unable to meet such expectations. It is also likely that the sexual promiscuity for which Lloyd George was notorious became intensified during periods of stress; such episodes, if they occurred, must have left her feeling depressed and inadequate. Whatever the cause, a number of gaps exist in the diary: those which occur between 1914 and 1922 are usually explained by Miss Stevenson as periods of illness or exhaustion, during which she and Lloyd George were irritable toward each other. It may be significant that the most regrettable lapses occur during the Prime Minister's periods of greatest stress: the entire year of 1918, in which his career reached its zenith and he, as one of the Big Four, helped to engineer the peace; and the period following June, 1922, during which his power structure collapsed and he fell from public life forever.

Except for one or two desultory attempts in 1926 and 1927, Miss Stevenson did not make any serious effort to keep a diary again until 1934, when Lloyd George's hopes for a return to power reached their highest point. The diary was kept faithfully for two years, followed by sparse comments in 1936 and 1937, and ends with a final—and rather moving —entry in May, 1944.

It may logically be asked at this point why Lloyd George did not divorce his first wife and marry Miss Stevenson during the early years of their relationship. The answer is simple enough. Lloyd George, with his customary astuteness, once pointed out to Miss Stevenson that if one adhered to minor conventions, the major ones could be flouted with impunity: in other words, so long as reasonable discretion was practiced, a mistress was entirely permissible and the open secret would not be capitalized upon; but if he obtained a divorce his destruction would be as complete and irreversible as Charles Parnell's had been. It may be argued that such considerations no longer applied once he was out of office, but Lloyd George never ceased to hope that he would be called to power again—and he was convinced that as a divorced man he would inevitably be barred from his goal.

The diary, fascinating as a record of human relationships, is equally so in its commentary on events of the day. Its reader will be appalled at the picture it gives of a government characterized by chaos, stupidity, and general ineptitude. He will be astonished by the continual infighting and intriguing, and he will be impressed by the fantastic agility displayed by those who managed to remain in control or to seize it. In short, he will wonder how Britain ever managed to wage a war. This is undoubtedly an accurate impression so far as it goes, but it should be remembered that the picture is somewhat onesided. Miss Stevenson set down the things Lloyd George thought worth mentioning, and these were either the things he fretted over or the things he crowed about. A vast amount of dull but constructive routine work was obviously accomplished and never mentioned at all. Moreover, Lloyd George was a man whose exaggerations and outrageous falsehoods were part of his charm, and there are indications that even his communications to Miss Stevenson were not always entirely free of them.

Among the many glimpses of other figures, those of Winston Churchill are probably the most interesting. He and Lloyd George were similar in many ways and the rivalry between them was apparently intense. It is significant that both were called upon to lead their country during a great war, but were considered too unpredictable and dangerous to lead it in time of peace. Churchill is portrayed as a shameless glory seeker who continually kept himself in hot water and whose efforts to gain power were doomed to frustration. In spite of his burning ambition, Churchill did have to bide his time, and did not find the greatness he sought until after the passage of a quarter century.

This is an immensely readable and interesting book, enhanced by the impeccable editorial contributions of A. J. P. Taylor. Never obtrusive, and a model of brevity, Taylor provides concise bridges across the various gaps and scrupulously identifies most of the many figures named within its pages. It is greatly to Lady Lloyd George's credit that this diary has been preserved and given to the public. Although it does not radically alter our concept of David Lloyd George the politician, it does bring him back to life so that we may view him in three dimensions and from a closer vantage point than before. He is still the nimble, ruthlessly astute leader whose efficient manipulation of people and of institutions brought him great eminence and important enemies. But he is also David Lloyd George, the man. Driven by hungers, subject to nervous upsets and uncertainties, he can exhibit a sunny disposition and is often kindly; he loves nature and flowers; he likes to give presents and to see the happiness they bring; he can inspire love and lasting devotion. To overlook these qualities is to overlook half the secret of his success.

Too often when we study the acquisition of power, we are inclined to disregard those appealing or endearing human traits that make the acquisition possible. To the extent that we have been guilty of this oversight in regard to Lloyd George, Frances Stevenson's diary will enable us to rectify the deficiency.

John W. Evans

LOCAL ANAESTHETIC

Author: Günter Grass (1927–   )
Translated from the German by Ralph Manheim
Publisher: Harcourt, Brace and World (New York). 284 pp. $6.95
Type of work: Novel
Time: The present
Locale: Berlin

A story, with parabolic and symbolic labyrinths, illuminating the spiritual stupor and suppressing complacency of a self-indulged, mechanically consoled society

Principal characters:
>STARUSCH, a middle-aged teacher
>THE DENTIST, his dentist, psychoanalyst, and adviser
>SCHERBAUM, one of Starusch's sensitive students
>VERO LEWAND, his girl friend
>COLONEL KRINGS, a one-time Field Marshal, now owner of a cement company
>LINDE, his daughter, Starusch's fiancée
>SCHLOTTAU, her other lover
>IRMGARD SEIFERT, Starusch's second fiancée

In Günter Grass's previous novels, specifically in *The Tin Drum* and *Cat and Mouse,* critics have recognized a major voice in Germany. With a diagnostic severity these novels registered the pulse of a sick German past and exposed a guilt which most nations in some way share. Now, in *Local Anaesthetic,* he turns broadly to the present and lays bare the nerve ends of contemporary existence, with its dissipated impulses and its Lotus-land will for easeful delivery.

Divided into three major parts, the story concerns a forty-year-old school teacher's adventures in a dentist's chair and his relationships with his fiancée, a student, and a female colleague. The first part, a mixture of truth and fantasy recollected desultorily from the dentist's chair, reviews Starusch's past, his fiancée's preoccupied opposition to her father, and Starusch's passive but bitter failure to hold her. The second part narrates Starusch's attempt to prevent his favorite student, Scherbaum, from burning his dachshund as a dem-

onstration against the use of napalm in Viet Nam. The third part tells of his second engagement and his interpretation of a dull present in terms of time-accumulated sensibilities.

Symbolically illustrative of the sustaining ennui of contemporary life, *Local Anaesthetic* is a drugged, slow-paced story of ineffectual synthetic humanity. Disregarding the activities in the dentist's office, the essential action of the first part takes place in a sand-box fantasy or in consoling daydreams. In this part the images of Starusch's part parade before him unrealistically on a TV screen set up to distract patients from their discomfort. His immediate need of anaesthetics shapes his perception of his former self. He sees his innocent boyhood in terms of his preserved milk teeth, and correlative to them he remembers his mother's death in a doomed troop transport in which she was fleeing the ravages of war. He romanticizes his vigorous period of youthful rebellion when he led a daring band and was known by the name

Störtebeker. He sees himself settled into respectibility as an engineer for the Krings Cement Company. In Krings himself Starusch sees confused images of his mechanically rational dentist and an inglorious Nazi failure who tries contemptibly to retain his lost dignity. In sandbox war games Colonel Krings unsuccessfully pits his military wits against his superior and relentless daughter, Linde, who, as the indifferent fiancée of Starusch, fuses with the revolutionary student, Vero Lewand, whom Starusch ambivalently finds both appealing and offensive. In her opposition to her father, Linde represents the modern spirit's rejection of Nazi pride.

As his review progresses, Starusch thinks of himself as having invented a dust-eliminating device of great value to his company. Yet Linde turns more and more to a young electrician, Schlottau, in whom is reflected, on the most obvious level, Scherbaum's opposition to Starusch. Linde's preoccupation with her war play and her collusion with Schlottau lead to the dissolution of Linde and Starusch's engagement.

With consolation money given him by his fiancée he prepares himself academically in history and German. As a teacher he is sensitive to his students and does not overestimate his effectiveness. His favorite student, Scherbaum, is an intelligent seventeen-year-old who, taking his world too seriously, responds with indignation at what he interprets to be insensitivity in his fellowmen. Like the role of Linde and all activists, his role is to sensitize, while Starusch's role, as a suppliant exponent of his society, is to desensitize. The second part of the novel develops this inevitable conflict.

The conflict begins with Scherbaum's declaration that he is going to burn his dachshund to awaken people to the atrocities of Viet Nam. Starusch feels compelled to dissuade his student from this unconventional and dangerous act. On the advice of his dentist he tries first to disillusion the young idealist by showing him from examples in history the futility of demonstrations. After threats fail, he suggests a different location from the one selected by Scherbaum. He suggests then a substitute for the beloved dachshund and finally a substitute form of protest. His principal defense, however, is simply dialogue. "Dialogue," his dentist instructs him, "prevents action." Starusch therefore reasons with Scherbaum endlessly. As another strategem he reviews with Scherbaum the proposed site, a street of pastry shops where bored ladies in furs entertain themselves with gossip and sickening sweets. In front of these self-humored, sugar-drugged ladies, Scherbaum regurgitates in disgust. Hopefully Starusch sees in this spontaneous protest a possible substitute for Scherbaum's original proposal.

Slowly, well into the battle, Scherbaum begins to weaken. Originally he had envisioned an act growing spontaneously out of himself without compromise or deviation. But he momentarily capitulates to the suggestion of a substitute dog; as a purer alternative he himself hits on the idea of anaesthetizing his dachshund. His environment further shapes him literally and symbolically when he submits to having his distal bite repaired. He comes at last to feel that no act among men can be perfectly pure. Even his own friends misunderstand his purpose. The final blow comes ironically from an unsuspected quarter of Starusch's personality, his habit of romanticizing his own youthful exploits. Repulsed by Starusch's romantic pretenses, Scherbaum cannot take a chance on what his deed could in time become to others, or even to himself. The forces of his world therefore stifle his pure will and convert him to a usefully conformed and easeful existence. It is left to him to assert his moral energies as a liberal editor of the censored school paper.

Throughout the Scherbaum episode another activist student, Vero Lewand, figures prominently. Lacking the simple purity of Scherbaum and therefore incapable of a creative act herself, she responds to the Establishment with restrained arrogance and bitterness. She supports Scherbaum, though she is too shallow for him, and defends him against the strategies of Starusch, even to the expedient sacrifice of her honor.

Vero too is a victim of the leveling forces of society, but her capacity is to resent rather than to resist. Her last scene is at the table of a pastry shop where, like the ladies of the fashionable world, she stuffs on cloying sweets, despising the world that possesses her. Like Starusch and Scherbaum, she too has a physical defect, enlarged adenoids, by which her personality is defined; but unlike them she makes no attempt to repair herself.

In the brief third part, the human capacities of both Vero and Linde are carried over in Irmgard Seifert. She too has had her youthful visions and has acted positively, though now she lives in regret and unfulfillment. She regrets her former unsympathetic idealism and particularly an impulsive incident in which she nearly caused the death of a peasant farmer. Yet she waits like Vero for the pure moral act

of a Scherbaum. Irmgard finds some satisfaction and hope in her companionship with Starusch. They agree without passion upon an engagement, which apparently is never to lead to marriage. It is and has been Irmgard's fate always to be promised but never fulfilled.

His relations with Irmgard and his dentist in this third part give enlarged perspective to Starusch's character and life. With confirming evidence the dentist offers another version of the story Starusch has told him. There was no Krings Cement Company, and Starusch was never an engineer. According to the dentist, Starusch visited Schlottau's wife in his new Mercedes convertible while the husband, the driver of a concrete mixer, was presumably away. The wronged husband returned unexpectedly, backed his truck up to the car and filled it with quick-setting concrete. To spare a scandal the owner of the cement company paid Starusch an indemnity with which he attended school and became a teacher.

Starusch maintains in rebuttal that the car belonged to Krings and that in revenge Schlottau had instigated the concrete sculpturing during one of Krings's heroic speeches. In revenge for the dentist's exposure of him, Starusch exposes the dentist's uncontrollable and hypocritical love of tooth-decaying sweets and suggests a clandestine relationship between him and his assistant. Starusch acknowledges his habit of imaginatively compromising with reality and illustrates this habit by allusion to the painter Möller, who was persuaded to compromise his art by using inappropriate models for his allegory and thereby distorting the relation of idea and form. He shows in revelries near the conclusion of the novel that his consciousness resides somewhere between reality and fantasy, reconstructing or repressing experience continuously, and that he suffers always the burden of humanity: "Nothing lasts. There will always be pain."

Günter Grass's accomplishments in *Local Anaesthetic* are considerable. He achieves penetrating perceptions of the modern world, mind, and spirit. His world very well illustrates that prophesied in the earlier anti-utopias, such as *1984* or *Brave New World*. The mechanical has displaced the dynamics of life; humanity has capitulated to synthetic pragmatism and complacency ruled, if not by Big Brother, by irresistible social forces. The dentist's philosophy, largely an adaptation of Seneca, emphasizes stoic resignation, relative moral tolerance, a clinical approach to existence. In a program he calls Sick Care, he advocates a socialistic panacea for all human needs, and he reduces life to a matter of maintenance and sustenance. He is dedicated literally to reshaping defective bites, symbolically to reshaping dissident social attitudes. At one time, so the dentist informs Starusch, the pain of dental work was relieved only by distractive pain in another area; for instance, he illustrates, the patient's finger was held over a flame while the dentist worked. Now the dentist eases his patients with anaesthetics. The novel illustrates that modern society comparably shapes men painlessly by simply taking away their sensitivity, consoling and conjoling them into weakly responsive, plastic identities.

Like most modern literature, in technique and form *Local Anaesthetic* illustrates the psychology of conscious knowing. Memory, fantasy, reason, and impulses interfuse as catalysts of the active mind. The dentist's chair is a psychoanalyst's couch too, and the TV screen over the dentist's shoulder, with its flash-picture flow of episodes, reflects the freely wandering mind of the patient Starusch. The three parts of the story convey three temporal perspectives by which life is normally realized—retrospection, perception, and anticipation. These correlate in a pattern of organic, accumulative awarenesses. Recurrent patterns of sensual, emotional and intellectual experiences give a kind of continuity to the fragmented episodes of the lives presented.

The state of the human spirit in this novel is partly to be assumed in a wasteland world. Nevertheless, vital, if ineffective, youth exists in this world. In fact a youth-spirit constitutes part of the accumulative being of every character. Those no longer young, having matured into sterility, recall the fiery spirit and moral energy of their bygone youth. Though at times misguided by impulses, the youthful spirit represents fundamental and positive human qualities, not to be found in the young alone, but in all humanity. In this novel, however, the vital comes to naught; humanity here is anaesthetized by selfish evasions, negative values, and relativistic tolerance. The tension between the active and passive humanity is made explicit in an early confrontation between Scherbaum and Starusch. To Scherbaum's expressed concern over the atrocities in Viet Nam, Starusch replies:

"Yes, Scherbaum, I've read. Bad. Very-very bad. But I must admit that this ache, this draft that always hits the same nerve, this pain, which isn't even so bad, but which I can localize and which never stirs from the spot, affects me, shakes me and lays me bare more than the photographed pain of this world, which for all its enormity is abstract because it doesn't hit my nerve."

Local Anaesthetic is a timely novel written with a powerful monotony that catches well the soporific drones of a drilled-in lethargy. Readers will get the message even if they do not understand.

Charles Workman

LOLITA

Author: Vladimir Nabokov (1899-   )
Publisher: G. P. Putnam's Sons (New York). 319 pp. $5.00
Type of work: Novel
Time: 1910-1952
Locale: Europe and the United States

A controversial, satiric novel, brilliantly written, which traces the love affair of a middle-aged man and a twelve-year-old girl

Principal characters:
HUMBERT HUMBERT, a specialist in nympholepsy
DOLORES HAZE (LOLITA), a nymphet
CLARE QUILTY, a playwright

Lolita is a girl's name, really a rather harmless name, but mention it almost anywhere and the firecrackers of controversy will begin to pop. For Lolita is a character in (and the title of) Vladimir Nabokov's best-selling novel which has produced responses that invariably seem to be in the superlative and range all the way from "Nastiest!" to "Funniest!" to "Most brilliant!" The popping of firecrackers and superlatives is not limited to literary circles only: Lolita as a recognizable character in fiction has penetrated into the miasma of television jokes and has stimulated imitations in the comic strips. At the moment Lolita is as well known as, for instance, Eliza or Scrooge. Such a character and such a book must be approached gingerly, perhaps crept up on from behind. Let us consider the story from the standpoint of three possible readers, whom we shall designate here, simply, as Reader One, Reader Two, and Reader Three.

After he has covered the first few pages, Reader One realizes that *Lolita* is the memoirs or confessions of Humbert Humbert, a middle-aged murderer awaiting trial. Humbert was born in France of well-to-do parents; at the age of thirteen, while on the Riviera, he falls in love with another thirteen-year-old, Annabel. There follows a fumbling, aborted love affair. The frustration, coupled with the death of Annabel within a few months (of typhus), has such a traumatic effect on Humbert that henceforward he can truly love only little girls between the ages of nine and fourteen, not just any little girl but those of special charm whom he calls "nymphets." If Reader One (the most sensitive of our three) feels a growing restlessness in his stomach at this point, he must steel himself for definite qualms to follow. Toward the end of an unsatisfactory marriage to a girl named Valeria (she was not as young as Humbert at first thought) he decides to move to the United States, where he must live if he is to benefit from a legacy. Here he spots a girl, Dolores Haze, nicknamed Lolita, who is the right age (twelve) and, in charm, is the nymphet of nymphets. Now comes the scene that makes Reader One's sensitive stomach begin to turn, like the slow roll of the earth. While sitting on a couch beside Humbert, Lolita impudently throws her legs across his thighs and he achieves secret sexual gratification. In order to make the full seduction of Lolita more convenient,

Humbert marries her widowed mother. Then comes his big break: the mother is knocked down by an automobile and killed. Lolita is his.

Humbert prepares carefully for his first night with the girl. He intends to give her sleeping pills so that she will not suffer the shock of what is being done to her. In one of the book's many great ironies, he finds his precautions unnecessary: she has already had sex-fun at a summer camp and so she becomes the willing aggressor. In the midst of the description of their night together, Reader One, whose stomach has orbited from apogee to perigee and who, incidentally, may have a sweet, teen-aged daughter, snaps the book shut, jumps up, shouts "Disgusting!" and tosses the book aside, never to read another line.

We now turn to Reader Two, a man of stancher stomach. Far from being disgusted by what he has read, he has enjoyed it all tremendously, if a little sheepishly. He decides *Lolita* is erotic, perhaps pornographic; and so when Humbert and his stepdaughter begin an aimless tour of America (Humbert cannot tarry too long anywhere, for people are suspicious), Reader Two starts skipping great chunks of the story, just skimming along breathlessly in search of more erotica. He does not find it. Sadly he formulates a critical judgment: not such a hot book after all. Author Nabokov himself, in an epilogue to the novel, admits the existence of Reader Two and is sorry for his plight. But he is not downcast. There is always Reader Three.

Reader Three is the intellectual type who reads on at least two levels at once. He may suspect, as others have done, that Humbert's affair with Lolita is an allegory on the corrupting of

America by that old devil, Europe; and certainly, even if he is only fairly perceptive, he will see in the couple's circum-American tour the unfolding of a wonderfully clever satire: through their eyes the America of motels, filling stations, and resorts is rather shabby and desolate. And Reader Three will spot a sharp jab at "progressive" education in the scene in which Humbert discusses with a teacher the matter of Lolita's "adjustment"—the adjustment of a girl who is having an affair with her stepfather!

Since he is a perceptive man, Reader Three will also recognize in this humorous satire a growing element of tragedy and disillusionment, which first appears when Humbert himself sees Lolita as an ordinary little girl picking her nose while reading the comics. The tragedy (like the irony) deepens when the girl is snatched away from Humbert by Clare Quilty, playwright and pervert, with whom she has been flirting on the sly. It takes several years of detective work by Humbert to find out the name of her "kidnapper," and by that time Quilty has dropped her because she was unwilling to gratify his peculiar sexual demands. When Humbert catches up with Lolita she is living in a clapboard shack. She is married (to a deaf veteran), monumentally pregnant, and, by Humbert's standards, very old— she is seventeen, rough-skinned and blue-veined and ropy. But Lolita is still the love of his life. And so, when she rebuffs him, the final act of tragedy seems preordained: he must seek out and kill Clare Quilty, the villain who broke up his "home."

As is usually true, all three of our readers are partially correct: at times *Lolita is* disgusting; in the early sections there *is* erotica; and, setting aside all foolishness about allegory, there *is* serio-comic satire of a high and subtle order. But what makes *Lolita* a near-classic is the magnificence of the writing. In this era of novels so loosely constructed that the reader's sense of form must be satisfied by a good, strong binding, Nabokov's taut and perfectly proportioned story makes us yearn for the old craftsmen; and his rhythmic, poetic diction, his ambivalence of touch that permits him to blend so many conflicting attitudes toward his characters (and thus produce our three disparate readers) are hard to match in any era. Possibly the only American writer equipped to produce this story, if he had thought of it, was the late Nathanael West. And, of course, whatever else he has accomplished, Nabokov has created one of those rare characters who slip out of literature into folklore: Lolita, Humbert's "Lo-lee-ta."

Sources for Further Study

Criticism:

Baker, George. *"Lolita*: Literature or Pornography," in *Saturday Review*. XL (June 22, 1957), p. 18. *Lolita* is a literary curiosity so skillfully done that it is more interesting than the average run of fiction, but not one of the great novels.

Beaver, Harold. "A Figure in the Carpet: Irony and the American Novel," in *Essays and Studies*. IV (1962), pp. 113-114. *Lolita* is a fine example of that select group of satire that becomes the highest art. The reciprocal flaw of irony as seen by this article gives to Nabokov's characters and surroundings the peculiar intensity that makes the novel's satire successful.

Josipovici, G. D. *"Lolita*: Parody and the Pursuit of Beauty," in *Critical Quarterly*. VI (Spring, 1966), pp. 35-48. This article analyzes Nabokov's accurate gibes at American pretensions and mores through an examination of the author's parodic style.

Malcolm, Donald. "Lolita," in *New Yorker*. XXXIV (November 8, 1958), p. 195. Malcolm sees *Lolita's* satire arising from the conjunction of a sense of humor and a sense of horror. Vice or folly is regarded not with scorn but with a tragic sympathy.

Reviews:

Atlantic. CCII, September, 1958, p. 78. 750 words.

Commonweal. LXIX, October 24, 1958, p. 102. 1,000 words.

New York Times. August 17, 1958, p. 5. 1,300 words.

Saturday Review. XLI, August 16, 1958, p. 12. 1,800 words.

Time. LXXII, September 1, 1958, p. 62. 1,300 words.

THE LONELINESS OF THE LONG-DISTANCE RUNNER

Author: Alan Sillitoe (1928-   )
Publisher: Alfred A. Knopf (New York). 176 pp. $3.50
Type of work: Short stories
Time: The present
Locale: Nottingham, England

A collection of nine stories by a vigorous young English author of arresting powers, portraying life from the point of view of the English working class in work that is young and angry but richly seasoned with salty humor and a relish for words

Alan Sillitoe's first book was a novel called *Saturday Night and Sunday Morning*. It was hailed as "brilliant," "ground-breaking," "exciting," and "uproarious"; it lent itself naturally to a comparison with the work of Arnold Bennett and D. H. Lawrence. *The Loneliness of the Long-Distance Runner,* his second published book (he claims to have destroyed hundreds of early poems, a few stories, and another novel), must arouse similar critical approbation.

Here, again, the writer reveals an acuteness of vision and a gift of language which are not to be ignored. The quality of Sillitoe's prose may indeed be superior to that of many of his more famous young contemporaries. The style is not absolutely fixed, but seems to vary to suit the story; the stories are not equally successful, perhaps because Sillitoe can render some subjects better in a style which is more immediately impressive than is the case with others. But the best of these stories are powerful, and taken altogether the collection is an imposing representation of a fine talent.

The title story is the longest. It is a picaresque tale told in the first person. The unnamed narrator is a roguish young citizen of Nottingham, a likable self-made criminal committed to the death to a war against respectable and complacent authority. After early experience in Remand Homes, he finds himself an inmate of a Borstal institution in Essex where he is told by the governor, who has a passion for athletics and a naïve belief in their efficacy as a method of criminal reform, that if he works hard and proves himself a good runner he will be sent back to the world an honest man. Such a promise only makes the boy laugh, for he knows he will always steal whatever he thinks the world owes him and never suffer any moral compunction. He goes into training, however, resenting as he does so the extra hour of effort before breakfast each day and resenting even more the implications of his coöperation. Because he wants to "get back at them" in his own way in his own time, he resists the temptation to run away while hoofing cross-country.

The second part of the story is a flashback to the events which luck ironically made his steps into the Borstal. He tells graphically but without sentimentality of the bloody death of his father from cancer of the throat, of the £500 insurance collected by his mam and promptly spent by her on a television set, clothes, ham sandwiches, and chocolate bars for the family, who lived a happy life as long as the money lasted while she made love with "some fancy-man" on a new bed upstairs. It is his pal Mike who dreams up the plan to rob the cash box of a neighborhood baker, a plan carried out to the whistled music of "The Teddy Boys' Picnic" on a foggy night. Cleverly they cache the proceeds of their theft in a drain pipe so as not to arouse suspicion through lavish spending.

But an equally clever policeman calls on the boy the next morning and demands to know where the money is. His act of innocence is good but unconvincing, and repeated searches are made for the loot. At last on a rainy morning, while a policeman is interrogating the suspect at the door, the money is washed down at their very feet.

The story resumes with life at Borstal. The personal ego and the penal theory of the governor are both at stake in a track meet between his institution and Gunthorpe. The long-distance hero of the story refuses to be a hero in the field. His revenge against his captors and against the smug ladies and gentlemen of society takes the form of deliberately losing the event at the last moment, right before their eyes. The hard labor which follows does not move him to repentance. He has won against them all. He remains a rogue.

The remarkable thing about such a story as this is that although it has a social bias, it has no sociological complexion. Sillitoe projects it as a literary reconstruction of experience, not as a special plea; out of the details of the narrative emerges the symbolic loneliness of the long-distance run which is a life; and it is all couched in a vital, slangy, powerful language. In effect, the story is a kind of transposed Salinger.

None of the other stories quite catches fire in the same way, perhaps because no other is developed with such rhetorical gusto or is imbued with such a magnificently impudent tone.

The very length of "The Loneliness of the Long-Distance Runner"—which by itself takes up a third of the volume of nine stories—may suggest that Sillitoe is a writer who, like Robert Penn Warren, is at his best in the larger forms. But if this story is superior, we should not overlook the fine qualities of the others.

It is indeed possible that the exuberance of "The Loneliness" effects a kind of overstatement, that its dazzling eloquence tends to blind a reader to the subtler and more delicate quality of its companion pieces.

Thematically, these fall into three groups: stories about the loneliness of bachelorhood, stories about the loneliness of marriage, and stories about the revelations of adolescence.

"Uncle Ernest" is about Ernest Brown the upholsterer—his name is always spoken so, in one breath—who in his middle age still has never adjusted to loneliness. His only recourse is drink, until one day he meets in a café two penniless female children. He buys them food and cares for them out of avuncular kindness, then one day is warned by two insensitive detectives to stay out of the café in the interest of public morals. Another kind of irony operates in "Mr. Raynor the Schoolteacher," the finely told story of a classroom martinet whose real depth of vision is sustained by his sight of the girls in the draper's shop across the road from the school. He observes them with phrases from Baudelaire in his mind, but each of them disappears into another man's arms.

Sillitoe handles the theme of pathos in marriage with the same scrupulous regard for just the right detail and the same aversion to sentimentality. "The Fishing-Boat Picture" is a strange and haunting love story told in the words of a postman about himself and his wife Kathy. She has never respected his reading, thinking it a sign of his ignorance that he needs to read, and finally, when he hits her for burning a library book, she runs off with a house painter. Ten years later she returns to Nottingham for a visit with her postman-husband and receives from him a fishing-boat picture which she admires. Soon thereafter he happens to see it in a pawnshop and redeems it. As her visits continue, she never refers to having sold it and eventually asks for it again. Again it appears in the pawnshop, but the postman leaves it there this time. Later, after Kathy's death, the picture serves to remind him of all that he had never done to salvage love from their psychological impasse. "The Match," one of the most impressive stories in the collection, is about two friends at a football game, and about how their civic pride in the Nottingham team becomes intricately involved in their domestic situations. The motivation of the quarrel which the one named Lennox has with his wife and family recalls Joyce's story "Counterparts." "The Disgrace of Jim Scarfedale" is about a complicated mother-son relationship, a ruined marriage, and eventually the exposure of Jim Scarfedale as a molester of young girls. The narrative is recounted by an eavesdropping neighbor boy who learns a lesson from his observations and concludes he

would rather pay his way around the British Isles by robbing gas meters than stay home tied to his mother's apron strings.

The loneliness of adults is a theme which takes perspective in this volume from the theme of the initiation of the young. "Noah's Ark" concerns the adventure of two boys stealing rides on a carousel at the Goose Fair. The rapidly paced story portrays the vertiginous world challenged by the reckless adolescent and the brutal thrust from "the Noah's Ark jungle [one of them] had ridden on free." "On Saturday Afternoon" is the apocalyptic account of a boy's experience with a man who insists on suicide. "The Decline and Fall of Frankie Buller" is a pathetic tale of a neighborhood gang leader, lionized by his followers but finally deprived of their support by wartime evacuation, and at last discredited in the community by the necessity of undergoing shock therapy. The narrator is careful never to let Buller know that anyone sees through his persistently juvenescent illusion and bluff.

Such stories as these take their significance as much from their subtlety of detail and their magic of language as they do from any mere sketch of "what happens." Sillitoe's achievement in this book is a kind of "Nottinghammers." It is not an exaggeration to say that one is reminded of Joyce's *Dubliners,* from which book Sillitoe seems to have learned.

THE LONELY HUNTER
A Biography of Carson McCullers

Author: Virginia Spencer Carr (1929-   )
Publisher: Doubleday and Company (New York). 600 pp. $12.50
Type of work: Biography
Time: 1917 to 1971
Locale: Southern and Eastern United States and Europe

A just and sympathetic definitive biography of an outstanding recent American writer

Recent biographies of American literary figures are chiefly remarkable for exposing their subject's awesome character failings. Carlos Baker's *Ernest Hemingway: A Life Story* reveals no *machismo* artist, but a self-indulgent bully who tried to destroy anyone he could not dominate. Mark Schorer in *Sinclair Lewis* portrayed a sick, whining man, whose hatred of humanity grew to morbid proportions as the years passed. Lawrance Thompson's biography of Robert Frost uncovered a gnarled old man who was no rude tiller of the soil and simple, patriotic voice of the people, but a sadist of psychotic proportions. Virginia Spencer Carr's *The Lonely Hunter: A Biography of Carson McCullers* may have halted this biography-by-assassination trend. Professor Carr treats McCullers with sympathy, understanding, and justice. What emerges in this lengthy, painstakingly documented study is the definitive portrait of a contradictory and intense human being. Carson McCullers was every bit as eccentric in real life as any of her vibrant, Gothic creations.

While she possessed neither William Faulkner's grand design of human interaction, nor Flannery O'Connor's penetrating philosophical vision, McCullers did write several novels and short stories set in the South which have become modern classics. Her first novel, *The Heart Is a Lonely Hunter* (1940), is a powerful story about a young girl's search for identity, and a deaf mute's search for acceptance. The setting is a small town in the Deep South, but the book's meaning, its interrelated themes of anguish and joy bound together by humor and the grotesque, transcend its location. *The Heart Is a Lonely Hunter* shows McCullers' command of precise language, ability to dramatize scenes, and insight into human nature. *Reflections in a Golden Eye* (1941) is a deeper penetration into the grotesque possibilities inherent in human relationships. *The Member of the Wedding* (1946) returned to the theme of adolescent feelings with as much perception as *The Heart Is a Lonely Hunter*. McCullers' last novel, *Clock Without Hands* (1961), is more abstract than her earlier work and has received less critical acclaim. However, *The Ballad of the Sad Café and Collected Short Stories* (1955) has been acclaimed as one of the very finest fiction anthologies ever assembled. Clearly this is no great body of major work, but Carson McCullers should be measured by the quality of what she wrote, which is considerable.

Carr's contribution to understanding McCullers is primarily biographical, not an estimation and analysis of her literary works. Normally, such an emphasis would be questionable at best, an invasion of privacy and the past to follow that Gothic notion that the dead owe us both their secrets and a living. Carson, however, turns out to be a rewarding subject. Her personal life was not only highly interesting, but instructive; her professional career was an important chapter of recent literary history. Carr's research is so thorough that serious students of McCullers' writing cannot help but find many passages in this biography that illuminate her writing. Carr consistently presents opposing views and contradictory evidence in an effort to document her subject's life rather than shape information to create an easy thesis and judgment.

With care and thoroughness, Carr debunks the public image of Carson McCullers, prodigy author and vulnerable, wounded writer. A good deal of work went into the fabrication of this image. The publicity picture of Carson upon the appearance of *The Heart Is a Lonely Hunter* revealed a round-faced adolescent girl with pug nose, small mouth, and scattered bangs looking all of fifteen years old. Carson was actually almost twenty-four, already a chain smoker, hard drinker, and deeply involved in several romantic entanglements. Projecting an aura of the genius who needed assistance, especially from older, established males, McCullers found very valuable. Sponsored by Louis Untermeyer and others, she gained entrance into the highest literary circles. During the 1940's, she

could count on paid summers at the Bread Loaf Writers' Conference or the Yaddo Colony, and she received two substantial grants from the Guggenheim Foundation. Carr reveals that during the 1950's and 1960's, Carson, while never wealthy, could effectively use her charms on those in a position to produce dramatic and movie versions of her prose works.

In reality, Carson was no hurt dove, but, in Carr's words, an "iron butterfly." True, she was painfully shy, introverted, and the victim of an inordinate number of debilitating physical illnesses. Throughout her life McCullers was plagued by serious respiratory ailments and alcoholism. At age thirty she suffered the first of several strokes which eventually paralyzed her left side. She underwent a mastectomy and numerous surgical operations for severe arthritis. Severe nervous tension was a constant McCullers characteristic. In spite of such handicaps, however, she possessed an iron will and unflagging determination. She was a highly contradictory personality, typically affecting people in opposite ways. Carr must be credited for establishing a clear and balanced portrait of a person whom almost everyone regarded as either a bitch or a saint.

Carr's problems do not end with the divided view of how others saw Carson McCullers, for her personal life was also contradictory as well as unconventional. Carson was an intense human being, capable of loving to the fullest either men or women. Carson's most passionate relationship was with Annemarie Clarc-Schwarzenbach, an adventurous, wealthy Swiss expatriate who, in turn, was enamored of Thomas Mann's daughter, Erika. Annemarie had lived the life of luxury and high adventure that Carson had dreamed of as an adolescent. According to Carr, Carson imitated and worshiped the women she loved, but these women seldom reciprocated with similarly intense feelings. McCullers' passion for women was an important aspect of her being that apparently everyone close to her recognized and accepted, except her husband.

James Reeves McCullers, Jr., grew up in Wetumpka, Alabama, the star athlete and writer of his high school class. Reeves met Carson in 1935 when he was stationed as an Army enlisted man at Fort Benning, near Columbus, Georgia, Carson's home town. In the early days of their relationship and marriage, Reeves shared the same high aspirations to be a novelist that his wife had. But with Carson's publication of *The Heart Is a Lonely Hunter* in 1940 and its subsequent success, Carson and Reeves became distant. Reeves provided a protective and competent masculine presence, and this Carson greatly needed. She did not need, however, Reeves's suspicious and sometimes dishonest nature; nor did she wish to be sexually involved with him. Intimidated as the husband of America's finest young woman novelist, puzzled and then terrified about their personal problems, Reeves found consolation, or at least attention, in alcoholic bouts of depression. Carson had become devoted to alcohol a little earlier when her relationship with Annemarie terminated.

Reeves and Carson had an unusual relationship, to say the least. They were married, divorced, remarried, and then separated before Reeves's suicide in 1953. Besides all the other problems, Reeves simply could not keep up with Carson's pace in acquiring famous new friends and gathering fame. Failure in his writing career and in his relationship with Carson, whom he desperately needed, weighed heavily upon him; his sexual failure with his wife led him to question his own masculinity. Eventually he fell in love with David Diamond, a composer who felt an unrestrained passion for *both* the McCullers. Carson took the news of a Reeves and David liaison very badly. According to Carr, Carson felt that Reeves could have sexual relations with anyone he pleased since she had so little to give in this area of their relationship; but he was not to fall in love with a mutual friend. Through periods of intense fulfillment and intense jealousy, these three remained close friends for years.

Carr argues that an insight into Carson's bisexuality provides meaningful insight into her personality and creative powers. This deep need and ability to love both women and men gave Carson the insight for her fine character portrayals and her profound understanding of human relationships, especially when they formed triangles. In this kind of interaction Carson felt that the selfish bonds of identity were replaced by empathy with others, what she called "the we of me." As the paralyzed victim of a stroke, Carson had a real understanding of alienation and the grotesque. Carr also establishes Carson's fixation on frustrated female adolescents. Tall, thin, and very youthful looking until her later years, Carson typically scorned dresses, preferring jeans and a man's white shirt; this outfit added to her unforgettable personal appearance and manner.

One of the most intriguing episodes in *The Lonely Hunter* concerns Carson's involvement in 1941-1942 with an artists' commune in Brooklyn. Living apart from Reeves at the time, Carson loved the disintegrating Old World neighborhood and the vast number of creative people who passed through this area under the Brooklyn Bridge. The commune was organized and run by W. H. Auden who ruled with what might charitably be called a very firm concern. Carson's friend Louis Untermeyer was in residence, as was George Davis, the owner and a noted conversationalist. When Gypsy Rose Lee joined the house, the whole tempo changed. Miss Lee was not only the most famous "interpretative dancer" of her era, but a warm and very literate human being. Carson was entranced. Eventually, several of Auden's friends moved in, including the poet Louis MacNeice, composer Benjamin Britten, and a talented tenor named Peter Pears. A magazine of art and criticism, *Decision,* was planned and

printed at the commune on 7 Middagh Street. The place was filled with excitement and confusion, but with all the drinking, parties, and all-night conversations, there was hardly any time for serious creativity. When Auden left for a teaching position at the University of Michigan, the commune folded. It had been a refreshing, stimulating experience, a community of displaced refugees during the hysterical early war days, but finally everyone wanted to resume his own work.

In *The Lonely Hunter,* Virginia Carr, by her thorough research and very readable style, significantly illuminates Carson McCullers the person and Carson McCullers the writer. The story is often not a pretty one, and there will probably always be unanswered questions about this talented and enigmatic individual. Yet, Carr explains her subject with such sensitivity and honesty that general readers can be grateful for a fascinating "life and times" account, and scholars will be able to spend years analyzing a mass of new data brought to light.

Patrick Morrow

THE LONELY PASSION OF JUDITH HEARNE

Author: Brian Moore (1921-   )
Publisher: Atlantic-Little, Brown and Company (Boston). 223 pp. $3.50
Type of work: Novel
Time: The present
Locale: Belfast, Ireland

The story of a lonely woman who fails to find a husband and who cannot find peace by recourse to friends, to her church, or to alcohol

Principal characters:
JUDITH HEARNE, a spinster
MRS. HENRY RICE, her landlady
BERNARD RICE, the landlady's son
JAMES MADDEN, the landlady's brother
PROFESSOR AND MRS. OWEN O'NEILL, friends of Judith
EDIE MARRINAN, another friend of Judith

Judith Hearne, a spinster living in Belfast, has three props to her lonely life, and they do not always serve: a silver framed photograph of her aunt, a colored oleograph of the Sacred Heart, and her "long pointed shoes with the little buttons on them, winking up at her. Little shoe-eyes, always there." Without sentimentality, without dramatic embroidery, but with a fine use of the techniques of realism as refined in the stream of consciousness methods devised by James Joyce and Virginia Woolf, Brian Moore *gives*—rather than simply tells—the lonely passion of Judith Hearne. For Judith's life is one of dreams never realized, of expectations never met, and of deceptions always discovered. Her petty hopes and lies alike lead to nothing but frustration. Her friends are mere acquaintances upon whom she imposes herself in such a way that neither she nor they ever come to understand each other. Her religion supplies ritual without a sign of truth. Her priest cannot understand her inmost troubles, but treats her as a long-winded parishioner whose confessions delay his golf game. The satisfaction of wine gives way to the stupor of whiskey and Judith, trying to hide her drinking from her landlady and the other roomers, is told that through the night she has been singing wildly in her solitary room.

This is the poignantly told experience of a spinster in her forties as she bolsters herself with illusions and whiskey. In the midst of her loneliness she makes a self-examination which, far from liberating her from her faults, merely confirms her suspicion that she is doomed in life and that nothing—not whiskey, not friends, not dreams, not "Mr. Right," not the priest, and not God—can save her. She settles down, without hope, into ugly despair. But, strangely enough, the novel is not depressing, for there is a clarity of vision here which compensates for the murkiness of the thing seen. In understanding Judith Hearne's departure from hope, we come to accept her as a person. Without sanctioning her attempts to escape, we acknowledge her worth and pity her for her unavoidable fate.

The novel introduces Judith as she moves into another apartment and unpacks the photograph of her aunt and the oleograph of the Sacred Heart. At first, as usual, she is encouraged by the friendliness of the landlady, Mrs. Rice, and her son Bernard. The son lives with his mother, has no job, and pretends to be engaged in the creation of a great poem. The characterization is vivid:

> He was a horrid-looking fellow. Fat as a pig he was, and his face was the colour of cottage cheese. His collar was unbuttoned and his silk tie was spotted with egg stain. His stomach stuck out like a sagging pillow and his little thin legs fell away under it to end in torn felt slippers. He was all bristly blond jowls, tiny puffy hands and long blond curly hair, like some monstrous baby swelled to man size.

The landlady's brother lives there too; he has just returned from America where he has made a modest "fortune" by having been awarded a ten thousand dollar settlement after being struck by a bus. James Madden takes an interest in Judith because he thinks she might have some money she would be willing to invest in an American coffee shop in Dublin. Judith, however, regards him as her last chance; her intense desire for a husband leads her to misinterpret his business proposal as a marriage proposal. Although she is disturbed by Madden's uncouth ways and American ideas—the result of his having been a "hotel man" in New York City—she is willing to compromise for the sake of being settled. However, when Mrs. Rice and her son suggest that Jim had been only a doorman, that he does not pay his rent, and that Judith is simply trying to take advantage of him, Judith retires to her room and opens the bottles of whiskey she has been hiding in her trunk.

Judith has been handicapped in her effort to find a husband by having had to take care of an ailing and neurotically tyrannical aunt who, playing upon her sympathies, drove Judith into caring for her even after the aunt had become unbalanced enough to be ordered to an institution. The pitiful aspect of Judith's dependence upon the pictures of her aunt and of Jesus, pictures she turns to the wall when she is about to settle down to her drinking, is that neither of the two answers her questions or prayers. From her point of view, both make demands without giving rewards, and yet there is nothing else to turn to, except whiskey.

While Judith is involved in what turns out to be a habitual pattern of disillusionment and retreat to alcohol, James discovers Bernard in the process of seducing the sixteen-year-old maid. The sight of the girl so excites James that a few days later, when he has a chance he slips into her room at night and, intimidating her with threats of seeing to it that she loses her job if she denies him, he satisfies himself.

Judith, faced by the landlady's accusations of drunkenness, tries to find comfort by making visits to her friends the O'Neills. The father is a professor who retreats to his study when she appears; the children sometimes stay to visit with her only because their mother orders them to do so. Judith no longer has her convent friend Edie Marrinan to chat and drink with, for Edie has ended up in a nursing home. The O'Neills do their best to foster the illusion that Judith is a member of the family, and that the children are her nephews and nieces—but Judith knows that the dream is not working.

She reveals this later when, thoroughly drunk, and having been unable to find any sign of hope from her priest or from Edie, she stumbles into the O'Neill home and confesses to Mrs. O'Neill that she has always hated her. After a violent scene in the church when Judith, having cried, "I hate you!" to God, tries to open the tabernacle on the altar and, with bloody hands, collapses before it, she too is taken to the nursing home.

As Brian Moore's portrayal concludes, we find Judith with the realization that between her and death there is nothing to count on except the portrait of her aunt and the oleograph of the Sacred Heart. Judith, looking at the picture of Jesus, asks, "And You. Were You ever? Is this picture the only You?" and she answers, "It is here and You are gone. It is You. No matter what You are, it is still part of me."

This is more than a realistic and moving image of the inner life of a disappointed and disillusioned woman; it is a critical insight into the problem of relating religion on earth to the needs of human beings. The slow disintegration of faith is shown as relentlessly as the disintegration of the dreams and the body of Judith Hearne. Prompted by despair and the skeptical suggestions Bernard makes, Judith suddenly sees nothing in the church but bread, painted statues, and all-too-human priests. Yet she makes the effort to recover something of the old glory, and she prays for a sign. She goes from person to person looking for one point of justification for her life, or one true companion. Disappointed, she ends with nothing but the images on the wall, pictures which are for her no longer representative of ideals beyond them, but which must be taken for what they are: merely pictures, her last and only companions.

The lonely passion, the solitary suffering, of Judith Hearne has been starkly presented by Irish-born Brian Moore. This is his first novel. His skill at rendering the soul of a woman with the clarity with which others reveal the outer slums of life—and with the same compassion and anger—will probably enable him to write other extraordinary and revealing books.

Sources for Further Study

Criticism:

Foster, John W. "Crisis and Ritual in Brian Moore's Belfast Novels," in *Eire: Ireland*. III (Autumn, 1968), pp. 66-74. The theme of the novel, according to Foster, is a primitive rather than a twentieth century dilemma —"The rites of passage."

Ludwig, Jack. "Brian Moore: Ireland's Loss, Canada's Novelist," in *Critique: Studies in Modern Fiction*. V (Spring-Summer, 1962), pp. 5-14. An analysis of characterization in *The Lonely Passion of Judith Hearne* as well as in some of Moore's other novels.

———. "A Mirror of Moore," in *Canadian Literature*. VII (Winter, 1961), pp. 18-23. Moore is compared to Joyce in his compassion by Ludwig, who also finds that *The Lonely Passion of Judith Hearne* provides the most complete examples of character development in Moore's novels.

Reviews:
Canadian Forum. XXXVI, August, 1956, p. 111. 1,700 words.
Commonweal. LXIV, August 3, 1956, p. 448. 800 words.
New Statesman. XLIX, May 21, 1955. p. 728. 480 words.
Saturday Review. XXXIX, July 7, 1956, p. 9. 420 words.
Time. LXVII, June 18, 1956, p. 104. 700 words.

THE LONESOME TRAVELER AND OTHER STORIES

Author: John William Corrington (1932–   )
Publisher: G. P. Putnam's Sons (New York). 286 pages. $5.95
Type of work: Short stories

A collection of quasi-related stories, set in Louisiana and spanning a period from 1868 to 1968, telling fascinatingly tragic and charmingly humorous truths about the South, its times, people, and problems

John William Corrington is one of the five or six most gifted Southern writers working today. In fact, in terms of quantity and consistently deepening quality of work, he is probably the best. He has phenomenal creative energies which find expression in his rendering of a complex breadth of perceptions and depth of concerns into novels, poems, and stories of rich character, persuasive narrative, and memorable theme. Part of Corrington's considerable strength as artist lies in his ability to tell new stories of the much-storied South in such ways as to avoid unpleasant comparison with the Southern giants who preceded him.

At the same time he is unabashedly Southern in his manner, in his technique, and in his innate sense of what a story really is. He makes Louisiana and Mississippi come whackingly, resonantly alive. Dealing with a section of the country treated previously by the formidable talents of Robert Penn Warren, Eudora Welty, Flannery O'Connor and Walker Percy, Corrington not only updates the material, but adds his own special qualities of humor, irony, and compassion for the Southerner of the past and of the present. In each story here, he shows his attitude toward the Southerner to be one of mingled fear, love, amusement, and fascination. For him the Southerner is a singular man trapped in Time, suspended in his attempts to discern between the good and the bad aspects of the present and the now-burdensome past; caught between sun-blaze and rich earth, he is victimized as well as heightened by his passions of hatred and love, both. He is a potentially violent man dozing on the fecund and equally violent earth, and both he and the earth can awake instantly, for strange, irrational reasons, and burst into violent expressions of pride, bitterness, hatred, or love.

In writing of such bafflingly complex subjects, Corrington is better than Warren at making *all* of his wide range of characters individually alive; he is better than Welty at humor when he wants to prompt laughter; he is better than Percy at showing the various kinds of existential isolation which the Southerner is prone to experience. Moreover, he is always exciting, vital, provoking; he is a consummately skillful storyteller in the traditionally Southern sense of that phrase, with the one admirable exception that he can confront and depict accurately the contemporary South as well as the old. In this collection of stories, he displays a judiciously clear, cool mastery of the demanding craft of rendering the South in short fiction.

Further, concerning Corrington's creative energy, it is worth noting that he has made the decade of the sixties his own. An industrious writer, he has already built up an impressive canon for a craftsman only in his late thirties. For instance, from 1962 to 1965 he published four volumes of poetry: *Where We Are, Mr. Clean and Other*

Poems, The Anatomy of Love, and *Lines to the South.* In 1964 came his first novel, *And Wait for the Night,* which was followed in 1967 by *The Upper Hand,* a novel which received consistently admiring criticism. Moreover, he wears at least two other professional hats: he is a professor of literature at Loyola University of the South, in New Orleans; he is the author of numerous scholarly articles, and, as an editor, he has co-edited an important brace of critical anthologies of fiction and poetry entitled *Southern Writing in the Sixties.* Somehow not slowing himself down as a writer of fiction, nor curbing himself stylistically toward too academic a tone, he took a B.A. from Centenary College, an M.A. from Rice University, and a doctorate from the University of Sussex at Brighton, England.

There are nine stories in *The Lonesome Traveler,* each labeled and placed sequentially in a specific point in time. For instance, the first story, "If Time Were Not/A Moving Thing," is labeled, "New Orleans: 1868–1968." Thereafter the specific labels are "Atlanta: 1864," "Gettysburg: 1913," "Shreveport: 1929," "Shreveport: 1933," "Mississippi: 1935," "Shreveport: 1946," "Shreveport: 1958," and "New Orleans: 1965." For Corrington's several themes and concerns, Time, as well as the various ways in which we are conscious of Time, obviously forms the central basis from which everything else extends. In "If Time Were Not/A Moving Thing," Corrington makes clear his fascination with Time through his device of sometimes ironic, sometimes moving juxtaposition of events in New Orleans, past and present. In that story, the shifts in time from 1868 to 1968 are calculated to shock the reader with the disparity of times, and, at the

same time, impress him with the sad similarity, the continuing relevance, of the times. Through this conjunction, the grace and charm of Marie DuCote, her adherence to a code is contrasted with the existential emptiness of contemporary man in a scene which also depicts the typographical device Corrington employs to "insert" the reader back and forth into the different periods of time:

By morning He had heard my promises and sent to me a sleep as free of trouble as a child's, as Emile's. So that, waking in early afternoon, I smiled at Emile, embraced him and sent him on his business. I knew whose bride I was, whose mistress I would have to be. And yet

> I
>> knew
>> that
>>> Mr. Posey
>>> almost
>>>> never

missed the six o'clock news on television. He would come stumbling into the hotel room he had occupied for the past nine years, strip off his greasy overalls, and stand naked except for his socks and brogans, staring out the dirty window down into heat-cramped traffic that never ceased to flow late or early along Terpsicore Street.

"Time," Corrington's technique reiterates, "*is* a moving thing" and is therefore a poignant human problem. It is his characters' very consciousness of the passage of time that often causes them to have strong feelings of the futility in their existences and to seek blind refuge in autocratic religious forms, traditional codes, or a kind of vague guilt over their involuntary involvement in all history. For instance, in "If Time Were Not/A Moving Thing," Marie DuCote resolutely lives in her own realm of consciousness and time, deeply religious, in love with "Him," removed from the real 1868, until she becomes pregnant. For a time then, her twins cause her to live for her "now," but when the boys die of fever the only meaning in her "time" goes with them to the grave. Set face to face against her retreat into keenly intellectual despair is the ignorant but equally compelling desperation of Mr. Posey, the locomotive engineer who, in 1968, is filling out his days, passively awaiting retirement. Frustrated, afraid, Mr. Posey senses time moving around and through him, and he feels himself uncomfortably a part of every facet of that movement:

> So he would sit, mouth open, and slowly absorb the day's quotient of the unspeakable, trying to see how the flaming crash of a Grand Prix car in Germany might be tied to twenty men trapped beyond hope in a West Virginia coal mine. Putting aside his rationalism, Mr. Posey would whisper almost below the threshold of sound as burning race car was followed by grimy men dragging wrapped bundles from a mineshaft elevator: *Oh, Christ. Oh, Sweet Jesus. Oh, I didn't have nothing to do with that. Never saw such. I never had no hand in nothing like that.* And it was true. . . . He had done none of it, and yet it belonged to him as if by some means of travel faster than light itself, he had dropped explosive into the mine and managed to get to Germany in time to loosen a steering knuckle in a certain car before the race began.

In another way, Time is of major concern to Corrington: particularly in the South does he see the burden of history choking men and land with old guilts, old passions. Several of these stories deal with the fact that the Civil War, even in 1968, is still a part of the

consciousness of many Southerners. They are at least subliminally conscious of their forebears' having fought nobly or ignobly, of having been defeated in a great war and of having suffered long and harrowing consequences. This consciousness of the past often asserts itself in various forms—a sense of family unity, a blind adherence to traditional ideas of responsibility and duty, a strong sense of belonging to a place, and a sense of the necessity of pride and self-reliance. Paradoxically, Corrington illustrates in nearly each story how the same Southerner who feels, for instance, a strong allegiance to his family may also be seethingly resentful of the confinements caused by such bonds. He may become confused about what his duty is; he may even come to see his sense of place as restrictive rather than comforting. Thus, because of his consciousness of Time, the Southerner is a figure who challenges fictional treatment; his very complexity, the dichotomies in his makeup, grow out of what Time does to him, or has done to him already before he is even born.

The traditional Southern reliance upon the wisdom of grandparents, old aunts, uncles, fathers; the belief and pride in the grandchildren, nephews, nieces, cousins—all that comprises the sense of family is a manifestation of the Southern consciousness of the sequence, the linear quality of Time. In each of these stories Corrington ironically juxtaposes characters who have different concepts of Time and different concepts of their places within a scheme of Time. Thus, they have difficulty in communicating with one another. They are isolated, caught in a trap of Time which has bereft them of any sure sense of self or religion or duty. The conflicts in each story have to do with the protagonist's struggles to apprehend what a viable role for him may be. In the lighter stories the past teaches, brings to the present valuable things; in the darker stories the values of the past prove futile when confronted with contemporary complexities. Also in each story, the conflict grows from the characters' attempts to decide what is a proper relationship between past and present. Some characters bitterly discard any heritage, finding it restrictive or empty; others take the old codes of conduct and revitalize them for their new day. The best example of such bold redefinition and utilization of the past is in "The Retrievers," a humorous story about two youngsters who find a buried treasure. The story's theme is obvious in its title: there are things of great value from the past which *can* be retrieved through intelligence and a redefined, modernized kind of faith. In this story, the youngsters, Malissa and Nathan Armistead, make use of an old map to "retrieve" a treasure which had been there in their yard in Caddo Parish for almost eighty years waiting for someone with imagination and faith to win it back. Malissa and Nathan use the instructions found on the old map, ignoring along the way the unsought and scoffing advice of parents and older siblings who cannot see beyond the snare of the mundane present. In addition, they utilize present-day scientific knowledge and—in spite of all odds—triumph in making their family's fortune. The story is a gentle, wry one with typically warm, insightful Corrington touches regarding the family relationships; it is basically a comic tale, but it does illustrate how the problem of Time runs through even the lightest of these stories.

In the more tragic title story, "The Lonesome Traveler," Time is personified by the traveler, the ubiquitous, near-mythic Mr. Able Gone. Observing the story's tragic events, participating in them and commenting, chorus-like, on them, Mr. Gone always gives the impression that he has been other places, seen worse things, and, moreover, *will* see more that is worse elsewhere at another time. He is outside the Time-scheme of the other characters in the story; he is Time-less—of all Time, and, paradoxically, is thus the *most* victimized of all the characters caught in Time.

Each of these stories has its psychological roots in the complexity of existence, what it is, why it is, and what—if anything—it means. When we read, story by story, from 1868 to 1968, the relativity and mystery of Time is made the book's only constant factor as it affects various individuals in their different moments in life. Strangely, Time, though moving frenziedly, inexorably, remains unchanged through each moment of fragmented reality in these stories. Everything else changes, goes.

In several ways, Corrington's stories are deeply satisfying. They are subtle and complex in characterization and motivation. They have a solid and effective texture of place and atmosphere, asserting their own pith, rhythm, and mood. He knows, for instance, when to employ the oblique, Southern "front-porch voice" and when to employ a detached, deft objectivity. Listen to the Southern, drawling voice of the narrator of "The Retrievers":

> But what I want to tell about is how we came to live on Fairfield Avenue without opening a plumbing shop or finding that we were the lost heirs of General Kirby-Smith. We came to be thought of as part of the old folks, one

of the families to be consulted, and we got that way overnight. No waiting period. We just overshot the whole gaggle of Heathertons, Priors, Richleys, and Gaineses who had bought in and were busily trying to live down the buying.

It all happened because of my young brother and sister. . . . They became, you might say, the true founders of the Shreveport branch of the Tennessee Armisteads. It was quite a trick, starting as an embarrassment and ending with a big legal thing complete to U. S. Internal Revenue sneaking around and every trimmer in the parish grinding his teeth and trying to figure a way to cash in on our good luck.

Which is getting ahead. Because it started in the summer of 1933, when we were living out off Highway 20. . . .

In contrast, listen to the detached, efficient voice of the more urban, more modern narrator of "The Night School":

I cannot hide things well. When I lie, I am always caught. My mother claimed it was because I was a good boy and could not learn to lie well. I lie badly, but it has nothing to do with being good. Lying is only a facility like perfect pitch or sensitivity to color: one has the ability or not. To compensate, I try never to become involved in a situation where only liars can prosper.

Consistently Corrington surprises and charms, much as Flannery O'Connor could, by his startling juxtapositions of unlikely characters and images. In "If Time Were Not/A Moving Thing," Mr. Posey goes into a tavern which

was dark with only a bored barkeep leaning half-asleep against the sagging backbar and two men huddled over beers in front. Above them in the

gloom a globe, blue and green and girdled with a wide lettered band, floated like a projection in a planetarium. On the band it said SCHLITZ. One of the men wore overalls with a rusty hammer caught in the tool strap at his side. Under the overalls he wore a shortsleeved T-shirt, and his hairy arms were gauded with flecks of white and azure and terra-cotta house paint. Mr. Posey wondered if he had been decorating some kind of Catholic church.

The importance of Corrington's fiction lies in his powerful gifts as storyteller conjoined with his keenly sensitive, intellectual range of discernment and statement. His stories finally not only delight but also instruct in the profound matters of man, his heart, his spirit. It is Corrington's strongest trait that he can so gracefully fuse these elements that he rescues his work from being *merely* one thing or the other. An indication of his craftsmanship which simultaneously produces delight and substance, is this scene from "A Time To Embrace" which displays his strengths as a creator of memorable character, dialogue, and setting:

My father stretched his legs. —I believe we have whiskey inside, he said. —Are you gentlemen old enough to share a glass with me?
—I know where it is, I said. But Bobby Lee was already up and walking into the house. My father rose and walked up and down the porch. —I expect this is a man's work. These are a man's hours, God knows. I hope Bobby Lee's folks won't object to the hours or the stimulant.
—We've—I began, and then fell silent.
—I'm sure you have, my father said.
—But not under my aegis.
—We'll be fine. We'll be just fine, I said pointlessly.

—I know. My father smiled, looking upward where the moon rode high, a handful of clouds racing across its face. Far away, I heard low thunder.
—We could use a night shower or two, my father said. —It's been dry.
—It'll drive the fish down. They won't feed if the water's troubled.
—The big ones will, he said as Bobby Lee reappeared with whiskey, glasses and a pitcher of ice water. —The big ones will bite anytime. You fish still waters to fill the frying pan. Fish troubled waters for sport.
We sat and drank. The evening was turning cool, and a sullen pulse of lightning showed through distant clouds.

There is in this collection a discernible, though often frail, thread of continuity from story to story in terms not only of Time but of character, place, and theme. In this sense the stories move through fluxions of time, families, and landscape. All of these elements change on the surface, but deeper down the changes are slow. It is too strong to suggest that the various stories show "progress" as the Time, characters, and land "progress" or change; they do not; their themes and concerns remain the same. Only the outward manifestations of material things change. Man's problems in these stories are the same in 1868 as they are in 1968; the last story makes the same point as the first: man is a mysterious and passing strange animal; he is a stranger to himself, and, only through love can he win even tentative victories over the incursions of the world and Time; for his spirit he can have faith—anything higher than that is beyond man's capabilities.

The only adverse criticism this collection might merit is the observation—and it is just that, a matter more of taste than of critical analysis—that at least three of the stories are really too long; intriguing and involved as they are, they are more properly novellas, and one has the feeling that he is reading material with which the author might have been happier had he developed it into a novel. This, however, is a minor observation, for the stories are quite strong, filled with humanity, incident, surprise, and an astonishing depth of feeling and insight. Corrington is already very good, but he has probably only begun.

Thomas N. Walters

A LONG AND HAPPY LIFE

Author: Reynolds Price (1933-   )
Publisher: Atheneum Publishers (New York). 195 pp. $3.95
Type of work: Novel
Time: 1957
Locale: Warren County, North Carolina

A realistically observed, quietly told, poetically styled first novel evoking the grace of innocence and the mystery of love

Principal characters:

ROSACOKE MUSTIAN, a country girl who dreams of a long and happy life

WESLEY BEAVERS, the headstrong, wayward young man whom she loves

EMMA MUSTIAN, called Mama, Rosacoke's widowed mother

MILO and

RATO MUSTIAN, Rosacoke's brothers

SISSIE, Milo's wife

MR. ISAAC ALSTON, a local landowner

MARY SUTTON, a colored woman, the mother of Mildred Sutton, who died in childbirth

SAMMY RANSOM, Mr. Alston's servant, believed by some to be the father of Mildred Sutton's child

MACEY GUPTON, a neighbor

MARISE GUPTON, his wife

FREDERICK, the Gupton's youngest child

By any standard of criticism Reynolds Price's *A Long and Happy Life* was the outstanding first novel published by a young American writer in 1962. Winner of the William Faulkner Foundation and Sir Walter Raleigh awards, it conveys in its coherent and unifying vision more than a bright promise for its author's literary future. The book is a wholly self-contained and admirably achieved work in its own right, and the point of praise is not the fact that Mr. Price has handled with great delicacy and skill a small group of lives against the background of his North Carolina setting, but that he has filled his limited scene with larger meaning. In his fable of inarticulate desire, lost innocence, and the wisdom of acceptance retrieved from despair he gives dramatic form to moral issues deeply embedded in character and conduct.

More important, perhaps, the novel testifies to a new spirit and a different, imaginatively personal way of looking at life that is beginning to reanimate writing out of the South. For the Southern renascence may now be viewed within a wider cultural perspective as another instance of the process by which, from time to time, works of the imagination give shape and life to a social picture or a moment in history, and in so doing enlarge and replenish our vision of the world. Some societies appear destined to be revitalized in art after they have ceased to function as historical fact. Disregarded by the mass, on the verge of change or extinction, they find renewal in poetry or prose. This is what happened in the case of New England Puritanism. What was vital in that theocratic society—its concepts of good and evil, the exercise and responsibility of purpose and choice, the working of consciousness and conscience—Hawthorne preserved indelibly in his moral romances, to the enrichment of our literature. The South contained another society—Faulkner called it the old order—brought to a second flowering by the poets and novelists who began to write in the Twenties and Thirties.

These writers appeared at a time when the family and community structures of Southern life were breaking up under the social and economic pressures of the twentieth century. A section of the country which had known almost no change for several generations suddenly found its landscape transformed by industry and urbanization. What Thomas Wolfe saw in Asheville during his boyhood, the growth of a mountain village into a briskly modern city, was not an isolated instance in the life of the region. The face of the South was changing and with it the beliefs and attitudes of its people. Unable to view the world with the same certainties their fathers and grandfathers had known, the poets and novelists of the Southern renascence discovered, like Wolfe, that they could not go home again. Like him, too, they were haunted by the knowledge of something "lost and stricken" in the far away and long ago. The more the old life with all its local ties receded from them in fact, the more they were conscious of its presence in memory. But what they no longer possessed, or were possessed by, could be re-created in art. The "South" about which they wrote was not so much an actual geographical region as a landscape of the imagination, out of time, out of reach, but not out of recollection in family tales and legends, if not in personal experience. Faulkner's true home place was not the real Lafayette County in Mississippi but his imaginary Yoknapatawpha County, and he made its Jefferson the center of a moral universe. Because he knew what the old order had once stood for, flawed as it was but satisfying to human needs, he could judge the descendants of his Sartoris, Compson, and McCaslin clans by their involvement in the Snopesian society of the present. Allen Tate could write in "The Mediterranean" about a rich land "where tasseling corn,/Fat beans, grapes sweeter than muscadine/Rot on the vine: in that land were we born." The writers of the renascence created in their books a region of lost effort, tragic vision, violent truth.

At the present time, however, there are signs that the resources of historic memory and evocative sense of place, the rich vein out of which these writers mined their books, is beginning to run thin. William Faulkner and Thomas Wolfe are dead. Eudora Welty no longer writes, apparently, or at least she has stopped publishing. Repetition of themes and images in the work of Robert Penn Warren gives almost the effect of parody to his recent novels. Katherine Anne Porter has entered a more public world. The years lengthen between the novels of Andrew Lytle and Carson McCullers. Flannery O'Connor continues to people a region of grotesques. At its best the fiction of this group probes deeply because it is both ancestral and prophetic, haunted alike by the beginnings of Southern culture and the threat of its extinction. But the young novelists who still work within this historical-aesthetic tradition can do little more than rework old materials now several times removed from their own time and place in the modern South. Without their own memories of the passing of the old order to sustain them, they yearn toward a time when that past and that place could be, not recovered in memory, but merely remembered. In their imitative books the flaws of the renascence literature become as apparent as its virtues. A sense of place can flower as picturesque genre painting, filling a landscape with images that do not function as symbols but merely stand as stereotypes: the ruined mansion, the Negro cabin, the redneck's shack, the statue of the Confederate veteran in the courthouse square, the dingy, porticoed house looming over garages and cotton gins. Absorption in character can become devotion to its oddities, and the grotesque is born. A sense of the past may direct attention backward, away from the dislocations of the present. Clearly a new and clarifying vision is needed if Southern writing is to maintain the vitality and validity it possessed twenty or even ten years ago.

Here is the point at which Reynolds Price and the writers of his generation appear upon the scene. He belongs to that small group of poets and novelists —others are George Garrett, Ellen Douglas, James Dickey, Shirley Ann Grau, Walker Percy, and Eleanor Ross Taylor—who are willing to take the risk of showing in a new light the fragmentation of Southern life and the disruption of the regional sensibility, to put their trust in some personal view of the world, to let their themes discover their own forms, to reveal the wonder and terror and loneliness and humor of being, not within the historical perspective or through the familiar techniques of their predecessors but as a record of experience directly and simply presented.

This is Reynolds Price's great achievement in *A Long and Happy Life*. The novel tells, in brief, poignant fashion, the story of a young girl's search for love. But to state the theme so baldly is to do great injustice to the writer's sense of truth concerning people and things and the skill with which he transmutes mood and feeling into action. With altogether unhackneyed means of character portrayal and deft economy of style he shapes on a purely domestic level a fable of compelling tenderness and compassionate insight that opens out upon universals. What he is really writing about is the idea of love and separateness in the human experience, the mysteries of personality which sometimes bring people together but more often hold them apart. This theme of isolation and the failure of men and women to understand one another or to communicate their loneliness and longing gives the novel a dimension of meaning beyond the immediate concerns of Rosacoke Mustian's touch-and-go affair with Wesley Beavers.

The story opens with Rosacoke on her way to Mildred Sutton's funeral. She is riding behind Wesley on his motorcycle, "her white blouse blown out behind her like a banner in defeat," for Wesley is merely showing off as he flashes past the few cars and the truck hauling the pine coffin, and Rosacoke still has no way of knowing whether she is his girl or isn't. Mildred had been her colored playmate and friend. Once they had packed a dinner and gone walking in Mr. Isaac Alston's

woods and there they had seen a horned
deer watching behind them. Now Mildred is dead, leaving behind her a
baby with no father that anyone knows
to give it a name. In Mount Moriah
Church the mourners sing " 'Precious
Name, Show Me Your Face,' and it
was Jesus they were singing to—meaning it, looking up at the roof to hornets'
nests and spiders as if it might all roll
away and show them what they asked
to see." But the sight of Wesley, who
is outside polishing his motorcycle,
throws his image between Rosacoke
and memories of her dead friend, and
she thinks of him as she saw him for
the first time six years before, perched
in a pecan tree and looking off into
the distance. When she asked him, he
shook nuts down on her. That was the
beginning of her thinking about Wesley—"him caring for nothing but the
smoke he couldn't see, wondering if
there was a fire somewhere, waiting."
After he enlisted in the Navy she
wrote him long letters and sometimes
got in return scrawled postcards as
casual as the dates they had had when
he drove her to picture shows in War-
renton.

Wesley is not one to declare himself. During his hitch in the service
he had known other women and can
remember the nights he spent with
them even if he no longer recollects
their names. Now he is out of the
Navy and about to return to Norfolk
to sell motorcycles. Rosacoke knows
about his wild life there, or at least
makes a shrewd guess. Her own problem is deciding how far she should
go in setting matters straight between
them once and for all; otherwise, she
has no prospect except her job with
the telephone company and a life at
home with her widowed mother, her

married brother Milo and his wife,
and her younger sister. Milo's broth-
erly advice in the form of a bawdy
jingle leads Rosacoke to the decision
that "There ought to be some way you
could hold him. Anybody who looks
like that—you ought to give them anything you have. Anything you have
and they want *bad* enough."

But Rosacoke discovers that the gift
of herself brings nothing in return,
certainly not her hope that "Wesley
would change some day before it was
too late and come home and calm
down and learn how to talk to me and
maybe even listen, and we would have
a long time together—him and me—
and be happy sometimes and get us
children that would look like him and
have his name and answer when we
called." Pregnant, she discovers that
her pride is stronger than her despair,
and she decides to bear her burden
alone, as Mildred had done. When
Wesley learns of her condition and
makes his offer of marriage, she rejects his proposal.

Nothing in the novel shows Mr.
Price's daring and resourcefulness to
better advantage than the closing scene,
the Christmas pageant at Delight Bap-
tist Church. Here the writer takes the
risk of a deliberate cliché—and brings
off his effect superbly. When the girl
who was to play the part of the Virgin
Mary runs away to be married, Rosacoke is forced to take the role. She
sits there with the youngest Gupton
restless in her arms and her own child
stirring within her. She looks at Wesley, who is one of the Wise Men,
watching her in the light of the can-
dles and waiting for a sign. Suddenly
she realizes that she will take Wesley's
offer after all, "because it was her duty,
for all it would mean." A scene that

might have dissolved in pure sentimentality is firmed and deepened by a writer whose tact in handling the simplest and homeliest materials is proof of his powers as an artist.

There is much more that one might say about *A Long and Happy Life*. This brief outline gives no indication, for example, of Mr. Price's power to evoke the sights and sounds and smells of a whole countryside, or the exactness of gesture and speech with which he sets his people clearly before us, or the power of a style tuned to a variety of effects but always simple and colloquial in idiom. Illuminating these is a vision of clarity and honesty that sees no littleness in the small scene or the limited experience. Mr. Price's novel is as stark and clear and simple as an old ballad, told with the same warmth and apparently as effortlessly. In the recent past Southern writers have concerned themselves with the mortality of man and the nature of evil. Reynolds Price points to the strength of love, the moral configuration of inocence.

Sources for Further Study

Reviews:

San Francisco Chronicle. March 26, 1962. 700 words.

Saturday Review. XLV, March 10, 1962, p. 17. 1,350 words.

Spectator. March 23, 1962, p. 376. 650 words.

Time. LXXIX, March 23, 1962, p. 88. 750 words.

Times Literary Supplement. March 23, 1962, p. 197. 950 words.

LONG DAY'S JOURNEY INTO NIGHT

Author: Eugene O'Neill (1888-1953)
Publisher: The Yale University Press (New Haven). 176 pp. $3.75
Type of work: Drama
Time: August, 1912
Locale: New London, Connecticut

An autobiography in the form of a "play of old sorrow, written in tears and blood"

Principal characters:
> JAMES TYRONE, a popular American actor
> MARY CAVAN TYRONE, his wife
> JAMES TYRONE, JR., their elder son
> EDMUND TYRONE, their younger son
> CATHLEEN, a maid

On the outskirts of New London, Connecticut, stands a house built in the New England Victorian style, complete with verandas, turrets, and a widow's walk. The Thames River is not far away, and there are nights when the fog drifts up from the water like "the ghost of the sea." Then residents in the old-fashioned houses on the avenue can hear all night long the sound of the foghorn and the chiming of ships' bells from the harbor. This was the house which James O'Neill, a popular actor famous for the role of Edmond Dantès in *The Count of Monte Cristo,* bought as a summer home for his family in the 1880's. It is also the setting of *Long Day's Journey into Night,* his son's "play of old sorrow, written in tears and blood."

The facts of Eugene O'Neill's early life are generally known. He was born in a Broadway hotel in 1888, and his earliest recollections were of life backstage, memories that became a succession of overnight hotels, long train rides, and hundreds of theaters between New York and San Francisco, New Orleans and Chicago. Later he attended various Catholic preparatory schools before entering Princeton in

1906. Meanwhile his education in more worldly matters had been conducted under the tutelage of his dissipated older brother James. Dropped from Princeton for his poor academic record, he married, went prospecting for gold in Honduras, and lived "on the beach" in Argentina and in New York water-front saloons after his return from South America. After another sea voyage, this time to England, and a short tour with his father's *Monte Cristo* company, he went back to Connecticut and became a reporter for the *New London Telegraph.* By that time hard living and dissipation had undermined his health. Ill with tuberculosis, he entered the Gaylord Sanatorium in 1912. There he read Ibsen, Strindberg, and Nietzsche, and determined to become a playwright.

These matters being common knowledge and *Long Day's Journey into Night* an admittedly autobiographical work, it is easy to understand its somber message that character is fate. In fact, O'Neill thought the play so personal and haunting in the nature of the truths it reveals that when he died in 1953 he requested that it be withheld from the reading and playgoing public until twenty-five years after his death.

Under different circumstances his wishes would probably have been carried out, but his father, mother, and older brother—the other characters in the play—had been dead for many years, so that there was no longer need to avoid injury to the living. Besides, as O'Neill had written in his letter of dedication to his wife, the play had been written "with deep pity and understanding and forgiveness for *all* the haunted Tyrones." Since a playwright lives only in the living theater, Mrs. O'Neill decided to add this important work to the O'Neill canon. The play had its world premiere in the Royal Dramatic Theater in Stockholm early in 1956. The reading text went into two printings before publication. The Broadway production, under the inspired direction of José Quintero, was to become one of the high spots of the 1956–57 season.

The connection between O'Neill's own ill-starred family and the doomed Tyrones of his play is clear but never consciously forced. As in real life, James Tyrone, the father, is a talented actor who has sacrificed possible greatness in the theater for the sake of a single romantic role which has brought him material success but no real happiness in his career. Grudging, hot-tempered, miserly, he lacks the moral insight needed to deal with the problems his family presents. The mother is a gentle, loving woman who has escaped from her husband's bohemian life into her own private world of fantasy. A drug addict, she needs the protection and sympathy her husband and sons are unable to give. James, the older son, is a cynical, drunken wastrel. Edmund, the younger brother, is a poet whose only outlet for frustration is drink and an attitude of morbid pessimism absorbed from his reading of the modern skeptics and realists.

The true natures of the Tyrones are not immediately apparent. The play opens on an August morning in 1912, shortly after the family has finished breakfast, and the scene is one of warm and cozy domesticity which almost prepares us for another comedy of confused adolescence and small-town life such as O'Neill presented in *Ah, Wilderness*. Before long, however, the atmosphere of cheerfulness and family familiarity has dissolved into something deeper and more sinister, the realization by husband and sons that Mary Tyrone has reverted to the use of drugs. Throughout the course of that fated day the underlying tensions, grudges, and ties of old but almost forgotten affections come slowly to light, so that between morning and midnight each member of the family makes his long voyage into night, which in this case is the black depths of the despairing, doomed human soul.

Like most of O'Neill's dramas, the play contains no plot in the formal sense. Instead, the playwright has given us the development of his characters to the point where each faces some truth from which there is no escape. When James Tyrone tries to persuade his wife to forget the past, she breaks in passionately, "Why? How can I? The past is the present, isn't it? It's the future, too. We all try to lie out of that but life won't let us." This passage carries the theme of the play and brings each of the characters closer to the moment when self-deception is swept aside and we see life in all its nakedness and torment. James Tyrone has tried to justify his miserliness as a course of prudence and wisdom, but his penurious habits are revealed as nothing more than peasant niggardliness and cramping memories of the grinding poverty of his youth. Mary Tyrone has given many excuses for her drug habit: the hardships of childbirth, the second-rate doctors who gave her drugs instead of the professional skill her husband was unwilling to pay for, the bad food, cheap hotels, and loneliness of the life she lived with him on tour. In the closing scene she betrays the convent-bred innocence which made life a terror she was unable to face. The older brother is betrayed by drink into confessing that mixed love and hate have led him to condone his own weaknesses by ruining the younger brother he envies. Edmund, the playwright-to-be, is in many ways the most unsparingly drawn figure of the play. Cynical, bitter, dissipated, radical, he blames the others for their lack of example and love. There is more than mere youthful pessimism in his despairing outburst: "It was a great mistake, my being born a man. I would have been much more successful as a sea gull or a fish. As it is, I will always be a stranger who never feels at home, who does not really want and is not really wanted, who must always be a little in love with death." Here, perhaps, is the clue to that tragic sense of life which makes Eugene O'Neill the most powerful and prophetic voice in the American theater.

But if *Long Day's Journey into Night* is a play of ancient sorrow, deep torment, and remembered anguish, it is also a work of compassionate insight and pity. The knowledge that Edmund has tuberculosis and must go to a sanatorium is the dramatic center which brings the emotional forces of the play into its focus of tangled family relationships. For at the end the Tyrones are still a family. Lives have been wrenched and illusions destroyed, but the final mood is one of understanding and calm. Here again O'Neill shows the grand simplicity he had in common with the old Greek dramatists in whose plays man's deeds of fury and terror were followed by moods of pity and calm.

On the stage *Long Day's Journey into Night* owes much to the combined talents of Frederick March, Florence Eldridge, Jason Robards, Jr., and Bradford Dillman, but it owes even more to O'Neill's undimmed genius for character drawing and situation. In *Mourning Becomes Electra* he showed man pursued by the furies of conscience. In this play he creates an equally moving drama from the grim hauntings of his own reclaimed past.

Sources for Further Study

Criticism:

Cerf, Walter. "Psychoanalysis and the Realistic Drama," in *Journal of Aesthetics and Art Criticism*. XVI (March, 1958), pp. 328-336. Cerf cites *Long Day's Journey into Night* as proof that psychological realism and artistic realism are mutually incompatible.

Finkelstein, Sidney. "O'Neill's Long Journey," in *Mainstream*. XVI (June, 1963), pp. 47-51. This is a general discussion of O'Neill's play prompted by the appearance of the motion picture version of it.

Krutch, Joseph Wood. "O'Neill's Last Play—Domestic Drama with Some Difference," in *Theatre Arts*. XL (April, 1956), pp. 89-91. This article views *Long Day's Journey into Night* as directly autobiographical and an arresting attempt to face those external circumstances which made O'Neill the desperate man he was.

Redford, Grant H. "Dramatic Art vs. Autobiography: A Look at *Long Day's Journey into Night*," in *College English*. XXV (April, 1964), pp. 527-535. It is as poetry and as dramatic art, says Redford, and not as autobiography that *Long Day's Journey into Night* should be judged.

Winther, Sophus Keith. "O'Neill's Tragic Themes: *Long Day's Journey into Night*," in *Arizona Quarterly*. Vol. 13, No. 4 (Winter, 1957), pp. 295-307. This drama combines in one action the great themes O'Neill developed in all his tragedies.

Reviews:

Christian Science Monitor. March 1, 1956, p. 11. 490 words.

Nation. CLXXXII, March 3, 1956, p. 182. 1,000 words.

New York Herald Tribune Book Review. February 19, 1956, p. 1.

New York Times. February 19, 1956, p. 1. 1,800 words.

Saturday Review. XXXIX, February 25, 1956, p. 15. 1,200 words.

THE LONG MARCH

Author: William Styron (1925–   )
Publisher: Random House (New York). 120 pp. $4.95
Type of work: Novel
Time: Early 1950's
Locale: A Marine training camp, South Carolina

A novel, both realistic and symbolic, dealing with military authority, endurance, and violence in a Marine training camp

Principal characters:
LIEUTENANT CULVER
COLONEL TEMPLETON
CAPTAIN MANNIX

This short realistic novel opens symbolically with an account of a grim accident in a Marine training camp: eight young marines are killed when some short rounds of ammunition are negligently dropped on a chow line. The event deftly foreshadows the horror, destructiveness, and fatigue inherent in a game-playing, simulated combat environment. Styron focuses sharply on the horrors of war by presenting what he sees as the grotesquely narrow-minded mentality of military life and procedure. Though the setting of the novel is a Marine training camp, and though the participants are reservists rather than regulars, all of the brutality and psychological strife of real war are sinisterly present.

The accidental death of eight men becomes the exciting force for the rest of the narrative: the accident is further proof that things are getting sloppy in the training camp, and thus the combat-trained, gung-ho Colonel Templeton ("Old Rocky") announces that the entire battalion, made up almost entirely of young reserves, will undertake a forced march.

The Colonel explains that his battalion, were it to meet an aggressor enemy right now, would do very badly. To strengthen his unit's combat readiness, and to inculcate a greater *esprit de corps,* he orders the long march of the title—hiking rapidly, and with packs, for thirty-six miles. The Colonel refuses to make any allowances for the central fact that most of his men are reserves, men suddenly torn away not only from the pleasures and softness of civilian life, but also from the military psychology. In an abrasive, tough, and demanding way, the Colonel explains:

"We've been trying to differentiate too closely between two particular bodies of men that make up the Marine Corps. Technically it's true that a lot of these new men are reserves—that is, they have an "R" affixed at the end of the "USMC." But it's only a technical difference, you see. Because first and foremost they're *marines.* I don't want my marines doping off. They're going to *act* like marines. They're going to be *fit."*

Flabby and helpless, the battalion organizes for the forced march as a symbolic (and, to Styron), idiotic test of endurance. As Captain Mannix, the heavy-set Jew from Brooklyn who, like most of the others, resents having been called back to duty, reacts:

"Christ on a crutch! Do you realize

how far that is? Why that's as far as it is from Grand Central to Stamford, Connecticut! Why, man, I haven't walked a hundred consecutive yards since 1945. I couldn't go 36 miles If I were sliding downhill the whole way on a sled . . . this silly son of a bitch is going to have all these tired, flabby old men flopping around on the ground like a bunch of fish after the first two miles."

Mannix' reaction and prophecy become fully believable as the reader witnesses each of the principal characters fight for his life merely to keep marching. And the march becomes much more than a physical challenge; the fears associated with the duress of the forced march activate other fears in each man, many of which have to do with the basic fear of simply being unable to do the sorts of things done easily six years earlier. The reserves are all men who have put war, real or simulated, out of their minds, and suddenly they are being coerced back into a wartime psychology. Values accepted without questioning now threaten both the physical and the mental stability of every participant. Each man privately wonders if he can "make it," and with even greater concern wonders whether Old Rocky will himself be able to carry out his own order. The forced march thus becomes a delicate contest between each of the reserves and their Colonel.

After describing the inner anxieties of various members of the battalion, Styron finally presents the picture: it is just about twilight as the battalion of over a thousand men stretches out in two columns over a mile long along the road. Mannix discovers a nail in his shoe, but at this point he is unwilling to admit to the slightest difficulty and, Culver's urgings aside, decides to march with the nail (rather than accept the Colonel's offer to let him ride in). Mannix argues: "He's a little sadist, but he's not gonna have All Mannix crapped out. I'll walk anywhere that son of a bitch goes and a mile further."

The reserves are all tired before they begin. They miss the comforts of private civilian life and, in particular, their wives (Mannix: "Now maybe it's all right for a kid to go without sex, but it's degrading for someone like me almost thirty to go without making love for so long. It's simply degrading.")

Culver is afraid that he won't make it but is at least partially comforted by knowing that Mannix is also afraid. The Colonel, in the lead, starts the march by establishing a rapid pace, "the pace of a trained hiker—determined, unhesitant, much closer to a trot now than a walk." Culver's first fears had been abstract. Now that the march has actually begun, his fears and those of the other reserves are concrete; each man becomes obsessed with only one idea: to last. To conceal their own anxieties the officers tongue-lash the men to keep moving and to stay away from their canteens. Hate keeps them all going, hate of the Colonel's unstated ambition to have "led the longest forced march in the history of the corps."

Mannix' foot becomes extremely painful as the nail wears through his shoe. After examining the foot, the Colonel concludes, after an embarrassingly long hesitation, that yes, perhaps Mannix had "better ride in on one of the trucks." With fierce pride and determination, Mannix responds: "No sir! . . . . No, sir! I'll make this frigging march."

At a quarter past four in the next morning—halfway through the march—Mannix continues to lash at the men in a hoarse, ill-tempered voice. Mannix seems to become as much a reflection of the obstinate mentality of the military as the Colonel has been from the start (who, while no longer leading the march, is nevertheless holding his own with the other, younger men). Less than one-third of the company is willing to continue the march, only the diehards, the athletes, and the few like Mannix who are determined not to give the Colonel the satisfaction of seeing them quit. With only six miles left to march, the battalion "was a seedy, bedraggled column of people: of hollow, staring eyes and faces green with slack-jawed exhaustion." Culver tries futilely to make Mannix see that for Colonel Templeton "the hike had had nothing to do with courage or sacrifice or suffering, but was only a task to be performed."

In an almost absurdist scene, the exhausted men, still virtually convinced that they cannot "make it," arrive back at the camp, to be confronted by the picture of Marines in neat khaki going to lunch and themselves dumbfounded at the sight of "the mammoth gyrating Captain so tattered and soiled who addressed convulsive fluttering prayers to the sky, and had obviously parted with his senses." Mannix whispers to Culver, "What the hell, we've made it."

Resting from the long, destructive march, each man slowly assigns his own meaning to the experience. The Colonel has had his march and his victory. Culver is unable to determine why he cannot hate the Colonel. Going down the hospital hall, Culver encounters a crazed Mannix. Standing before several Negro maids, Mannix drops his towel, his only clothing, and admits to being in very great pain. He has neither the strength nor the desire to reach down and pick up the towel. For all practical purposes, he is dead. But the long march is over.

Christopher R. Reaske

THE LONG SHIPS

Author: Frans G. Bengtsson (1894-1954)
Translated from the Swedish by Michael Meyer
Publisher: Alfred A. Knopf (New York). 503 pp. $4.50
Type of work: Novel
Time: The years just before and after A.D. 1000
Locale: Scandinavia

A new Scandinavian saga, but enough like the old ones to have been composed in A.D.1000 when its hero Red Orm went a-viking

> Principal characters:
> RED ORM, a viking
> TOKE, Orm's lifelong friend
> ARE, Orm's brother
> BLACKHAIR, Orm's second son
> KING HAROLD BLUE-TOOTH, Orm's overlord
> YLVA, Harold's leader
> KROK, a viking leader
> SOLOMON, a silversmith from Cordoba
> BROTHER WILLIBALD, a priest
> ALMANSUR, Caliph of Cordoba

The Long Ships is Frans G. Bengtsson's first novel. Before its publication, Bengtsson had already become known in Sweden as a poet, a man of letters, and a historian. The characteristics of these three lines of activity are blended in this novel, which is enough like a genuine saga to be mistaken for one. It has in it enough voyages, fights, carouses, and intrigues to satisfy any saga-lover. It even takes the reader into attendance at a Thing, the early Scandinavian equivalent of trial by jury and government by the people.

The Long Ships is a tale of the Vikings in the years just before and after A.D. 1000, that date on which Christians expected the world to come to an end. Scandinavian Christians prepared for the end by indulging in all those pastimes that meant most to them, but their pagan selves believed the end of the world would never come while their cattle and women continued to produce. Religion has a major part in this book, as indeed it did in the lives of Scandinavians of that time when St. Olaf and others persuaded their subjects, sometimes brutally, to embrace Christianity. Nor is Christianity the only religion offered as a change from the worship of pagan gods. In one of his adventures Red Orm was forced to bow down to Mohammed three times daily as part of his duty to his master, Almansur. But religion is only one of the subjects touched on in this tale of Red Orm, the Swede who traveled through most of the world then known.

Red Orm went on his first Viking expedition unexpectedly. Defending his mother's sheep from raiding Vikings, he was overpowered and thrown into a boat headed out to sea. He showed enough spirit for Krok, the leader, to give him more freedom on shipboard than a prisoner might expect. Krok and his men, dissatisfied with their raids in Wendland and the islands off the coast of Sweden, headed west. Off the coast of France they encountered four Jutish ships. During a parley between the leaders, Orm and his lifelong friend Toke fished out of the water a man who begged to be taken on board. This was the Jew Solomon, a silversmith from Cordoba. Incensed against a rich Christian who had sold him into slavery, Solomon led Krok into an attack on the Christian's castle in the north of Spain. Krok's men found more booty than they could carry off, but they never got it past the mouth of the river. Ships in the service of the Caliph of Cordoba routed Krok's fleet and put most of the Scandinavians as slaves into the Caliph's galleys.

The Jew Solomon escaped to Cordoba, where eventually he sought favors from the Caliph Almansur for Orm and Toke. They were taken from the galleys and put in the Caliph's bodyguard. There they served, waiting to find the man who had killed Krok. When they did find him six years later, they killed him and sailed out of the Caliph's kingdom.

The ship they used for escape contained a bell from the church in which the apostle James was buried. Almansur had intended to take it back to Cordoba. Instead, Orm and Toke used it to bell their way to St. Finnian's Isle, just off the Irish coast, after they had despaired of reaching harbor safely while their galley slaves still lived.

On their way home, Orm stopped to pay his respects to King Harold Blue-Tooth, his overlord. There he fell in love with Ylva, Harold's daughter, during a long Yule festival that included feasts, duels, story-tellings, a miracle, and a convalescence for Orm from a sword cut. Then he went home, ending his first Viking expedition.

In his second he raided King Ethelred's land, receiving more silver than he knew existed. There, too, he came across the priest who had previously served in Harold Blue-Tooth's court. To induce the priest to lead him to Ylva, who was then in England, and to perform a marriage ceremony, Orm embraced Christianity. Then to insure his men their share in the silver, he persuaded them to become Christians too. This was a milder form of inducement than many Vikings used to spread the gospel, though not as ingenious as that used by the Erin Masters when they refused to perform their magical tricks at the christening of Orm's first son unless the audience were baptized first.

Coincidence plays a large part in this novel, a point that might be questioned if the characters were anything but wanderers in a roving age. Orm runs into the priest, Brother Willibald, in Harold Blue-Tooth's court in Denmark and again in a group of besieged men in England. The Erin Masters appear at Orm's home in Sweden and later among the Patzinaks along the Dnieper River. Orm's brother Are left Sweden to roam the seas. Twenty-nine years later Orm found him on a Gotland salt ship.

Are, in the Viking tradition, sailed from home to plunder. After many adventures he found a place for himself among his countrymen in the bodyguard of the Byzantine emperor. In the intrigues of court he discovered the treasurer stealing the emperor's gold. After stealing and hiding the gold himself, he was also discovered, tortured, and set free. He arrived home without eyes, tongue, or right hand. The priest fashioned a rune stick. Fingering it, Are could make the priest understand what words he wanted to tell the story of his wandering. Are knew where the Bulgar gold was hidden. He wanted Orm to know.

Orm needed little persuasion to make his third and last expedition. To bring back the Bulgar gold he gathered a trustworthy band, including his thirteen-year-old second son Blackhair, and hired an expert river man to run the Dvina and Dneiper rivers. As they started out Toke said, "It is strange that we Northmen, who . . . are more skillful seamen than other men, sit at home as we do, when we have the whole world to plunder."

That was the feeling of all the men in the band. With plenty of adventure and a chance but fortuitous meeting with one of the Erin Masters, they came back with much loot—silver, gold, and marvelously worked rings, necklaces, chains and bracelets. The Bulgar gold was treasure enough for all. They had so much luck that Orm worried.

They arrived home five days after Orm's house had been looted, his church burned; and one of his daughters carried away. After avenging those misfortunes, Orm settled down. But Blackhair was not content with a single expedition. He went back to the Bulgar regions, leading his own men. Later in England, he sailed in the same ship with Canute.

The reading of any of the Scandinavian sagas makes one realize that the tenth-century Viking was in many respects a more widely educated person than the term generally implies. "Viking" carries the suggestion of wayward plunderer, but it actually represents a man who was brave, clever, eager, well-traveled, and learned in languages, geography, history, and religion, as well as the nautical sciences. A Viking may not have been civilized in the modern sense, but he reflected an age of courage, curiosity, and adventure.

THE LONG STREET

Author: Donald Davidson (1893-1968)
Publisher: Vanderbilt University Press (Nashville). 92 pp. $4.00
Type of work: Poetry

A volume of excellent poems, written with prophetic insight and dealing with the nature and cause of man's loss of security and identity in the modern world

The Long Street is a collection of thirty-seven poems, ranging in length from four lines to fourteen pages and covering a period of composition of more than thirty-five years. During this time, the author has published two other volumes of poetry, *The Tall Men* and *Lee in the Mountains,* and several other books, including *Attack on Leviathan, Still Rebels, Still Yankees and Other Essays,* and *Southern Writers in the Modern World.* As these books and many articles reveal, few writers have demonstrated so clear an understanding of contemporary society and of the traditions and forces which lie behind it. Few have written with such conviction and such prophetic sense of purpose.

The unifying theme of *The Long Street* is essentially the same as that which constitutes the basis of the other books here mentioned and which Mr. Davidson has stated in *Still Rebels, Still Yankees* as: "The impact of the modern regime upon the great vital continuum of human experience to which we apply the inadequate term 'tradition.'" In *Southern Writers in the Modern World,* Mr. Davidson has further defined this conflict as "the cause of civilized society, as we have known it in the Western World, against the new barbarism of science and technology controlled by the modern power state. In this sense, the cause of the South was and is the cause of Western civilization itself." Put briefly, it is "individualism" versus "collectivism." Speaking of the Agrarian movement, with which he was associated between 1930 and 1940, he explains: "Our quarrel was not with industry or science in their proper role, but with industrialism as a tyrant enslaving and ruling science itself, thus reducing all principles to one principle, the economic, and becoming a destroyer, ready to break the continuity of human history and threatening the very existence of human society."

One of the frequently recurring themes in *The Long Street* is the idea that change does not necessarily mean progress. In "The Ninth Part of Speech," a verse letter to a Bread Loaf School of English colleague who once lived at the remodeled Schoolhouse not far from the Davidson's Vermont home, the author expresses concern about changes which have taken place in American education during the transition from the one-room schoolhouse to the "glass-front life-adjusted schools/Where Dunce and Master sit on equal stools." In "A Barren Look," two people (apparently an older man and a younger man) are crossing Vermont by auto and stop at a bridge. The older man speaks first:

"Here is the bridge where a trout pool used to be.
Step softly, look, and tell me what you see."

"Bright water coursing through an unreaped meadow

And my own face mirrored in a boulder's shadow."

"So there is water still, and water is
good!
But look hard where that boulder stems
the flood
And, whispering, say if any living shape
Floats in its lee or, darting, seeks
escape."

"Only the empty water moves and the
deep-tufted slender grasses
Dowse their tips and sway where the
eddying ripple passes;
White birch and jewel-weed tremble
along the strand;
No track of man or beast or bird on the
gray sand."

"Once all were here, but now you read
their fate,
And that is why I feared a barren
look."

"I read only a bridge and a mountain
brook
That could be much more desolate
Beside this good road entered on our
map
As fully paved through Middlebury
Gap."

"No fish in the stream, no light in the
head,
And what if, next, the land be dead!"

The first speaker is not, as one reviewer has supposed, a blind man. He
sends the other to look and report
merely because he dreads to look, himself. It is the younger man who cannot
"see." He cannot see that a land which
serves primarily as an obstacle to be
crossed is a dying land. All he can
"read" is the "good road . . . fully
paved," a fact which he mistakes for
the sure sign of progress.

The book's central theme (encompassing the idea of change) is the importance of the past to the present and
the future. Any complete or sudden
break with the past, the author implies, is disastrous to both the individual and the general culture. In "Soldier and Son," the son is not truly the
son until he has been told of the past
experiences of his father. In "Relic of
the Past," when the city is lost and
all the "landmarks" perish, the moon
(the relic of the past) still serves as a
guiding "skymark." "On Culleoka
Road" opens with reference to the
"Girl in the blue sports car that floats
across the bridge" who is ignorant that
generations of lovers have preceded
her; "Joe Clisby's Song" states that the
older lovers have learned a few things
and still "Can tune the lips of youth/
As they did mine before/To sing the
truth." In "Late Answer: A Civil War
Seminar," one of Mr. Davidson's colleagues at Bread Loaf reprimands him
not only for seeing any connection between the world situation of 1961 and
the issues of 1861 but also for still har-
boring "these dank Faulknerian memories" of the Civil War, which all
sensible people have "long forgot."
Purely as a matter of curiosity, another
Yankee colleague asks Mr. Davidson
to explain what the Rebel Yell really
was. Mr. Davidson says that it was
"The sound of valor where it dwells
with sorrow," and he describes the
conditions under which the yell develops or fails to develop:

"The whispering in the marrow spreads
to the brain;
The remembering heart carries it round
again
Till it beats in the throat, the lips, the
weeping eye
And is born at last in a blazing wordless
outcry.

"But if that whisper's fettered in the
  brain,
The heart, forgetful, takes not back
  again;
Throat and lips are cool; the eye is dry;
Speech clear and perfect and there's no
  outcry."

The Rebel Yell, he says, was essentially no different from the sound of
valor expressed during the battles of
the American Revolution.

The function of the poet, Mr. Davidson feels, is to keep fresh the memory
of valor by interpreting the past to the
present, to relate the present to the
past, and, on the basis of this understanding, to point the direction for the
future. When functioning properly,
the poet is mythologist, historian, and
prophet:

Happy the land where men hold dear
Myth that is truest memory,
Prophecy that is poetry.

Yeats fell short of the poet's ideal be-
cause he "clutched the abstract Bird/
Of charred philosophy until he lost/
Usheen."

To emphasize the relation of the
present to the past, and also to subli-
mate a contemporary or even commonplace subject, Mr. Davidson often
makes use of Biblical and mythological
parallels. "A Touch of Snow" deals
with a very commonplace fact: The
appearance of a small patch of snow
on a Vermont mountain peak is a signal to the inhabitants in the valley below that, even though the end of
summer may seem far removed, "the
turn of the year" has already taken
place and they should make preparations accordingly. Something more
profound than local weather lore, however, is suggested by the poet's reference to the house painters as "two

wise men" and by his designation of
the patch of snow as nature's way of
"writing MENE there on our mountain height." A further hint of the extended meaning is contained in the
mention of "new" stars, apparently an
allusion to recent, man-made satellites.
These "higher warnings" suggest that
the poem deals with something far
more serious than the mere approach
of winter in Vermont.

"The Case of Motorman 17" makes
extensive use of the Greek myth of
Orestes. As the ancient Orestes had
committed the crime of killing his
mother, so Orestes Brown has in a
sense slain his past. Leaving his home
in the hill country, where individuals
are still individuals, he comes to the
city and takes a job as streetcar motorman, where people are only "fares"
and he himself is no longer a human
being but only "a function and a number, Motorman Seventeen." He becomes acquainted with the Reverend
Doctor Brown, a distant relative, also
named Orestes, who has likewise slain
his past by turning to "liberal religion."
After hearing his cousin preach a "liberal" sermon, Orestes thinks he sees
"the very Hounds of Hell" following
both himself and the preacher, but the
latter "hardened his heart and would
not listen." Finally these warnings culminate in fires in the streetcar and the
minister's home. Taking the matter to
court, the minister maintains that
Orestes must have set the fires.

Although the Streetcar Inspector
declares his faith in the truthfulness
and sanity of Orestes, and a Poet
makes an impassioned plea in his behalf, the Judge declares that "Poetry
has no standing in this Court," accepts the testimony of an Alienist (representing "modern science") and of

the Reverend Doctor Brown (representing "liberal religion"), and signs the commitment papers. In an Epilogue, the Poet suggests also a parallel between this case and the myth of "insane Orpheus torn by the more insane" and concludes:

> But if Orpheus bleed
> His singing head
> Will drift on the stream
> To redeem men
> Till poetry
> And justice come again
> Unless the world be dead.

It would not be difficult to see Mr. Davidson in the roles of both Orestes Brown and Orpheus. Like Orestes, Mr. Davidson is likely to be pronounced insane by those "distant cousins" whom he is trying most desperately to warn of impending doom. Like Orpheus, however, he will continue trying to "redeem men" through his poetry, for Mr. Davidson is a sound scholar of history, and he knows that no civilization which has ignored its poet-prophets has long survived.

Besides the thirty-seven poems, the volume contains also seven excellent engravings by the author's wife, Theresa Sherrer Davidson.

THE LONG VOYAGE

Author: Jorge Semprun (1923-   )
Translated from the French by Richard Seaver
Publisher: The Grove Press (New York). 236 pp. $4.50
Type of work: Novel
Time: Several nights in 1943, with glimpses into times several years before and after
Locale: France

*In an attempt to understand and to shape the significance of the past a resistance
fighter recalls, at a remove of sixteen years, his journey to a concentration camp in a
crowded boxcar and tells also of events occurring several years preceding and following
that experience*

Principal characters:
> GERARD (MANUEL), the narrator, a twenty-year-old resistance
> fighter
> THE GUY FROM SEMUR, Gerard's comrade in the boxcar
> JULIEN, a French resistance fighter on a motorcycle
> HANS (PHILLIPE), a German Jew who doesn't want "to die a
> Jew's death"
> MICHEL (JACQUES), a resistance fighter
> DR. HAAS, the Gestapo chief of the Feldenclarmerie region
> THE MOUSE, the executioner in the Auxerre Prison
> A GERMAN GUARD, in the Auxerre Prison
> RAMAILLET, a prisoner who refuses to share with his cellmates
> HAROUX, a resistance fighter freed with Gerard
> SIGRID, a German girl who suffers the guilt of her nation
> THE JEWISH WOMAN, on the rue de Vaugirard

Jorge Semprun's *The Long Voyage* is the third winner of the Formentor Prize, an international award for new writing. Born in Madrid shortly after World War I, Semprun fought against Franco, then served in the French resistance, and finally in 1943 was sent to Buchenwald. There he remained until the liberation. (He translated *The Deputy* for the Paris production.) His autobiographical hero, Gerard, survives a five-day train trip with 119 other prisoners in a padlocked boxcar.

In *The Long Voyage,* the classic night journey form has a profound twentieth century validity. Gerard's journey, like Marlowe's, becomes a quest into "the heart of darkness," and Gerard is greeted at the gates with the cry of that disillusioned idealistic imperialist, Kurtz: "Exterminate the brutes!" Like Conrad, Semprun feels that it is not enough merely to chant, "The horror! The horror!" Unlike the shadowy, reticent stand-ins of much modern fiction, Gerard is forceful, vibrant, and resourceful, and he earns the name of hero.

Beginning on the long fourth day of the journey, the novel is carefully executed in relation to its spinal image, the moving train. The conception and the structural device arise naturally out of the situation: night trains are expressive of the encompassing reality of Gerard's experience as exile and saboteur. As in the movie *Hiroshima, Mon Amour,* intricate and meaningful juxtapositions of past and present and significant anticipations of the post-liberation future are done with acute relevance of detail. Transitions are smooth. Gerard tells his German guard:

> "I hope the German army will be annihilated. And I hope that you will come out of it."
> He looks at me, he shakes his head, he says, "Thanks," he tugs on the strap of his rifle and leaves.
> "Are you asleep?" the guy from Semur asks.
> "No."

We are in the prison, then suddenly in the boxcar with the question, "Are you asleep?"

Gerard's unnamed, ordinary neighbor in "the little ease" of the boxcar asks many times, "Will this night never end?" His dying words are, "Don't leave me, pal." This enforced voyage obliges Gerard to venture upon a second sixteen years later, compelled by a knowledge that the night has never ended, that he has never left his comrade, that the millions of prisoners, and thus the so-called survivors, have not been liberated. "I forgot this voyage while realizing full well that I would one day have to take it again. . . . It was all there, waiting for me." Past and future are *now*, and the train is still moving. While one of the novel's strengths is the apparent spontaneity of these juxtapositions, a more controlled fusion of theme and form could have evoked more profound and awesome intuitions of inevitability and eternity.

Twenty when he makes the voyage, the narrator wisely waits sixteen years for the talk to die down so that his more controlled voice may be heard. He realizes that while he remembers perfectly the relatively uneventful voyage itself, it is difficult to recall the memories and dreams which sustained him in the period of greatest extremity, the long final night of the journey that killed the man from Semur next to whom he happened to be standing. The boxcar is already a tomb, crammed with future corpses; herded into boxcars, they are later herded into the barracks, then into the shower stalls to be gassed, then stuffed into the furnaces. As the train moves over the peaceful landscape we sense the dead-aliveness of them all. Gerard's personal tactic of endurance is to reconstruct certain books, like *Swann's Way*, in his head and to will himself back into a bookshop where he was once content. A rather literary saboteur, Gerard reads Valéry, Larbaud, Marx, Giraudoux, and Faulkner (in technique, this novel resembles *Absalom, Absalom!* and *The Sound and the Fury*). And he seizes on this voyage as a chance to evaluate the life he is liable to lose.

Semprun contrasts the man from Semur with Gerard in many ways. Unlike his neighbor, who has an elementary black and white concept of life and of the war, Gerard can see the absurdity of some of the notions of the Allies and he finally achieves compassion for the enemy. While the guy from Semur contains the voyage within his death, Gerard's life is devoted to expanding that voyage; thus, in a sense, the guy from Semur never dies. In Gerard's arms, his body becomes infinitely heavy, an eternal burden. When he lays the man down, he lays down his own past, as told to the man; but sixteen years later he takes it up again by telling *us* the same story. The burden becomes lighter with every moment that Gerard's life justifies itself in thought and action. The dead "need a pure, fraternal look. What they need, quite simply, is for us to live, to live as fully as we can." And Gerard *does* live imaginatively and actively, with a fullness that is heroic. To Gerard's research into atrocities dead and past, but never buried, Semprun contrasts a Jewish woman whom Gerard had befriended years before in Paris; she has survived, but, "immured in her solitude," she has willed Gerard and the camp itself into oblivion.

To achieve distance from his experience, Gerard seizes spontaneously on many devices. He conducts two beautiful French nurses on a tour of the liberated camp; to tell about the camp is to see it from the outside, that is, for the first time. He tries to understand the mind of a lovely German girl who, like him, strives, though out of guilt rather than suffering, to "will into oblivion" the facts of the camps. Viewing the crematorium chimneys from the living room window of a German housewife who mourns the loss of her sons in the war, Gerard feels not hatred but compassion for her. But he also sees that the camp was too much for the villagers to take in "since they had decided to let it be too much for them," and that all German villages and cities were ante-chambers to the compounds.

For Gerard "the unreal and the absurd became familiar." With Byron's prisoner of Chillon, he could say, "My very chains and I grew friends,/So much a long communion tends/To make us what we are;—even I/Regained my freedom with a sigh." His release was such a shock that he "missed the unique moment" in all its limpid purity, that long imagined moment when one is to experience what it is like to be outside, looking in. But many other insights he does not miss. He perceives the nature of the resistance fighter who dreads the hour when the searchers "catch you cold, your mouth filled with sleep," and he sees that "things being what they are, the possibility of being a man is bound to the . . . possibility of yielding to torture." His being on the train, he realizes, is not a question of freedom: he is on the train of his own free will because he was free not to do what led to his being on the train. All that matters now is that he is outside, not inside.

With his German guard in Auxerre Prison, who professes a desire to "understand," he discusses the "reasons for living and the reasons for dying." "I'm in prison because I'm a free man, because I found it necessary to exercise my freedom, because I accepted this necessity." The German soldier is there "because he did not feel the need to be somewhere else. Because he is not free" his life has "always been an overwhelming 'fact,' a 'being' outside himself which he has never been able to take possession of, to make it habitable."

Gerard sees his life's place in nature as the train moves through the Moselle valley, which appears to his vision more like a Brueghel winter scene than a Corot. "Even if all of us in this boxcar were dead, stacked in dead standing up . . . the Moselle valley would still be there before our dead eyes. I don't want to lose sight of this fundamental certainty. . . . I am nothing but this Moselle which invades my being through the eyes." Later, a free man, he has a similar moment: "That dull paralyzing joy takes root in the certainty of the absolute contingency of my presence here, of my radical uselessness. I'm not necessary for this rustling forest to exist, therein lies the source of that muted joy."

His experience provides insights into death: "dying is the only thing that can happen to me which I shall never experience personally." But the death of his comrade, Hans, "was indeed something that had happened to me, that would henceforth be part of my life." Another comrade is hanged in the compound square as an "example": "We are busy dying this pal's death, and by doing so we negate it, we cancel it, from his death we are deriving meaning and purpose for our own lives. A perfectly valid plan for living, the only valid one at the present time. But the SS are a sorry lot and never understand such things."

Gerard is in a position to perceive certain banal truths: that in such places as the camps a man is capable of stealing another's bread, thus his very life, from his weak hands. And there is the banal truth that "when you start off on a journey like this you have to know how to behave and know what the score is," not only for the sake of dignity, but for practical reasons. A heart attack in the boxcar is "a banal accident. . . . Except, of course, for those who have heart conditions." The victim's last question is, "What do you know about that?" Gerard goes on answering that question. *What* indeed *does* he know about *that*—about life? His purpose in this book is to let others know.

The Long Voyage has the kind of fictive life only a preoccupation with death can evoke. Although there is little sequential story, many moments are memorable. Just as Gerard is often caught off guard like Melville, who suddenly remembered images of the Encantades in the midst of a polite dinner party, the reader will be smitten by his memory of the way the Polish Jewish children were killed. They emerged from a frozen mass of standing corpses, that had to be pried loose from a boxcar, only to be slaughtered by dogs and SS guards as they ran, expecting some haven, for the gates of the camp. "Beneath the empty gaze of the Hitlerian eagles" above the entrance, the Jewish children were cut down, "their hands clasped for all eternity." Gerard can never forget his own arrival: "No one is paying us any heed, the living and dead welded together, and with a great clatter of brakes we arrive, motionless voyagers, into an area of harsh lights and the barking of dogs." The Wagnerian operatic setting, the sense of ritual, ceremony, and efficiency is magnificently hideous. Semprun leaves the reader with a disturbing sense of what the Nazis were like. Devoted to "hygiene, pedigreed dogs and Wagner's music," the guards left standing in the middle of the camp a beech tree in whose shade Goethe used to sit.

Semprun depicts the ingenuity of the damned: in the boxcar they use urine to revive those who pass out in a panic near the end when, ironically, they become eager to arrive at the camps, unaware of the crematoriums; in the camp, prisoners prop up the frozen dead at roll call to get extra rations. Gerard's personal tactics for survival range from the practical to the sublime. He slowly tastes toothpaste to prevent thirst. He relies on the power of imagination; hanging by his wrists from a tree, he endures by contemplating a rose in his torturer's garden. Imagination enabled him to survive; now, sensibility demands that he understand his experience.

Semprun has a tendency to cavort with language somewhat in the manner of Günter Grass, but with less justification. And we find the sort of clowning in dialogue that Jake and Bill exhibit in *The Sun Also Rises*. But repetition as a device is not displayed in language alone; dictated by the nature of his experience, it is essential to Semprun's theme as well as his technique. He is adroit in his use of clichés; his experiential context moves Gerard to examine such clichés as "go up in smoke." This is only one way in which he attempts to reify the mysteries of his experience. No rhetorical passages obtrude, and Semprun's lyricism is earned because it never approaches the self-indulgence one might expect and possibly forgive in such a book.

Semprun, striving rigorously for focus, excludes memories of his childhood before the war and of his life after the liberation, except as they relate to the war. The absence of chapter breaks emphasizes the continuity of the experience and the simultaneity of all moments relevant to it. That the reader may identify more intensely with the evaluating Gerard, Semprun shifts to the third person for a last impression of the hero; this shift also sets off the voyage, with its mingling of memory and imagination, from the pure reality of the arrival at the camp. Gerard speaks in the present tense most of the time; Semprun shifts to past tense as he senses opportunities for emphasis; but the shift also has thematic relevance: all time is one in the consciousness that evaluates and shapes its own raw material.

Semprun overcomes the subject matter fallacy (heavy reliance on the inherent interest of a subject to the neglect of artistic considerations) that must threaten anyone who writes about concentration camps. In *The Long Voyage* craft and subject join. In Gerard, the victim's compulsion to testify is combined with the artist's impulse to prevent it all from slipping into oblivion as some mere matter of record. Years after the war, Gerard hears from an eyewitness the story of the Taboo massacre in which his comrades were killed; but this man, in contrast to Gerard, tells a very dull, disordered story, intent as he is upon simply purveying the facts. Although Gerard is annoyed that he himself is unable to "seize completely" his experience, "to provide a second-by-second account," it is Semprun's refusal to *try* that helps make him an artist, rather than an impassioned reporter only.

Amid the many fictionalized reports, only a work of art embodying the significant shape, essence, and meaning of that massive experience can ultimately concern us both as life *and* as literature. Assailed though he is by "absolutely vivid memories that arose from the willed oblivion of this voyage," Semprun is no slave to the extraordinary; while he acknowledges the banality as well as the incredibility of the most *human* of history's massive atrocities, he defies oblivion with form and speaks in a passionate, authoritative voice, alive with rage and conviction. Like Stephen Crane in "The Open Boat," Semprun fulfills the obligation of the survivor to be an "interpreter," not merely one who testifies.

David Madden

THE LONGEST DAY: JUNE 6, 1944

Author: Cornelius Ryan (1921-   )
Publisher: Simon and Schuster (New York). Illustrated. 350 pp. $4.95
Type of work: History
Time: June 4 to June 6, 1944
Locale: France, England, Germany

The story of the Normandy landings on D Day

On April 22, 1944, Field Marshal Erwin Rommel remarked to his aide: "Believe me, Lang, the first twenty-four hours of the invasion will be decisive . . . the fate of Germany depends on the outcome . . . for the Allies, as well as Germany, it will be the longest day." Rommel's phrase has given Cornelius Ryan the title for his story of what happened on that "longest day," June 6, 1944, when a coordinated air, sea, and land attack breached Germany's formidable Atlantic Wall and permitted a flood of men and matériel to pour through. This initial breaching did decide the fate of Germany, as Rommel had predicted. By the end of June Rommel would report his casualties for the month as "28 generals, 354 commanders and approximately 250,000 men." Ten months later Germany would surrender unconditionally to the Allies.

Mr. Ryan employs in *The Longest Day* a journalistic technique that has become familiar to readers of such books as Walter Lord's *Day of Infamy,* the story of Pearl Harbor. Making use of official reports, numerous published works, and many personal interviews, as well as his own recollections of D Day (he covered it as a war correspondent), Ryan lets us glance briefly in upon a number of individual military personnel and civilians in France, England, and Germany during the two days before D Day. Then, as the action develops, he returns to these *dramatis personae* from time to time.

In addition, he introduces many new characters from privates to generals on both sides, even up to the Führer himself, who sleeps through most of the book.

Occasionally Mr. Ryan employs what in fiction is called "foreshadowing," so that the reader may anticipate a coming action, as when the German Major General Wilhelm Falley decides, against Seventh Army orders, to leave the Cherbourg peninsula for Rennes to the south, and Ryan adds, "His decision was to cost him his life." General Falley dies some one hundred and fifty pages later, shot by an American lieutenant. When Chaplain John Gwinnett parachutes into the marshes near the Dives River, however, Mr. Ryan overdoes his foreshadowing a little. He says, "Gwinnett did not know it now, but it would be a full seventeen hours before he found his way out of the swamps." How could anyone have known it at the time?

Ryan has a trained reporter's eye for specific details, and the ability to group these details into a vivid composite picture, as in his description of Omaha Beach when the second wave of American troops arrived:

> Piling up along the shore was the flotsam and jetsam of the invasion. Heavy equipment and supplies, boxes of ammunition, smashed radios, field telephones, gas masks, entrenching tools, canteens, steel helmets and life preservers were strewn everywhere.

Great reels of wire, ropes, ration boxes, mine detectors and scores of weapons, from broken rifles to stove-in bazookas, littered the sand. The twisted wrecks of landing craft canted up crazily out of the water. Burning tanks threw great spirals of black smoke into the air. Bulldozers lay on their sides among the obstacles. Off Easy Red, floating in and out among all the cast-off materials of war, men saw a guitar.

Many things went wrong for the Allies on D Day, but they were greatly aided from the beginning by the fact that the date finally chosen (Eisenhower called off a June 5 attack) was the birthday of the wife of Field Marshal Rommel and that he had left France to be with her in Germany on June 6. In addition, a number of other senior officers were absent from the front. "All of them had reasons," says Ryan, "but it was almost as though a capricious fate had manipulated their departure." Later, Hitler even considered investigating whether British secret service might have influenced such multiple coincidences.

Another detail of extreme importance to the Allies was that two panzer divisions which might have been rushed to repel the invasion could not be released for action without Hitler's personal permission. This permission was not given until after a conference between Hitler and his senior officers at Berchtesgaden. It came at 3:40 P.M., ten hours late.

Although the absence of Rommel and his officers and of the panzer divisions did perhaps contribute materially to the remarkable success of the first day's action in the invasion, this success was also the result of elaborate planning by General Eisenhower and his staff, and it was achieved by the combined skill, labor, and valor of a mighty force of men from the United States, Great Britain, Canada, and several of the occupied countries.

The invasion began in the early morning darkness with the dropping of thousands of parachutists who were to attack from the rear of the German coastal fortifications, destroy communication lines, hold open key roads and bridges, and cause confusion which would perhaps weaken the defensive action on the coast itself.

H Hour for the invasion from the sea, where a tremendous fleet of five thousand ships had waited, amazingly undetected, in the darkness twelve miles offshore, was set at 6:30. The first wave landed only five minutes behind schedule. The Channel waters were rough, and most of the soldiers had been miserably seasick for hours before the time came for them to move in. A violent naval barrage from several hundred warships was intended to immobilize at least some of the German coastal batteries, and permit landing craft to discharge their loads at the shoreline.

But Marshal Rommel had not only armed the Atlantic Wall with batteries of big guns and soldiers with various types of small arms; he had also placed thousands of obstacles at the shoreline to prevent or at least delay the landing of assault craft so that these could be sunk and their occupants drowned or otherwise killed by fire from the beach fortifications. These obstacles were mined and the waters beyond them contained floating mines. Still more mines had been distributed about the beaches to take care of any soldiers who managed to reach land. The use of mines was a passion with Rommel.

In such a complex operation as the D-Day assault it was inevitable that errors would be made or that unforeseen circumstances would delay or prevent planned actions. In the darkness many airborne soldiers parachuted into the English Channel or into marshland which Rommel had flooded to guard against just such an attack. Big bombers dropped bombs three miles behind the coastal batteries they were trying to knock out. Engineers who were to destroy Rommel's obstacles and mines were hampered by successive waves of infantry-loaded craft that moved in on them. Some assault boats arrived at the wrong destinations. One group of men sent to knock out a battery on a hundred-foot cliff at Pointe du Hoc finally reached the clifftop after heavy losses from small-arms fire, and found no guns. They had never been emplaced.

In spite of such errors as these and despite a heavy casualty list of at least ten thousand men, the Allies won the great beachhead which they had sought. General Eisenhower had written a communiqué to be sent out in case the assault failed. In it he took the blame for failure since he had chosen the day. The communiqué finally issued, however, was one of triumph, not defeat. Much hard fighting still remained for the Allies after D Day, and even a few setbacks; but they had entered Hitler's Fortress Europa and they would not be thrown out.

In his brief foreword to *The Longest Day* Mr. Ryan says his book is not a military history but the story of people. That is its principal virtue. History lives again in these people; and, reading of them, one feels he knows what it was like to be in Normandy on one of the most significant dates in all modern military history.

Sources for Further Study

Reviews:

Christian Science Monitor. December 17, 1959, p. 13. 600 words.

New Statesman. LIX, April 9, 1960, p. 530. 800 words.

New York Herald Tribune Book Review. November 22, 1959, p. 4. 900 words.

Saturday Review. XLII, December 26, 1959, p. 19. 500 words.

Spectator. April 15, 1960, p. 549. 950 words.

Time. LXXIV, November 23, 1959, p. 107. 1,000 words.

Times Literary Supplement. June 10, 1960, p. 373. 500 words.

THE LONG-LEGGED HOUSE

Author: Wendell Berry (1934–   )
Publisher: Harcourt, Brace and World (New York). 213 pp. $5.95
Type of work: Essays

In a series of essays Wendell Berry reflects on man's present inhumanity to man and man's abuse of the earth

In nine eloquent essays Wendell Berry, a Kentucky teacher, farmer, and writer, explores themes that are of the utmost concern to everyone today. Man's behavior toward his fellow man, man's behavior toward the world, citizenship and conscience in the time of an unjust war, and some autobiographical solutions and suggestions about these problems are the major concerns of *The Long-Legged House*.

In the first essay, "The Tyranny of Charity," referring to a specific man and his family of eastern Kentucky's Appalachian region, Berry looks at an unintentional kind of oppression. A furniture maker, who lives in an old scale house that was once used by a coal company to weigh trucks, depends upon the government for welfare benefits. The tools he uses are primitive; the market for his handmade products is small. If he sells any of his chairs, his welfare payments are reduced. However, because he loves his craft he continues to make furniture. What this man and men like him need, says Berry, are tools instead of food stamps.

The gift of food alone, whether or not limited to an established minimum, can lead only to endless dependence on governmental charity—in which case charity becomes no more than a subtle form of oppression. If a man continues long in direct and absolute dependence on the government for the necessities of life, he ceases to be a citizen and becomes a slave.

Agencies, bureaus, and institutions, unlike individuals in a community, do not deal with the particular needs and abilities of people. They treat people as abstractions. They are not motivated by love or compassion; they cannot "exercise taste and judgment," and they cannot "value a man for his industry or his art or his pride." Governmental institutions are abstractions that deal with people as abstractions. Their conception of man is one that deprives him of a sense of his own individuality. They debase him by treating him as a statistic of his class or condition.

What can the government do? Berry tells us that it can eliminate the "political fraud" and "bureaucratic paralysis" that seem to contaminate each problem that it attempts to solve. It can "create a condition in which personal effort is meaningful." It can give a man the tools instead of the food stamps.

The next essay, "The Landscaping of Hell: Strip-Mine Morality in East Kentucky," takes us from the small house of the furniture maker to a pastoral home where a man has taken "a proud stand." The writer lovingly describes the details of the house and its yard. Overhanging the house on three sides is a spoil bank, waste material from a coal mine. Soon the rains will loosen the muddy spoil and send it down upon the green yard and the mountain home. Lax strip-mining laws have created this sword of Damocles. Berry asks, What are the assumptions and attitudes behind such abuse of the land?

Many of our attitudes toward life and toward the earth are assumptions that we have inherited from our frontier forefathers. The frontiersman saw the natural world as an enemy to be plundered. For him the riches of the earth are inexhaustible. For him economic license and political freedom are the same. A corollary to these axioms is "that a free man is somehow morally obligated to get rich, his worth directly proportionate to his wealth." He was willing "to be subsidized by posterity, to become rich at the world's expense."

Federal intervention, states Berry, is not the ideal solution to the abuse of the land by coal companies. A local problem should be corrected by the local people. If men are forced to do what is right by outside authority, they forfeit their initiative; they are debased. "The right itself is debased as an aim and incentive."

From this bleak dilemma we move to a more placid setting for the next essay. "The Nature Consumers" brings us to Wendell Berry's home which stands on a slope overlooking the Kentucky River a few miles from where it flows into the Ohio at Carrollton, Kentucky. From the quietness of his "long-legged house," raised on stilts to avoid the perennial floods, he often observes the restless vacationers in their pleasure boats in pursuit of some contact with nature. From his observations Berry concludes that man can be as destructive to the earth while pursuing pleasure as he is while working.

The filling of the river with their trash and noise destroys the very thing that they seek. For nature reveals herself only to those who are willing to be quiet and listen. She speaks only to those who have silenced the noise inside themselves. As the writer says, it is

a "sad paradox." These people come in search of peace, solitude, and quiet, some "restorative contact" with the natural world, but they destroy the object of their search by their own restlessness and their destructive behavior towards the earth. Using one of his many rural similes, Berry says their pursuit is "like going in search of a forest with a logging crew."

In concluding this essay Berry warns us that men can relate to nature in one of two ways.

Man cannot be independent of nature. In one way or another he must live in relation to it, and there are only two alternatives: the way of the frontiersman, whose response to nature was to dominate it, to assert his presence in it by destroying it, or the way of Thoreau, who went to the natural places to become quiet in them, to learn from them, to be restored by them. To know these places, because to know them is to need them and respect them and be humble before them, is to preserve them. To fail to know them, because ignorance can only be greedy of them, is to destroy them. . . . [T]he world must live in men's minds if men are to continue to live in the world.

The "Loss of the Future" is an apocalyptic essay. We are coming to the end of the "possibilities inherent in the youth of our nation: the new start in a new place with new vision and new hope." That which was given us, the land and the hopes, is soon to be dissipated. Future possibilities will depend upon a wiser use of what we have left.

Instead of communities where people share a "place," have concern for one another and trust one another, we in America have ghettos of rootless people. We are a society of ghettos—

The Long-Legged House/BERRY

"ghettos of the rich, the intellectuals, the scientists, the professors, politicians, etc." People in these ghettos are constantly migrating, seeking better jobs, pursuing happiness, and trying to escape unhappiness. As a result very few people have a real relation with the "place he thinks of as his home," and very few have a real relation with one another. We have lost a sense of community, a sense of wholeness.

Many people have abdicated their personal responsibilities. Their duties to their fellow men have ceased to be personal. In many cases they have been taken over by governmental institutions. In this respect Berry agrees with Jefferson and Thoreau that the best government governs least, but a logical corollary to that statement, says Berry, is that the best citizen is one who needs least governing.

There are three principal reasons for the abdication of our personal responsibilities, according to Berry. The idealistic guidelines of Christianity and democracy place an "extraordinary burden on the individual." We have some tough rules to play by. Second, the problem is compounded because these ideals have been offered to the young as absolute solutions instead of the experiments which they are. "Christianity and democracy are by definition problematic." They are not panaceas to all the problems of man.

Another reason that he offers to explain the loss of human concern is that in the minds of many people "the ethic of success which holds that the highest aims are wealth and victory" have replaced the "ideals of service and excellence."

What we need for a healthier and happier life are communities instead of ghettos. A community, as defined by Berry, is

the mental and spiritual condition of knowing that the place is shared and that the people who share the place define and limit the possibilities of each other's lives. It is the knowledge that people have of each other, their trust in each other, the freedom with which they come and go among themselves.

The next essay is the text of a speech that Berry gave on February 10, 1968. "Statement Against the War in Vietnam" was delivered to the Kentucky Conference on the War and the Draft at the University of Kentucky. In criticizing our behavior in Vietnam Berry states that we must have lost faith in the vitality of our ideals because we are trying to preserve them by force. The diversion of seventy percent of our revenue to arms indicates that we consider violence the most efficacious means to preserve our ideals and to evangelize in their behalf. But violence destroys a sense of community:

If I solve my dispute with my neighbor by killing him, I have certainly solved the immediate dispute. If my neighbor was a scoundrel, then the world is no doubt better for his abscence. But in killing my neighbor, though he may have been a terrible man who did not deserve to live, I have made myself a killer—and the life of my next neighbor is in greater peril than the life of the last. In making myself a killer I have destroyed the possibility of neighborhood.

At the end of his essay-speech Berry states: "The revolution that interests me and that I believe in is not the revolution by which men change government, but that by which they change themselves."

Don Pratt, a student at the University of Kentucky, was jailed because he refused to participate in a war that he considers unjust, unnecessary, and immoral. Pratt's sacrifice, fate, and nobility stimulated Berry to clarify his own thoughts on citizenship and conscience in an essay written in honor of Pratt.

A man is first a citizen of a community or a place. Citizenship begins at home. As his devotion widens it begins to weaken. Berry cares more for his household than for the town of Port Royal, more for his county than his state, more for his state than the United States of America. But he *does not* care more for the United States than the world.

> I must attempt to care as much for the world as for my household. Those are the poles between which a competent morality would balance and mediate: the doorstep and the planet.

Men are bonded together by the earth, and it is here that they must pay their allegiance. "We are still as dependent on the earth as the earthworms."

Berry himself has rejected the artificial needs of urban life for life in the country where he attempts to "Live out a decent and preserving relationship to the earth." He has not "dropped out." He has dropped "in" to nature. He is truly implementing in his life the ideas that he promotes in his writings.

The last three essays in *The Long-Legged House*, "The Rise," "The Long-Legged House," and "A Native Hill," are more poetical, mystical, and autobiographical than the preceding six.

In the middle of December on a gray, cold Sunday Berry and a friend canoed six miles on the swollen, muddy Kentucky River which flows in front of Berry's home near Port Royal,

Kentucky. The river had moved out of its banks covering trees and familiar paths. In "The Rise" the writer's prose style, his senses and reflexes, moves, like the river, out of the ordinary into poetry.

Descriptions of movements and sounds are woven together in this essay to produce a splendid lyricism. After the rise, the "great singular flowing of the river" becomes several currents that braid together. Eddies, whirlpools, and cross currents "suck and slur" as they move around trunks of trees and branches. Juxtaposed to this violent movement and noise along the shores is the majestic silence in the middle of the river and in the fields where the river had overflowed.

The title essay of this fine collection is an autobiographical sketch interwoven with a biography of the author's "heron like house" which is made for wading at the edge of the water. It is a story showing how a person can come to belong to a place. "We are the belongings of the world not its owners." In detail he describes the stages of his relationship with his great-uncle Curran's camp, Berry's present home.

At first the "camp" is a place to get away from the dismal activities of the military school he attended, a place to camp and fish with his teenage friends. Later it is a sanctuary where he reads Thoreau, Marvel, Kenneth Rexroth, and William Carlos Williams; a cottage where he takes his new wife after he finishes graduate school at the University of Kentucky in 1957; and a study where he can write seriously. For five years he lives away from the camp in Europe, California and New York, and the camp is a place where he spends his summers. At last it becomes a place to live "within" rather than upon. Berry now lives here with his wife and two children.

A writer is always looking for a place where he can use and enjoy the power of silence, the power of attentiveness, and the power of the permanence of interest. Berry seems to have found his "place on earth."

In "A Native Hill," Berry, walking down a stream bed towards the Kentucky River, reminisces about the flow of his life. Remembrance of his past life and observation of the present natural surroundings enhance each other. He has left the streets of New York City for the paths of the Kentucky countryside despite the warnings from his literary friends that the young writer's talent would stagnate in this provincial atmosphere. However, states the author, instead of the predicted stagnation there has been an exhilaration.

> My language increased and strengthened, and sent my mind into the place like a live root system. And so what has become the usual order of things reversed itself with me; my mind became the root of my life rather than its sublimation. I came to see myself as growing out of the earth like the other native animals and plants. I saw my body and my daily motions as brief coherences and articulations of the energy of the place, which would fall back into the earth like leaves in the autumn. . . . As I slowly fill with the knowledge of this place, and sink into it, I come to the sense that my life here is inexhaustible, that its possibilities lie rich behind and ahead of me, that when I am dead it will not be used up.

Berry's noble thoughts and feelings, as expressed in these essays, are in the great tradition of Thoreau. In the woods of Kentucky he lives next to the pulse of life, and in a gesture of true concern he shares with us what he has learned. If we can learn to treat one another as individuals instead of abstractions; if we can learn to let the earth restore us instead of destroying it; if we can learn to create communities instead of building ghettos; if we can learn to let our ideals prove themselves instead of enforcing them with violence, then we can have healthier and happier lives. In the darkness of the present disorder and destruction these essays are lanterns that can help us find our way through the night.

Charles E. Fothergill

LONGTIME CALIFORN'
A Documentary Study of an American Chinatown

Authors: Victor G. Nee (1943-   ) and Bret de Bary Nee (1945-   )
Publisher: Pantheon Books (New York). Graphs and map. 410 pp. $10.00
Type of work: Sociological study
Time: 1830-1970
Locale: California, China, and Hong Kong

The development of a Chinese community from the earliest immigration of Chinese into California to the present, and their contributions to the culture of the American West

Principal personages:
SUN YAT-SEN, the Chinese leader, who visited California in 1910
WARREN SUEN, a gardener of Portsmouth Sq., San Francisco
JOHN JEONG, one of the oldest (eighty-four years) interviewed
LELAND CHIN, one of the people who witnessed the
    San Francisco earthquake
LEW WAT GET, an officer of the Suey Sing Tong
GERALD WONG, the ex-president of the Six Companies
LILAC CHEN, an eighty-four-year-old former prostitute
FONG, a thoughtful worker
GINARN LAO, a wealthy banker
CLIFFORD FONG, a seventeen-year-old hippie
FRANK CHIN, a novelist, playwright, and essayist

Two American Chinese brothers, educated at the University of California and Harvard, here offer a social study of San Francisco's Chinatown. They interviewed representative English-speaking citizens and used interpreters when the informant knew only the Cantonese dialect. Spending the summer of 1970 in Chinatown, they returned to Harvard to work over their findings, then on a Ford Foundation grant went back to Chinatown from May, 1971 to April, 1972.

In their five-part, fifteen-chapter study, their practice is to introduce a topic, discuss it historically, then quote extensively from the inhabitants of Chinatown to supplement and corroborate. Charts also show the structure and relationship of various Chinatown organizations.

Before beginning their more lengthy presentation, the authors mention three current struggles in Chinatown. Social workers, trying to develop an anti-poverty program to meet social and economic problems caused by the tremendous immigration since 1965, struggle with the "Six Companies" who have controlled the community's traditional institutions. Radical students from neighboring universities struggle for greater political and economic justice for what they regard as a downtrodden minority. And finally, the local teenagers rebel in frequent outbreaks of crime in a struggle against what they consider the backwardness of the "old ones."

Causes of the present situation lie, according to the Nee brothers, in the community's past history, so they present a study of the three generations who have lived there. Chronologically, they provide histories of the "bachelor society" made up of immigrant male laborers who dominated Chinatown in the past century; the "family society" that evolved when Chinese women were finally allowed to enter the United States following Roosevelt's repeal of the Chinese Exclusion Acts of 1882, 1899, and 1924; and an emerging society of the new immigrants from China and Hong Kong who have poured in since President Johnson signed the Act of Oct. 3, 1965.

In the prologue, entitled "Portsmouth Square," the authors set the tone of the rest of the book. They picture the center of life of Old San Francisco, now occupied by the Chinese. Here the survivors of the "bachelor society" play checkers, sleep shaded by a newspaper, or talk to while away the hours.

Underscoring the authors' observations here is an interview with the gardener of Portsmouth Square, Warren Suen, who brings peace in the knife fights of drug addicts and hands out a few coins for food to the "sad bunch of old men. . . . There's no future and there's no past, so they're stuck, waiting for the box."

Part 1, "The Bachelor Society," explains the origin of the book's title. To restrain the influx of Orientals, the United States made entry difficult for newcomers. Poor families in China used to save up to send an eighteen-year-old member to America. He would work hard, save money to send back to China, then at the age of thirty would return to China to marry a village girl and start a family. His reentry into the United States would be easy. He would tell the Immigration official, "Me longtime Californ'." After one or two more round trips to China, he would die in America, and his bones would be returned to the village cemetery in a tin box.

Some of those interviewed had, indeed, enjoyed long ties with America. The authors talked with old-timers whose fathers had lived in California during the Gold Rush of 1849. Others had worked on the transcontinental railroad when the Central Pacific, seeing itself outdistanced by track-laying crews of the Union Pacific, imported shiploads of Chinese "bachelors" who worked long hours to place the ties. Yet, the authors declare, when the eastern and western sections were connected by a gold spike on May 10, 1869, orators who praised the French, German, English, and "light-hearted Irish" rail layers, made no mention of the Chinese.

And when the Burlingame Treaty of 1868 was establishing reciprocity in privileges, immunities, and exemptions between citizens of China and the United States living or traveling in one another's countries, nothing was about permitting those Chinese to become U.S. citizens. In fact, the conversations of many of the "bachelors" detail many instances of cruelty and injustice by the whites.

Practically all the Chinese came at first from the revolutionary Kwangtung Province, of which Canton is the chief city. The authors provide a map of this area of coastal China and say that the sections from which the immigrants came practically determined their status in the U.S. Those from the wealthy Sam Yup district, west of Canton, set up as small merchants and skilled craftsmen. Those from the heartland, south of the Pearl River Delta, turned to fish and flower markets or making ladies' garments. The rest frequently became domestic servants.

Concerning the makeup of Chinatown, the Nees say that by the beginning of the century, Chinese clans grew up along family lines. The Wong, Lee, and Chin clans, formed of kinsmen of the same last name, were the largest and most powerful.

There were also associations based on their origin in China, the first, in 1851, being the Canton or Sam Gup Company, followed later in the year by the Sze Yup Company. Then came others. In 1880, representatives of the six most powerful formed the Chinese Consolidated Benevolent Association of America, better known as the Chinese Six Companies. Since these were mostly merchant groups, others formed a network of tongs modeled after secret societies of seventeenth century China to back their members. They gave rise to lurid and false reports of underground tunnels and opium joints that terrified white California and brought about the anti-Chinese violence between 1890 and 1900.

The truth about the tongs comes out in an interview with Lew Wat Get, born in 1887, an officer of one tong. Another informant of the same age was John Jeong, who comments on the tribulations of the Chinese. Leland Chin, age 73, narrates his experience during the San Francisco fire and earthquake, when his people were moved to safety. One interview was with Lilac Chen, who as a child was sold in Chinatown to be a prostitute, but ended up as interpreter at the Presbyterian Mission House.

Part 2, an interlude called "The Refugees," deals with Chinese who studied in America, returned home, then came back to the United States during the Chinese Civil War of the 1940's. Representative is the wealthy banker Ginarn Lao, born in 1895, who fills eight pages telling how he applied American "savvy" in Chinese problems, then Chinese honesty in America as he founded the first Bank of Canton on Wall Street.

Part 3, "The Family Society," concerns the second sociological sequence in Chinatown's history and opens with the description of a Chinese laundry operated in the basement by a family inhabiting the first floor. Historically, this period began slowly about 1913, when about 150 wives of merchants were admitted to California annually. Then after the 1924-1930 period, when all Chinese women were again excluded, came another time when sixty Chinese wives were allowed to join their husbands each year. The family society that eventually came into being caused the decline of tongs and the end of what the Nees' call "The colorful life involving unmarried male laborers."

Now mothers and fathers worked together in a business, and children were required to help as soon as they were old enough. Remembering the handicap of their own ignorance, parents sent their offspring to public schools as well as requiring several hours a day in Chinese schools to keep their original language alive and to instruct them in Chinese history and classics. However, the second generation was more influenced by American practices around them.

The result, according to the au-

thors, was that pressure by parents
and eagerness to learn brought about
the highest percentage of college
graduates among any California ethnic group, as well as the highest percentage of near-illiterates (among the
older ones).

Several informants told the Nees
of the gradual transformation from
loyalty to old China into approval of
Nationalist China. During World
War II, America's alliance brought
new prestige to American Chinese
and the first major entrance of the
American-born generation into white
and blue-collar jobs, though few have
been able to rise to the decision-
making level. Again the testimony of
a dozen men and women is offered at
the end of the explanatory and historical sections.

Changing conditions in Chinatown
received their greatest momentum
with Kennedy's Presidential Directive
of May 25, 1962, permitting Hong
Kong refugees immediate entrance as
"Parolees" into the United States. In
four years, 15,000 arrived, a number
increased by President Johnson's Act
of October 3, 1965, abolishing national origin quotas. By the end of
1966, permanent residence status had
been achieved by 9,165. This brought
about what the authors, in the section titled "The Rebirth," call the
emergence of a "Working Class
Society."

For much material on this period
since 1965, the Nees had to depend
on translators, because many of the
newcomers who reached California
of Old Chinatown had not learned
and spread beyond the boundaries
English. Two of the interviews to illustrate the final section are especially
interesting as showing the mingled

optimism and despair about the outcome.

Seventeen-year-old high school
hippie Clifford Fong believes that the
chief problem of the Chinese is that
white people have no realization that
the Chinese have problems. They
have heard vaguely of the good family structure and the absence of crime
except for minor tong clashes. They
may know of Chinatown's Old Chinese Hospital with sixty beds, though
unaware it must serve a population of
40,000. They have heard of the Ping
Yuen apartments built between 1951
and 1961, with 400 housing units for
single people earning less than $2,300
annually and families with an income
of less than $7,300.

Whites often base their judgment
of Chinese living conditions on the in-
expensive food at many Chinatown
restaurants, ignorant of what Chinese
told the authors, that their cheapness
represents a sacrifice of profit by the
owners to provide the only sort of
work that many ignorant Chinese immigrants can do.

The most eloquent section of the
study is perhaps the twelve-page report on his thoughts provided by a
thirty-two-year-old writer, Frank
Chin, fifth generation of his family
born in America, whose father was
president of the Six Companies. He
tries to "legitimize the Chinese-
American sensibility," and describes
his feelings about attempting to write
of his people, though confessing that
"No American-born Chinese-Ameri-
can writer has ever published and become even slightly known, and still
lives in Chinatown." They do not
identify with it any longer. They see
Chinatown as backward. He accuses
them of leaving their people and try-

ing to achieve a second-class white status.

But reading the Nees' book, the Chinese can be proud of their own status; and white readers will finish it with a new idea of Chinatown, far truer than a tourist's impression. They will share the authors' indignation over injustices and their pity for the people who make up ten percent of San Francisco's total population, with nearly half of them below Federal poverty level standards. Yet they will agree with the Nees' assertion in the Introduction: "They have pride, they try to keep themselves looking half-dignified, and they don't beg."

Willis Knapp Jones

LOOK AT THE HARLEQUINS!

Author: Vladimir Nabokov (1899-   )
Publisher: McGraw-Hill Book Company (New York). 253 pp. $7.95
Type of work: Novel
Time: 1899-1974
Locale: Primarily Russia, France, and the United States

A witty, elegant, ambiguous mock "autobiography" of a Russian émigré writer whose career in many ways parallels Nabokov's own

Principal characters:

> VADIM VADIMOVICH N————————, the narrator, a Russian émigré writer
> IRIS BLACK, his first wife
> ANNA "ANNETTE" IVANOVNA BLAGOVO, his second wife
> ISABELLA "BEL," their daughter
> DOLLY VON BORG, Vadim's mistress for a brief time
> LOUISE ADAMSON, his third wife
> "YOU," his fourth wife, recipient of the memoir

The title of *Look at the Harlequins!* is derived from a short scene near the beginning when the hero, Vadim Vadimovich N————, reminiscing about his early years, recalls a time when his grandaunt chided him for being "sulky and indolent":

> "Stop moping!" she would cry: "Look at the harlequins!"
> "What harlequins? Where?"
> "Oh, everywhere. All around you. Trees are harlequins, words are harlequins. So are situations and sums. Put two things together—jokes, images — and you get a triple harlequin. Come on! Play! Invent the world! Invent reality!"

Thus, Vladimir Nabokov defines the basic function of the "artist": with his imagination and his facility with language, he creates a superior reality out of the inferior raw material at hand. Trapped in a mortal body, thrust into a reality that is shifting, ambiguous, even downright unreal, the human being has only his own creative powers to give order and meaning to the chaotic world.

Consequently, almost all of Nabokov's writings focus on a main character who is particularly adept at the "making of harlequins." He (always a "he") is brilliant, rootless (generally an exile, usually from Russia), talented, witty, and as a rule teetering on the edge of madness. He always possesses the "artistic temperament," although only four of the novels deal explicitly with the professional writer: *The Gift* (1952, 1963), *The Real Life of Sebastian Knight* (1938, 1941), *Pale Fire* (1962), and *Look at the Harlequins!* Indeed, this latest novel may well be Nabokov's definitive statement on the nature, role, and fate of the artist.

The book reads like the conventional memoir of an aged, sophisticated man of letters summing up his life and career. Vadim briefly chronicles his birth in Russia (1899), his flight during the Bolshevik Revolution (when he kills a Red soldier), his Cambridge education, the growth and development of his literary career, his three unsatisfactory marriages, his exile to an American university, the birth of his daughter and subsequent loss of contact with her, his commercial success, and, finally, his nearly fatal stroke and retirement with a fourth spouse. As in all Nabokov novels, the narration is elegant, witty, allusive, and discursive. Chronology is casual and leisurely as the story frequently shifts back and forth in time and space, although an overall linear progression is maintained. Vadim intrudes to comment, digress, and recount seemingly irrelevant details and anecdotes. He dwells with almost loving irony on his own idiosyncrasies, such as one of his "oldest and naughtiest pleasures: circulating stark naked all over a strange house." Vadim's predilection for mirrors is significant in this novel, since the entire "memoir" is itself a mirror; and that is what makes the book peculiarly Nabokovian: the novelist has given us a funhouse looking glass. Vadim is neither an autonomous character nor a fictionalization of the author. He is a distorted, fragmented, incomplete, clownish collection of Nabokovian traits and accomplishments trying to bestow some order on his personality.

Thus, the uniqueness of *Look at the Harlequins!* lies in the way the author manipulates, sometimes seriously, sometimes ironically, the self-conscious parallels between himself and his fictional counterpart. Although only alluded to in passing, Vladimir Nabokov's presence in the book is real and continuous; he is as much a character as are the creatures of his imagination who populate it.

Explicit parallels between Vadim's life and his creator's are underlined.

Both are Russian aristocrats born in 1899; both flee Russia after the Revolution; after living in a variety of European locations, both migrate to America to teach at a major Eastern university (Quirn for Vadim; Cornell for Nabokov); and, following the enormous financial success of a sensational book, both retire from teaching and return to Europe.

Their works can likewise be compared. Vadim is periodically mistaken for his creator; there are frequent allusions to, and borrowings from, other Nabokov works; brief summaries of Vadim's novels resemble Nabokov's; and the list of Vadim's works that prefaces the novel almost duplicates Nabokov's. To cite only a few, Vadim's *Tamara* echoes Nabokov's *Mary; Camera Lucida (Slaughter in the Sun)* suggests *Camera Obscura (Laughter in the Dark); Dr. Olga Repnin* resembles *Pnin;* and *A Kingdom by the Sea* is Vadim's equivalent of *Lolita*.

But, although Vadim is a recognized, honored writer, his works, especially those detailed in the novel, are at best gross parodies of Nabokov's. The living parallels are important, but the real meanings of the book probably lie in the differences. Vadim's father was a rake and gambler killed in a pointless duel; Nabokov's father was an enlightened liberal aristocrat who was murdered by fanatics while defending a friend. Vadim describes his childhood as "atrocious, intolerable . . . inhuman"; in his autobiography *Speak, Memory!,* Nabokov pictures his childhood as happy and contented. But the most important differences lie in their relationships with women and in their emotional and psychological makeups. While Nabokov has remained happily married to the same woman for half a century, Vadim's marital and familial history is frantic, frustrating, and chaotic. While Nabokov has always been an emotionally and intellectually stable individual, Vadim is a psychological wreck who flirts with madness throughout the novel; and the novel is primarily the story of Vadim's attempt to find that unity of perception and being which presumably his authorial double already possesses.

Vadim's precarious mental equilibrium shows itself in a number of ways. He wakes up at night "momentarily mad"; frequently he experiences "the friends of my incurable ailment, 'flayed consciousness' . . . shoving aside my harlequins"; he cannot go swimming for fear that he will be drowned because of a "fit of *total* cramp—the physical counterpart of lightning insanity"; and, most diastrous of all, he is unable to reconcile a personal obsession with time and space.

Prior to each marriage, he describes his malady to each of his prospective brides via an imaginary situation. For instance, with Iris, his first wife, Vadim postulates a scene in which they are walking slowly from one point to another, carefully noticing everything as they proceed. Upon reaching the destination, Vadim asks her to make an about-face imaginatively in order to return the same way. She does so.

"Shall we start walking back?"
"You may, I can't! This is the point of the experiment. In actual, physical life I can turn as simply and swiftly as anyone, but mentally, with my eyes closed and my body immobile, I am unable to switch from one direction to the other. Some swivel cell in my brain does not work . . . if I do not cheat, some kind of atrocious obstacle, which would drive me mad if it persevered, prevents me from imagining the twist which transforms one direction into another, directly opposite. I am crushed, I am carrying the whole world on my back in the process of trying to visualize my turning around and making myself see in terms of 'right' what I saw in terms of 'left' and vice versa."

This obligatory "confession" that he makes to each of his brides-to-be is actually a test of their potential value as wives for him; each of their reactions predicts with fair accuracy how and why the marriage will fail. Iris is threatened by the story and pushes it out of her mind; Annette pays no attention to it at all; Louise dismisses it as a joke.

Thus, Vadim brings his creative impulses and his psychological obsessions to each of his first three wives. Each of them fails him in different ways for reasons partly his own fault, partly theirs. Because he can communicate neither his artistic designs nor his psychological aberrations to his wives, they can neither help him find artistic fulfillment nor secure emotional stability. Consequently, Vadim's "autobiography" is, until very near the end, a chronicle of progressive loss of meaning and emotional fragmentation.

All of this makes Vadim sound dangerously like the sensitive, "tormented," neurotic "artist" figure of so many contemporary novels. Nothing could be further from Nabokov's intentions. His view of such fictional characters, and of the psychological milieu, largely Freudian, which has spawned them, is thoroughly contemptuous ("Let the credulous and the vulgar," he once remarked, "continue to believe that all mental woes can be cured by a daily application of old Greek myths to their private parts. I really do not care"). For all of his intelligence and artistic productivity, Vadim is a weakling and a clown. His actions provide the makings of grotesque comedy, not tragedy or even sentimental melodrama.

This is not to say that Vadim's preoccupations are frivolous. His experiences as an artist are central to Nabokov's fiction, and his obsession with time and space echo Nabokov's own. And the fact that he comes to terms with these two problems, his buffoonery notwithstanding, brings the book together thematically.

Approximately two-thirds of the way through the book we realize that this is not merely a personal memoir, but is, in fact, a narrative directed at a specific listener, identified only as "you." "You," it develops, is one of Vadim's daughter's former classmates whom he meets during his last days at Quirn; she is to become his fourth wife. Thus the narrative becomes more than a life story; it is an attempt to define that life in order to communicate its meaning to the person who has given it a new direction. "You" is clearly the one capable of bringing Vadim out of his emotional confusions, even if she has arrived on the scene somewhat late. Alone among his women, she reads and understands his fiction. And it is "you" who finally resolves his Time-Space obsession. Her response to the "confession" is as follows:

"His mistake . . . his morbid mistake

is quite simple. He has confused direction and duration. He speaks of space but he means time. His impressions along the HP route (dog overtakes ball, car pulls up at next villa) refer to a series of time events, and not to blocks of painted space that a child can rearrange in any old way. It has taken him time — even if only a few moments — to cover distance HP in thought. By the time he reaches P he has accumulated duration, he is saddled with it! Why then is it so extraordinary that he cannot imagine himself turning on his heel? Nobody can imagine in physical terms the act of reversing the order of time. Time is not reversible."

Vadim's response is ecstatic. He proclaims himself "cured"—even though he adds that "your explanation . . . is merely an exquisite quibble—and you know it." The book ends on a typically Nabokovian note of irresolution. Has Vadim found a kind of serenity in an explanation that resolves his Space-Time dilemma? Or, because he has finally found a woman who can understand him and speak to his needs, is it no longer a sick obsession? Vadim has at last put the fragments together, although it is too late to make an appreciable difference in his career (well over seventy, he is slowly recovering—hopefully—from a serious stroke).

But why the elaborate Vadim-Nabokov doubling? Why not just tell the story of Vadim and leave it go at that? One obvious answer lies in Nabokov's taste for playing "games" with his readers via cross-references, literary allusions, wordplay, and sophisticated ironies—practices that stimulate his advocates and irritate his detractors. Perhaps the criticism that *Look at the Harlequins!* is an elaborate in-joke which can be fully appreciated only by certified Nabokovians is not entirely unfair; a knowledge of Nabokov's own life and works is *de rigueur* to a full understanding of this novel.

More importantly, however, the intrusion of Nabokov into his own novel reinforces his view of the artist as conscious manipulator of his fictional reality and, through that, of the world beyond it. Vadim emerges, finally, as a kind of Nabokov gone wrong. By playing with this grotesque, comical "reflection" of himself in the framework of a parody-autobiography, Nabokov is able to examine "obliquely" implications and issues that are central to his vision, while maintaining the detachment of his elegant, ironical, witty verbal surface. Parody is raised to the level of aesthetic and philosophical speculation. In this novel Vladimir Nabokov has, at the very least, written a quadruple harlequin.

Keith Neilson

LOOK BACK IN ANGER

Author: John James Osborne (1929–   )
Publisher: Criterion Books (New York). 96 pp. $2.75
Type of work: Drama
Time: The present
Locale: The English midlands

A gifted young Englishman lacerates himself, his wife, and his friends in his fruitless struggle against a barren modern world

Principal characters:
JIMMY PORTER, dissatisfied working-class intellectual
ALISON PORTER, his wife
CLIFF LEWIS, his friend and business partner
HELENA CHARLES, his mistress
COLONEL REDFERN, Alison's father

The first major work of one of England's "Angry Young Men," this electric and violent play centers around sensitive, emotional, and abusive Jimmy Porter, whose mistress says of him,

there's no place for people like that any longer—in sex, or politics, or anything. That's why he's so futile. Sometimes, when I listen to him, I feel he thinks he's still in the middle of the French Revolution. And that's where he ought to be of course. He doesn't know where he is or where he's going. He'll never do anything, and he'll never amount to anything.

This member of a more intellectual English equivalent of America's "Beat Generation," who ranges from street invective to literary references, is a scurrilously combative husband, friend, and lover who can nonetheless plead, "Was I really wrong to believe that there's a—a kind of burning vitality of mind and spirit that looks for something as powerful as itself?" Full of contradictions, Jimmy Porter has been to a university yet makes his living running a sweet-stall; passionately on the side of the working class, he marries one girl from the well-to-do class and becomes the lover of another; agonizingly vulnerable himself to real and fancied slights, he is violently caustic to others, both those who love him and those who do not.

At the play's start Jimmy and his wife Alison are seen living in the large but drab and crowded attic of a large Victorian house. Across the landing but one of the family is Cliff Lewis, an even-tempered young Welshman who is Jimmy's old friend and partner in the sweet-stall and who says of himself, "I've been a—a no man's land between them." Part family friend and part buffer, he cushions Alison as much as he can from the constant shocks and violence Jimmy continually offers her as a kind of obverse side of the laceration he inflicts upon himself. Alison is pregnant, but she is unable, because of their conflicts, to bring herself to tell Jimmy. Later, when the presence of an actress friend, Helena Charles, has tautened the tension and increased the abuse, Alison is unable to stand it. Helena sends for Alison's father, who, like her mother, had violently opposed her marriage to Jimmy.

Look Back in Anger/OSBORNE

He takes her away. When Jimmy returns to the flat, desolate from the death of a surrogate mother figure, he takes Helena, whom he had previously villified, as his mistress.

The beginning of the last act, on a drab Sunday evening several months later, is a duplicate of the first except that Helena has taken Alison's place, making a seemingly better adjustment to Jimmy despite a fundamental repugnance for his views and the conditions of their illicit life together. When Alison visits them on an impulse, ill, worn, having lost her child, Helena sees that she must relinquish Jimmy for his sake, for hers, and for Alison's. Alison then begs him to take her back. He does, and they call each other by the private names they had used—his "bear" and hers "squirrel." Earlier Alison had described this playful fantasy: "We could become little furry creatures with little furry brains. Full of dumb, uncomplicated affection for each other. Playful, careless creatures in their own crazy zoo for two. A silly symphony for people who couldn't bear the pain of being human beings any longer."

This is an ending, and a drama, in which the characters seem beyond any strong affirmation, in which they seem capable only of shifting defensive alliances against the environment in which they live. And despite Jimmy's sadism and neuroticism, Osborne makes out the times to be the villain. Jimmy's father had died from injuries he received fighting in the Spanish Civil War. Like a vocal and intellectual Miniver Cheevy, Jimmy complains that

"There aren't any good, brave causes left. If the big bang does come, and we all get killed off, it won't be in aid of the old-fashioned, grand design. It'll be just for the Brave New-nothing-very-much-thank you. About as pointless and inglorious as stepping in front of a bus."

It is a world in which superannuated people like Alison's parents look back, wistful and bewildered, at a bogus Edwardian dream, and in which prematurely aged and crabbed young people like Jimmy look forward to a vision of boredom or annihilation. At one time Jimmy says, "The Big Crash is coming, you can't escape it," and at another he reflects, "I must say it's pretty dreary living in the American Age—unless you're an American of course. Perhaps all our children will be Americans. That's a thought, isn't it?"

The play is not wholly an unrelieved vision of squalor and hopelessness, however. At times it is lightened by Jimmy's passion, Cliff's good humor, or Alison's love. For one brief time Osborne uses an amusing, vintage vaudeville skit staged by Jimmy and Cliff. But in its dominant tone, the play is a cry, harsh, passionate, and impotent, against a world of which Alison says, "Something's gone wrong somewhere, hasn't it?" And her father, speaking in the voice of the older generation, answers, "It looks like it, my dear." Osborne's talent seems to be a real one, and his play is vital and dramatic in spite of its theme and its import. It will be interesting to see if his view of his world will permit him to sustain the same level of vitality in his future work.

Sources for Further Study

Criticism:

Dyson, A. E. "Look Back in Anger," in *Critical Quarterly*. I (Winter, 1959), pp. 318-326. *Look Back in Anger* is a play which increases understanding of the tormented and their torments. Dyson analyzes the intertwined themes which make up this drama.

Faber, M. D. "The Character of Jimmy Porter: An Approach to *Look Back in Anger*," in *Modern Drama*. XIII (May, 1970), pp. 67-77. A study of characterization in *Look Back in Anger* which notes that Jimmy Porter projects his own psychological shortcomings onto the external environment.

Groef, Hilda. "Why All This Anger?," in *Catholic World*. CLXXXVIII (November, 1958), pp. 122-128. Deals with the concept of anger in John Osborne's *Look Back in Anger*.

Huss, Roy. "John Osborne's Backward Half-Way Look," in *Modern Drama*. VI (May, 1963), pp. 20-25. Huss looks at the dramatic context of Osborne's social protests in *Look Back in Anger*.

Weiss, Samuel A. "Osborne's Angry Young Play," in *Educational Theatre Journal*. XII (December, 1960), pp. 285-288. This close analysis of *Look Back in Anger* finds that the play takes on a coherence and shape that reveals a tight core of related thinking and feeling.

Reviews:

Booklist. LIV, October 15, 1957, p. 98.

Library Journal. LXXXII, December 1, 1957, p. 3122.

Spectator. February 1, 1957, p. 150. 900 words.

LOOKING UP AT LEAVES

Author: Barbara Howes (1914–   )
Publisher: Alfred A. Knopf (New York). 61 pp. $4.00
Type of work: Poetry
   The fourth collection by a poet of established intellectual toughness and technical brilliance

With the publication of *Light and Dark* in 1959 Barbara Howes established herself as a poet of fine sensibility and intelligence, and toughness, in the sense that she looks at all things in an effort to see what is really there. She uses nothing as an excuse to say something "pretty," though what she says is often beautiful. In the opening stanza of "Portrait of an Artist," from *Light and Dark,* she appears to characterize her own approach to the world:

> For dear life some do
> Many a hard thing,
> Train the meticulous mind
> Upon meaning, seek
> And find, and yet discard
> All that is not of reality's tough rind.

In *Looking up at Leaves,* Miss Howes carries her fine perception and poetic craft into examinations of love, nature (observed and contended with), art and poetry, and home and its power to hold one fast.

The book is divided into two parts, "A Short Way By Air" and "Vermont Poems—A Cycle." The first section contains a number of poems about the Caribbean. The obvious contrast between the two sections, then, is that between the comforts and pleasures of the exotic and the unpredictable, and the comforts and pleasures of what is familiar.

But the organization of the book is more complex than it at first appears. What keeps it from being two barely related groups of poems is the selection and arrangement of the poems in the first part. While "A Short Way By Air" includes a number of poems which grow out of experiences of the Caribbean, there are several New England poems here too, and a few in which geography is not important. The whole section moves roughly between two poems, one near the beginning, one near the end, which make it clear that "A Short Way By Air" is a round trip. The first of these is called "Dead Toucan: Guadeloupe":

> Down like the oval fall of a hammer
> The great bill went,
> Trailed by its feather-duster body
> Splat on cement.
> His mates fell out of countenance,
> All listened, shivering in the sun,
> For what was off, amiss:
> In his pretend haven under a flame tree
> The agouti crouched, chewed on his
>   spittle, shook,
> The porcupine rolled in his box, the
>   parakeets
> Chattered regrets,
> Knowing something was wrong in their
>   hot Eden:
> That their King had followed his
>   heavy fate to earth;
> And his superb
> Accomplishment,
> His miracle of balance,
> Had come to nothing, nothing. . . .
> A beak with a panache
> Chucked like an old shell back to the
>   Caribbean.

There is no nonsense here. Miss Howes, as usual, by-passes an excellent opportunity to romanticize, and instead gives us the matter-of-fact "splat" which signals something wrong, as there always must be, in anything like Eden.

In "What Bird," which is not restricted to the Caribbean by any evocation of a particular landscape, or by any exotic nomenclature, Miss Howes, near the end of the first section of the book, varies the theme slightly, to a similar end:

What bird is that, in the corner,
The cat brought in? I resurrect
No more than this scatter of dark
Plumage, household graffiti
To add to the lore of the dump.
Colorless, bodiless, less the bird
That inhabited this costume
And which proved its former mastery
Of air, by failing that once;—
Like anyone else who does badly
Sometimes: feathers in the corner: a
   dunce.

This poem, along with "My Dear, Listen:," "A Stand of Birches," and others, effects a gradual transition into "Bermont Poems" which the mechanical division of the book belies.

The result of this arrangement is a tension between what seems to be and what is, and it is this tension, rather than the ostensible scheme, which holds the book together, so that the whole, including both sections, may be divided according to the subject matter.

Miss Howes approaches love almost tentatively. She knows enough not to define it (though she will make it the subject of a sentence with the verb *is*), and she rarely permits the reader to draw, from one of her descriptions of a situation, the conclusion that This Was It. Most often, she expresses a hope for love, or declares a receptiveness to it, as in "The Bay at West Falmouth":

. . . The heart's serenity is like the
   gold
Geometry of sunlight: motion shafting
Down through green dimensions, rung
   below rung
Of incandescence, out of which grace
   unfolds.

Watching that wind schooling the bay,
   the helterskelter
Of trees juggling air, waves signalling
   the sun
To signal light, brings peace: as our
   being open
To love does, by this serenity of water.

For Miss Howes, love is something more than the powerful attraction of two people for each other, something less than the all-inclusive love expressed by such poets as Whitman or Roethke. It is a thing to be approached with caution. Any statement about it pushes the idea of it farther back in the mind. This is what happens in "Footnote":

Love is a great leveller.
Some of us
May fancy we have mastered desire—
Not likely; it's too imperious. For many
Love is a great
Barrier; some are ill
With fear of it. Few, really,
Have ever breathed its blue oracular air
Deep in their lungs. Love is a bell
That sounds and bodies forth the whole
   being.
We need own
So little: half a bed;
So much: hope that love is, will be
Love.

"Dead Toucan: Guadeloupe" and "What Bird" exemplify one of Miss Howes's approaches to nature: the act of observation, the statement leading out of such observation. In other poems she explores certain struggles between men and nature, presenting personal

4522   *Looking Up at Leaves*/HOWES

experiences without making epic struggles of them. In the opening poem,
"Out Fishing," the speaker sets the
scene, as a good day in the Caribbean,
and tells us that not much has happened for several hours, until

> The great one struck that twine-
> Wrapped flying-fish hard, turned and
>   bolted
> Off through the swelling sea
> By a twist of his shoulder, with me tied
>   fast; my rod
>
> Held him, his hook held me,
> In tug-of-war—sidesaddle on the ocean
> I rode out the flaring waves,
> Rode till the great fish sounded; by his
>   submersion
>
> He snapped the line, we lost
> All contact; north, south, west, my ad-
>   versary
> Storms on through his world
> Of water: I do not know him: he does
>   not know me.

Here are the facts, their intrinsic interest added to by poetic craft, not by
mystical tinkering. Miss Howes lets
her speaker tell what really happened,
and allows the facts of the experience
to do what they can. She avoids sentimentality almost to the point of coldness. In the opening lines of "Headlong," for example, she gives us only
the facts:

> Setting off home, I ran over a wood-
>   chuck.
> He lunged out—no sleight-of-wheel
>   could have missed
> His pepper-and-salt wedge head; a young
>   fellow,
> For whom the graveled roadside pro-
>   vided
> A grainy banquet. Well, he was quite
>   dead
> When I backed up to see what I had
>   done.

That Miss Howes sticks to the facts
does not make her a poetic Joe Friday;
rather, it keeps her closer to the truth
toward which she is always moving.
She continues:

> This is an old story. Only wisdom
> Can read the plane geometry of this
>   tale . . .

Then a restatement of what happened:
the intersection of two paths, the result. All she adds is this, also a fact, to
which she has led the reader inexorably:

>   . . . I ran
> A gauntlet of chill air the long way
>   home.

Home, together with its power to
draw one to it, is another subject explicit in a number of poems and implicit in the structure of the book as a
whole. But for Miss Howes, home
seems to be whatever place one can
make himself belong to. The Vermont
cycle is one process by which Miss
Howes makes her home in New England. The vents of a place ("Town
Meeting Tuesday," "The Snow Hole,"
"Headlong," "Running Into Edgar Bel-
lemare") and one's participation in
them make that place home. And this,
in a sense, is one of the things meant
by the ambiguous ending of "Troy
Weight Taken," one of the poems in
"A Short Way By Air":

> We do not need to comb
> Arkansas to find
> Rubies; loneliness
> Vanishes in this crystal-
> Clear actual air,
> And one by one makes one.
> Love tempers us, and every
> True embrace is carved
> In ivory, lasts; although

My eyes are shut, I learn
Each golden day that golden
Moorings hold me home.

Finally, Miss Howes meditates on works of art, and on art in general, as a means of following facts to ultimate truth. Among the best of these poems is "Ode to Poseidon," subtitled "Lines on a Grecian Urn Recently Acquired By the Williams College Museum of Art." And in "My Dear, Listen:," she restates the problem of the poet, as set forth in the opening stanza of "Portrait of an Artist":

More than other beings
An artist should keep
The pathway open
To his inward life,
To that native self
That must daily be fed,
Pondered and watered
If what might be
Is to turn—by grace, by craft—into
    poetry.

The craft is here, and grace. This grace is of one kind. The other is in the hands of the gods, who have been generous to Miss Howes.

Henry Taylor

LOOKOUT CARTRIDGE

Author: Joseph McElroy (1930-   )
Publisher: Alfred A. Knopf (New York). 531 pp. $10.00
Type of work: Novel
Time: The present
Locale: London, New York, Corsica, Wales, Stonehenge

An elaborate intellectual mystery, filled with symbols, allusions, and often vivid portraits of the violence of the modern world

Principal characters:

> DAGGER DI GORRO, an American amateur film maker, living in England
> CARTWRIGHT, an American businessman and amateur film maker, living in England
> LORNA CARTWRIGHT, his wife
> JENNY CARTWRIGHT, his nineteen-year-old daughter
> WILL (BILLY) CARTWRIGHT, his younger son
> SUB, Cartwright's boyhood friend
> MONTY GRAF, British friend of Cartwright
> CLAIRE, Cartwright's American contact

Set mainly in London and New York, *Lookout Cartridge* concerns a film made by two Americans living in England and the forces that are threatened by the film and by Cartwright's diary of its shooting, as well as by his inquiry into why the film was destroyed. But the plot of this long and demanding *tour de force* is merely an excuse for the stylistic and philosophical gymnastics of the author. The question is whether the reader is willing to follow narrator Cartwright's obsessive mental process as he puts fragment after fragment of information together to find out what others think he already knows—and why it is valuable enough for them to threaten his daughter's life for it. The story's clothesline of suspense, hung here and there with tough situations and tougher talk, is conventional, but McElroy brings a certain amount of freshness to his contemporary imagery, including that of film cutting, the supernatural, scientific toys, and the jargon of the modern world. There are glints of comedy beneath the calculated convolutions of the novel's language, but *Lookout Cartridge,* like Pynchon's *Gravity's Rainbow* and other recent novels, obtains its symbolic and allusive formulae from science and technology rather than from literature and art. It is a special kind of game that only the initiated can play.

The author has a fine sense for detail, for observing the minutiae of everyday life. He fills his narrative with closely observed descriptions of street scenes, with sudden glimpses of contemporary life styles. But his characters are stylized to the point of flatness; they are puppets, manipulated for the plot, rather than full-bodied men and women who cause the plot to happen. The reader cannot believe in them as human beings or care about their fates. Possibly the author has done this deliberately, believing that the time has come to leave the traditional novel with its emphasis on characterization behind. But to capture the emotions of the reader, a novel must be more than an ingenious jigsaw puzzle of elaborate metaphors and clever symbols. For all of its intellectual artifice, this book does not deeply engage the reader's sympathies. One admires it as a construction, but one remains essentially aloof from it.

Diary and memory work together in the narrative, and sometimes at odds, trying to reconstruct the past, to find the reality of life. The diary and memory, and the fragmented and mostly destroyed movie which are their subject, belong to Cartwright, the protagonist of the plot. Memory is perhaps the real subject of *Lookout Cartridge,* for everything important seems to have happened in the past, and the necessity which drives Cartwright is that of recalling this past. "Bring back a memory," his daughter Jenny tells him, when he travels.

Also at the heart of this unusual novel is the scientific tradition as it is embraced in science fiction, in industry, and in the popular imagination. There is a revolution at work in the world, the characters agree, but it is more scientific than social. "Are you part of the film-making revolution?" Cartwright asks some young film makers, but he is told that anyone who *is* part of the revolution would not have to ask. The narrator-hero tells his children the tale of "Beauty and the Computer." The connections in the novel, flashing and vanishing almost at random, suggest the alternating connections of a vast computer. Little attempt is made to hold the reader's interest through conventional methods; like a switchboard ablaze with signals, the novel hurls fragments of conversations and brilliantly illuminated but tantalizingly brief scenes at the reader, who can only struggle to unify these images into a meaningful whole. The scraps of incident and shards of memory do eventually add up, but one person's summary might be quite different from somebody else's. The novel is like a fun house mirror, reflecting the viewer as well as the author and his characters.

One of the foremost themes in this book is that of violence in the modern world. Near the opening of the novel the reader is deliberately shocked by a scene of gratuitous violence. The selfish callousness of the contemporary citizen is shown when the narrator witnesses the accidental stabbing of a man in the street with a car radio antenna and, after watching the man collapse in a pool of blood, wanders into a camera shop to look for a new camera for his daughter, apparently undisturbed by what he has witnessed. Cruelty, various forms of brutality, and the constant bombardment of mechanical violence give the novel a kind of nervous vitality, but at the sacrifice of sympathy. No one in the novel emerges as genuinely admirable or sympathetic.

Like the novels and stories of Thomas Pynchon, Donald Barthelme, and John Barth, *Lookout Cartridge* is a novel to study, a novel written for academics to explore rather than for the general reader to read. The book is filled with devices to make it seem *avant-garde,* such as not using quotation marks around the dialogue and breaking into the action with random thoughts and disjointed phrases. However, difficulty or obscurity is no guarantee of either profundity or quality. Fascinating as this novel often is, the author seems to have deliberately set out to construct a puzzle rather than a coherent narrative. The reader follows the ironies, follows the coincidences which dot the story line, such as it is, and suspends disbeliefs as the hero battles obscure and menacing forces, but despite the energy put into the tale, it is never quite convincing.

Influenced as the book is by the movies, it is possible that it was inspired, at least indirectly, by the several movies dealing with the notorious underworld figure Dr. Mabuse, directed in the 1920's and 1930's by the great German film maker Fritz Lang. Certainly, the technical pyrotechnics of the novel suggest the dazzling genius of the movies, and the tale of the power-hungry Mabuse and his many faces and vast organization has many similarities with *Lookout Cartridge*. In this century, novelists and movie makers both seem fascinated by the subject of great, hidden powers which are striving to take over the world. These organizations are seldom clearly defined, but their presence is *felt,* and more than a few protagonists have suffered at their hands. Actually this startlingly *avant-garde* novel is part of a pattern in twentieth century narrative fiction, both cinematic and novelistic.

The novel suggests a montage of countless movies of the past and present and future, a splicing of scenes and film clips and newsreels into a dazzling but not always coherent whole. The labyrinthine narrative tracks Cartwright's efforts to separate occurrences from imaginings, splicing together at random figures and scenes enigmatically recalled, including Welsh hippies around a bonfire, an art-gallery intrigue, an Olympian softball game, and assorted acts of grotesque violence. In the end, Cartwright has gained a kind of wisdom, possibly, about himself and the truths which rule mankind, but these visionary axioms, for the most part, escape the reader. The scenes of violence and grotesque comedy linger longer in the reader's imagination than the bits of wisdom thrust forward along the way. McElroy should trust more to his talents for describing characters and their actions than to his predilection to philosophize.

Ultimately, it is the nature of truth which is being explored in *Lookout Cartridge*. Ironically, in this age of great scientific and technical skills and massive information retrieval systems, of mass media and instant communications, truth is more elusive than ever. We cannot look to scientific advancements or to technical growth to help us find truth, any more than we can look to movies or other giants of communication. The only place where we can and must look for the truth is in ourselves. All of us, like Cartwright, race through life, searching for the answer, but the end of the steeple chase is within us. Actually, the message, if such it is, of this dazzling and experimental novel, is almost conventional, unless the message *is* the medium.

Bruce D. Reeves

LORD BYRON'S WIFE

Author: Malcolm Elwin (1902-   )
Publisher: Harcourt, Brace and World (New York). 556 pp. $8.75
Type of work: Biography
Time: 1792-1860
Locale: England

A fully documented biography of the wife of the famous poet and a detailed study of the break-up of her marriage

> *Principal personages:*
> LADY BYRON (nee Anne Isabella Milbanke)
> LORD BYRON, her husband
> AUGUSTA ADA BYRON, their daughter
> SIR RALPH AND LADY MILBANKE (later Noel), Lady Byron's parents
> THE HON. AUGUSTA LEIGH, Byron's half sister
> LADY CAROLINE LAMB, Byron's mistress
> LADY MELBOURNE, Byron's confidante

The publication in 1961 of Doris Langley Moore's *The Late Lord Byron* and the ensuing controversy that raged for months in the staid columns of the London *Times Literary Supplement* demonstrate that the Byron mystery refuses to die. So here we have yet another book, the heart of which is that perennial question: what really caused the separation of Lord and Lady Byron that rocked London society in 1815-1816? Once again there has been a flood of interpretations and reinterpretations of the letters and remarks of these long-dead people.

The opening, for the first time, to scholars of the vast accumulation of Byron papers assembled by the poet's grandson, the second Earl of Lovelace, and now in the possession of the Earl of Lytton, has made possible this revival of the mystery. The papers had been used by members of the family; and, indeed, the mere history of their use, involving family loyalties and feuds, sympathies and antipathies, presents to the reader, unless he be a Byron specialist, an almost impenetrable labyrinth. Mrs. Moore and now Mr. Elwin are the first outsiders to be given access to all of these documents. As a result, we know a vast deal more about the day-by-day happenings in that tempestuous ménage in Piccadilly. But has the heart of this mystery been at last plucked out?

The flamboyance of Byron's personality, even more than his fame as a poet, has tended to push his wife into a somewhat minor role in the story of his life. He dominates the scene; she appears and disappears in accordance with the waxing and waning of her relations with him. Yet she had a life both before and after her brief marriage. The present volume, then, is a full-length attempt to present this life and to view the fatal marriage somewhat more from her side of the story. The almost unbelievable mass of documents that she preserved—sometimes as many as twelve letters a day—is the basis for the book.

Her father was Sir Ralph Milbanke, the sixth baronet, whose sister, for whom Byron had the greatest fondness, was Lady Melbourne, mother of the future Prime Minister, whose wife, in turn, was the notorious Lady Caroline Lamb. The Duchess of Devonshire called Milbanke "old twaddle Ralph," but his portrait by Reynolds shows a man with an interesting, almost handsome face. He was well-to-do and had a small but respectable political career. Anne Isabella's mother was the Hon. Judith Noel, a name which her husband took in 1815 in accordance with the will of Judith's brother, Lord Wentworth, so that the reader must adjust himself to the fact that the parents were called Noel after that date. Byron's feelings towards his mother-in-law can be judged from a comment, in 1821, in a letter to Augusta Leigh, that ". . . the old b——h will live forever because she is so amiable and useful." He always blamed Lady Milbanke for the breakup of his marriage.

Annabella, as the future Lady Byron was called, from a contraction of her two Christian names, had the usual upbringing of a daughter in an aristocratic family of that period. But two important facts emerge: she was the only child of rather elderly parents —both her father and mother were past forty when she was born—and she was intolerably spoiled. Whatever its other failings may have been, the spoiling of children was not among the weaknesses of Regency society. She seems to have been somewhat less than attractive: indulged, precocious, and from early childhood convinced that she could never be wrong in anything. One of her older friends referred to her as an "icicle." She went through two London seasons without attracting any great number of suitors. And then an ironic destiny caused her path to cross that of Byron.

The history of their meeting, their courtship, and their marriage has long been well known in its larger outlines, though never before has it been so thoroughly documented. It was inevitable that the two should meet, for the London society of those days was small, and everyone knew everyone else. Byron, in spite of his gaucherie, was a social lion at the time. He had already published the first parts of *Childe Harold* and had engaged in a hectic affair with Lady Caroline Lamb. Annabella met him in April of 1812. He felt free to marry, for the possible sale of Newstead Abbey promised a solution of his financial difficulties. These were great, for Byron was even more careless of money than was the usual young nobleman of the period. But to his surprise and, perhaps, relief, Miss Milbanke refused him, and he plunged into an affair with Lady Oxford. The period from July of 1813 to September of 1814 the author calls "Annabella in pursuit." Having rejected the lion of London society, the fashionable poet, the great lover, she changed her mind and began the game of luring him back. She succeeded all too well; he returned and was accepted in September of 1814, and in December he "reluctantly" traveled north for his wedding, loitering on the way. The fatal marriage was solemnized on January 2, 1815.

Here the reader may pause to consider the question of why such an unlikely marriage ever took place, for surely no more ill-suited couple could be imagined: a temperamental, undisciplined rake with a gift for poetry wedded to a solemn, humorless puritan with a gift for mathematics. Why did he ever marry her or she him? The answer is perhaps not too obscure: like all dissipated men, he was attracted by a woman who was the opposite of the sensual mistresses he had known; like all women, she had the ambition to reform a profligate and the conviction that she could do so. Such marriages have been countless and have inevitably ended in disaster; this one has become famous because of the fame of the husband.

The largest part of the present volume deals with the brief period of April to December of 1815, during which the Byrons were living in a much too expensive house in Piccadilly. Because of the vast documentation that has now become available, we can follow the events in this miniature lunatic asylum day by day, even at times hour by hour. It was an incredible scene: duns at the door, Byron deeply involved with the affairs of Drury Lane Theatre and with brandy, the birth of Augusta Ada, whom he called "sole daughter of my house and heart." Finding the situation intolerable, Annabella investigated the possibility of having Byron declared insane; failing in this attempt, she left him forever on January 15, 1816. But—and this is one of the strangest events in this strange affair—she wrote him an affectionate letter from her parents' home, so that the subsequent news that she had gone for good came as the greater shock to him.

Then followed the terribly involved legal question of the separation. By leaving her husband, Lady Byron had put herself in an awkward position. Divorce in those days, though possible, was not easy; it could be granted only by the ecclesiastic court, and to appear before that tribunal would mean the presentation of evidence that might prove extremely embarrassing to the parties involved. On the other hand, since Annabella had deserted Byron, the possibility always existed that he might successfully claim custody of the child, a possibility that she regarded with horror. So there

was a vast amount of maneuvering in an attempt to manipulate Byron into agreeing to a legal separation without a divorce, while well-intentioned friends were trying for a reconciliation. Byron was finally worn down; the decree of separation was signed, and, on April 25, 1816, he left England forever, in the midst of a scandal that, obviously, has not subsided after nearly a hundred and fifty years.

The great mystery, of course, has always been: what was the real cause of the separation? From 1816 until her death in 1860, Lady Byron devoted herself to but one purpose: to justify herself in the eyes of society for having left her husband. In accomplishing her purpose, she so beclouded the issues, laid so many false trails, that it is now almost impossible to get at the truth, and even Byron specialists are still busily arguing the case.

This much is clear: in this marriage were joined two such incompatible personalities that only disaster could be the outcome. Mr. Elwin, granting that Byron made an impossible husband, discounts most of the lurid "confessions" that the poet made to his wife on the grounds that Byron, realizing that Annabella had no sense of humor whatever, could not resist pulling her leg. And yet some overt act took place. What was it?

The story of incest between Byron and his half sister was first given wide currency by the meddlesome Harriet Beecher Stowe in 1870, and the tale was supported by Lord Lovelace in his *Astarte* in 1905. Yet Mrs. Moore, in *The Late Lord Byron*, pointed out that the "minutes" of the conversation between Lady Byron and Lady Caroline Lamb cannot be relied on because of Lady Caroline's well-known inability to tell the truth. In our own time, the tenth Lord Byron (a descendant of the poet's first cousin, George, who succeeded him as seventh baron), said that he was one of the few who knew the truth, that the cause of the separation was not incest, but that the true cause could never be divulged —a statement that brings us up against a stone wall. Two other causes for the separation have been advanced, each with its supporting evidence: that Byron compelled his wife to listen to minute descriptions of his affairs with prostitutes or that he compelled her to submit to unnatural sexual relations. If the second of these theories is true, one can understand why Lady Byron shuddered at the prospect of bringing the case into the ecclesiastic court. Among the three possibilities the reader must make his own choice.

There is one minor but interesting fact about Lady Byron after the separation, a fact that has been noted but not emphasized. In 1827 the death of Lord Scarsdale called the Barony of Wentworth out of abeyance, and Lady Byron became Baroness Wentworth in her own right. The Barony of Wentworth, created in 1529, was much older than that of Byron, created only in 1643; yet Annabella never claimed it and continued to be known as Lady Byron. Could she really have so deeply hated the memory of her husband if she chose to be known by his title rather than by her own much older one? Could she really have believed Augusta Leigh guilty of incest and yet continue to see and correspond with her almost daily for years?

This book is intended for the Byron specialist rather than for the general reader. Yet the author presents a memorable portrait of a woman whose lifelong conviction was that she must always be right in everything and that everyone else must be wrong. Mr. Elwin ends his story abruptly with the signing of the deed of separation and passes over Annabella's remaining years in but a few paragraphs. One would like to know more about those years and more about the daughter, Ada, Countess of Lovelace, that strange mathematical genius who must have shocked her mother by insisting upon being buried in the Byron vault beside the father whom she could not remember. Ada died in 1852. Lady Byron lived for eight more years, to complete what Mr. Elwin aptly calls that "unique monument of self-justification known as The Lovelace Papers."

Tench Francis Tilghman

LORD GRIZZLY

Author: Frederick F. Manfred (1912-   )
Publisher: The McGraw-Hill Book Company (New York). 281 pp. $3.75
Type of work: Novel
Time: 1823-1824
Locale: The American West and Northwest

A novel relating the adventures of one of the West's greatest mountain men, Hugh Glass

Principal characters:
HUGH GLASS, a mountain man
GENERAL ASHLEY, a militia general
BENDING REED, Hugh's faithful Sioux squaw
MAJOR HENRY, another officer
JIM BRIDGER, a mountain man
JOHN S. ("FITZ") FITZGERALD, another mountain man

A generation ahead of the settlers, the farthest reaches of the American West were explored by wilderness-loving trappers who called themselves mountain men. It was they who searched the river valleys of the West, even beyond the continental divide, for the furs that styles demanded. Those men lived alone or in small groups, trusting to hard-earned wilderness lore, personal strength and vigor, skill with weapons, and luck to carry them through the dangers of terrain, weather, savage beasts, and Indians. In all the annals of the mountain men there are no names more deserving of the stories—legendary and true—that surround them than the names of Jedediah Smith, Jim Bridger, and their fellows. One of the most honored names is that of Hugh Glass, who is the Chief White Grizzly of Frederick Manfred's *Lord Grizzly*.

Among the tales of the mountain men, adventures filled with fury, excitement, hate, lust, and brawling, there is probably none quite so appropriate to a novel as that of Hugh Glass after he had been mauled by a grizzly bear while hunting in what is now the northwestern portion of South Dakota.

The author points out in his Preface to *Lord Grizzly* that the book is a novel, but that it is a novel based on the real-life adventures of his hero. Before he began to write, Manfred collected all the extant accounts and legends that related to the life of Hugh Glass and especially those dealing with the battle with the grizzly, the desertion by comrades, the crawl back to Fort Kiowa, and the showdown with the men who had left him helpless in tne wilderness to face a cruel death.

The story, even in its bare outlines, is a heroic affair as Manfred tells it. Hugh Glass or, as the Indians named him, Chief White Grizzly, long before his famous adventure had deserted his wife and two children in Pennsylvania to lead a wandering life in search of freedom. Throughout Hugh's life he often became embroiled in trouble because he hated laws and all other restrictions. No one knows exactly what he did in the years after he left his family until he became a mountain man. Apparently he served for a time as a buccaneer under the notorious Jean Laffite.

In *Lord Grizzly*, the reader meets Hugh Glass as a man in his fifties, somewhat older than most of the mountain men, in June, 1823. Hugh is a member of a party of men working under General Ashley, a militia general, on a fur-trading expedition up the Missouri River. Attacked by Indians, the party retreats by boat to Fort Kiowa, where Hugh finds his faithful Sioux squaw, Bending Reed. Soon after the retreat, Hugh sets out with another party under Major Henry to establish forts for the beaver trade. When the party of whites is attacked by Indians, Hugh covers up the fact that the two sentinels, Jim Bridger (then just a lad) and John S. "Fitz" Fitzgerald, had been asleep.

The next day Hugh Glass, in a fret because he has been ordered to shave off his whiskers, leaves the party to do a little meat hunting on his own. While afoot he meets a female grizzly with cubs. Although the bear mauls him terribly, he finally kills her with his knife. The rest of the party find him apparently dying. In fear of Indians, they leave him with two comrades—Jim Bridger and Fitz. The two men are also forced to desert him when Indians attack, but they manage to draw the savages away from the helpless Hugh. Glass, left without food, medicines, water, or weapons, miraculously recovers, sets his cracked leg bone, and crawls and hobbles back toward Fort Kiowa, almost two hundred miles away. Believing he was treacherously deserted by his two companions, Hugh Glass vows revenge. Barely recuperated, he leaves Fort Kiowa, believing himself on a God-sent mission of vengeance on his supposedly treacherous friends. He travels northwest up the Missouri to Fort Tilton and on to Major Henry's outpost on the Yellowstone river in what is now Montana. There he finds Jim Bridger. Hugh

"loans" Bridger his life, but swears to seek out the older Fitz and kill him.

By this time the spring of 1824 has arrived and Hugh starts back eastward to Fort Atkinson in charge of a party carrying beaver pelts. Near the border of what are now Nebraska and Wyoming, on the banks of the North Platte River, the men are attacked by Indians. Hugh escapes and works his way back to Fort Kiowa after crossing the famous Badlands, and then goes down the Missouri to Fort Atkinson. Word of Hugh's search for vengeance has already arrived. One day Hugh finds Fitz, also an escapee from Indian attack, stumbling afoot into the fort.

Two days later, almost a year after the desertion, Hugh Glass has his showdown with Fitz, who has recovered from his ordeal. Fitz returns Hugh's famous rifle and the bag of money left for Hugh by the men in Major Henry's party. Hugh, sensing Fitz's sincerity, is unable to bring himself to shoot; he remembers his own mistakes, including the desertion of his family, and the many comrades he has already lost as a result of accidents and Indian attacks.

Those brief paragraphs carry only the outlines of a story already famous and cannot tell the story, as Manfred does in the novel, by relating the tale in all its grim determination, hardship, and fearsome detail. Here the mountain men come to life again, and with Hugh Glass one goes through the agonies of the battle with the female grizzly—a skinning knife and the strength of one man pitted against the bestiality of the two-inch claws and the immense teeth of the enraged bear bent on protecting her cubs. One endures also with Hugh Glass the mental anguish of being left alone to die beside his own grave by comrades thought sincere. One endures with Hugh the pain of splinting the broken bone, the grimness of the crawl across the prairie wastes, the bottomless hunger that is alleviated only partially and occasionally by eating rattlesnakes, gophers, tops of grass, and wild berries, and one endures with the hero the fear of facing Indian savagery and torture if he is caught, horribly wounded and crippled, without even a weapon to forestall by his own hand the awful agonies of death at the hands of savages.

Only in the novel, too, does Hugh's desire for vengeance come alive. By boat, afoot, and on horseback, day after day, month after month, Hugh Glass relentlessly follows the trail after Jim Bridger and Fitz. It is almost with horror that one reads of Hugh's determination, guided as he is by his belief that he has a divine mission to perform. When spring comes early, when he miraculously escapes Indians, and when he manages to cross the Badlands afoot, Hugh feels that God has helped him. Such assumption of divine assistance cannot help changing Hugh. It is not age alone that turns his hair and beard white in less than a year.

The novel is not without its pleasanter side. Even some comedy is present in Bending Reed, Hugh's squaw, who believes herself possessed by a contrary god. There are marvelously written scenes of buffalo hunts on the prairies, of the camps that the trappers make at night and the feats of eating that go on after fasting all day on the trail. It was a picturesque as well as a dangerous life that the mountain men led, but they would have no other. They were a race that could not outlast the coming of the settlements and civilization, but they are a vivid page in American history. Who is there left on the American scene who can say that he has pleasure as they did with a breakfast of whiskey and pancakes—the whiskey to wake him up and the pancakes to weight him down?

Many readers will be delighted to discover that the author, Frederick F. Manfred, is Feike Feikema, author of *The Golden Bowl, Chokecherry Tree, The Primitive,* and other books. Manfred used the pen name of Feike Feikema from 1944 to 1951. This is his first novel published under his own name, but it is as full of vitality and richness as the others.

LORD ROCHESTER'S MONKEY

Author: Graham Greene (1904-   )
Publisher: The Viking Press (New York). Illustrated. 231 pp. $15.95
Type of work: Biography
Time: 1647-1680
Locale: England

A biography of John Wilmot, Earl of Rochester, by one of England's foremost novelists

Principal personages:
JOHN WILMOT, Earl of Rochester
ELIZABETH MALLET, his wife
ELIZABETH BARRY, his mistress
CHARLES II, King of England

Written between 1931 and 1934, Graham Greene's biography of John Wilmot, Earl of Rochester, was originally rejected by his publisher, Heinemann, and was laid aside until its belated publication in 1974. At the time of its composition, the only available collection of Rochester's poems was John Hayward's somewhat unreliable Nonesuch edition; the only modern life of Rochester was the 1927 biography by Johannes Prinz, which not only was inaccessible to English readers but also was weakened in several places by inaccuracies and omissions. Previously, Rochester's literary reputation, along with that of Restoration poets such as Richard Lovelace and Sir John Suckling, had been dimmed by the brighter light of John Dryden; considered minor figures, Rochester and the other "Cavalier poets," if covered at all in anthologies, were represented by a mere handful of love songs. Since the 1930's, critics have given serious consideration to Rochester's poetry, but biographers, with the exception of Professor Pinto in his *Enthusiast in Wit,* have largely ignored the life of one of the most notorious participants in the colorful, often bizarre drama of Charles II's reign.

In part this neglect has undoubtedly been due to the fact that records from John Wilmot's life are often scanty or difficult to authenticate; verifiable evidence, irrefutable facts, and documented dates are almost absent from the biographer's available material. Greene is faced with this dilemma at every turn. Almost nothing can be stated with certainty, while a great deal must be based on conjecture. Working thus with a very shaky skeleton of proven data, the author must rely on a variety of secondary sources to flesh out his subject and bring him to life for his readers. In many instances, for example, he must propose a chronological sequence based upon such ephemeral information as the state of the Earl's relations with his wife or mistress, the condition of his health, the political or religious sentiment expressed in a poem, or the mood conveyed in a letter.

To readers familiar with Graham Greene's "entertainments" (*The Third Man*) or with his serious fiction

(*The Power and the Glory; The Heart of the Matter*), the relatively undistinguished prose of *Lord Rochester's Monkey* may come as quite a surprise. The distinctive and polished style of the novels does not grace the biography, the text of which even lapses at times into obscure, awkward, or confusing constructions. Whether this lack of smoothness reflects a creative writer's difficulty working within the expository prose medium, or is simply an object lesson in the change that forty years of experience can work in an author's style, can only be guessed; that *Lord Rochester's Monkey* would have benefited from judicious revision is certain.

Stylistic weaknesses in the text, however, are compensated for by the excellent artistic layout of the book. Greene's biography is profusely and beautifully illustrated by more than a hundred original photographs and reproductions of paintings, engravings, and manuscript pages. With their captions, often accompanied by pertinent quotations from Rochester's poetry, these illustrations could almost stand alone as a photographic essay of one poet's life and the portrait of an age.

Beyond simple problems of style, and notwithstanding the merits of its artistic format, *Lord Rochester's Monkey* suffers from serious flaws of both content and organization. Chapter One, "Landscape," fails to provide sufficient thematic direction for the rest of the work. The bulk of the chapter is devoted to describing the character and political intrigues of the poet's father, Henry Wilmot, while the remainder briefly summarizes young John's childhood and

schooling. Inordinate space is given to a father who saw his son perhaps once or twice and died before the boy was ten years of age. On the other hand, inadequate treatment is given to the character of the poet's mother, Anne St. John, Countess of Rochester, who was to outlive husband, son, and grandchildren and figure so critically in all the lives she touched. Likewise, the few pages devoted to the earl's brief stay at Oxford leave unanswered crucial questions regarding his personal and moral development, although the dearth of records from this period probably makes such omissions unavoidable.

The remaining ten chapters of the book are arranged topically rather than chronologically, and cover such areas of Rochester's life as his naval experiences during the English-Dutch sea battles of the 1660's; his curiously paradoxical friendship with King Charles; his courtship and marriage; his relations with a long progression of mistresses; his literary career; and his deathbed religious fears and repentance. Such a method of organization is disconcerting in places, since the reader misses a sense of time continuity and tends to lose his bearings amid some of the sudden shifts between periods of the earl's life. On the other hand, some of the individual chapters are excellent character studies in which Greene's subject comes alive both through his own actions and writings and through the range of responses that his behavior provoked in friends and enemies. "The Poet and the King," for example, a particularly fascinating chapter, explores Rochester's lifelong relationship with the Restoration monarch.

Rochester's career as one of the inner circle of dissolute courtiers surrounding the king began early. He first came to Charles II's attention as a youth of seventeen, when he was recommended by the king as a suitor to the sought-after heiress Elizabeth Mallet; three years later he insisted upon seating his young friend in the House of Lords although he was not of age. Throughout his life Wilmot benefited from numerous royal favors, including such appointments as Gentleman of the Bedchamber (which carried a yearly pension of £1,000), Keeper of the King's Game in the County of Oxford, and Keeper and Ranger of Woodstock Park (where Rochester spent much time and eventually died). In return Charles was rewarded for all these gifts with countless satiric lashes as the object of biting wit and scathing criticism in Rochester's poetry. Time and time again, Rochester would be banished from the Court as a result of a particularly brutal satire, and it was during these periods of exile that he would live in London disguised as an innkeeper or a quack physician. But always he would be forgiven and reinstalled in the Royal circle. As the recitation of such incidents progresses, the reader gains as much insight into the king as into the poet; he begins to understand the man whose "abysmal cynicism" was so pervasive that he never expected to be loved by anyone, but appreciated wit and gaiety above all—even when they were exercised at his expense.

Other sections of especial interest are those dealing with Rochester's famous mistress ("Elizabeth Barry") and with his wife and children ("Still-Life"). In the latter, Greene examines the unhappy union of two young, witty, and intelligent people in a marriage that could satisfy the needs of neither party; he traces the husband's development from affection, to constant infidelity, to resentment of his wife's forgiveness, to anger and finally bitter guilt and remorse. In "Elizabeth Barry," the reader sees the cynical seducer of so many women himself succumb to the actress renowned for her stage performances and notorious for her sexual license. Greene arranges a series of key letters between the lovers—all undated—in a sequence based on the progression of Rochester's feelings from blind infatuation, through the tortures of jealousy, and eventually into complete disillusionment and the pain of unreturned passion. In these as in all the chapters of *Lord Rochester's Monkey,* the author buttresses his text with extensive quotations from the earl's poetry. But, contrary to what a reader might anticipate from a biographer who is himself a literary figure, there is no literary criticism of the poems; Rochester's work is cited merely for the biographical evidence which its subject matter affords.

In the final provocative chapter, "The Death of Doriment," Greene recounts events from the earl's last months, during which his health declined steadily toward what he knew was certain death. Drawing much of his data from records left by Rochester's confessor, Dr. Burnet, the author outlines the arguments on the nature of the universe, the existence of God, and the value of Christianity which allegedly occurred between dying cynic and fashionable cleric. As we read of Rochester's final repentance and resignation in the face of death, however, this biography's most disturbing weakness becomes apparent: we have come full circle to the end of a life whose central motivations have never been identified. The crucial question, which is raised on several occasions throughout the book, is never answered: What caused young Rochester, after a childhood of such bright hope and promise, suddenly to shift his course into a debilitating life of drunkenness and debauchery? At the close of Greene's biography, the reader is left with the riddle unsolved and George Etherege's poignant description of Rochester fresh in his mind: "I know he is a Devil, but he has something of the Angel yet undefac'd in him."

Nancy G. Ballard

LOSING BATTLES

Author: Eudora Welty (1909–   )
Publisher: Random House (New York). 436 pp. $7.95
Type of work: Novel
Time: A summer in the 1930's
Locale: The hill country of northeast Mississippi

A seriocomic Southern novel of family and place, of youth and age, of life and love and death

> *Principal characters:*
> ELVIRA JORDAN VAUGHN, "Granny"
> HER BEECHAM GRANDCHILDREN: Nathan; Curtis, m. Beck; Dolphus, m. Birdie; Percy, m. Nanny; Noah Webster, m. Cleo; Beulah, m. Ralph Renfro
> THE RENFRO CHILDREN: Jack, m. Gloria; Ella Fay; Etoyle; Elvie; Vaughn
> LADY MAY RENFRO, Jack and Gloria's baby
> MISS LEXIE RENFRO, Ralph's sister
> BROTHER BETHUNE, a Baptist preacher
> CURLY STOVALL, a storekeeper
> MISS ORA STOVALL, his sister
> AYCOCK COMFORT, Jack's friend
> JUDGE AND MRS. OSCAR MOODY
> MISS JULIA MORTIMER, the former teacher of Banner School

Eudora Welty's new novel, her first since 1954, contains many of the characteristics of content and style present in her writing since her early short stories. Also, it is partly reminiscent of her second novel, *Delta Wedding*, published in 1946, since most of its characters belong to one large family gathered together for a particular occasion. In *Delta Wedding* the Fairchilds and numerous relatives from nearby are present for the wedding of Dabney, the second of her parents' eight children, to a plantation overseer. In *Losing Battles* the descendants of "Granny" Vaughn (along with many in-laws) make up most of the large gathering at the home of Beulah and Ralph Renfro in Banner Community to celebrate Granny's ninetieth birthday and simultaneously the return from Parchman, the Mississippi prison farm, of Jack Renfro, the eldest of the five living Renfro children. The immediate action covers the hot, dry summer Sunday of Granny's birthday and a part of the following day. But, because much of the novel is made up of reminiscences and recountings of earlier events, the complete time span covers many years.

Miss Welty has employed varied techniques in developing her several novels and her many short stories. *Delta Wedding*, for example, uses a shifting point of view so that the reader perceives events, people, and themes through the separate and diverse minds of several characters. In contrast, *The Ponder Heart* is an extended monologue to an unnamed listener by a chatty Southern woman whose mind and heart color with love and humor the story she is telling. In *Losing Battles* the author is the external observer who gives needed facts, describes scenes, and reports dialogue, leaving the reader to interpret for himself what he has mentally seen and heard. This technique has the advantage of keeping the author screened in the background, thus making the book seem to progress by itself. But, in a novel of more than four hundred pages peopled by a large number of talkative characters, the technique sometimes taxes one's patience and his attention-span. The talk, true and entertaining as so much of it is, often makes one feel like leaving the garrulous older folks and joining the children at their games or, like some of the well-fed elders toward the end of the hot Sunday, just snoozing away while the tongues continue to wag.

The cast of characters in *Losing Battles* is so large that one is grateful to Miss Welty for listing all of the significant ones in several groupings at the beginning of the novel. One often finds it necessary to turn back to the list to learn again who belongs to which group and his or her relationship to the others. Even a few of the characters themselves, who see one another only at the big annual reunions, have to have their memories refreshed regarding details of family relationships and past occurrences.

A key question in the diffused story line of the novel involves the relationship of Gloria to the Vaughn-Beecham-Renfro clan. A foundling, she was called Gloria Short until she married Jack Renfro the night before he began a two-year term at Parchman for the theft of a safe from Curly Stovall's store. In the repeated (and often cruel) teasing she is made to endure from various members of the family, she is mocked as the daughter of Rachel Sojourner, who had put up with similar teasing

when for a while she helped Granny Vaughn care for the orphaned Beecham children. Though granting that Rachel may have been her mother, she resents the suggestion that her father was Sam Dale Beecham, the only one of the Beecham boys who never teased Rachel and who may (or may not) have married her before he died in World War I.

Just why Gloria is so opposed to being a Beecham, she does not specify, though there is a clear hint of her reason in what she says to Jack at the end of the novel: "And some day, some day yet, we'll move to ourselves. And there'll be just you and me and Lady May." She knows the clannishness of Jack's family and she has apparently learned long ago what is made evident to the reader during the lengthy discussion of Miss Julia Mortimer and her lifetime dedication to learning and teaching: to the Beechams education is largely a foolish waste of time. Miss Julia tried to inspire the Beechams long ago and lost the battle. As Uncle Dolphus says, "Yes'm, she taught the generations. She was our cross to bear." He, like several of the others, seems proud of his own ignorance.

But Miss Julia *was* an inspiration to Gloria, her prize pupil who grew up and became the teacher in Miss Julia's old school at Banner, aspiring to follow in her footsteps until she fell in love with her oldest pupil whom she had determined to get through the seventh grade anyway. But the conception of Lady May, the marriage to Jack, and Jack's jailing (in that order) put an end to her plans. Jack's answer to Gloria's wish to be alone with him and Lady May is: "And a string of other little chaps to come along behind her. You just can't have too many, is the way I look at it." As Miss Julia lost her battle against ignorance in Banner, so Gloria will apparently lose her battle to escape from the Beechams and the Renfros. She seems doomed to live out her life in the community that Judge Moody calls the "very pocket of ignorance."

As in much of Miss Welty's writing, the events and conversations in *Losing Battles* alternate in mood: from laughter to tears, from comedy to pathos, from high spirits to anger or to sorrow. As the various family members arrive for the reunion, there are shouted greetings, jesting remarks, questions, and bits of news. The reminiscences begin with the account of Jack's theft of Curly's safe in order to regain his dead grandmother Ellen's wedding ring which simple-minded Ella Fay had traded to Curly for candy. There is comedy in the recalling of Jack's struggles with the heavy safe and more comedy in the trial before Judge Moody (though the hilarious absurdity of the trial in *The Ponder Heart* is missing). Jack's joy at his return home (in order to get to the reunion he escaped one day before he was to be released) is lessened by his learning of the deaths of Grandfather Vaughn and of Jack's stud horse Dan. Gloria's happiness in having Jack again with her and Lady May is followed by her tears over the news of Miss Julia's sudden death and her troubled memory of the warning Miss Julia gave her against marrying Jack, a warning followed by Miss Julia's laughter. Jack tenderly and lovingly tries to comfort and reassure his wife, who bitterly comments, "But everybody finds us. Living or dead"— and they return to the noisy, hungry crowd at the reunion dinner which ends the long day.

The atmosphere of a semi-rural Southern community infuses *Losing Battles* through the plentiful talk, the place names (Foxtown, Flowery Branch, Free Will), and such reminders of the natural world as the dust which lies everywhere, a mocking bird "letting loose for all he was worth, singing the two sides of a fight," yellow butterflies "as wild and bright as people's notions and dreams," and lightning that "branched and ran over the world with an insect lightness."

Miss Welty's felicity of style has been evident since her earliest stories. It is seen intermittently in *Losing Battles* when she as author takes over from the talkative Banner residents and their visitors. Gloria's hair is "wedding-ring gold" and her baby's as "red as a cat's ear against the sun." Gloria's freckled cheeks are "speckled as sweet warm pears" and she sees herself in Lady May when she notices "the first freckle lying in the hollow of the baby's throat, like a spilled drop of honey." The backs of aged Granny's hands "showed their blotches like pansy faces pressed into the papery skin." Mr. Renfro spanks the watermelons lined up on his porch and they resound "like horses ready to go." In the August sun the wooden cover over a well has "the heat of a platter under the Sunday hen." Here and there one finds the beauty of an impressionist painting in such a passage as this which pictures the reunion scene toward the end of the day:

> Around them the white tablecloths, clotted with shadows, still held the light, and so did old men's white shirts, and Sunday dresses with their skirts spread round or in points on the evening hill. The tables in their line appeared strung and hinged like the Big Dipper in the night sky, and the dia-

monds of the other cloths seemed to repeat themselves for a space far out on the deep blue of dust that now reached to Heaven. Now and then a flying child, calling a name, still streaked through everybody, and some of the die-hards turned themselves round and round or rolled themselves over and over down the long front hill, time after time, toward an exhaustion of joy.

With *Losing Battles,* Eudora Welty has shown again the rightness of her reputation as one of our finest authors of fiction.

Henderson Kincheloe

THE LOSS OF EL DORADO
A History

Author: V.S. Naipaul (1932–   )
Publisher: Alfred A. Knopf (New York). 335 pp. $7.50
Type of work: History
Time: Sixteenth to nineteenth centuries
Locale: Trinidad

> *An account of the colonization of the island of Trinidad*

This book intends to confront the present appearance of Trinidad with its history. The island now seems the archetype of all that is placid and hedonistic, but its history is a compendium of violence, conquest, and tragedy. Naipaul begins with the conflict of English and Spanish over the primitive island. The two civilized nations had a good deal less trouble with each other than with the native inhabitants of the island and the fearsome tropical conditions that protected them from invaders. A small Spanish garrison was annihilated by troops under the command of Sir Walter Ralegh, who then set about making the island a part of the English dominions. His journals are used to very good purpose by Naipaul, whose research in general seems far better than that of the usual amateur historian. Ralegh's speech to the assembled native tribes is worth remembering:

> I made them understand that I was the servant of a Queene, who was the great casique of the North, and a virgine, and had more casiqui under her than there were trees in that yland: that shee was an enemie to the Castellani in respect of their tyrannie and oppression, and that she delivered all such nations about her, as were by them oppressed. . . .

Deliverance and oppression were in fact to be the theme of the next phase of the island's colonization. Ralegh, having triumphed over the Spaniards, then developed his invasion of the entire area of "Guinea," that part of the Caribbean containing Trinidad and other potentially rich resources. His first attempt was a disaster that has become famous, and has lingered in the Western imagination. A landing on one of the rich shorelines of Guinea resulted in an appalling defeat of the expeditionary force. They were impaled by poison arrows, devastated by the heat and humidity, and finally overcome by the multitudinous sicknesses of a tropical coast. The first phase then of Trinidad's history ended with conquest by the English, but at a tremendous cost both to themselves and to their dream of a New World abounding in gold and jewels.

The next phase was perhaps more cruel, though more pedestrian. The heroic conflict gave way to a different kind of enterprise. The native Indians, "dulled by defeat and disappointments," gave up the unequal battle against the representatives of civilization. They were in the future to pose great problems for government, but none of a military nature. A great shipping trade was built up and plantations began to make their appearance. The produce of Trinidad became famous, especially in the form of rare woods, in the marketplaces of Amsterdam and London. As Naipaul puts it, "the New

World as medieval adventure had ended; it had become a cynical extension of the developing old world, its commercial underside."

In this phase the face of the Caribbean and of Trinidad changed entirely, for there were new forces beyond the conception of the original adventurers now straining for dominion of this rich part of the earth. Because there were merchant navies now populating these waters a whole new economic situation presented itself: it was easier to get a share of El Dorado at second-hand than at first. The buccaneers left it to the miners and merchants and priests of the Caribbean to accumulate the wealth; they took it only after it was in transit. Perhaps the counterparts of the buccaneers were the planters, who took over entire islands and converted them from fishing societies to vast sugar plantations based on the institution of slavery. Under these circumstances the original tribes had no chance to maintain their form—or even to exist.

It was not surprising that there should be sporadic attempts at rebellion. These were impulsive, unplanned responses to the kind of conditions imposed by the new masters. These revolts did not have political ends in mind, nor were they even directed by some sense of strategy or function. When a condition became intolerable the decimated remains of the original tribes took on for a moment their original bravery. Such outbreaks were quickly and with relative ease repressed, leaving behind only a barbarous toll of seventeenth century justice. By the close of this century the island was depopulated, as much as nine-tenths of its native population having succumbed to disease, warfare, difficult conditions of labor, and judicial extermination. Trinidad lapsed into the quiet of the grave.

Once more under the rule of Spain, the island remained quiet and barren, its principal activities being restricted to some planting, trade, and the development of a religious mission. But the advent of slavery promised a vast and unpredictable change for this and other islands of the Caribbean. A great many French citizens were invited to settle the island of Trinidad, and they brought with them large establishments of slave Negroes from Africa. The island, originally the home of the Carib Indians, then conquered by England, governed by Spain, was now the mixing vessel of still two more civilizations. It was not a peaceable arrangement. When, to a colonized area was added the conflict of national powers and the character of slave culture, the results were almost certain to be dangerous and hostile to any form of community.

Perhaps the center of Naipaul's narrative is the long civil war that ensued. The planters, at the head of the island's economy, naturally wished for the greatest profits imaginable and the most static conditions of social life. The slaves, who formed the vast majority of the social pyramid, declined into superstition and criminal gangs. The central institution of the island became the jail: "it could not be otherwise: the planters of the commission, entering the jail, faced the tortures, confessions, and rotting bodies like the African darkness that might overwhelm them all." From this point begins the appalling account of judicial torture that characterized an entire century of the island's development. The author believes that this institution of judicial torture was, in fact, the central matter of importance. It defined the relationships of two conflicting classes of humanity.

Under Spanish, and later under the new English authority the process of judicial torture was carried to a very wide degree indeed. The details, which are harrowing, were discovered by Naipaul in long-buried records of depositions and interrogations in the Public Records Office. They involved imprisonment, fettering, flogging and other corporal forms of punishment, mutilation, torture, and a variety of painful kinds of execution. These punishments were applied regardless of age or sex. In fact, the most celebrated case, that of Luisa Calderon, demonstrated the impartiality of that particular form of justice. This case, which was gone into in detail, proved to Lord Castlereagh's government that a very great number of atrocities had been legally committed in a territory under the mandate of Great Britain. But no great public reform was stimulated, and no new system of legislation was designed to cure these desperate ills. Trinidad was simply too remote, its population too heterogeneous for a world empire to be concerned.

The ironies, as Naipaul sees them, are these: the notion of history on Trini-dad defeats the imagination, since after the traumatic actions of conquest and settlement came the long periods of neglect and decadence. Great—and infamous—things were done, but they disappeared into the maw of time. The great acts of heroism of Ralegh and his opponents resulted in the creation of a desert. The shift of interest to the northern islands allowed Trinidad to disappear from public view; one of the most bitterly comic things in this book is the ignorance of the Spanish government at one time, and of the British Foreign Office at another, as to where the island was, and who "owned" it. The development of a slave civilization resulted in appalling cultural limits, the bottom of the social pyramid being separated from the top by a fantastically vicious judicial system operating under Spanish laws of the conquest. The end of slavery early in the nineteenth century meant only that the island could once again be ignored. With none of its problems ever rationally confronted or settled, it became a place for tourists—after once having been a functioning culture of its own.

Ronald Berman

THE LOST HONOR OF KATHARINA BLUM

Author: Heinrich Böll (1917-   )
Translated from the German by Leila Vennewitz
Publisher: McGraw-Hill Book Company (New York). 140 pp. $7.95
Type of work: Novel
Time: February, 1974
Locale: Germany, possibly Bonn

> *The story of the destruction of an intelligent, sensitive, and morally pure woman by a corrupt and amoral society*

Principal characters:
> KATHARINA BLUM, a self-employed housekeeper and caterer
> HUBERT AND GERTRUDE BLORNA, her employers; the former, also her lawyer
> ELSE WOLTERSHEIM, her godmother and friend
> LUDWIG GOTTEN, the man Katharina meets at a dance and falls in love with
> ALOIS STRAUBLEDER, an eminent industrialist, a friend of the Blornas and would-be lover of Katharina
> WERNER TOTGES, reporter for the *News*

The Lost Honor of Katharina Blum by Nobel Prize-winner Heinrich Böll is a complex study of the quality of human life in the world today. The novel's subtitle, "Or: How Violence Develops and Where It Can Lead," indicates its primary thematic concern; it is an investigation which eventually involves all aspects of society.

The primary level of the plot is almost a traditional murder mystery, a genre generally equated with sex and violence presented in a sentimental and sensational manner. The attitude of this narrator, however, differs obviously: there is a detached, objective, repeated desire to avoid the usually overplayed blood, guts, and sex, and an insistence upon accuracy of fact and detail. In addition, the reader is immediately told the bare facts of the murder and the identity of the murderer, who turns herself in only a few hours after the crime. The focus of the novel becomes, then, not the traditional "Who did it?" but "Why was it done?"

With such a focus, the character of the murderess, Katharina Blum, assumes major importance in the final impact of the novel. Katharina is almost an archetypal dream: the poor but virtuous girl who, because of her own intelligence, drive, and virtue has achieved an independent financial status, an apartment she owns, a business she owns, and the respect of all who know her. Married early to escape her family home, Katharina left her husband because his attitude toward her compromised her sense of human dignity. Although considered attractive by the socially and economically powerful men she meets in her profession, like Clarissa, she holds herself morally pure for the man she can truly love.

When Katharina accidentally meets Ludwig Götten at a dance the night before Carnival, they immediately and totally fall in love. Unfortunately, he is sought by the police, who trace him to her apartment. Her assistance in his escape, the arrests of both at different times, the attendant publicity, the murder, the couple's determination to reunite after their prison terms—these events form the basic plot around which the thematic concerns are structured. Although the plot may be reminiscent of a soap opera, as in all great works the telling difference comes in the reverberations, in the treatment of problems inherent in human nature, and in the conflict between the individual's sense of values and self-worth and the amoral or corrupt social system.

The honorable but defenseless world of Katharina is impinged upon first by police suspicion, then by the press accounts of her "lost honor." As the obscene phone calls and mails mount, as the newspaper's stories grow more lurid, referring to her as a whore, a Communist conspirator, and the murderer of her mother, Katharina's self-control breaks in a frustrated act of violence: she smashes things on the walls of her immaculate, once-treasured apartment. As public insults against her morality and invasions of her privacy —encouraged by the *News*—increase, the almost inevitable result of outrage and frustration occurs: the act of utmost violence, murder. Premeditation is not proven; provocation is. With no one else to protect her honor, the act, as stated in the opening of the novel, seems "not inexplicable, but almost logical." From beginning to end, Katharina has no moral misgivings about her deed. She feels no remorse, an emotion which can only result from the betrayal of one's inherent moral code, one's "honor";

Katharina has not betrayed her code. No remorse, therefore, is felt, either by the heroine or by society, which has no moral code to violate. Katharina's concept of "honor" is obviously an unfashionable anachronism. This upside-down world in which morality becomes a stigma is recognizably the world in which we all might find ourselves trapped.

The innate morality of Katharina serves as a standard by which the rest of the representatives of society are judged. Her insistence on precision and correctness far exceeds that of the policemen who question her. The Police Commissioner casually invades her privacy by wiretapping with no moral or legal hesitation; he even publicly praises the *News* for collecting and publishing information which the police could not legally obtain.

The press, as exemplified by the *News* and its star reporter, Tötges, is a sensational exploiter of half-truths and fabrications, and cares only for its own profits. Even Tötges' murder and funeral are used as an occasion to extol a "victim of the profession" who has, ironically, victimized Katharina, her mother, the Blornas, and, potentially, Else. Only the economically powerful Sträubleder, who tried to force his attentions on Katharina, and who has the political contacts to control the paper, escapes—by turning attention on his friends, the Blornas. Katharina's murder of the reporter, of course, can only have symbolic value: he is immediately replaced. The paper's sensationalistic exploitation will continue because the public will pay for such stories.

This novel, then, becomes not

simply a "new twist" in the murder mystery genre, but an indictment of the "lost honor" of modern society. The crimes of Katharina and Götten are clearly less than those of their "civilization." Götten steals from an already corrupt system—the Army—with the collaboration of some of its admired, well-known leaders; Katharina lies to protect the man she loves and kills to avenge her honor. The true indictment is brought against the establishment itself. The narrator, almost hysterically, remarks at one point that no one is excluded: the Church, which takes no moral stands; the lawyers; the "industrialists who are professors or politicians on the side"; the Crime Commissioner; and the system of justice which does not worry about the moral and psychological effects of wiretapping, even on the men who are paid to eavesdrop. Even the rejects of society, the prisoners, will reject Katharina for the same reason society sent her to jail: her moral incorruptibility. The narrator clearly has a hard time attempting to bring the order of a well-constructed novel to bear on a world which no longer has the sense of order and cohesiveness which comes from shared moral values. Furthermore, Böll indirectly suggests that most modern art, like the *News,* panders to the worst of human nature. The indications of deterioration and collapse in the lawyer Blorna at the end likewise seem to apply, not primarily to him, but to his society, which at best lacks any concern for morality, and at worst persecutes the true moralists, be they housekeepers like Katharina or artists.

The full ironic significance of the setting of the novel, the Christian festival of Carnival, is seen only in retrospect. The traditional spiritual meaning of the festival, in which man both celebrates the joys of the world and the flesh and prepares to bid them farewell for Lent, can only be recognized in the attitudes of Katharina and Götten. In contrast, society (as epitomized in the Carnival "officials," the town's leading businessmen) worries about the "sacrilege" of the murder because it might damage business profits—the only reason Carnival has been restored and promoted.

At one point in the novel, a character questions whether the *News,* the most obvious villain of the novel, operates as it does because of the structure of society. The answer is yes. Blame lies with society's lack of morality: the whole establishment, in one way or another, commits "acts of violence" against the individual's sense of privacy, decency, and morality, acts which are accepted as normal or even commendable procedures. *The Lost Honor of Katharina Blum* may exaggerate the problem, but exaggeration is an effective traditional tool used by morally indignant masters of social satire such as Jonathan Swift. As the narrator comments after one brief eruption of violence settled by an artist, "From this occurrence plus the preceding acts of violence it should be possible to deduce that Art still has a social function." Böll's novel becomes a case in point, analyzing as it does the causes and effects of acts of violence in our civilization.

Ann E. Reynolds

LOST IN THE FUNHOUSE

Author: John Barth (1928–   )
Publisher: Doubleday and Company (Garden City, New York). 201 pp. $4.95
Type of work: Fiction for print, tape, live voice
Time: The twentieth century and antiquity
Locale: The Maryland coast and anywhere

A "series" of short humorous fiction pieces, experimenting with media, which offers musings on existence and life as fiction itself

John Barth's reputation has already been established by *The Sot-Weed Factor,* a comic epic set in seventeenth century America, and by *Giles Goat-Boy,* a humorous but somewhat ponderous multilevel satire on the university and on civilization. *Lost in the Funhouse,* although it also contains many comic elements, differs greatly in form and subject from both of the above-mentioned works. Barth himself calls this work a "series"; this series of short and individually unified fiction pieces has its unity in its arrangement. Not all of the pieces were composed, points out Barth, for the medium of print; tape and live voice are the other media to be employed, and in a prefatory note the author lists the items along with the most desirable medium, or media, for each. The expressed means of delivery are given specifically; "Autobiography," for example, is "for monophonic tape and visible but silent author." Certain of the series' pieces appeared in various periodicals as early as June, 1966. Audio effects, such as apparently senseless (when received in print) repetition, pervade nearly all the pieces.

"Frame-Tale," the initial piece, is in one sense not a tale at all, but rather a visual pun, which involves cutting and gluing part of a single page. Directions on where to glue are inside the dotted line which is to be cut. A sort of twisted circle results (assuming that one follows the directions correctly),

and it is an excellent metaphor for the construction and arrangement of *Lost in the Funhouse.*

"Night-Sea Journey," the second item of the series, is a dramatic monologue with musings on existence. The point of view is that of a sperm, which is journeying to an ovum. The sperm worries that life may be merely a fiction, and he narrates philosophical opinions of his own and of his fellows who have drowned along the way. Latent in the narration is the idea of the author's psychological biography, of man living his postnatal life with the conceptual, or perhaps intuitive, knowledge of his end, his goal, his death, continually in his consciousness. "Is the journey my invention?" he asks. "Do the night, the sea, exist, or is this a dream?" The narration closes with the orgiastic summons: " ' 'Love! Love! Love!' ' " The entire work, *Lost in the Funhouse,* is allegorically latent in this piece.

"Ambrose His Mark" is the third piece, and again Barth presents a biographical first-person narrative, which as the title indicates, deals with identity and existence. Ambrose, the narrator, is an infant of a few months, and he is conceivably the result of the successful journey of the sperm in the preceding narration. Possessor of a bee-shaped birthmark, Ambrose recounts how he finally got his name when he was several months old. Ambrose's father is in an insane asylum, and his mother has alternating spells of being extremely attached to him and of being totally ignorant of him. Her favorite pastime is to nurse Ambrose publicly: "For in one humor she would fetch out her breast in any company and feed me while she smoked or strolled in the garden—nor nurse me quietly at that, but demand of Aunt Rosa whether I hadn't Hector's eyes. . . ." Viewing this pastime was Grandfather's delight and Uncle Konrad's embarrassment. Grandfather, with an intention of making a quantity of mead, needs honey; he fashions hives and erects them opposite those of the neighbor, Willy Erdmann. Grandfather persuades Andrea, Ambrose's mother, to nurse the infant near the empty hives. Erdmann's bees are drawn to cluster on the nursing Ambrose and the exposed breast, and this situation, along with Erdmann's protestations of thievery, leads to a great explosion of slap-stick humor. This leads also to the naming of Ambrose at last; the members of the family mention Plato and Xenophon, when infants, as having been lit on by bees, but Andrea rejects those as names for her child. Then Uncle Konrad's assertion that the same thing happened to Saint Ambrose brings the family to choose that for the child's name. Thus, the gift of speech becomes associated with the narrator, and, as with "Night-Sea Journey," with the author himself, musing on his identity, his vocation, his life as fiction.

The next piece, "Autobiography," reinforces this idea. The media play is strong, and the narration is once more in the first-person singular. Again the narrator, not specifically Ambrose, puzzlingly searches his identity: "You who listen give me life in a manner of speaking." The piece ties in with the preceding ones: "Among other things I haven't a proper name. . . . I don't recall asking to be conceived!" There are no events, only musings in "Autobiography."

"Water-Message," which comes next, treats of Ambrose as a now older child, one of about ten years, and the title itself, by its water image, serves also to connect the series so far. The somewhat sissyish Ambrose (the narrator is omniscient) has trouble identifying with his peers and escapes into fantasies of his death and of sexual triumph. While playing on the Maryland beach near his home, he finds a message in a bottle which brings up once more the problems or questions of existence and identity: the paper which was in the bottle is blank, except for two phrases: "TO WHOM IT MAY CONCERN" and "YOURS TRULY."

Juxtaposed to this piece is "Petition," an epistolary request to "His Most Gracious Majesty Prajadhipok," which concludes, "Yours truly," and is unsigned. Again the questions of identity and existence come up. The petitioner describes his wretched experiences with his Siamese twin, to whose back the petitioner's belly is fastened. The request is for money to pay surgeons to separate the two. In the life of the twins is a girl named Thalia, and the petitioner suspects there are two of her also, a Thalia within a Thalia.

Ambrose reappears in the next item of the series, now as a child of thirteen. "Lost in the Funhouse" tells of Ambrose's and his family's holiday at Ocean City, Maryland, but at the same time it presents many apparent intrusions (it is ambiguous as to when they are Barth's and when they are Ambrose's) on how to write fiction, again with the underlying idea of the author and protagonist possibly living fiction.

The interplay of media is strong: "Ambrose was 'at that awkward age.' His voice came out high-pitched as a child's if he let himself get carried away; to be on the safe side, therefore, he moved and spoke with *deliberate calm* and *adult gravity*. Talking soberly of unimportant or irrelevant matters and listening consciously to the sound of your own voice are useful habits for maintaining control in this difficult interval." There are intrusive directions on point of view, metaphor, and other tools and devices of fiction. More and more strongly, Barth entertains the idea of life as fiction. Ambrose, while in the amusement park, has sexual fantasies about the girl who has accompanied the family to the beach. He tells himself, "You think you're yourself, but there are other persons in you." Thus, this piece also relates directly to the series, Ambrose seeing himself as the petitioner sees Thalia. In the funhouse, as on the boardwalk, "Nothing was what it looked like."

In the following four pieces, which are abstract and non-Ambrosian, the media play and the toying with the concept of identity, fiction, and reality, become overt. "Echo," "Two Meditations," "Title," and "Glossolalia" are diverse and rather brief; unfortunately, these qualities do not save them from being tedious. The lengthier piece, "Life-Story," which follows these four, is, perhaps, the presentation of the mature author's life, although he is no longer identified as Ambrose. "Life-Story" presents the author's life as the author is in the process of writing fiction, identifying the life and the act of writing as one. It, too, is quite tedious, but perhaps intentionally so.

"Menelaiad," the following piece, goes a step farther: ". . . this isn't the voice of Menelaus; this voice *is* Menelaus, all there is of him. When I'm switched on I tell my tale, the one I know, How Menelaus Became Immortal, but I don't know it." Imagining he has Telemachus for a listener, Menelaus talks on about his frustrating experiences, sexual and otherwise, with Helen. As did Ovid in the *Metamorphoses*, Menelaus gets speakers within speakers *ad infinitum*. At one point there are six sets of quotation marks around a single word. Speaker identity is being lost.

The completion of this loss is in the last of these pieces, "Anonymiad," which brings the twisted circle of the work to its starting point, "Frame-Tale" and "Night-Sea Journey." Alone on a rock in the sea, nowhere in particular, the anonymous narrator gives an account of being cuckolded and marooned by his wife and friends.

Despite occasional tedium, *Lost in the Funhouse* is both clever and delightful; virtuosity in media and fantasy, and incisiveness in introspection make the latter two qualities predominate.

Quentin Gehle

THE LOST ONES

Author: Samuel Beckett (1906-   )
Publisher: Grove Press (New York). 62 pp. $4.95 (paperback)
Type of work: Novella
Time: The present
Locale: The inside of a cylinder

A brief, highly compressed story of the existence of two hundred persons within a cylinder fifty meters round and eighteen high

> *Principal characters:*
> UNNAMED SEARCHERS, CLIMBERS, WATCHERS
> THE SEDENTARY
> THE VANQUISHED

The Lost Ones is Beckett's first nondramatic piece since *How It Is,* and the first to appear since he was awarded the Nobel Prize in Literature in 1969 when, as we have it, he was so little concerned about the Prize, remaining aloof and what now seems to have been "in hiding," that the Nobel committee was unable to deliver the announcement of the award for several weeks.

Beckett began the novella in 1966 but did not finish it until early in 1970, a fact which, considering its brevity, would be astounding in itself were it not known widely that Beckett has been heading toward an elegant, elaborate silence. *The Lost Ones* is only about nine thousand words, or more nearly a short story in length, published in exceptionally large type and running but sixty-two pages. The *Evergreen Review* number 96 reprint, set in normal size type, ran twenty-three pages, half of which were split in half by superb pen and ink illustrations. In *The Unnamable,* his always verbose and rattling style led directly to such a silence:

> *The fact would seem to be, if in my situation one may speak of facts, not only that I shall have to speak of things which I cannot speak, but alas, which is even more interesting, but also that I, which is if possible even more interesting, that shall have to, I forget, no matter. And at the same time I am obliged to speak.*

Perhaps less obvious is the point that Beckett's dramatic and prose situations lead to the same circular nowhere as his literary style. That is, waiting (*Waiting for Godot*), the desert act (*Act Without Words*), the uninhabited seashore (*Molloy*), the nebulous place of the mind an instant before death (*Not I*), preoccupation with a wasted past (*Krapp's Last Tape*). Paradoxically, Beckett's short plays and prose works are long on dialogue, whereas the long works (*Malone Dies, Molloy,* for example) are short on situation, continuing maddeningly in circularity while the reader-viewer who has caught on long before suffers the complete route in full knowledge of where it will go and how little if anything will be "delivered."

The Lost Ones is set in the same static waiting situation as *Waiting for Godot*; nothing can be gained because one's final and total loss came at the time of his birth. The world the lost ones inhabit is a cylinder fifty meters round and eighteen meters high. There are two hundred people inside—searchers, climbers, watchers, the sedentary, and the vanquished. There are fifteen ladders that lead to niches in the upper half of the cylinder into which the people, with support and much waiting below, seek some strange piece of themselves, or perhaps just an awareness. Just what is sought, other than a kind of necessary peace, is never made clear. What *is* clarified in the familiar Beckett geometric detail are the rules for searching. Indeed, searching seems an end in itself, all roads leading back to the beginning, and whether the reader sees it as attempted escape from a trapped life or a mere pastime, he is inevitably forced to release his impression and begin again (as do the searchers in the story), looking here and there for the elusive symbolic chain.

There seems to be none. At the very moment when the rules seem clearly a play on religion, a way to God, or else seeking as a state of virtue, at that very moment Beckett, perhaps in the middle of a sentence, turns the whole huddled mess into something far more human where shoulders rub shoulders and people become ordinary suffering people. And when the reader has given up the religious parody, he will begin speaking of ethics and "doing unto others," and we are back where we began. Beckett manipulates his reader as searcher even as he manipulates his two-dimensional cylinder people —a mad game of the mind in which the soul suffers, but not as much as the skin:

The effect of this climate on the soul is not to be underestimated. But it suffers certainly less than the skin whose entire defensive system from sweat to goose bumps is under constant stress. . . . For skin in its own way . . . has not merely one adversary to contend with.

The reader is back to "flesh against flesh," wherein the suffering becomes physical. Beckett, it seems, suggests the real difference between an agony of knowledge and one of the body, as though the mind led the body to its pain rather than the true anatomical theory that pain is felt only *through* the brain. The mind, then, is the body. Or at least the mind contains the body, Beckett seems to be telling us; and the cylinder itself is the collective mind of man and his condition. It therefore contains his body.

The rules, the search, the waiting, all seem to be Beckett's understanding of the condition of our lives, and if one begins seeing something hopeful in the search for an exit, one need only remember that contemporary space exploration offers the same pointlessness about it for us as the niches have for the inhabitant of the cylinder.

The condition within the cylinder is more standing in line than climbing or searching. One waits in line for what seems like years before arriving at the base of the ladder. And the rules for queueing are strict and one may lose his place in line easily. Others merely watch. Still others examine the limp and vacant vanquished. The major tone is that of waiting, however, and Beckett has returned to his hellish situation in which he has cast so many of his characters who have nothing whatever to do while waiting for what may never come, and which, if it did, would not be recognized anyway. They pass their hats back and forth, or jump up for water perpetually out of reach, or, as in the case of the woman in *Not I,* become reduced to a mere mouth taking a last breath before dying, and, not to stilled for that moment, senselessly rattle on in horrific human tones of fear that lead now and then to uncontrolled, ghastly screams of the terror surely ahead, desperately attempting to put off the only other human state besides waiting—oblivion.

There is of course nothing in this novella to suggest that Beckett is trying to make anything realistic. That is, unlike Krapp, who has depth of character, and Molloy, who, we believe, sucks real stones, the lost ones are of the same statistical quality as the dimensions of their universe. Yet, the book is not so abstract as all that, in that the suffering is recognized by the reader as his own, of another kind perhaps, with similar causes. Herein lies the clue to why it took Beckett double, even triple the length of time that seems necessary to write nine thousand words: It reads as though it were written in one sitting. The narrative is sustained in a single concentrated tone that must be read with the same concentrated attention. Rather than a distillation, *The Lost Ones* seems, as does the dialogue in *Not I,* to come in a single last breath. The connection is made between writing technique and reading technique; it is then made between the condition of suffering of the inhabitants and the same condition in the lives of Beckett's readership. Experience is gained without verisimilitude, through the

mind, not the senses, and Beckett has again shown us that his territory is the brain.

Throughout Beckett, we find worlds without vegetation, without the beauty of growing things. The cylinder is in this way an unnatural land. But as before, the lack of trees or green mountains, except for the symbolic one-leafed tree in *Wating for Godot,* should have signaled us that the land is the interior of man. The exterior? It doesn't exist. Characters live in the mind of the beholders, or not at all. We do not then bear witness to men in their environment; rather, we see in to what we also see in ourselves.

Several times in the narrative an illustration of searching or queueing-up ends with the searcher or climber being free to do this or that, usually to leave his long-sought place in line, or leave a zone. That is perhaps the key to how Beckett interprets freedom. It seems to be a new look at the word, for within this cylinder one has the freedom to move *providing* he does not feel the *need* to move about. When ruled by his nature, he has no choices. One must conclude that Beckett sees freedom of thought and activity as that very limited time when we can do nothing else. He tells us that the passion to search is such that no place may be left unsearched, so that one is driven by the method, not the goal. And the freedom to react means one may give up, "unable to endure it any longer," renounce the ladder and resume the search "in the arena." Then, aren't the lost ones, like Sisyphus who also had the "limited freedom" to react to his condition, aware of their trapped existence? Beckett is very careful to avoid the question of awareness, as though it either did not bear on his theme or else was irrelevant, since man can never know where he is or why. One must conclude that a certain ignorance is what condemns the lost ones to their frustrations.

But it is simplistic to view the drives and passions of Beckett's lost ones as examples of ignorant man going about his life like the poor blind ants unaware of approaching feet, for one must conclude from the novella that, should they become aware of the conditions of their existence, they would nevertheless be driven by their natures as passionate searchers to act out what cannot any more be avoided than any other natural phenomenon in the universe subject exclusively to physical law.

Beckett permits a single hopeful image within the tight confines of the law-ridden geometric condition of man: He is the only object in the universe capable of real suffering. It is all he has and it is that very thing which makes the whole of creation matter.

John Herrmann

Sources for Further Study

Reviews:

Best Sellers. XXXII, January 1, 1973, p. 449. 650 words.

New Republic. CLXVIII, January, 1973, p. 29. 400 words.

New York Review of Books. XIX, December 14, 1972, p. 42. 700 words.

New York Times Book Review. October 29, 1972, p. 4. 1,450 words.

Times Literary Supplement. August 11, 1972, p. 935. 750 words.

THE LOST REVOLUTION

Author: Robert Shaplen (1917-   )
Publisher: Harper and Row (New York). 404 pp. $6.95
Type of work: History
Time: 1946-1965
Locale: Vietnam

The history of Vietnam from World War II to the intervention of the United States

> *Principal personages:*
> BAO DAI, Emperor of Annam
> HO CHI MINH, Premier of North Vietnam
> NGO DINH DIEM, Premier of South Vietnam from 1954 until his assassination in 1964
> NGUYEN KHANH, Premier of South Vietnam in 1964
> NGUYEN CAO KY, the present Premier of South Vietnam
> THICH TRI QUANG, the leader of the Buddhists in South Vietnam

A whole series of books on Vietnam has appeared which concentrate on the political chaos and corruption in that state. *The Lost Revolution* must be added to the work of Browne, Halberstam, and Lacouture, all of which attempt to account for the present nature of the Vietnamese war in terms of its political past. Shaplen begins by considering the condition of the country after World War II; it is his contention that the decline of Vietnam began with the re-entry of the French at the end of that war. As he sees it, the plans of the French for an Indochina Federation and their idea of a French Union were simply "contrived theoretical devices by which the French hoped to regain their military, political, and economic position in Indochina."

Cochin China—which we now know as South Vietnam—had been under the cultural influence of the French before World War II. It was during that war, however, that the Vietnamese attained a new sense of their identity and began to resent the power of the outsiders. The return of the French to power did nothing to assuage this resentment. Shaplen is particularly acute in summing up the reasons for the increasingly uncomfortable relationship of subjects and colonizers. The policies of the French were politically unrealistic; the economics of colonization were based on prewar ideas; the men sent to rule the government and furnish the forces of occupation were largely ignorant of the nation they had come to oversee. The great variable, of course, was that Tonkin China—which we now know as North Vietnam—had undergone a revolutionary change under Ho Chi Minh during the war. This change the French were not willing to accept.

After a long series of misunderstandings the French sent General Jean de Lattre de Tassigny to take command of the Indochinese province. As Shaplen sees it, this plan resulted in an unfortunate infusion of ideology into a precarious enough situation. One may feel that De Lattre was essentially correct in his analysis of the danger posed by the Communists to the North, but Shaplen finds the opposition of the General to be ideological and very nearly mystical. As he puts it, "De Lattre was convinced that he was leading a crusade against Communism." Shaplen is, however, balanced in his judg-

The Lost Revolution/SHAPLEN

ment otherwise, and he points out that, before his death, De Lattre very nearly solved the political problems of Vietnam through his intelligent military tactics.

After Dienbienphu and the Treaty of Geneva in 1954, the government was taken over by Ngo Dinh Diem. Diem is certainly one of the most controversial figures of the last generation, universally regarded by the left as a tyrant and religious bigot and by the right as a valuable assistant in the war against Communism. Shaplen is critical of Diem, but not doctrinaire. He notes that, aside from matters of ideology, there are personal, familial, and political elements to be assessed by any critics of Diem. For example, the sheer administrative problems of running a broken country were nearly insurmountable. Diem had no real program and was not assisted by an able cabinet. These facts, in addition to "his stubbornness . . . his refusal to delegate authority and to take advice from anyone but his family, and . . . his imperious habits and ways," combined to unseat him.

There is an interesting account of the coup which toppled Diem; the real villains of the piece are Madame Nhu and her husband, Ngo Dinh Nhu. The language of conspiracy is heavily used by Shaplen to describe this pair, whom he finds "paranoid," "megalomaniac," and involved in "duplicity . . . counter-duplicity . . . machinations." The Nhus are heavily criticized, but one should like to see a more intensive analysis of their programs. The collection of anecdotes that Shaplen presents are of considerably less use than a short history of their actual political moves. As for the assignment of responsibility, this is the weakest part of the The Lost Revolution. Shaplen is

content to accept a statement by Henry Cabot Lodge culled from the *New York Times* that the United States was not involved in the overthrow of Diem. True or not, one does not go to an interested party to find out the causes of a dispute of this nature. Lodge's position, and his ambitions, both prevented him from being more open. On one point, however, Shaplen is clear enough: "it may be assumed that what took place in Saigon between the time the coup was planned and mounted and the date of its successful conclusion would not have occurred without the prior approval of one man in Washington, President John F. Kennedy."

Those parts of *The Lost Revolution* which deal with the American commitment after the death of Diem are already somewhat dated. The vast increase in American men and arms makes Shaplen's view of the war seem strategically unfocused. The story of the fighting ends with the North Vietnamese advantages of 1964 and 1965; for this reason the strategic picture tends to be more pessimistic than it now is. There is, however, a sensible appreciation of the nature of the battle: the difficulties of terrain, supply, and tactics. The increased commitment of the last year, however, demands a much deeper account of the military picture and much more attention paid to the strategic and political effects of escalation.

Shaplen's summary of the "lost" revolution seems true enough, but based, after all, on hindsight. Most readers will in fact acknowledge that "Vietnam has become both the conscience and a belated cause of the United States." It is not so easy to say that we encouraged a spurious nationalism against a true one. These terms are relative, and the corruption, stupidity, and incompetence of the rulers of South Vietnam have, after all, no connection with the "truth" of their nationalism. Shaplen believes that we could, through aid and sympathy, have obviated the entire war. This view leaves out one very important question. What if the ultimate pressures on Vietnam came from *outside* that country? Would foreign aid and expressions of our sympathy for nationalism have had a real effect on Communism? One is not so certain. Shaplen's conclusion on the nature of our ideology and the foreign policy which reflects it are not going to win much agreement: "The sad truth of the matter, it seems to me, is that we have lost our revolutionary zeal; we tend not to think so much in terms of change and revolution as of adjustment and accommodation." When we think of the support given in the past decade to revolutionary governments—to Tito, to Nasser before he rejected it, to Castro before he chose his own side—it seems that such a generalization is out of place. One is likely to conclude that as a principled statement it is extremely dangerous, if only because its corollary—that we should by definition welcome revolution—is no more satisfactory than the original.

Ronald Berman

THE LOST WORLD

Author: Randall Jarrell (1914-1965)
Publisher: The Macmillan Company (New York). 70 pp. $3.95
Type of work: Poetry

The last book by a master of the American plain style in poetry is compassionate, moving, and humane

The year in which *The Lost World*, his seventh book of poetry, appeared, was the last year of Randall Jarrell's life. The pleasure of reading these accomplished poems, each of them plain yet inimitable, is mingled with the sad recognition that the career of a major figure in recent American poetry came to an end at a time when his powers were at their full. Perhaps his papers will afford materials for a posthumous collection: all who value poetry will hope so; but for the moment *The Lost World* must be regarded as the last testament of Randall Jarrell.

Jarrell's unornamented style, his preference for colloquial diction, and his disinclination to write in definable prosodic structures have occasionally prompted critics to charge that, whatever the authority of his perceptions, his command of the music of language and of the techniques of verse was deficient. Passages in several of the poems in *The Lost World* should go far toward silencing that criticism. In "Woman," for example, the speaker addresses his beloved in these words:

> O morning star,
> Each morning my dull heart goes out
> to you
> And rises with the sun, but with the
> sun
> Sets not, but all the long night nests
> within your eyes.

In these lines, and in the concluding lines of the poem as well, Jarrell had occasion to employ his special, muted lyric voice. Nevertheless, the long poem from which these lines are drawn is dominated by the analytic, not the lyric impulse. An examination of the ambiguities and contradictions which play their parts in the relations of man and woman is the poem's central concern. The lyric passages are merely one element in an essentially dialectic development.

Jarrell's view of the world allows his lyric impulse full scope only in the poems he addresses, at least ostensibly, to very young readers. Three such poems, which first appeared in *The Bat Poet*, a storybook for children published in 1964, are repeated in *The Lost World*. "Bats," the longest of the three, opens:

> A bat is born
> Naked and blind and pale.
> His mother makes a pocket of
> her tail
> And catches him. He clings to
> her long fur
> By his thumbs and toes and
> teeth.
> And then the mother dances
> through the night
> Doubling and looping, soaring,
> somersaulting . . .

The spirit of the poem soars with the bat, but its subject, indisputably, is dun and unromantic.

The unromantic, the unlovely, the everyday were always Jarrell's best subjects. In them he saw—and helped his readers to see—the extraordinary, even the beautiful. He wrote of the joy of unexpected discoveries made close to home in "Well Water," the shortest of the twenty-two poems in *The Lost World*.

> What a girl called "the dailiness of life"
> "Adding an errand to your errand.
>   Saying,
> "Since you're up . . ." Making you a
>   means to
> A means to a means to) is well water
> Pumped from an old well at the bottom
>   of the world.
> The pump you pump the water from is
>   rusty
> And hard to move and absurd, a
>   squirrel-wheel
> A sick squirrel turns slowly, through
>   the sunny
> Inexorable hours. And yet sometimes
> The wheel turns of its own weight, the
>   rusty
> Pump pumps over your sweating face
>   the clear
> Water, cold, so cold! you cup your
>   hands
> And gulp from them the dailiness of
>   life.

The daily experiences of an unexceptional life are the subject of the three-part poem which gives its title to the book. "The Lost World" is the world of childhood, a childhood of the 1920's. The quotidian experiences of the boy who is Jarrell's *persona* in this poem acquire a special vividness because they are set against the background of Hollywood in the heyday of the movies. The child, walking home from school, sees

>   a star
> Stumble to her igloo through the howl-
>   ing gale
> Of the wind machines. On Melrose a
>   dinosaur

And pterodactyl, with their immense
>   pale
> Papier-mâché smiles, look over the
>   fence
> Of *The Lost World*.
>   Whispering to myself the tale
> These shout—done with my schoolwork,
>   I commence
> My real life: my arsenal, my workshop
> Opens, and in impotent omnipotence
> I put on the helmet and the breastplate
>   Pop
> Cut out and soldered for me. Here is
>   the shield
> I sawed from beaver board and painted;
>   here on top
> The bow that only Odysseus can wield
> And eleven vermilion-ringed, goose-
>   feathered arrows.

"The Lost World" is the second poem in the book. The last poem, "Thinking of the Lost World" is a moving meditation on the impossibility of recovering the world of childhood. Thirty-five years after his Hollywood schooldays, the man that boy had become laments,

>   My bow
> Is lost, all my arrows are lost or broken,
> My knife is sunk in the eucalyptus tree
> Too far for even Pop to get it out,
> And the tree's sawed down. It and the
>   stair-sticks
> And the planks of the tree house are all
>   firewood
> Burned long ago; its gray smoke smells
>   of Vicks.

And yet the poem ends not in the awareness of something lost but of something gained.

In some sense these two poems seem autobiographical, but it is the special virtue of Jarrell's poetry that it frequently initiates us into the inner experiences of believable people unlike the poet and equally unlike the typical poetry reader. The poems expand the range of our human experience; indeed, they seem to have as their objective the humanizing and broadening of our perceptions. "Next Day," the first poem in the collection, has much in common with the memorable title poem of Jarrell's prize-winning 1960 collection, *The Woman at the Washington Zoo.* Both poems are monologues, both are spoken by women, and both by women on the brink of unutterable despair. The speaker of "Next Day," a financially comfortable wife and mother, is in a supermarket, "Moving from Cheer to Joy, from Joy to All." What comes to her is the recognition that her life is "commonplace and solitary." But the poem redeems her life by compelling us to share it, to sense its tragic desperation, to value its largely wasted humanity.

In another moving monologue, a mother thinks of her two daughters, one who died in childhood, the other now a grown and married woman. The poem opens with the mother's dream of "The Lost Children":

Two little girls, one fair, one dark,
One alive, one dead, are running hand
    in hand
Through a sunny house.

Moving from the dream of playing with the irrecoverable children to painful waking experiences which reinforce the mother's sense of loss and back again to dream, "The Lost Children" seems always to balance itself on the brink of sentimentality. Jarrell's earlier poetry has often been justly crit-icized for falling from the tragic into the sentimental, but in *The Lost World* his sense of decorum is sure. The boundary between deeply felt poetry and sentimental verse (the boundary which every poet who attempts to express profound emotion must walk) is narrow and indistinct, but Jarrell's wit, his sense of irony, and his self-discipline sufficed in his mature poetry to keep him on the safe side of the mawkish, even when he moved in the bordering realm of genuine pathos.

They did not, however, keep him from projecting himself into maimed and miserable lives. In "The One Who was Different," Jarrell says of himself:

I identify myself, as always,
With something that there's something
    wrong with,
With something human.

The distinguished poems in *The Lost World* compel the reader to identify himself as well with all that is human.

Jarrell's subjects are not restricted to the day-to-day realities of life in the neighborhood. "A Hunt in the Black Forest," a narrative in which a mute and a dwarf revenge themselves upon a cruel king, derives its ambience from the chilling Märchen of the brothers Grimm, and another atypical poem, "The House in the Wood," leads us toward a confrontation with inner terror. Yet most of his poems demonstrate that it was the particular, not the archetypal, which most often arrested Randall Jarrell and which in poem after poem he rendered startlingly arresting.

Robert Regan

LOVE & FAME

Author: John Berryman (1914-1972)
Publisher: Farrar, Straus and Giroux (New York). 96 pp. $6.50
Type of work: Poetry

The final work published during the life of the poet, dealing with artistic beginnings, early experiences with love and fame, and his return to the idea of a God of rescue, culminating in a series of "Eleven Addresses to the Lord"

Love & Fame, the last of Berryman's books to be published during his life, is suspended between *77 Dream Songs* and the final posthumous work *Delusions, Etc.* which Berryman prepared himself before his death. The centrality of *77 Dream Songs,* the structure which gave them body, is missing here. Henry, The protagonist of *The Dream Songs,* is not to be found in this work and occurs only fitfully in *Delusions, Etc.* Neither do we have the grim and demonic work of *Delusions, Etc.,* the culmination of Berryman's use of syntactical inversion to achieve a powerful intensity of language, nor the confrontation of "I faint for some soft & solid & sudden way out . . . the sweet cold numbing upward from my burning feet."

What *is* central to this book is the tension which exists between the parts of a dichotomy. There is a division, a duality, both personal and theological, throughout the book. It is directly approached earlier in the *Dream Songs:*

I notice at this point a divided soul,
headed both fore & aft and guess which
    soul
will swamp & lose:

that hoping forward, brisk & vivid one
of which will nothing ever be heard
    again.

In *Love & Fame* we are given a bareness of view which is naked and painful, no longer projected outward onto another figure (Henry alias Mr. Bones) but taken back onto the self. Of this work Berryman allows that: "the subject was entirely new, solely and simply myself. Nothing else. A subject on which I am an expert. Nobody can contradict me . . . I am a scholar in certain fields, but the subject on which I am a real authority is me, so I wiped out all the disguises and went to work." The book was xeroxed and sent out ahead of printing to friends for reassurance, criticism. Told by Edmund Wilson that the book was "hopeless" despite "fine lines and striking passages" Berryman comments that it is like saying to a beautiful woman who stands naked as Venus that she has a nice left small toenail. Not until the age of thirty-five did he look at reviews of his work for fear of "being killed by some remark."

The book begins wih a dedication to Tristan Corbière, the Breton poet who managed in his 29 years to produce a highly original book of poetry, important for its irony and use of a familiar spoken voice. Sometimes referred to as a poet of frustrations (not unlike Berryman), he set up a battery of sporting guns at his window one Sunday and alarmed churchgoers by firing a simultaneous volley. (One thinks here of the suicide of Berryman's father, which the boy witnessed from his window at the age of 12.) Berryman speaks in the dedication to Corbière of his "mockery of the pretentious great," his "self-revelations."

The book is divided into four parts, the first concerned with early loves, artistic beginnings, memories. The first poem in this section, "Her & It," wants to serve as a reduction for "Love & Fame" and calls to mind the poem by Yeats "He and She" ("I am I, am I;/ The greater grows my light/ The further that I fly."). In Berryman we find:

> I fell in love with a girl.
> O and a gash.
> I'll bet she now has seven lousy children.
>
> I wish she'd read my book & write to me. . . .

Of that early fame, of those early loves: "I have traveled in some high company since/ but never so dizzily./ I have had some rare girls since but never one so philosophical. . . ." Here we meet Elspeth's "haggard unsuccessful lover" who receives "elephant cheques" from his publishers here and abroad, who with his scholarship restored is "the Prodigal Son/ welcomed with crimson joy." This is the same person whose fantasy it was to "satisfy at once all Barnard & Smith/ & have enough left over for Miss Gibbs' girls."

After college commencement and "some wandering days in Montreal" and other parts, Berryman prepares for the journey to England (by dint of a fellowship): ". . . I pulled myself reluctantly together at last . . . headed for Pier 42—where my nervous system/ as I teetered across the gang-plank/ sprang back into expectation . . . off to the strange Old World . . . & visit by hook or crook with W. B. Yeats." (And he does take high tea with Yeats, his mouth dry, his heart in his mouth.)

The second group deals essentially with those years in England. In "Away" the ship pulls out, "the jammed dock slides away backward" and the poet calls: "Yeats, Yeats, I'm coming! it's me. Faber & Faber,/ you'll have to publish me some day . . . I swamp with possibility." The voice is young, hopeful, overzealous. Tucked in among the Elgin marbles, Keats's letters, Blake's Prophetic Books and Picadilly is the alternate voice of Berryman in the present looking down as though through a long hallway at those years:

> Images, memories, of a lonely & ambitious young alien.
> Buildings, buildings & their spaces & decorations,
> are death-words & sayings in crisis.
> Old masters of old Cambridge, I am listening.

And a voice answers from the midst of those earlier days:

> Black hours over an unclean line.
> Fear. Of failure, or worse, *insignificance*.
> Solitudes, sometimes, of an alien country
> no book after all will ever read me into.

From "Monkhood": "I don't show my work to anybody, I am quite alone."

Much of the third section was written during a hospitalization. In the first poem of that section even the most benign of reviewers feels discomfort in these lines:

> I dreamed a dream to end dreams, even my dreams:
> I had died—no problem: but a mighty hand
> was after my works too, feeling here & there,
> & finding them, bit by bit.
> At last he found the final of all one, & pulled *it* away, & said 'There!'

These are poems on despair ("It seems to be dark all the time./ I have difficulty walking."), poems about need, suicide. Here the issues become more central, the confrontation more intense.

The last of the book is composed of eleven addresses to the Lord. Of these Berryman says: ". . . there is a grave piety in the last poems, which is going to trouble a lot of people. . . . They are the result of a religious conversion . . . I lost my faith several years ago, but I came back . . . into the notion of a God who, at certain moments, definitely and personally intervenes in individual lives, one of which is mine. The poems grow out of that sense. . . ."

If, as A. Alvarez tells us, the series of songs "Opus Posthumous," are to mourn and celebrate beforehand Berryman's own death, almost as though he must write an elegy on himself because there is no one else he can trust with the task, it would not seem terribly far-fetched to think that in part the *Dream Songs* are the central work of mourning, that what comes afterward represents a different phase in that same process. Elizabeth Kubler-Ross, a physician who has worked with the terminally ill, describes some of the ways in which people confront their own deaths. At first there is a strong denial and afterward rage, anger. Later still, there comes depression, and finally a kind of resolution and acceptance and a putting in order of the human house if there is time. This book, *Love & Fame*, feels as though it wants to live somewhere on that continuum, well after the rage, long after denial, yet the decision for death having been made. If along this continuum we look at a poem from 77 *Dream Songs* which seems the nearly perfect embodiment of a life-long unresolved rage:

The marker slants, flowerless, day's almost done,
I stand above my father's grave with rage,
often, often before
I've made this awful pilgrimage to one
who cannot visit me, who tore his page
out: I come back for more,

I spit upon this dreadful banker's grave
who shot his heart out in a Florida dawn
O ho alas alas
When will indifference come, I moan & rage
I'd like to scrabble till I got right down
away down under the grass
and ax the casket open ha to see
just how he's taking it, which he sought so hard
we'll tear apart
the mouldering grave clothes ha & then Henry
will heft the ax once more, his final card,
and fell it on the start.

and then look at a poem which is clearly one of resolution in his final book *Delusion, Etc.*:

He Resigns

Age, and the deaths, and the ghosts.
Her having gone away
in spirit from me. Hosts
of regrets come & find me empty.

I don't feel this will change.
I don't want anything
or person, familiar or strange.
I don't think I will sing

any more just now;
or ever. I must start
to sit with a blind brow
above an empty heart.

we can begin to place the work of

Love & Fame. For it is in this book that we see a last-ditch effort at saving himself. Here there is a kind of dialogue with the self, which sometimes takes the form of self-aggrandizement (and has led critics to write harshly of the work), but seems to be a stroking of his narcissism in an effort to discover again, to recover reasons for remaining alive. There is an overriding sadness as though the dialogue is not really working, as though he knew beforehand that it might not. In "Death Ballad" two girls in the psychiatric ward have decided to end it all:

> . . . in their present mental weather,
> no power can prevent their dying. . . .
>
> Only . . . take up, outside your blocked
>   selves, some small thing
> that is moving
> & wants to keep on moving
> & needs therefore, Tyson, Jo, your
>   loving.

The dichotomy seems to be based in the complexity of the warring instincts for life and death. We can say with fair certainty that Berryman was last seen waving as though to his friends in a last gesture of parting (or was it greeting?) as he flew towards the Mississippi frozen in winter, but it is what a man gives language to, what he names as he pauses, that we are left with and where we must go. It is in the poetry that we come to know the groundswell which moved Berryman along to that final act and the struggle with which he held off that motion. Hugh Kenner says that "like primitive astronomers we are free to note recurrences, cherish symmetries and seek if we can means of placating the hidden powers: more for our comfort than for theirs."

Love & Fame. Love and/or fame. One or the other. A dichotomy. A collection in the language of alternates, opposites, opposing forces. The uncertain marriage of such opposition in these words: "You must perhaps both pray for & abandon. . . ."

Myra Sklarew

LOVE AND ITS DERANGEMENTS

Author: Joyce Carol Oates (1938–   )
Publisher: Louisiana State University Press (Baton Rouge). 66 pp. $4.50
Type of work: Poetry

The second volume of poems by the author of them, *winner of the National Book Award for fiction in 1970*

Ten years ago Joyce Carol Oates' first stories opened out on grim rural landscapes populated by intensely solitary characters. In flight from, yet entangled in, family and personal history, her people collided anonymously, often violently. Strangers curiously familiar with each other were propelled into an actual or figurative sexual embrace made to contain all the angry momentum of the escape. The scene changed to small towns and migrant camps, the inner city and the suburbs, but in every setting generations of a family succeeded one another, with all the haphazard intimacy imposed by proximity, with the constant estrangement and the plurality of inexpressible urgencies—the whole relentless inheritance from fathers to daughters, mothers to sons, that made the family so intolerable and so inescapable. Her characters lived out on the existential edge, where landscapes became mirrors of near-delirium, and rooms in splendid houses and sagging shanties turned into ovens of heat and light to terrify their inhabitants. Her people were continually seeking or creating or being thrust into some experience—sudden, brief, feverish, orgastic, random—some expression of desperation adequate to their private cataclysms of love and pain. They might have seemed absurdly grotesque and implausible had they not been so piercingly accurate and in a way ordinary, so like the selves one may try to confine to the padded cells of one's mind. Her charac-ters might have been less capable of lodging in one's consciousness had her vision of the bare, basic, and unmitigated, the primal in the everyday, been less acute.

In much of her work we have seen in the last two years—last year's first volume of poems, *Anonymous Sins,* and the selection of stories from the last five years, *The Wheel of Love,* now along with *Love and Its Derangements*—she has increasingly sharpened her focus on the abrasive process of living with the compromise of one's younger notions of what the world is like, what one's life can be. It is seldom a monumental compromise—her characters were never very naïvely hopeful in the first place, and when they were, they weren't for long. Even her children were ageless with knowledge. Rather, it is the solid weight, the density of time itself against which her people hurl themselves now. She is largely absorbed in what it means to turn thirty or so and find that you haven't quite been consumed *or* consummated in the initial anarchy of passion, or that you have survived even the absence of it, your renunciation of it. She is absorbed in what it means to find yourself married—to a person, to art, to the Church, or to your past—and wish whole- or half-heartedly you weren't, then to try fitfully, ambivalently, to break away and finally perhaps to opt for a slower death in stasis. Miss Oates is exploring, in short, what it means to have tried to sustain love.

She stated the dilemma in four lines of a poem called "A Woman in Her Secret Life" in *Anonymous Sins:*

> If I forget my family it is
> to pollute myself in the bone
> of strangers, of men, to give up
> my face to their face's imprint.

These lines signal her concommitant absorption in articulating what it is like to be a woman, a woman's body being what it is, love in the Western world being what it is. The two strands of thought are never far apart; they mingle and merge.

Love and Its Derangements is not strikingly different from the earlier *Anonymous Sins.* The earlier collection included a few efforts at rhyme and versification. More importantly, there were more long poems and compact cycles of poems, and these in their dramatic and narrative techniques were characteristically more transparent, more accessible. The first book may seem fuller, as indeed it literally is, but instead of setting the two selections against each other, it is more insightful to understand that they belong together, if not between the same covers, then certainly together in one's reading. Taken together, they more nearly constitute a whole. And they bear witness to a transition, perhaps concurrent with her artistic passage from rural to urban and suburban milieus, which domesticated the pressure of her raw material without in the least diminishing it. Yet since these poems have appeared in a number of widely diverse places over the last few years, brought together in two volumes now they really constitute a spatial intensification of an ongoing personal and technical task of clarity.

The poetry is of a piece with the fiction—it is jerky, occasionally awkward, but always penetrating, often startling. The poems are composed of hard, stark, simple words and are not abundantly musical. They *are* visual and tactile, as is the fiction. Many of the poems seem to be meditations on or corollaries to the stories, and probably the best poems are three with tiny, intently focused plots—"The Sirens," "The Struggle to Wake from Sleep," and "Passing an Afternoon"—which need to be *read* more than they need to be talked about here. When some of the poems seem unstylish, I keep recalling the successful woman poet in the story "Accomplished Desires" who realized "how reality was too violent for poetry and how poetry, and the language itself, shimmered helplessly before the confrontation with living people and their demands." While that realization may be worthless for rationalizing away the failure of any poem, it is nevertheless true, and significant to appreciating the level of feeling on which Joyce Carol Oates writes.

The emotional range of *Love and Its Derangements* is suggested immediately in the first two poems; it extends from the most frenzied scramble of love-making in midair to the sensuous haze of sleep. Landscapes for this exploration of love and its confusions vary through the poems from beach to city to asylum to ordinary rooms. The repetitive experience of love animates the psyche into an inexorable pattern of rising and falling, projected in one poem as the soaring and plummeting of sea gulls. In the habit of passion gravity is the ultimate and abiding natural force. These are the barest elements in the definitions of love and its mutations.

Love is first shapeless, formless; it is an anarchy we don't know how to contain or when to release. We exalted love as the human mission, and then made it elusory; now we careless zealots pursue it with a vengeance:

> We in love skate
> over the knuckles of others.
> They say, "Why did you do that?"
> We reply, "We are accomplishing certain
> difficult turns."

Love is always flight and descent, and we are still questing after that old, promised transcendence, that orgastic reach for the infinite, when in fact "we love/in rooms":

> Geometry created us.
> Perfect of proportion, we love
> in rooms; doors chaste
> as blank foreheads open
> to our private keys. . . .
>
> Outside our rooms are
> fences that sink into the earth:
> roots curling in that darkness
> are cut in pieces, unliving.
> Our earth is filled in with
> broken bricks, boards, and old nails.
>
> In a box we maneuver
> from a set of walls
> to another set of walls—
> no space in between.
> Our stories, told quickly,
> are symbols of ourselves, the people
> we must be, the lovers, inspired
> to an infinite love
> in a series of boxes.

Love is above all a chaos out of which we try to make sustenance. So we lovers evolve a dubious symbiosis for which the price of union—the appearance of completion—is a certain obliteration of self.

What then is this old romantic love but a fabrication, a whole world made out of words breathed into the air? Lovers envelop themselves together in an invisible protective sac of words, a kind of placenta, their privilege. But once the sac is punctured and the lovers are borne separately out into the world, Joyce Carol Oates must remythologize love according to her own unrelenting vision.

> it is not a baptism
> or a fury from an old god's beak
> but an ordinary violence
> framed by windowsills
> the loosing of fresh blood
> an ordinary violence
> girls strain from windowsills
> to achieve

While she discards the old mythology, she preserves the patterns of ritual. Love is that which happens over and over again, the same old tyranny reborn, invariably *déjà vu.* Passion is periodic and finally habitual, and for lack of knowing what else to do with it we canonize it.

We are faintly absurd genuflecting in that ritual, sensing as we do after awhile that one is no more than a fixed point somewhere on a wheeling cycle of love, hurtled around through the familiar exhilarations and atrocities of passion by the demands of one's body and one's loneliness. Volition is debilitated—"We are loving in pantomime/ It is a scenario we have inherited." We are acting out "a frayed drama," she calls it elsewhere, the denouement of which is depletion and bewildered paralysis. It is the experience of reaching one's capacity for boredom, which for her characters means reaching the limits of one's tolerance for anonymity and stasis. Love prolonged is attrition; lines from *Anonymous Sins* expose it as the biggest dream-cheat of them all:

> . . . Marriage auspiciously
> Drapes you in white, and then
>   rapes you with hung
> Bodies of broken birds. . . .
>
> I never thought I'd disband
> My youth so young.

Distilled from this monotonous process of loving and recovering is the obstinate fact of aloneness. Despite the protective sac of words, despite the symbiosis, lover is existentially separate from lover, and perhaps the best we do is to share the fudamental condition of estrangement. "The beloved is a cage/you cannot enter," she says of the absent lover; but it is probably true as well of the beloved who is present.

Women *alone* then. It is here that Joyce Carol Oates delineates with controlled anger and perfect clarity a definition of who and what woman is. And the definition is less the conventional indictment of men than it is an apocalyptic confession simply of what it is like to be an intensely conscious woman.

> women lose too much blood
> and are then incompetent
> of judgment
> they become translucent
> and see too much . . .
>
> they lose blood enough
> to write their names everywhere
> initialing a city
> in bright drying red

And all this wear and tear of body and spirit that goes by the name of love leaves women to "contemplate their bodies/silent and baffled as bandages."

All this for a woman amounts to mutilation—"an ordinary violence." It amounts to turning into someone else, possessing words, thoughts, even a face, only half your own. A woman's skin is rubbed raw with the skin of men, so that touch itself, however gentle, can only be a stinging agony; and finally when enough layers of one's organ of sensation have been rubbed away, touch will be nothing at all, no feeling, only bleeding.

Love is voluptuous self-destruction, but a woman, as long as she can, must regard its most ravaging consequences with composure and a certain detachment:

> You have broken me up into pieces.
> Chunks of flesh hand-sized
> and bite-sized have fallen from
> one another is surprise.
> Look, they are pulsing. . . .
>
> All this mess, this bleeding
> of puzzle parts, will have to
> be cleaned up.
> The parts must be forced back together.
> They must add up to the shape
> of a woman, a topographical map,
> with proper directions of North and
>   South.

This mutilation is rehearsed in every kind of experience, as it is in a poem depicting the routine carnage on the expressway. The rush-hour exodus from the city is infused with sexual metaphor. The inevitable collision of glittering machines sends shards of glass flying back into an open mouth— an astonishing image of conception itself. If this is the "ordinary violence" with which we are conceived, and if this is the unembellished picture of our acts of love, what *is* the connection between men and women? It is a question that echoes insistently through the last story in *The Wheel of Love,* without answer.

A woman's body comes to be an insupportable burden, especially if it is judged beautiful. A woman struggles between that heavy impassiveness and the compulsion to perpetual dance. In one of the most extraordinary passages in all of Joyce Carol Oates' writing (from the story "Unwritten, Unmailed Letters"), her character confesses the compulsion:

> . . . I am wearing a mask, I am never naked. My nakedness, with my lover, is a kind of mask—something he sees, something I can't quite believe in. Woman who are loved are in perpetual motion, dancing. We dance and men follow to the brink of madness and death, but what of us, the dancers?—when the dancing ends we stand back upon our heels, back upon our heels, dazed and hurt. Beneath the golden cloth on our thighs is flesh, and flesh hurts. Men are not interested in the body, which feels pain, but in the rhythm of the body as it goes about its dance, the body of a woman who cannot stop dancing.

This passage has reverberations in the poem "Mirage": "men have no idea of your body/they do not see the body," because, as she perceives elsewhere, men are simply inept, embarrassed before a woman's pain. But these are merely the conventions of love. A man is driven to the brink of madness and death, and a woman, to longing for self-mutilation:

> I wish I could take a knife and cut out an important piece of my body, my insides, and hold it up . . . on a street corner, an offering. Then will they let me alone? . . . I want to cut up my body, I can't live in this body.

Miss Oates' is a poetry of love as we have known it (once we have had the nerve-endings of perception rubbed raw into sufficient acuteness), rather than a poetry of love as it might be, out there beyond the fantasies of popular songs, out there beyond the revels of narcissistic romanticism, or even out there beyond the daily, incremental violences of intimacy. If indeed there *is* anything out there. Perhaps it was our old propensity for dreaming what's "out there"—beyond the horizon, over the rainbow—that lent us the bravado to live as though man and woman could come together without murdering each other. When we are tempted to see through our self-mystification, we stand staring at seagulls floating and dipping through air, "as near as we know to the shapes of love."

> If we could tear open those bodies and unwind
> from them their fatal guts
> would they tell us anything about ourselves?

Even the task of understanding human love will require acts of mutilation.

Margaret Myers

LOVE AND WILL

Author: Rollo May (1909–   )
Publisher: W. W. Norton and Company (New York). 325 pp. $6.95
Type of work: Psychoanalytical philosophy

An inquiry into the interdependency of love and will and why they have become problems in our time

"The striking thing about love and will in our day is that, whereas in the past they were always held up to us as the *answer* to life's predicaments, they have now themselves become the *problem*."

Thus begins one of the most profoundly affecting books in the past few decades. It is a book difficult to classify. It is part psychology, part philosophy, but through it all is the very real concern of a man for Man in trouble. Dr. May does not preach, but the book is highly ethical in its probing, questioning, and suggestions.

Dr. May draws on the experience of more than twenty-five years of psychoanalytic practice and a wide and thoughtful reading. He tells us in the Foreword that *Love and Will* was eight years in the writing. That much is evident on reading the book, for almost every sentence is packed with information and meaning, so that the book often seems a distillation of a much larger work. What appears to be Dr. May's guiding concern every step of the way is that the study be readily accessible to as wide an audience as possible. While more than passing acquaintance with psychology helps in understanding the concepts discussed, the book can be read and understood by the average reader. That Dr. May has succeeded is evidenced by the fact of its reaching the nonfiction best-seller list. The editors of the magazine *Psychology Today* thought *Love and Will* so important that they devoted one whole issue to it.

It is almost impossible to quote at random from a work of this kind. Dr. May has structured his work tightly, and any one concept flows logically from preceding ones so smoothly that to take a sentence or paragraph out of context would be rather like showing a jawbone and saying, "This is what Man looks like." One could, with profit, reproduce the Table of Contents and urge that the book be read, and read again.

The book is divided into three sections: "Love," "Will," and "Love and Will." There are three concepts, none of them particularly new, but they are related in ways that may not have been suggested before. They are: "Eros," the "Daimonic," and "Intentionality." Dr. May has a great deal to say about sexual love, but it is Eros, in the larger Greek sense of "the drive of love to procreate or create—the urge . . . toward higher forms of being and relationship" to which he directs most of his attention. It is the loss of the sense of Eros in our mechanistic world that Dr. May mourns and which he seeks to re-introduce into our culture. "Eros is the center of the vitality of a culture—its heart and soul," he says. He sums up: "And when release of tension takes the place of creative eros, the downfall of the civilization is assured."

That is just one of the many highly explosive bombs that Dr. May lets fall on his unsuspecting reader. It is interesting to note that the letters to the editor of *Psychology Today* after the issue devoted to *Love and Will* were concerned with what Dr. May had to say about sex. In this day of enlightened discussions of sex and the casual sexual liaisons formed, it would seem that sex itself has become a problem. Dr. May understands that very well when he says that "what underlies our emasculation of sex is the *separation of sex from eros*. Indeed, we have set sex over *against* eros, used sex precisely to avoid the anxiety-creating involvements of eros." It is the re-combination of eros with sex that Dr. May is pleading for:

> The daimonic is *any natural function which has the power to take over the whole person*. Sex and eros, anger and rage, and the craving for power are examples. The daimonic can be either creative or destructive and is normally both. When this power goes awry and one element usurps control over the total personality, we have "daimon possession," the traditional name through history for psychosis. The daimonic is obviously not an entity but refers to a fundamental, archetypal function of human experience—an existential reality in modern man and, so far as we know, in all men.

The second of Dr. May's concepts is one that he very naturally sees as a view to which objections will be raised. He makes his case for recognizing the daimonic in our lives and learning to live with it rather than trying to repress it. Through a step-by-step guide, he shows us that love and the daimonic are allied, and that by making the impersonal daimonic personal, we can go on to a transpersonal understanding of the meaning of love in human life.

Dr. May's concept of intentionality is the most difficult to understand. He gives us a history of the word, beginning with Greek thought, then progressing through Arabic philosophy to the Western world, particularly in the Middle Ages, and on up to the present. It is a word and a concept that has come in and out of vogue for centuries. Dr. May says: "By intentionality, I mean the structure which gives meaning to experience. It is not to be identified with intentions, but is the dimension which underlies them; it is man's capacity to have intentions. It is our imaginative participation in the coming day's possibilities. . . . out of which comes the awareness of our capacity to form, to mold, to change ourselves and the day in relation to each other." Tillich defines intentionality as "being directed toward meaningful contents." It is this concept that Dr. May uses to bridge the gap between love and will.

Another book, published shortly after *Love and Will*, gives an excellent short history of Phenomenology and discusses in the chapter devoted to Edmund Husserl the phenomenological and psychological implications of intentionality. The book, *Existence and Love*, by William A. Sadler, is a companion volume to *Love and Will* and is, in its way, as important a book as *Love and Will*. It is a more scholarly work and therefore not as accessible to the average reader, but one which gives a concise background to many of the things Dr. May mentions in passing.

It is interesting to trace the influences on Dr. May's thought. It was largely through his efforts that Americans were introduced to the European existential phenomonologists. In the book *Existence: A New Dimension in Psychiatry and Psychology*, which he edited with Ernest Angel and Henri Ellenberger, the vehicle of thought is Heidegger as expanded by Binswanger, the Swiss psychiatrist. This book is quite technical and was not intended for the general reader, but it is essential in understanding Dr. May's thought. Dr. May's *Man's Search for Himself*, published in 1953, accurately predicted the violence and destructiveness in the 1960's that were the outcome of the emptiness and apathy of the '50's. Dr. May scrupulously credits the men whose ideas he uses to explain his own version of what has happened to modern man. Dr. May expands and furthers their ideas with a very evident concern. It is this concern, or care, which unites love and will. As Dr. May says, "Care is a state in which something does *matter;* care is the opposite of apathy. Care is the necessary source of eros, the source of human tenderness." In his book *The Courage To Be,* the late Paul Tillich says that the minister must, at times, take on the function of psychotherapist, and that the therapist, by communicating the courage to be, can perform a ministerial function. Tillich possessed a pene-

trating understanding of psychoanalysis, and was, we assume from reading May, a valued and respected friend. Tillich brings up the concepts of the daimonic and intentionality in *The Courage To Be.*

Dr. May draws interesting psychological insights from the world of art, literature, and music, and says that "Art and neurosis both have a *predictive* function. Since art is communication springing from unconscious levels, it presents to us an image of man which is as yet present only in those members of the society who, by virtue of their own sensitized consciousness, live on the frontier of their society— live, as it were, with one foot in the future." Dr. May's own thoughtful readings, and the insights he draws from them, are presented in this definitive work. If the field of psychoanalysis is ever to go beyond the witch-doctor stage, it will be because of men like Rollo May, a man living on the frontier of psychotherapy.

Dennis Pendleton

LOVE AND WORK

Author: Reynolds Price (1933–   )
Publisher: Atheneum Publishers (New York), 143 pp. $4.50
Type of work: Novel
Time: The present
Locale: North Carolina

A probing story of past and present and of a man attempting to find the meaning and direction of his own life in a world of memory, imagination, and fact

Principal characters:
THOMAS EBORN, a teacher and writer
JANE EBORN, his wife
MR. AND MRS. TODD EBORN, his parents
MISS IDA NOLEN, his mother's friend
TED, one of Tom's University friends
ALIX, Ted's fiancée

Reynolds Price's third novel, *Love and Work,* probes the thoughts and actions of a young man as he experiences the death of his mother, the effect of the chaotic drift of the past on the present, and the reality of total failure as a husband, son, teacher, and author. Tom Eborn nourishes knowledge of something nebulously defined and seemingly lost in his hidden psyche. The faster the bonds are severed with the past, the greater emphasis Tom's conscious mind places on its presence in his memory. The omniscient narrator blends occurrence with dream in such a skillful manner that the dreams of Tom become real for the reader and relay deeper insight into the main character's unsettled state of mind. Tom exists emotionally "between two worlds—one dead and the other powerless to be born." This novel, then, deals primarily with the first of these two worlds and presents a series of actions in four days that plunge Tom into the depths of despair, where Kierkegaard believed man discovers either salvation or suicide.

The major concern in this novel is Tom's recognizing and categorizing satisfactorily the degree and quality of love that had existed between his mother and father. Tom's dead world comes alive in his consciousness when his worries, doubts, memories, and dreams finally collate into a pattern of vivid awareness that love had manifested itself in his past. The chapter written on his parent's imaginary courtship and Ida Nolen's final message reconciles in his mind what had plagued him as a gaping discrepancy glimpsed between the young couple's courtship and the closing years of their life together. The problem thus posed leads Tom to bury himself in his work in order to escape the reality of total despair.

The novel opens with a ringing telephone that Tom refuses to answer. The continuous ringing makes him remember how the death of his father and four friends had been announced earlier in his life and that thirty miles away gropes his mother who daily grows blinder because of an optic aneurysm. Yet Tom remains in his study insensitively pounding out an essay, work for a student publication, because Jane, his wife, had promised to protect his privacy from the intruding world. Tom's essay supports his belief that work frees a man from any dependence on other human beings and shields mankind from final doom. Jane, troubled by the telephone call from Mrs. Eborn to Tom, interrupts her husband's thoughts in order to convey her concern. Tom, realizing that his literary effort had been terminated for the morning, decides to join his mother and her television-addicted friend Ida for lunch.

It still seemed home, from miles away —the safe place, the goal (no, the *end*) of all wanderings. He had driven these thirty miles perhaps a thousand times in the past sixteen years, beginning as a college freshman himself, home each weekend as the nearest refuge from roaring dorms, sour cafeterias. The road then had been almost country road— two narrow lanes laid through round pine hills, a house or a gas station every few miles (country gas stations, no pennants or beacons). Yet clear or cluttered, and though he now mostly drove it in duty, a knowledge had always come upon him, at about halfway, that forces stronger than his own guilty will had taken control and were reeling him in—not flapping and gasping but willing and soothed, *won* not *caught*. It came upon him now. More than willing, he yielded; raced in.

Upon arriving at the old family home, he finds no one; so he decides to occupy himself by nostalgically reminiscing over things past. There Tom reads an account of his father's death, recorded twelve years earlier by his mother. His introspection is again disturbed, this time by Ida who brings news of Mrs. Eborn's collapse and hospitalization. Tom arrives at the hospital within minutes of his mother's death. After funeral arrangements have been completed, Tom drives back to his work—not Jane or home. There he

concludes the essay and attempts sleep.

After the funeral, Tom submerges himself into teaching and grading the final semester work. This university drudgery for most teachers becomes a sacred guide to solitude and calm for Tom. Having graded the last examination, Tom drives home only to discover Jane weeping over his essay. As feeble consolation for her hurt, Tom offers to renew their marriage contract; Jane accepts. The following day Tom drives to his mother's home to sort the family papers.

The house still looked disturbingly clean. Though uncontrollably neat himself, he'd made early peace with his mother's disorder (dishevelment not squalor) and had been, only weeks before, touched by her saying as she gestured toward corners—"One more thing about blindness, Tom—you never see cobwebs." So now, as he opened blinds and light flooded corners cleared at last for her funeral, he felt a little freed, another knot loosened—the house now entirely *house*, no longer his, no more hung with emotion (threat, demand) than his automobile. The chance for disinterest stood in him suddenly, amazingly—"I can clear all this, myself, today."

Returning home late in the afternoon, he rounds a curve to see a car that had smashed into a light pole minutes before. After the authorities have been notified, Tom remains helplessly immobile. The police arrive in time to watch the young driver die in Tom's arms. Tom drives home, his sight focused on the road, trying not to think of the dead boy, his mother, the novel he is writing. That evening at supper Tom, cowardly, excuses himself from dinner with his wife and friends by escaping to his bedroom in order to hide from the shocking effects of the day.

Next morning Tom throws himself into literary reconstructions of imaginary scenes from the courtship of his parents. Much of the story is spent unfolding the appealing nature of the girl, his mother, who captivated the suave, sure-of-himself young man his father was pictured as being. Tom seems to gain some psyche satisfaction from his fictious portrayal of his parents' courtship.

Ida calls the following evening to inform Tom that Mrs. Eborn's house had been broken into. Tom and Jane immediately leave for the family home. There they meet Ida, and she relates what Mrs. Eborn had called to tell Tom the morning of her death. Ida's story concerns Mrs. Eborn the night before she died when she found her husband, dead for twelve years, sitting in his chair in the living room. Moments later he vanished. Ida clears the mystery of Mrs. Eborn's house being entered by suggesting that Tom's mother and father had returned home together after their twelve-year separation.

Because of all these events, Tom has learned to bury himself in his work as therapeutic salvation from the futile rationalization of his past. He is highly introspective, reflecting upon insights into life, literature, and the art of writing, but totally unable to express effectively any of his thoughts:

All he knew was the answer, no antidote yet, no reparation. "The wreck, that boy—the woman was right of course. My hands are clean. I am not mad yet. But coming today, the wreck was an emblem of my own cruel waste. Surely not intending it, the boy very easily demolished himself. My act was intended, but easier still. In an ashcan

fire I destroyed all I had of my parents' lives, denied them the dignity of their passions. The boy is my parents, may also be me. Mistakes can be permanent. Perhaps I've destroyed what cannot regrow; hacked all of us—Father, Mother me and therefore Jane—loose from our only tether, the past; our proofs of a constant need and use for love, however less strong, less lasting than our skins the love must be." That seemed the thing he was sorry for, the wreck against which these past weeks had warned him—dreams, his mother's death, Jane's instant discovery of the hole in his essay; then the boy's death, too late, mere confirmation, mockery of his waste. But the thing was done—his own life free and, worse, adrift; his parents' lives fouled and stopped by him.

Jane, on the other hand, seems to manifest stability, but her character is not totally developed in this novel. Also, for some reason Tom has lost a sense of chivalry toward Jane. Had he ever had such a feeling toward her? Like Huck Finn, Tom is motivated to see tragedy in possibly harmless situations of life. Ambivalent feelings toward his parents are often expressed. His father's death, for which he was totally unprepared, had left him emotionally crippled and distraught; he almost wished for his mother's death in order to erase his inadequate feelings of unfulfilled sonship duties. Tom's feeling for his father is one of adoration, even twelve years after their separation by death. His feeling for his mother has become a strange mixture of tender concern, conscience pangs, and resentment. When his mother dies, his subconscious thought finds freedom which enables him to discover that the marriage of his parents was firmly based on mutual love.

He saw the change and meant it; it was true—"What I'd granted *us*. It began with you—what you said that night when you'd read my piece on work. I had stripped Mother's life; your life—and ours. There were pure kinds of work that involved no products so were hardest of all, being fueled by nothing more visible than love. These scenes will be a chart of one kind, a work of love which will find exactly that—that love can be work."

This solution of the novel seems adequate for the author. But for the reader the conclusion is not so simple; the problem is at best only half solved. Tom has not yet realized the larger of his two worlds: that other one, "powerless to be born." Perhaps the author means to imply that now Tom can live in a mature relationship with his wife and his friends, not afraid of what danger a ringing telephone may suggest, and not forced to work simply to escape frustrations that overpower him. Probably Mr. Price intended no such implication—to him the problem is Tom's desire to discover the true perspective of his father and mother's love for each other.

Only after a sequel story of Tom's subsequent attitude toward life would most readers believe that the problems of the plot have been adequately treated. As the story begins, Tom, escaping life by means of work, is a highly unsuccessful caricature of a husband, teacher, friend, or individual. Why should he be so concerned about the degree of love his father and mother felt for each other when his own feeling for his wife is hardly mentioned, if non-existent? What degree of manliness does a man possess who leaves his wife as host of their friends while he, almost physically sick, keeps to his bedroom. What chivalry has a man who without stated cause neglects his wife emotionally, consigning her to the menial practicality of life? The entire relationship of Tom and his wife suggests that he feels superior to her, that her feelings do not matter to him, and that their having to get along together in daily, commonplace routine becomes a hindrance to his actual existence.

In fairness to Reynolds Price, we must admit that he shows us ourselves in our moments of weakness, our moments of selfishness, our moments of seeking escape from unsoluable difficulties. Has Mr. Price showed us a modern Hamlet who is able to conclude differently from Shakespeare's Hamlet that the envisioned wrongs of his mother toward his father did not exist—that the fact of their love for each other becomes for him the cornerstone of his new faith in life? Tom has no Claudius to kill, and henceforth he can devote himself to the business of living positively according to the formula he has discovered from the relationship of his parents. His present depends upon his past, which he inherited, and only after the major links with the past are broken can Tom Eborn be born again, as his name suggests, into the present. Before the realization of his parents' love for each other, work was Tom's salvation. Now through the lessons of experience, work can regain its proper perspective in a reality balanced by love.

Jane Litton

LOVE IN THE RUINS

Author: Walker Percy (1916-   )
Publisher: Farrar, Straus & Giroux (New York). 403 pp. $7.95
Type of work: Novel
Time: 1983 or the none-too-distant future
Locale: Louisiana

As satire of our times and alarming prophecy for the future, Walker Percy's third novel makes a radical departure from the style and subject matter of his earlier books, The Moviegoer *and* The Last Gentleman

Principal characters:

DR. THOMAS MORE, who loves "women best, music and science next, whiskey next, God fourth, and (his) fellowman hardly at all"

ELLEN, his lusty Presbyterian nurse

LOLA, a big, beautiful, talented girl who teaches cello at Texas A. & M.

MOIRA, a romantic secretary from the LOVE clinic, where human sexual response is measured

ART IMMELMANN, a curiously diabolic and knowledgeable drug salesman

It is Walker Percy's contention that the anxiety of our times comes, not from the threat of the bomb's fall, but from the possibility of its not falling. In other words, the threat of imminent extinction adds savor to our existences. In Kierkegaard's terms, in times of dread, one forgets ends and wants only *to be.*

And so Walker Percy sets his third novel in the South "at a Time Near the End of the World" (specifically, 1983). At the book's beginning, Percy's protagonist Dr. Thomas More (a collateral descendant of Saint Thomas More) is found barricaded in an abandoned ruin (an orange-roofed former Howard Johnson's motel) with three women. More tells the entire tale in the first person, supposedly speaking to posterity from his barricade by way of a tape-recorder. The book is, however, too introspective (and too long as well) to maintain for long the illusion that More is speaking extemporaneously. The recorder is simply a device Percy uses to introduce his

story; he abandons it almost immediately.

More's dilemma is seen at first in rather simplistic terms: "surviving with three girls, all of whom like you and each of whom detests the other two, is both horrible and pleasant." Provisions are set in so that the four may survive a catastrophe which promises to demolish the entire western world. The end of the world is, however, as much promise as threat; and More is aware of the ambivalence of his position: "Either I am right and a catastrophe will occur, or it won't and I'm crazy." As it turns out, More is not crazy and the catastrophe does materialize; the Troubles fail, however, to annihilate the modern world.

The end-of-the-world threat forms the novel's narrative framework, yet it is merely a scaffolding. For Percy knows that "in every age there is the temptation to see signs of the end," and so his concern is not so much with the end itself as with the psychological and philosophical phenomena which do indeed threaten, most urgently in this age, to precipitate the world's end. The book then takes upon it something of an encyclopedic quality as our narrator catalogues the "manifold woes of the Western world" by introducing us to a multitude of characters, some presented as little more than case histories, who repeatedly illustrate the malaise of the times.

The malaise includes exacerbated cases of alienation, bad faith, everydayness, empiricism, and severe polarization. The society of the future is dichotomized into mutually exclusive groups of businessmen and scientists, conservatives (or Knotheads) and liberals (or LEFT-PAPASANEs). Conservatives suffer from delusions of conspiracies and large bowel complaints, while liberals "are more apt to contract sexual impotence, morning terror and a feeling of abstraction of the self from itself."

In somewhat more theoretical terms, however, the polarization which Percy depicts in *Love in the Ruins* epitomizes a deep schism in the consciousness of Western man. Conservatives really suffer, as Dr. More theorizes, from aggravated cases of bestialism or adjustment to the environment, while liberals are afflicted with angelism or excessive abstraction. Their problem, of course, is the legacy Descartes left us: "the dread chasm between body and mind that has sundered the soul of western man for five hundred years."

In other words, polarization is the chief symptom of manifold woe. But the humor in *Love in the Ruins* emerges less from the book's larger implications than from its smaller touches —such as an ex-priest reading *Commonweal* at the vaginal console in the

LOVE clinic. And the book is successful satire because it is so discomfitingly familiar to us. For though Percy sets his novel at a time near the end of the world, clearly the maladies of the times are those of today, heightened, to be sure, just slightly. In Percy's projected 1983 world, vines grow on the freeways and around the bottle of Southern Comfort in the country club bar; machinery is abandoned because no one can repair it; and the hottest political issue of the day is euthanasia, or the right of oldsters to peacefully and pleasantly terminate their own existences. A divisive war in South Ecuador continues. The system (or what is left of it) is threatened by enclaves of militant Black Bantus on the one hand, and communes of peaceful hippie swamp people on the other. And in the American Catholic Church the priest prays for success on the golf links in the name of the "greatest pro of them all." The church celebrates Property Rights Sunday, and the parishioners are reminded that "Our Lord himself, remember, was not a social reformer."

Even the church, then, has become rational and pragmatic. Mysteries, such as God and the human soul, are embarrassments to an emancipated priest and his parish. But not to Dr. Thomas More, who repeatedly shocks his medical colleagues by diagnosing behavior in terms of "perturbations of the soul." More, in fact, has invented "the first caliper of the soul and the first hope of bridging the dread chasm that has rent the soul of Western man ever since the famous philosopher Descartes ripped body loose from mind and turned the very soul into a ghost that haunts its own house."

More's device promises to bridge the chasm and restore soul to body so that man might once again "coincide with himself." The machine is called "More's Qualitative Quantitative Ontological Lapsometer," and it works—that is to say, it correctly diagnoses the maladies, though it cannot cure them. With his lapsometer, More hopes to win the Nobel Prize and to be remembered, with Newton and Einstein, as a man whose discovery changed the consciousness of the Western world. Significantly, after the rather abortive catastrophe, precipitated by diabolic misuse of his lapsometer, More cares no more for prizes. He realizes that "In the last age we planned projects and cast ahead of ourselves. We set out to 'reach goals.'" But More learns better. He wants only to live in love, and perhaps in faith as well. In other words, he wants only *to be*.

If then the end-of-the-world threat is an insufficient device around which to organize the novel, the growth of the protagonist is not. And Dr. More progresses from a man who must gulp down a daily concoction of Tang, Vodka, and duck eggs to overcome morning terror and who cannot differentiate between his love for three, perhaps four, women, to a man who eats grits, hoes a garden, and takes his wife to bed in the morning "twined about [her] as the ivy twineth, not under a bush or in a car or on the floor or any

such humbug as marked the past peculiar years of Christendom, but at home in bed where all good folk belong."

In *Love in the Ruins* Percy is doing several things at once. First of all, he is satirizing an age which lionizes Spiro Agnew and Jacqueline Susann and devotes all its energies to developing ever better golf courses. More importantly, though, Percy studies the malaise in man's soul and implies that it lies beyond objective diagnosis and clinical cure. Percy convinces us that an empirical approach, founded upon the assumption that only the visible is real, cannot presume to heal the sickness of the soul when empiricism, by definition, denies the soul's existence. And most importantly, Percy presents us with a protagonist, a "spotted Christ," a "maculate Christ," a "sinful Christ" who can "reconcile man with his sins" by showing him that one copes best with the modern world through love and faith.

Love in the Ruins is superb satire which, while debunking the foibles of the present moment, manages also to clarify some of the universal dilemmas of human existence. It is not so tightly integrated a book as *The Moviegoer*, winner of the 1962 National Book Award for Fiction, but perhaps that is only because it is written on a larger scale.

Panthea Reid Broughton

LOVE POEMS

Author: Anne Sexton (1928–   )
Publisher: Houghton Mifflin Company (Boston). 67 pp. Paperback, $1.95
Type of work: Poetry

The most recent collection of poems by the Pulitzer Prize winner of 1967, author of Live or Die, All My Pretty Ones, *and* To Bedlam and Part Way Back

The theme of love, which reaches its greatest intensity when paradoxically opposed and threatened, is the controlling passion of this sequence of twenty-five poems. Miss Sexton quotes from an essay by William Butler Yeats:

> One should say before sleeping, "I have lived many lives. I have been a slave and a prince. Many a beloved has sat upon my knees and I have sat upon the knees of many a beloved. Everything that has been shall be again."

One might add that these poems themselves reveal a personality, a speaker who is audacious and intense and determined to live at great risk.

Many paradoxical qualities give to these love poems their shape and color: tenderness and ferocity, joyous rebirth and mordant death, magnetic attraction and repulsion, return and departure. There is a continuity to the sequence and because of this linkage the lover is presented in several metaphoric guises. He is a carpenter who reconstructs the emotive framework and rebuilds the potential joy of the woman-speaker; and it is no accident symbolically that the woman says in her joy:

> . . . for this is the kingdom
> and the kingdom come.

In another instance the image of the lover is that of a boat builder who hoists and rigs the rundown body of the woman—a resurrection theme recurs throughout the sequence. Then the lover becomes a musician:

> Pure genius . . . the composer has stepped into the fire.

The lover becomes an architect. As architect and carpenter, the lover is questioned at one point about the identity of the woman he holds in his arms, and in a passage modeled on "The House That Jack Built" he replies:

> She's the one I carried my bones to
> and built a house that was just a cot
> and built a life that was over an hour
> and built a castle where no one lives. . . .

and

>   . . . Not my real wife.
> She's my real witch, my fork, my mare,
> my mother of tears, my skirtful of hell,
> the stamp of my sorrows, the stamp of my bruises. . . .

Frequently, as in the passages above, the singsong lilt carries a rather frightening content: a sense either of emptiness or of impending injury dominates the tone. Anne Sexton is kin to Diane Wakoski in her sense of the grotesque, the potential horror of the mordant elements that lie just below the skin of beauty. Here is a passage from Miss Sexton:

> For months my hand had been sealed off
> in a tin box. Nothing was there but subway railings.

Perhaps it is bruised, I thought,
and that is why they have locked it
up. . . .

and here is a passage from Miss Wakoski:

> I leave my white hand
> a jeweler's dummy
> with oval nails
>
> . . . .
>
> on the rim
> on the shade
>
> . . . .
>
> for days,
> the white hand cut off at the wrist
> holding the blind delicately. . . .

And Miss Sexton's metaphors of injury are reminiscent of Sylvia Plath:

> My mouth blooms like a cut.
> I've been wronged all year. . . .

and

> Her wings are fastened onto
> her shoulders like bandages. . . .

Yet once in a while there is a pleasing kind of freedom and gusto, unmarred by mixed feelings or hypercon-
sciousness, which permits the poet to
sing wholeheartedly:

> Sweet weight,
> in celebration of the woman I am
> and of the soul of the woman I am
> and of the central creature and its de-
> light
> I sing for you. I dare to live.

Possibly the most impressive passages in the book are those which express deep and unreserved eroticism,
such as the following:

> I am alive when your fingers are.

. . . .
So tell me anything but track me like a
climber
for here is the eye, here is the jewel,
here is the excitement the nipple learns.

I am unbalanced—but I am not mad
with snow.
I am mad the way young girls are mad,
with an offering, an offering. . . .

and

> I was wrapped in black
> fur and white fur and
> you undid me and then
> you placed me in gold light
> and then you crowned me. . . .

Again:

> Draw me good, draw me warm.
> Bring me your raw-boned wrist and
> your
> strange, Mr. Bind, strange stubborn
> horn.
> Darling, bring with this an hour of un-
> dulations, for
> this is the music for which I was born.

But unalloyed eroticism cannot win
the day of this complex kind of love
poetry, which is full of the recognition
of brevity, a sense of loss. The woman
speaker realizes her lover will depart
and the two of them will be shipped
home from summer's love in separate
crates. She attempts to face this realistically:

> Let's face it, I have been momentary.
> A luxury. A bright red sloop in the har-
> bor.
> My hair rising like smoke from the car
> window. . . .

and she compares herself with the wife
to whom her lover will return:

> She is the sum of yourself and your

dream.

   . . . .

She is solid.

As for me, I am a watercolor.
I wash off.

As for the pain of departure, it is handled under heavy influence of Sylvia Plath and is imitative of Plath's father poems, particularly when Miss Sexton calls her lover, "Oh, my Nazi,/ with your S.S. sky-blue eye." In fact, one senses a strong desire to emulate Plath's techniques of building pain and terror, but Miss Sexton lacks Miss Plath's stony anger, her devastating hatred.

The last poem in the book is obviously the most ambitious, a lonely document of twenty-one pages entitled "Eighteen Days Without You." It brings together all the thematic elements of the volume. It is loose and ultrapersonal, rather like a diary; yet some of the sections possess a remarkably successful compression and unity, and at times a lovely lyricism. But the structure is defective. References to historic events are hastily stitched on the basic fabric of a love poem, and some of them are embarrassingly shallow. The poet recalls the day she and her lover met:

   . . . It was Harvard Square

at the kiosk with both of us crying.
I can thank that *there*—
the day Jack Kennedy was dying.

   . . . .

And we both wrote poems we couldn't
   write
and cried together the whole long
   night. . . .

Other sections begin with mere taglines such as "That was Oswald's November" and "Pearl Harbor Day." It's as if the writer suspected an unfortunate thinness in this book of love poems and were trying to attach weights of some larger significance to the scale-pans of love. Some parts of the poem are suffocated with trivia which do not convey a sense of *sincerity* to the reader.

This latest collection is certainly what anyone would call good verse, for the most part. But its successes are minor compared to Miss Sexton's strongest writing of a few years ago. These love poems are skilfully wrought, both sensuous and sensual, and most often sing themselves well; yet they lack a genuinely tragic air that might have created the resonance of greatness. In this sense Anne Sexton has suffered at least a slight decline very similar to that of Denise Levertov after she began to imagine herself vessel and repository of love.

Robert Hazel

LOVE STORY

Author: Erich Segal (1937–   )
Publisher: Harper and Row (New York). 131 pp. $4.95
Type of work: Novel
Time: The present
Locale: Cambridge, Massachusetts, and New York City

A frankly sentimental story of marriage between two college students who learn the meaning of love

> Principal characters:
> OLIVER BARRETT IV, a Harvard senior, scion of a wealthy Boston family
> JENNY CAVILLERI, a Radcliffe senior, daughter of a pastry baker
> OLIVER BARRETT III, Oliver's "stuffed shirt" father
> PHIL CAVILLERI, Jenny's widowed father, a foil to Oliver Barrett III

A reader looking for the motivating principle in Erich Segal's *Love Story* will find it best expressed in the last words of the novel: "Love means not ever having to say you're sorry." Although that thematic statement seems to be an overly simplified definition of a more complex emotion, it is nonetheless valid in terms of the author's plot. By excluding from his novel any psychological implications of a love relationship, Erich Segal has written a simple novel about a childlike love which requires no verbalization. Ironically, however, the very simplicity of both the plot and the theme frustrates a reviewer. How does one criticize a book which is based on the apparently unsophisticated idea that the love of two people grows out of their uncomplicated, often unspoken emotional responses? It is tempting to dismiss *Love Story* as a basically sentimental portrayal of a "boy-meets-girl, boy-gets-girl, boy-loses-girl" situation. However, Segal's characters, unlike those in traditional sentimental novels, do not consciously overindulge in emotions for their own sake. Rather, the seemingly sentimental actions and words of the characters in *Love Story* reflect Segal's belief in an ideal which, like the novel itself, mocks analytical critical probings.

Ideal love, Segal believes, cannot be verbalized or analyzed. It is dependent neither on wealth nor on social position for its existence. But love can completely alter a person. In its expression of these beliefs, *Love Story* reads like a fictional representation of Erich Fromm's theories in *The Art of Loving*. Love, Fromm writes, is the "active concern for the life and growth of that which we love." In other words, love means giving, not receiving. But, Fromm carefully explains, love as an act of giving depends on the character development of the person who is loving. The only person who can truly give has "overcome dependency, narcissistic omnipotence . . . and has acquired courage to rely on his own human powers."

To understand how Segal has not only echoed Fromm in the plot of *Love Story* but has also kept conventional sentimentality from intruding upon its action, one must look at the opening line of the book. As the last sentence summarizes the novel's theme, so the first establishes its restrained tenor and its basically cyclic structure: "What do you say about a twenty-five-year-old girl who died?" What Segal says literally is that Oliver Barrett IV, Harvard Dean's list "jock," met, fell in love with, and married Jenny Cavilleri, a Radcliffe music major. And then, three years after their marriage, Jenny died of leukemia. Structurally, however, Segal transcends the latent sentimentality of the simple story. By relating the story in retrospect through Oliver's first-person narration, the author enables the reader to experience the transforming power of Jenny's love for her young husband.

That a plot based on the theme of initiation through love should achieve best-seller popularity in an age of fiction which often celebrates only grotesque, lonely, and alienated individuals is curious, but not totally inexplicable. The reason for the success of *Love Story* must be attributed to its author's perceptive, honest, and often exhilarating description of two young people in love. In other words, Segal's delineation of Jenny and Oliver's feelings toward each other evokes an almost *déjà vu* sensation in a reader who recalls that in his youth love could be as simple and uncomplicated as the clichéd "I love you." Ironically, though, a cliché did once represent truth. Only time and misuse have forced that truth to lose its original vitality. What Segal perceives is that for many readers of *Love Story* there still resides some vestigial response to the vitality and honesty of the original truth. The value of the novel, then, resides not so much in its fictional

achievement, but rather in its universal, albeit somewhat clichéd, belief that "love conquers all."

What plot there is to this novel grows out of Oliver's inability to see that love is indivisible and that love for Jenny and love for his father should stem from the same source. The conflict between the two loves is precipitated by the socio-economic distinctions between Oliver, the descendant of a wealthy Boston banking family, and Jenny, daughter of a Cranston, Rhode Island, pastry baker. Jenny's refusal to accept Oliver's estrangement from his father, who disapproves of their marriage, only irritates her husband. Oliver regards Jenny's continual efforts to effect a reconciliation as reflections of "some atavistic Italian-Mediterranean notion of papa-loves-bambinos." Nonetheless, Jenny's determination to reunite father and son never weakens. After a violent argument about Oliver's rejection of an invitation to attend his father's sixtieth birthday party, Jenny rushes out of their apartment. Suddenly aware of what he has done to her, Oliver frantically searches the Cambridge area for her. Returning alone to the apartment, he finds Jenny sitting on the steps:

> I stood there at the bottom of the steps, afraid to ask how long she had been sitting, knowing only that I had wronged her terribly.
> "Jenny, I'm sorry—"
> "Stop!" She cut off my apology, then said very quietly, "Love means not ever having to say you're sorry."

It is apparent from his words that Oliver has not yet learned Jenny's lesson about the silent, forgiving communication which is part of love. However, the same statement about the unconditional quality of love is eventually repeated by Oliver to his father in an emotional reconciliation scene after Jenny's death. Her words, then, not only resolve the conflict between Oliver and his father, but also work as a backdrop against which to evaluate the depth of characterization in the novel.

Although Jenny is the more memorable of the two main characters, she is also the more static. A totally rounded character from the beginning of the novel, she acts as a normative referent for the development of Oliver. Often flippant, occasionally sarcastic, but never unkind, Jenny is, according to Fromm's definition, a fully developed human being. Always actively concerned about her husband's growth as a person, she never alters her opinion that Oliver's treatment of his father is disgusting and immature. Like a catalyst or an initiator, Jenny's love eventually forces Oliver to grow up.

Recalling their trip back to Cambridge after Jenny was introduced to his parents, Oliver recognizes Jenny's awareness of his own immaturity and acknowledges her completely rounded personality:

> What I had loved so much about Jenny was her ability to see inside me, to understand things I never needed to carve out in words. She was still doing it. But could I face the fact that I wasn't perfect? Christ, she had already faced my imperfection *and her own.* Christ, how unworthy I felt!

From this "unworthy," self-centered, somewhat shallow boy who had grown up with "the notion I had to be number one," there emerges a man who understands that love is kindness, respect, and acceptance. In the moments after Jenny's death, Oliver finally realizes the true significance of the words Jenny spoke after their first quarrel:

> "Oliver," said my father urgently, "I want to help."
> "Jenny's dead." I told him.
> "I'm sorry," he said in a stunned whisper.
> Not knowing why, I repeated what I had long ago learned from the beautiful girl now dead.
> "Love means not ever having to say you're sorry."
> And then I did what I had never done in his presence, much less in his arms, I cried.

By telling the story in retrospect, Oliver finally brings the novel back, full-cycle, to the beginning. And the reader understands that Oliver has realized from his opening question how one-sided and selfish was his attitude towards love. Thus, the end of *Love Story* reveals Oliver as the same round and completely developed character that Jenny was. Consequently, the cyclic structure of the novel further reinforces Segal's uncomplicated but universal belief in love's transformational qualities.

Like Oliver, many readers have finished *Love Story* with tears in their eyes. Contributing to this unabashed response is the total meaning of the novel: love, although delicate and frail, can effect powerful changes. Admittedly, such a view is not part of the twentieth century literary mainstream. As popular fiction, however, *Love Story* successfully creates conflict and emotional response. As philosophy, it offers a simple statement that may assuage the perplexity and loneliness that a large segment of humanity feels today. One cannot really demand more from a popular best seller.

Dorothy A. Lukas

Sources for Further Study

Criticism:

Spilka, Mark. "Erich Segal as Little Nell, or the Real Meaning of Love Story," in *Journal of Popular Culture*. Spring, 1972, pp. 782-798. Spilka compares in a tongue-in-cheek way, the heroine of *Love Story* to Charles Dickens' Little Nell.

Reviews:

Atlantic. CCXXV, June, 1970, p. 124. 400 words.

Best Sellers. XXIX, March 15, 1970, p. 414. 450 words.

Christian Science Monitor. April 30, 1970, p. 13. 430 words.

New Statesman. LXXX, August 28, 1970, p. 249. 270 words.

Newsweek. LXXV, March 9, 1970, p. 960. 400 words.

THE LOVE-GIRL AND THE INNOCENT

Author: Aleksandr I. Solzhenitsyn (1918—   )
Translated from the Russian by Nicholas Bethell and David Burg
Publisher: Farrar, Straus and Giroux (New York). 131 pp. $4.95
Type of work: Drama
Time: Autumn, 1945
Locale: A labor camp somewhere in the European U.S.S.R.

A play in four acts, telling the story of a political prisoner in a Stalinist labor camp who finds his spiritual freedom through an affirmation of love

Principal personages:
>
> RODION NEMOV, a prisoner, the "Innocent" of the title
> LYUBA NYEGNEVITSKAYA, a prisoner, the "Love-Girl"
> PAVEL GAI, a prisoner, Nemov's friend
> GRANYA ZYBINA, a prisoner, a woman in love with Gai
> BORIS KHOMICH, a prisoner, profiteer, and production chief of the camp
> TIMOFEY MERESHCHUN, a prisoner, the camp doctor
> KOSTYA, a prisoner, professional criminal, work allocator of the camp, Nemov's friend

The Love-Girl and the Innocent, a play by Aleksandr Solzhenitsyn, 1970 winner of the Nobel Prize for literature, was first published in the West in 1969 and performed in Minneapolis at the Tyrone Guthrie Theater in 1970. It is a portrayal of that most exquisite of human sufferings, endless degradation, and despair.

The play is set in an unnamed labor camp somewhere in central Russia in the Autumn of 1945. Its action is focused on the love that arises between two prisoners, Rodion Nemov, a former Red army officer imprisoned for unspecified political crimes, and the woman prisoner Lyuba Nyegnevitskaya, imprisoned for anti-Soviet agitation. Both Nemov and Lyuba were convicted under the infamous Article 58 which allowed such inclusive width of interpretation that the labor camps of the Stalinist era were kept filled with its victims. It is Lyuba who is the "love-girl" of the title, a Russian euphemism for prostitute, for she has survived her years in the labor camps by selling her body to the camp officials for food and favors. Nemov is the "innocent" of the title. New to camp life, he has not yet learned its sharpest lesson: that constant terror and brutality can be endured or survived only through accepting brutality and adding to the terror. Initiative, efficiency, integrity, and human decency are neither desirable nor possible within Solzhenitsyn's vision of the system of tyranny. Nemov, supposing at first that honesty and the efficiency of military order can subdue and put right the chaos of greed and self-interest that keeps the labor camp in constant turmoil and lowers its productivity, has accepted from Camp Commandant Ovchukhov the post of production chief, or prisoner in charge of the internal organization of the camp. He quickly discovers his own error. For the order of camp life is not chaotic, but only infernal, founded upon human greed and sloth. Each man, from the lowest, most helpless prisoner to the camp commandant himself, grubs after whatever little bit of satisfaction and material comfort he can obtain at whatever cost to those around him. The prisoners' often-repeated watchword is, "You die today, I'll die tomorrow." Nemov is soon deprived of his powerful position by the other entrenched prisoner office-holders and their retinues of "shivers," or hangers-on because he will not play their game of embezzlement and extortion for personal profit. The camp commandant, himself deeply involved in the business of personal profiteering from the sufferings of his prisoners, is easily convinced that Nemov should be removed from his post and replaced by the venal and sycophantic criminal Khomich. Only when Nemov is forcibly returned to the ranks of helpless prisoners does he discover his first sense of freedom. Later, he says of his days as production chief, "I was still trying to get in with the authorities. A sudden crash and there I was still trying to pull myself back at the last step. In those days I preferred to bend others than to bend myself. But I feel freer now I'm an ordinary black-faced working man."

The love that grows between Nemov and Lyuba comes as a surprise to them both and to Nemov as a kind of grace beyond hope. He tells her, "Ever since I was arrested, I've felt as if I was living in a cloud of black smoke. I haven't been able to smile, but it's so wonderful now, now I'm with you. It's as if you've released me, let me out into freedom." But Lyuba has lived longer in the prison camps and replies to him only, "Go on talking," enjoying, but under no illusions about the dream world spun by his words for her. The crisis for both comes soon upon their discovery of each other. For Lyuba, Nemov's love for her in all its innocence is a chance for a long-lost self-respect; she says to him, "Look, wouldn't it be better if I stayed your sister? I'll be a good sister, you'll see. . . . If only I could change back again, just for you become clean and pure." That of course can never be, any more than the leveling tyranny of camp life can fulfill the dream of brotherhood and prosperity that was the goal of the Revolution. As the profiteer Khomich has cynically said earlier in the play, "This isn't a State, this is Campland!" Lyuba knows that the realities of existence under tyranny leave no one clean and pure, and she fears for her beloved innocent Nemov in a world his idealism cannot comprehend. She says to him:

> Darling, tell me one thing. Are you hungry? I mean now? Because I am. All my life I've been hungry. How will we be able to survive this camp? You'll never be able to fix things up for yourself, you haven't got a trade. By yourself you might be able to keep afloat, but with me round your neck you'll sink. In a little while you'll want to get rid of me.

The camp doctor, the prisoner Mereshchun, propositions Luyba to join his harem of "nurses" in return for food, special favors, and his protection. She tells Nemov of the doctor's proposition and offers it as a source of survival for both, if Nemov will only consent to share her with another man. But Nemov will not go down like the other prisoners in venal compromise, for he has discovered that there is for him something more valuable than his life: it is his conscience. He tells her, "Lyuba, I could never share you, not the smallest piece of you, with anyone." As she frees herself from his embrace, she speaks sadly, "Well, you must give me up then. You'll lose all of me, all of me." Nemov returns to his work and as if in justification of her fears for him, he is badly injured when a faulty ore bucket falls on his head. The last scene of the play sees a group of prisoners embarking on transport vehicles for the even-more-hopeless camps of the Siberian wastes and Lyuba climbing the steps of the doctor's warmly-lit cabin, her head bowed.

Despite the flowering and sudden end of the love story that is the central subject of the play, *The Love-Girl and the Innocent* has no dramatic shape in its four acts. The drama of the play is not in any story or plot development, but rather in the constant violence done to the human sensibilities by what is unfolded before the audience. There is created a sense of constant terror, of the absurdity of all actions, of an all-pervasive grime, and an inescapable injustice. The audience endures unrelieved outrage in sympathy with the prisoners of Campland. We are reminded repeatedly of a great dream ruined, a noble experiment betrayed. The brutality of the camp guards is not so much a source of that betrayal as is the venality of both brutalizers and brutalized. The question is raised, "What do we need to survive?" And we are struck by the similarity of form between Nemov's "I couldn't share you with anyone," and the greed of the others in Campland, for their venality is also a refusal to share. Where, then, is virtue? And of what nature is Nemov's "conscience"? For Nemov, sharing Lyuba would be to prostitute the only beautiful thing he has found in this world of hell. He can not spoil this unexpected grace of love which has come to him only after he has freed himself from the desire to grub, to bend others and not himself be bent.

Nemov's refusal to share his beloved has the same form as the action of the profiteers, but its essence is radically different because it rises from a deeper value—the value of moral absolutes. Though Nemov apparently loses what he would not share by refusing to share it, he does not in fact lose it at all; for it is his freedom to choose a path of action beyond necessity which is the essence of his love, and this freedom he has not bartered for a mitigation of suffering. In his refusal he has ceased to be an innocent and he has released Lyuba from being a love-girl, even when she is later forced to seek the doctor's cabin. Nemov's innocence lay in his ignorance of his own capacity for evil and his potential for freedom; his refusal is an exercise of that freedom and a recognition of the possibility for its venal opposite within him, which must be refused. By Nemov's choice Lyuba is freed from her former degradation, no matter what her future surrender to that degradation, because she has been recognized for at least one moment in time as a human being, worthy of another's sacrifice for her, not as a dehumanized instrument of pleasure.

Solzhenitsyn's stagecraft belongs to the tradition of Gorky, not that of Chekhov. It follows a strict naturalism of presentation with no interest in psychological subtleties or nuance. The effort to reproduce the realistic detail of the camps is carried to the extent of copious stage directions as to the set designs and staging. Which is to say that Solzhenitsyn's play is in many ways an archaism, belonging to the conventions of the Twenties and earlier, not those of the Sixties. But in some far more essential way, *The Love-Girl and the Innocent* is an even greater archaism—it is part of the Russian spiritual tradition, an element which has been almost entirely overlooked by the reviewers in their zeal for celebrating Solzhenitsyn's denunciation of the Russian political system. Solzhenitsyn in this play and in his novels is an obvious inheritor of the spiritual wisdom of Dostoevsky, though not, like him, an adherent of Christianity. It was in "The Legend of the Grand Inquisitor" that Dostoevsky framed the terms of the question of human suffering. All humanity is subjected to suffering; we all live in the prison camp of ourselves from which there is no release, save death. But we all have, as Dostoevsky's Jesus assures the Inquisitor, the great gift of Freedom. A refusal of freedom, an acceptance of tyranny would mitigate suffering. But to refuse one's freedom is to repudiate man, to repudiate oneself; thus, suffering is the price of freedom, and freedom the mark of humanity. In the acceptance of suffering rather than slavery to illusions of well-being, Dostoevsky's and Solzhenitsyn's heroes assert the spirit and the human and gain themselves. Even Dostoevsky's "Underground Man," who prefers his own lowest impulses, debasement, and cruelty to the crystal palace of an illusory universal harmony, finds himself still in possession of his "own stupid will." Amid the unrelieved terror of Solzhenitsyn's Campland, the humanity of Nemov's "own stupid will" is the assertion of a higher and more complex innocence.

Rollin Lasseter

THE LOVELY AMBITION

Author: Mary Ellen Chase (1887-1973)
Publisher: W. W. Norton and Company (New York). 288 pp. $3.95
Type of work: Novel
Time: Early twentieth century
Locale: England and Maine

An unpretentious but moving novel about a Methodist minister who brings his wife and three children from England to downeast Maine

Principal characters:
JOHN TILLYARD, a Methodist minister
MRS. TILLYARD, his wife
THE NARRATOR, his daughter
ANSIE TILLYARD, twin brother of the narrator
MARY TILLYARD, the older daughter of the Tillyards
MRS. GOWAN, a mental patient
KATIE, the Tillyards' housekeeper in England
MRS. BAXTER, the Tillyards' housekeeper in Maine
MR. PLIMSOLL, a primitive Methodist minister

The Lovely Ambition is an atypical novel for our times. In its depiction of the happy and relatively uneventful life of a family and in its graceful and lucid style, it more closely resembles the novels of the last century. It is, however, decidedly more than a warmed-over serving of nineteenth century sentimentalism. Miss Chase admires a former way of life, but she is careful not to present a too romantic view of it. And she is clearly aware of the currents of our own era that have swept away this earlier mode of living. In writing of a time when simple virtue was socially acceptable and more easily attainable than it is today, Miss Chase is not being simply nostalgic but, in her unassuming way, is examining universal values.

Set in England and New England, *The Lovely Ambition* describes the life of the Tillyard family. There are clashes of interest among the members of the family and annoyances from the outside, but the fundamental tranquillity is never seriously threatened because of the spirit of love and generosity that binds them. The personality of John Tillyard is the source of the trials of the family and of its strength. Gifted with an unusual intellect, he might have aspired to a position of more renown than that of Wesleyan parson in Saintsbury, Cambridgeshire. To be a Methodist in that part of England was somewhat disreputable, as was shown by the careful distinction made between the *chapel* of the Methodists and the *Church* of the Anglicans. To his friends and even to his own family, Tillyard's selection of denomination remains a mystery. He is little interested in the fine points of theology. He has a feeling for tradition, but he is not so bound by it that his background in Methodism would provide a sufficient motivation for his choice. The true reason appears to be his strong, but unostentatious, love for the weak and the lowly. His life is a constant testimony to his kind-heartedness. The occupation in farm life he loves most is lambing. In season he spends night after night nursing the newly born lambs to strength. He seeks the company of common people—the farmers, the workmen—and derives deep pleasure from learning of their lives.

While John Tillyard lives on a plane that makes him largely unaffected by the petty inconveniences and indignities that his station in life may impose on him, his family is less fortunate. Mrs. Tillyard leads a life that is often uncongenial to her nature. A practical woman, she frequently has reason to regret the unworldliness of her husband. But love and stanch loyalty prompt her to forego her own wishes when they conflict with Tillyard's. It is in school that the children feel most strongly the effects of their father's position. Small everyday acts and occasional bursts of open conflict remind them that they are *chapel* folk, not respectable Anglicans.

Their decision to move to America is the most momentous one in their lives. Tillyard has long admired the United States. An avid reader of Tocqueville, he has been struck by those passages in which the French writer speaks of the promise of American democracy. A copy of *Walden* is his constant companion in Saintsbury and the book has filled him with the desire to visit the country of Thoreau. A more practical consideration that influences their decision to move, however, is the fact that America will provide a better opportunity for Ansie to receive a good education. The offer of a pastorate in Pepperell, Maine, comes just at the time when the Tillyards are becoming concerned about Ansie's preparatory schooling.

A world unlike both what they have known in England and what they are to know in New England is revealed to them on the ship crossing the Atlantic. Tillyard, unwilling to miss an opportunity to mingle with the common people, chooses to travel steerage. Here

the family is thrust suddenly out of a world governed by kindness and courtesy into one ruled by primitive emotions. Confronted for the first time with the spectacle of drunkenness and violence, the children are puzzled by the behavior of their fellow travelers. They wonder about the Greek girl who willingly submits to the kisses of a dozen or so men who struggle to lie beside her. They observe with shocked curiosity the gambling, the cursing, the discomfort, and the despair that surround them. Not the least interesting, nor the least repulsive, of the passengers are the Plimsolls. Like Tillyard, Plimsoll is a Methodist minister who is leaving England to accept a pastorate in America. Here the comparison ends. Plimsoll is proud of his lack of education, which he makes up for in missionary zeal. Like a vulture, he descends upon unsuspecting persons, bringing to them his narrow theology. The ridicule and persecution that he receives in return are his chief delight in life. Mrs. Plimsoll is a silent and imperturbable person who performs her domestic duties with efficiency and with no show of affection. Their fourteen children are, at best, sullenly quiet; at worst, unctuously pious. The teachings of the same John Wesley helped to shape the lives of the Tillyards and the lives of this unlovely and unloving brood.

While the Tillyards feel some nostalgia for Cambridgeshire and are occasionally dismayed by the different customs in America, they find their lot, in general, an improved one. No longer are they subject to discrimination because of their religious denomination. Materially, too, they are better off. A pleasant farmhouse is provided as a parsonage, and they are able to carry on light farming. The inhabitants of

Pepperell are, once their customary reticence is overcome, generous and open-hearted. Coöperative efforts in such things as haying are a special enjoyment for the Tillyards. They are fortunate in having Mrs. Baxter as a housekeeper. A perfectionist in managing the house, she is at first a rather unapproachable person, but the genial influence of her employers brings out her humanity and she comes to exert an influence on the psychological as well as the physical well-being of the family. Tillyard's efforts as a preacher are well received, and it is not long before he is being considered for a position of greater responsibility.

An important new element is brought into their lives by Tillyard's being employed to make a series of visits to the mental patients in an Augusta hospital. This endeavor more than any other in his life gives him a chance to realize his "lovely ambition" to aid those in need of help. Successful in his first efforts, Tillyard decides, despite the misgivings of his wife, to have certain of the inmates visit at the parsonage. After two experiments that end in embarrassment and failure, he brings Mrs. Gowan, an elderly lady who spends her time making flags under the delusion that she is Betsy Ross. Her life had been one of many trials—mistreatment by a fanatically religious mother, marriage to a petty thief, loss of her only child—but in spite of these experiences she has retained a zest for living that most "normal" people would envy. Brought back to sanity by her association with the Tillyards, she approaches each experience with childlike wonder and delight. The Tillyards, as they help her, discover that their own lives are enriched.

Ironically, it is through Tillyard's "lovely ambition" that tragedy is brought to the family. As they are bringing a load of hay into the barn, Ansie, attempting to steady Mrs. Gowan, is struck by a beam, thrown to the ground, and killed. Mrs. Gowan, shattered by the experience, begins to talk again about General Washington's visit.

But the book does not end on a note of defeat. Miss Chase leaves us with the feeling that, however unpredictable the consequences of action, a good man's life has a value that external events cannot destroy.

LOVERS & AGNOSTICS

Author: Kelly Cherry (1940-   )
Publisher: Red Clay Books (Charlotte, N.C.) 74 pp. $3.00 (paperback)
Type of work: Poetry

The first collection of poems by a remarkably promising and exciting young writer

Kelly Cherry's first novel, *Sick and Full of Burning* (1974) was praised for its wit, its intricate structure, and its humor. This favorable comment appeared in fashionable places, such as the *Chicago Tribune* and the *Atlantic Monthly*. This book of poems, on its own terms, is every bit as good as the novel, but it is with wry resignation that one imagines how it would strike the fashionable reviewers.

Lovers & Agnostics is almost fiercely unfashionable in its display of technical and thematic ambition. As Fred Chappell says in a brief and somewhat feisty Foreword to the collection:

Ms Kelly Cherry . . . has purposely written a poetry of intellection (not an "intellectual poetry," which is a different kind of thing and often a rip-off), and by this means has widened, if not obliterated, the boundaries of her sympathies; she has gained the freedom of the observer, having quite seen through the easy pose of the false confessor. She has abjured notions in order to attain to ideas.

Cherry has also attained remarkable feats of characterization, of both men and women, and the creation of a more extended world than poetry usually contains, in a long sequence called "Benjamin John." In scope and technical accomplishment, this is a splendid collection. Even its few flaws are noteworthy, as being the consequences of considerable risks.

The collection is arranged in four sections, the second and third being sequences. The first section, "Among the Mighty Dead," opens with a chilling soliloquy, "The Bride of Quietness," spoken by a woman who has become her husband's creation; when she departs in various ways from the classical outlines in which he has imprisoned her, he departs from her. However,

> He always found poetic justic
> Amusing, and he knows I wait my turn.
> The artist dies; but what he wrought
>   will last
> Forever, when I cradle his cold ashes
>   in this urn.

The most ambitious poem in this first section is "In Memory of Elaine Shaffer," a flutist who died in 1973. There are small lapses in this poem which are evaded by the shorter "Song for Sigmund Freud," or "Advice to a Friend Who Paints," but this elegy is still an achievement of much greater magnitude. Its first stanza states its theme:

> *They lie—all those who so smartly insist*
> *That any correlation can exist*
> *Between meaning and music. There is*
>   *none.*
> *Only a point at which the audience*
> *For both stands and reveals itself as one.*

The poem moves through five sections, whose varying prosodies and lengths make them suggestive of the movements in a musical composition; but for the reasons quoted above, the parallel is not labored, not insisted upon. And, while the poem's major theme is the nonexistent correlation between meaning and music, its subject is, of course, the poet's world as it appears now that Elaine Shaffer has been removed from it.

The first section, after the italicized first stanza, proceeds to establish the personal dialectic between the poet and the musician; the second is a brief list of those great women, like Sappho, Elizabeth, and Curie, who "survive/ In the unconscious"; now "another of our sex, forever freed,/ Wakes from life to this lament of the unliberated." By this time the reader is aware that he is in the presence of an elegy composed along surprisingly classical lines. In an aesthetically satisfying transition from Section II to III, a lament in rhymed tercets, the customary questions are posed: Why the musician instead of the poet? What was the nature of her uniqueness? Where is she now? These questions are put in personal and distinctive ways: tradition serves the poem, rather than the other way around. The fourth section returns to the major theme, regret over the inadequacy of poetry to express the poet's present ideas and emotions. The strong final section contains a brief digression on the plight of the poet, cosseted in a tame college, and a tentative consolation in the motion of opposites toward harmony. The concluding lines are themselves a splendid harmony of the poem's thematic ambition and its emotional pressure:

> O Elaine, Elaine,

> In that progression toward the plane
> of spirit
> You and I, however unalike, move
> Hand in hand, the poet and musician,
> Behind the curtain's formal bow, and
> know
> That when it closes for the final time
> Our audience has always been the same
> Demanding dream, the shadowy critic
> Whose fearful standard fathers short-
> lived sisters
> In sound, related through our haunting
> chorus:
> The silence in the wings that waits for us,

> *The silence in the wings that waits for us.*

If the poem is not flawless, it is because the poet has tried something that few have the nerve or the knowledge to attempt. In the third section, the lament, for example, there is a use of the musician's last name which strikes an odd note, as in Wordsworth's address to the "Spade! with which Wilkinson hath tilled his lands." Even so, this is a remarkable poem, worth keeping around for a long time, just as we keep, say, "Kubla Khan" complete with its "fast thick pants" or the Intimations Ode, complete with its "six years' Darling of a pigmy size." It takes less nerve to mention this poem in the same paragraph with Coleridge and Wordsworth than it did for the poet to achieve it in the first place.

The usual custom in arranging the poems in a collection decrees that things shall not go steadily downhill after a point one third of the way through the book. That rare reader who goes straight through this collection will therefore wonder how he will fare following "In Memory of Elaine Shaffer." It turns out that the author of the next section, "Benjamin John," could have written the elegy with relative ease. This sequence is one of the rarest achievements in recent American poetry.

The sequence concerns the life of an academic; it begins in his youth, and takes him through graduate school, marriage, a career, and on toward death, though it stops just short of reporting that inevitability. The tone of the sequence as a whole is splendidly ambiguous, as individual poems range from compassionate portraiture to satirical cartooning.

Benjamin John emerges as one of those men for whom almost everything is a burden, especially personal attachments and responsibilities. He is continually hounded by the everyday, by the attractiveness of his female students, and by occasional visions of the Green Queen, a shadowy figure who may be a woman he might once have been able to win, and whose departure into realms of the unattainable he is not quite prepared to acknowledge. It would be unfair to quote from the sequence; it must suffice to say that it never falls below the expectations aroused by the first part of the book, and when it exceeds them, as it often does, it achieves magnificent flights of intense characterization. It is the work of a highly accomplished poetic technician who is also at home with fiction; it has the novelist's breadth and depth of empathy.

"A Lyric Cycle" of eleven short poems makes up the third part of this collection. It is notable for the chiseled, smooth precision of its language; lyrical in the classic sense of the word, the poems have been set to music for soprano solo by the Soviet composer Imants Kalnins. Though the poems recount and respond to various moments, painful and otherwise, in a love affair, they have been purified of background, like certain kinds of Oriental paintings, so that the moments and feelings that are delineated hang suspended, ringing like tapped crystal, as in "Circe," the concluding poem of the cycle:

"But as the fading sun clips you from
    my sight,
I will remember you.

"When you have gone,
the sun
like a silent song
will burn up the far side of night."

The book concludes with the title section, which contains nine poems more nearly miscellaneous in theme and manner than those assembled in the earlier sections. It is here that Cherry revels most explicitly in her debt to classical literature; there are translations from Catullus, remarkable for their understanding of the originals, and for the boldness with which they avoid literalness in order to convey that understanding. A witty monologue in deft stanzas jostles with more "subjectivist" visions in more open forms. But the voice is always there, always true to itself. Many books are greeted with excessive praise, as if only shouting could be heard above the rumbling of the inexhaustible presses; but when the shouting dies down, it is safe to predict that this book's voice will still be audible. It is a remarkable example of rare devotion to craft, rare integrity of purpose.

Henry Taylor

LOVE'S BODY

Author: Norman O. Brown (1913–   )
Publisher: Random House (New York), 276 pp. $5.95
Type of work: Prophecy
Time: The apocalyptic Now
Locale: Here

A post-Freudian duodecaphonic song of experience, pogromed in a multiplicity of voices, which attempting to redeem and redream the innocence of many, his flesh and the world, as if in a Finnegans Wake of contemporary Apocalyptic thought

Those who read Norman O. Brown's *Life Against Death* in 1959 were hardly prepared for *Love's Body* in 1966. There was really no place to go after *Life Against Death*. A smoldering, brooding intelligence, trained in the Classics, had fused itself with Marx and Freud, and the blueprint of the immediate past and the inexorable future had been etched with an undeviating line that sketched the acceleration of human history in an irrefutable rhetoric of academic doom. The wholesale rationalization of man's institutional life and the concomitant desexualization of his private clandestine (libidinous) life were analyzed, interpreted, signed, sealed, and held ready for delivery. But there was no place to go.

Life Against Death was a remarkably volatile examination of moribundity—a merciless document of our hypersensitive age, an addition to the voluminous reading lists of the sophisticated, the culturally prurient, of both the yea- and the nay-sayers of our contemporary babble. It was a truly impressive secondary source, worthy to be shelved next to Herbert Marcuse's *Eros and Civilization*. But like that latter book (as well as Freud's *Civilization and Its Discontents* from which both books spring), it was a text which could be consigned to the peripheries of one's attention, useful for a reference or a footnote, a depository to be

tapped when one needed a particularly devastating argument against the future of hope or humanity. These, of course, are uses which, in practice, become techniques for dismissing a book. The modern mind has no compunction about being educated in the intricacies of its own doom. Our absorption power is nothing short of miraculous, or how could we possibly stand the ordeal of our daily newspaper? *Life Against Death* proferred a powerful thesis, but a tolerable one. It was just one more example of man's capacity to analyze his own death with dispassion and deliberate awe. No exit. No place to go.

Love's Body holds no brief with such nonsense. It leaps, as Brown says, from history to mystery. A place to go. Not pyramidically or linearly, laying square-hewn blocks of logic as the reason builds, but directly, immediately, for the first time—as the escaped desperate mind flies. The first time, all over again; new, the good news: ". . . unless we are born again, we are not born at all." And Brown would be one of the midwives to this new second birth. "All the Lord's people to be prophets. Prophets, or poets: sing unto the Lord a new song." He would be the smasher of our spiritual idleness. "Literal meanings are icons become stone idols," he says. *Love's Body* is a grotesque sledgehammer of iconoclasm. It cracks the brittle bones of rational discourse, fragmenting itself into sixteen arbitrary segments and further dividing each segment into flying shards of isolated paragraphs—"to be divided, to be eaten, to be drunk."

But what an artful formlessness it makes! It can be read backwards, forwards, or in a helter-skelter skim; bits and pieces, it is all of a piece. "The unity is not organic-natural unity," says Brown, "but the unity of fire." *Love's Body* is a searing and a sere book, a dismembered shambles of a book, a wasteland of dead seeds and worn-out relics that our civilization has shored against its ruin. But there is another book which rises silently, almost invisibly, out of these fragments. Not some splendid multi-tiered city of the ancients which the excavator envisions to have once stood on the crumbled framework which he fastidiously uncovers, but a new, never-existent city that the reader grudgingly discovers already abuilding in his own accustomed bones. "Broken flesh, broken mind, broken speech." These are Brown's construction materials. "Broken speech; speech broken by silence. To let the silence in is symbolism." And Brown constructs aphoristically, muttering forth a journal for the dawning, filtering the silences in between his sentences and paragraphs, creating resonant shapes out of air and light and the hollow distances between the nerve-endings.

At the same time the book is cranky, violently opinionated and one-sided, perversely self-indulgent, arrogant, stubborn, humorless in its prophetic megalomania. And it is an uncomfortably "physical" book, almost kinetic in its impact, without charm or grace or the elegance of distance. It seems to have been blurted out from the pit of the throat rather than written. It would clutch at you in its savage writhings—a twisting Laocoon of a book without the warmth or weakness of human expression in its unmediated directness. One supposes, however, that those Athenians who were the first audiences at Sophocles' plays must also have felt that their basic good natures and innocent desire for entertaining edification were being rather badly abused by the intransigent playwright who trafficked so unconcernedly in terror. Brown puts no trust in the rational ambiances of persuasion; he has no energy to spare for seduction. *Love's Body* proceeds in the stacatto rhythms of successive rapes. The oracle is in too urgent a harmony with the deepest volcanic vibrations of its mountain to be concerned with good or bad manners. *Love's Body* is direct vatic utterance. It sounds the silences at the end of *Colonnus*; it appropriates the artistic prerogatives of the dark outlawed priest; its blood-dimmed vision is as uncompromisingly awful and ecstatic as that of Revelations. But it swears that these old bones can live.

There is a thesis in *Love's Body*, to be sure—a skeletal argument for the need and the possibility of metamorphosis; but the ultimate validity of the argument is subordinate to the occasion that it provides. The body and the world's body are identical; each is the other, and both together are love's body. Change the one and you change the other. Organize the body politic into more and more repressive and centralized systems of hegemony; exploit, pollute, and exhaust the natural fecundity of the physical-organic world; inevitably the psycho-physical bodies of men will reflect the same twisted depletion and fatal blockages of energy that are so manifest in the "objective" world. But the lines of forces are reciprocal in their influence. "Wheresoever a man comes, there comes revolution," said Emerson. *Love's Body* is a passionate incantation that would invoke the long-heralded appearance of that rough beast, the new man who will put the world and himself to the torch and turn all order into a flaming dance of life. The new man will recognize no boundaries, no rigidities, no masks and deceptions of representation. His name will be Everyman's, or no man's; he will be polymorphous, perverse, Blakean, in an orbit of vital existence far beyond the reality-principle, beyond tragedy, comedy, or religious exaltation. His world will be a palpable garden of delights, his body to be love's body and the world to be love's body:

> Carrying our seed in our head; like flowers, flaunting our sex shamelessly; as in Bosch's Garden of Earthly Delights, upside down; an end to uprightness, the way up is the way down. Erect is the shape of the genitally organized body; the body crucified, the body dead or asleep; the stiff. The shape of the body awake, the shape of the resurrected body, is not vertical but perverse and polymorphous; not a straight line but a circle; in which the Sanctuary is in the Circumference, and every Minute Particular is Holy; in which
> > "Embraces are Conninglings from Head even to the Feet,
> > And not a pompous High Priest entering by a Secret Place."

However, Brown's argument—his abrupt analysis of the parallel developments in the bureaucratization of sociopolitical structures and the tyrannical genitalization (rationalization) of modern man—is not, one believes, the really significant business of *Love's Body*. His thesis may or may not stand wholesale verification under the attacks of those competent to judge in all the widely scattered disciplines through which his thought so trenchantly ranges. From one viewpoint, it doesn't actually matter. The undeniable power of *Love's Body* is not dependent on the validity of the material from which it emerges. The power stems from the poetry of Brown's fierce juxtapositions, from the swelling changes and possibilities of meaning which he uncannily rings on the grudging spirit of his listener. One must be clear and unequivocal about this: *Love's Body*—whatever else it may attempt to be—is primarily a poem of excruciating moral seriousness. It is entirely possible that it may be our equivalent of a major epic poem. Like the great epics of the past, it does highest justice to the profoundest strengths which men possess; at the same time, it is never unaware of men's frailties—particularly those which we conceal murkily in the deceitful trappings of fate and limitation. There is an unflagging battle in each of its paragraphs, but the end-effect of all the struggles finds each mortal wound miraculously healed on a higher plane of physical symbolism. And, above all, *Love's Body* is a rhapsodic celebration of the founding of a new city and the engendering of a new race of heroes. Brown chants a nativity hymn to postmodern heroic Man, perhaps still unborn, perhaps never to be born except in mens' dreams of themselves, perhaps already born and merely awaiting history's laggard recognition. On this level of accomplishment—the word, "aesthetic" is indicative of the paucity of our rationalized language to describe significant experience—there can be no serious misunderstanding. *Love's Body* attains a sublimity all the more intense and enduring because of the unexpectedness of its form.

One final matter should be touched

on as well. Brown's employment (necessarily) of psychoanalytic terminology and our age's unhappy capacity to vulgarize thought and symbol to the lowest and most diluted level may conceal the nature of the new/old energy-source which is the focal center and final justification of his effort. "Action at a distance" is Brown's phrase for that deepest demiurge which has unceasingly revealed itself throughout the time of man as love, charisma, presence, beauty, grace, animal magnetism, and the like. "Action at a distance" is the living refutation of self-enclosing, self-perpetuating, cause-and-effect mechanisms. It actively demonstrates the breakthrough of all fictitious boundaries, as well as the breakdowns of all so-called "permanent" systems of order. Frustrated in its freedom to act, it is also the root-cause of man's sickness when he resists the spontaneity of his own responses. But the Dionysian release that Brown propounds is not a release to a spurious license which is, in its own way, as restrictive and tyrannizing as the formalistic restraint which it opposes. Not either/or, but both/and is the major theme which *Love's Body* articulates: both/and, spontaneously, and simultaneously. Brown exhorts man to release himself to that distance which he naturally encloses—himself in contiguous, interpenetrating wedlock to the world's body where the creative flow of energies between the both will be only and always one.

Earl Rovit

Sources for Further Study

Criticism:

Erikson, Kai T. "A Return to Zero," in *American Scholar*. XXXVI (Winter, 1966-1967), pp. 134-146. Erikson looks critically at Brown's notion that repression is the natural consequence of social organization.

Marcuse, Herbert. "Love Mystified: A Critique of Norman O. Brown," in *Commentary*. XLIII (February, 1967), pp. 71-75. A generally complimentary explication of Brown's main arguments in *Love's Body*.

Reviews:

Book Week. July 10, 1960, p. 5. 1,050 words.

Commonweal. LXXXV, December 23, 1966, p. 353. 650 words.

Harper's Magazine. CCXXXIII, November, 1966, p. 138. 950 words.

Nation. CCIV, March 27, 1967, p. 405. 2,200 words.

New York Review of Books. VIII, May 4, 1967, p. 3. 3,100 words.

New York Times Book Review. July 24, 1966, p. 3. 700 words.

LOW'S AUTOBIOGRAPHY

Author: David Low (1891–   )
Publisher: Simon and Schuster (New York). Illustrated. 387 pp. $5.00
Type of work: Autobiography
Time: 1891–1956
Locale: New Zealand, Australia, England, the Continent, the United States

A self-portrait of David Low's life in art and politics, among his friends and the world figures he has characterized and caricatured, together with behind the scenes commentary on the world at points of crisis

    Principal personages:
      DAVID LOW
      MADELINE KENNING LOW, his wife
      G. W. RUSSELL, owner of the liberal *Spectator* who gave Low his first major job
      WILLIAM McLEOD, artist and co-owner of the Sidney *Bulletin,* to which Low contributed his first political cartoons
      W. M. HUGHES ("OUR BILLY"), Prime Minister of Australia, praised and lampooned by young Low
      ARNOLD BENNETT, English author and Low's friend
      H. G. WELLS, another writer and friend
      LORD BEAVERBROOK, newspaper magnate and Low's employer and friend
      HERBERT HENRY ASQUITH,
      DAVID LLOYD GEORGE, and
      RAMSAY MACDONALD, British political figures caricatured by Low
      F. W. THOMAS, English humorist and Low's co-worker on the London *Star*

"I started out to be a comic artist. Curiosity to find out how the wheels went around led me to the world of ideas and I became a graphic satirist. Circumstances made me a political caricaturist." So David Low comments on looking backward over his sixty-five years, half of which were attended by fame, even though he declined fortune. His life is a minor document, a cartoon history of his beloved Empire at the crossroads, as one critic has suggested aptly. No reader should be misled to think that the book reveals the artist-writer-satirist-politician-cartoonist at home, although he is an old-fashioned family man, for this is his manifesto.

His life remains private, but his public life is a matter of documentation which he reveals penetratingly and with as clean lines as ever he drew with a brush or pen.

He inherited his disputatiousness from his father, a dour Scotsman whose latter years were blighted by Calvinistic interests brought on by the unfortunate death of a son. From his mother's family Low's legacy was indomitability, a frontier-style independence which allowed him to go straight down the path to a kind of Lincolnian democratic belief, avoiding rightist and leftist beliefs or embracing elements of either as long as the cause was served.

This is his credo:

> I had been to a limited extent a signer but rarely a joiner. It seemed to me that a public commentator should be unattached, a being sitting apart, perched in the blue. I had never felt called upon to join any party; I was positively uncomfortable in crowds, and I felt no need to pump up my own enthusiasm with mass emotions. Parties there had to be if aims were to be realized, but my place was always on their flanks, doubting, careful lest loyalty be perverted from the ideas to the organizations which existed only to carry out the ideas. Being skeptical particularly of ideology identified with the permanent success of one party organization exclusively, I was unsympathetic to those whose reaction to the brutalities of he Nazi Party and the Fascist Party was to pop headlong into the Communist Party. . . . No doubt the Capitalist system had within itself the seeds of its own disintegration, as the Marxists said; but so had all systems—if they didn't burst new buds now and then. . . . I banked on the British political genius for mixing oil and water. . . .

Low grew up in New Zealand and took his first important job in Australia, where oil and water had been mixed in a radical way. He had so little formal education that he felt called upon to apologize for the mistakes in his life brought on by sheer ignorance; he once failed a college entrance examination because he was unable to place his wide experiential knowledge in scholastic pigeonholes. But he made his own way from the time he was fifteen, when he was paid for a satiric sketch, and by 1907 he was working for Fred Rayner, artist-proprietor of the New Zealand *Sketcher,* for two pounds a week at the age of sixteen. He advanced a year later to the liberal *Spectator,* and then emigrated to Australia at the age of twenty to accept a job on the *Bulletin,* in Sidney and Melbourne, at five pounds a week.

In Australia, a country whose social reforms at the turn of the century have only recently been acceptable in England and America, the artist as a young man learned of politics. His association with artists and writers—especially the writer-artists who are the satirists, caricaturists—helped him find his medium, the clean-lined drawing of essence. He once walked in eight weeks the several hundred miles between his two cities as an exercise in independence; he then became a peripatetic cartoonist practicing his art and perfecting his style on Australian VIP's. His cartoons, for this term best describes his early work, caught the attention of Arnold Bennett, who somehow managed to get Low to London—though he did not intend for him to get to Ernest Parke's *Star.* Low, that simple but bold signature, then became legion and legend.

The two most fortunate friendships of his life were formed with two very different men, H. G. Wells and Lord Beaverbrook. The former had early shaped the artist's philosophical viewpoints, while the latter sustained the artist's integrity in this all too physical world. After years of beseeching, Beaverbrook happily gave in to very strident demands by Low to remain independent of the former's *Evening Standard* policies. In twenty-three years only one cartoon was withdrawn from the paper (and this on grounds not at all connected with Low's politics or Beaverbrook's beliefs), a period spanning more than two artistically satisfying decades made up of excruciating crises and upheavals of all types. This serves as a monument and a guide mark to free speech in dictatorial times.

Asquith, Lloyd George, Ramsay MacDonald, Stanley Baldwin, Neville Chamberlain, and always Winston Churchill moved in and out of Low's vision, and he drew as he saw and believed. All the dictators came and went under his pen, which helped to destroy them. Novelty characterizations of the literati passed in cartoon review, as did all the important persons whom Karsh has caught in photographs, with Low always catching from the inside out. He also wrote brilliantly about them in the same way, catching essences.

Only two men refused to sit for a portrait by the master craftsman: John Galsworthy who objected to caricature on grounds of conscience, and Rudyard Kipling, who had been pinioned by Max Beerbohm. Among the humorists, Low discovered little surface humor, and here he draws an analogy to the writer's and the caricaturist's approach. The latter aims at satire through wit tempered by criticism whereas the former often dwells on the surface or slightly below; the master in either case catches more than fun and the reader should get more than amusement. No one has written more lucidly or convincingly than Low does of the uses of cartoon and the need for political caricature.

Arnold Bennett, who considered himself the discoverer of Low, caustically criticized his protégé's journalism, his failure at crisp diction, and his grammar. Low cheerfully submitted to this criticism and seemed thereafter to try, but indifferently, to improve. If his writing did not live up to Bennett's standards or failed to compare favorably with his drawing, no one need be greatly concerned. *The Best of Low*, a previous book and an anthology of cartoon and caricature, preserves the art; this book preserves the artifacts, in the form of letters to and from friends, relevant drawings which mark important transitions, and excellent photographs of himself, his wife, and such good friends as Wells, Asquith, and Beaverbrook.

"Style," said Frank Harris, "is the way great men speak." Here is a book with style, the voice of a spokesman against tyranny everywhere, the underlining in brilliant prose of a great artist's life.

LUCE AND HIS EMPIRE

Author: W. A. Swanberg (1907-   )
Publisher: Charles Scribner's Sons (New York). 529 pp. $12.50
Type of work: Biography
Time: Twentieth century
Locale: China, the United States, Italy

A readable but biased study which accords Henry Luce tremendous power and accuses him of its grievous misuse

Principal personages:
HENRY ROBINSON LUCE, founder of Time, Life, Fortune, Sports
    Illustrated
BRITON HADDEN, co-founder of *Time*
CLARE BOOTHE LUCE, his second wife

Imagine the world minus *Time* magazine. Better? Maybe. Worse? Perhaps. Different? Certainly. Our language, our attitude toward most historic events, and perhaps even those events themselves, have been shaped and toned by the slim weekly periodical which calls itself a newsmagazine and which critics classify in less flattering terms.

W. A. Swanberg's *Luce and His Empire,* a biography of the cofounder of *Time* and the father of *Life, Fortune,* and *Sports Illustrated,* amply demonstrates Luce's—and *Time's*—widespread influence. Reviews of the book have challenged Swanberg's conceptions of the motivations and direction of that influence, but most have admitted that Swanberg is entirely justified in seeing Luce and his publications as one of the dominant forces of our century. Estimates are that, at its peak, Luce's empire weekly reached more than a third of the nation's literate adults.

Ironically, however, while Swanberg's main thesis describes Luce as a brilliant fanatic who mixed fact and fancy to further his own so-called Christian and patriotic causes, the book itself is as biased as the man it chronicles. Swanberg, well-known for his fair and accurate appraisals of Theodore Dreiser and William Randolph Hearst, charges Luce with no petty crimes. Luce, he claims, helped to create the climates which permitted Hitler's rise, the Cold War, and even the Viet Nam conflict. His hatred for the Communists was based, Swanberg says, on a twelve-day visit in 1932 which, "closing his mind with a sharp final click, was historic." But, however well-founded Swanberg's accusations may be, he has in attempting to build a strong case against Luce instead made the reader call for a mistrial. The evidence is simply inadmissible because of the way in which it is presented. Every page and even the section titles ("'Oh, Harry,' spake the Lord"; "The Lucepress Pollution"; "Christians, to Arms!" for example) reveal Swanberg's utter lack of objectivity.

Swanberg criticizes *Time* for continuously inserting opinion under sly guises. A politician, for example, may be "trim-figured" and "keen-brained" or "flabby-chinned and gimleteyed," depending on his standing in the Luce private poll. Yet Swanberg resorts to exactly the same tactics. His opening scene—mostly an imaginary reconstruction—reveals his plan. He places Luce in China in October, 1945, gloating over the Allied victory and considering the status of Chiang Kai-shek. In this single scene Swanberg outlines the Luce defects—all by presenting Luce's musings. We are meant to see that he worships Chiang ("in a sense the most important man in Luce's Life"); that he is willing to change dispatches from his own correspondents when they do not portray Chiang as sufficiently heroic ("It was his magazine, after all."); that he has a bent for propaganda which allegedly confused the whole question of China; and that he is unable to see China as it is rather than as his dreams make it. Swanberg asserts that Luce's attitudes here—prejudice and unconscious dishonesty—are the same as those he exhibits on all occasions.

Born April 3, 1898, Henry Robinson Luce was the son of missionary parents in Tengchow, China. "They were superior people except for the Christian prejudice without which they never would have gone to China," says Swanberg. Their son, who would later demand a private elevator so that he might pray while riding the thirty-six floors to his office, early received the training which would make him a man confident of God's unerring support.

The man destined to change journalism was introduced to the field when he edited the weekly paper (circulation thirty) at his boarding school. Later, as a scholarship student at an exclusive Connecticut prep school, he met Briton Hadden, a student with whom he would compete for school and college literary honors and who would later serve as co-founder of *Time*. Although the two were equally talented, Hadden outranked Luce in an easy ability to make people like him. His "Look out, Harry, you'll drop the college," a jibe at Luce's continual seriousness, underlined their basic difference.

After a brief newspaper career, the two young men boldly conceived a weekly magazine aimed at bringing together in brief form the week's events. In a phrase which would later be cited as defense for their bias, they promised "fair news treatment *without* objectivity," and *Time* appeared March 23, 1923. It was dedicated to a number of platitudes such as a "respect for the old, particularly in manners," and "faith in the things which money cannot buy."

From the beginning, its jaunty personal style ("Backward ran the sentences until reeled the mind") and its desire to jazz up the dull news it so freely rewrote from conventional news sources marked it as an original. "It was of course not for people who really wanted to be informed. It was for people willing to spend a half-hour to avoid being entirely uninformed," Swanberg says.

When Hadden died in 1929, Luce gained total control, and, Swanberg claims, "an important effect of Hadden's death was its liberation of Luce the ideologist-missionary-propagandist."

Although Luce's personal life as described in the book seems totally secondary to his magazines, he apparently could be as romantic as he was ruthless. After years of a seemingly happy marriage, he decided in 1934—on the basis of a few casual meetings—to abandon his wife for Clare Boothe Brokaw, a young divorcee then working for *Vanity Fair*. As he declared à la the Duke of Windsor, he simply could not exist without the woman he loved.

The second Mrs. Luce excelled her husband in ambition, patriotism, and the ability to offend as well as to charm. She was celebrated for her *bon mots,* but criticized for her coldness and tendency to talk too much. A sometimes successful playwright whose lesser efforts caused *Time* reviewers to anguish over what to say about a flop by the boss's wife, she would later be elected to Congress and serve as ambassador to Italy. The Senate and the Vice-Presidency were also on her list of goals, Swanberg says, appropriate offices since Luce himself hankered after the Presidency. Although the two often did not see each other for months, their marriage was a success of sorts. The normally egotistical Luce even yielded the spotlight with grace when attention was directed at his wife.

Throughout Luce's life, Swanberg says, he had little concern for people. Again and again he met and social-ized with most of the famous people of the world, yet had little interest in them except as sources of ideas and stories. The intricate politics among staff members of his magazine who were competing for his favor revealed this same lack of ability to form true friendships. He respected many men professionally (if they knew how to "compete with him and make him like it"), but his employees were generally valued only for what they might produce.

Active and involved almost to the minute of his death in 1967, Luce had relinquished the title but not the power as head of his magazines. On his death, his face appeared for the first occasion on *Time's* cover. And, says Swanberg, his spirit still permeated its pages. Inside was a story praising his journalistic "fairness."

Swanberg has presented an exhaustive look at Luce's life. Although the reader who has not done research elsewhere would be ill-advised to accept his version of more than the basic outline of Luce's career, the book is a valuable example of the strong reaction aroused by a man who himself did not believe objectivity existed.

Judith Bolch

LUCIFER IN HARNESS
American Meter, Metaphor, and Diction

Author: Edwin Fussell (1913-   )
Publisher: Princeton University Press (Princeton, N.J.). 182 pp. $9.50
Type of work: Literary criticism

A provocative sequence of three long essays which define and explore "the fundamental dilemma of American poetry"

Edwin Fussell, as he himself demonstrates, is not the only person who knows that the fundamental dilemma of American poetry is the difficulty of writing a new poetry in language which can rarely shrug the burden of English sensibility. The American poet has almost always seemed either English (Bryant, Eliot) or barbaric (Whitman, Williams), whether his situation is examined in terms of meter, metaphor, or diction. It is a problem which has driven some poets to distraction, yet few critics have contended fruitfully with it.

Fussell's learning is large, and his memory astonishing. It seems simple-minded to praise a literary critic's memory, but without it connections cannot be made, echoes cannot be heard. The sinuous thread or the tangled web become snarls of frustration in the hands of readers who have not Fussell's gift for keeping several things in mind at once, over a long period of time.

Part of this book's provocativeness is in its style, which is aggressively nonacademic. The impulse is admirable: "If I have offended this common sense or good taste of the well-disposed reader, I am genuinely sorry. If I have made even a slight dent in the bulwarks of the American literary establishment, I am delighted." Most of the time, the informal and sometimes poetically compressed style seems exactly right, but there are a a few moments when it seems sophomoric and self-indulgent. Some readers will find more of these moments than others will; it is a matter of taste. And of course it is also a matter of holding the reader's interest. The bulwarks of the American literary establishment are thick, heavy, and, in spots, impenetrable. Even when he is letting himself go, doing a little grandstand playing, Fussell is sharp, and his argument clear and persuasive.

Each essay is divided into six or seven wittily titled subdivisions. The first essay, "The Meter-Making Argument," establishes the American poet's ambivalent attitude toward the prosodic traditions of the "mother tongue," and reminds us of the political nature of the dialectic between English and American poetry: "Given the nature of poetry in English and the facts of American history, free verse is as inevitable as the Declaration of Independence." Fair enough: the nationalistic American poet is often forced to be anti-British. But because the seductive and authoritarian British tradition is so hard to dispense with, many poetry-writing Americans are hardly nationalistic. Fussell's prime example of the Loyalist is William Cullen Bryant, who believed not only that English and American poetry were one, but that

The Faerie Queene represents the English language ('so far as the purposes of poetry require') in a state of 'perfection' not subsequently improved upon." So the dialectic, both sides of it, comes ashore in America; without a conservative party, there can be no radical tradition.

Fussell places Whitman, Pound, and Williams in the radical tradition; anyone else would do the same. But Fussell takes some time to reveal the disparity between Williams' actual debt to Whitman and his sense of it; Williams mistakenly believed that Whitman's chief contribution was to overthrow the pentameter; he could not hear the measure in Whitman, any more than he could count the stresses in his famous "variable foot." Nevertheless, these three poets made it possible for American poets to hear a new rhythm, absorb it, and return to regularity from time to time "with a diminished sense of discomfort, a greater feeling of freedom and mastery, broader possibility, wider choice. . . . Sometime between Whitman and Pound, the English tradition became—insofar as we care to use it—ours."

The chapter on meter concludes with an examination of America's assimilation of the English tradition. In "Radical Explosions and Conservative Reassertions" Fussell shows how, and why, Frost's regularity is not Bryant's, but a post-Whitman metric. Robert Lowell's early pentameter couplets, too, were distinctly American, even to Williams' ear. Finally, in "The United States as Poem" it is shown that the American tradition is neither the English way nor some impossible opposite, but both, "in provocative antithesis and alternation . . . in . . . harmony continuously on the edge of dissolution and re-articulation."

"The Constituting Metaphor," the second essay, is a largely successful attempt to discover, define, and name the means by which the American poet, cut off from unity of form and diction, can yet unify his poem. The term "constituting metaphor" seems to refer to the overall metaphoric thread of a poem; it is set in contrast to local metaphor and extended metaphor. Here again Fussell takes his cue from Whitman, who said of Dante's *Inferno,* "One simple trail of idea, epical, makes the poem"; and from Pound, who added, "The *Divine Commedia* is a single elaborated metaphor."

Fussell goes on to draw an analogy between the constituting metaphor and the "single effect" which Poe sought in the writing of short fiction. This whole concept is useful, but not, it seems to at least one reader, revolutionary. It is hard to see the distinction between the constituting metaphor and a term such as "actual subject," as employed in Wallace Stevens' dualism, nominal subject and actual subject. Fussell must see a difference, for he says that "Stevens does not compose within the tradition of the constituting metaphor." Clearly, not all actual subjects are metaphorical, but many are. Nevertheless, Fussell's formulation provides him with a very useful way of connecting Whitman's practice with later examples, such as *The Bridge, The Waste Land, The Cantos,* and *Paterson.* His readings of these poems are sensitive and suggestive, if not thorough; but this book explicitly avoids the detailed close reading of texts.

"What the Thunder Said" takes up the problem of diction: "Lacking his rhythm or his form, a man is gauche and uncontrolled; lacking a language, he is nearly out of his mind. The final agony of the American poets is of course poetic diction." And in a footnote to these sentences, Fussell explains that his broad use of the term "poetic diction" will range "from such relatively inconsequential matters as word choice to such ultimate issues as the question whether a human being can maintain his integrity unless he can modulate and hear the true sound of his own voice and his neighbors'."

Returning to Bryant as exemplary Loyalist, Fussell shows how the American language's slow growth away from English aroused in American poets an increasing dissatisfaction with the smoothness of traditional poetic diction. Prior to Whitman, in an era labeled (in the meter essay) "The Age of Growing Discomfort and Inadequate Remedy," Poe, Emerson, and James Russell Lowell contended in various ways with the problem of diction. Fussell makes the sensible point that much of Poe's awkwardness—unlikely and repellent rhymes, archaic and self-destructive word choice—is not the result of ineptitude, but of "an aggressive movement made against an intolerable situation."

The situation continued to be nearly intolerable through the age of Eliot and Pound, for whom diction was still one of the front lines of the struggle between American and English po-etry. But as in the instance of meter, American diction underwent the cycles of "radical explosion and conservative reassertion," to the point that when Williams faced the question of English, his poetic reply can almost be taken at face value:

> At City College, New York . . . I was defining our right as Americans to our own language, saying that English, its development from Shakespeare's day to this, does not primarily concern us.
>
> "But this language of yours," said one of the instructors, himself an obvious Britisher, "where does it come from?"
>
> "From the mouths of Polish mothers," I replied.

Fussell quotes this passage from Williams' *Autobiography* with obvious relish, but also with a clear sense of where Williams was not quite on target. The American dialectic includes English from time to time, as it must in order to stay dialectical.

As an exploration of the radical tradition in American poetry, *Lucifer in Harness* is hard to beat. Its chief flaw is that its scheme prevents Stevens, Robinson, Frost, and a host of other "conservative" poets from getting a fair shake; despite his steady insistence on the open-endedness of American poetic tradition, Fussell comes perilously close to erecting a closed critical system. But the book is still valuable to the practicing poet, and indispensable to the serious student of American literary history.

Henry Taylor

THE LUCK OF GINGER COFFEY

Author: Brian Moore (1921-   )
Publisher: Atlantic-Little, Brown and Company (Boston). 243 pp. $4.00
Type of work: Novel
Time: 1956
Locale: Montreal, Canada

The story of a foolish impostor who is finally made to face his true self

> *Principal characters:*
> JAMES FRANCIS (GINGER) COFFEY, an Irish immigrant
> VERONICA (VERA) COFFEY, his wife
> PAULINE (PAULIE) COFFEY, his daughter
> GERRY GROSVENOR, a bachelor political cartoonist in love with Veronica
> MR. MACGREGOR, managing editor of the Montreal *Tribune*

Brian Moore's first two novels may be described as two variations on the theme of isolation. Judith Hearne, in *The Lonely Passion of Judith Hearne* (1956), is a Dublin spinster in her forties who seeks but does not find love and understanding. In *The Feast of Lupercal* (1957), Diarmuid Devine, a schoolmaster in his late thirties who teaches in a Dublin school for Catholic boys, attains a long-desired opportunity for love, but is defeated both by himself and by fate.

In a sense, Mr. Moore's third novel repeats the theme of isolation, though the garishly dressed dreamer, Ginger Coffey, is a very different person from either Judith Hearne or Diarmuid Devine. Also, the circumstances of his life contrast sharply with those of Mr. Moore's two earlier protagonists. Ginger is a Dubliner in a strange land, an Irishman whose speech stamps him at once not only for natives of Montreal but also for those of his countrymen who preceded him to Canada. Though he has been married for fifteen years and has a fourteen-year-old daughter, he feels isolated from Veronica, who cannot forgive him for his many broken promises to her, and from Pauline, who only intermittently reveals a brief suggestion of the closeness she once shared with her father. During the few weeks covered by the action of the novel, Ginger discovers himself betrayed first by Veronica and then by Pauline, so that for a short while he thinks of himself as completely alone. No one cares whether he lives or dies, and few people are even aware of his existence.

The pity is that Ginger is a habitual liar who cannot control his lies. His isolation from his wife and daughter is far more his fault that it is theirs. He lives by choice in a Walter Mitty type of dream world in which he becomes by the force of his fancy the kind of person he can never be in reality. Lies are needed when danger signs begin to hint that what he has imagined is not true. He fibs to himself; he telephones Veronica or Pauline and fibs again, stalling for time. What is not strictly true now may be true tomorrow or next week. Or if things don't turn out that way, perhaps there will be something else just as good. There *must* be because it's not fair for one man so deserving as Ginger Coffey to have bad luck all the time. Things are bound to change, and then Vera and Paulie will see how fortunate they are in having him as a provider. So goes Ginger's mind despite one defeat after another. Staggered by one blow of fate, he reels while his mind clears and his eyes begin to make out the rosy vistas in the valley of the future. Into the battle he plunges again, evading, temporizing, willing his lovely dreams into being, until his final miserable disillusionment, when he cannot continue the deception any longer. Or can he?

There is nothing tragic about Ginger, for he is too small a man for tragedy. But he is woefully pathetic. Essentially he is a good man, though a pitifully weak one. What he does he usually does with good intentions, and he means no real harm to anyone. When provoked to harm by desire or anger, as when he assaults Vera or later when he slaps Paulie, he is immediately sorry, a humiliated penitent who pleads for forgiveness. Accused of selfishness, he denies it, he will not, cannot see it. He is misunderstood. Will no one ever grasp that?

When the story opens, the Coffeys have been in Montreal for six months. After a succession of jobs in Ireland and in Canada, none of which he kept very long or thought very highly of, Ginger is unemployed. Dejected, Vera insists that he buy tickets for passage back to Ireland with money that has been saved for an emergency. The truth is that Ginger has dipped secretly into this fund in the anticipation that something would finally turn up. The day of reckoning is delayed when Gerry Grosvenor, a political cartoonist for the Montreal *Tribune*, falsifies Ginger's shabby record of employment and arranges for him to apply for a reporting job on the *Tribune*. Mr. MacGregor, the canny and tough Scotch managing editor, quickly discovers the deception but grudgingly offers a proof-

reading job. This Ginger takes in desperation, with the vague prospect of being made a reporter later on. To increase his income, he adds to this (to him) degrading nighttime job a daytime one as the driver of a diaper service truck. One night, when Vera mumbles in her sleep, Ginger learns that Gerry's interest in the Coffeys has been more than altruistic, and he leaves, taking Paulie with him and allowing Vera to do as she wishes.

Though his faith in Vera has been shattered—he accepts no blame for her turning from him to Gerry—he sets up apartment housekeeping with Paulie and agrees to fake an adultery scene so that Vera can divorce him. He reneges on the plan, however, when his mind revolts in disgust at what he is doing, and he returns early to the apartment where he is angered to find Paulie dancing erotically with one of a group of Montreal punks whom she has invited to a party. When Paulie threatens to marry Bruno, Vera, who has secured a dress-shop sales job through Gerry, asks to come back to watch over Paulie, but with one major restriction: no marital intimacies.

Deciding to stake all on his envisioned promotion to work as a reporter for the *Tribune*, Ginger chucks his diaper service job (and a promotion to an office job too), learns he will not be made a reporter, gets drunk, commits a nuisance in public, is jailed overnight, is given a six-months' sentence (suspended), is fired by the *Tribune*, and is again unemployed. In a rather unconvincing sentimental conclusion, Vera says there was never anything really improper in her relationship with Gerry (who, she discovered, wanted her physically only), argues Ginger into asking for the diaper service office job, and the Coffeys are together again

—after a fashion.

Mr. Moore's well-constructed narrative moves rapidly; his dialogue is effectively handled, and his characterizations are for the most part nicely differentiated, though Gerry remains a little vague as a villain. Ginger, who dominates the novel, is portrayed through his youthfully ridiculous dress —he is nearing forty—his alternately aggressive and hesitant actions and talk, and a simplified stream-of-consciousness revelation of his mental meanderings into dark pits of misery or fields of conquest. Ginger is easily the best part of the book. Though the concluding sentences suggest that Ginger, having tried and failed to be a big man, will be content to "die in humble circs," one cannot help feeling that it will not be long before his mind, like incurable Walter Mitty's, will be soaring again in the airways of romance.

LUNAR LANDSCAPES
Stories and Short Novels 1949–1963

Author: John Hawkes (1925–   )
Publisher: New Directions (New York). 275 pp. $5.95
Type of work: Stories and short novels

Six short stories and three short novels which demonstrate not only the connections between surrealism and naturalism but also the redeeming possibilities of acceptance of life's essential absurdity and brutality

John Hawkes' *Lunar Landscapes* is a collection of stories and short novels in which the usual Hawkesian terror, ambiguity, and grotesquerie are gathered in a Walpurgis Nacht celebration of that world which, like the moon, haunts the night air of the subconscious mind. The nine landscapes of the collection are unearthly in the vagueness of their location; specific settings are only hinted at by language and general environment—Germany, England, Western United States, New England, and Italy—all Western, all combining the physical and spiritual paradoxes which clash tragically in the death-ridden world of Hawkes' works.

"The Traveler" (1962) and "The Grandmother" (1961) are companion pieces in which an essential purity or redemption is sought, first by traveling away from home, from humanity, toward the sea; "what is the sea if not for the washing of dead relatives and for the swimming of fish and men?" Justus, the traveler away from the sordid past of an adulterous affair with his brother's wife and the painful memories of a stillborn child of his own dead marriage, seeks the mechanical purity of a racing automobile, money, and fresh white linen on his bed at night. He shies away not only from his own human qualities, but also from the earthiness of woman, as seen in the grotesque hump-backed milkmaid, the

grandmothers, and his wife, Sesemi. He floats upon the sea, life: "Creatures that float are indestructible and children beware of them." He is a "rationalist thriving upon the great green spermary of the earth." Yet Justus is burned by the sun, a purgatory which awakens him to the spiritual need for sacrifice: "The whole lamb . . . for my brother. For Lebrecht! You see, Sesemi, I am the father [of Lebrecht's child] after all."

Justus' money proves counterfeit at the sacrificial meal in "The Grandmother"; his mastery over his brother's wife, Metze, is also painfully destroyed as Lebrecht, urged on by Metze, finally carves the meat and serves it to her. The adulterous Metze consummates the sacrifice when she lies down on the couch and begins to talk to her dead mother. "Bring him [the son] to me, Metze. Bring him to his Grossmutter."

The horrible irony of men's actions is surrealistically displayed in "A Little Bit of the Old Slap and Tickle" (1962). Sparrow the Lance Corporal, "wearing his old battledress and a red beret," comes home to his family living in "the sweeper lying straight and true in the mud up to her water-line, his salt and iron house with chicken wire round one portion of the deck where the children played, the tin pipe at the stern with a breath of smoke coming up. . . . It was like living in a war memorial . . . ten windy miles of devastation." But "love, not beauty, was what he wanted," and Sparrow feels that his deserted mine sweeper is as "respectable as a lighthouse keeper's station," that living "with a woman worn to thinness, wiry and tough as the titlings on the cliff" brings a love which is even greater for its being in the midst of a scene of desolation. It is real, "and love was even better when they were sick, the heart of it more true with aching arms and legs." Sparrow is not perverse, not in the ethical context of Hawkes' works; he is victorious by virtue of his enduring values.

"Death of an Airman" (1950) is the most conventional story in the collection; the plot unfolds chronologically and the description is naturalistic rather than impressionistic. However, it is the most horrifying and unredeemed story in the book. An enlisted man, under the direction of a Disinterment Officer, is busy as a member of the Graves Recording Group, digging up the body of a decorated airman from the beach in order that it can be reburied elsewhere. The inhumane theme of the story is evident in the statement by the D.O.: "The odor's the same behind any army cook house. . . . Out of an old can or from the sand, the smell's still the same." The Group's attitude, and that of society by extension, toward the dead heroes is one of brutal indifference: "Number twelve, twenty-two, ten, sixty-six, coming up for the last time. . . . When you go down now, you'll stay." Hawkes teases our sensibilities by having children and swimmers playing on the beach alongside the morbid scene. He punctuates the naturalistic irony in the last sentence when he tells us that the enlisted man has idly forgotten to pin the dead airman's medal on the transferred corpse. Instead, he has left it pinned over his own heart.

Hawkes' ability to evoke mood through description is apparent in a troubling story called "The Song Outside" (1962), a song of death which is never sung, only "hummed, and without melody, planting one harmonic structure upon another." The absurd men in the desert sit in the abandoned patio of an adobe house and evoke "a bitter terrifying image of the vulture landing and sliding head first across the sand to devour its prey." As in his novel, *The Cannibal*, Hawkes uses a ghastly opening scene to elicit an immediate fear. In this instance, he uses a vulture wheeling over the earth below. The men call this figure of death a "taboo," a "mistake." Although the story leaves one rationally unsatisfied, as do most of Hawkes' works, the naturalistic implications can be felt just as powerfully as those outlined in "Death of an Airman." The desert scene remains unredeemed, either by man or nature: the stillness, the heat, the humming—that is all there is.

A much more complex and tantalizing idea is presented in "The Nearest Cemetery" (1963). The title is typical of Hawkes; it must be understood before full comprehension of the work is possible. In this case, the "nearest cemetery" is the mind; people are buried in one's mind and the sounds of them echo in the ears. "Every object . . . and every place already contains its fill of sound and the ear is its own coffin, its own little reverberating casket that hears everything it was ever meant to hear." The story takes place in a small state penitentiary in New England where the narrator, a barber, tells of the confused, but powerful, events of the past in which he, the fourth lover of the Princess, killed her. Now, in his "wordless life," he listens to those sounds: "the ear is the coffin that can't be closed or nailed or buried. . . . So the mind lies between the echoing coffins of the ears," the echoes of death, of organ music, and the Lord. The narrator is imprisoned in his own mind, buried alive with the past.

Compared to the short stories of this collection and his other novels, the novella "Charivari" and the two short novels, "The Goose on the Grave" and "The Owl," are disappointing. The various elements within these three works never fuse into any meaningful whole or sustained mood; they seem confused and amateurish in their inconsistent searching, impotent scatterings of misdirection and false starts.

"Charivari" (1950) is valuable only to the Hawkes scholar. It is a story of an immature married couple, estranged not only from each other but also from the idea of pregnancy. The first three sections of this earliest of Hawkes' works are impressionistic, but quite conventional in the use of language, boring in their airy examination of marital psychoses. Yet, suddenly, in the last part, "Rhythm," section fourteen, the style changes into that concrete, visceral style which only the later Hawkes commands. Overall, the theme and content of "Charivari" are sterile; Updike has covered the same ground, in a much more fervent manner, in *Rabbit, Run*.

Both "The Owl" and "The Goose on the Grave" attempt to dramatize in surrealistic terms the brutal sterility of unending sacrifice; the characters of both novels are bound within a reoccuring system of institutions, activities, and values which crushes them in their unawareness of cause and effect. The religious spirit of sacrifice is indulged in continually as an unaware attempt to find redemption from a binding circularity; the effect is self-defeating. Il Gufo, the hangman of "The Owl," rules over the wasteland of Sasso Fetore. It is his job to perform the pentecostal rites of sacrificial execution: "Thus stands the cause between us, we are entered into covenant for this work." At the last supper before the prisoner was hanged, "there came the effulgent memory of execution, step by step, dismal, endless, powerful as a beam that transcends our indulgence on earth."

The same problem of unredeemed circularity, endless sacrifice, informs "The Goose on the Grave." Sacrifice is a "continuous dream, warm and without waiting and despite the presence across the valley of the enemy." Yet, both short novels are failures; they do not concentrate on this central point of sacrifice in any discernible pattern. The various elements are rather like excited molecules in an uncontrolled medium. Hawkes traditionally deals in confusion, but it is fallacious to think that fiction must reflect this fact in form.

In the best of these nine stories, the heavy confusion of strong images, presented with impressionistic candor, wraps the reader in a mood, but appears to desert him intellectually. It is a landscape of alien figures, or at least we would like to think so; yet, once the provoked mind of the reader catches up with his emotions, he finds that the landscape is actually his own. His emotions, his desires, his darkest longings, like those of Hawkes' characters, have outstripped his rational faculties and left him, subconsciously a savage, bewildered with the environment. The moon is not foreign; it is, like the fictional world of Hawkes, attached to earth, our own real world.

J. J. Johnson

LYRICAL AND CRITICAL ESSAYS

Author: Albert Camus (1913–1960)
Translated from the French by Ellen Conroy Kennedy and edited and annotated by Philip Thody
Publisher: Alfred A. Knopf (New York). 365 pp. $6.95
Type of work: Autobiographical, lyrical, and critical essays; interviews
The first appearance in English of Camus' earliest published writings and of some of his important critical statements made over the years

Albert Camus seems to have suffered as a result of the incomplete image the public had of him. He considered himself to have been cast too readily in a narrow, inflexible mold by journalists in a hurry to meet a deadline or eager to simplify for the sake of their readers. He regretted being trapped within the narrow dimensions of the characters of his best-known works. Meursault, for example—the protagonist in *The Stranger*—contained only a small part of his creator's personality, but there was some tendency to identify him with Camus. The publication of *Lyrical and Critical Essays,* after that of Camus' *Notebooks,* goes a long way toward deepening our understanding of the author's complexity and toward changing the stereotype.

Three separate collections of essays make up the *Lyrical Essays* of the title. The last of these, *Summer,* was first published in 1954, whereas the first two, *The Wrong Side and the Right Side* and *Nuptials,* date from much earlier, having been published in 1937 and 1938 respectively, when Camus was still a very young man. A common thematic thread—Camus' preoccupation with the Mediterranean sensibility, the problem of the Absurd, and an acute consciousness of the inevitability of death—runs through all three groups of essays. Before he finally relented, Camus was unwilling to have his early essays republished in France. Although Camus' reputation has per-

haps declined in recent years, a circumstance that seems inevitable for many writers immediately after their deaths, his doubts about the artistic merits of *The Wrong Side and the Right Side* and *Nuptials* seem unfounded. Although they are essays in the etymological sense of the term—experiments in writing, a trying out of ideas, a testing of form—they in no way strain the reader's indulgence. Intrinsically they are highly readable, while at the same time they have the added merit of shedding light on the physical and emotional climate out of which *The Stranger* and *The Myth of Sisyphus* grew.

Like Gide or Mauriac, but unlike Malraux, Camus was a writer who, as an adult, could still relive in intense, imaginative fashion within the world of his childhood. Although Camus took pains to disguise details of his intimate, personal life when writing his works of fiction, the indelible memories of his early years in Algeria are transparent even in those works written long after he had crossed the Mediterranean and settled in Paris. In several of the *Lyrical Essays,* Camus speaks very revealingly and with obvious pleasure of his native Algeria. The sun, the sea, and sensuality are shown to be at the heart of a personal mythology which played a large part in shaping the author's sensibility and even his intellectual development.

If the *Lyrical Essays* are taken as

factual, they will help dispel some of the gloom which has built up around the portrait of Camus the man. Camus was somewhat amused at having acquired the reputation of being a somber, ascetic personality, attributes resulting, no doubt, from the tragic dimension of his writing. Right up to the time of his unfortunate death in an automobile accident in 1960, Camus protested that he had a prodigious appetite for all that life had to offer, an inheritance, he claimed, of a confluence of joyous elements which made of his formative years a near-perfect idyl. Life in Algiers, Camus declared, was life spent among a people indifferent to the mind, but with a very lively admiration for the body. Camus even goes so far as to affirm that he discovered the sad, gray face of wretched poverty only after he made his first contact with the industrial cities of Europe. His own very humble background—his father was killed in World War I, leaving his uneducated wife to work and earn the family bread—was no time of hardship. The author insists that his poverty as a child was amply redeemed by the happiness of companionship and the brilliance of the Algerian sun: "Poverty, first of all, was never a misfortune for me: it was radiant with light." Camus' theory that favorable climatic conditions can easily counterbalance material poverty would find few defenders among the sociologists or political scientists, but it does serve to emphasize how deep the author's affection for his native land was.

The solar paganism propounded in the *Lyrical Essays* implies tragedy as the complementary aspect of joy. Just as everything appears black after one has gazed up into the sun, so a life of joy appears even more absurd, when confronted by the inevitability of

death, than one of melancholy. For in the latter case, death might even be welcomed as a form of release. The permanence of the Mediterranean landscape, of sun and sea and rock, more than the shifting seasons and the mellow light of the North, underlines the brevity of man's life. And the men of the shores of the Mediterranean, Camus claims, are endowed with a deep sense of the tragedy of existence.

Whereas Camus successfully convinces the reader of the importance of the Mediterranean in his own vision—and the sense of place is very strong not only in *Lyrical Essays* but in most of his fiction—he is less able to translate this personal mythology into a general doctrine. It is patently simplistic to resurrect Mme. de Staël's theories about Northern melancholy and Southern joy, or to propose new theories entailing a rigid dichotomy between North and South. Camus seems unwilling to recognize that the Mediterranean area has been the cradle of the most diverse opinions, ideas, and doctrines. One wonders on what authority Camus holds the Mediterranean to be "the very denial of Rome and Latin genius." It seems unreasonable to admit Spain to the inner circle of Mediterranean values, one of the first of which is moderation, while making no mention of the excesses of the Inquisition, the Spanish Civil War, or the government of Franco. Here, the author's enthusiasm and his love of Algeria, which serve him so well in conjuring up the atmosphere of Oran or of Algiers, deny him the possiblity of objectivity which other Mediterranean writers such as Paul Valéry were able to attain.

The second part of *Lyrical and Critical Essays* is made up of a large number of generally short essays spanning the years from 1937 to 1959. They discuss authors of several nationalities. Camus reveals himself to be a discerning critic, guided by his intuition rather than by any dogmatic or doctrinaire approach to literature. Unlike Jean-Paul Sartre, Camus offers no overall theory of literature. He considers each work on its own terms, always as literature, never as sociology or history or psychology. Surprisingly, perhaps, the author's tastes in literature seem generally conservative, though he is unstinting in his praise of René Char, an outstanding, living French poet whom Camus knew well. Camus displays a good knowledge of and respect for the tradition of French literature, although this does not prevent him from being very receptive to Herman Melville and penetrating in his understanding of William Faulkner.

Many readers will be intrigued to find among the critical essays the very first review of a work of Sartre's by Camus. This essay, on *La Nausée,* was written and published in 1938, when Camus was only twenty-five. It is significant in several respects. Camus had not yet met Sartre, but he immediately shows an understanding of the latter's ambitious attempt to present philosophy in the form of fiction, as a novel. Defining the novel as a genre expressing a philosophy in the form of images, Camus reproaches the author of *La Nausée* for leaving his ideas insufficiently clothed or disguised: "The novel in question today is one in which . . . [the] balance has been broken, where the theories do damage to the life." While admiring *La Nausée,* Camus has some reservations about its meeting the criteria of pure fictionality. This criticism seems significant. On many occasions in the critical essays of this volume, Camus dis-

plays a marked interest in style and technique and problems of fictionality. It would seem that Camus the thinker has caused Camus the creative artist to be neglected, although Camus himself had a high notion of art.

The third and final section of *Lyrical and Critical Essays,* entitled "Camus on Himself," is by far the shortest. It consists of a well-chosen selection of interviews and letters in which the author talks about himself, his work, his relationship to other writers, and his feelings about the public.

When Camus was alive, the similarities between his thought and that of Sartre seemed remarkably striking. Now, with some critical distance between them, it seems much more difficult to place their names together under the general heading of "existentialism." It no longer seems inappropriate that Camus should declare in one of the interviews in the third section of *Lyrical and Critical Essays* that he is not an existentialist:

"No, I am not an existentialist. Sartre and I are always surprised to see our names linked. We have even thought of publishing a short statement in which the undersigned declare that they have nothing in common with each other and refuse to be held responsible for the debts they might respectively incur."

"Camus on Himself" includes as its final chapter an interview dated 1959, the year before Camus was killed. The author was asked to formulate his wish for the future. His reply is particularly moving, in view of his tragic death shortly thereafter:

"Within a superabundance of life-giving and restoring forces, even misfortunes have a sunlike glow and engender their own consolation." This remark of Nietzsche's is true, and I have experienced it myself. And all I ask is that this strength and this superabundance should be given to me again, even if infrequently. . . .

The publication of *Lyrical and Critical Essays* brings still further proof, if any were needed, that Camus' talents were multiple, and that his sudden death seems no less tragic with the passing of time.

James McNab

LYTTON STRACHEY
Volume I: The Unknown Years (1880–1910)
Volume II: The Years of Achievement (1910–1932)

Author: Michael Holroyd (1935–   )
Publisher: Holt, Rinehart and Winston (New York). Illustrated. Vol. I, 479 pp.; Vol. II, 754 pp. $21.95
Type of work: Biography
Time: 1880–1932
Locale: England and the Continent

A full-scale critical study of the eminent biographer and his association with the Bloomsbury Group and other important artistic, political, and social personages of the time

Principal personages:
LYTTON STRACHEY, biographer, critic, and essayist
SIR RICHARD and
LADY STRACHEY, his parents
JAMES STRACHEY, his psychoanalyst brother and confidant
DORA CARRINGTON, a Bloomsbury painter in love with Lytton Strachey
RALPH PARTRIDGE, her husband and Strachey's friend
VIRGINIA WOOLF, novelist
LEONARD WOOLF, her husband, a writer and publisher
JOHN MAYNARD KEYNES, economist
LADY OTTOLINE MORRELL, the fashionable London hostess of an important intellectual and artistic salon

By the time Lytton Strachey died in 1932, he had performed a great service for the art of biography. After his dazzling and controversial works, no longer could the life of an eminent Victorian be celebrated in two staid volumes of over-rich prose that presented only the public face, the official acts, the aspects most representative of copy-book maxims. Strachey cleared all the eulogistic misrepresentation away, added a readableness which was part art and part artful trickery, and prepared the way so that a major biographical work such as this present book could be written.

Michael Holroyd has used few, if any, of the Strachey techniques. This is not an "impressionist" biography. Conversations are not reconstructed from edited correspondence. Since the author has had unrestricted access to first sources, he has been able to report rather than infer the uttermost privacies of his subject's life. The result is an eminently readable as well as scholarly examination of a curious, eccentric, peppery, yet winning man whose reputation as an artist is sure to be stimulated toward renascence.

Lytton Strachey was born into a distinguished upper middle-class family with traditions of service to his country, leadership in Anglo-Indian and military affairs, and literacy. Members of this class in nineteenth century England proceeded naturally into public service, into the Church, to scholarly lives at Oxford or Cambridge. They were related to one another and had cousinship in the aristocracy. There was enough money—at least in youth

—to give them leisure; there were opportunities to which birth entitled them; there was a tradition of literacy and individualism that gave them courage to direct their lives away from the establishment. The Huxleys, the Darwins, the Stephens family that produced Virginia Woolf all shared a Victorian respectability enlivened with genius.

Lytton Strachey was one of the ten children of Sir Richard and Lady Strachey. Always a sickly child, his education was unusual for his age and class. When he finally entered Cambridge, he was able for the first time to escape the stifling restrictions of the Victorian schoolroom and the omnipresence of his aggressively protective family.

At Cambridge, where his intellectual interests were matured, he was able to initiate the associations and friendships that influenced his life. As a member of "The Apostles," a Cambridge secret society of intellectuals, wits, and exotics, he became friends with Leonard Woolf, E. M. Forster, Rupert Brook, Bertrand Russell, and John Maynard Keynes. Here, too, his initiation into the homosexual world took place.

Holroyd had placed at his disposal the uncensored correspondence and diaries of Strachey and many of his friends. Strachey's brother James, who had studied under Freud and became himself an important English analyst, gave the author every assistance in ferreting out the most personal aspects of Strachey's life. From this material emerges a picture of the sexuality of the times—sexuality apparently as free as today's, with that freedom accepted in many intellectual, artistic, and social circles. The only difference between those times and these—a difference of

degree only—is that these sexual secrets were kept within the circles where the participators belonged.

When Strachey emerged from school and became an active member of the Bloomsbury Group, all of them were aware of his homosexuality. They knew he and Maynard Keynes were rivals for the affection of the young painter, Duncan Grant, as well as they knew that Bertrand Russell was the lover of Lady Ottoline Morrell, that fashionable lady who with her salons bridged the gap between *la vie de bohème* and English society.

How the Bloomsbury Group came into being and who they were are delightfully delineated. The two Stephens sisters, Virginia, who later married Leonard Woolf, and Vanessa, who married the art critic Clive Bell, were the initiators, together with their brothers, Adrian and Thoby. When Vanessa married, she set up another Bloomsbury salon. "The drawing-room has no carpet or wall-paper," wrote Lytton to a friend, "curtains some blue and some white, a Louis XV bed (in which they lie side by side), two basket chairs, a pianola, and an Early Victorian mahogany table." There were also pictures by Picasso and Vlaminck, a new moral code that repudiated Victorian insincerity, and an atmosphere of intellectuality and fun that was an enchanting substitute for the delights of university life.

"The group is said to have comprised an alert and original band of man and women whose splendidly unfashionable and undemocratic enlightenment proved too strong for our universities and too subtle and idiosyncratic for our unclutured, unimaginative society," writes Holroyd. "The much derided Bloomsbury voice, believed to symbolize in some mysterious way all that the movement stood for, came naturally to Lytton Strachey in whom it was so delightful and captivating that it charmed everyone and soon spread equally naturally to his friends. Occasionally it might be put on a little to tease—for there was perpetual gaiety in Bloomsbury—and sometimes, by the sly cadence of a single word—'Really?' or 'extraordinary!' an outsider's truism was horribly crushed—for Bloomsbury could never gladly suffer fools."

All the "Bloomsberries," as the group was nicknamed, met constantly, discussed interminably and with ribald malice one another's works and sex lives, and reported minutely the progress of their love affairs in witty and candid letters. Strachey, quite carried away with the atmosphere of mutual involvement and intrigue, once proposed to Virginia Stephen, before her marriage to Leonard Woolf, and was quite relieved to be refused.

During this period, Strachey wrote a number of brilliant reviews and essays for *The Spectator*. It was not until after the war, however, that *Eminent Victorians* was published, and Strachey was bathed in the limelight of a national and even international literary fame.

Strachey's interpretations of Cardinal Manning, Florence Nightingale, General Gordon, and Dr. Arnold "are not painted with the grandiloquent formality of sentimental portraiture, the falsity of which can be apprehended by an ordinary knowledge of human nature, but they are rendered with the acuteness of true caricature," writes Holroyd. "They are not photographs in literature, and some of the lines of character in their make-up bear only misshapen resemblance to the originals. But seen as creatures of parody and extravagance, each one constructed around a few easily recognizable and strongly developed traits, they each convey the impression of an authentically lifelike countenance."

The success of this brilliant book gave Strachey the money and the self-confidence to live the life he wanted.

In 1915, he had met the young ex-Slade student, Dora Carrington—boyish, intuitive, not well-educated, but with a kind of dynamism and youthfulness that was touchingly attractive.

Not long after meeting Strachey, "Carrington," as she was always called, fell deeply and eternally in love with him, even though knowing that he was homosexual. Their relationship was one of the strangest emotional entanglements in the history of all unusual complications among talented people. She later married Ralph Partridge, with whom Strachey was infatuated, and all three lived together in the country, supported by Strachey. Their mutual dependence was touching. Carrington ran the house and nursed and adored Strachey. Ralph attended to the practicalities of chopping wood and mending light cords while he adored Carrington. Strachey, though occasionally having more or less transient love affairs with young men, depended utterly on Carrington's affection while remaining, at the same time, still rather in love with Ralph.

As the years passed, their emotional lives became even more involved. Ralph had a mistress who stayed in the house also, while Carrington enjoyed occasional love affairs with both men and women. Strachey himself was deeply in love with a temperamental young man who never gave sufficiently of himself to be a satisfactory love object.

Strachey's publication of *Queen Victoria* was another triumph, and he became a literary lion of London in the 1920's. He was caricatured by Max Beerbohm, entertained by duchesses, envied by literary friends, and attacked by critics—all indicative of how famous his work had made him.

Unhappily, his health continued to deteriorate. After the publication of *Elizabeth and Essex,* which was not received with the enthusiasm given his two earlier major works, he did not have the strength to undertake another. After one last visit to France, one final foray into the glamorous world of London—visits with Lady Cunard, Noel Coward, Somerset Maugham, the Guinesses—Strachey returned to his country house to suffer quietly and gallantly a lingering death from cancer.

Carrington was distraught with grief. Less than two months later, at the country house he had willed her, she donned Strachey's yellow silk dressing gown, rolled up a favorite Oriental rug so it would not be damaged by her blood, and shot herself.

Not only is this an engrossing, "tell-all" biography of a fascinating, eccentric, and important artist, but it is also an excellent social history of the times. One can see that the seeds of "swinging London" were sown in the 1920's and even earlier, as restrictive Victorian moral codes disintegrated and the establishment began to lose its sacrosanct aura. Strachey's witty, irreverent work contributed to this destruction of pomposity. Michael Holroyd's book should go far in re-establishing Strachey's reputation as an artist as well as humanizing him as a man.

Leclare Ratteree

MACAULAY: THE SHAPING OF THE HISTORIAN

Author: John Clive (1924-   )
Publisher: Alfred A. Knopf (New York). Illustrated. 499 pp. $15.00
Type of work: Biography
Time: 1800-1838
Locale: England and India

A sensitive and sympathetic study of the childhood, youth, and young manhood of the British man of letters and statesman

Principal personages:
THOMAS BABINGTON MACAULAY (1800-1859)
ZACHARY MACAULAY, his stern, overbearing father, a famous
    Evangelical and anti-slavery crusader
SELINA MILLS MACAULAY, his mother
HANNAH MACAULAY, later LADY TREVELYAN, and
MARGARET MACAULAY, later MRS. EDWARD CROPPER,
    his beloved sisters

The "Whig interpretation of history" regarded the past from the vantage point of the power, prosperity, and material and moral progress of nineteenth century Britain. Whig historians could afford to be complacent and self-congratulatory during the *pax Britannica,* the Industrial Revolution, and the political reform era. Believing in the inevitability of progress, they judged the past confidently by the crude criterion of success. Whig history merged into teleology, and the principles of the great Reform Act of 1832, which the Whigs believed had reconciled order and liberty definitely, seemed to form history's apparent design and imminent end. Hence events, personalities, and institutions which had advanced the now triumphant cause of orderly liberty—Magna Carta, the Reformation, and the Glorious Revolution, for example—were "progressive" necessarily and thus "good"; and those like the Stuart monarchy or the radical Levellers and Diggers which had failed were for that reason alone "bad" as representatives of the his-

torically doomed forces of either anarchy or tyranny. Whig historians gloried in Britain's greatness, and this greatness in turn appeared to validate the entire Whig historical view, value system, and optimistic prognosis for continued human progress.

Thomas Babington Macaulay was the greatest of the Whig historians. He identified historically with the rise of Whig principles, and indeed as a Member of Parliament in 1832 he assisted at their triumph. Macaulay expounded the "Whig interpretation of history" in his widely read essays, orations, and magisterial *History of England.* His literary efforts enshrined the Whig viewpoint in British consciousness so that it became almost the ideology of the age. With "propulsive historical imagination," perfervid rhetoric, a technique of painting the past in glaring colors, violent forms, and striking textural contrasts, and his very cocksureness about everything, Macaulay brought the Whig view of English history into not only the popular awareness but also the historical canon, where it would remain dominant for most of the next century and where even today in standard textbook accounts it still holds its own.

As Whig history tended to evaluate every cause by historical success, so in self-appraisal Macaulay tried to reckon his attainment of wealth, honors, rank, power, and fame the measure of felicity. Not seldom, however, did Macaulay realize the emptiness of such crude and superficial materialism. Even the proverbially cocksure Macaulay had tormenting doubts. Outside Macaulay wore the protective armor of aggressive intellectualism and unshakeable confidence in himself and his opinions, but inside he remained soft, insecure, and what can only be termed "childlike." For all his success Macaulay remained profoundly unhappy, emotionally stunted, and incapable of giving or receiving affection except in his pitifully immature romantic relationship with his two youngest sisters, Hannah and Margaret.

Macaulay was the historian of English progress, and yet at times he articulated a deeply disturbing historical pessimism—like his celebrated vision of a future New Zealander sketching the ruins of St. Paul's from a broken arch of London Bridge. His writing of history stressed "circumstance," the relativity of historical situations and the necessity for understanding the past in its own terms; and his imaginative works like the poem "Epitaph on a Jacobite" displayed remarkable sympathy for the very lost causes which he most deplored ideologically. In a series of essays Macaulay delivered a devastating critique of Utilitarianism among other reasons for its failure to do justice to the complexity of human nature.

John Clive analyzes the complexity of Macaulay's personality and historical thought in this exemplary biography. Clive sets out "to trace some of the forces—familial, intellectual, political, and personal—which helped to shape the man and the historian," and he succeeds admirably. Concerned with Macaulay's formative years, Clive ends his study in 1838—the year of Macaulay's return to England from India and the beginning of his work for the great *History of England*. Clive does not deal with the last twenty years of Macaulay's life, which saw the completion and publication of his greatest works, his career in the British Cabinet, and his elevation to the peerage as Baron Macaulay of Rothley. Although Clive clearly states his rationale for this truncated biography, this does not allay the reader's disappointment and nagging sense that Macaulay did not cease to develop intellectually and personally when he approached forty. It is testimony of the excellence of Clive's study that the reader hopes he will follow soon with the complementary volume covering the remainder of Macaulay's life.

Clive describes Macaulay with understanding and sympathy, but without partisanship. He examines Macaulay's personality critically but gently and without the cant of psychohistory. The task is not easy, for Macaulay was hardly the romantic protagonist. He was sedentary, obese, personally untidy, and proverbially ugly and odd. He took part in no military campaigns, duels, love affairs, or heroic ordeals. Clive confronts not an adventurous life but the far more subtle and intriguing drama of the mind. The conflicts in Macaulay's formative years were inward and indeed with himself. Clive argues unobtrusively but persuasively that the crucial determinant in Macaulay's intellectual and personal development was his relationship with his father Zachary.

The dynamic of Macaulay's formative years was repressed hatred of his father which he never dared to express openly but rather translated into aggressiveness in the world of letters and politics. Outwardly the model of self-assuredness—Lord Melbourne would observe that he wished he were as sure of anything as Tom Macaulay was cocksure of everything—inwardly Macaulay struggled unsuccessfully against crippling resentment and his sense of unworthiness that would keep him emotionally "childlike" for his entire life.

Macaulay was the eldest of the eight children of the stern and unbending Evangelical father Zachary and the gentle mother Selina. From infancy he failed to live up to his father's expectations, and in fact the first wholly extant letter from Macaulay to his father sets the tone. The six-year-old wrote,

My Dear Papa,

I am sorry that my writing did not please you. I hope that I shall improve in it. . . .   (July, 1807)

He never could please his father. Perhaps the paradigmatic incident was Macaulay's debut as a public orator in 1824 when he spoke before the Society for the Mitigation and Abolition of Slavery which his father had founded. It was a brilliant oration, and seeing his son moving a distinguished audience in behalf of his sacred cause ought to have been the fulfillment of Zachary's dream. But on their walk home from the triumph, Zachary said to his son, "By the way, Tom, you should be aware that when you speak in the presence of royalty, you should not fold your arms."

Understanding the overpowering influence of his father helps to explain Macaulay's prodigious intellectual achievement, which he always hoped, in vain as it turned out, would please his father. It helps also to explain Macaulay's pathetic emotional dependence on his sisters, traits such as his untidiness, forgetfulness, and lack of introspection which were muted expressions of rebellion against his father's most conspicuous virtues, and even perhaps his tolerant liberal politics which may have been shaped by respectful dissent from his father's tough-minded, moralistic, and authoritarian manner. Brilliant successes during Macaulay's formative years always appeared to Macaulay himself as frustrating partial failures. His precocious intellectual development and distinguished academic record at Trinity College, Cambridge, his celebrated early literary efforts in *Knight's Quarterly Magazine* and the *Edinburgh Review,* his election to the House of Commons in 1830 and splendid political career, and even his distinguished service overseas where as legal member for the Supreme Council of India in 1834-1837 he drew up the famous plan for a Westernizing educational system for India and created a uniform Indian code— all somehow fell short of what Macaulay expected that his father expected of him. Although Clive prudently does not emphasize the point, and Macaulay would never have let himself think it, the real watershed in Macaulay's life was the death of his father in 1838.

Terence R. Murphy

THE MACKEREL PLAZA

Author: Peter De Vries (1910-   )
Publisher: Little, Brown and Company (Boston). 260 pp. $3.75
Type of work: Novel
Time: The present
Locale: Avalon, a suburban town in Connecticut

A satirical account of a liberal preacher's efforts to remarry, in defiance of a congregation bent on perpetuating the memory of his dead wife

Principal characters:
> THE REVEREND ANDREW MACKEREL, pastor of People's Liberal Church
> HESTER PEDLOCK, his housekeeper, sister of his dead wife
> MOLLIE CALICO, a young woman he wishes to marry
> PIPPA CALICO, her mother
> FRANK TURNBULL, one of Mackerel's parishioners

The Mackerel Plaza is a very amusing novel, its pages liberally salted with puns and witty paraphrasings, and the story and characters are replete with humorous possibilities, presumably their chief reason for existing at all. The hero is the Reverend Andrew Mackerel, of People's Liberal Church ("the first split-level church in America"). From the pulpit he makes such statements as "It is the final proof of God's omnipotence that he need not exist in order to save us" and "the Bible is at worst a hodgepodge of myths, superstitions and theologies so repugnant to a man of taste and sensibility, let alone a true Christian, that its culmination in the latter ethic is perhaps the greatest miracle we know," statements enthusiastically received by his suburban congregation. He is dedicated to the belief that "faith is a set of demands, not a string of benefits; that a man is under some obligation to better himself," and he is ardently opposed to any taint of fundamentalism in religion, as spiritually and aesthetically vulgar. Not unbelievers, but parishioners who have "got religion" are the bane of his existence. One of his chief duties is to talk them into a more reasonable frame of mind.

The reader is first introduced to the Reverend Andrew Mackerel as he is in the act of telephoning an irate complaint to the Zoning Board: someone has just erected a "Jesus Saves" sign in the restricted-property area near his parsonage.

But Andrew Mackerel is also faced with a more personal kind of frustration. His wife, the "Jane Addams of the East," has been dead three months, and he wishes to remarry. His choice is the very good-looking Zoning Board secretary, Mollie Calico, who spent several years unsuccessfully trying to make good on Broadway and who is now perfectly ready to settle down with a husband. It is not Mollie's slightly interesting past which stands in the way, however, but the town's determination to canonize the first Mrs. Mackerel.

When, after secret meetings in disreputable parts of another town, Mackerel finally decides the time has come to take Mollie to the annual church Harvest Supper, he learns that the entertainment this year is to be specifically in honor of his departed wife. Of course, he cannot bring a prospective second wife to a banquet where there will be speeches made about his first.

Chief among Mrs. Mackerel's worshippers is her sister, Hester Pedlock, temporarily acting as Mackerel's housekeeper. Only Mollie and the reader are sharp enough to recognize immediately that Hester's devotion is not to her sister's memory, but to Andrew Mackerel himself.

Just as Mackerel, having finally disclosed to Hester his plans concerning Mollie, is hoping that he may reasonably expect to be married inside a few months, he receives another blow: Turnbull, a parishioner who has got religion, has convinced himself that Mrs. Mackerel was drowned in an attempt to save his life. In memory of her, he will give the town a fountain, and as the civic leaders take up the idea, the project booms into a whole downtown shopping area, the "Mackerel Plaza." Because the cornerstone cannot be laid until spring, Mackerel's plans for remarriage must be postponed indefinitely.

In desperation, he persuades Mollie to spend a night with him in a seamy hotel. The evening proves a total fiasco; moreover, he—but not she—is recognized. Her mother, scenting scandal, decides that he's not the man for her Mollie, and forbids him to see her at all. To make things completely dismal, Mackerel's book on man's martyrdom to society is rejected as exaggerated by his publisher.

At this point, determined to prove his thesis by becoming a self-made martyr to society, Mackerel begins to crack up. So does the coherence of the novel as it moves toward its mildly demented but foreseeable conclusion. Trying to convince the town that his wife was wholly human, he arouses considerable suspicion that he might have killed her. He tells two off-color stories from the pulpit, resulting in his

being given a temporary "vacation" and nearly in his loss of the church altogether. Mollie runs away with People's Liberal's dramatic director, and Hester leaves Mackerel without a housekeeper. Mrs. Calico, having learned of her daughter's complicity in the hotel episode, is so filled with remorse at her former injustice to Mackerel that she takes on the job of housekeeping, but before long Mackerel is convinced that *she* has matrimonial designs on him. To get rid of her, he hints that he may actually be a wife-killer. She leaves and goes directly to the police station with the report of his confession. To make matters worse, the townspeople's prayers for rain are answered, and Mackerel's faith, which did not admit of such cheap miracles, is shattered.

Finally, however, order is restored. Mackerel marries Hester instead of Mollie, and is perfectly happy with the substitution. It develops that Mrs. Calico's matrimonial designs were not upon Mackerel, but upon Turnbull. A home movie, taken the day of the fatal accident, proves that, far from having drowned his wife, Mackerel himself was attempting to rescue Turnbull at the time. In gratitude, Turnbull makes the Mackerel Plaza over to the minister, who is then reinstated in his pulpit and whose faith is even expected to recover from the crushing blow of the miracle.

In reading *The Mackerel Plaza*, the reader receives the impression that Peter De Vries was often wasting his cleverness. Whole sections of the novel seem to have been developed with no other purpose than as preparations for a witticism. The prayed-for rain is a case in point. De Vries appears to have been carried away with the joke of a miracle's resulting in loss of faith, for the miracle here seems no less contrived than if it had been seriously presented with the opposite effect in mind. Moreover, as the reader follows the account of the thunderstorm, he gets the uneasy feeling that the *real* reason for it is to give Mackerel a chance to put his hand out the window and say, "Jehovah's wetness."

The characters, too, sometimes give the appearance of having been created in illustration of a joke. Mollie Calico's mother is a homey little person, whose cozy house reminds Mackerel—rather too often—of children's animal stories.

> She looked precisely like some clothed and bespectacled forest creature sniffing and philosophizing in its chimney corner. She was Mrs. Tiggy-winkle, who did the washing in the Beatrix Potter books. Or Tabitha Twitchett, who ran the grocery store and did not give credit; or Goody Tiptoes, or all these rolled into one: an anthropomorphic thing in a ruffled gown and, at night of course, a lace cap. Already I could see her pushing moss under the thatch with her nose to keep us snug all winter.

At first, this sort of thing seems a good piece of characterization, but after Mackerel has been reminded of the forest folk three or four times, and refers to Mrs. Calico as "Tabitha Twitchett" almost as often as by her own name, the reader has the sensation that she was created chiefly for the purpose of the comparison.

Mackerel's name is another bit of jocular contrivance, which cannot be viewed in the tradition of naming characters according to their personalities, for there is nothing particularly fishy about the Reverend Andrew Mackerel. The name suggests nothing except the expression "Holy Mackerel"—an appellation which our hero was happily able to shake off upon leaving the theological seminary.

Despite its faults, *The Mackerel Plaza* does have elements of real satire. The trouble is that the author moves so rapidly from irony to farce and then to fantasy that some of his effects are dissipated by the galloping pace at which his story progresses. Yet the serious element is there, beneath the puns and jokes and contrived comedy, and what appears to have begun as absurd caricature and irresponsible comedy ends on a note of rational, almost dignified, religious belief.

THE MAGIC BARREL

Author: Bernard Malamud (1914–   )
Publisher: Farrar, Strauss and Giroux (New York). 214 pp. $5.95
Type of work: Short stories
Locale: New York, Rome, Stresa

A collection of thirteen short stories dealing with commonplace human misadventures which provide profound insights into human nature

Bernard Malamud, dealing masterfully with the human dilemma in several different situations in *The Magic Barrel,* is extremely adept in providing a depth of characterization in order to furnish perceptive moral insights into human nature in general. Malamud does concern himself with particular ethnic sensibilities: those of the Jew, the Italian, and the Negro. He expands upon a particular consciousness in order to draw a more universal parable. The characters range in type from Feld, the poor old shoemaker in "The First Seven Years" to Fidelman, the errant artist-student (of sorts) whom we find wandering through Italy in "The Last Mohican." Malamud's artistry lies in his ability to take these characters and to build on a certain passion or emotion inherent to them in order to depict a certain dilemma. He then derives an ironic moral observation from the resolution of that dilemma.

In "The First Seven Years," Malamud gives us Feld the shoemaker and well-meaning father, his helper Sobel, and the shoemaker's independent daughter Miriam. Naturally the papa tries to match Miriam up with the "right" boy and dreams of Max, "whom he so much respected because of the sacrifices he had made throughout the years—in winter or direst heat—to further his education." The story begins on an ironic note as Feld mentally reproaches Sobel for the latter's insensitivity in hammering away at a piece of shoe leather, thus interrupting Feld's reveries of Max.

Feld busily makes moral judgments of the other characters throughout the story. Sobel, he feels, stays on as his helper, working for low wages and with no possibility of advancement, "no doubt because of his terrible experiences as a refugee" and because he "was afraid of the world." Miriam, although "she was always with a book in her hand," has no desire for a college education, and therefore Feld is convinced that she will never be able to better her situation in life because she is essentially an uneducated person. He judges Max to be a man of great cerebral proportions and yet Miriam says, "I was bored. Because he's nothing more than a materialist. He has no soul. He's only interested in things."

The great visions Feld has had about his Miriam marrying the college boy Max fall through. Another misfortune occurs when Sobel, upon hearing Feld make the arrangements with Max, grabs his coat and rushes away from the shop. Feld has always found Sobel to be a bit bizarre and temperamental and so attributes his desertion to these personal traits. Finally, realizing that a man with his weak heart cannot take on all of the work by himself, Feld goes to Sobel to beg him to return and learns that Sobel has stayed only because of Miriam. The father becomes reconciled and Sobel is back at work the next morning, "pounding leather for his love."

The actual act of pounding leather is

indicative of Sobel's tenacity concerning the quest of Miriam. Malamud well illustrates how both Feld and Sobel are insistent, Feld because Miriam is his beloved daughter and Sobel because she is a potential wife. Sobel, ironically, is the one hope for Miriam, for although papa is interested in a man of education for his daughter, he manages to find one who is interested "only in things." Feld ignores Sobel, for he is ugly, too old, and is only a shoemaker. He completely disregards Sobel's profound spirituality and can think only of his daughter's impending life with a poor shoemaker. The story ends optimistically, in spite of Feld's dark feelings about Sobel, for the poor shoemaker's helper is spiritually rich and is truly devoted to the daughter.

The other stories in *The Magic Barrel* present just such ironic moral observations of life itself. Just as Feld ignored what was under his own roof, Gruber, the landlord in "The Mourners" does not recognize his own plight until Kessler, his poor old tenant, illuminates the situation at the conclusion of the story. Kessler, having lived in a decaying tenement for ten years, is virtually unknown to the other tenants. The vindictive janitor takes offense at the way Kessler piles his garbage bags, complains to Gruber, the landlord, and an eviction notice is given to Kessler. The story consists of the futile efforts of the janitor, the landlord, and the city authorities to oust Kessler from his rat's nest. At one time all of his furniture is actually moved into the street, whereupon the tenants move it back to his rooms. We find Gruber at the end of the story watching Kessler mourn for his past misdeeds, sitting in the middle of the floor. Gruber realizes suddenly that it is *he* who is being mourned: "Then it struck him with a terrible force that the mourner was mourning him: it was *he* who was dead." Finally, the spiritually dead Gruber sits down and joins Kessler, guilty of having deserted his family years ago, and the landlord, overcome by his own sense of guilt and shame, becomes a mourner too.

In the three stories, "Angel Levine," "Take Pity," and "The Loan," Malamud realizes the coming-together of real and unreal elements. Manischevitz the tailor is beset by innumerable trials. The Angel Levine, a Negro Jewish angel, is sent to aid the tailor in his tribulations. Manischevitz loses faith, cannot accept the fact that a Jewish angel can actually be black, and Levine retreats to the depths of Harlem. Prejudice almost defeats the tailor; however, as a last resort, when everything is going worse than ever, he goes into Harlem to seek out the angel, thereby ultimately saving his wife's life and the angel himself from going astray. The commonplace problems of poverty, family illness, and lack of faith are joined with the supernatural saving powers of the improbable angel, thus making both the mundane and the fantastic in the story extremely memorable.

"Take Pity" involves a conversation between Davidov, the census taker and Rosen, a man who has committed suicide and speaks to Davidov from another world. Rosen had been rejected all his life by a neighboring widow. In order to leave his entire fortune to her in spite of her protestations in the one life, he arranges for a deed leaving everything to her in the event of his death. He then kills himself and is compensated for his rejection in life. The theme is one of unrequited love and its commonness is enhanced and made memorable by Rosen's speaking from another, more fantastic, world.

In "The Loan," Kobotsky, the old friend of Lieb the baker, comes back after fifteen years, asking for money for his late wife's gravestone. Bessie, Lieb's second wife refuses to permit her husband to lend his friend the money; she is afraid of the man who was once the friend of her husband's *first* wife. Lieb attempts to reminisce with Kobotsky, only to be interrupted by Bessie's "Lieb, the bread!" Ironically the baker goes over to the "gas oven" and takes out the bread. This symbol is to recur at the story's conclusion, reminding us of the other fantastic world of degradation and destruction which haunts the three principals in "The Loan." As Bessie tells the stories of her past life's agonies, "Bessie raised her head and suspiciously sniffed the air. Screeching suddenly, she ran into the rear and with a cry wrenched open the oven door. A cloud of smoke billowed out at her. The loaves in the trays were blackened bricks—charred corpses." Kobotsky and Lieb embrace each other and the old friend leaves the baker, both men being deprived somehow by the memory of past events.

In "The Lady of the Lake," we find Henry Levin, a floorwalker in Macy's book department, changing his name to Freeman and traveling to Italy. The change of name is in itself ironic, in that Levin actually imprisons himself in becoming a "free man." He spends all of his time pretending to be something that he is not—a gentile. A lovely girl, with whom he falls in love, asks him if he is a Jew and he denies his race consistently throughout the story, believing the girl will abandon him if he speaks the truth. The story is full of ironies and that may be its weakness. Although Henry misjudges characters and the implications of their speech, it is obvious to us that he is mistaken and will lose his Isabella. When she tells him that she is the daughter of a caretaker and not a member of the aristocracy, he bitterly accuses her of pretending when it is he who is the true pretender. The story is also full of not-so-subtle symbols and this fact further weakens the too obvious irony. Of course, we discover that Isabella is a Jewess and that she has been testing Levin all along. It is simply that he has been too much of a dunderhead to recognize the signs.

Fidelman is another kind of "schnook" whom we find in Italy. Malamud picks up on Fidelman in two stories in a later collection of short stories, *Idiots First*, in "Still Life" and "Naked Nude." Fidelman is always being taken in by one type or another. In this case it is Susskind, the "schnorrer," as Fidelman first calls him. Susskind pursues Fidelman throughout the story, constantly asking for money, and when he receives it, asking for still more money. Fidelman moves from one hotel to another, trying to elude the persistent Susskind but somehow turning up in places where the little Jew finds him. Fidelman is at first hard and callous to him; however, each approach of Susskind's is more persistent than the last, and Fidelman gives in each time. Finally our hero draws the line: "Am I responsible for you then, Susskind? . . . Without prejudice, I refuse the obligation. I am a single individual and can't take on everybody's personal burden. I have the weight of my own to contend with." Susskind, in revenge, steals the first chapter of Fidelman's work on Giotto and the rest of the story is devoted to Fidelman's compulsion to say in Rome and his attempts to find Susskind and the missing chapter. He finds the beggar lighting his candle with chapter pages, flies into a rage, and pursues the refugee in the streets, only to be stopped by the insight that, as Susskind puts it, "The words were there but the spirit was missing." However, the refugee keeps on running. Art as art still evades Fidelman, the self-confessed failure of a painter, and he pursues his "Virgilio Susskind," the nemesis and yet the seer whom he has so long overlooked.

As seen in these stories, Malamud is a masterful scene-painter and observer. His characterizations are superb, his principals always searching for meaning in life, even if at times along crooked paths. The moral truths are evident and universal, and Malamud's characters manifest them best when they *show* and do not tell the reader what these truths should be.

Toni Harris

THE MAGIC STRIPTEASE

Author: George Garrett (1929-   )
Publisher: Doubleday and Company (Garden City, New York). 272 pp. $7.95
Type of work: Short novels

The Magic Striptease, *a comic-strip fable about Jacob Quirk, called Proteus, Prince of Impersonators;* Noise of Strangers, *a story about law, order, and injustice in a small town; and* The Satyr Shall Cry, *a movie soundtrack in various tongues and voices about a double murder and everybody's account of it*

"Three novels making up a phantasmagorical three-ring circus," the dust jacket reads. "And only George Garrett, as ringmaster, knows what's real in this virtuoso display of fantasy and illusion."

To have conceived the novels that make up *The Magic Striptease* is proof enough of the fantastic imagination of a writer who has been on all fronts of literature in a remarkable career while he is still a young man capable, it seems, of yet doubling or even tripling his already abundant output, while getting better as he continues. To have followed his masterwork, *Death of the Fox,* with such a startling display of wit, levity, irony, and humor in language that ranges from Southern seedy to funny-paper farcical to barroom bawdy (Garrett serves as his own censor and bleeps out the bleepables) firmly establishes Garrett as what he has been for some time to those who have known him and his work: a writer of true and rare versatility, able at any time to break the barriers of language and launch a full-scale atack against the dull, the commonplace, the mere traditional.

Take, for example, the title work. *The Magic Striptease,* subtitled *A Comic-Strip Fable,* deals with the misadventures of one Jacob Quirk and is told throughout fifteen sections that range back and forth between the entries in Quirk's secret journal and the third-person narration that itself changes to first-person in the last few pages. Even the tense shifts with the present-tense entries of the journal, the past-tense anecdotes and soliloquys of characters, and the present- and past-tense storytelling of the narrator. If ever imitative form were used to good purpose, it is here, where change and shift, question and quest, guise and guile *are* the story.

Jacob Quirk, from infancy, has had "a natural inclination towards mimicry," a talent his tired father looks down on and one which his gin-swilling, hell-raising mother encourages and relishes. Young Jakey (as his mother calls him) spends his childhood in front of a mirror practicing his face-making while the other children his age are out playing and romping. One of his best imitations is of his father, and when his mother sees it she breaks out into uncontrollable guffawing.

At supper one evening the father has had enough and takes up the carving knife, chasing his braying wife around the kitchen table. When the woman retaliates with a gin bottle and a swinging door, the weary man dies of a stroke just before he receives the fierce blows. Jakey, to please his mother, makes the father's face again, so hilariously successful to the mother that she falls into paroxysms of laughter, takes a long pull from the gin bottle, and plunges the knife into her heart.

Thus Jacob Quirk is launched into the world, taking up residence at the State Orphans' Home, where he is encouraged by the Director to cultivate his art of caricature and to remain where he is appreciated. Once out and in the world, however, he finds that caricature alone will not suffice. The more he polishes his art, the less successful he becomes. He feels, though, that he is on the verge of something big, something really startling. In the meantime he fails to satisfy his agent, who denounces his acts as no longer funny and who tells Quirk that "this is a business! Art is for kids . . . !"

Then it is that Jacob Quirk begins the "work towards the goal of total self-transformation." He perfects his art, at last able to sculpt himself into the shape and substance of any known human form. All he has to do is to study a character long enough and he can become that person. From one of Quirk's journal entries we are given a clue to the ultimate meaning of the story: "No poet or novelist can ever manage to blend himself, to wed himself so completely, into the flux and flow of an imaginary creature's being. I can, if I choose, drown myself in the stream of consciousness of a purely fictional character." He goes on to explain in his journal that his characters are always purely fictional, that the only limits he will know are the boundaries of his own ability to imagine and create. He feels now that since he knows his own limitations (which are few, to say the least!), he has become, by his own definiiton, a rational man.

Subsequently, he proceeds to make himself into a kind of human camera. He takes on the forms of postmen, fruit peddlers, milkmen, laundrymen, and policemen, among others. And in each comic situation someone gains by his transformation, not the least of whom is Agon the fruit peddler. Despised for his looks and his niggardly ways, Agon is redeemed when Quirk becomes Agon and gives away fruit to the neighborhood, so that when Agon "returns" he is a hero.

Quirk has been operating on what he calls the "pleasure principle" and taking pleasure where he can find it, but finally he calls the principle into question, realizing that he can never be loved for himself. He concludes that carnal knowledge is the only true knowledge, "the only true communication," but with the conclusion he reasons further that what he has been looking for all along is simply himself. The battle with himself rages, and in moments he sees himself as becoming a "monster."

After a wild escapade which results in a young woman's madness, Quirk decides that he must do penance by teaching. It is not long until he winds up in the "booby hatch." The final excerpt from the journal includes the statement that "all the world's a mental hospital, and we are only patients in it." But "just like a light bulb in a comic strip" Quirk realizes that what he has been pursuing has been limited to the human form.Why not tackle the world of the beasts? And then, quite logically, why confine oneself to mere living things at all?

So Quirk disappears, becomes inanimate, haunting old adversaries in various forms, including a fountain pen and a cuckoo clock. Cults spring up, experiments are conducted, foundations fund special studies—all to the memory or the study of the Quirk syndrome. His spirit is everywhere, although no one knows where the real Quirk is. And so he is omnipresent. As the narrator emerges as a character in the last pages, talking to a bishop about Quirk—The Master—the Christian parallels to Quirk's life and death are explicitly pronounced, and embellished. The novel ends with the possibility that Quirk might, even now, be the very book that we are reading.

The story is baffling, interesting, and terribly funny. But if it is read as a kind of parable, perhaps the moral is something like this: literature has reached an impasse largely because it has limited itself to a study of the human character, and that study always ends in the great abstractions. All that can save it is to free the creative imagination to deal, not just with the facts of a person's life to show the person, but with the artifacts that surround us all so that the abstraction itself can be dealt with objectively. One thinks of the work of Ionesco and of Robbe-Grillet, and especially of an older *dictum,* that of Plato, who saw in the natural forms of the ideal world what he called "ideas," that must rise above mere mimesis to give a wholeness to the shape of things. For only then could the poet be allowed a special place—as a teacher—in Plato's Republic. Garrett's created world here is far from the Platonic state, but Garrett himself may be one of the first writers Plato would admit, though even then probably on probation.

In the second piece, the "straight" story called *Noise of Strangers,* the heretofore stereotypical sheriff of a small town (here called Fairview) is given new dimensions. Sheriff Jack Riddle is a thoughtful man who is admired by the townspeople, who shows compassion for the town drunk, who is considerate enough to allow his wife to sleep mornings, and who is cast against his will as godlike protector of a town that just wants to die in peace. He might *look* the part of Rod Steiger in *The Heat of the Night,* but he shows qualities all along that are only hinted at in Steiger.

Riddle's young deputy, Larry Berlin, hardly a new centurion, has shot and killed a speeder who turns out to be a hood who has recently robbed and killed in a nearby town. It is Berlin's first "kill," and he thinks no more of it than he would if he had bagged a six-point buck, except that forms must be typed out in six copies because, as Jack says, "Everything serious comes in six copies." So nonchalant is Berlin that he has stopped for breakfast at the diner before bringing in the corpse . . . and the live prisoner, Ike Toombs, who was in the speeding car when Berlin shot the driver.

Toombs is a wandering, guitar-playing cynic, going to fat, getting old, and getting more lost, who is beset at odd times with an incongruous laughter that drives the hothead Berlin up the wall. But Sheriff Riddle is, for the most part, patient with him, and what ensues is a sad question-and-answer period between Toombs and Riddle that might stand as a Mickey Spillane version of the grilling of Raskolnikov by Inspector Porfiri or the tepid culmination in our time of what Koestler showed in *Darkness at Noon*.

The point of view character shifts in the story so that we get the filtered third-person account of Berlin, Riddle, and Toombs—and even a sort of composite view by the town itself, of itself. We see the brazen Berlin and know what he thinks of weakness (closely allied to goodness in his small mind) in a sheriff; we finally learn in overhearing Toombs's thought-words that he was indeed merely hitchhiking and had no part in the crimes of the driver; and we come to know the real reason why Sheriff Riddle books the unfortunate Toombs. Like Camus' Meursault, convicted not for murder but for feeling no love for his mother, poor Toombs is jailed because Riddle must maintain an image for and control over his deputy, lest he be replaced by him.

The Satyr Shall Cry is called in its subtitle *A Movie Soundtrack in Various Tongues and Voices*. It is a multi-viewed mystery of sorts that takes place in Paradise Springs, Florida. Alpha Weatherby, a sexy bankteller, and Dan Lee Smathers, a tent revivalist known as Little David, are murdered, and what takes place in the story is a complicated chapter-by-chapter account by virtually everybody remotely connected with the victims—all in an unraveling, winding, intersecting narrative that rivals (and may be indebted to) *As I Lay Dying*.

The chapter titles tell us who is speaking, and what each speaker says reveals his own connection to the victims—some of which are remote if not trivial. There is, to begin the tale, the "testimony" of Dudley Hagood, editor of the local paper. From him we get "the facts." From Sheriff Prince we get a subjective account of his theory about the "pattern" of the crime, of which there is none. Then there are Darlene Blaze, who could just as easily have been named Candy Barr or Blaze Starr; Penrose Weatherby, young brother of Alpha; Martin Pressy, who is making a book in pictures called *The Magic Book of Woman* and who, while living with his mother, will photograph any woman in the nude who will allow him access. There is Debbi Langley, who grants Pressy photographer's privileges, among others. There is the version of Billy Papp, one of the convicted murderers (though innocent). There are chapters dealing with the preface of Pressy's book and the checklist of an "anonymous stranger who flew the Twin Cessna" who accidentally figures into the crime.

And there are others. But in the short chapter revealing the entries in Penrose's secret diary, we learn that Alpha's brother has done just about everything except pull the trigger. And then, finally, Geneva Laseur, the other convicted murderer, reveals all in a desperate letter to the Governor.

What is most amazing about the plot is its invention and the handling of the point of view. Just when a particular chapter seems farthest away from illumination, there is an intersection with a piece of information picked up earlier so that in sparse, dense, and intense viewpoints we get from George Garrett in one hundred pages what it would take a lesser writer hundreds to unfold: a plethora of characters and a porno-religious-love-hate-murder plot that hangs together until the last page.

It has been written that "George Garrett, like Quirk, seems able to transform himself into anyone and anything—with magical results." He proves it in this book, as he has in his others. It would be interesting to try to fit these seemingly disparate novels together, to see just why they are housed together. One can be certain that there is a reason, but perhaps only the Garrett-Quirk, who not long ago "became" Sir Walter Raleigh and wrote a brilliant book, can tell us what it is.

Joseph Maiolo

THE MAGIC WILL
Stories and Essays of a Decade

Author: Herbert Gold (1924-   )
Publisher: Random House (New York). 304 pp. $7.95
Type of work: Short stories, essays, and memoirs

A collection of stories, essays, and memoirs written by an active man with an active mind and an active heart

"Society and the public life are as they may be, and moving in," Herbert Gold writes in the title essay of this book, "but the private will remains." And of course the private will is that magic one that brings messages from our mysterious sources—what we have been, are, and yearn to be. For all its romance and mystery, however, it is tough. "My magic will still insists on its desire," Gold has told us earlier in the same essay.

And this report is confirmed again and again in the book. Gold conveys eagerness more often than urgency in his essays into both real and imaginary worlds. This fact changes the air, and gives a special tone of light to his testimony. We are relieved to escape the apocalyptic nay-sayers and the articulate neurotics who suck on crises as if they were their own juicy thumbs. The reason is, Gold has a way of liking people; he is even *interested* in them —not as emblems, or vessels you can pour *caritas* into—but as people. There is, in this eagerness, that sort of innocence that comes from intelligence and knowledge: he suspects, standing knee-deep in a crisis, that we really *have* been here before, and because of this there is no way to be sure we are doomed.

This is all impressionistic, and it would be wrong to suggest that Gold is glib or facile in the midst of suffering. Quite the contrary: his various accounts of experiences in Haiti and

Biafra have risen in passion, anguish, and sympathy. His sensitive story, "A Death on the East Side," and his article, "A Survival," telling of his being in the Paris airport that day in 1962 when a jet crashed, killing all aboard who had only minutes before surrounded him in the terminal—these pieces probe deeper than what the average sight-seeing mind desires; and furthermore they reveal that death is not simply a political or social problem.

But even in the modern ghetto of *Angst,* humor abides. And humor has its styles; which is to say, Gold's humor, spiraling in a thousand configurations through these essays and stories, is always his very own. The stance is ironic, usually self-ironic, so that again and again we hear that sad, funny, woefully recognizable sour note: "And it ended with love, true love, Donna Smith sheltered by my strong arms in a light which held my hickies," and "Repressed, suppressed, tormented, unconscious, the desire to kill is a part of the risk of city life, like postnasal drip." Such artful and irreverent bathos sounds like a symphony of naughty noises through the pages, and would keep the reader amused and turning pages, if there weren't enough already to keep him going.

But of course there is a plenitude of effect, and the reader will keep going, because these are not really pages at all, but a three-ring circus in which mind, sense, and heart are happening all at once. The wit is there, always: "The future is a slightly disagreeable consequence of the present, following it by association as 'liver' follows 'cirrhosis of the.'" Such gags as this are expendable, to be sure; and there are readers who cannot reconcile the gag man with the bringer of messages; but these are the people who tend to be humorless in the face of serious joy.

Anyway, the wit—the voltage behind the gags—is lavishly used. If Gold will travel to the next township for a gag upon occasion (rather than "upon a horse or motorcycle"), it is nevertheless simply true that this same wit turns suddenly, mercurially to good use, and produces the insight we ask for. "Powerlessness corrupts; absolute powerlessness corrupts absolutely," he says, stating a counter truth whose corrective virtues are always needed. On the very next page (this is in an essay titled, "Let's Kill the First Red-Haired Man We See"), regarding one aspect of the Youth Revolution, he says, "But the grooviness ended with thievery, fights, jealous rage, and a contagion of breakdowns. A Panglossian reaction might be: Okay, let's work out the violence, it's the price we pay for superorganization. The trouble with this is that violence *expresses* other feelings, but *communicates* itself—the desire to hurt."

I do not know of anyone who sees more clearly into the murky and tangled realities of Happening Now. As he proved in his novel *The Great American Jackpot*, Gold's diagnoses of the epidemic manias are viciously accurate. And it is as ridiculous to ask for prescriptions at this stage as it is to ask that Gold stop spinning off gags. They are part of the message, too; we ought not to be too owlish about humor.

"I wouldn't have chosen this trip, he says, regarding his "Summer Vacation" in Biafra; "but neither could I refuse it." A writer spends a lot of time choosing between things he wants to do and things he wants to write; as Hemingway's career showed, they both derive from the center of a man, his style. In this sense, Gold seems always, instinctively, to find out where to stand so he cannot refuse. He has an omnivorous appetite for the out-of-the-way, the humanly irregular. He loves the ragged glamour of Haiti, and goes there frequently (at least once since this book was published). He is intent upon "programming the peculiar things" (the title of one essay), and this intensity, appetite, love all show through the words, making them luminous a little more often than a reader has a right to expect.

The Magic Will is a good harvest of experiences—both the real ones, focused in the lens of an interesting man's sensibility, and those hypothetical ones of fiction. The binding force of the book is this testimony of one man. In addition to the values mentioned, there are the gallery of characters that are vividly presented: a narcoleptic Minister of Tourism (Haiti); a wealthy old Italian who, as a young man, knew Proust (this is a funny/sad story, reminiscent of "Death in Venice"); the "First and Last Beatnik" (a San Francisco black man suffering from logorrhea); and a woman named "Sheila" (in a short story titled "The Older Woman") who is right out of *The Great American Jackpot*.

Then, too, there is the style: not merely the wit, the horseplay, a sort of non-precious, unabashed camp—but the presiding wit, and the voice that has an unmistakable cadence and point. It is elliptical, asyndotic. It turns again and again to anaphora: "She didn't answer. She couldn't answer. She was asleep."

In the midst of accumulating information, Gold takes time to feel his way around the bulges and ruptures of the world. He is abnormally sensitive to the lock-step of generations, the casual cruelties we scatter in our wake like shells from peanuts. He seems to believe that with enough care and thought and information and understanding we might become wise; and it is good to report that he is a writer with a mind who therefore thinks wisdom is worth having. And of course, too, there's the magic will itself, which we dare not forget: "Peculiar things happen to all of us, especially if we are paying attention. The first is being born, the last is dying. And in between, the magic will works to give us eyes and a heart, a register and a judging apparatus constructed over the millions of years by fishy juices and sponges, a history and a soul. Of course, it's helped by genes and habits, but these we can take as natural, like the smog we breathe."

These are the words of a man who pays attention splendidly.

Jack Matthews

THE MAGUS

Author: John Fowles (1926–   )
Publisher: Little, Brown, and Company (Boston). 583 pp. $7.95
Type of work: Novel
Time: August, 1952–October 31, 1953
Locale: London and Greece

A novel which examines the mystery of human love and existential responsibility in the twentieth century

Principal characters:

NICHOLAS URFE, a young Englishman
ALISON KELLY, an Australian girl
MAURICE CONCHIS, the mysterious owner of Bourani, a villa on the island of Phraxos; the Magus
LILY DE SEITAS, an English girl; also known as Lily Montgomery and Julie Holmes
ROSE DE SEITAS, Lily's twin-sister; also known as Rose Montgomery and June Holmes

John Fowles, who in addition to *The Magus* is also the author of *The Collector* and *The French Lieutenant's Woman,* as well as *The Aristos* (a "self-portrait in ideas"), is possibly the most talented and serious living British novelist. His work exhibits continuous growth, not merely in the craft and art of fiction, but also in philosophic maturity and thematic complexity.

The Magus is not easily described. It is the first person retrospective account of Nicholas Urfe's journey into the labyrinth of himself. It is also a recapitulation in evolutionary terms of the development of Western man. Like Ferdinand, the psychotic lepidopterist of Fowles' first novel, Nicholas exists in an emotional vacuum, regarding people as objects in an egocentric universe, using and then discarding them in an apparently endless cycle of temporary relationships. In the beginning of the novel he is a rather typical graduate of Oxford, a dabbler in poetry, a cynic with precise and limited emotional gauges. But then he meets Alison at a party and they pick each other up. The difference is that while

Nicholas Urfe regards Alison as merely one more pleasurable conquest, she (like her predecessor in Chaucer's *The Canterbury Tales*) is concerned with relationships.

Nevertheless, Nicholas soon wearies of Alison and decides to go to Greece to teach English: "The truth was that I was not a cynic by nature; only by revolt . . . but I hadn't found where I loved, and so I pretended there was nowhere to love." In search of himself and somewhere to love ("I needed a new land, a new race, a new language; and . . . I needed a new mystery."), Nicholas goes to the Lord Byron School on the island of Phraxos. There he finds all he says he needs and more.

Nicholas is first carried to the brink of suicide because of his isolation: "I hated myself. I had created nothing, I belonged to nothingness, to the *néant,* and it seemed to me that my own death was the only thing left that I could create. . . . It would validate all my cynicism." But he is drawn back from suicide by the singing of an unseen shepherdess: "It seemed intensely mysterious, welling out of a solitude and suffering that made mine trivial and absurd." The word "mysterious" is possibly the key to the entire novel, for Fowles insists in *The Magus* on the necessity of submitting, finally, to the mystery of ourselves and the world, to an anti-gnostic perspective in which "objectification" is a dangerous and even criminal illusion.

Following his aborted effort at suicide Nicholas meets Maurice Conchis, a Prospero-like figure combining the resources of an Onassis with the imagination of a Picasso. Conchis (the name has semi-allegorical overtones) involves Nicholas in a series of calculated and sometimes bizarre confrontations with myth, mystery, *ménages à trois*, magic, pornography, and history. Conchis is the director of a type of radical, experimental "living theater" in which the actors play complex and treacherous roles designed to lead Nicholas (only one of a series of subjects) to self-understanding. Conchis' theater in some ways resembles in its scope and totality a huge international intelligence operation stretching from the London offices of the British Council to Greece (Athens, Phraxos, Mount Parnassus), Italy, and back to Regent's Park, where the novel ends. Chapter Two, for example, opens with Nicholas remarking, "I heard that the British Council were recruiting staff." Retrospectively, one can see that even this vague, anonymous "tip" is probably part of a design calculated to push Nicholas towards his meeting with Conchis, for the latter asks (when they meet for the first time), "I choose well?" Nicholas protests that he has only come for a drink of water, but the older man states omnisciently, "You came here to meet me. Please. Life is short."

Thus Nicholas from the start is the subject (or perhaps the victim) of what is labeled the "godgame." He is "guided" to Conchis and in the same fashion toward a series of carefully structured "experiences" which force him to examine his values as well as his sense of sanity and equilibrium, and to ask himself the old Socratic questions of identity and purpose. These questions, of course, are posed in twentieth century terms, with an intense awareness of the spiritual, sexual, intellectual, and political desolation of contemporary Western civilization. The point of the godgame is to lead Nicholas to an understanding of human life, love, and its ultimate responsibilities.

The figure of Conchis dominates the novel and at the same time presents the reader with a difficult problem, for if Conchis is credible within the context of *The Magus,* how should one regard him morally? For Conchis (like Nicholas himself in the beginning) is a manipulator of people. His purpose, of course, is excellent, but we never see Conchis risking or revealing anything vital in himself in his experiments. Conchis displays not merely the omniscience and invulnerability of a god, but often approaches the intensity and sometimes the cruelty associated with tyrants.

Nevertheless, in *The Magus,* Fowles has given us, in terms suitable to the post-Freudian imagination of the later twentieth century, a renewed statement of the need, even the inescapability, of human love which goes beyond sexual coupling and the casual affair. Human beings are (because they must be) more than "mere machines for sensations" and must therefore transcend the monstrous character of our times. Perhaps Fowles will eventually go on to dramatize in his fiction the endurable, intractable processes of love, to show us what modern love truly looks like. If he does so, then *The Magus* will be a sort of prologue, a strange and wonderful masque dealing with the mystery of human consciousness, the last and greatest of our mysteries, and perhaps akin to God's.

Marcus Smith

Sources for Further Study

Criticism:

Berets, Ralph. *"The Magus*: A Study in the Creation of a Personal Myth," in *Twentieth Century Literature*. XIX (1973), pp. 89-98. Berets analyzes the fantasies of the hero within the development of the plot.

Presley, Delma E. "The Quest of the Bourgeois Hero: An Approach to Fowles's *The Magus,"* in *Journal of Popular Culture*. VI (1972), pp. 394-398. Presley shows the main character in the novel to be a representative of the newly popular hero of the middle class, and analyzes the hero's motivation.

Reviews:

Book Week. XXV, January 9, 1966, p. 4. 1,750 words.

New Republic. CLIV, February 19, 1966, p. 26. 900 words.

New York Times Book Review. January 9, 1966, p. 4. 1,100 words.

Times Literary Supplement. May 5, 1966, p. 381. 400 words.

THE MAIAS

Author: José Maria Eça de Queiroz (1843-1900)
Translated from the Portuguese by Patricia McGowan Pinheiro and Ann Stevens
Publisher: St. Martin's Press (New York). 633 pp. $7.95
Type of work: Novel
Time: 1875
Locale: Lisbon and its environs

The account of the moral decay of a promising young nobleman in the decadent Lisbon society of the late nineteenth century

Principal characters:
> AFONSO DA MAIA, an aging Portuguese aristocrat
> CARLOS DA MAIA, his grandson, a wealthy, intelligent young man of great promise
> MARIA EDUARDA, his mistress who is later discovered to be his sister
> JOÃO DA EGA, his closest friend, dilettante and would-be writer
> ALENCAR, an aging poet of the romantic tradition
> COUNTESS DA GOUVARINHO, another of Carlos' mistresses
> DAMASO SALCÊDE, a young fop, first Carlos' most admiring friend, then his bitter enemy

The works of Eça de Queiroz, distinguished nineteenth century Portuguese novelist, have become widely known only recently, with their translation into English, but their reputation seems certain to rise. The author is a masterful painter of society on a wide canvas, as well as a gifted satirist.

The Maias is a long, leisurely novel depicting the decadence of the upper classes in Lisbon toward the end of the nineteenth century. Symbolizing this society is the central figure, Carlos Eduardo da Maia, the heir of a noble line, who returns to Lisbon after completing a fine medical education, with excellent intentions of setting up a flourishing practice, doing brilliant research, and writing definitive medical books on the side. Instead, he devotes most of his time to setting the fashion in men's dress, carrying on casual intrigues with the Countess da Gouvarinho and other women who pursued him unashamedly, and planning great literary productions with his friends, none of whom manage to do much

more than talk about their future achievements.

Although much of the book is thinly veiled social criticism, the plot itself is highly romantic, even melodramatic. The early chapters, which form a prologue to the central intrigue, chronicle the lives of Carlos' grandfather, Afonso, and his father, Pedro. Afonso endured an unhappy marriage with a beautiful but melancholy Portuguese noblewoman, who passed on to their son Pedro her highly emotional temperament. Pedro defied his father's wishes to wed the daughter of a slave trader, Maria Monforte, a dazzlingly lovely woman who repaid his affection by running away with an Italian and taking her daughter with her. Pedro delivered his baby son to his father and shot himself. Afonso made inquiries about his lost granddaughter and heard eventually that she had died. Struggling to recover from his grief over the death of his son, he devoted himself to the young Carlos, providing him with the best possible education and resting all his hopes in the boy's promise.

When Carlos decided to settle in Lisbon, Afonso renovated the old family home, Ramalhete, at the same time ignoring warnings that the place always proved fatal to the Maias. It was there that the two men lived as Carlos began his dilettante's career, gathering around him a circle of witty friends.

Then came Carlos' fateful encounter with the wife of a Brazilian diplomat, Castro Gomes. Irresistibly drawn to her after a chance meeting, he haunted the streets of Lisbon and nearby resorts in the hope of seeing her again. The fortuitous illness of the governess of Maria Eduarda's child took Carlos into her home as physician, and they soon became lovers. Maria's husband left for Brazil on a diplomatic mission, leaving her free to move into a little house Carlos provided for her.

One crisis follows another as the plot unfolds. Castro Gomes returned and told Carlos that Maria was not legally his wife; the child was that of her first lover, an Irishman. Repelled by her deceit, Carlos at first wanted to reject Maria altogether, but she won him back and he proposed to marry her. Then his friend João da Ega made the shattering discovery that Maria was, in fact, the lost sister abducted by her mother long before. Carlos was horrified, but he could not at once find the courage to tell Maria what he knew, and he once again entered into an incestuous relationship with her. This deliberate sin sickened him and his love turned to disgust; the knowledge of it killed Afonso, who quickly perceived the whole truth. Carlos sent Maria and her child to Paris and set out around the world with João.

Were this melodramatic series of events all Eça de Queiroz had to offer, the novel would be little more than a sensational potboiler. But in the context of the book as a whole the affair of Carlos and Maria Eduarda becomes a metaphor for the whole of Lisbon society, where all is sensual, but sterile. It is this larger society that interests the author most; Maria Eduarda does not even appear during the first third of the book, and the development of the plot often takes second place to the depiction of Lisbon life.

Eça de Quieroz works in an interesting structural pattern, linking a succession of vivid scenes with passages of narration. Many of these scenes could almost stand alone as sketches portraying society: Carlos as a boy at tea in his grandfather's home, playing with two neighbor children as two aristocratic ladies and the village abbé look on; Lisbon society gathered for rather chaotic horse races; Carlos and João at the theater, listening as "Rufino, transmontane lawyer, swarthy and bearded, flung open his arms as he extolled an angel, 'The Angel of Alms,' whom he had glimpsed far up in the blue, beating its satin wings."

Settings are frequently used to reinforce characterizations or to convey a moral judgment on a scene. The depth of Carlos' dedication to his profession is made clear before the character himself is revealed in any detail. The reader learns of him first through the furnishings he brought to Ramalhete; "the quilted furniture, the silk-covered walls, made Vilaca [the family steward] remark that these were not the rooms of a doctor—but of a chorusgirl!"

The author's characteristic irony underlies his description of the house that Carlos rented for Maria. She protests at the "sensual luxury" of the decor, but each detail foreshadows the revelation of the truth of her relationship with Carlos:

> But the strident air of sensual luxury of the room which was to be hers did not please her at all. It received its light from a room lined with tapestries, where the loves of Venus and Mars were worked into the weave of the wool; over the communicating door hung a heavy wrought-iron lamp of the Renaissance, and at that hour, illuminated by a shaft of sunlight, the place shone like the interior of a heathen temple which had been converted into a lascivious harem.

Eça de Queiriz' characters are all seen from the outside; there is almost none of that psychological probing that we have come to expect in modern novels. These figures are, as one reviewer has suggested, slightly caricatured. They are not "type characters," but they are drawn with an extravagant hand that shades many of them into the comical. Carlos and his friend João, a would-be literary genius, are too self-conscious, too preoccupied with the figure they cut in society to be tragic heroes, though the situation in which they find themselves has tragic elements. João postures extravagantly when his liaison with the glamorous Rachel Cohen is broken off by her husband, but his grief is too theatrical to be truly moving. Even Maria Eduarda, initially seen as the epitome of all that is beautiful and virtuous, is a much less sympathetic figure after her past becomes known.

Many of the minor characters are comic, satirical gems. Damaso Salcêde is a pompous fop, full of references to his family's wealth and fame, which exist chiefly in his own mind; he never

acts with moderation. Impressed with Carlos' chic—the quality he valued above all else—he attached himself to him like a leech:

> If Carlos appeared at the theatre Damaso immediately sprang from his seat, even if it was in the middle of some lovely aria, and, treading on gentlemen's toes, crushing ladies' dresses, he would suddenly rush away and come and install himself in the box at Carlos's side, with his cheeks aflame, a camellia in his lapel and displaying his cuff-links shaped like two enormous balls.

His adoration was dimmed when Carlos became Maria's favored lover; Damaso had fancied himself in that role, and he revenged himself by writing to Castro Gomes of the affair, then sending the details of Maria's past to a scandal sheet. His courage, however, extended only to anonymous letters. When the indignant João called upon him to explain his insults against Carlos, he hastily retracted his statements with the defense that he was drunk when he made them, a distinctly ungentlemanly confession in an era when a man's honor was his great possession.

Count Gouvarinho, characterized by João as "a downright ass," exemplifies all that is wrong with the government of the time. One character explains:

> "My dear fellow, politics today are a very different matter from what they used to be. We've done the same as you literary people. In the old days literature was all imagination and fantasy and ideals. Now it's reality, experience, positive facts, documents. Well, here in Portugal politics have taken up the realist trend. In the time of the Regeneradores and the Historicos, politics meant progress, transport, liberty, ver-

biage. We've changed all that. Today it's plain fact—money, money!"

The Count is amply qualified for the political office he wins if money is the criterion, but his narrow vision is evident in very line he speaks. He opposes a proposal to teach gymnastics in schools with this crashing retort:

"Senhor Presidente, I should like to say just one word. Portugal will for ever leave the path of progress where she has shone so brightly, the day we substitute with impious hand the trapeze for the cross in our schools."

Perhaps the best of the author's comic figures is the aging poet, Alencar, a passionate romantic, adherent of love, liberty, and democracry, and the foe of naturalism in literature and modernism in general:

Was not naturalism, with its alluvial obscenity, threatening to corrupt social decency? Well then he, Alencar, would be the paladin of morals, the gendarme of good habits! And thus the poet of

Voices of Dawn, who for twenty years in song and ode had proposed erotic commerce with all the ladies of the capital; . . . he, Tomas d'Alencar, who . . . had himself experienced a deplorable life of adulteries, voluptuousness and orgies amid the velvets and wines of Cyprus, now turned austere and incorruptible, all of him a monument of prudery.

The Maias, long though it is, has little of the structural looseness that characterizes so many nineteenth century English novels. Eça de Queiroz uses every resource at the novelist's command to build a coherent picture of Lisbon society. The dialogue reveals the emptiness of the city's intellectual life and the pretension of the characters; the settings intensify the reader's impression of cloying luxury; and the plot underlines the decay of morals and ambitions. The author's sweeping vision, his satirical and ironic perception of life, and his control of his narrative should lead readers in search of his other works.

Elizabeth Johnston Lipscomb

THE MAIL BOAT

Author: Alexander Randolph (1922-   )
Publisher: Henry Holt and Company (New York). 179 pp. $2.50
Type of work: Novel
Time: The present
Locale: A small island in the Tyrrhenian Sea

A short novel, told in a series of letters, relating the experiences and revealing the emotions of a naïve young American girl and her worldly, cynical lover

Principal characters:
MARTHA BAKER, an American girl
OSCAR TOWER, a young American novelist
JENNY, Martha's friend and confidante
THOMAS, Martha's former suitor
ANDREW McCLOY, Oscar's friend
MARIO, a native boy

The Mail Boat is completely deceptive in its brevity and its uncomplicated line of plot development, for within its narrow scope it deals with far more important matters than do many novels whose value may be measured by bulk as much as by literary merit. An exquisitely proportioned novel by a young Middle European now living in this country, the book presents a Henry Jamesian situation in a Norman Douglas setting.

This is not to say that Mr. Randolph is a mere imitator of these older writers. But it was Henry James who first drew for us a portrait of the unsophisticated, intuitively innocent American girl brought face to face with the decadence and corruption of the Old World; this was one of the themes by which he conveyed so forcefully a sense of the moral evil and guilt pervading modern society. And Norman Douglas has shown in his books the enervating effect of idyllic Mediterranean islands on the Anglo-Saxon character and temperament.

In a way that is difficult to explain, Alexander Randolph resembles both of these quite dissimilar writers and yet preserves a clear-cut literary identity of his own. For one thing, he brings the European sensibility to a revealing study of the American abroad. His Martha Baker is no latter-day Daisy Miller, as a paragraph of comment on the book jacket suggests. For another, the young American novelist, Oscar Tower, rootless, and almost deracinated, is more typical of the age than he is of any particular place in the modern world. Nor is Mr. Randolph's approach to his material at all like James's method in its subtlety and indirectness. Here the writer has deliberately adopted the old-fashioned epistolary form in order to have his principals tell their stories directly and in their own words in the letters they write. As a result the characters in this novel are outlined with sharp, clean edges, prototypes of reality as true and recognizable as though cut with labeled patterns from varicolored papers.

There are evasions and subterfuges revealed, of course, but these are the result of situation rather than of characterization. Martha Baker, the heroine, has broken away from her sheltered life in America and the standards of the prosperous, middle-class society in which she had grown up. In Rome, during a tour of Europe, she had gravitated to a group of drifting, expatriated esthetes—writers, painters, sculptors hedonistically pursuing their personal pleasures in that ancient and tolerant city. Half-attracted, half-repelled by what she found there, she was drawn in particular to a talented but shallow, cynical young novelist named Oscar Tower. When they go off together to a small island in the Tyrrhenian Sea, Martha expects to act as a combination of secretary, housekeeper, and mistress while he completes a novel for which he has taken copious notes.

The Mail Boat opens as they are settling in the house Tower has rented away from the village. Having thrown her bonnet over the proverbial windmill, Martha cannot let her mother at home in America know the truth about her escapade. Consequently, her early letters to her mother are a strange blending of apology and evasion. Other letters to Jenny, her friend and confidante, and to Thomas, a former suitor and a professor at Yale, present Oscar as she sees him. To Martha this interlude on the island promises a great romance. As she describes it at first, the island is a place of beauty and solitude, with only the mail boat to bring its inhabitants back to the realities of the outside world each third day. Oscar, in his own letters to Andrew McCloy, a friend living in Paris, betrays a different view. Oscar is self-centered, shrewd, and sophisticated; his temperament is as dry and brittle as the book he is planning to write. To him the island is dull, dirty, and uninteresting, but he hopes that it will serve as a retreat for an amusing love affair and provide the quiet he needs to get ahead with his novel. Thus a contrast is established at the outset. Oscar assumes, without putting the matter bluntly into words, the inevitable ending of such an affair. Martha, on the other hand,

hopes for marriage and reveals her ignorance of the consequences likely to follow her breaking of conventions and taboos.

Evil enters their Eden with the introduction of Mario, a physically beautiful but corrupt native boy to whom Oscar finds himself unaccountably, and at first unwillingly, attracted. There are no direct revelations, only hints and suspicions in Martha's mind. She detests Mario, is suspicious of his motives in making seemingly innocent visits to Oscar. When quarrels and accusations follow, both Martha and Oscar reveal their disappointments and broken hopes in their letters. In her innocence Martha even writes to Thomas with complete candor, begging his advice and assistance, and is crushed when he replies to tell her that he can offer no help and that he is engaged to another girl.

Suspecting that she is pregnant, Martha eventually writes a desperate, frightened letter to her mother but changes her mind and sends off another letter in which she asks only for her return fare home. Then Mario dies suddenly, and Martha learns of his death during her daily trip to the village market. Shocked, she transfers the blame for his death to herself and is totally unprepared to convey the news to Oscar. Although deeply moved by the tragedy, he in turn is moved to a more open awareness of Martha and tries for a time to give her the affection and attention she had resented in his friendship with Mario.

This reversal of situation is presented subtly and with telling economy of means. It is significant that Martha is the one to pursue Mario's family with expressions of sympathy and that Oscar becomes impatient with the hours spent in this way. As small events and details pile up in their daily contacts it becomes evident that the fascination and happiness of their idyllic interlude cannot be recaptured. Martha wishes to leave but cannot bring herself to take so decisive a step. Oscar wishes he could get away from her but lacks the initiative to make the first move. At last Martha departs on the mail boat, leaving only a written note of farewell. The shock of finding her gone makes Oscar feel that he must follow her. But tragedy intervenes. He receives a wire from the embassy in Rome stating that Miss Martha Baker is dead, apparently by her own hand.

In *The Mail Boat*, Alexander Randolph has attempted a difficult task and has brought it off with considerable success. The book lives not only in its characterizations and the involvement of plot but also in scores of revealing touches—descriptions of setting, insight into states of mind, a skillful evocation of background figures like those to whom the twenty-four letters of the story are addressed, the harsh yet colorful peasant life, the passing of time. One hesitates to think how another writer might have buried this material under all the literary paraphernalia dear to contemporary psychological novelists. By ruthless pruning of all non-essentials Mr. Randolph has produced a work of much promise which in character portrayal, moral subtlety, and atmospheric power shows the tautness and compactness of a major theme within a relatively simple form. Projected between two angles of vision lighting up a single situation, the novel gives new dimensions to the modern theme of moral innocence victimized by emotional sterility.

THE MAKEPEACE EXPERIMENT

Author: Abram Tertz (Andrei Sinyavski, 1925-   )
Translated from the Russian by Manya Harari
Publisher: Pantheon Books (New York). 192 pp. $3.95
Type of work: Novel
Time: The present
Locale: Lyubimov, Russia, USSR

*A novel dealing with the rise and fall of an idealistic dictator, told in a story which
is both a Russian political allegory and a broader human parable*

Principal characters:

LEONARD MAKEPEACE, a bicycle mechanic, ruler of Lyubimov
SAMSON SAMSONOVICH PROFERANSOV, his ancestor, a nineteenth
century humanist, scientist, and theosophist
SAVELY KUZMICH PROFERANSOV, Leonard's very distant cousin, a
librarian and the narrator of the novel
SERAFIMA PETROVNA KOZLOVA, a school teacher from Leningrad,
later Leonard's wife
VITYA KOCHETOV, a spy from Moscow, later Leonard's most loyal
aide
SEMYON GAVRILOVICH TISCHENKO, the Party's First Secretary in
Lyubimov

On February 14, 1966, Andrei Sinyavski was sentenced in Moscow to
seven years at hard labor for having
published abroad literature which was
hostile to the Soviet Union and the
Communist movement. Using the traditional Russian pseudonym Abram
Tertz, Sinyavski published, first in
France and then in England and
American, from 1959 to 1965, two
novels, *The Trial Begins*, in 1960, and
The Makepeace Experiment; a collection of five stories, *Fantastic Stories*, in
1963; and an extended essay in aesthetics, *On Socialist Realism,* 1960.
The six hundred pages of these books
do constitute an indictment of the Soviet Union, but of a nature which demands analysis, for Sinyavski, like the
often attacked but finally safe Yevgeni
Yevtushenko, is both a loyal Russian
and a believer in Communism. His
criticisms of the government were from
within, written with a painful sense of

betrayed faith, which is perhaps the
reason why the Soviet government
made such an unprecedented display
of his trial and punishment. That
Sinyavsky is being treated so harshly
speaks for the clarity of his vision; like
Boris Pasternak, he is an artist of integrity and ability, a credit in his refusal
to ignore his artistic lights, his intense
and passionate Russian spirit. It is that
spirit which shone in the work of Dostoevski and Tolstoi, Gogol and Maya-
kovski, but which was nearly snuffed
by the artistic betrayals of later writers
such as Ilya Ehrenburg, who are sensitive to political currents but not to
what William Faulkner called "the old
verities and truths of the heart."

It is to the service of and the quest
for these truths that Sinyavski dedicated his art in *On Socialist Realism,* a
work that is perhaps the logical extension of Leon Trotski's *Literature and
Revolution,* which in 1924 first clearly

defined socialist realism and which Sinyavski was probably never allowed to read. His analysis of recent Russian literary history led him to the belief that Stalin's Communism had successfully given to men the first completely ordered world since the Middle Ages and that socialist realism was an art form totally suited to that world view and to Stalin himself, "mysterious, omniscient, all-powerful," who "needed only one quality to become God—immortality." The death of Stalin destroyed the religious unity of the Communist vision and ended absolutely the usefulness of socialist realism. In the new era, a new art must be shaped to discover truth in a disorderly and painfully "real" world. Sinyavski hoped to find such a new direction:

> Right now I put my hope in a phantasmagoric art, with hypotheses instead of a Purpose, an art in which the grotesque will replace realistic descriptions of ordinary life. Such an art would correspond best to the spirit of our time. May the fantastic imagery of Hoffmann and Dostoevski, of Goya, Chagall, and Mayakovski (the most socialist realist of all), and of many other realists and nonrealists teach us how to be truthful with the aid of the absurd and the fantastic. . . . We don't know where to go; but, realizing that there is nothing to be done about it, we start to think, to set riddles, to make assumptions. May we thus invent something marvelous?

Sinyavski's first novel and his book of stories are both reasonably successful attempts to invent something marvelous. Both books are Russian in their very essence. Fatalistic, phantasmagoric, and comic, they are, like Gogol's stories or Dostoevski's *Notes from the Underground* before them, artificial

and passionate at once, fantastic only to be more fully realistic. They are often similar to the Russian novels of Vladimir Nabokov in manner and form, but they lack his overwhelming genius and they are more despairing, darkly comic and oppressively fatalistic, reflecting the restrictive and frightening artistic world from which they spring. A scene in *The Trial Begins* exemplifies these elements of Sinyavski's manner. Two secret agents are searching the narrator's room and his papers:

> He ran his hand over the first page and, presumably by way of censorship, scooped up all the characters and punctuation marks. One flick of the hand and there on the blank paper was a writhing heap of purple marks. The young man put them in his pocket.
> One letter—I think it was an s—flicked its tail and tried to wriggle out, but he deftly caught it, tore off its legs, and squashed it with his fingernail.

This scene, fantastic and comic, contains the agents of fate, secret agents who are as comic in their fallibility even as they are frightening in their final infallibility. There is no escape for a man who acts in the face of fate, whether he is a man doomed to death by the face of fate, whether he is a man doomed to death by a falling icicle ("The Icicle") or the writer doomed to be caught and imprisoned, as is the narrator of *The Trial Begins*:

> The Court is in session, it is in session throughout the world. And . . . all of us, however many we may be, are being daily, nightly, tried and questioned. This is called history.

The Makepeace Experiment is Sinyavski's richest and best work, a novel which is a full expression of his thinking and an artistic figuration of that thinking in a parable of great subtlety and complexity. It is the story of Leonard Makepeace (Lenya Tikhomirov), a bicycle mechanic who gains the power of psychic magnetism by means of the ghostly influence of his idealistic ancestor, Samson Samsonovich, and uses that power to turn Lyubimov into an earthly paradise in which mind does control matter. Makepeace's illusions bring happiness to all: the people eat toothpaste and water, believing them to be caviar and champagne; they work without tiring; and the new utopia is secure from Soviet interference because it is invisible to outside eyes.

Leonard is, then, Lenin the dreamer and Stalin the near god (the city's name is changed to Makepeace) and Khrushchev the humanitarian; he gives order to his world and happiness to his people. But the order fails, as Sinyavski believes all order must, and Leonard loses his power. The illusions fade and reveal themselves as shams; the Soviet government moves in tanks; Leonard, losing control of his last great effort at restoring his power, plunges his utopian world into a chaos of violence and disorder.

The old government is restored, but the people dream of another Leonard, stronger and more perfect, who will give them order and meaning once again. They are, however, alone. Even the narrator, Proferansov, who tells the story in unhappy partnership with the spirit of Samson Samsonovich, is left at the end, dreaming of Makepeace, fearing the government's punishment for his writing the book, and abandoned by Samson and the nineteenth century idea of progress and humanism which he represented.

The novel may be read simply as political allegory (as apparently the Russian judges did) or more fully as a parable of man's continual struggle for order and his continual failure. Only Leonard's mother maintains belief at the novel's end, but hers is an older belief, a belief in God and the Christian faith. But Sinyavski's God is neither Christian nor Communist; his is a God of eternal metamorphosis, changing like the world of His creation, like the long process of history and the procession of man's dreams and ideas. *The Makepeace Experiment* is an attempt by art to reveal for a moment a face of God, imaginary and artificial but by the force of that imaginative act, realistic and true.

Two novels, five stories and an extended essay may be all of Sinyavski's work that we shall ever have. He is a young man, a serious writer just reaching the maturity of his talent. The poems of Andrei Voznesenski, although perfectly in tune with Soviet policy, would seem to indicate a loosening of the restrictions against fantastic art. Perhaps Sinyavski may find the freedom to write again. If not, these few volumes remain a testament of his artistry and a monument to the courage and strength of his spirit.

R. H. W. Dillard

THE MAKING OF CHARLES DICKENS

Author: Christopher Hibbert (1924–   )
Publisher: Harper and Row (New York). Illustrated. 321 pp. $5.95
Type of work: Biography
Time: The nineteenth century
Locale: England, principally in and around London, Continental Europe, and America

A study of the childhood, youth, and young manhood of Charles Dickens as they affected his literary career (with an Epilogue summarizing the rest of his life)

> Principal personages:
> CHARLES DICKENS
> JOHN DICKENS, his father
> ELIZABETH BARROW DICKENS, his mother
> MARIA BEADNELL, his youthful sweetheart
> CATHERINE HOGARTH DICKENS, his wife
> MARY HOGARTH, his beloved sister-in-law

Charles Dickens was a productive phenomenon. His staggering output of fictional words rose numerically into millions. His surviving letters add to the prodigious mass; and although not part of the monumental survival, his ephemeral writings as a legal clerk and professional journalist are part of the total body of writings. But it is not copiousness of words that gives him his place in literary history. His books teem with life: multitudinous characters appear, make their vigorous impressions, and vanish to make way for other multitudes. The works contain comedy (from gross farce to subtle humor), realistic observation, romance, unabashed sentiment, and tragedy. They offer something for practically every reading taste. Even Dickens' most ardent admirers admit his faults: his careless stylistic lapses, his excesses, his violations of taste; but even hostile critics are hard-pressed to deny his greatness, which towers over his faults —indeed, perhaps grows out of them. In commenting on his behavior when he was trying to promote the sale of *Pickwick Papers,* Christopher Hibbert touches on characteristics of the man and the writer:

Dickens, though, cared nothing for these customary proprieties. He wanted Pickwick to make money, and to reach as wide a public as possible, and if it could be helped to achieve those ends by coming out as a serial and by being advertised by his personal appearance on the stage of the St. James's Theatre, he was certainly not going to be conventional or modest. It might not be in the best of taste to behave in this way, but, then, as George Santayana has said, Dickens had more genius than taste. Besides, he liked appearing on the stage, anyway.

Hibbert's unifying theme in *The Making of Charles Dickens* is that Dickens made use of his own childhood and young manhood as subject matter to a degree that few other authors have, that he shaped his work from his own disappointments, frustrations, sufferings, and enjoyments in a way that makes biographical study particularly important for those who wish to understand and appreciate his works. This is not, of course, an original idea; and Hibbert gives handsome acknowledgment to his predecessors in Dickens studies, particularly to Edgar Johnson, whose two-volume biography (*Charles Dickens. His Tragedy and*

Triumph) is generally accepted as the definitive study on Dickens down to the present. Nevertheless, Hibbert has composed a sound, readable book with its own individuality. By his choice of inclusion and emphasis he has modified somewhat the portraits presented in earlier works.

Writers on Dickens have pointed out that the great creator of characters was himself a most interesting figure; and even readers who do not care greatly for the powerful, exaggerated novels may enjoy reading about the life of the author. Hibbert has divided the main part of the book into eleven chapters, each designed to cover a portion of the life having a particular bearing on some aspect of the writer's work. The final section of the book proper is an epilogue covering with a rapid summary the last quarter-century of Dickens's life. Copious notes are included and a bibliography, in which about half of the items appear also in Johnson's bibliography. Many of the other items were not in print when Johnson's work was published. The illustrations are of two distinct kinds, printed differently: reproductions of early illustrations to the works of Dickens interspersed throughout the text and a separate section of halftone reproductions of portraits and pictures of places associated with Dickens. The last two photographs present a cruel contrast. One is the picture of Ellen Ternan, the pretty young actress with whom Dickens was in love late in life; the other is of Mrs. Dickens at the time of her separation from her husband. In the latter portrait Mrs. Dickens appears excessively dumpy, fat, and ugly. Hibbert has also included the reproduction of a painting of Mrs. Dickens, a work done early in her married life, which furnishes almost as startling a contrast.

The reader is advised to look up a still earlier portrait reproduced in the first volume of Johnson's work to appreciate the overwhelmingly lovely girl Dickens married, and to look again at the aging, pathetic creature who had small cause to rejoice at her life with the great genius. The story of Ellen Ternan and the separation from Catherine belongs to the Epilogue, not to the main story; nevertheless, there were many signs in the early portion of the life to make the unhappy ending of the marriage no surprise.

According to Hibbert, the first ten years of Dickens's childhood (1812–1822) were happy ones; but even in those days he had horrifying experiences. For example, his nurse, Mary Weller, filled his mind with gruesome stories that captured his vivid imagination:

> All his life he was to be fascinated by the sinister and the grotesque, the fanciful, the morbid and the occult, those dark corners of the mind that he felt irresistibly drawn to explore. His work . . . is full of the fruits of this festering imagination, this disquieting, insatiable curiosity which was to lead him, almost against his will—'dragged by invisible forces', as he put it himself—to wander at night into the slum quarters of London and into the morgues of Paris, fearful, as so many of his characters are, not only *for* himself but *of* himself.

From these early years also dated another profound influence on the future novelist: the popular theater. The stage had a triple fascination for Dickens: delight in being a spectator; joy in taking part in theatrical performances; and absorption in theatrical dialogue which displayed itself in comic and melodramatic passages throughout his works. For an example of this third debt to the theater: much of Sam Weller's dialogue in *Pickwick Papers* is traced to specific comedians.

The happy childhood ended in 1823. John Dickens was an improvident man; the family fortunes went down and down. Small Charles was put to work at Warren's Blacking, shoe-polish manufacturers. Shortly afterwards the elder Dickens was arrested for debt and sent to the Marshalsea Prison. The boy hated his lowly employment and never forgave his mother for feeling that he was better off working. The sad truth is that forgiveness was not a strong part of his nature. He liked his father better, even though the elder Dickens was more directly responsible for the family poverty. John Dickens served as model for Mr. Micawber, William Dorrit, and perhaps other characters. Mrs. Dickens was the model for Mrs. Nickleby and Mrs. Micawber. The miseries of Oliver Twist, David Copperfield, and other Dickensian boys are no doubt young Charles's miseries seen through self-pitying lenses. The masterful passages on prison life, the "gloomy, decaying, vaguely menacing" London, and the "dreadful" River owe their vividness to these early years as well as to more mature observation.

After his father's release from the Marshalsea, Charles spent three years in school, perhaps gaining more from acting and writing for its publications than from academic work. He then went to work for a firm of solicitors at Gray's Inn, and still later he became a parliamentary reporter. At that time amateurs paid for the privilege of acting in the private theaters, and Hibbert is certain that the young clerk appeared in private theatricals. Indeed, for a time he considered a professional stage career; and in his later years he was a type of actor-producer for a company that devoted its proceeds to charity.

During the years from 1829 to 1833, an interest outside his embryo professional career furnished him with more grist for the novelist's mill: he met and fell desperately in love with Maria Beadnell, a pretty, coquettish young woman. The novelist fudged his autobiographical story by bringing his hero and irresponsible heroine to the altar and then bringing her to the grave. In his account of Maria, Hibbert departs from his time scheme and furnishes a postscript about a meeting with Dickens some twenty years later, when she was fat, far from pretty, and married. She was still trying to play the ingenue —thereby getting herself into another novel. Her middle-aged cuteness cured Dickens of any remnants of his grand passion; but his youthful infatuation left scars on his sensitive nature. He seems never again to have dropped his protective shell, even with his wife.

The year 1836 was a memorable one for Dickens and the literary world. In it he published his *Sketches by Boz* and began the serial publication of the *Pickwick Papers*. On the rebound from Maria, he married Catherine Hogarth; he was twenty-four, four years her senior. In Hibbert's book, she becomes a pathetic heroine, as badly battered as many of the novelist's own feminine creations. Hibbert, indeed, finds echoes of her in several Dickensian characters. He more than hints that in *The Old Curiosity Shop* she was the model for Mrs. Quilp, that Mrs. Hogarth unwittingly sat for her portrait as Mrs. Jiniwin (Mrs. Quilp's mother), and that the hideous dwarf Daniel Quilp was a Mr. Hyde version of the novelist. It has been suggested before that the quarrels between Quilp and his mother-in-law echoed squabbles between Dickens and his.

Catherine's sixteen-year-old sister Mary came to stay with the couple soon after the honeymoon; but she died about a year later. Dickens was in a passion of grief, for he seems to have been more fond of her than of her less bright and alert elder sister. Her death led to an unwholesome idolatry which damaged both the life and works of Dickens. At her death he apparently became conscious of his incompatibility with Catherine, and his blameworthy unkindness to her increased steadily. Both Johnson and Hibbert believe Mary responsible also for the "Little Nell" syndrome in the novels.

Catherine bore her husband ten children—not counting miscarriages. Hibbert remarks acidly:

> Though a fundamentally kind and sympathetic man where others were concerned, he wrote of her pregnancies in those facetiously exaggerated letters of his as though he had nothing to do with them, as though they were yet another example of her lazy ineptitude.

Hibbert's book is a convincing presentation of Dickens' use of his experiences and emotions in creating his fiction; but of course creative genius is not explained by uncovering sources, personal or literary. Much happens to the originals to transform them when their likenesses appear in the novels. As noted before, even *David Copperfield*, the most nearly autobiographical novel in the whole series, is far from true autobiography. Hibbert has upheld his thesis without damaging the interest in his own story and characters. The book is as fascinating as a novel—to many tastes, no doubt, more fascinating. A major virtue of it is that it stimulates reading or re-reading of the works of Charles Dickens.

George Burke Johnston

THE MAKING OF THE PRESIDENT, 1960

Author: Theodore H. White (1915-   )
Publisher: Atheneum Publishers (New York). 400 pp. $6.95
Type of work: Political history

A very detailed study and analysis of the campaign of the two major candidates in their bid for the election to the office of the presidency in 1960

Principal personages:
JOHN F. KENNEDY
RICHARD M. NIXON
HUBERT HUMPHREY
LYNDON B. JOHNSON
NELSON A. ROCKEFELLER
SENATOR BARRY GOLDWATER of Arizona
ROBERT KENNEDY, Democratic campaign manager
THEODORE C. SORENSEN, chief Democratic political writer
EMMET HUGHES, chief Republican political writer

Theodore H. White has made a significant contribution in the field of political reporting. This work is unique in that almost all of the materials utilized by Mr. White comes as first-hand information or impressions. The subtitle of the volume might well be History While It Is Hot or History in The Making. The style of writing employed by the author is clear, concise, and colorful. He writes with objectivity and has a keen ability to analyze both the candidates and their audiences. No stranger to the political scene, Mr. White has used his many years of experience as a political reporter to its fullest advantage, and the end result is a fascinating and profound study of the most recent presidential campaign. The book will most likely serve as a model for future political reporting, with many of Mr. White's techniques being utilized.

This study of the presidential race in 1960 gives a clear insight into the campaign of the leaders of both major parties and of the attempts they made to reach the voting public. The author weaves into the story much of the eye-witness material which he collected during the months that he was personally associated with both candidates. Many of the behind the scenes discussions of strategy are revealed. These matters, plus the little verbal portraits of the major political figures, combine to make delightful reading for the amateur or the professional in politics.

The study, which begins on election day, follows John F. Kennedy until he retires after a night of frustration over the failure to gain a definite victory. Then the reader is taken back to the earliest maneuvering among the Democrats for the role of standard bearer for the election in 1960. One of the earliest candidates for the nomination was Hubert Humphrey. As early as 1958, Humphrey had begun to permit his name to be mentioned as a possibility for the next presidential election. In 1959 he had traveled to Russia in an attempt to be recognized as one having first-hand knowledge of Russian affairs. On the home front Humphrey had contacted several of the outstanding leaders of the party in hopes of acquiring the necessary backing. This reviewer is of the opinion that Humphrey was the choice of the author. Other candidates for the party nomination were Senator Stuart Symington, of Missouri; Senator Lyndon B. Johnson, of Texas; and former Governor Adlai E. Stevenson, of Illinois. Only Kennedy and Humphrey entered the state primaries, while the other candidates chose to wait for the nomination, which never came, at the national convention.

The Republican Party had only two or possibly three open aspirants for the nomination: Richard M. Nixon, Senator Barry Goldwater, of Arizona; and Nelson A. Rockefeller, Governor of New York. Nixon was the choice of President Eisenhower and most of the conservative wing of the party. Rockefeller had the backing of the liberal group within the party, while the conservatives were supporting Goldwater. According to Mr. White, all of these men had actively been seeking the endorsement of influential party leaders since 1956.

After a brief discussion of the possible candidates, the reader is taken to the grass roots of American politics, the primary. Both Kennedy and Humphrey entered the Wisconsin primary, which in the opinion of the author was the most dangerous of all primaries because of the political diversity within the state. Although neither candidate had much time to concentrate in the state, both campaigned in each of the Congressional districts. The power of the Kennedy organization becomes apparent immediately, with the vastly superior Kennedy machine in complete control of the situation. During the primary Senator Humphrey described the two organizations by stating that they were like "the corner grocer running against a chain store."

After the indecisive victory in Wisconsin, Kennedy realized that he must enter the primary in West Virginia.

This predominantly Protestant area, in addition to being in a severe economic depression, was almost completely immersed in the Southern flavor of Democratic politics; all of the factors combined made the state extremely difficult for Kennedy to carry. As a result, the West Virginia victory, which completely ended Humphrey's presidential hopes, clearly placed Kennedy in the front as the leading candidate of the Democratic Party.

Kennedy went to the National Convention in California with 600 pledged votes, only 160 short of enough to secure the nomination. The Kennedy machine had worked to secure the additional votes needed, and his backers were confident that the nomination would be won on the first ballot. As the roll was called the opposition began to melt away, and Kennedy secured the desired nomination on the first ballot. The convention was one of the dullest in years; the only events which served to make things come alive were the demonstrations for Stevenson and the surprise acceptance of Lyndon B. Johnson for the vice-presidential nomination.

The Republican convention was even duller, for the nomination of Nixon was a foregone conclusion. Only the brief Rockefeller attempt to force the Republicans to repudiate the administration and the policies of President Eisenhower promised to enliven the convention, and after this short-lived flurry of excitement the rest of the program continued according to schedule. Nixon was nominated unanimously on the first ballot, after the ten ballots which had been cast for Senator Goldwater had been changed. The Republicans then permitted Nixon to select Henry C. Lodge as his running mate.

After telling of the nomination of the

two candidates, Mr. White devotes the balance of the book to the campaign for election, which is by far the most interesting portion of the study. The author begins this phase with an excellent chapter comparing and contrasting present and past political problems. The growing population, the population shift, and occupational changes and trends are thoughtfully considered. The role of the Negro in the politics of the Northern cities is analyzed. The problem of urban and suburban populations is discussed, with great insight into the current economic ideology as contrasted with economic ideology in the earlier years of our national history.

The reader is then carried back to the political arena to follow the early plans and operations of each candidate. The full value of the Kennedy machine is demonstrated, and the outstanding organizational ability of Robert Kennedy is discussed. The Kennedy campaign got off to a slow start, but a monumental milestone was passed when the candidate attacked the religious question head on in Houston, Texas, and won out over a hostile audience of Protestants. After this victory Kennedy began to show needed confidence, and this newly gained self-confidence spread to the other members of his staff. Each public appearance began to have more personal charm and sincerity, and the candidate was able for the first time to project his personality to his audiences.

By way of contrast, Nixon opened his campaign on July 28, 1960, with no apparent indication of uncertainty or indecision; he appeared supremely confident, and the Republican campaign began in high gear. Within ten days after his nomination, Nixon had made speeches in six states, including Hawaii. The immediate value of this di-

rect and active approach was noted in the Gallop poll, with Nixon the popular favorite for the first time since the national conventions. Later the Nixon schedule was to be dealt a severe blow when the Vice-President became disabled because of an infected leg. This injury was blamed for the lost rhythm of the Nixon campaign.

The strategy of the Nixon forces was to reflect the theme of the Eisenhower years—peace and prosperity. This plan, according to Nixon, was under attack by the Republican regulars because they considered "kid-glove" tactics to be ineffective. The regulars were of the opinion that the only way victory could be obtained was to get tough and to hurl charges at the Democrats, Kennedy in particular. Nixon refused to embrace this approach; he wanted to dissociate himself from the Herb Bloch conception of a dirty gutter-brawler. Kennedy, on the other hand, attacked the Republicans for being standpatters and for not advancing any new social legislation during their eight years of leadership. Kennedy promised to lead the nation to a better life with his "New Frontier" approach.

Mr. White devotes a chapter to the four television debates in an attempt to show their effect on the American voter. The decision to debate with Kennedy, in the opinion of the author, was disaster for Nixon, a decision giving a great advantage to Kennedy because it raised him to the level of the Vice-President, put Nixon on the defensive. In analyzing the debates, White reaches the conclusion that Nixon won the debates but that Kennedy won the voters, and ultimately the election.

As the election entered the final weeks of campaigning the author was able to notice a complete reversal of the earlier mental attitudes of the two men and their organizations. The Kennedy touring unit was relaxed, confident, orderly, but not inflexible in its program to reach the White House. On the other hand, the Nixon entourage was gloomy, shot through with the feeling of defeat. Newspapers encountered no problems when seeking out Kennedy, but Nixon and his closest advisers were unavailable to the press. Nixon waited until the eve of the election to use President Eisenhower, a delay which, according to many Republicans, cost Nixon the election. Then, too, the Martin Luther King incident lost Nixon many Negro votes. Mr. White is of the opinion that Nixon was afraid to get involved in the incident, hoping by inactivity to keep the Negro vote and those of the Southern whites. Kennedy, on the other hand, acted quickly upon learning that King had been given a jail sentence. He telephoned Mrs. King, indicating his concern over the turn of events, and assured her that, as president, he would intervene, if necessary. This move marked a turning point, for many Negro leaders openly left the Republican Party and carried large blocs of the colored vote over to Kennedy. Mr. White states that this action enabled the Democrats to carry Illinois, Michigan, and possibly South Carolina. The author attributes Nixon's defeat to his failure to capitalize on events such as the King incident, his inaccessibility, his indecision, his leg injury (which occurred at the height of the campaign), and above all, his inability to project himself to the American people during the television debates.

This work is more than a profound study of the election of 1960; it is also a penetrating study of the two parties and their leaders and a model for future campaign reporting. Possibly the greatest single weakness of the volume is the lack of information concerning the background maneuvering of the two candidates between 1956 and 1960. However, this is a minor consideration, and the many excellent points completely overshadow this minor detail. On any count this book must be recommended both for the interest it generates and for its complete presentation of the election of 1960. It is a must for anyone who is interested at all in American politics.

THE MAKING OF THE PRESIDENT, 1964

Author: Theodore H. White (1915-   )
Publisher: Atheneum Publishers (New York). 431 pp. $6.95
Type of work: Political history
Time: November 22, 1963 to November 3, 1964
Locale: The United States

A narrative history of the battle for the Presidency of the United States between two unevenly matched opponents, Barry M. Goldwater and Lyndon B. Johnson, recounted day by day by a leading journalist who followed the campaign trail of each man

> Principal personages:
> JOHN F. KENNEDY
> LYNDON B. JOHNSON
> BARRY M. GOLDWATER
> NELSON ROCKEFELLER
> WILLIAM SCRANTON
> HENRY CABOT LODGE
> GEORGE ROMNEY
> RICHARD NIXON
> HUBERT H. HUMPHREY
> WILLIAM E. MILLER
> DWIGHT D. EISENHOWER
> CLIFTON WHITE

When did the tide turn against Barry Goldwater? One of the Republican candidate's campaign aides, replying to this question, said it reminded him of an old football story: "The tide turned when the other team first appeared on the field."

This inevitable lack of suspense in the 1964 election undermines the natural drama inherent in most major political campaigns. The close Kennedy-Nixon race, subject of White's *The Making of the President, 1960,* did not present a similar obstacle. In telling the 1964 story, White was faced for the first time with unexciting material and foregone conclusions. If the result is less compelling than the 1960 book, it nevertheless repays study. Despite a quality of inevitability in the unfolding plot, the characters in this history —seen in numerous close-ups—are engrossing political archetypes.

White's story opens, properly, on November 22, 1963. His vivid report of the assassination of President John F. Kennedy is told with eloquence and tasteful control, qualities often slighted in the rest of the book.

"Lyndon Johnson Takes Over" is the title of the second chapter. In workmanlike prose, White outlines the new President's performance. The story, in its multitude of detail, seems complete; yet we learn little that could not be gleaned from a review of the year's news reports. Well-worn tales of Johnson's early background are conscientiously reported: "Hungry, brawny, standing in line in employment offices, waiting for a job assignment, footing a shovel with a highway gang for a dollar a day, dawn to dusk, he was finally persuaded by his mother to go back to school."

After tracing Johnson's early development from youthful New Deal administrator to Senate majority leader, White finally gives us Johnson the man. From the moment he accepts the nomination as Vice-President, Johnson is portrayed as a thin-skinned, often humiliated, proud, "premature elder statesman" who was forced by circumstances to stay in the background while a group of younger men experimented with the federal government. In agonizing detail, White relates the indignities inflicted on the Vice-President, mostly casually and unthinkingly by the Kennedy staff. (At meetings of the National Security Council, for instance, Johnson was observed listening in silence, "his fingers locked and working together until sometimes the knuckles were white.") Yet the late President took special care for the dignity of his sensitive Vice-President, and Johnson was grateful. More important, Kennedy saw that full information on secret and emergency planning for continuity of America government in case of nuclear attack was provided for the Vice-President, thus preparing him to assume control over all resources of command and communication. Beneath this preparation, White comments, were thirty years' observation of the federal government in action, and beneath that the instincts "of a Texas hill-country boy."

Years earlier, the uphill drive to nominate Barry Goldwater for this job had begun in earnest. White traces the birth of the Goldwater movement to the 1960 GOP convention, when party conservatives protested the Rockefeller-Nixon compact of Fifth Avenue in a mood of near violence. Goldwater, as spokesman, had angrily denounced the agreement as a "betrayal" and soon found himself the champion of the Re-

publican right. Yet it was nearly three years before he claimed leadership of the disgruntled conservatives.

Leadership they found, however, in the person of a young businessman named Clifton White, head of the national Young Republicans. This group, the author points out, "seized control of the Republican Party, turned it over to Barry Goldwater, then lost it to Goldwater's inner circle." In the fall of 1961, White gathered leaders from Young Republicans groups all over the nation to plan the seizure. The carefully conceived series of coups accomplished by these non-professionals is one of the most astounding stories of the election. Scarcely two years after their initial meeting, they sponsored a Draft Goldwater rally that attracted 7,000 people from all parts of the nation; the Arizona senator suddenly became the leading GOP candidate.

When Goldwater began to work with the volunteers in 1963, he found formal campaign organizations already set up in thirty-two states, with several states "locked up completely." Although temporarily dissuaded by the assassination of the President, who was his close friend, the author believes that Goldwater was moved to try for the nomination by his sense of duty to the conservative cause. White adds that the massive campaign already beautifully set up by the indefatigable volunteers may also have influenced Goldwater's decision to run.

Meanwhile, Republican party chiefs were desperately seeking an alternative to Goldwater. White supplies a remarkably full history of pre-primary campaign maneuvering that reveals much about the techniques parties use in nominating a man for the world's most important job. Providing well-chosen background material, White breathes life into the doomed efforts of Goldwater's Republican opponents.

The omnipresent availability of Richard Nixon, the author asserts delicately, "brought a wrinkling of the nose in Manhattan." Romney, "ensnared . . . in provincial futilities" with the Michigan legislature, is dismissed here as having little appetite for the Presidency.

The Presidential primaries of 1964, White marvels, exceeded "in savagery and significance any other in modern politics" and ended with the Republican Party "desperately wounded." He details the deadly blows Rockefeller dealt Goldwater in these battles. Yet it was his own image Goldwater had to fight, for he had come to the campaign with a heavy burden of public statements that did not endear him to voters. "For mismanagement, blundering and sheer naïveté, Goldwater's New Hampshire campaign was unique in the campaigns I have seen," concludes White.

In one stunning paragraph, the author reveals how the divorce and remarriage of Nelson Rockefeller cost him the nomination. The scene: a typical midmorning rally in a high school gymnasium in Hollis, New Hampshire, late in the primary campaign. Rockefeller had brought his new wife, now heavy with child, and someone produced a folding chair for her; everyone else stood. As she sat, as if in a witness chair, the television crews flooded her with lights, while her husband stood at her side. The townspeople, in a semicircle, as if they were a jury, all stared fixedly at the woman as her husband spoke. "They might have been a gathering of Puritans come to examine the accused." Hollis, along with most of Republican New Hampshire, was to favor Henry Cabot Lodge.

To the four high-spirited young amateurs who ran this primary campaign for Lodge (then serving President Johnson in Viet Nam) victory was unexpected and exhilarating. White relates this political escapade as a hilarious aside.

More in the mainstream was the painful farce of William Scranton's vacillating candidacy. Armed with Eisenhower's endorsement, how could he lose? Yet the indecisive former President apparently offered and withdrew support from both Lodge and Scranton in a bewildering series of moves. White can only attempt to explain them by saying that "he was for a wide-open discussion of issues by *all* possible candidates . . . he was only pursuing his high-minded civic duty . . . the distinction between being 'urged' to run and the implicit promise of support if one did run was always obscure."

While White does not take the five-week Scranton campaign too seriously, he does suggest that "as an exercise in gallantry it may have saved the soul of the Republican Party."

The entire Scranton caper took place during "the time of the power broker," that period after the primaries were over and before the convention. One stage for the frantic maneuvering to nominate anybody but Goldwater was the June Governors' Conference in Cleveland. White adroitly captures the mood of pandemonium that characterized that conference for the Republicans; candidates were thrust in and yanked out as if they were puppets, while party chiefs pulling the strings appeared foolish, fickle, and callous.

The GOP convention four weeks

later belonged to Barry Goldwater as surely as the Democratic convention was to belong to Lyndon Johnson. Almost unnoticed in the wild exuberance of the predominantly Goldwater delegates were the weak thrusts of the disorganized anti-Goldwater leaders, Scranton, Rockefeller, and Romney.

Nevertheless, what Rockefeller had begun that spring in New Hampshire, Scranton finished in June and at the convention: "the painting for the American people of a half-crazed leader indifferent to the needs of American society at home and eager to plunge the nation into war abroad." It was here, as White sees it, that Goldwater won the battle and lost the war, with his unforgettable thrust at the moderates who had tried so hard to stop him: "Extremism in the defense of liberty is no vice! . . . Moderation in the pursuit of justice is no virtue!"

In a chapter entitled "Riot in the Street: the Politics of Chaos," the implications of the Negro revolution on this election are probed. Although the problem of equal opportunity for all was not debated by Goldwater and Johnson, the violence with which the issue exploded on the scene could hardly be ignored in this campaign, and White's lengthy analysis is useful.

The "vast incoherence" that enveloped the proceedings as the Goldwater campaign staggered on is reconstructed skillfully. Meanwhile, the genial President was inviting crowds to "Come down an' hear the speakin'." Peace and Progress were his themes, and as a sure winner he decided both to broaden the base of his support and to shape the mandate. To the captivated White, the President is "Fair-Shares Johnson," "Preacher Johnson," "Old Doc Johnson," and so on, each

role richly illustrated with examples. (Apparently there were fewer Barry Goldwaters: chiefly "Goldwater the Prophet" and "Goldwater the Patriot," with Goldwater the frustrated intellectual offered more tentatively.) The fragmenting device is more irritating than useful.

The book is also marred by hasty writing, which cannot be excused simply because the writer is a journalist. Certainly there was ample time before the publisher's deadline to correct such giddy phrases as this: "like a club sandwich of ice cream and pickles, the Goldwater and Scranton forces were interwoven" on floors of the same convention hotel. Another example of first-draft writing opens the chapter on the Republicans' first stirrings: "It was impossible to foresee, as the calendar turned the pages of the new year, just how great would be the Republican disaster of November to come."

The election itself, the actual Goldwater-Johnson contest, is pictured as a mere mopping-up operation. All the issues had been raised (and answered, for most Americans) as early as March, in the New Hampshire primary. Yet the author considers the 1964 campaign a rare thing in American politics, "a campaign based on issues."

He defines the significant issues rather well: war and peace, the nature and role of government, the morality of society, and the quality of life. White's grasp of the overall strategy of each party is impressive. How did the Democrats grapple with the Goldwater crusade against mushrooming federal power? They chose a specific response, social security, and managed to place Goldwater on the defensive. The author gives credit to the Republican candidate for making people begin to consider the elusive issue of quality as a proper concern for politics.

Goldwater's running mate, Congressman William E. Miller, is unaccountably slighted in this history. His name appears only as an infrequent reference. Much is made of Johnson's choice of a running mate, but the carefully detailed story of his decision against Robert F. Kennedy provides scant insight into practical politics; the two men simply were not personally compatible. The warm, in-depth portrait of Hubert H. Humphrey, Johnson's hardly unexpected choice, is a valuable aid to an understanding of the political scene.

As a profound study of a quadrennial American phenomenon, this history is unique; as a re-creation of half a dozen human dramas, it is absorbing; as a history of one of the most significant elections in this century, it is indispensable.

Roberta Madden

THE MAKING OF THE PRESIDENT, 1968

Author: Theodore H. White (1915–   )
Publisher: Atheneum Publishers (New York). 459 pp. $10.00
Type of work: Political history
Time: January, 1965–January, 1969
Locale: The United States

A narrative history of the contest for the American presidency against the violent background of 1968, by a reporter who had close access to the major political leaders

The day-to-day history made during a few months of each presidential election year has become Theodore H. White's special province. In the third of his narrative accounts of American presidential politics, this experienced journalist has set out to relate "what happened to the American people in 1968," a politically grotesque year. The reader who expects White to make sense of the chaos will find no logical pattern in this history—nor possibly in any book written at such close range. Much of what happened was simply irrational: this happened, and then this happened, and then this. What distinguishes White's treatment of the familiar story is the wealth of "inside-dope" details, as well as his peculiar insights into the behavior of major political figures. No other reporter has enjoyed such close access to the important leaders in the big campaigns, and White discusses these men with candor and perceptiveness.

The author decided to tell the story, not chronologically, but by grouping events around "a dominant personality or a dominant disturbance." Overlaying the traditional political rituals in 1968 were widespread anguish over the Viet Nam War and anxiety over rioting and crime in the streets and over the assassinations of Martin Luther King and Robert Kennedy. Discussion of these two key issues permeates each chapter, for every major candidate—

except Eugene McCarthy—felt compelled to speak on *both* issues.

The controversial war in Viet Nam led President Johnson to retire from presidential politics, and his act brought new candidates into competition. Yet the volatile issue was poorly understood by the leaders and the public. Until recently, experts on Asia were amazingly scarce in this country. White dramatizes this grave lack by revealing that as late as 1950, the State Department's source materials and information on southeast Asia filled only half of one file drawer. Up until April, 1968, he estimates, "American statecraft possessed . . . probably 40 men with a crude understanding of Viet Namese language and culture, with less than 20 of those in the field, responsible for guiding half a million American troops, of whom 25,000 had died in battle." White, having specialized in Chinese at Harvard and served as *Time's* first regular correspondent in the Far East, thus speaks with special authority. Yet he can only speculate that the agonizing national problem the war had become by 1968 had originated somewhere in the vast official ignorance about Viet Nam and Asia in general.

American politics turned upon countless contradictions between appearance and reality all through the year. For example, the preceding fall, Ambassador Bunker and General Westmoreland reported to the nation that the war was going well. In his State of the Union address President Johnson had taken the same line—instead of warning the people of the horrors he knew were soon to occur. Because Americans had believed dimly that with half a million superbly equipped troops, the costly war was slowly being won, color television pictures of the "blood, gore, and flame" of the Tet offensive in January came as an overwhelming shock. The enemy's military effort proved to be a "complete failure," as the President announced, but the enemy had scored a "psychological victory." Within two months, the President himself would be the chief victim.

At about the same time in 1965 when the U.S. course in Viet Nam had been irrevocably set for the next three years, an incident occurred in the Watts district of Los Angeles that led to the other half of the great issues of the 1968 campaign. Before order was restored to Watts, 34 persons lay dead. Similar riots wracked every large city in the land in the following summers. White observes that the word "integration" thereafter lost its force in American politics, and was never used seriously again. In the spring of 1968, the assassination of Martin Luther King snapped a symbolic bridge between the militants and the more moderate Negroes.

In the new climate of domestic violence, the chief actors were blacks and students, "the two largest underprivileged groups in the nation." The students, a major new pressure group, were to overwhelm the politics of 1968. By that year, what the author terms "the campus proletariat" had grown to nearly seven million persons—"the largest working-class group with a single interest in the United States." This new force inevitably began to exert itself in a quest for power—a quest symbolized in the dominant personality of Eugene McCarthy. Few reporters penetrated the mystery that encompassed this unique leader, for McCarthy was always his own man, lacking any political obligations and exhibiting little concern for the traditional public rituals. The least accessible of the major candidates, he regarded newsmen as "amusing animals" and preferred to talk to poets, novelists, and essayists. White admits his own reaction: "All through the year, one's admiration of the man grew—and one's affection lessened." Two major decisions appear responsible for the considerable power McCarthy achieved in the fragmented Democratic Party—the decision to utilize the huge support of youth and the decision to enter the key New Hampshire primary. Bored by organizational details and strategy, McCarthy let both decisions be made by his campaign manager. The influence of "the McCarthy kids" is a familiar story. One of the interesting details White provides is the effort of an Amherst French major who translated the candidate's literature into French, for 100,000 Hampshiremen—nearly a sixth of the state's population—were of French-Canadian descent. Despite the invaluable contributions of such enthusiastic amateurs, the McCarthy campaign is pictured as a chaotic operation. One staff member said he had never worked with so many people who hated one another. McCarthy did act decisively to try to keep his innocents from going to the convention, and he ignored his own nomination and the balloting to care for those wounded in Chicago.

McCarthy's chief rival as anti-Establishment Democrat, Robert F.

Kennedy, was a victim of that same brutal political year. The reporter was Kennedy's friend, and he offers a tender, sympathetic portrait of the man others called "ruthless." (The book is dedicated to the memory of the late President Kennedy and Robert Kennedy.) White discloses that Bobby regarded McCarthy as "vain and lazy" and not suited for the presidency. Unable conscientiously to support McCarthy, even as a pre-convention ploy, Kennedy himself was forced to run. McCarthy's offer to step aside after one term and turn the presidency over to Bobby left him incredulous, for Kennedy believed in winning and using power to the utmost. Robert Kennedy was a "disturber," White observes, yet his program was substantially the same as that offered by Nixon, the exponent of non-excitement. White believes that if Kennedy had lived, he would have won the Democratic nomination in Chicago.

Especially after the death of Robert Kennedy, the old politics lacked appeal for many Americans, including Theodore White. Nevertheless, his discussion of the campaign of Hubert Humphrey amid the clash of old politics and new is engrossing and conscientiously done. No one was more shocked by the Tet offensive than the Vice-President, who had been excluded from the top-level councils where military analysts had warned of the new enemy action. White reveals that the Vice-President first learned the news in the morning papers. From Humphrey's deep reservations about the systematic bombing of North Viet Nam years earlier, to the Pyrrhic victory he won at the Chicago convention, to his final surge in the last weeks of the campaign against Nixon, the story is presented fully. Several minor incidents and details are espe-cially interesting: the rumor that President Johnson was reconsidering his renunciation and would run; Johnson's iron control of the convention, so that Humphrey's son-in-law had to wait in line for tickets to seat the Vice-President's own family in the galleries; Humphrey's letter to Mayor Richard Daley of Chicago, urging that the demonstrators be granted permits (Daley did not reply); the President's casual remarks revealing an apparent contempt for Humphrey; the brief Edward Kennedy "boom" at the convention.

White reports that the Vice-President bitterly resented the television coverage of the convention. For instance, while Cleveland's Mayor Carl Stokes, a leading Negro politician, was seconding Humphrey's nomination, the networks ran their tapes of the violent demonstrations that had occurred more than an hour earlier in the streets of Chicago. The delegates, watching on their portable TV sets, along with people across the nation, believed that Humphrey was being nominated "in a sea of blood"—a reasonable but false assumption, White remarks. His discussion of the question that has haunted many Democrats—why did Humphrey do nothing to stop the violence of police and demonstrators?—is helpful, if not entirely satisfying. The Vice-President was unaware of much of what was going on, "too busy on another, older level of American politics," and he lacked control over the convention.

The significance of money is emphasized again and again in the discussion of each candidate's campaign. Humphrey's effort limped along until the final weeks, largely because there was no money to pay the bills. Only the AFL-CIO contributed handsomely to the Vice-President's cause—by getting his message across, by providing experienced manpower to do the work, and by giving money. At last, other sources began to contribute dollars also. Humphrey's campaign manager believed that if the Democrats had had ten million dollars, instead of five or six million, they could have won. He points to the "fantastic cost of the media," attributing Humphrey's last-minute upturn to the surge of money at the end of the campaign. "If you figure that by setting up a twenty-five-million-dollar media budget, and making a game of who gets the best time slots and who hires the most creative media talent— and if you elect a President that way, what the Hell's the country coming to?" For 1968 was the year of television "spots." One minute on "Laugh-In" or on the World Series was considered more valuable than a half-hour major address.

Yet money was no problem for a perennial Republican candidate, Nelson Rockefeller. Popular with the public but not with the decision-makers within his party, Rockefeller is presented by White as a talented and visionary leader who lacked the organization Nixon had built upon the loyalty of grass-roots supporters. White pictures Rockefeller pulling out of his pocket a small paper on which was written the total amount of money—a very large sum—that the Rockefeller family had contributed to the party in New York over the years. Unfortunately for him, Rockefeller vacillated between candidacy and non-candidacy during 1968. At first he supported George Romney as the logical opponent for Nixon. Later he himself challenged the power structure of the GOP, just as McCarthy and Kennedy were doing in the other major party. In

the weeks preceding the Republican convention, Rockefeller and Ronald Reagan developed a symbiotic political relationship. Although the two men were at opposite extremes of the Republican spectrum, Rockefeller the liberal and Reagan the conservative, they needed each other to try to stop Nixon.

White believes that his fellow journalists "savagely massacred" Romney in his campaign for the presidency. The candidate's evangelical earnestness and "cloying naïveté" offended the men of the media, and they brought him down, the author claims. As an instance of the "relation between the reality of politics and its distorted reflection in the media," White discusses Romney's notorious "brainwashing" remark. A slip of the tongue, uttered on a local television program, appeared five days later in a New York *Times* headline. That night the major TV network news shows picked up the story and ran the thirty-second film clip, isolated from its context—"the part presented as the whole, the fragment presented as reality." Soon, *Time* magazine wrote Romney off as a fool not qualified for the presidency, and before long his strength, as reflected in elaborate opinion polls, began to slip drastically. At last he withdrew from the race—"an honest and decent man simply not cut out to be President."

If money is needed to win, along with skillful manipulation of the media and a computer-like organization, another factor may be decisive too—a lack of bitterness on the part of the candidate. Only Nixon, of all the leaders in both parties, had shed his resentment over the unfairness, the humiliations, the wrongs that seem inevitable in the political process. White had observed Nixon eight years earlier from a distance and had felt "suspicion and dislike"; the man's intensity offended him. But he found that Nixon had changed during the interim; he had relaxed, found time to listen to good music, to read and study, to exercise his unusual curiosity. More important, during 1966, he had traveled 30,000 miles and visited 82 congressional districts, gaining experience and poise, and earning the loyalties of appreciative candidates, which "was solid money in the bank of politics." The next year, he traveled abroad, building an image as a foreign affairs authority. While Nixon was thus sheltered from the American press, Romney, "like a missionary sacrificed to the cannibals," preoccupied the media all year. When Nixon returned, he had only to perfect his organization, for he was "of the fiber and bone of the Party." Contrasted with "the aching woes" of Humphrey's finance chairman, Nixon's chairman found money flowing in freely, and the GOP finances were impeccably programmed.

Like any professional reporter, White scrupulously observes and reports the details of significant events. His attempts to analyze the ideas and emotions that swirled through the land in 1968 tend at times to be facile, but his closeups of political personalities and places are superb. Of the Miami auditorium, site of the GOP convention, he noticed that the shallow seating arrangement spread thin the emotional charge—"as if it were a saucer, not a cup." On the other hand, the scene of the Democratic disorder, the Chicago amphitheater, with its high galleries, made the floor "a pit for gladiators" and encouraged conflict and drama. Looking at the Republican delegates, the reporter saw that the dominant color was gray, not the gray of Wall Street, but the gray of Main

Street. The Democrats were more varied, and their delegations showed new blood—as many college professors as farmers or labor leaders. White's sketch of Mayor Daley is unusually generous: "the best old-fashioned mayor of the country," a firm but kindly believer in authority. Incidentally, White judges "equally guilty" the National Mobilization Committee to End the War in Viet Nam and the police for the bloody confrontation in Chicago.

White might fruitfully have spent more time examining the George Wallace phenomenon, a "major force" in the 1968 election, and a force by no means defunct. White sees Wallace as a demagogue appealing to Americans who felt their government had sold them out. Yet finally, many voters were ashamed to support Wallace. Unfortunately, White is sometimes patronizing in his assessments of groups of people he does not know well. For example: "The South these days is no longer one, but twain; there is the Deep South, racist and Wallacite, living in its nightmare of fears; and the Middle South, or Border South, where here and there one can detect under its permanent conservative frost a first feeble spring of human tolerance." This simplistic statement overlooks the fact that two Deep South states preferred Nixon to Wallace, and that several northern states—including Michigan, Alaska, Arizona, California, Nevada, Indiana, Ohio, and Wisconsin—gave the Alabama candidate percentages ranging from 6.8 to 13.2 of their total vote.

Except for such lapses, however, White has seen steadily and clearly the complexities and vicissitudes of presidential politics in a year that may well have marked a turning point in the American style of self-government.

The Making of the President, 1972 promises to record a new departure for the American people, for their leaders, and for Theodore H. White, chronicler of campaigns.

Roberta Madden

THE MAKING OF THE PRESIDENT, 1972

Author: Theodore H. White (1915-   )
Publisher: Atheneum Publishers (New York). 391 pp. $10.00
Type of work: Political history
Time: 1969-1972

A narrative history of the United States presidential election in 1972

Beginning with the presidential election of 1960, in which John Kennedy barely defeated Richard Nixon, Theodore White established a quadrennial institution of political writing which has since been copied by many reporters. White, who won the Pulitzer Prize for his first "Making of the President 1960," is a careful storyteller. Television viewers will remember his informal dialogues with Eric Sevareid at the last conventions in Miami. A *summa cum laude* graduate of Harvard, he still calls himself a liberal. His writing is dramatic, and provides inside stories of various candidates for the presidency, all against the background of historical contrasts.

This, then, is the fourth of a series. This volume, like the others, is destined to become a classic volume on Presidential elections. In this election, Richard Nixon won by the greatest "landslide" in modern American political history, a victory of greater margin than anyone else before him. Readers will wish to compare this volume with its predecessors, particularly because Nixon's tremendous victory was so quickly followed by efforts to impeach him. They may find it less exciting, though, since it was clear from the very beginning that Nixon would be the inevitable winner.

White knows from experience how to document what goes on prior to an election. He narrates the whole process, showing that this specific election was different in at least one respect: it offered the voters a clear choice, not "an echo." Nixon, the incumbent, carried 49 of the 50 states, receiving more than 17 million more votes than George McGovern, the Democratic candidate. A Nixon watcher of long standing, White gives a brief preview:

Obviously, in the politics of 1972, two entirely different stories are intertwined. There is the story of Richard Nixon, and how he, as President, read the nation's mood to win the greatest margin of votes in American history. But then there is the rival story of the various Democratic parties, whose inheritance from the Rooseveltian past had given them one of their greatest grass-roots victories at local and state level across the country — but whose choice of national leader to oppose Richard Nixon totally failed to catch the spirit of the times.

All along, this story provides thumbnail sketches of the Democratic nominees, men like Muskie, Lindsay, and Humphrey. Little is said, incidentally, of George Wallace, who urged the voters to "send them a message," but who was catastrophically wounded in a shopping center during his campaign for the nomination.

One of the helpful descriptions in

this book is that of "the absurd way the United States selects its Vice-Presidents." The volume also provides helpful background for what turned up later in the mess called "Watergate." Since the book was published, Congressional Committees and Grand Juries, not to mention media reporters, have been revealing some of the previously unpublicized happenings concerned with the 1972 election. Even White notes this in his preface:

> I have had to write this book in a moment of passage which happens but rarely in American life — when the passing of a generation coincides with a crisis of conscience. As this is written, two former members of the Nixon Cabinet await trial; Federal grand juries in several cities are pursuing the trial of the greatest political scandal in American history; a Senate investigation is already exploring the entire political process and crimes of which the Nixon administration has been accused. And all this takes place against the background of another crisis, a change of ideas, at a time when the thinking of one generation has been worn out and the next system of ideas is not ready to replace it.

This, then, is the story of a historic election in depth. It describes how both major political parties go about getting the votes, including their shabby campaign practices, and explains the meaning behind the voting results which are broadcast about midnight on election day.

White has a way of picking up and elaborating on unguarded conversations. He is good at describing the machinations of the "open" convention of the Democrats, which turned out to lack adequate control, and the

following Republican convention, which was characterized by too much efficiency and even obvious manipulation. He is at his best when he shows how George McGovern worked for the nomination. (McGovern told him once that he first decided to run for President in 1962 while reading White's story of the campaign between Nixon and Kennedy).

White's picture of McGovern, however, is not very attractive. The Democratic candidate was a "nice guy" but he was never really in control of his troops. He describes the fruitless pursuit of Ted Kennedy for the party's Vice-Presidential candidate, and shows real sympathy for Senator Eagleton, who had to be dropped from the slate and replaced by Sargent Shriver.

White goes into great detail in explaining the erosion of old line Democrats from the party. He debates such issues as the alienation of labor, the exclusion of powerful mayors and Congressmen, and the utilization of quotas for blacks, women, and young people. McGovern, according to White, was so moralistic that the people seemed to feel that such "purity" was unsafe for the country. The McGovern campaign, then, was a "movement" in which the leaders saw things as too oversimplified. As a result, the campaign, according to White, was "disastrous." The Democrats were idealistic, but so absolutist as to alienate the regular Democrats as well as many of the majority voters. Their candidate's vacillation and indecisiveness, his careless phraseology (backing Eagleton a "thousand percent"), his stated willingness to beg Hanoi "on his knees," and the misunderstood plan to refund "a thousand dollars for every citizen," all convinced the voters that he was not solid enough for the job.

Whereas the Democratic Convention was wild and unpredictable, the Republican gathering was neat and dull. Its contrast, according to White, was one of "business suits against bluejeans."

Nixon's triumph in the election of 1972 was won by a single man, adjusting America's role to the new world with an almost exquisite recognition of the passage of time, and a diplomatic finesse of conciliation and killpower. He recognized best, and spoke most clearly, for he persuaded an astounding majority of Americans that he understood their emotions and needs better than his rival. With this victory, he believed in all sincerity that he had been given a mandate to reorganize the American government to make it more responsive to what the voters had shown they wanted.

The result was never really in doubt. Nixon's staff was trained primarily in public relations and advertising; they projected the image of his being too busy to campaign. While his critics accused him of being afraid to reveal himself, Nixon remained quietly in the White House, confident of victory from the very moment McGovern was nominated.

White even admits a grudging respect for Richard Nixon. He accompanied Nixon to China in 1972 and was invited to fly back to Washington with the President from San Clemente on election day. He recalls:

I remember walking the beach of the Pacific at San Clemente in November on election weekend, as Kissinger tried to unwind from the negotiations

going on between Hanoi, Saigon and the President's office. As we left his villa for a stroll, Kissinger was indulging in a momentary burst of anger at the government of Thieu, which was then obstructing negotiations, and at George McGovern, who was denying the sincerity of the Nixon-Kissinger quest for peace.

This volume provides about as good a picture as one could get, at the time, of President Nixon. White obviously is much more charitable to the President than to his Democratic opponent. He even implies that Nixon will go down as one of the major presidents of this century —this, in spite of his tension with the press. Nixon was a pragmatic, solitary, patriotic individual, but White should know all this after three personal interviews. Like most strong Presidents, he tended to grab power, striving to be the central figure, even in growing conflict.

Of all those who, in the weeks thereafter, reflected on the election of 1972, perhaps the solitary President understood it best. It meant that if he were to make his mark on history permanent, he would have to do it with greater individual boldness, with greater personal exercise of authority, than any victorious President before him.

Nixon's negative obsession with the liberal press was mutual. His repudiation of the intellectuals and idea men in Washington was part of his natural makeup. He avoided reporters, and instead took his message directly to the people by television.

According to White, the basic issues of this and other campaigns were three—war and peace, bread and butter, black and white. The particular central issue at this time, however, was power. Should ultimate power be concentrated in the executive, in congress, in the press, or in the people?

> In this writer's opinion, it is possible that at least three or four million Americans were so disillusioned by both candidates that they chose not to vote at all. Had it not been for Watergate, it is quite possible that Richard Nixon's margin would have been increased by another three or four million votes — that, indeed, his stunning 61-38 victory might have gone as high as 65-35, for a record that might never again be approached in American two-party history. The Watergate affair blew that opportunity.

One of the election's paradoxes is that Nixon promised the voters to put more restraint on Federal power. He attacked centralized power and promised to tighten the controls. What actually happened, of course, is that he accumulated even more power, demonstrating an arrogance toward Congressional legislation.

> Richard Nixon campaigned in 1972, as he always had, against central power, against the idea of the omnipotent President doing his will from Washington. He was for returning home power to the people in their communities. But in practice he took to himself more personal power, delegated to more individuals of his staff the use or abuse of that power, than any other President of modern times. Faced by a hostile intellectual world, a hostile vanguard of the press-television system, a recalcitrant party of his own, and a Democratic Party committed by definition to opposition, he

abandoned all the old conventions of party politics.

This election, of course, as later events revealed, was tragically climaxed by Watergate, termed by White as "that family of obscenities." As an unintended result, his book provides background for readers debating the issues of impeachment. White, incidentally, added an additional chapter on Watergate, and apparently revised the rest of the book, making minor changes immediately before publication. He insists, though, that Nixon would have won anyway, in spite of Watergate, and in spite of the embarrassment caused his loyal supporters. This experienced reporter perhaps did not know the extent of such things as the bugging of Democratic headquarters, the use of dirty tricks, the later coverups, pay-offs, and so on.

No view of a situation can be as accurate as later views when all the information is in. This book, therefore, suffers, in that most readers will know more about Watergate than White did at that time. Still, even though most citizens are now aware of the misuse of power by the White House staff, the public seems to prefer President Nixon to the possibility of his opponent, George McGovern. White says little of CREEP (Committee for the reelection of the President) or the Plumber's Group (the term given a group instructed to plug up leaks from the White House). And of course, he was not aware that John Ehrlichman, Nixon's Number One domestic adviser, would be convicted of lying and conspiracy, or that Nixon would resign his office in August of 1974.

The story of Watergate was only one of a number of major stories in the election of 1972. As it unravelled it was to become a story of 1973 and would fit better, someday when all was known, into a story of the use and abuse of power in a modern state.

White, then, paints an understandably positive portrait of President Nixon, even though the Republican Vice-Presidential candidate was forced to resign for receiving illegal kickbacks. The question will be raised whether the Nixon staff told Theodore White the truth, or whether the author of *The Making of the President 1972* really was "taken in." White says very little, for example, about the controversial milk deal, the alleged manipulation by the ITT, or the possibility of financial skullduggery between Howard Hughes and "Bebe" Rebozo.

It would be no less than a national tragedy if men came to regard the election of 1972 as fraud; or attempted to reverse the verdict of the people at the polls on the technicalities of a burglary, in a spasm of morality approaching the hysterical.

Theodore White, whose opinions on the matter should be respected, is now advocating a national primary, rather than the dreary process of state primaries and national conventions. Furthermore, he still makes a strong case for sympathetic understanding and support for the man in the White House. His book will hold the attention of readers for all of its 480 pages. White is a fine storyteller; and if he seemed to miss out in some different spots, we should realize that no single reporter can be everywhere.

Alfred C. Payne

MALCOLM

Author: James Purdy (1923-   )
Publisher: Farrar, Straus and Cudahy (New York). 215 pp. $3.95
Type of work: Novel
Time: The present
Locale: A large American city, probably New York

A fantasy in which a motherless, abandoned fifteen-year-old boy is guided by an astrologer through a series of grotesque adventures involving deviant characters in modern society

Principal characters:
MALCOLM, a placid, handsome boy innocently facing life
PROFESSOR COX, an astrologer
ESTEL BLANC, a Negro undertaker
KERMIT RAPHAELSON, a midget artist
LAUREEN, his Amazonian wife
GIRARD GIRARD, a billionaire
MADAME GIRARD, his wife
JEROME BRACE, an ex-convict
ELOISA, his alcoholic artist wife
MELBA, a frequently married Negro jazz singer

James Purdy is that recurrent figure in our national literary life, the young writer absolutely devoted to his art but uniformly rejected by American commerical publishers until after he has established some measure of success abroad. After a number of futile attempts to publish his first novelette, *63: Dream Palace,* and a collection of short stories, *Don't Call Me by My Right Name,* a group of his friends had them printed and privately distributed. Thus they came to the attention of Victor Gollancz in London, who published them to the tune of high praise from Edith Sitwell and others. Only then, retitled *The Color of Darkness,* did they appear in America. A violent and passionate book, the collection peeled away the civilized surface of life and flashed a harsh light on the horrors and grotesqueries beneath: a boy dies in a bug-infested, abandoned house and his brother deposits his decaying corpse in an attic trunk; a boy, unable to explain to his indifferent mother why he spends all his time looking at pictures

of his dead father, is dragged to the cellar and forced to watch the pictures burning in the furnace; a lonely motherless boy tries to swallow his father's wedding ring, and when the man attempts to recover it the boy kicks his father in the groin. These strange, surrealistic effects were extravagantly praised, but Purdy's new book, *Malcolm,* has had a rather mixed reception, possibly because his admirers were expecting a full-length work of Dostoevskian proportions and got instead a brief picaresque novel in an old tradition by a young writer of great but still unfulfilled talent.

The structural base for *Malcolm* is as old as *The Golden Ass, Don Quixote,* or *The Knight of the Burning Pestle,* and it has been exploited in modern terms by such writers as J. D. Salinger, Saul Bellow, Nathanael West, and Raold Dahl. It consists of taking a character—often an adolescent or a pre-adolescent—having some force strike him loose from the normal processes of living, and sending him hurtling through a series of bizarre adventures which in the end become a form of initiation into adult society. But new graftings on the picaresque tradition do not wholly explain the world of odd perspectives and hallucinated reality in *Malcolm*. Readers of the novel may well feel that somewhere they have experienced this sort of thing before—the spectacle of people behaving in a strange and amusing way that on the surface seems quite meaningless but which nevertheless suggests that beneath it all there is some profound significance. The likeness, although it exists in a different climate of man's haunted dreams, may soon suggest itself: *Alice in Wonderland*.

But Purdy's wonderland is not entirely conjured up from his own imagination. It exists in out-of-the-way corners, the Bohemias and Gold Coasts of American society, and no doubt the writer could take his readers on a guided tour of New York, San Francisco, or any of a half dozen large cities to point out the places and people Malcolm has visited.

At the begining of the novel we find Malcolm seated on a golden bench before one of the most palatial hotels in the world. He is a fifteen-year-old boy, "a cypher and a blank," whose father has either died or left him, whose wealth is just beginning to dwindle, and who has no human ties. That is all we ever learn, and that vaguely, of his antecedents. Professor Cox, a mysterious astrologer, intrudes on the emptiness of the boy's life. He talks with him and decides to guide Malcolm through a series of awakening experiences to be effected by visits to addresses supplied by the astrologer. The sequence of these visits determines the episodic structure of the novel as Malcolm begins his pilgrimage to doom.

The first address to which Malcolm goes is that of Estel Blanc, a retired Negro mortician whose hobby is writing songs for Cora Naldi, his platinum blonde mistress: "And is it so that you were there? And is it so you were? And is it so that while you were, Cherries were your ware? Pale cherries were your ware?" But Estel Blanc, puzzled by Malcolm's "coolness, detachment, and lack of receptivity" to his mistress' singing, sends the boy away to Professor Cox's second address. This happens to be the studio apartment of Kermit and Laureen Raphaelson. There Malcolm becomes involved in the marital strife of the midget artist and his Amazonian wife, who tries hard to serve her husband but is constantly abused with foul language and relegated to a back room which she shares with fifteen cats. Kermit, infuriated by the fact that his wife will not support him as an artist should be supported, provokes her into a fight that reduces the apartment to a junk heap. Laureen then leaves him and runs away with a Japanese wrestler.

At this point in the novel a pattern of meaning begins to take shape. Just as Estel Blanc suggests an image of death and Malcolm's visit to the Raphaelsons possibly stands for the self-centered concerns of the artist, so his next encounter takes him into the world of money. At the third address he finds Madame Girard, an imperious, dipsomaniac *grande dame* surrounded by a coterie of dandies and solicitously hovered over by her billionaire husband, Girard Girard. Completely charmed by Malcolm's innocence, they plead with him to stay with them at their summer home in the country. Malcolm, finding the Girards almost too imposing in their wealth and power, insists that Kermit also be invited. But Kermit, partly because Professor Cox absolutely forbids the visit and partly because he too finds the Girards overwhelming, hides in a closet when his would-be host and hostess come for him.

Malcolm then goes on to address number four. There he is entertained by Jerome Brace, an ex-thief and former convict, while his artist wife entertains jazz musicians. Eloisa, too, is charmed by Malcolm and insists upon painting his portrait, which she expects to sell to the Girards for a small fortune. Meanwhile, in a hilariously melodramatic scene, Girard Girard tires of his wife's haughty commands, declares his independence, and, although she kisses his beautifully shined shoes in supplication, leaves her to have six sons by Laureen Raphaelson.

From the cluttered home of the Braces, where "no matter at what hour, one felt that it was afternoon," Malcolm ventures into life on his own and accidentally is led toward love—or, more specifically, sex. While waiting to meet Girard at the horticultural gardens, he is picked up by Gus, a leather-jacketed young Negro and whisked away on a motorcycle to join the "contemporaries" at a night club. There he meets Gus's ex-wife Melba, a *chanteuse* who immediately announces her willingness to marry Malcolm. He agrees, but Melba decides to postpone the wedding for a few days so that Gus can take Malcolm into town and arrange to have the boy "matured." After they have been tattooed by Professor Rabinolte, they go to a house of prostitution where Gus dies from the effects of the tattooing needles. Lying about his age, Malcolm marries Melba:

Too young for the army, too unprepared to continue his schooling, too untrained for ordinary work—what was left for him but marriage? And in his case marriage supplied him with everything that he had up to now lacked, and also gave him his unique way of leaving the world, in which he had perhaps never belonged (as some people said) in the first place.

For Malcolm marriage becomes a one-way road to death after he proves to be such a magnificent lover that Melba, although she is otherwise bored by him, remains insatiably faithful. One night, in a night club, Malcolm seizes a man whom he believes to be his long-lost father. In his weakened state he is thrown violently to the floor and suffers a gash in his head. Neglected by Melba, he is nursed by Madame Girard. Soon she reports that he is dead and arranges a grandiose funeral, including an order for a half a ton of roses and violets to drown out the smell of burnt tomatoes from a nearby ketchup factory. The magnificence and solemnity of his funeral are ruined when the coroner and the undertaker insist that there is no corpse. Although there are rumors that Malcolm is still alive, he is soon forgotten by all except Madame Girard, who cherishes his 300-page diary of conversations. Professor Cox soon finds another protégé.

This brief outline can only suggest meanings which crisscross and blur images like cracks in a shattered mirror. One has the feeling, however, that something portentous is indicated, even though never clearly presented. What kind of meaning this all adds up to is anybody's guess, but for those who do not insist that it add up to a neat sum the individual parts should prove immensely entertaining and even illuminating in terms of the excesses and grotesqueries of modern American life. With moods alternating between fantastic hilarity and grim horror, *Malcolm* is by no means as profound or as artistically successful as *The Color of Darkness*, but it is easily as insightful as the fiction of Nathanael West or as comic as Thomas Mann's *Confessions of Felix Krull*. James Purdy's first book was no mere flash in the pan.

MALCOLM LOWRY

Author: Douglas Day (1932-   )
Publisher: Oxford University Press (New York). 483 pp. $10.00
Type of work: Biography

An outstanding literary biography of the author of Under the Volcano, *considered by some to be one of the greatest novels of the twentieth century*

Principal personages:
MALCOLM LOWRY
ARTHUR OSBORNE LOWRY, his father
STUART OSBORNE LOWRY, his older brother and only family
    member to attend his funeral
JAN GABRIAL, his first wife
MARGERIE BONNER, his second wife
CONRAD AIKEN, a famous author and Lowry's longtime mentor
JUAN FERNANDO MARQUEZ, a close friend of Lowry during his
    days in Mexico
JOHN DAVENPORT, a literary critic and Lowry's lifelong friend
ARTHUR CALDER-MARSHALL, a novelist and friend in London
DAVID MARKSON, a young New York novelist
ALBERT ERSKINE, Lowry's editor at Random House
MARTIN, RALPH, and ROBERT CASE, three brothers, Lowry's
    friends and drinking companions during their London and
    Cambridge days

Vladimir Nabokov once wrote that biography is the lowest form of fiction, that biographers are essentially frustrated novelists who cannot make the final imaginative leap from the so-called real work of personal experience (remember, too, Nabokov says that "reality" is perhaps the only word in the English language that should never be found without quotes around it) to the final created world of the true novelist. This is both a profound and silly statement—silly in that it asks us to believe, for example, that writers of limericks (a "low" form of poetry) are frustrated sonneteers. Even if this is true, it may finally be unimportant: people will continue to write limericks and others will continue to enjoy them, and a good limerick is probably better than a bad sonnet.

However, like many of Nabokov's seemingly outrageous pronouncements, this one also touches on an important truth, and that is that the processes involved in creating biographies and novels are in important ways very close. So, too, for that matter are the processes of enjoyment and evaluation on the part of the reader of the end results. A biographer reshapes the life of the man he deals with by way of the choices he makes about what he will include in his book, what degree of significance he will accord a particular event or character trait, and the like. Again, it is one choice after another, ultimately adding up to some truth that stretches beyond the mere facts and dates of a man's life.

Douglas Day's *Malcolm Lowry*, then, is surely one of the higher expressions of the biographer's art, for among other things this work serves to bring into greater prominence a writer who might otherwise have remained in relative obscurity. Day believes and finally convinces us that his subject deserves a better fate. Certainly one comes away from Day's book with a strong desire to read more of Malcolm Lowry, and this result is perhaps the highest index of the literary biographer's success.

As so many novelists have done, Day begins his biography with the death of his hero. The opening pages unfold almost cinematically; a wide, establishing shot of the village of Ripe in England where Lowry died; a gradual moving of the camera-eye into the town where it finally comes to rest in dramatic fashion with a close-up on the hero's grave-stone:

Malcolm Lowry
1909-1957

Then the "dissolve," as it were, and Day picks up on the events of the last few years leading up to the evening of Lowry's death, and the death itself (by "misadventure" according to the coroner). This all occupies the first of nine chapters. The second chapter begins with a further discussion of the circumstances surrounding the death, a discussion of the various differing versions of the death, and a final settling on the one that seems the most accurate. After that, Day proceeds in fairly strict chronological order begining with Lowry's birth and early boyhood.

Towards the very end of the biography Day concludes about his subject: "Lowry was a great author who happens to have written only one

great book." The book, familiar to some, is *Under the Volcano*. The main thrust of the biography is towards these ultimate conclusions: that *Under the Volcano* is ". . . the greatest religious novel of this century . . ." and that Lowry, a man beset by the demons of alcoholism and self-torture, was nonetheless able to withstand their onslaughts long enough to allow his genius to show through, and that such genius should not be allowed to be forgotten. This, then, is the essential service (if such a limited word may be used) that the biographer has provided us.

Because of the importance of *Under the Volcano* to Lowry and to those around him, and because of its claim to greatness, Day devotes a large amount of space to an exhaustive treatment of the novel—its creation (the seemingly countless revisions), its major and minor themes, its multi-dimensionality, its rejection and acceptance by publishers, and its final killing and saving effect on Lowry himself. This last is hopefully not an easy paradox, for the one thing that stands out almost more than anything else is Lowry's essentially paradoxical nature: his manic lows and equally manic highs, his degrading cruelties and wonderful kindnesses, his tremendous capacity for self-destruction and for recuperation. Day convinces us in the end that it is only out of this kind of deeply divided self that a marvelous and grotesque novel like *Under the Volcano* could erupt.

Malcolm Lowry is compelling reading. Lowry wrote furiously when he wrote, and when he was not writing he drank, and when he drank he wrote incredible letters to friends about how and why he was not writing. These letters are often minor masterpieces themselves:

> I have to confess . . . that I am going steadily and even beautifully downhill: my memory misses beats at every moment & my mornings are on all fours. Turning the whole business round in a nutshell I am only sober or merry in a whisky bottle, & since whiskey is impossible to procure you can imagine how merry I am, & lucid, & by Christ I am lucid. And merry. But Jesus. The trouble is, apart from Self, that part which used to be called: consciousness. I have now reached a position where every night I write five novels in imagination, have total recall (whatever that means too) but am unable to write a word. I cannot explain in human terms the incredible effort it has cost me even to write this silly little note, in a Breughel garden with dogs and barrels & vin kegs & chickens & sunsets & morning glory with an approaching storm and a bottle of half wine. And now the rain! Let it come, seated as I am on Breughel barrel by a dogs grave crowned by dead irises. The wind is rising too, both on ocean & in the stomach. And I have been kind to in a way I do not deserve. I have to write pretty fast. . . . A night dove has started to hoot & says incessantly the word "dream, dream." A bright idea. I remember always your kindness and generosity.

This letter, Day tells us, reflects the essential Lowry, the Lowry desperately afraid that his powers as a writer were slipping away and yet capable of expressing that fear with honesty, intensity, and even humor.

In his final assessment of Lowry as artist and man, Day enlists the help of Jung, especially Jung's ideas about the artistic temperament. Here Jung departs from Freud's idea that neuroses are the very wellsprings of an artist's creativity. Jung says there are two radically opposed modes of artistic creation: *psychological* and *visionary*. The *psychological* artist is the artist of consciousness, the one who by way of a conscious, reason-oriented mind deals with ". . . crucial experiences, powerful emotions, suffering, passion, the stuff of human fate in general." The *visionary* artist deals with " . . . primordial experience which surpasses man's understanding," experience which is "glamorous, daemonic, and grotesque." In short, he is the artist of the irrational, the artist of chaos. Jung says that for an artist to be totally one or the other ultimately causes him to fail as an artist. As Day paraphrases Jung: "To reside absolutely at one or the other pole means at the very least artistic death: either sanity bought at the price of sterility, or immediate experience of the unconscious at the price of psychosis." Of course, Lowry gravitated strongly toward the visionary, and as long as he could go there for his inspiration and return to the psychological pole and make his vision coherent, he was a successful artist (even a genius); but, as the vision began to overwhelm him, as he began to be more and more trapped by his own neuroses, he lost his ability to *shape* his art, and it no longer communicated coherently.

Even as Lowry disintegrated as an artist and a man, he could still exert a kind of magic on those around him, even strangers in bars. An anonymous voice was once reputed to have said that, "The very sight of that old bastard makes me happy for five days.

No bloody fooling." It is no wonder, then, that the biography of such a man should be so entertaining, and at times, deeply moving. Douglas Day has succeeded in writing a compassionate and scrupulously fair biography of an exceedingly fascinating man, and has shown himself to be a discerning and convincing literary critic as well. *Malcolm Lowry* received the 1974 National Book Award for Biography.

Al Zolynas

Sources for Further Study

Reviews:

Commonweal. XCIX, February 1, 1974, p. 445. 1,100 words.

Critic. XXXII, May/June, 1974, p. 63. 2,950 words.

New Republic. CLXIX, November 3, 1973, p. 25. 1,450 words.

New York Review of Books. XX, December 13, 1973, p. 28. 4,850 words.

New York Times Book Review. November 4, 1973, p. 3. 2,300 words.

Times Literary Supplement. April 19, 1974, p. 417. 1,400 words.

Virginia Quarterly Review. L, Summer, 1974, p. 441. 800 words.

THE MALEFACTORS

Author: Caroline Gordon (1895–   )
Publisher: Harcourt, Brace and Company (New York). 312 pp. $3.95
Type of work: Novel
Time: 1946–1948
Locale: Bucks County, Pennsylvania, and New York City

A novel about a poet who faces the problems of being unable to write, after many years of success

Principal characters:
>   TOM CLAIBORNE, a forty-seven-year-old poet
>   VERA, his wife
>   MAX SHULL, a close friend of the Claibornes
>   GEORGE CRENFEW, Tom Claiborne's cousin, a psychiatrist
>   MARCIA, George's second wife
>   CATHERINE POLLARD, George's ex-wife
>   CYNTHIA VAIL, Vera Claiborne's younger cousin
>   ED ARCHER, Tom's longtime friend

At the time *The Malefactors* was published, in 1956, Caroline Gordon had been a writer of fiction for a quarter of a century. One of her earlier novels, *Alex Maury, Sportsman,* had been considered a classic and a masterpiece by such highly regarded critics as Arthur Mizener and William Van O'Connor; but despite critical praise, and despite the excellent quality of her fiction, the work of Miss Gordon has gone largely unnoticed in the academic world and also among general readers. As Arthur Mizener noted in the New York *Times Book Review,* when *The Malefactors* first appeared, Miss Gordon had been given only a sentence in *The Oxford Companion to American Literature,* and that sentence appeared at the end of the entry on Allen Tate, who was Caroline Gordon's husband. Miss Gordon has simply gone unnoticed, although her novels and short fiction have showed, ever since *Penhally* (1931), a growing skill and care in writing, and a continued and strengthened ability to perceive the problems of human life.

The Malefactors is the story of a poet, Tom Claiborne, born in Tennessee, who has traveled far from his childhood home and environment. Thanks to a legacy from an uncle, Tom Claiborne went to Europe in the 1920's, like many another young American of the time, where he became established as a successful poet and as the editor of *Spectra,* a "little magazine" which attracted the new and the older literary lights of the time. At the time the novel opens, in 1946, Claiborne has given up the magazine to another editor and retired to a farm in Bucks County, Pennsylvania. His wife Vera is the rich daughter of an Irish-American mother (heiress to an industrial fortune) and an Italian-American father, a painter. Vera Claiborne's wealth supports the household, Tom Claiborne's modest inheritance having long since disappeared.

The Claibornes live in a large and somewhat magnificent Pennsylvania Dutch farmhouse which they have restored at great expense; the Yankee house and the Yankee money which have come to him seem to Tom Claiborne a just return for what Union soldiers had done to his family's house and fortune during the Civil War. Vera Claiborne has achieved modest fame and responsibility as a breeder of Red Poll cattle (derisively referred to as "muley cows" by her husband) and as president of the Red Poll Breeders' Association. Her husband, on the other hand, has seen himself become in his own eyes a failure: he finds he can no longer write. Though he tries, poetry is beyond him, and even his efforts at critical writing are insufficient. Although he goes regularly to his study to work, he spends his "work hours" taking naps or worrying about the failure of his creative and critical powers. Almost a part of the household, since he lives in a cottage on the farmstead, is Max Shull, a painter and a homosexual whom the Claibornes have known for many years, in Europe as well as in America. Max Shull simply no longer takes his painting seriously. And that, as Tom Claiborne sees it, is really the whole household's problem—that their lives are only a party every day, with nothing taken seriously enough to make it meaningful.

On the day the story begins, Vera Claiborne is having a party, much like a country fair, in honor of her prize bull, Blencker's Brook's Best Man. One of the guests is Cynthia Vail, Vera's younger cousin. Cynthia has run away from her husband, a Midwestern college professor who, in her eyes at least, has condemned her to a stodgy life symbolized by her having to be "at home" one afternoon to receive college students' visits. Within a few days, on Tom Claiborne's birthday, Cynthia and Tom have become lovers. For a time they meet in New York City when they can, but Vera's discovery of the affair gives the lovers the push they

need; Tom Claiborne leaves his wife to take an apartment with Cynthia, who has established herself as a poet, thanks to her lover's help, and is becoming well-known in New York literary circles.

Having to earn a living, Tom Claiborne accepts the editorship of a new literary magazine to be published by a company which also publishes a mass-interest magazine named *Parade,* a firm managed by Tom Claiborne's long-time friend, Ed Archer. Work with the magazine, life with Cynthia Vail, and the separation from his wife all prove to Tom Claiborne that he has made a mistake once again. Tormented by strange dreams and hallucinations, Claiborne turns for help to his psychiatrist cousin, George Crenfew. Crenfew, who had given up painting years before, counsels Tom Claiborne and, finally, tells him where Vera is staying, on a farm which is an unofficial Catholic retreat begun by Catherine Pollard, George Crenfew's ex-wife. The novel ends with Tom Claiborne's apparent desire to be reconciled with his wife and, with her help (and that of Catholicism) to find a new and satisfying life.

As is so frequently the case in twentieth century fiction since Henry James and James Joyce, not a great deal happens in this novel. It is not action that is important; what is important is what people think and how they solve the psychological dilemmas life presents to them. Tom Claiborne's problems are, as Caroline Gordon sees them, not merely problems of an ordinary psychological nature; rather, they are problems of a philosophical and spiritual nature, problems which can be solved only by Tom Claiborne's accepting a new view of man and his relationship to the Deity. Slowly, as he reviews his life and values, Tom Claiborne comes to the realization that all humans are malefactors, including himself, and that he must accept a truly Christian view of people he has known, be they homosexuals, drunken priests, senile old men and women, or his own somewhat rascally father. Perhaps the word "sinners" might better have been used in the book's title, for it is Tom Claiborne's realization that, while all are sinners, all can serve God in some way, including Tom Claiborne, and be reconciled to God, whatever they may do in life. In a very real way, Tom Claiborne learns, every man and woman must be viewed and helped as if he were the Christ, not merely as if he were a Christian.

Having been a part of the literary scene in her own right and as the wife of Allen Tate, the poet and critic, Caroline Gordon had ample opportunity to observe the generation of literary people and artists she describes. Other attempts have been made to write full-length fictional portraits of poets, but few have succeeded as well as Caroline Gordon in her portrayal of Tom Claiborne. It must be noted, however, that the reader can be haunted by the feeling that the characters are in some ways based upon real persons, or combinations of real persons, that the author knew. This feeling is reinforced when the reader discovers that, for example, a dead poet mentioned many times in the novel committed suicide by jumping from an ocean liner and was also fascinated by the Brooklyn Bridge. The similarity of the fictional person to Hart Crane is impossible to overlook, especially if the reader remembers that Crane's first volume of poetry, *White Buildings,* was published with a foreword by Allen Tate. As has been pointed out before, however, the realistic detail which fills the novel, making it a literary re-creation of the period 1920–1948, is not given for its own sake. Everything in the novel is used to present a perception of man and the world. By reading all the detail carefully one comes to understand how the novelist has shaped her work to present Tom Claiborne's entire life, not the problems of his late forties alone, as problems which can be analyzed and solved only by appeal to spiritual, rather than worldly, considerations. Tom Claiborne at first is repulsed by Catholicism as he meets it among the people he encounters, but he finds eventually that only this particular perception, held by Catholics, can help him. His resistance changes to acceptance, as symbolized by his discovery that his wife, unknown to him, has been a Catholic since childhood.

Gordon W. Clarke

MALTAVERNE

Author: François Mauriac (1885–1970)
Translated from the French by Jean Stewart
Publisher: Farrar, Straus and Giroux (New York). 195 pp. $5.95
Type of work: Novel
Time: 1901–1903
Locale: Bordeaux and the estates of the Gironde

Alain Gajac's notebooks from his seventeenth through his twenty-second year, his relationships to his God, his friend, his fiancée, his mother, and his identification with his estate, Maltaverne

Principal characters:
> ALAIN GAJAC, narrator of the tale and heir to Maltaverne, an estate in the Gironde near Bordeaux
> MADAME GAJAC, his mother and manager of the estate
> SIMON DUBERC, the son of the Gajac family's bailiff
> MARIE, a clerk in Bard's Bookstore at Bordeaux, Alain's first love and fiancée

The late François Mauriac's last novel, *Maltaverne* (*Un adolescent d'autrefois*), is presented in the form of confessional notebooks, the testament of Alain Gajac from his seventeenth through his twenty-second years. The notebooks, intended originally by Alain for his schoolfriend André Donzac, contain the record of those years' events, both of Alain's outer relationships and his inner speculations; and they become for him, in the last weeks recorded therein, a repository of material for his future writing career—"the substance of a three-franc paperback."

François Mauriac's "young man of long ago" is our contemporary in all but dress. Alain Gajac is a man who thinks himself in love with God, who cannot do without God, as so many thousands of our own "sensitive young men" think themselves in love with this or that spiritual ideal—sincerity, peace, honesty, freedom, love; but like them, Alain Gajac is a man in love only with himself, who sees even his God as the reflection of his own face in the mirrors of his relationships with others. Alain Gajac's God is his own ego. Mauriac's last "sensitive young man," a figure familiar to readers of his earlier works, is that character so often met in the literature of the nation of Molière and Pascal—the "angel" who is in truth a demon of pride and spiritual blindness. Alain's expressed identification with his estate, Maltaverne, a great acreage of arid heathland and bleeding pine forests, is the emblem of his inner state.

On first inspection it would seem that the form, these confessional notebooks, betrays Mauriac in this last work. There is almost no story line; the events of the boy's four years are told in no conventionally chronological order and the personal revelations device allows for little character development of the secondary figures and very little of the narrator himself. Because we see Alain Gajac only through his own images of himself, we see mostly his posturing and self-deception, seldom relieved by moments of honesty. In truth, the narrator at twenty-two years is as much a monster and as unsympathetic figure as the narrator at seventeen. He is of interest to the reader only as a kind of nauseating case study in the psychology of moral idiocy. Nothing profound happens within him. All things seem only to happen to him—or rather to the people around him. The form, as Mauriac's spare style limits it, enforces so objective a light on the narrative that only the aridity of the narrator is visible. What is not given us by Alain—his dream life, his visions, his love, his wonder and awe, his conversations with his God, the whole poetry of a living man's experience—becomes of much more compelling interest to the reader than what is actually in the novel—the record of the ego-fantasies of a shallow, loveless, self-deceiving bore.

The flap-blurb on the American edition argues that "so personal and revelatory is it that there can be no doubt that Alain is largely Mauriac himself." If *Maltaverne* is autobiographical, replaying the major thematic motifs of Mauriac's early masterpieces—the land-hunger of empty lives, the demands of social position and religious allegiance, the struggles of the young with powerful matriarchs—let us hope the novel is not autobiography, for it would betray a major failure of self-understanding in a prose-poet of otherwise profound insight into the state of his characters' souls. We must conclude that Alain Gajac is not the youthful Mauriac, but one of Mauriac's most ingenious creations, a refinement of that character who haunts French literature since Molière defined him—the dreadful, irreligious *dévoté*, a Tartuffe who believes his own cant.

"I am unlike other boys," Alain, the narrator, begins. "If I were like other boys, at seventeen I should go shooting with Laurent, my elder brother . . . instead of pretending to be a dog." With this confession, not so unexpected of "sensitive young men" in the century of *The Sound and the Fury* and *The Tin Drum,* this boy who is, despite his protestation, so very much like a hundred other fictional boys with "sensitivity" in our literature, opens the story of his involvement with the seminarian Simon Duberc, son of the Gajac family's bailiff.

Alain's story is his involvement with three people important to his conception of himself in the years of the notebooks: and its action is his utterly unconscious betrayal and devastation of them all, the wake of his imperceptivity into the hearts of others and his nonlove for anyone but himself. His bailiff's son—Simon Duberc; his fiancée—Marie; and his mother—Madame Gajac—have no other existence for him than their roles in the dramas of his own ego-fantasies. Simon Duberc, the bailiff's son, is tempted by the seventeen-year-old Alain first to the mortal sin of ambition for sainthood and two years later to the venial sin of security at the price of integrity. Marie, his "first love," is used first as a source of sympathy and ego-flattery by Alain, and then as a weapon against his mother in a temporary "engagement." When she has fulfilled her usefulness, he insults, discards, and forgets her without a qualm of conscience. His sin he sees always as the one sexual act between them, never as his attitude towards her or his treatment of her; and that sin of incontinence he knows to have given him the masculine confidence he lacked, so that he interprets it as a grace and no source for guilt, thus relieving himself of the necessity of considering Marie any longer.

Behind all of his encounters there is the continuous battle with his mother, Madame Gajac, that stiff, aloof, lonely, and formidable widow, as unrelenting in the attainment of her goals as is her son. To free himself from her control and establish himself in his own right, Alain insults, mocks, scorns, and humiliates his mother as meanly and lovelessly as he uses others against her. They part at last only after the old woman is exhausted, bereft by a gruesome murder of her only real love—a neighbor's young daughter—and driven to utter despair. "I need nobody any more," she cries; and Alain responds first with scorn, then hurt feelings, and finally with the suggestion that he go away, for "from a distance you'd be able to put up with me, you'd get used to me again."

For Alain, other people exist only within his own fictions, never in their own reality. Simon he sees as the pathetic power-hungry peasant who loves his young master despite all insults and neglect. He never sees Simon as the limited, bumbling, tactless, but loving young man he is, who despite Alain's abrupt dismissal of their acquaintance tells the young master that his reclaimed vocation will save "both our souls." As he watches his mother's grief and growing despair after the loss of her neighbor's daughter who had cheered her otherwise lonely life, he subjects her state of mind to an arid and loveless, even if accurate, analysis: "Thus Mother was being stripped, day by day, of all her certainties. Nothing was sure of all she had believed, but the falsest thing of all was what she had mistaken for revealed truth."

"I cannot do without God," the seventeen-year-old Alain says. "That's what makes me different, deepdown,

from all the rest." And near the end of the notebooks, at twenty-two, he repeats the impassioned claim: ". . . I cannot do without You—ah, that I know! You know: born in different surroundings, I might perhaps have been able to do without everything else but not without You." But it is exactly at this point that Mauriac centers the novelist's objective eye—Alain not only *can* do without God, he does do without Him.

To Simon Duberc he confesses that "Pascal's total surrender to his director was the thing that I should find most utterly impossible." Despite his continual reveries over the reality of the inner life, the existence of God, the key to the absurd universe, the difference between his own religious certainties and what his mother "had mistaken for revealed truth," he records in the notebooks only his ego-fears and inflations and his second-hand theology. Nowhere can one find that deep and pervasive love for others and for God that characterizes the truly religious spirit. Nor can a mind that returns to "the inner life" only on occasion, as does Alain Gajac, impress us as seriously convinced of a deep faith. In his nineteenth year he wrote: "O God, passionately as I have loved my mother, it's not for her that I feel a love greater than my love for You. . . . The truth is that, like herself, I love Maltaverne better than I love You. . . ."

Alain Gajac might better have said, "I love myself better than I love You" —for as he says to Simon Duberc, "And Maltaverne means myself." Maltaverne, the estate of Bazalais pine forests that is the source of the Gajac wealth, the object of Alain's passion, and the cause of his contention with both mother and fiancée, is Mauriac's symbol for Alain's state of soul. Near the end of his narrative, he sees Mal- taverne as Mauriac has seen his soul: "a bleak, arid heathland, which will end as scorched earth."

Rollin Lasseter

A MAN AND TWO WOMEN

Author: Doris Lessing (1919-   )
Publisher: Simon and Schuster (New York). 316 pp. $5.00
Type of work: Short stories
Time: The present
Locale: England and Africa

A varied collection of short stories detailing the predicament of the individual in terms of his human relations and his environment

Doris Lessing's *The Golden Notebook* was one of the most impressive fictional performances of 1962, an exhaustive account of a twentieth century woman novelist's emotional and intellectual plight which attempted to convey the problematic relationship between life and art by alternating the personal entries of her notebooks with chapters from the novel which she was presumably writing. In her latest collection of short stories, *A Man and Two Women*, Mrs. Lessing again demonstrates those qualities of prose fiction which render her not only one of the most important women writing today but one of the significant voices, regardless of sex, in contemporary fiction. The short stories in this collection do not, unlike *The Golden Notebook*, individually represent Mrs. Lessing as a technical innovator, but, taken in the aggregate, they do suggest the range of her accomplishment and the degree of technical control she maintains throughout that range.

To say that Mrs. Lessing's voice is a distinctly feminine one is neither to denigrate her achievement nor to imply that the masculine mind is a closed book to her, though it may be one which on occasion makes for unpleasant reading. The centers of consciousness in most of these stories are women, women as diverse as the lower-middle class heroine of "Notes for a Case History," the professional mistress of "Between Men," and the prosperous, intelligent neurotic of "To Room Nineteen," but Mrs. Lessing is quite capable of tackling the masculine ego, as the initial story in the volume, "One off the Short List," devastatingly testifies. Its hero is Graham Spence, "a member of that army of people who live by their wits on the fringes of the arts," a failure in career and in marriage who attempts futilely to salvage the shards of his fragmented ego by projecting an image of himself as a bon vivant and seducer, seeking in the non-forthcoming recognition of that image compensation for his feeling of personal failure and defeat. The story concerns his one-day pursuit of Barbara Coles, a rising young stage designer whom he is interviewing for the B.B.C., and details his strategy of seduction, the collapsing ploys he uses to ingratiate himself and establish an easy familiarity with Barbara and her theatrical set, his conversational fumbles before and during the interview, his prolonged and desperate pass to which the girl finally submits only out of boredom and exasperation, his ultimate sexual failure, and finally his embarrassed attempt to pass himself off before Barbara's co-workers as her successful new lover. The irony is fierce, but so thorough is Mrs. Lessing's rendition of Spence's subterfuges and rationalizations, his willful self-blindings to the reality of his pain and humiliation, that pity and recognition almost measure with contempt.

"A Woman on a Roof" is another study of male frustration, but it is the other side of the emotional coin. A young man working on a roof is attracted to a woman who sunbathes daily on a roof several buildings away, but the romantic fantasies which he centers upon her are destroyed when, upon his trying to make her acquaintance, they meet with the stony opposition of her total indifference. The situation is a nascent version of "One off the Short List"; however, what is self-delusion in Spence is innocence in the boy, and what appears understandable disgust in Barbara Coles becomes inevitable callousness in the nameless woman.

"Before the Ministry" deserts the relation of the sexes for the masculine world of politics. Two members of the rival factions of an African government meet before the Ministry in London and discuss which of their leaders, Mr. Devuli, the alcoholic leader of the old guard, or Mr. Kwenzi, the left-wing representative of the new order, is to represent the country in an interview with the Minister. The two exchange insults under the guise of formal diplomatic parlance until the arrival of their two leaders, Devuli, a tottering titan who accuses his adversaries of having attempted to poison him, ultimately submitting to the smooth pressures of Kwenzi while the latter's underling mouths irrelevant platitudes of statesmanship. Mrs. Lessing, trenchantly underlining the crumbling of human dignity before political expediency, views the frustrations and absurdities of public life with as keen an eye as she does those of private experience.

It is essentially the private life, however, which occupies Mrs. Lessing, and it is here that her talent most character-istically shines: in "Between Men," the increasingly drunken conversation of two kept women who are between affairs; in "Each Other," a scene between an incestuous brother and sister who preserve the pseudo-sanctity of their relation by refraining from climax; or in "Notes for a Case History," the record of a middle-class girl who knowingly rejects her own integrity and the man she is drawn to for a conventionally successful marriage. The longest and possibly the best piece in the volume is "To Room Nineteen." In it the seemingly happily married Susan Rawlings gradually becomes obsessed with the triviality of her married existence as well as the burden which everyday life with her husband and children imposes upon her and withdraws from them, seeking isolation and a mindless satisfaction of solitude, first in the anonymity of a seedy hotel room and finally, when her husband has pursued her even there, in suicide. "To Room Nineteen" is striking as an unconventional twist on the by now nearly bromidic theme of isolation, but even more so as a revelation of the madness which exists in the midst of the ordinary pattern of life, a madness induced by the realization of that pattern's blankness.

In "How I Finally Lost My Heart," Mrs. Lessing resorts to a rather fey symbolic gimmick which vitiates the story's effectiveness, but it is about the only time her hand falters. Her ability to render the very quality of environment is strong, particularly in the African stories, and in "The Sun Between Their Feet," a story in which nothing happens other than a woman's observing the activities of a dung beetle, she manages to convey the tremendous disparity between the human imagination and the reality of nature. But it is basically the human imagination and its ordinary frustrations which concern Mrs. Lessing. And it is in her revelation of the extraordinariness and the rich individuation of the ordinary that her authentic gift lies.

Donald L. Mull

MAN IN MOTION

Author: Michael Mewshaw (1943–   )
Publisher: Random House (New York). 247 pp. $5.95
Type of work: Novel
Time: The present
Locale: Maryland, the Southwest, Mexico

Horrified by the sudden death of his stepfather, a directionless young writer flees his home town and heads for California with a gorgeous girl

Principal characters:
WALKER HAWLEY, an aspiring writer
LILA CAINE, his traveling companion
DADDY DICK MURDOCK, Walker's stepfather
MRS. MINA MURDOCK, Walker's mother
GRANDMOTHER HAWLEY, Walker's rich grandmother
DEDE CLINTON, Walker's girl friend

Walker Hawley, the young, tormented writer-hero of this excellent first novel, suffers from an almost unbelievable number of modern complaints. The things he feels inside—weariness, depression, nausea, anxiety—place him on a par with Sartre's Roquentin. Everything in the world grates on Walker's nerves. In fact, he is so classically screwed up, so utterly miserable, that one is tempted to laugh at him at times rather than cry.

The reason is that Walker's misery is so repetitive and predictable. Every time Walker makes a move, every time he even eats or drinks or thinks or sleeps, he ends up griping and grumbling, feeling sick to death and cheated inside. Life is always bothering him and tricking him, always letting him down.

Walker is confused about everything: about himself (he has a glaring identity problem), about his family (his mother's in a lunatic asylum; his stepfather is a drunk), about religion (the brothers at his parochial school wanted him to become a priest), about his writing (he's blocked), about sex (he gets a lot but isn't satisfied), about

love (he has a hard time loving anyone but himself).

He is also alienated. Alienated from the lower class, the middle class, the upper class. Alienated as much by the hip, pot-smoking members of his generation as by the loud, hard-drinking fraternity boys. He is, without really having chosen to be so, an outsider, and also a dangling man—in much the same position as Saul Bellow's dangling man or Thomas Merton (in *Seven Story Mountain*) before he became a Trappist monk. Like both these frenzied characters, he feels sad, empty, worthless, frustrated, and absolutely desperate to come to a decision about his life. He also resembles them in his towering self-pity and self-concern. Like them, he is oppressed by the ugliness and emptiness of America. His final resemblance to them is that he is a frustrated writer—an ambitious young man getting nowhere, eating his heart out, anxiously biding his time.

Here, thankfully, the resemblance ends. It might be going overboard to say that *Man in Motion* is the best book of the three, but it is by far the most enjoyable and humane—the most forgiving, the most innocent and fresh, the most healthy. Although brilliantly written and certainly more serious than Mewshaw's book, *Seven Story Mountain* sticks in the mind as the work of an icy, neurotic, self-hating, and life-hating man. Almost the same description can be applied to *Dangling Man*. Both books seem to be over-absorbed in the suffering they describe, as if their authors were as trapped within themselves as their creations. What sets *Man in Motion* apart from them (and from nearly all the anguished literature in this vein) is not only the distance Mewshaw keeps from his character, but also his wonderful sense of humor —his ability to laugh at Walker Hawley at certain crucial points where other writers would wince or cry.

When it comes to existential *angst,* there is such a thing as suffering too much, suffering to the point where it becomes ridiculous. This is the surprising thing we learn when the book is at its funniest and best. At other times, Mewshaw falls into as disappointed, futile and self-serious a mood as the next writer in this genre. Luckily, however, it is the humor which prevails. In fact, it is hard to think of another novel which treats anxiety and despair in quite the same way—with quite the same earnestness and compassion, and yet also with the liberating ability to stand back and laugh, laugh hard, when in reality things could not be worse.

As the novel begins, there is nothing funny about what is going on, and nothing funny happens for a long time. One almost suspects that Mewshaw set out to write a deadly serious book, then experienced a change of humor in midstream. If so, it is fortunate he felt both ways. Although slow and even boring, the sourness of the opening chapters sets us off our guard.

The novel opens under gray November skies in the depressing town of Cottage City, Maryland, a decaying, lower-middle-class suburb of Washington, D.C. Cottage City is where Walker spent his childhood and where he still lives (at home, with his step-father, Daddy Dick) in spite of the fact that he is twenty-six years old. It would be exaggerating to say that Walker "grew up" in Cottage City, because his main problem is that he has not grown up at all. Walker mopes around the house, worries about his writing, agonizes that time is passing him by; but he desperately lacks the ability to take the bull by the horns and figure out a way to change his life.

And what does he do with his life?

Well, he lives such a banal existence he could scream. By day, Walker is a cashier in a supermarket. At night, if he is not writing (and usually he is not), he sees his girl friend, Dede Clinton, a seemingly ideal mate, whom he supposes he loves but isn't in any hurry to marry. Otherwise, his only love in life seems to be driving his Carolina-blue TR-3. Walker is addicted to getting in it and taking trips, "month-long hauls to Canada, Alaska, the West Coast" or just "short sprints down Bladensburg Road to Jerry's Hot Dog Stand." In other words, he doesn't know what he wants, and, as a result, he can't stand still.

Walker may be feckless and mixed-up, but he isn't a fool. One believes in his potential as a writer, just as one believes in his frustration at not being able to write. It is a familiar story: "With only a short story to his credit, he wasn't a writer at all. Just barely an aspiring one. And 'Drowning Voices' (which he published as an undergraduate) seemed almost like a mistake, a cruel one at that, for it'd made him think a career in writing lay ahead. . . . Now he no longer wondered whether he could do it again but, instead, how he'd done it in the first place."

To increase his anxiety, his mother has recently had a nervous breakdown and is in a mental institution. As the story begins, Walker has come to tell her that he plans to leave home and go to San Francisco. She reacts to the news in a predictably neurotic manner, lashing out at him, accusing him of being the reason why she had her breakdown. The confrontation ends with Walker feeling miserable and guilty but still determined to go.

The reasons why he wants to leave are obvious. He feels trapped. He finds the ugliness of Cottage City unbearable. It is like Dublin was to James Joyce, filled with associations of failed lives, petty minds, anger, and stupidity. For another, he is afraid he will become like Daddy Dick, a lovable but depressing man, a big beefy construction worker "lobotomized by beer and TV." And there is also the fact that his rich paternal grandmother has offered him $5,000 to get away from Cottage City (which she looks down on as if it had plague), go to San Francisco and get to know his real father, who lives there. So it is actually Grandmother Hawley, a hard-headed realist and snob, who plants the poisonous seed of escape in Walker's mind—and also gives him the wherewithal to do it. Walker submits because he is completely outer-directed and lost.

As things turn out, Walker suddenly gets inspired to place an ad in the Washington *Post* for a rider to accompany him to San Francisco. The next day, a sexy-sounding girl with the ominous name of Lila Caine calls him up. They arrange to meet. She turns out to be both beautiful and hip—and now the novel seems about to take wing. In an exalted mood, Walker decides to leave the Monday after Thanksgiving.

But first comes an horrendous Thanksgiving dinner at home. Walker spends the day being yelled at by his nagging sister, Nancy, who lectures him and tells him to grow up. Daddy Dick passes out in the basement in front of the TV. Walker's mother calls Walker up and weeps over the phone. Finally, stuffed to the gills with turkey and thoroughly depressed by everything on earth, Walker climbs wearily through the dark to his attic bedroom and falls asleep. Sometime during the night, however, he wakes up and starts worrying about Daddy Dick. He calls down the stairs. There is no answer. In a panic, he rushes to the basement and discovers that Daddy Dick has fallen backwards down the stairs and is stone-cold dead.

Suddenly, his whole life seems at stake. If he stays for the funeral, he will probably be trapped in Cottage City forever. He is so repelled by the thought that he throws up his entire turkey dinner. "I won't do it," he shouts. Hysterical, he packs a suitcase, rushes out into the snow, gets in his car, drives maniacally to pick up Lila Caine, and they're off.

The rest of the book is a brilliant description of their trip across America (which eventually terminates in complete disaster in Mexico). To Walker's delight—and later his despair—the only thing that interests Lila is getting into bed. As a result, they spend more time in motels than on the road.

But in spite of the sexual pyrotechnics, the novel remains brooding and glum. Walker cannot forget the death of Daddy Dick and cannot forgive himself for evading his responsibilities. As he and Lila proceed West, he grows more and more anxious, until finally he becomes terrified. The ugliness and emptiness of the Southwest depress him just as much as the atmosphere of Cottage City. Lila Caine turns out to be shallow and only pseudo-hip, a cheerleader in disguise. But what really scares him is his growing awareness that he is totally lost. Time is running out, and he still doesn't know where he is going or why he is going wherever he's going or what he's going to do whenever he gets there. Dismissing San Francisco as his objective, he decides to venture into Mexico, where he imagines everything will be lush and beautiful and green.

At this point, the TR-3 breaks down, forcing Lila and Walker to spend the night in the desolate hamlet of Cottula, Texas. They find a basement room in the house of a buxom redhead aptly named Phoebe Looney. Later in the evening, they go out to skate at Beegee's Roller Skating Rink, the only place of entertainment in the town. And now the first of several screamingly funny incidents occurs. A bunch of townies hijack Lila and lock Walker in the washroom. Enraged, Walker careens around the restroom on his skates, punching a prophylactic machine, which promptly spits out a cellophane package of New Formula, Double Strength Linger Ointment. Walker gets out of the scrape, but the next night he tries out the ointment to his discomfort and dismay.

Utterly dejected, he continues into Mexico, where he and Lila immedi-ately begin to fight. At one point, they start their squabbling while the TR-3 is climbing a mountain. Walker slams on the brakes, orders Lila out of the car, then gets out himself and follows Lila up the road, commanding her to come back and get her bags. Unfortunately, he has forgotten to apply the emergency brake, and the car rolls down the hill and plunges off a cliff. Here, with Walker at his nadir, the reader finally *really* looks at him and laughs.

These three incidents—the bathroom, the ointment, and the demolished car—serve to humanize Walker for us, so that we begin to accept him for what he is. No questions asked. We admire him simply for being alive. This is an extremely rare accomplishment for any novel. Walker's justification for being alive, simply alive, is somehow very much our own.

The book has other funny incidents, of course, and all of them are the kind one wants to retell. For instance, Walker gets dysentery in Mexico and must spend a whole day on the john. He runs out of toilet paper and turns to using pages out of books. But he has brought only two books with him, one by Thomas Merton, *The Sign of Jonas,* and the other *Best Short Stories on Campus,* which contains his only published short story. First, he uses Merton (bravo!) and then every story in the college anthology but his own (long live Walker Hawley!).

Two athletic Sigma Chis from the University of Alabama also figure heavily in the closing chapters. They pick Lila and Walker up after the demise of the TR-3 and stick to them like glue for the remainder of the trip. Eventually, they steal Lila away. The last night he is in Mexico, Walker gets horribly jealous and drunk and ends up being sick all over them.

By now it should be apparent that the dominant images in the book are all completely visceral. Whenever Walker vomits, one can assume he is about to make up his mind. Getting it all out, cleaning himself out, he feels lighter and ready to go. The upshot of the book is that he boards an airplane and flies back to Cottage City into the arms of his old girl friend, Dede Clinton. It is not what you would call a happy ending. But for Walker it represents a definite change of mind. Renouncing his hard-headed grandmother, renouncing his real father (who writes him terse, business-like letters and lectures him to grow up), he decides that he will try to be a spokesman for the miserable, the screwed-up, the frustrated residents of Cottage City.

One hears much about sympathizing with the underprivileged these days, but rarely has one encountered such real sympathy for humanity at large. *Man in Motion*, in spite of its myriad and obvious flaws, is really a first-rate book.

M. Cronan Minton

THE MAN IN THE GRAY FLANNEL SUIT

Author: Sloan Wilson (1920-   )
Publisher: Simon and Schuster (New York). 304 pp. $3.50
Type of work: Novel
Time: The present
Locale: New York and Suburbia

A novel about a bright young man in a gray flannel suit who loses his desire to become a big executive

Principal characters:
> TOM RATH, a bright yet sad young man, 1955 model
> BETSY, his wife
> RALPH HOPKINS, president of United Broadcasting, Tom's boss
> BILL OGDEN, a man headed up the ladder toward a vice-presidency
> CAESAR GARDELLA, an ex-G.I. Tom had known in Italy
> MARIA, Tom's Italian sweetheart and mother of his child
> SAUL BERNSTEIN, a wise judge

This is the kind of novel that can be taken as speaking for an age. Perhaps the gray flannel suit will become for us as important a symbol as Babbitt. For this is a novel of human bondage, and the slave uniform is the gray flannel suit.

Tom Rath, who has a job with the Schanenhauser Foundation, finds out that there is an opening at United Broadcasting. He is interested because he cannot see that there is much value in anything unless a man's income is more than the $7,000 he is already getting. His wife Betsy, in complete agreement, hopes that they can sell their small house, get rid of the old car, and at last begin to live. Tom puts on his neatly pressed gray flannel suit, leaves his Connecticut home, and goes to the city on the commuter's train. From here on out everything seems to shine like gold and smell like money, but Tom becomes increasingly dissatisfied with the values of the life he leads. He begins to think about his G.I. days and the girl he left behind, pregnant, in Rome. His personal problem becomes that of relating the values he knew then to the hard, impersonal values of big business.

This book is something more than a satire, for it neither exaggerates nor falsifies the kind of life in which thousands of young men contend for power and money. The novel has warmth since Tom is not callously conditioned to accept the life he is forced to lead, but responds to it as an intelligent, although somewhat confused, young man.

Nevertheless, in writing about Tom's boss, Ralph Hopkins, the author has had to face a problem which confronts everyone who tries to create a realistic picture of the *big* big businessman. How can a person who devotes every moment and every human relationship to the problem of building the scope and influence of a mighty corporation be made understandable or sympathetic to readers who, through choice or necessity, are not practicing the same fantastic art? Sloan Wilson has done his best, and his best is good enough.

The multi-millionaire executive, Hopkins, president of United Broadcasting, wants to start a big campaign to make himself head of a committee on mental health. The problem is to give a number of respectable physicians the illusion of having thought up the idea by themselves. To this end, Hopkins enlists the aid of the top men in the corporation. He knows that if he can slip into the humanitarian role he dreams of, all the magic-making power of modern advertising media are at his disposal.

Strangely enough, the health project does not seem to be simply another bid for power or even for fame, although one of Tom's friends cynically suggests that it is. The implication of the book is that Hopkins cannot rest; he is for some reason compelled to take on big jobs, one after the other. His psychoanalyst tells him that he has a guilt complex and is trying to punish and kill himself by working, and that the guilt complex is probably based on a fear of homosexuality. Whatever the cause, Hopkins probably wants to justify his way of life, and he cannot take the ordinary way of giving his life content by going home, helping his children, and loving his wife. He must take the complex, big business, big power way of justifying himself: he must become head of a national mental health committee.

His first step is a speech to be given to a convention of physicians in Atlantic City. Tom Rath is hired as Hopkins' personal assistant, at a compromise salary of $9,000, to work on the speech and handle the details. This job is difficult because Bill Ogden, avidly striving for a vice-presidency, rejects every draft of the speech. Hopkins praises the drafts but, in effect, rejects them also. The whole business of turning out a speech seems to become the number one problem for the corporation until Tom finally decides to start being honest. When Tom tells Hopkins that the company is trying to sell mental health like cigarettes, a new line of attack becomes possible and

Tom is able to turn out an acceptable draft which turns the trick of getting Hopkins the chairmanship he wants.

What is important to the reader is not the question of whether or not the speech will ever get written, although satisfying suspense develops here, but the study of personalities in conflict. Perhaps one can account for the sucsess this novel is enjoying by pointing to the legions of gray-flanneled men whose daily business lives involve just such foolish and bitter contests of opinion and power. Tom is fortunate enough, because of his successful commitment to honesty in his dealings with Hopkins, finally to escape from Hopkins' plan to make Tom a big executive like himself. But one realizes that in actual life not everyone has the kind of sense and the kind of saving circumstances which enable Tom to get out of the race for the big money.

Tom's final rejection of Hopkins' hopes for him is preceded by a series of events which follow his recognition of one of the elevator operators as Caesar Gardella, whom he had known in the army. Caesar had loved a girl in Rome, too, and had married her. When he and Tom get a chance to talk, Caesar shows that he no longer holds an active grudge against Tom for having left Maria pregnant in Rome when the move to the Pacific came, and for never having returned. But Caesar suggests that Tom should help Maria, for she and her husband, with Tom's son, are near poverty in Italy. Tom wants to help, but he is afraid of the consequences. When he decides to be honest with Hopkins, he finds it easier to be honest with his wife about wanting to send money to Maria and the boy. Problems having to do with his plan to have a housing project on the property left to the Raths by Tom's grandmother are also resolved when in a town meeting Tom makes a direct, rather than a clever, approach to the situation.

The novel contains a number of flashbacks dealing with Tom's love affair with Maria and his experiences as a paratrooper. These passages are effective and moving, making credible Tom's decision not to become simply another frightened member of the gray-flanneled army.

When Tom tells Hopkins that he will not go to Hollywood to learn more about that end of the business, Hopkins agrees to let Tom keep the job with the mental health committee. But Hopkins explodes for the only time to cry, "*Somebody* has to do the big jobs! The world was built by men like me! To really do a job, you have to live it, body and soul! You people who just give half your mind to your work are riding on our backs!" And Tom re-

plies, "I know it."

Interwoven with Tom's story is the portrait of a small-town judge, Saul Bernstein, who seeks justice by personal inquiry into the lives of those he is called upon to judge. He does so even though it makes his stomach ache to take the destinies of human beings in hand. The reward comes when Tom tells him that he and his wife want to send money to Italy for Maria and the boy.

Tom says, "I suppose that may be a little unconventional, but to us it seems like simple justice." The judge then refuses to accept payment for handling the matter because, as he says, "I like what you call 'simple justice.' The kind I generally deal with is so complex."

From gray flannel to simple justice: this is the course of Sloan Wilson's neatly written, highly effective, and pertinent novel of our muddled times.

Sources for Further Study

Criticism:

Kelly, James. "The Man in the Gray Flannel Suit," in *Saturday Review*. XXXVIII (July 23, 1955), p. 8. Kelly views the novel as an autobiography of the commentator that makes allowances for the man inside the uniform.

Reviews:

Commonweal. LXII, August 26, 1955, p. 525. 550 words.

New Republic. CXXXIII, August 8, 1955, p. 19. 1,050 words.

Time. LXVI, July 18, 1955, p. 102. 700 words.

Yale Review. XLV, Autumn, 1955, p. 157. 300 words.

THE MAN JUST AHEAD OF YOU

Author: Robert M. Coates (1897-1973)
Publisher: William Sloane Associates (New York). 192 pp. $4.00
Type of work: Short stories
Time: The present
Locale: Contemporary America, mainly New York

Thirteen stories treating men caught in moments of crisis

Robert Coates is already well known to readers of *The New Yorker,* in the pages of which all thirteen of these stories originally appeared. Along with five novels and three "general" works, two earlier collections of short fiction bear Coates's name. The sort of professionalism demanded of a man so prolific is quite apparent in *The Man Just Ahead of You,* marking both the excellence and the weakness of these stories.

In *The New Yorker* vein, the real violence of these tales is that of the mind: incident is subordinated to the echoes and evaluations which stem from an impelling event, and there is a fine polish to the occasionally too-slight substance underlying each tale. All these traits are present, well-handled, finely turned. Yet what is merit in a single story becomes mannerism in its being present in all; thirteen stories in the same key would be too many.

Happily, Coates manages to provide enough variety in subject matter, if not in manner, to keep one from feeling trapped in a gray flannel maze. But each of his characters is trapped, in one way or another. In "Encounter in Illinois," a tourist and his wife are insulted and threatened by a trio of hoodlums dressed in the expected leather jackets. They are followed down the highway and almost forced off the road, until the tourist asserts himself and "wins" a game of highway "chicken" by forcing the boys' car into a ditch. He succeeds only by beating the hoodlums at their own game, sinking to their level.

More clearly defeated is Buck in "When the Big Barn Burned." His barn, crops, and tools go up in a blaze that attracts the neighbors—some who come to help, to sympathize, or merely to stare, and some secretly to gloat that the misfortune is not theirs—and even an insurance salesman who tries to take advantage of the moment to remind Buck how much better off he might have been with greater coverage. Crushed under the load of this catastrophe, Buck drives his car headlong into the burning barn, destroying his last valuable possession; it might as well go with the rest.

Two other stories, "Memento" and "Getaway" hinge upon the actions of a man behind the wheel of a car. In the first, a man and wife strike and kill a dog while driving to a party at their friends' home in Suburbia. He has had a few drinks, and she maintains an obviously practiced silence until he makes the final mistake of offering money to the owners of the dead dog in an attempt to assuage his conscience. Then the couple's marriage splits open at the seams as recriminations fly back and forth. Although an uncomfortable truce is achieved, the husband has learned for the first time how little his wife respects him, indeed, how little about him there is to respect.

The second, "Getaway," details the involved and ineffectual flounderings of a man who hits and kills a pedestrian on a lonely highway, then drives off in an instant of panic. As he wanders country roads and tries to think of a way clear, even rationalizing that his "position" and "family" are better served by his cowardice, his conscience drives him finally to a sudden, retributive death.

In all four of these stories, men seek to escape an impersonal, mechanistic world in the very machine representative of that world. Another character, Harry Burgess in "Storm," probably should be grouped with these other protagonists, for his inability to drive his car through a blizzard to the hospital where his wife lies ill seems to him a personal failure, cowardice.

The complexity of today's world proves too much for Carter Johnson in "Return." Desperately trying to get to the bank before it closes, trying to cover his weekly payroll, Johnson cracks and loses his sense of direction, literally as well as figuratively. He climbs through a nearly empty building to mount the water tower atop it. There he hopes to stand as "the happiest man on earth," the world at his feet and the serene blue sky around him. That hope is of course doomed, because there collects a crowd who refuse to allow him the peace of his tentative sanctuary. His wife comes to plead with him, embarrassed and willing to promise anything to draw him down; yet she lunges away from him horrified when he does set foot again on the roof, on "reality." He ends struggling in a sea of tightening arms as the people who pleaded with him to descend suddenly hold him fast.

Another "Captive" is young Perry Balding in his hospital bed in the Special Care Ward, a boy who sees the people around him dying, who comes near to death himself, but finally finds comfort in his "love" for an older woman also in the large ward. Unaccountably, just at the moment when Perry and his companion seem on the verge of total recovery, she dies while the super-efficient nurses administer probably the wrong treatment to another patient and fail to respond to her need. Perhaps the real tragedy of this tale is that Perry, because of his throat operation, cannot easily communicate with anyone. And the woman who dies depends for help upon an automatic, mechanical device which is intended to signal her plight. When communication fails, and the machines built to replace it fail, there is little room for hope.

"Listen, Paul" displays Coates's ear for precise and revealing dialogue, as a would-be divorcee tries to regale a bartender with her problems, pretending to ones she lacks as she unintentionally reveals those she has. She gains a sudden insight into her own future as she catches the eye of an old barfly who mistakes her glance for a come-on and is embarrassed. Her voice grows more and more shrill as she tries to make herself heard by someone who will take responsibility for what she comes to see is the result of her own actions. Another of Coates's characters, Billy in "The Citadel," learns the disappointments which accompany responsibility as he is forced to enter an adult world in an unwanted encounter.

Not all these tales, however, are quite so somber. There is the fantasy of "The Return of the Gods," in which the gods take to a mother-of-pearl Olympus certain mortals who believe in them. "The Downfall of Travis Penniman" is a fine spoof of a kind of ego which so often infects a certain type of public man, the kind Coates calls "the war correspondent, novelist, political authority, and lecturer." "The Happy Hour" is part fun, part fantasy, yet it treats as well a mammoth "identity problem," as its hero wanders into a bar and "becomes" someone else who once frequented the place, ran up a bar-bill, and jilted a girl who now sits at a back table, waiting.

The title piece of this collection is the least easily described, perhaps because it is more essay than story. The first-person narrator offers a theory to account for the rudeness which meets one in the actions and attitudes of clerks and bus drivers, of all the people of "the city," New York. He suggests that traveling around the city just ahead of each of us is a man who irritates, insults, or offends the very persons with whom we must come in contact. The rudeness which we each meet is in every case the legacy of that man just ahead of us. The narrator even reports his once having come upon the man just ahead of him at a newspaper stand as a quarrel broke out between that man and the newsstand attendant, only to discover that the anger apparently stemmed from the actions of someone yet one step further ahead of *him*.

It becomes impossible to assign the blame for the tensions that seem to grow in the very air of the complex world in which each of Coates's characters struggles. Coates does not really try; he merely pictures that struggle with clarity and precision. Not to be read at one sitting, *The Man Just Ahead of You* will reward a leisurely reading with unfailing craftsmanship and excellence.

Richard E. Peck

MAN OF LA MANCHA

Author: Dale Wasserman (1917-   )
With lyrics by Joe Darion and music by Mitch Leigh
Publisher: Random House (New York). 82 pp. $3.95
Type of work: Musical drama
Time: End of the sixteenth century
Locale: The common room of a prison in Spain

A warm, earthy musical presentation of Cervantes' Don Quixote

Principal characters:
DON QUIXOTE (CERVANTES), in real life Alonso Quijana, a
    country squire,
SANCHO (THE MANSERVANT), Don Quixote's squire,
ALDONZA, the kitchen wench,
THE INNKEEPER (THE GOVERNOR),
MARIA, the innkeeper's wife,
FERMINA, a servant girl,
THE PADRE,
ANTONIA, Don Quixote's niece,
DR. CARRASCO (THE DUKE), Antonia's fiancé,
THE HOUSEKEEPER,
PEDRO, the head muleteer,
ANSELMO,
JOSE,
JUAN,
PACO, and
TENORIA, muleteers, and
THE BARBER, in reality all prisoners of the Inquisition
GUARDS AND MEN OF THE INQUISITION

"I shall impersonate a man . . . enter into my imagination and see him! . . . No longer shall he be plain Alonso Quijana . . . but a dauntless knight known as—Don Quixote de La Mancha!!!" With this invitation the members of the audience, as well as the prisoners awaiting the action of Inquisition, are invited to join Don Miguel de Cervantes in his attempt to save his famous manuscript from destruction by presenting a "charade." Dale Wasserman first created the play for television. The production won him several awards, but left him dissatisfied. At the suggestion of one of his friends, he decided to turn it into a musical play for the Broadway stage.

Man of La Mancha was first presented on November 22, 1965, at the ANTA Washington Square Theatre in New York City. The majority of the reviews that followed in the next few days were tepid, some even hostile. The musical drama was considered as dead as the age of Cervantes and a failure to honor him; it was suggested that the drama should be centuries away from Broadway instead of several blocks. The dialogue and lyrics were considered vulgar, the choreography was of the "cootch" variety, and the stage similar to a record turntable. One review did give it more pluses than minuses, but only one review actually praised the production. The reviewer must have written with some degree of foresight: *Man of La Mancha* won the New York Drama Critics Award for "The Best Musical of 1966."

As the play opens, Cervantes and his manservant are being placed in the common room of a stone prison to await their turn before the Inquisition. The stage is unique in that it stands free; the only access to it is from a drawbridge which lowers for the guards to allow them to bring in a prisoner or take one before the Inquisition. The stage is fully utilized. The audience's imagination is aided by the lighting and the props which are sections of the stage used in various scenes to give as much realism as the parts of a prison can allow. One fine example is the entrance to the cells below the common room the grating is used to form the screens for the confessional scene and then again as Quixote's bed in the death scene.

Once the guards have left Cervantes, the other prisoners attack him and begin to loot his trunk, which is full of acting props. The wrapped package he holds under his arm is taken, but after the prisoners discover that it contains only paper the Governor of the prisoners heads toward the fire to burn it. When Cervantes tries to save the manuscript from being thrown into the fire, the Governor announces that there will be a trial and the Duke of the prisoners will act as prosecutor. Cervantes pleads guilty to the charges, but when the Governor again starts for the fire Cervantes cries:

> Your Excellency! What about my defense?
> THE GOVERNOR But you just pleaded guilty.
> CERVANTES Had I said "innocent" you surely would have found me guilty. Since I have admitted guilt, the court is required to hear me out.

Cervantes then presents his defense

as the charade in which all the prisoners will take part. The Governor becomes the Innkeeper; some of the men are muleteers, and some of the women take on various roles—kitchen wenches, the innkeeper's wife, Don Quixote's niece, and his housekeeper. As Cervantes invites them to join in his charade, he proceeds to create the characters of Don Quixote and his manservant, Sancho. While Cervantes speaks he dons the makeup and costume of Quixote from the props in his trunk.

Mr. Wasserman has Cervantes slip in and out of his new character so well that there is no strain on the audience as he makes the transition. The prisoners become their charade characters under Cervantes' direction, each prisoner seeming to fit the role he has been given and taking delight in a chance to break the monotony of prison life.

In many many musicals the actors appear to burst unaccountably into song; this is not the case in *Man of La Mancha*. The songs further the action, continue the story, do not create an interruption, or slow the pace of the play. One excellent example occurs when the muleteers at the inn announce that they have come to Aldonza for love. She replies:

> Love!
> One pair of arms is like another. . . .

She continues:

> I do not like the life I live,
> But I am me, I am Aldonza,
> And what I give I choose to give!

This declaration is an integral part of the play, explaining her place and role before her meeting with Don Quixote.

The original story by Cervantes is never forgotten by Wasserman, but what Wasserman has managed to do is present both men at once in the body of one man. We are given the full meaning of the two men, the real and the unreal. Cervantes' novel is a masterpiece of multiple effects suggested and carried into the play. The story has been told on several levels. We are shown Don Quixote's warped or sane desire of life, Cervantes' view of life as it was and is; and we can see the prisoners' views as well as realize our own.

Don Quixote battles the windmill in a scene which is comic and pathetic at the same time. Even though the windmill is represented by lights, it is easy for the audience to imagine the setting. Don Quixote needs to become a knight before he can fight the "Great Enchanter" who turned into the windmill before the don could battle with him. Seeing an inn in the distance, Don Quixote believes that it is a castle and feels that it is there that he can be dubbed a knight.

The knight-to-be enters the inn in a state of anger, for there was not a single dwarf in the battlements to announce his arrival. The "lord of the castle," who is the innkeeper, is coaxed by his wife to get rid of the madman, but he states that "Madmen are the children of God." He ushers the knight and his squire into the dining area where Don Quixote meets Aldonza. He asks her speak her name. When she pronounces it he feels that she is jesting, for as he sings:

I have sought thee, sung thee, dreamed thee, Dulcinea!
Now I've found thee, and the world shall know thy glory.
Dulcinea . . . Dulcinea!

After Don Quixote leaves to be shown his quarters the muleteers chide Aldonza. When they are finished, Cervantes hustles the mock jury into another scene, that of Don Quixote's neighborhood church, where Antonia, his niece, and his Housekeeper have confronted the Padre at confession. They tell him of the rumors they have heard, at the same time saying, "I'm only thinking of him." In the confession the niece says, "Oh, I dearly love my uncle but for what he's done to me / I would like to take and lock him up and throw away the key!" Her fiancé, Dr. Carrasco, is disturbed by the actions of her uncle, for he feels it is bad to have a madman in the family and therefore he may have to break off the engagement. The wily Padre challenges him to cure the old man and he accepts. As they march off to find the uncle they again state, "We're only thinking and worrying about him!"

It is in this kind of scene that we are shown the hypocrisy which Cervantes satirized in his novel. On the stage it becomes quite clear who is being thought about. The Padre quickly realizes this, as do the members of the audience. This is not the only example of the way in which Wasserman carries the true Cervantes into his play and onto the stage. For Mr. Wasserman never lets us forget that this is Cervantes' story and that it is actually his manuscript, his life's work, which is in danger of being destroyed; so we are ushered out of the Quixote story back into the common room by outbursts from the prisoners. Cervantes must justify his manuscript and he is hard put in trying to do so.

The Padre and Carrasco arrive at the inn. As they confront Don Quixote, a barber enters. The old man decides that the barber's shaving basin is the Golden Helmet of Mambrino. The barber complains that it is not golden and will not make him brave, but Sancho answers, "Well at least he'll find it useful if he ever needs a shave!"

Don Quixote, under his own impression that the innkeeper is lord of the castle, asks him to make him a knight. The Padre realizes that there is little hope at the present for saving the old man. Carrasco argues, "Not necessarily. We know the sickness. Now to find the cure." The Padre reflects, "The cure. May it be not worse than the disease." He then sings the beautiful "To Each His Dulcinea" which ends:

> There is no Dulcinea,
> She's made of flame and air,
> And yet how lovely life would seem
> If every man could weave a dream
> To keep him from despair.
>
> To each his Dulcinea
> Though she's naught but flame and air!

"There is no Dulcinea" states the song. But need there be a physical Dulcinea, must there be more than a dream,. a quest? Every man envisions something which cannot be grasped by the hand. The world is built on dreams and imagination; Mr. Wasserman has taken us into *his* imagination and thrust us even further into that of Cervantes'.

While Don Quixote stands his vigil Aldonza appears and asks him what he could desire of her. He states "Nothing," but she calls him a liar. He then admits that he wants to serve as her knight and if necessary to die gloriously, giving his life "in the sacred name of Dulcinea." This confession disturbs Aldonza; she starts to leave, then turns and questions him further. Don Quixote states that he must follow

the quest. She asks:

> What does it mean—quest?

The song ends:

> DON QUIXOTE The mission of each
> true knight . . . his duty—nay, his
> privilege! (*He sings*)
> To dream the impossible dream,
>
> . . . .
>
> To love, pure and chaste, from afar,
> To try, when your arms are too weary,
> To reach the unreachable star!

The song ends:

> And the world will be better for this,
> That one man, scorned and covered
>   with scars,
> Still strove, with his last ounce of cour-
>   age,
> To reach the unreachable stars!

These lyrics are true to the heart of Cervantes' novel. In this one song the power, majesty, and humility of the don are brought home to the audience.

Following this discussion of the quest, Don Quixote, by some miracle, defeats the muleteers in their attempt to get Aldonza. Don Quixote is then dubbed a knight in a most hilarious scene in which he is given the added name of "Knight of the Woeful Countenance." Aldonza has almost succumbed to Don Quixote's madness when she is raped by the muleteers, breaking the illusion and bringing her back to the reality of the world in which she lives.

Don Quixote is brought back to reality by Dr. Carrasco in an amazing scene in which Don Quixote is faced by knights carrying shields made of mirrors. Everywhere he turns he sees no one but himself and he realizes how foolish he is. A broken man, Don Quixote allows Carrasco to take him home.

Wasserman gave the novel *Don Quixote* his full attention in writing his play. The fact is quite apparent at this point in the action, for the author has carried us through the full idea of the novel by using only a few samplings from the work and yet he has adapted these so well to the stage that his presentation has a tremendous impact on the audience. There is no intermission, and yet it is not necessary; if there were one it would tend to destroy the building inter-involvement of the audience, prisoners, and Cervantes.

The Don Quixote story ends when he is taken back home—Cervantes had not completed his manuscript. The prisoners become angry and prepare to burn the work, for they have seen themselves pictured and realize the horror of their lives. Cervantes has not given them any answer to their predicament and they know it is necessary to have at least a ray of hope to survive. Cervantes begs them not to burn it: "A few moments only! Let me improvise. . . ." Quickly he sets up a scene in the broken knight's bedroom. The family is gathered around his bed, and the Padre feels that there is little time left for the old man to live. Sancho appears and talks to the dying man. Because of Sancho's "little gossip . . . a little chat . . . a little idle talk . . . of this and that," Don Quixote seems

to revive somewhat from his delirium. Aldonza enters and begs him to bring back the dream of Dulcinea. The old knight revives after remembering the "Quest" and he plans to begin his search anew but he dies. While the Padre sings the last rites the Captain of the Inquisition comes to take Cervantes away. Meanwhile the prisoners have been so moved by his story that they return his manuscript and the Governor says, "Plead as well there as you did here and you may not burn." Cervantes is led away as the prisoners join in singing "The Impossible Dream."

Mr. Wasserman has written a stirring and beautiful drama which brings us the man Cervantes as well as Don Quixote. Cervantes strives and reaches the audience as well as the prisoners. Quixote fights the windmill, meets his "lady," and goes through several of the incidents in the novel. In addition to capturing much of the spirit of the novel, the play also gives us some light into the background of Cervantes himself. But another quality of the play is difficult to explain in words. It is the spirit, the emotional impact of his work, something which was carried from his first creation, through his collaborators and actors, into the response of the audience. *Man of La Mancha* is experienced and should be remembered as one of the finished and noteworthy musical dramas of this or any other decade of the past fifty years.

Lee Petrie Ruddle

THE MAN WHO CRIED I AM

Author: John A. Williams (1925-   )
Publisher: Little, Brown and Company (Boston). 403 pp. $6.95
Type of work: Novel
Time: 1930's–1960's
Locale: New York, Africa, Europe

A wide-ranging story of the black man in the white world of the present

Principal characters:
MAX REDDICK, a black American journalist and author
MARGRIT WESTOEVER, his white Dutch wife
LILLIAN PATCH, his first love, a black from New York
HARRY AMES, Max's friend, also a successful black American writer
CHARLOTTE, his white wife
BERNARD ZUTKIN, Max's literary mentor
JAJA ENZKWU, an African diplomat who first discovers the King Alfred Plan
MINISTER Q, a militant black nationalist

John A. Williams' novel moves with great energy over a wide landscape. The protagonist, Max Reddick, takes part in such diverse events as literary cocktail parties in New York and shoot-outs in Europe; he converses with the President of the United States, and he reports a Congolese revolution. Our attention never flags as the plot hurries from one interesting happening to another. Yet, the novel is not merely a slick adventure story: its themes are important and its conclusions ominous.

One can only guess to what extent *The Man Who Cried I Am* is autobiographical. Both author and protagonist struggled through difficult times establishing literary careers. Of the three novels written by Williams prior to *The Man Who Cried I Am,* the first, *The Angry Ones,* was compared unfavorably with the works of Ralph Ellison and James Baldwin, and the third, *Sissie,* was published during a New York newspaper strike, thereby eliminating publicity and reviews. The second novel, *Night Song,* won for him a year at the American Academy in

Rome, but because he was black and rumored to be marrying a white woman, the unanimous vote of the panel was reversed. This scandalous event is re-created in the novel when Harry Ames, under similar circumstances, is denied a European sabbatical. The kind of bitter indignation Williams must have felt when his award was revoked runs throughout the novel. If he fears the power a racist America has over its blacks, he even more hates the cruel injustices that have already taken place.

The novel begins in Amsterdam where Max Reddick sits in a café. His eyes glazed over from the librium, alcohol, and other drugs he has taken to dull the constant, agonizing pain of rectal cancer, he is dying and knows it. He has no idea that the next day he will be dead, not from cancer, but at the hands of an American agent. Nor does he realize that it will be his decision alone whether a bloody revolution will engulf America, and that in making the decision, he will cause his own death but gain a sense of self that has eluded him all his life.

The central theme of the novel concerns Max's seeking out his unique identity. His problem is more complex than that of an ordinary man because both his color and his occupation demand passivity. Always defined by others, he is unable to define himself. As a black, he must play the game of accommodation and compromise, forced by white society to assume unauthentic postures. As a writer, he cannot act in any way that has real consequences, but must simply provide commentary on those who do act. So he sits in the Amsterdam café, proud of nothing he has done, tired, and bored with writing, politics, and people. He is waiting to see his ex-wife, but only to say goodbye. His existence is affirmed, ironically, only by the thing that is killing him, the fatal pain deep in his bowels. "He was sure of one thing: that he was; that he existed. The pain in his ass told him so."

During the next twenty-four hours Max reflects on his life, on those events and people who have contributed to what he has made of himself. We might wish that the characters in the novel (excepting Max) were portrayed with more fullness, as more completely rounded persons. That they fail to achieve this stature is lamentable, but they do serve a crucial function in Max's search for his identity. Most of the characters, the blacks in particular, have formed distinct ideologies in coping with a racist society. From this wide variety of life styles that Max encounters, his own philosophy is formed, his own identity is molded.

Lillian Patch, Max's first love, seeks to accommodate herself completely to the values of American society. She expects Max to give up the economically unstable life of a novelist so that they might live a comfortable middle-class life. Max looks for a job but finds only hate for both the employers who discriminate against him and for himself for prostituting his real talent as a novelist. Lillian becomes pregnant; rather than force Max to marry her, she has an abortion which, done illegally and recklessly, kills her. Max is filled with a bitter loathing for a white society that has seduced Lillian and him into sharing its values, and then because of mindless prejudice, denied them the realization of their hopes.

As a reporter for *Pace Magazine*, Max encounters two Negro leaders whose opposing philosophies delineate clearly the differences between a violent and nonviolent ideology. Covering a boycott in Altea, he meets the Reverend Paul Durrell (a close fictional resemblance to Dr. Martin Luther King, Jr.). Max is impressed with Durrell's quiet determination, leadership, and organizational ability, but there is something about the man that puts him off; Max senses that his nonviolent approach will only invite even more oppression. Max also meets Minister Q, a militant Black Muslim who preaches that blacks should eschew passivity to assume a posture of violent defense. "I call now for black manhood. Dignity. Pride. Don't turn the other cheek any more. Defend yourselves, strike back. . . ." Not for a long time will Max's life reflect the choice he makes between the ideologies of Durrell and Minister Q, but the intellectual decision is clear: his own life and his knowledge of American history tell him that militancy is the only answer.

Late in the novel, Max will have to make a decision he knows will cost him his life. A character he meets early in the book makes that same kind of choice to die. Moses Boatwright, a graduate in philosophy from Harvard, affirms his identity by plumbing the depths of his own evil, committing the absolutely antisocial act of murdering a white man and then eating his heart and genitals. Like Max, he knows he will be killed for his action, but he takes the existentialist consolation that he is master of his fate by determining his own death.

The Man Who Cried I Am is more than a critique of black life within the confines of the United States. Max's job sends him to Africa where he finds different, though equally destructive, white influence. There is, of course, the blatant oppression of the European countries who doggedly cling to their colonial realms. But Williams chooses to describe in more detail and with much scorn the elite of the newly independent countries whose antics mirror all that the white society had stood for.

In Europe, Max joins a colony of Negro expatriates where he hopes to find an environment of literary creativity. Despite great deprivation, Max realized it was better for black writers in Paris, for there they would simply go hungry—in America they would starve and be oppressed as well.

Interracial love is another theme that Williams treats with great sensitivity. Though the status-conscious diplomats who chase after white women are dismissed with contempt, those who marry white women out of love are given ample sympathy and pity because their relationships cannot survive the tensions of a racist society where both whites and newly militant blacks condemn interracial marriage. Max's marriage to Margrit, a fine, loving Dutch woman, exposes him so often to the undisguised hate and hostility of American whites that he realizes he can no longer suffer passively. In this realization he comes close to finding what he really is: Max Reddick, a black American, ready now to kill rather than be degraded. He buys guns, polishes them, and practices again and again. As a later decision will cost him his life, this decision to arm himself costs him his marriage. What is deadly real to Max is to Margrit paranoid fantasy. They quarrel and she leaves him to return to Amsterdam.

The final episode of the novel finds Max in Leiden. Through some papers left by his friend, Harry Ames, Max learns of the King Alfred Plan, a "final solution" devised by high U.S. government officials, whereby a massive mobilization of police and army personnel would either export to Africa or exterminate the twenty-two million black Americans. Max is stunned momentarily into inaction. Before him is documented proof of what Minister Q has said all along about the evil of the "white devil." To release the King Alfred Plan would be to turn America into a nightmare of violence, but for Max the truth must be told and the dreadful consequences accepted, even welcomed. "Black bodies will jam the streets. . . . Those people are going to tear up that unreal tranquility that exists in the United States. . . . I am going to loose those beasts, black and white, and when they are through . . . we will know just where we stand. It will be a start." Max's beliefs suddenly become personally relevant, his purpose clear, his identity finally found. Significantly, it is Minister Q, whose philosophy most closely resembles his own, to whom Max releases the news. Max is prepared to die for his actions; following an automobile chase and a shoot-out, he is murdered by American intelligence agents.

Some critics have complained that Williams has cheapened an otherwise fine novel by tacking on an implausible and melodramatic denouement. In defense of Williams it must be admitted that in terms of the logic of the novel, and with an eye to recent world history, the ending is horrible and frightening, but certainly not impossible.

The Man Who Cried I Am is more than a condemnation of a racist society. Williams touches with great concern on the agonizing problems of interracial love and treats extremely well the loneliness and anxiety of a committed writer. He is at his best, however, when he transcends completely topical and political problems to portray the most basic and human theme of all, that of conquering self-doubt to realize who one truly is.

Timothy H. Gunn

THE MAN WHO LOVED CHILDREN

Author: Christina Stead (1902-   )
Publisher: Holt, Rinehart and Winston (New York). 527 pp. $5.95
Type of work: Novel
Time: The 1930's
Locale: Washington, Ann Arbor, Harper's Ferry, Singapore

A study of the collapse of a very unusual family which ultimately embodies all families

> *Principal characters:*
> SAMUEL CLEMENS POLLIT (SAM), the man who loved children
> HENRIETTA COLLYER POLLIT, Sam's second wife
> LOUISA, Sam's daughter by his first wife
> ERNEST,
> EVELYN,
> SAUL,
> SAM,
> THOMAS, Sam's children by his second wife
> BONNIE and
> JO, Sam's sisters
> OLD ELLEN, Henrietta's mother
> HARRIET, Henrietta's sister
> MADELEINE VINES,
> GILLIAN ROEBUCK, and
> MRS. VIRGINIA PRESCOTT, Sam's loves
> BERT ANDERSON, Henrietta's lover
> NADEN, Sam's Malayan secretary

Christina Stead's novel, first issued in 1940, has enjoyed a rebirth during the past year, when the attention of some of the United States' most distinguished writers and poets brought to a new edition a new respect. The book jacket carries plaudits from no less important figures than Hortense Calisher, Robert Lowell, Elizabeth Hardwick, Jean Stafford, and Peter Taylor. The introduction, which is both a commentary and an appreciation, is by the late Randall Jarrell, who says that this novel "knows as few books have ever known—knows specifically, profoundly, exhaustively—what a family is: if all mankind had been reared in orphan asylums for a thousand years, it could learn to have families again by reading *The Man Who Loved Children*." The kind of praise that is given this novel is hard for any work to live up to.

This is actually four stories in one, not in the sense that there are four parallel stories, but that there are four different plots which are all part of one plot; for in this book what happens to one character happens to all. Thus, in the final analysis, the collapse of the Pollit family is the collapse of all of the Pollits and all of those who revolve, in one way or another, around the Pollits.

The personality that fills the book and shapes the personalities of the other characters is that of Sam Pollit, a scientist working for the government. Sam, who was born into poverty, has sought ever since to rise out of it. He is engaged in the eternal search for happiness, which consists, for him not in material gain, but in the illusion of material gain. He is happy to live in a huge house he cannot afford, in the midst of a large family he cannot really support. As long as he can build for himself an illusion that he owns the world he is satisfied.

Mr. Jarrell says that "Kim was the Little Friend of all the World; Sam is its Little Father." This is indeed the keystone of Sam's personality; his life is a fight to replace the Earth Mother with Sam the Little Father. He wants to become the Pied Piper of the world, and he creates the illusion of his success out of the whole cloth of his family. Jarrell says that "We can bear to read about Sam, a finally exasperating man, only because he is absolutely funny and absolutely true." The reason why this man built of illusion becomes real for the reader is that he is constantly seen through the eyes of children, to whom illusion is reality. And if ever a man was perfectly constructed for the world of children, it is Sam. Nowhere is this more evident than in his language:

> Bring up your tea, Looloo-girl: I'm sick, hot head, nedache [headache], dot pagans in my stumjack [got pains in my stomach]: want my little fambly around me this morning. We'll have a corroboree afterwards when I get better.

What destroys Sam, finally, is that he becomes so much a part of childhood that he is too much even for the children.

Sam searches for love in an ever widening circle of loves. He collects lovers in relationships that are as sterile as his life. Madeleine Vines, Gillian Roebuck, Mr. Virginia Prescott, and his wife Henrietta are all unable to fill his void; he can only satisfy himself with the memories of his dead first wife Rachel, as he escapes once more into illusion. The only time that Sam even approaches an objective realization of his situation is in his conversations with Naden, his Malayan secretary on a scientific expedition. But Sam is unable to escape his predicament; he is unable to avoid telling the world, in effect, to ravish him—to crush him. And the world, in its usual way obliges.

As much as this is Sam's story, it is also Henrietta's. In her suicide is the dissolution of the Pollits objectified. Where Sam reacts positively to the world, she exemplifies a negative reaction which can only culminate in her taking her own life. Her wealthy background is her cross, for she is unable to make even a minor adjustment to Sam's improvidence. Her legacy is her trump, and when it fails to take the trick, the only world she has ever been able to trust has failed her. The shock is too great.

Her marriage to Sam is by no description a happy one. She resents having to worry about money. She resents the children with whom she has been saddled. Most of all, she resents Sam's ability to escape into a world of illusion when she has nowhere to escape to. She tries to escape into a pitiful affair with Bert Anderson, from which she garners five dollars now and then, but no answers to her despair. The only course she finds left is to drink a cup of tea loaded with cyanide. This, ironically enough, is her only authentic act.

Both Sam and Henrietta have their counterparts among the children. Sam's is Louisa, his daughter by his first wife. This ugly duckling, the workhorse of the family, forced to take over the motherhood that Henrietta has abdicated, wraps herself in an illusion every bit as insidious as Sam's. Even as she must act the mother, she herself longs to be mothered, and she ultimately convinces herself that Henrietta (who actually hates her) is a true mother to her. The irony of Louisa's situation is that in her mother's family there is a place for her, and love, but she has a compulsion to make Henrietta her mother. Interestingly, it is Louisa who emerges as the only character who has any real strength. Yet she seems at the end as destined as any for unhappiness.

Henrietta's reflection can be seen in Ernest. Henrietta's longing to regain a position of wealth is reflected in Ernest's obsession with money. Ernest must not only acquire money, but also he must hoard it, and manipulate it, and manipulate others with it. If, as at the end of the story, he has to face a temporary setback, he nevertheless remains undaunted.

The Man Who Loved Children has a strangely gothic character about it. It is not that the characters or the plot are fantastic, for the novel pictures a very real (if somewhat exaggerated) world. It is rather that the reality itself seems fantastic, as if it were something one does not *want* to be real. Mr. Jarrell says in the introduction: "The book has an almost frightening power of re-membrance; and so much of our earlier life is repressed, forgotten, both in the books we read and the memories we have, that this seems friendly of the book, even when what it reminds us of is terrible." Indeed, the thrill of this novel is very like the delicious thrill of a particularly frightful horror story.

The writing in the book is not without flaws, and it is because of the writing that the book may be a great failure. In her attempt to picture the Pollit family in its totality, Christian Stead tells too much; a more judicious selection of details would be a relief. The style is a curious adaptation of stream-of-consciousness technique into a kind of stream-of-action technique. Every scene is given second by second, with one action flowing into the next, no matter how minor. The novel is like a motion picture with no editing, no cuts, and there is a great lifting of tedium each time the scene changes.

Nevertheless, the book is a compelling one. The fascination of discovering how this incredible, yet incredibly real, family will work itself out is inescapable, and the result is a significant statement about the human condition.

Vincent Stewart

THE MAN WHO NEVER WAS

Author: Ewen Montagu (1901-   )
With a foreword by Lord Ismay
Publisher: J. B. Lippincott Company (Philadelphia). 160 pp. $2.75
Type of work: Narrative of espionage
Time: World War II
Locale: England and Spain

The account of an elaborate wartime hoax that tricked the German High Command and prepared the way for the Sicilian invasion, in a spy story which proves that truth is often stranger than fiction

To confuse and mislead the enemy has always been one of the prime objectives of war. The first instance on record is the episode of the Trojan horse—or "Operation Equine" as it would probably be called in the code books of modern strategy planners. The most recent is the story of "Operation Mincemeat" as told in *The Man Who Never Was,* one of the most fascinating yarns to emerge from behind the veil of secrecy which continues to hang over the maze of plots and counterplots staged behind the scenes during World War II.

The Man Who Never Was holds no pretensions to literary merit. It is straightforward and factual in material and style. But it is, for all that, one of the best spy stories in years, more fantastic than anything from the pen of E. Phillips Oppenheim, that old master of espionage in fiction, or in the novels of younger, more realistic Eric Ambler. The true facts can now be revealed, perhaps, because the central situation, the planting of false information on a body cast ashore on the Spanish coast, has already been given fictional treatment in *Operation Heartbreak,* the late Duff Cooper's short novel which disturbed certain British officials when it appeared several years ago. The great virtue of Ewen Montagu's book is that every improbable detail is simple truth, so improbable and yet so simple, in

fact, that it deceived German General Intelligence, Hitler, and the German High Command to the extent that troops and materiel were diverted from Sicily well in advance of the Allied invasion.

The idea of "Operation Mincemeat" occurred to Lt.-Comdr. Ewen Montagu, R. N. V. R., while he was serving on an inter-departmental committee dealing with questions of security at the time of "Operation Torch," as the invasion of North Africa was designated. Plans for "Operation Husky," the invasion of Europe, were also well under way, with Sicily as the logical objective. Although Winston Churchill had declared, "Anybody but a damn' fool would know it is Sicily," there was every need to keep the enemy in the dark and prevent them from pinpointing the invasion spot by holding out such possibilities as Sardinia, Yugoslavia, Southern France, and Greece. Commander Montagu's scheme was to make sure that false information would reach the Germans seemingly by accident and so convincingly that all circumstantial evidence would appear genuine and the information real. He reasoned in this fashion:

What you, a Briton with a British background, think can be deduced from a document does not matter. It is what *your opposite number,* with his German knowledge and background will think that matters—what construction *he* will put on the document. Therefore, if you want *him* to think such-and-such a thing, you must give him something which will make *him* (and not *you*) think it. But he may be suspicious and want confirmation; you must think out what enquiries will *he* make (not what enquiries would *you* make) and give him the answers to those enquiries so as to satisfy him.

It was with these facts in mind that Commander Montagu planned to secure a body, give it the identity of a British officer bearing messages and letters, and let it float ashore in supposedly neutral Spain, where German secret agents were especially active at the time. In this way, with official approval, the fictitious Major William Martin, Royal British Marines, came into existence. The first and most difficult step was to obtain a body. One was found at last, that of a man who had died of pneumonia after exposure, a form of death that would not be inconsistent with the condition of a man supposed to have died after an airplane crash at sea; it was necessary, however, for Montagu and his fellow officers of the Naval Intelligence Division to promise that the man's real name would never be disclosed.

This account of the creation of a personality for a man who had never lived has all the qualities of a mystery thriller. It was decided, after much consideration, to make him an officer of the Royal Marines on the staff of Lord Louis Mountbatten, Chief of Combined Operations, a billet that would explain his role as a trusted emissary. Three "official" letters were prepared. One, signed by General Sir Archibald Nye, Vice-Chief of the Imperial General Staff, was informally directed to General Alexander at 18th Group Headquarters in Africa. In it Nye indicated that "Operation Husky" would be directed against Greece and a second, "Operation Brimstone," against Sardinia, with a diverting operation against Sicily as a cover target for the invasion of Sardinia. Another letter, from Lord Mountbatten to Admiral Sir Andrew Cunningham, commander in chief of the Mediterranean fleet, explained Major Martin's mission and by a pun also suggested that Sardinia was to be the invasion point. A third letter, also from Mountbatten, was directed to General Dwight Eisenhower at Allied Headquarters, Algiers, and asked him to write a brief foreword for a pamphlet to be distributed throughout the U. S. Army.

The next step was to create a personality for Major Martin. On his person he carried such items as love letters from Pam, his fiancée, a snapshot of the girl, a letter in which his father stiffly disapproved of a sudden wartime engagement, an unpaid bill for the engagement ring, a dunning letter concerning an overdraft of seventy-nine pounds at Lloyds Bank, naval identification cards, theater ticket stubs, a St. Christopher medal—stage properties that would build up a convincing picture of Major Martin, R. B. M. The body was then put aboard the submarine *Seraph* and set afloat in an inflated Mae West off the Spanish town of Huelva. Attached to the body by a courier's chain was a briefcase containing the letters from top British officials.

The plan succeeded beyond all expectations. The supposed Major Martin was buried in Huelva and in time his papers were returned to London through official channels. Because there was evidence that they had been tampered with while in the possession of Spanish authorities, it seemed certain that the information they contained had been passed on to German Intelligence. Winston Churchill was in Washington at the time; the British Chiefs of Staff sent him a cryptic message, "Mincemeat swallowed whole."

So it turned out. General Rommel was ordered to Greece to take command of forces assembled there in preparation for an invasion assault on the Greek islands, and the 1st German Panzer Division was sent from France to Tripolis in the Peloponnesus. A group of German R-boats was also dispatched from Sicily to the Aegean. Meanwhile fortifications and reinforcements had been increased on Corsica and Sardinia. Even after the invasion of Sicily had been launched, the German High Command continued to regard it as a cover attack to divert men and supplies from the expected attack on Sardinia. In Sicily, at least, Winston Churchill's description of the "soft under-belly of Europe" was proved true in part because of the role played by a man who never existed except in the minds of some Naval Intelligence officers.

This book is a genuine story of suspense, not of curiosity as to the outcome, however, since that is known well in advance, but in the ingenious and patient dovetailing of one bit of evidence with another to make every circumstantial detail ring true in inventing a man, a mission, and a personality. Since absolute secrecy had to be observed, only a few people could be in on the scheme; consequently awkward questions were asked when some service departments accepted Major Martin as a bona-fide officer and reports of his death reached the Naval Wills Department and the Medical Director-General's Department. But Naval Intelligence had enough prestige to cover its tracks and halt further inquiries. For this reason the true story of Major Martin was never revealed until it could be told by the man who invented him and carried out the hoax in which the man who never was played so important a part.

THE MAN WITHOUT QUALITIES: VOLUME II

Author: Robert Musil (1880-1942)
Translated from the German by Eithne Wilkins and Ernest Kaiser
Publisher: Coward-McCann (New York). 454 pp. $5.00
Type of work: Novel
Time: 1913-1914
Locale: Vienna

A comedy of ideas analyzing the consciousness of modern man and set in Vienna, 1913-1914

Principal characters:
ULRICH, the Man Without Qualities
LIEGE-COUNT LEINSDORF, moving spirit of the Collateral Campaign
DIOTIMA, Ulrich's cousin, an aspiring intellectual
HERR DR. PAUL ARNHEIM, a Prussian tycoon
GENERAL STUMM VON BORDWEHR, another member of the Campaign Committee
MOOSBRUGGER, a carpenter, a sexual maniac and murderer

Robert Musil planned to write *The Man Without Qualities* in four sections, but had completed only two in their entirety when he died suddenly in 1942. This fact, however, does not interfere seriously with the interest or significance of the novel, for it is not a story in the usual sense; rather, it is an extended analysis and exemplification of the ideas, emotional states, and social behavior of modern man.

Ulrich, the Man Without Qualities, is so designated because he perfectly epitomizes *all* qualities of modern man. He is, as the translators of the book remark in their Foreword, "the man in whom all qualities merge spectrally into the whiteness of none." Ulrich, like Musil himself, was a man of versatile accomplishments, trained in military science, engineering, mathematics, philosophy, and psychology. Consequently, his awareness of diversity revealed to him that no unifying ideas and values underlay the Central European civilization he belonged to. In the Austria of Emperor Franz-Joseph the appearance of significant order was a formal illusion, an anachronism, like the emperor himself.

Actually, modern life was a chaos of cliques and individuals at cross-purposes; under superficial order was a profound disintegration, and society, like a shattered vessel, kept a precarious habit of arrangement amongst its splintered particles before falling into shards. So many of these segments of reality were comprehended in Ulrich's consciousness that they neutralized one another and left him uncommitted to anything in particular. His nihilism was confirmed by his belief that real things are just a kind of unstable and inadequate metaphor for possibility, that realities should therefore not be taken literally. When he considered how little even those persons who "believed in" reality agreed upon what it was or what was worthwhile about it, his detachment became philosophically inevitable.

The story or "fable" of *The Man Without Qualities* is an ironic, endlessly digressive parable of intellectual nihilism. There is a pervading irony in its essential situation. On the eve of the first World War, which was to bring about the dissolution of the decadent Austro-Hungarian Empire, a

"Collateral Campaign" was instituted to plan a year of grandiose celebration, in 1918, of the seventy-year reign of Emperor Franz-Joseph.

Accordingly, the Man Without Qualities, although skeptical about the values of reality generally and of his own society especially, was maneuvered into becoming Secretary of this campaign and its presiding intelligence. The sponsors of the campaign hoped to redefine Austrian greatness and to inspire the Empire to a rededication, and incidentally to intimate to the world that Prussian might was a less significant phenomenon than Austrian culture (this incidental purpose accounted for the word *Collateral*). Ulrich, who undertook unwillingly the office of Secretary, saw that both its occasion and its purpose were hollow, misconceived, and intrinsically incapable of being made significant. Also, he soon found that the persons and organizations whose aid was solicited or accepted were all in monomaniac pursuit of particular and conflicting interests, and were all seeking to convert the campaign into a scheme for promoting them.

Nearly all the characters of the novel were connected in some way with the Collateral Campaign. Its moving spirit was the Liege-Count Leinsdorf, who wanted the Campaign to define and give prestige to the great traditions of Austria. Unfortunately, he had merely a sentiment rather than a conception of the noble traditions of the Empire, and his part in the campaign consisted mostly of trying to find persons who might produce more definite ideas on the subject. "Something must be done!" was his constant slogan, but he could think of nothing to do but set up more committees and call for more suggestions. All the grand ideas produced

were nebulous; all the definite ideas were trivial; it seemed impossible to frame an idea to animate the Campaign that was both grand enough and definite enough. Ulrich morosely remarked that "one can realise demands for an Emperor-Francis-Joseph-Jubilee-Year-Soup-Kitchen, or fulfill those of the Society for the Care and Protection of Domestic Cats, but one can no more give solid and enduring form to great thoughts than to music!"

Another leader in the enterprise was Ulrich's cousin "Diotima," wife of a leading government official. She was a statuesque but vacuous woman, fond of speaking of "soul," not because the word meant anything to her but because uttering it was accompanied by sensations of sublimity. She sought for a suggestion which would give soul to the enterprise.

Diotima brought into the Campaign Herr Dr. Paul Arnheim, a Prussian tycoon, whose immense wealth, international connections, Prussian nationality, partly Jewish origin, universal but not altogether sound learning, and suave cosmopolitanism made his colleagues in the Campaign regard him as a man too complex and ambiguous to be fully trusted. In addition to being an international financier, Arnheim was a "superman of letters," a kind of promoter and stock-broker of intellectual enterprises. "The superman of letters is a successor to the prince of the intellect, a substitution corresponding in the sphere of mind to the replacement of princes by rich men that has taken place in the political sphere." Arnheim is Musil's ironic embodiment of the notion that what popularly passes for an intellectual genius in the modern world is an enormously successful intellectual mediocrity—power in combination with the commonplaces that pass current as wisdom to ordinary minds. "Arnheim would advise the Lord to organise the Millennium on business principles and entrust the administration of it to a big business man, one, it went without saying, who must also have encyclopaedic knowledge and a philosophic outlook."

Another personage assisting in the Campaign was the fatuous, literal-minded General Stumm von Bordwehr, who sought a grand idea to inspire the Campaign by applying methodical military procedures. The Jubilee Year was to be, among other things, a "Peace Year," and the General argued at first that on this account it ought to be dedicated to building up Austria's military strength, according to the familiar argument that military might deters nations from going to war —or at least makes wars shorter if they do occur. When this logic was rejected as dubious, he visited the State Library, intending to read all the books in order to abstract possible ideas from them, but desisted when he saw how many books there were. Later he proposed that the Campaign Committee should undertake to collect and classify all the great ideas of history, in order to sift them and select the grandest of all to animate the Campaign.

Against this attempt to bolster monarchial pride, Musil presents the story of a carpenter named Moosbrugger, a sexual maniac under sentence of death for murdering a streetwalker. His arrest and trial have created public interest throughout the Empire. Many of the other characters are fascinated by this man, who apparently represents to them their subconscious and suppressed desires. "If mankind could dream collectively," reflects Ulrich, "it would dream Moosbrugger." He reminds civilized and thoughtful and moral man, who tries to make reality conscious, rational, and controllable, how much of it is essentially unconscious, irrational, and uncontrollable.

Given these persons and this situation, the great Collateral Campaign gets nowhere; it merely brings to light the uncertainties and disagreements among its agents. The book is a comic view of the modern Wasteland, as many-vistaed and inconclusive as Sterne's *Tristram Shandy*. Musil unpacks the consciousness of Twentieth-Century Man. The writer has a modern view of history: he feels that men are involved in history, but do not make it; that the order of history is all in the past. He has a modern sense of time, like Bergson's or Whitehead's—a belief, stated by Ulrich, in an emergent reality more important than the Here-and-Now appearance which reality takes on relatively to any particular generation. Finally, Musil's book could not have been written without Freudian psychology and modern science. It psychoanalyzes modern society and finds God and Devil to be psychological metaphors and civilization to be a precarious artifice which by no means accounts for all of human character and behavior. Although it is often boringly digressive, a sophisticated reader will find this book a formidable and challenging intellectual adventure, replete with epigrammatic irony.

MANCHILD IN THE PROMISED LAND

Author: Claude Brown (1937-   )
Publisher: The Macmillan Company (New York). 415 pp. $5.95
Type of work: Autobiography
Time: The 1950's
Locale: Harlem and Greenwich Village in New York City

Memoirs, in which the author recounts his childhood and early manhood on the streets of Harlem

Principal personages:
    CLAUDE BROWN, the author
    MAMA, his mother
    DAD, his father
    PIMP, his brother
    THE BOYS, on the streets, in the jails, and in the reform schools
    THE STAFF OF THE WILTWYCK SCHOOL FOR BOYS
    MR. PAPANEK, the director of the Wiltwyck School for Boys
    JUDY, the white girl

The opening sentences of *Manchild in the Promised Land* are startling, but they are no more startling than the story that Claude Brown has to tell, the true account of what it is like to grow up in an atmosphere of poverty, violence, and fear. Using the age-old principle of the narrative hook, Brown begins with the most important incident in his life, when "there was a bullet in me trying to take my life, all thirteen years of it." The bullet that threatened Brown was merely one more shot fired in the war that engaged all of the young Harlem Negroes of Brown's generation, the war they fought as they tried to come to terms with a ghetto world.

The significance of Claude Brown's story in a time of ghetto riots, freedom marches, and political bickering over problems of race relations is clear. The insight that the book offers into the sources of these riots is only one of many reasons why the book is worth reading. Claude Brown shows the despair, the hopelessness, the directionlessness of lives which can result in senseless rioting; he demonstrates the valuelessness of lives which have no ethic to restrain them when the opportunity to riot arises.

The picture that Brown paints is all the more effective because it is written in a readable and exciting style. In the first place, he is in full command of his medium; he is able to call on all the resources of syntax and rhetoric to produce a clear, readable exposition and at times a moving evocation of the passions that consume the Harlem youth. In the second place, the lexicon on which he draws is often the lexicon of the streets, so that the flavor and sound of Harlem life are always with the reader. The result is a fast-paced narrative which, if it has a fault, tends at times to overpower the reader. The high emotional pitch maintained throughout sometimes makes one wish for a short low-key passage for relief.

The promised land of the title is that sought by the parents of Brown's generation when they immigrated to Harlem from the South. What they found instead of milk and honey was squalor, unemployment, and more prejudice. The plantation owner of the South

was replaced by Goldberg, the landlord, and the unfeeling policeman
(there is more than a hint of anti-
Semitism, but it may be that the Jew
simply became the symbol of White to
the inhabitants of the Harlem ghetto).
Consequently, they merely entered
into a situation more hopeless than the
one they had left.

These immigrants had, if anything,
a worse world to offer their children.
And as these children grew older the
rift between them and their parents
grew wider. Their lives no longer had
the stability of the plantation; they
were on their own without the social
and ethnic pillars of morality and
ethics to sustain them. The younger
generation were able to taste just
enough of what freedom means to
want a better life, while their parents
were satisfied with the *status quo*, or
feared what a fight for change might
bring:

> The slang had changed. In this day
> when somebody would say something
> about a bad cat, they meant that he
> was good. . . . I couldn't get it over to
> Mama that things were changing. The
> bad nigger to my generation was a cat
> like Paul Robeson. To Mama, that was
> a nigger who was crazy, who would go
> out and marry some white woman.
> Mama and Dad would associate a nig-
> ger like this with the ones they saw
> hanging from a pine tree down in the
> Carolina woods with blood on his pants.
> They'd say this wasn't a bad nigger to
> them, this was a crazy nigger, one that
> was going to get himself hanged.

The result was that childhood in the
Harlem ghetto was not childhood at
all. As Brown describes growing up in
Harlem, it was like some sadistic sort of
fraternity hazing to which there was
no end. The environment was not one
which inspired good citizenship:

> When I was very young . . . I would
> always be sitting out on the stoop. . . .
> Because there was so much out there in
> that street.
>
> You might see somebody get cut or
> killed. I could go out in the street for
> an afternoon, and I would see so much
> that, when I came in the house, I'd be
> talking and talking for what seemed
> like hours. Dad would say, "Boy why
> don't you stop that lyin'? You know you
> didn't see all that. You know you didn't
> see nobody do that." But I knew I had.

The lack of any opportunity for a full
childhood is pointed up by one of
Brown's friends, a young con artist
whose life ran from one jail sentence to
the next.

> "Man, Sonny [Brown], they ain't got
> no kids in Harlem. . . . I've seen some
> real small people actin' like kids. . . .
> But they don't have any kids in Harlem,
> because nobody has time for a child-
> hood . . . kids are happy, kids laugh,
> kids are secure. They ain't scared-a
> nothin'. You ever been a kid, Sonny?
> . . . I don't ever remember being
> happy and not scared."

Brown is, indeed, at his best when he is
describing childhood in Harlem. He
demonstrates relentlessly that the children of his generation were cheated
from the first, that the only opportunity they had was the opportunity they
took and that only when by some miracle they realized there was an opportunity to take.

Nevertheless, Brown reveals that
there was a kind of search for values,
but that search was almost always unsuccessful. It was next to impossible to
keep young men in school; the accepted game was escape-the-truant
officer. And if the schools were not
given a chance, the homes had nothing
better to offer, for too often the parents
had either never begun or given up the
search:

When I was a little boy, Mama and Dad would beat me and tell me, "You better be good," but I didn't know what being good was. To me, it meant that they just wanted me to sit down and fold my hands or something crazy like that. Stay in front of the house, don't go anyplace, don't get into trouble. I didn't know what it meant, and I don't think they knew what it meant, because they couldn't ever tell me what they really wanted. The way I saw it, everything I was doing was good. If I stole something and didn't get caught, I was good. If I got into a fight with somebody, I tried to be good enough to beat him. If I broke into a place, I tried to be quiet and steal as much as I could. I was always trying to be good. They just kept on beating me and talking about being good. And I just kept on doing what I was doing and trying to be good.

The lack of any firm moral basis from the home is, evidently, what Brown considers as one of the primary causes of the crime that is an accepted part of **ghetto life. The recent studies of** Negro family life seem to be supported by Brown's own experiences.

Brown spends some time discussing the attempts of many Harlem people to find a system of values in religion. His picture of the subjective, evangelical Christianity into which many escaped (particularly the older generation) is not an encouraging one. He pictures this faith as a source of emotional release rather than of any enduring ethic; his description of his own reactions to such services (he was attending to please a girl) proves how little relevance Christianity seemed to have to his life. The Coptic faith, with its emphasis on a Negro Christ and Ethiopia as the land of milk and honey, was able to offer him a more attractive commit-

ment, but even the Coptics were unable to hold his attention for long. Brown was never attracted to the Black Muslims, but his attitude toward them is interesting. According to Brown, the extreme militancy of the Muslims is a relatively recent development. He describes them as one more attempt to catch the imaginations of Harlem Negroes, but as a group which was gradually being filled with the disillusioned refugees from the reform schools and the jails.

The real system of values operated in the streets; the real ethic was an ethic of the streets. The rule was "do unto others when they do unto you or to your women":

I suppose the main things were the women in the family and the money. This was something we learned very early. If you went to the store and lost some money or if you let somebody gorilla you out of some money that your mother or father had given you, you got your ass beaten when you came back home. You couldn't go upstairs and say, "Well, Daddy, that big boy down there took the money that you gave me to buy some cigars." Shit, you didn't have any business letting anybody take your money. You got your ass whipped for that, and you were supposed to.

The principal goal of Brown and his fellows was to be the most masculine and the most deserving of the title "bad nigger." Brown points out that the best way to prove one's manhood was to kill whoever had threatened that manhood. Consequently, the ethic of the streets demanded murder and celebrated the man who killed. The heroes were those who were martyred in the electric chair because they had proved themselves:

But I think everybody was curious about whether or not it was worth it to kill somebody and save your name or your masculinity, defend whatever it was that had been offended—whether it was you or your woman or someone in your family. It seemed as though nobody would know this any better than the cat who was going to pay with his life, and he wouldn't know it any better than when he was getting ready to pay. If a cat could say it was worth it at the time he was going to give his life for it, who could challenge it? Who could say that it wasn't worth it? This was what everybody wanted to know.

The moment that somebody heard that anybody had gotten cooked, they would say, "Well, man, what did he say?"

I never heard of anybody ever saying it was worth it. They said a lot of things, but nobody ever said it was worth it.

Brown obviously decided it was not worth it, and it is in his description of his search for the road out of Harlem that he shows there is some hope, even in the ghetto. While most of his fellows were escaping into narcotics, crime, and/or death from police guns, execution, or overdoses of heroin, Brown was finding a way out through education. His escape started when he was sent to the Wiltwyck School for Boys; how important that step was is testified by his dedication: "To the late ELEANOR ROOSEVELT, who founded the Wiltwyck School for Boys. And to the WILTWYCK SCHOOL, which is still finding Claude Browns." It was at Wiltwyck that Brown met Mr. Papanek, who taught him that there could be an escape. Even after he left Wiltwyck, he still went to talk to Mr. Papanek, who had the qualities that may eventually solve the problems of slum delinquents:

> It was about this time that I discovered Papanek's secret. It was really very simple. He had the ability to see everybody as they really are—just people, no more and no less. Also he saw children as people, little young people with individuality, not as some separate group of beings called children, dominated by the so-called adult world. Having this ability alone made him a giant at understanding people; being Papanek . . . made him irresistibly likeable.

Papanek was able to convince Brown of what the public schools could not: that his hope lay in education, in learning.

So it was that Claude Brown left home, got a job, and started going to high school in the evenings. He left Harlem for Greenwich Village and found a world that he had not known existed. He began to discover what his opportunities could be, as well as the limitations that a white society insisted on imposing on him. He even dated a white girl for six months, until her parents found out and sent her away. Eventually he made his way to college and into law school—out of the ghetto and into the world.

This is not to say that Claude Brown's story has a completely happy ending, for the ghetto still exists. Harlem continues to take its toll, including Claude Brown's own brother, Pimp, who escaped into the illusory world of heroin. But *Manchild in the Promised Land* does offer hope: Claude Brown is real, and there may be more where he came from.

Vincent Stewart

Sources for Further Study

Reviews:

Best Sellers. XXV, September 1, 1965, p. 225. 850 words.

Book Week. August 22, 1965, p. 5. 1,450 words.

Commentary. XLI, January, 1966, p. 82. 1,800 words.

New Republic. CLIII, September 25, 1965, p. 26. 1,800 words.

New York Review of Books. V, August 26, 1965, p. 8. 2,050 words.

New York Times Book Review. August 22, 1965, p. 1. 1,450 words.

Reporter. XXXIII, November 4, 1965, p. 53. 1,400 words.

THE MANDARINS

Author: Simone de Beauvoir (1908-   )
Translated from the French by Leonard M. Friedman
Publisher: The World Publishing Company (Cleveland and New York). 610 pp. $6
Type of work: Novel
Time: Late 1940's
Locale: France and the United States

A first-hand study of the manners, morals, and political activities of a group of easily identifiable French intellectuals

> Principal characters:
> HENRI PERRON, novelist, editor, and hero of the Resistance
> ROBERT DUBREUILH, an embittered idealist, writer, and fellow traveler
> ANNE DUBREUILH, his wife, a psychiatrist
> NADINE, their daughter
> PAULA, Perron's mistress
> LEWIS BROGAN, an American novelist

Let the reader be warned: *The Mandarins* is not a novel to be read for mere entertainment as that word is generally understood in connection with a work of fiction. In fact, in some ways the book is the dullest novel of 1956—plodding and unimaginative in the story it tells, exasperating in its digressions and the lengthy arguments in which the characters engage, wooden in structure. There are enough entries on the credit side of the ledger, nevertheless, to overbalance for any thoughtful reader the weaknesses of this massive exegesis of existentialist personalities, beliefs, and attitudes. The novel is almost painfully sincere in its revelations of spiritual crisis and moral compromise, brilliant in its handling of dialectic, rich in characterization, accurate in its charting of the political geography and its recordings of the intellectual climate prevailing among the literary mandarins of postwar France.

Most Americans, to many of whom the word "intellectual" is a term of ridicule or reproach, have little conception of the position of privilege and responsibility held by the intellectual in French society. He is the spokesman, often the leader, of groups active in the political, social, and literary life of the nation, and in this connection the example of his private life may be as important to his followers as his public utterances and actions. This is the mandarin class. The intellectual elite indicated by the title of Simone de Beauvoir's novel. Mlle. de Beauvoir writes with the complete familiarity of one who has shared the life she describes, for in existentialist circles today she stands second only to Jean-Paul Sartre, leading figure of this bleak philosophical cult and her long-time associate in public and private life. Although her book passes as fiction, she seems to have changed little except the names of her characters; otherwise we have a clear picture of what Sartre, Camus, Koestler, the author, and a host of lesser figures were thinking, saying, or doing in the period of letdown and readjustment following World War II, when they were no longer united in a common cause by the hardships and ardors of the Resistance. The author's thin disguise makes *The Mandarins* the most thoroughgoing *roman à clef* of modern literature, and for this reason important as a political, social, and personal document.

At least this is the way French readers and critics viewed it. In France the novel received the Goncourt Prize, almost won for its author a chair in the Goncourt Academy, and had a sale of more than a quarter of a million copies. American readers, removed from the intellectual turmoil and political dissension of Mlle. de Beauvoir's mandarin group, are likely to be more temperate in their judgment. Most will give it a place between the biased reporting of this writer's earlier *America Day by Day* and the brilliance of her pamphleteering in *The Second Sex*.

The novel has been built around five key figures: Robert Dubreuilh, a pro-Russian, anti-American writer and philosopher who believes that this is the century of the intellectual and that "politics should never again be left to the politicians"; Henri Perron, a younger writer, editor, and hero of the Resistance who shares many of his older friend's views but who is less an extremist in his political convictions; Anne Dubreuilh, Robert's wife, a psychiatrist and the part-time narrator; Nadine, the Dubreuilhs' daughter, a creature of guilt complexes and moral waywardness, and Paula, Perron's mistress, a woman of profound sexuality who believes naïvely that with the war's end the clock can be turned back while she recaptures the passionate, idyllic spirit with which their love affair began.

The central situation in which these people are involved is undoubtedly the now historic quarrel between Jean-Paul Sartre and Albert Camus. The novel opens in Paris shortly after the Liberation, when the German armies in the field are moving desperately toward their final collapse. The intellectuals and heroes of the Resistance who gather for a victory celebration face a crumbling world of their own, although they are still unaware of their predicament. Their experiences in the Resistance movement have given them a concept of political thinking and intellectual attitudes in terms of absolutes: the traditional Left which looks to the future and is therefore the hope of mankind, the traditional Right, corrupt, impotent, which has become the tool of international power politics: the Proletariat and the Bourgeoisie. To the European intellectual, of course, these concepts are easily identifiable with the dominant nations of the contemporary world, the Soviet Union and the capitalistic United States. Morose, despairing, Sartre-like Dubreuilh is an intellectual Jacobin who sees in Russia the only possible political and cultural hope for all men of good will. To this end he organizes an anti-American political group, the S.R.L.

Perron's influential paper is associated with this group, but, less committed to a program of political action, the young writer finds it difficult to close his eyes to the fact that Communist ideology and the totalitarian practices of the Party are one thing in theory but far apart in actual fact. Moved by the dictates of his own conscience, he prints a story which reveals the truth about Russian slave labor camps, thereby wrecking the S.R.L. and bringing down on himself the wrath of Dubreuilh, whose attitude is expressed in these words: "My duties as an intellectual, my respect for the truth—that's all so much idle chatter! The only question is to know whether, in denouncing the camps, you're working for mankind or against it." Here we have an illustration of the moral compromises so common in European intellectual life today, results of a state of spiritual blindness or political credulity that most Americans find impossible to understand.

Anne Dubreuilh, meanwhile, has tried to find her own way out of this muddle of tension and feud by an affair with an American novelist, Lewis Brogan, whose speciality is the wilder and more sordid aspects of slum life. But this experience proves unsatisfactory in the end and Anne returns to Paris to face the existentialistic emptiness of her life there. She is driven close to suicide by realization that life holds no meaning or purpose except that which each human must find for himself, but she finally makes her own compromise with her situation through a decision to be useful to others. Paula, disappointed in the possessive nature of her love for Perron, goes mad. Nadine marries Perron, for Dubreuilh and the younger writer have rather despairingly reconciled their personal differences and are willing to be rather wary friends as well as relatives by marriage. As publishers of an intellectual journal they are trying once more to serve the twin causes of politics and culture, even though they know that in present-day society the two are often incompatible.

Simone de Beauvoir uses these people and their friends and hangers-on to dramatize an age of tension and crisis. If the novel does nothing else, it helps to explain those aspects of French life and culture which have puzzled Americans over the past decade: the nature of existentialism and the secret of its appeal among the café cultists; the suspicion of America that is balanced by an equally strong attraction Russia holds for the European artist; the attitude of a literary generation represented by Perron, a man of intelligence and conscience who saw his country shamed and himself "an insignificant citizen of a fifth-rate power"; the ability of men like Dubreuilh to make adherence to Communist ideology, at least in theory, a moral duty; the identification of the intellectual with the revolutionary Left as an example of the credulity which extreme skepticism often breeds.

These matters give *The Mandarins* its substance and depth. On the level of private experience the novel becomes a study of the manners and morals of an important element of modern European society. On a more public plane the book is a carefully documented political and moral history of our time in its picture of the Parisian mandarins caught between a world which they have repudiated and one which they are trying to shape.

Sources for Further Study

Criticism:

Reck, Rima Drell. "Les Mandarins: Sensibility, Responsibility," in *Yale French Studies*. 27 (Spring-Summer, 1961), pp. 33-40. *The Mandarins* achieves a complexity which Simone de Beauvoir's earlier novels often lack and examines the author's techniques.

Reviews:

Atlantic. CXCVII, June, 1956, p. 77. 550 words.

Commonweal. LXIV, June 15, 1956, p. 279. 1,200 words.

Nation. CLXXXII, June 9, 1956, p. 493. 1,750 words.

New York Times. May 27, 1956, p. 1. 1,700 words.

New Yorker. XXXII, September 15, 1956, p. 156. 2,100 words.

Saturday Review. XXXIX, May 26, 1956, p. 17. 800 words.

Time. LXVII, May 28, 1956. 1,100 words.

MANDATE FOR CHANGE, 1953-1956
The White House Years: Volume I

Author: Dwight D. Eisenhower (1890-1969)
Publisher: Doubleday and Company (Garden City, New York). Illustrated. 650 pp. $6.95
Type of work: Memoirs
Time: 1953-1956
Locale: Washington and the world

Memoirs in which the thirty-fourth President of the United States tells of the events, as he sees them, leading up to the sweeping mandate, and describes the problems and personalities of his first administration

Principal personages:
DWIGHT D. EISENHOWER
KONRAD ADENAUER
GEORGES BIDAULT
WINSTON CHURCHILL
ANTHONY EDEN
NIKITA KHRUSHCHEV
RICHARD M. NIXON
HERBERT BROWNELL
ALLEN DULLES
MILTON S. EISENHOWER
MAMIE EISENHOWER
JAMES C. HAGERTY
HERBERT S. HOOVER
HARRY S. TRUMAN
JOSEPH R. McCARTHY

The account of the stewardship of President Eisenhower began officially on January twentieth, 1953, when he took the oath of office in Washington as the thirty-fourth president of the United States. So he declares in the first sentence in Chapter I. Chapter XXIV ends with his decision, on February 29, 1956, to run for a second term. In the intervening pages the author discusses with freshness mingled with humor and philosophy his many problems during those crowded years in the White House.

Although a number of the ex-Presidents of the United States, including the last three, have left useful memoirs, one critic calls this present volume something unmatched in presidential literature. Its honest writing reveals a personality differing greatly from his portrait by newspaper reporters and political associates. In looking not only at his victories but also at his partial and complete failures and in telling why he took the steps and what he thought he was accomplishing, Eisenhower reveals himself as a decisive, courageous man who, without arrogance or vanity, was motivated by deep faith and by a carefully evolved philosophy. Throughout the book, however, he never questions his judgments or goes back to reflect on those decisions.

For politicians who complained that he did not give enough help to candidates of his party in off-year elections, he states: "It is doubtful whether a President should intervene too intensively and directly. The President has a duty to exercise leadership in behalf of all the people." His role, he believed, was to explain issues, programs, and achievements in the hope that the majority of Americans would approve and would support the party's candidates and program.

To clarify the situation he faced, the author goes back in time in Chapter I, titled "Prelude to Politics." To a newspaper correspondent, Virgil Pinkley, he gives credit for the earliest suggestion, in 1943, that he run for the presidency. At the time he laughed off the idea, but in 1945 the proposal was repeated by President Truman, who offered support to Eisenhower in order to insure continuity of his own ideas. In view of that statement, the title, *Mandate for Change*, is a bit puzzling.

At the suggestion of Walter Winchell, twenty thousand communications flooded his office during one week in 1946, when he was President of Columbia University, urging him to run, with another deluge as time for the 1952 convention approached. However, rather than the voice of the people, it was the voice of his conscience, he says, as well as his feeling that many politicians were trying to limit the power of the presidency in matters vital to America and the world that persuaded him to enter the New Hampshire primaries of March 11, 1952.

Something of the strain as well as the humor of campaigning appears in the pre-election chapters. This chatty book is full of anecdotes that are both amusing and dramatic. We also get new sidelights on events after charges

had been brought against his running mate, Richard M. Nixon, and on Eisenhower's share in steps taken to present the truth to the voters.

Chapter IV explains Eisenhower's thinking on international problems and the reasoning back of his earliest appointments and acts. His attempts to use Army methods in delegating power, both at the White House and in administration, explain some of the charges against him of failing to push his policies.

Book II opens with an account of Eisenhower's inauguration. Vainly the new President sought to make the inaugural parade short because he had, as he said, "marched in too many parades myself." (He had been among other things, a member of the West Point contingent in Wilson's inaugural in 1913.) He had better success in replacing the tall silk hats by Homburgs for the ceremonies, and he silenced those who stressed tradition by remarking that an even longer-standing tradition decreed tricornered hats and knee breeches. He explains that his lassoing by Roy Rogers during the parade had been prearranged several days before, as part of the high jinks of the Republicans' return to power. However, one quoted incident of the following day was to reveal to him the essential seriousness, as well as the loneliness, of his new office. General Omar Bradley, with whom he had been on an "Ike" and "Brad" basis since 1911, telephoned him and began the conversation with a formal salutation, "Mr. President."

Throughout the book the words "integrity" and "efficiency" contained in his first State of the Union Message are frequently repeated. The dedication to peace of this military man and his religious faith are also constantly reiterated.

He knew he would have problems. Herbert Hoover, from his own experience, had warned him: "Some people will want you to lead them back at full speed to the 'good old days.' Others will want you to initiate welfare programs regardless of their effect on federal financial affairs and the nation's economy. To go back is impossible. Yet to allow present trends to go on is unwise; they will lead to disaster. All you can do is to turn away gradually from the path leading to paternalism until it takes a central course, and then stick to it. And both sides will dislike you."

Eisenhower's path, as he outlines it, was the "Middle of the Road," a course "that preserves the greatest possible initiative, freedom, and independence of body and soul to the individual but that does not hesitate to use government to control cataclysmic economic disasters that can be even more terrible than convulsions of nature."

His political promises continually occupied his mind, despite the slim Republican majority and its lack of practice in coöperating with the Chief Executive. His feeling that a leader should use reason and not force explains why so many of his projects met with only partial success. Too many cowardly Congressmen, he says, put their jobs and their constituents ahead of the country, and he offers as examples the fiascos in taxes, tariffs, and post office efficiency.

Problems of security concern him in Chapter XIII. Earlier he expressed his concern over the casual U.S. attitude toward communism. He writes of his feelings about the Rosenbergs and Dr. Oppenheimer, as well as the 8,008 cases of security lapses discovered during 1953-1954, but mostly the chapter deals with McCarthyism. Accusing newspapers and television publicity of encouraging the senator's career of baseless accusations, he explains his own refusal to inflate McCarthy further by personal combat.

Much of the book, of course, deals with the many extensive foreign problems faced by the President during his first term. How and why he acted are explained with generous praise for those who aided him. "American political, military, and economic influence was being used to help solve old problems, preserve freedom, eliminate traditional antagonisms, and give confidence to weak and exposed nations. We had inherited many problems out of the past. In company with good friends and allies around the globe, from Seoul to Guatemala City to Teheran to London, these problems we have solved." In Latin American problems he acknowledges the assistance of his brother Milton, "a dedicated diplomat with such exceptional capability that were it not for the accident of his being my brother, he would certainly have been asked to occupy a high cabinet post in my administration." Throughout his book, Eisenhower takes particular pains to avoid suspicions of attempting to form a family dynasty. His son John would not have attended the inaugural had not President Truman ordered him temporarily returned from Korea.

National defense is the theme of the last part of Book IV. Because they wanted a military man in charge of national security, many had voted for Eisenhower in 1952. He wryly reports the difficulties of deciding on what sort of defense to spend the national money, to keep equipment up to date in the face of the slogan: "If it works, it is obsolete." His conscientious efforts brought many charges that he was wrecking the Army and the Navy.

The story of any man's life gains in interest through the people with whom he becomes involved. Eisenhower had an unrivaled opportunity to meet and judge people. For this reason, his opinions of Churchill, Robert Taft, Arbenz of Guatemala, Mossadegh of Persia, Marshal Zhukov, and others offers much quotable material. Of the Russian Premier he says: "Khrushchev does not want peace, save on his own terms and in ways that will aggrandize his own power. He cares nothing for the future happiness of the peoples of the world—only for their regimented employment to fulfil the Communist concept of world history."

These memoirs were organized by Eisenhower's son John and Dr. William B. Ewald, Jr., who worked two years on the basic research. Helpful in understanding the text are sixteen appendices listing the members of the Cabinet under Eisenhower and providing the texts of Constitutional amendments, reports, and letters. Thirty-two illustrations and nine maps are also included. *Mandate for Change* is an engaging, personal, intimate book that reveals a man true to his concepts of morality. Perhaps he is too friendly to make a good historian, for his viewpoint is rosy and he is unwilling to condemn anybody. The book is not a great literary effort; some may find it monotonous and repetitious. But it is genuine and invaluable for those interested in knowing how the government is run.

Willis Knapp Jones

THE MANDELBAUM GATE

Author: Muriel Spark (1918-   )
Publisher: Alfred A. Knopf (New York). 369 pp. $5.95
Type of work: Novel
Time of plot: Summer, 1961
Locale: Jerusalem

In cool, controlled prose, Miss Spark's ninth novel details a religious pilgrimage to Christian sites in the divided sectors of the Holy Land; and illustrates the meshing of human lives and motives across all arbitrary barriers

Principal characters:
> FREDDY HAMILTON, a British foreign service officer
> BARBARA VAUGHN, a spinster teacher and pilgrim
> JOANNA and
> MATT CARTWRIGHT, friends in Jordan
> ALEXANDROS, a curio shopkeeper
> JOE RAMDEZ, an Arab entrepreneur
> ABDUL and
> SUZI RAMDEZ, his children
> MISS E. RICHWARD (RICKY), an English headmistress

A contemporary novelist exploring what separates and unites men might choose to write of East-West Berlin, divided China, or even Harlem-New York.proper, and many have; but few settings seem so tailor-made to this theme as Jerusalem during the hot summer of the Eichmann trial.

A sacred city for Jews, Christians, and Moslems, Jerusalem has been split between the Israeli and Jordanian governments since 1950. Despite an uneasy peace, both nations post armed guards along the joint border. Spies and smugglers who cannot obtain visas through the narrow Mandelbaum Gate move back and forth around it as easily as if international osmosis were the natural consequence of sealed boundaries.

Miss Spark applies this same osmosis to a cast of wildly divergent characters, brought together in the Holy City by coincidence and contradictory motives. Hardly has she detailed their striking differences before she shows these to be permeable membranes, and sets in motion a cloak-and-dagger plot which will entangle their lives to an almost ludicrous degree. Her two chief characters —one polite, one impassioned—are so temperamentally unlike that the most they can share on first meeting is a "good English giggle" over bad wine served with ice cubes in the Jerusalem Hotel.

Freddy Hamilton, a fifty-five-year-old British consulate officer in the Israeli sector, is a predictable, undistinguished bachelor who believes it is "one's duty in life to be agreeable." An ideal weekend guest on both sides of the gate, he composes his bread and butter notes in precise verse, sends long faithful letters to his aging mother in Harrodgate, England, and equates anti-Semitism with poor etiquette.

These qualities are summed up by Barbara Vaughn as "lukewarm," and she does not mind citing a verse from the Apocalypse to him: . . . "neither cold nor hot, thou wilt make me vomit thee out of my mouth." Barbara, a spinster English teacher, half-Jewish by birth, has come from Britain to tour the holy sites of her convert Catholic faith, and to visit her fiancé, an archaeologist working near the Dead Sea. "Afflicted by the beautiful and dangerous gift of faith," she is determined to make her religious pilgrimage, although there is personal risk to anyone of Jewish blood found on the Arab side of the city.

The tension of the novel is established in the first two chapters which present these characters. Freddy's life is a card file, arranged in neat categories of caution, bureaucracy, and uninvolvement. Barbara's is a missal. In middle age, Freddy is static; Barbara, a latecomer at thirty-seven to her first serious love affair, has already crossed half a world moving toward the human and divine objects of her love.

In *The Comforters*, published in 1957, the convert character was previously used by Miss Spark, herself a Catholic convert whose father was a Scottish Jew. The earlier characterization is smaller scaled, as if she were practicing for this larger and more complex work. In some of her earlier books a single quality has seemed to outshine the others; in *The Mandelbaum Gate* her skills are equally blended and are all subordinated to total impact.

Here, too, she continues to use Catholicism as a way of seeing life steadily and whole; but she has the advantages of a naturally fragmented setting. The real atmosphere of life in modern Jerusalem, accurately captured, turns into symbol almost of itself.

Over Freddy's objections, Barbara makes her stubborn pilgrimage and abruptly vanishes in the Jordan sector. While she is being sought by spies, friends, and three governments, a series of intricate flashbacks enlarge on these things which join and separate human lives. Most separate of all is defendant Eichmann, enclosed in a bullet-proof glass cage for his trial, denying responsibility for mass murder of Jews on grounds that he simply followed government orders. Other orders are awaited from the Catholic hierarchy in Rome, which may or may not bless Barbara's marriage to the divorced archaeologist. A forged document finally helps them make the right decision for the wrong reasons.

When Freddy Hamilton steps completely out of character that, too, is like a forged signature to actions which could not have been his own. Fearing for Barbara's life, he masterminds a bizarre rescue so atypical of himself that the wrench is too great, and a four-day bout of total amnesia falls in upon him like a blaze of sunstroke.

The pattern continues as other characters pass through their own Mandelbaum Gates. Barbara's possessive friend from England, Miss Richward, arrives with the intent of breaking up the unsuitable love affair and is betrayed by her long denied femininity into her own affair with an unlikely Arab businessman. In the same Jericho where Old Testament walls came down to the sound of trumpets, the characters astonish themselves: Barbara recovers from fever and beats her nurse with both fists; Freddy uncovers espionage and makes love to a blue-eyed Arab. The entanglement of all these lives, Miss Spark seems to be saying, is here carried to an extreme absurd enough to match the absurdity of their earlier timid uninvolvement.

In addition to sharp scrutiny of each character and an almost austere wit in describing the comeuppance each receives, the novel is notable for excellent descriptions of famous Christian shrines. Barbara, disguised as a mute Arab servant, finds herself part of a

motley group of worshippers and tourists, all of them solicited by an equally
motley set of competing religions. Miss
Spark looks down on these jealous
sects which surround traditional scenes
of Jesus' life with much the same aspect of Jehovah eyeing from Sinai the
golden calf; and she sets down their
competitions for grace as if she were
watching soldiers gamble for a seamless
robe.

One of her most memorable scenes
takes place where Golgotha is surrounded by rival altars. Coming to
worship are Copts, Syrians, Gregorian
Armenians, plain tourists, Franciscan
monks, and others, each carrying the
"prestige of the 'One True Church'
upon his shoulders." When an English
priest pauses to sermonize, much to the
distress of watching monks, Miss
Spark pauses to compress her novel's
theme. This kernel scene from which
many of the others seem to radiate
opens Part II, "The Passionate Pilgrims." The effect is as if the theme
of an entire mural were to be echoed
in an artist's miniature, painted and
half hidden in its center panel. Such
an effect is heightened by the structure
of the novel, which after a straightforward beginning has since been
wheeling out like a spider's web in a
series of concentric flashbacks.

By the time Barbara, half-drugged
and wearing a stolen nun's habit, is
spirited back through the gate in company with "a spoiled Arab, who could
not take any propaganda seriously,"
Miss Spark has held up to subtle ridicule all rules—internal and external—
which are not flexible enough to bend
with the human spirit. She makes love
triumph over orthodoxy, decency over
decree, and humor over hauteur. She
is too candid to pretend every outcome
of risk-taking is pleasant. Freddy's unmailed letter, for example, may be part
of the displaced chain of events which
ended in Harrodgate with his mother's
murder.

A writer without Miss Spark's
classic sense of form and structure
would have let the theme diffuse as it
diversified. Her near-perfect control of
subject matter and tone round the novel's last curve without a wasted word,
as she ends with her first stated definition of what the Mandelbaum Gate actually is, an artifical opening in an artificial wall:

"He [Freddy] walked round the city
until at last, fumbling in his pocket for
his diplomatic pass, he came to the
Mandelbaum Gate, hardly a gate at all,
but a piece of street between Jerusalem
and Jerusalem, flanked by two huts,
and called by that name because a
house at the other end had once belonged to a Mr. Mandelbaum."

Doris Betts

THE MAN-EATER OF MALGUDI

Author: R. K. Narayan (1906-   )
Publisher: The Viking Press (New York). 250 pp. $3.95
Type of work: Novel
Time: The present
Locale: Malgudi, India

A humorous and quietly unstressed novel about a tigerish blusterer and bully who ravages the calm of a town in southern India

Principal characters:
    NATARAJ, the printer of Malgudi, the narrator
    H. VASU, M.A., a taxidermist
    SASTRI, the printer's assistant
    SEN, a would-be journalist
    THE POET, author of a life of Vishnu in monosyllabic verse
    MATHU, a tea shop proprietor
    RANJI, a temple dancer and harlot

R. K. Narayan is a major Indian writer, a novelist whose books contain a diverting, touching blend of comic vision and tragic sensibility. Herein lie the reasons for his growing reputation abroad and the sometimes troubling anomalism of his literary situation at home.

There is every reason to expect that an emerging national literature, such as that taking shape in India today, will reflect the temper of the society and the age to which it gives expression. Most of the novels out of India in the past ten years or so have not proved disappointing in this respect. Their writers have examined the present conflict of tradition and change, the cases of conscience to which political decision and its moral consequences have given rise. From these books we get our picture of a nation trying to define itself in a period of transition when a total society is being forced to readjust its way of thinking and feeling to the weights and pressures of a different mode of life.

Among Indian novelists, however, R. K. Narayan is a notable exception to the current literary trend. Some of his critics insist that he is not serious enough in his presentation of the cultural scene. Certainly his novels make it clear that his primary interest is not directed toward abstract problems of society or politics illuminating the internal struggle between the old and the new that agitates Indian life today. Perhaps he feels that such problems are essentially of the time and therefore temporary. In similar fashion, he does not write about picturesque India of romantic tales or Mother India of mystical vision. He is as remote from Kipling as he is from E. M. Forster. His true subject is more fundamental and timeless. He writes about man, or, more specifically, the comedy of humanity as it is revealed by the comings and goings, the connivings and evasions, of tradesmen, petty officials, peasants, temple sages, and village poets. The India of his novels is not Nehru's or Gandhi's or even the *raj* of the British occupation. His quiet, unpretentious art transcends the political experience to touch upon the larger world and sweep the whole of life before it.

The amazing thing is that it is all so

The Man-Eater of Malgudi/NARAYAN

effortlessly done. Narayan writes as a man perfectly aware of his powers and limitations, without a trace of that fussy self-consciousness common to most novelists who are aware that they are making literature.

Like his earlier books, *The Man-Eater of Malgudi* shows from the first page to the last the easy grace of a master storyteller. There is no need for the writer to shape his material to this or that effect; merely to tell it is sufficient. The scene is again Malgudi, the small town in southern India that Narayan has transformed into a province of the imagination, a place almost as patiently and lovingly landmarked as Hardy's Wessex or Faulkner's Yoknapatawpha County. The story is told by Nataraj, a job printer of the town. Nataraj is not a type, the product of present-day social or psychological influences. He is superbly himself, brisk, easy-going, unambitious, timid, kind. These qualities make him a man worth reading about, for they make him a person easily put upon by more forceful personalities or those who wear the badge of authority. Nataraj prides himself on his industry, but he is not a good businessman. Wedding invitations go unengraved and labels for bottles of aerated soft drinks remain unprinted while he interests himself in the affairs of friends who gather daily in the anteroom of his shop. These include a poet who is writing the life of God Krishna in monosyllabic verse—"Girls with girls did dance in trance" is a good example—and Sen, an aspiring journalist who spends all his time talking about the editorials and articles he never gets around to writing. Sastri, a diligent printer's assistant, keeps innocent, muddled Nataraj from going bankrupt.

But Nataraj's happily confused life is shattered when H. Vasu, M.A., makes his abrupt appearance. Vasu, a bone-crushing strong man in his younger days and now a taxidermist, is a bully capable of cowing timid Nataraj by his presence alone. When he speaks, the little printer quakes. Vasu begins by ordering five hundred name cards and letterheads; he ends up by taking rent-free possession of the loft over the print shop and driving Nataraj's friends away from the anteroom. Before long Vasu is poaching in the Mempi jungle (for a taxidermist must have animals to stuff), filling the area with the rank smells of his operations, entertaining the town's disreputable women in his quarters, and abusing Nataraj's meekness and kindness in every insulting way he can devise. Soon the little printer is in trouble with his scandalized neighbors, the public health authorities, the rent control office (Nataraj is never able to explain that Vasu pays no rent), and suspicious wardens from the Mempi game preserve. Narayan sums up the situation with aphoristic humor and vigor: "Up to what age can a tiger be kept as a pet?" "Until it starts licking the skin off the back of your hand." For Vasu is the man-eater of Malgudi, the tiger in human form munching away at the town's social, economic, and moral life until there is almost nothing left for him to devour.

A typical episode in this amusing and persuasive novel is Nataraj's account of his adventures in the Mempi Hills. One day, on a sudden impulse, Vasu announces that he will take the printer for a short drive around the block. In spite of Nataraj's protest that a customer is waiting for some invitations to be delivered, he is propelled into Vasu's jeep and driven at furious speed to a small village a hundred miles away. There, hungry and penniless, he is put down unceremoniously before a fly-blown tea room while Vasu drives away into the jungle on one of his poaching raids. Mathu, the proprietor of the shop, feeds the abandoned townsman. While there, Nataraj hears about Kumar, the ailing young elephant of a nearby temple. Nataraj suggests that the animal—surely the most enchanting elephant in literature since Babar—be sent to the World Quadruped Relief League clinic in Malgudi for treatment. Later he returns home on the bus, a ride that, like most of the events in Nataraj's unusual day, sets before the reader the signts, sounds, and smells of Narayan's India.

The little elephant precipitates the crisis of the novel. Acting on Nataraj's suggestion, its keeper brings it to Malgudi and bustling Nataraj arranges for its care and cure. Meanwhile plans are being made for a great temple celebration. The first printing of the poet's monosyllabic life of Krishna will be presented to the god and afterward there will be an illuminated religious procession in which Kumar will have a place of honor. Then Nataraj hears rumors that Vasu is planning to shoot the elephant as the parade moves past the print shop. By this time the printer believes that Sastri was right when he called Vasu a *rakshasa*, "a demoniac creature who possessed enormous strength, strange powers, and genius, but recognized no sort of restraints of man or God." To deal with such a monster, according to the old saying, "one must possess the marksmanship of a hunter, the wit of a pundit and

the guile of a harlot." Desperate, Nataraj decides to shoot Vasu, but he is neither marksman nor hunter, and his effort ends absurdly. There is a harlot, one of Vasu's lights of love, but her attempt to poison the taxidermist fails also.

Kumar is not killed. Instead, Vasu is found dead among his smelly broths and molds in the loft over the print shop. His death casts suspicion of murder over the establishment until the mystery of the taxidermist's end is finally explained and Nataraj becomes a free man—freed of his bondage to tyranny, that is—once more.

The conclusion of this humorous novel of misadventure and miscalculation deserves special attention in view of the claim that Narayan slights the greater issues of his time. One wonders. Surely he is commenting in this novel on the tyranny of the strong, the corruption of power, the bewilderment of the good confronted by evil, the resiliency of the weak. The discovery that Vasu was the agent of his own fate implies more than an act of poetic justice. Power turned back upon itself is power exercised for self-destruction. Narayan manipulates no obvious symbols, documents no theme. Everything in the novel is organized within its own terms as a self-contained work of fiction. Yet it has always been the novelist's privilege to mirror the world in the minute particularities of mankind. Behind the comic vision which makes *The Man-Eater of Malgudi* a ruefully funny book a thoughtful mind is constantly at work.

MANI

Author: Patrick Leigh Fermor (1915-   )
Publisher: Harper and Brothers (New York). 320 pp. $6.00
Type of work: Record of travel
Time: The 1950's
Locale: Greece

The story of a trip to the Mani, a Greek peninsula, together with an account of the people who live there and of their culture

At one time or another every educated person, having been exposed to the literature of ancient Greece, must wonder what modern Greece is like and whether the people who inhabit the land of Homer, Aeschylus, Plato, and Aristotle are at all like their ancestors of long ago. Patrick Leigh Fermor's book gives some insight into the answer to such a question. The author himself is a lover of Greece, and he has spent much of his life there. The present volume records his observations on a recent exploratory trip through the Greek peninsula formed by the Taygetus Mountains, a finger of Greece that reaches farther south than any other point in Europe, ending in Cape Matapan, site of a legendary entrance to Hades. In the beginning *Mani* was intended by its author to be but a single chapter in a volume describing "the stages and halts, the encounters, the background and the conclusions of a leisurely journey—a kind of recapitulation of many former journeys—through continental Greece and the islands." When he came to write, however, Patrick Leigh Fermor found that to reduce his wealth of material to a single book was impossible. *Mani*, then, is the first of a projected series of books.

This volume has two expressed aims. One is to describe for the reader the modern Greeks of the mountains in relationship to their land and their history in a remote area where the past and the present still have a meaning for each other. The second aim is to transmit to the reader the feel of the Mani as the author experienced it. He writes:

All of Greece is absorbing and rewarding. There is hardly a rock or stream without a battle or a myth, a miracle or a peasant anecdote or a superstition; and talk and incident, nearly all of it odd or memorable, thicken round the traveller's path at every step. It seemed better, therefore, in writing to abandon the logical sequence of the journey; to avoid a thin spreading of the gathered material over the whole rugged surface of Greece; to attack the country, rather, at certain chosen points and penetrate, as far as my abilities went, in depth. Thus I could allow myself the luxury of long digressions, and, by attempting to involve the reader in them, aspire to sharing with him a far wider area of Greek lands, both in space and time, than the brisker chronicle of a precise itinerary would have allowed. It absolved me from perfunctorily treading many well-beaten tracks which only a guilty and dutiful anxiety to be complete would have made me retrace in print; there was now no need to furnish this free elbow-room with anything which had not filled me with interest, curiosity, pleasure, or excitement.

Fermor believes, too, that if a picture of Greece as it has been is to be presented, it must be done now, for he notes that in the quarter century he has been familiar with the country much that is precious has been destroyed, caught, as he puts it, between the butt of a Coca-Cola bottle and the Iron Curtain.

The Mani, the land Fermor describes, is a land of rugged mountains which reach down to the very edge of the sea and divide the Gulf of Messenia, part of the Ionian Sea, from the Gulf of Laconia, part of the Aegean. These mountains, all the more imposing because they rise abruptly from the waters, tower as high as eight thousand feet. It is a land of sun, heat, and stones, the kind of land to breed a hardy people. Communication and travel are difficult, so that the mountain people of the deep Mani are isolated from the world and from one another. So rocky is the coast that even the sea offers little chance of communication, harbors being few and far between. Through the rugged land Fermor traveled on foot, on muleback and, ocasionally, by bus or boat. In his travels he found, contrary to prediction, that the mountain folk were friendly and hospitable, offering food, drink, and rest to the traveler, happy to see a stranger and eager to exchange news, gossip, and other talk. The hospitality he constantly encountered reminded Fermor of the ancient hospitality recorded in Homer's *Odyssey*. Even before asking a stranger's name, the people provided for his needs, the entire household, Fermor noted, putting itself to service at a moment's notice without fuss, looking after the guest with utter simplicity and kindness.

The great amount of folklore retained by the Maniots was of special interest to Fermor, who absorbed as much of it as he could; he presents considerable commentary on it for the reader. He has long passages on centaurs, nereids, *kalligankantzaroi*, and other supernatural creatures found in Greek folklore, mythology, and literature since long before the time of Homer. For example, at the southern tip of the Mani, on Cape Matapan, is a cave fabled to be one of the entrances to Hades. Fermor went by boat to the entrance of the cave. Since the caïque could not sail very close to the shore, the author swam to it and into it, exploring a place known to man for millennia and fabled as a very entrance to the land of the dead. Here, as Fermor fully realized while floating in the waters and gazing about the cavern, was the very place, according to legend, Psyche had been sent by Aphrodite, the place where Orpheus had entered Hades on his search for Eurydice, the place where Herakles had dragged to the surface triple-headed Cerberus.

Seldom does a Western European or an American come so close, literally, to the geography of the age of fable. Also of interest to Fermor was the way in which, among the Maniots, formal religion and folk superstition have overlapped and merged. Here was a land in which a priest could go to a sorcerer to have the evil eye taken from him and then return to his Christian church to light a votive candle in thanks.

As the writer discovered, the Mani is also the cradle of Greek patriotism. In this bleak region men like Petrobey Mavromichalis and Theodorus Kolokotronis, almost as legendary now as heroes of the age of Theseus or the Trojan War, led the hardy peasants in uprisings against their Turkish masters during the long struggle of the Greeks to achieve national independence.

Another aspect of Maniot culture which interested Patrick Leigh Fermor was the Maniots' attitude toward death and funeral customs. He devotes many pages to telling about these matters, showing how the mountain people of Greece still have an attitude toward death which is much more akin to the beliefs of their ancient ancestors than to those of other modern people. They believe in an afterlife and an afterworld more like the Hades of ancient Greek culture than like the Heaven of traditional Christianity. Death, Fermor points out, is to the typical Maniot a time for emotion, especially a time of tearful release for the women, who keen and wail after the dead in an intense fashion alien to the tight-lipped and firm-jawed expressions of grief common among Europeans further north. The author notes also that the *mirolay*, the Maniot dirge, is among the few formal compositions of a literary nature to be found in the mountains and that this death chant retains many of the attributes of the Greek elegy borrowed from ancient Greek literature and found today in modern elegiac poetry of Western Europe. Fermor found the Maniots often to be articulate about their poetry. They made observations about it which he declared equivalent to a Cornish peasant's ability to discourse learnedly about the variations of the sonnet to be found in English literature at the end of the sixteenth century.

Mani is no ordinary book, and it lives up to the unusual aims its author set for himself. Rather than a mere narrative of a journey, it is a literary picture of the little-known Mani peninsula, a picture which brings the present—its geography, people and culture —into relationship with the rich texture of Greek history, not alone the ancient past but the recent past as well. Obviously the author was unusually well-equipped to write such a book. In addition to travel over much of Greece, he knew the language well, both the official Greek and the many dialects. Not once does Fermor record any difficulty in communication with the people he met. Rather, one is surprised by the number of learned notes he slips into his pages, notes explaining points about the nature of Greek words and phrases and their historical development. One is also impressed by Fermor's knowledge and understanding of Greek cultural history, which gave him the ability to understand and relate clearly what he observed. Yet the amazing learning displayed does not burden the book. *Mani* moves forward easily, in a flowing fashion that will captivate any reader interested in matters of style and well-written prose.

Fermor seems instinctively to know how to handle both language and tone in his writing. Reading his prose is much like hearing a violin played well. One is conscious that it is done well and with an easy grace that belies the effort being made. *Mani* reveals that its author is more than a traveler: that he is a literary artist, a scholar-historian, a philologist, and a man of action who enjoys meeting strange people in far-away lands, even at the cost of great physical effort and more than a discomfort.

MANJIRO
The Man Who Discovered America

Author: Hisakazu Kaneko (1900-   )
Publisher: Houghton Mifflin Company (Boston). 149 pp. $2.75
Type of work: Biography
Time: 1827-1898
Locale: Japan, the United States, Europe

The true story of the shipwrecked sailor boy, Manjiro, whose exciting life was to culminate in the opening of feudal Japan to the Western world

Principal personages:
>MANJIRO NAKAHAMA, the "Man Who Discovered America"
>CAPTAIN WILLIAM H. WHITFIELD, skipper of the *John Howland*

The history of the emergence into modern world affairs of the Japanese people is a remarkable and significant story, not merely for Japanese nationals, but also for Occidentals as well. Only a century has passed since the American naval commander, Commodore Matthew C. Perry, made his two official visits, in 1853 and 1854, which culminated in the justly famous treaties for intercourse with the Japanese nation, agreements which opened the way for extensive trade between the Eastern and the Western worlds. Moreover, this same decade marked the beginning of the development into a world power of a nation which formerly had been torn by internal dissension, dominated by suspicion, fear, and bitter hatred of anything in the least foreign or external to the home islands.

At present it is not at all easy for modern readers to realize just what the conditions were when Commodore Perry began his negotiations. Japanese scientists, industrialists, diplomats, and scholars now demonstrate before international congresses and conventions how fully their people have become members of the society of forward-looking and responsible nations. In commerce, in various branches of pure and applied science, the Japanese have come far and have performed amazing feats of ingenuity and skill within the past century.

One means of acquainting himself with this remarkable story of Japan's development as an extraordinarily thriving and industrious nation and of its swift assumption of Occidental modes is afforded the thoughtful reader in Hisakazu Kaneko's *Manjiro: The Man Who Discovered America.* Although his name and exploits are little known to most Americans, Manjiro is considerably more significant to the history of the Japanese people than Commodore Perry. Two aspects of this remarkable career have particularly fascinated the writer of this biographical sketch: the great appeal of its elements of high adventure, and the part that Manjiro played in preparing the Japanese leaders and people for the American offer of cultural exchange and commercial trade with the rest of the world. Hisakazu Kaneko, professor at the University of Tokyo, recounts the story of this memorable life in a simple but absorbing story which has many of the elements of the folk tale and which gives more detail to the early years of Manjiro's adventures than to those of his later public career.

When Manjiro was living in honorable retirement forced by severe illness during the 1880's and 1890's, he must have relived in memory many times some of the exciting years of his youth, scenes of the first act, as it were, in a stirring drama of endurance, luck, persistence, and intelligence. The first scene shows a poor fisherboy, who at the age of thirteen was shipwrecked on an uncharted island, existed for more than six months on a rocky islet, and was finally rescued on June 27, 1841, by Captain Whitfield of the American whaler *John Howland*. The next episode takes young Manjiro from the Pacific to the home port of the *John Howland*, New Bedford, Massachusetts. There he was renamed John Mung. This second portion of his career extended over a period of three years, during which the young Japanese absorbed all the education he could from Occidental schoolteachers and his New England associates. It was a quiet period, all the more remarkable because the young man was shrewd enough to recognize his need for formal training and intelligent enough to apply himself industriously to all the sources of information available to him. The final scene in this first portion of Manjiro's life presents him successively as a deck officer on an American whaler, a fortunate participant in the gold rush to California, and a traveler returning to his native land. The first act of this heroic life story ended in January, 1851, with Manjiro's return to Japan.

Act Two comprises Manjiro's activities in the next two decades. These years cost him many a rebuff, for he had a long, hard road to follow in acquainting his superiors with the many benefits for the Japanese people to be derived from the forsaking of a traditional policy of isolation and from the assumption of Western practices. Instead of a welcome as a returning hero, the first scene in this second period of Manjiro's life shows him subjected to interrogations, trials, and detentions for nearly two years. But Manjiro persisted. At length his practical and shrewd advice was heeded: the man who translated American books on navigation, who taught navigation and marine engineering to Japanese naval cadets, who instituted a national whaling industry, became an official delegate of his country both to the United States and ultimately to Europe. The episodes of this portion of Manjiro's career fuse and blend into a triumphal climax. At last he sees anti-foreignism diminish; he observes Japan attempting to remodel herself extensively along European lines.

Thus the drama of Manjiro's life comes to an end, with his final years spent in retirement, in honor, and in partial recognition of his tremendous feats as a pioneer of technology for his people and his homeland. The dreams of a simple fisherman's son who had unbelievable adventures that led him to positions of international significance were at last realized.

Kaneko's own summation of Manjiro's remarkable emergence from obscurity into national and even international prominence is expressed in a compact and dignified statement suggestive of the restrained tone of the entire book: "Thus ended the life of a man who, when a boy, was shipwrecked and rescued and taken to America as the first Japanese to be educated and live there, who became a voice in the wilderness and patiently taught his countrymen to open their eyes to modern science and Western civilization, who participated in the slow and turbulent development of his country from feudalism to democracy."

Though replete with dramatic and stirring episodes, this record is not of the swashbuckling-hero type of biography. For Hisakazu Kaneko is plainly not a polished professional writer, with a calculating eye cocked in the direction of motion picture rights for the Japanese counterpart of the Hollywood producer or director. Instead, the biographer has chosen to set forth in bare and unmannered style, with frequent understatement rather than melodramatic terms, the simple, unvarnished version of Manjiro's complex and historic career.

Biographies of courageous seafarers and of outstanding personalities in political and social history are legion. But even those readers who have specialized in the life stories of rather obscure marine heroes and lesser political figures have a treat in store for them in this tale of the "Man who discovered America" for the Japanese people. This biographical sketch opens up new vistas of human courage, ingenuity, and foresight, and reveals from a new point of view the details of Japan's earliest years as a modern nation.

THE MANOR

Author: Isaac Bashevis Singer (1904–   )
Translated from the Yiddish by Joseph Singer and Elaine Gottlieb
Publisher: Farrar, Straus and Giroux (New York). 442 pp. $6.95
Type of work: Novel
Time: The years immediately following 1863
Locale: Poland

*An engaging and dramatic novel which depicts life in Poland following an unsuc-
cessful uprising, a novel which looks toward progress and revolution while describing
in detail the relationships and inter-relationships of people who come into contact
(directly or indirectly) with a single manor in Poland*

Principal characters:
> CALMAN JACOBY, a Jewish grain merchant
> ZELDA, his wife
> JOCHEBED, Calman's oldest daughter, who marries
> MAYER JOEL, an earnest young business man
> SHAINDEL, another daughter of Calman's, who marries
> EZRIEL, a free-thinking young man who becomes a doctor
> MIRIAM LIEBA, another daughter, who becomes an apostate by
> marrying
> COUNT LUCIAN JAMPOLSKI, an impoverished aristocrat
> TSIPELE, the youngest of Calman's daughters, who marries
> JOACHANAN, a young but important rabbi
> CLARA, Calman's second wife
> ZIPKIN, who becomes Clara's lover

In this novel Isaac Bashevis Singer shows himself to be a master of fiction by achieving precisely what every great novelist accomplishes, the creation of a small but complete and viable universe, a living microcosm. Part of the interest we find in the novel is generated, naturally enough, by the similarities between this small fictional universe and the "real" one which each person meets in life. It is not the purpose of this review to show what the analogues are, except to indicate that the experience one shares as he reads the novel frequently suggests those experiences which are characteristic of human life in general: some characters are well developed, others are only sketched; some characters see their environment clearly, others find it blurred and foggy. Most of all, it is a world that visibly contains inter-relationships, people moving in orbits which are touching at times, orbits which are moving, themselves, away from some characters, toward others. As in life, some characters appear frequently and regularly during one stage of the novel, only to slip away absolutely during other portions. Some characters appear occasionally, some only once, and some we only hear of. But the one thing that the characters have in common—and the single fictional device which gives the novel unity—is their association, direct or tangential, with a single manor in Poland. Consequently the novel tends to focus on a group of characters who share mutual friends, acquaintances, experiences, and problems.

Calman Jacoby is the pious Jew who serves more than anyone else as the central character, and most of the other characters have some connection with him, even if that connection is through someone in Calman's family. Calman is the single character whom we follow closely through experiences accumulated during the progress of approximately one generation; he is the character who appears most regularly and who is most fully developed. Yet, he is not the norm or a type by which the other characters are to be measured; he is too highly individualized to fall into a type. Instead, Singer makes Calman human.

It is Calman who gains control of the manor near the beginning of the novel. Members of Calman's family are kept most constantly in view for the reader, though there are some interesting side excursions into the lives of minor characters also. Almost every character in the novel is associated in some way with Calman's family, so that the author keeps a fairly consistent field of vision at all times. The narrative line is good; that is to say, it is a good story. We follow the progress first of the various Jacoby daughters who are married off, one by one, as regularly as ritual. Jochebed, the eldest, is married to Mayer Joel, and thereafter they play minor, though not nonexistent, roles. Shaindel marries the slightly heretical Ezriel, somewhat of a freethinker in this novel which focuses closely on a fairly homogeneous Jewish culture. Miriam Lieba is the apostate whose fate becomes wretched almost from the moment she marries Lucian, the son of Count Jampolski, who controlled the manor prior to the 1863 uprising. As Miriam Lieba rejects her faith by turning Christian, she also rejects the comfortable and secure life she has always known. Tsipele, the youngest daughter, marries Joachanan, a young Hassidic rabbi. The marriages

and respective fates of the Jacoby daughters receive varying degrees of attention in the narrative, but the context—late nineteenth century Poland —remains the same in each case, so that a careful portrait is sketched of the culture in which the characters move. Also, the vision of revolution and reform remains in the background, growing with each generation, beginning to touch the lives of everyone.

The characters are set as well in a Hebrew tradition and the response of each Jewish character to his religion is examined. For some the religion is part of their consciousness and permeates their lives; for others, especially in the new generation, there is more inconstancy, some fleeing from what they feel are the restrictions of a highly ritualized life.

Such subplots as there are in the novel are significant and interesting, though they need not be discussed here. It simply may be stated that these subplots add to the novel rather than detract from it; they provide more richness and fullness than the novel otherwise would have, and they help to make this miniature fictional universe more realistic and concretely developed. After all, the incidental characters are as organic to life as the major characters.

Although the novel is intricate and highly detailed, it nevertheless achieves unity. And the style is generally good, though the translation seems a bit awkward and stiff near the beginning. If this is the case, in fact, stylistic problems are remedied quickly and smoothly, so that the result is a novel most readable in English.

Part of Singer's technique is to introduce some characters without indicating those who are important and those who are not. We never know until we proceed to the conclusion of the tale. This kind of forced detachment also makes the novel similar to life.

In addition to giving a moving and detailed description of the Polish culture during the 1860's and 1870's, Singer provides a fair amount of action and some fine characterization. Clara, Calman's second wife, is a remarkable portrait of a complex woman. Al-

though she tends to be malicious and inclined toward looseness, she is never a flat character with only two dimensions, but is simultaneously attractive as well as repulsive, weak at times, at others very strong. There are other villains as well, and there is a great deal of faith implied in the novel. Altogether the work stands as a fine artistic achievement.

Duane Schneider

Sources for Further Study

Criticism:

Buchen, Irving H. *Isaac Bashevis Singer and the Eternal Past*. New York: New York University Press, 1968, pp. 173-194. By the end of *The Manor,* the Jewish way of life has come into collision with modern skepticism. Buchen discusses this conflict as part of his overview of the author and his book.

Chametsky, Jules. "The Old Jew in New Times," in *Nation*. CCV (October 30, 1967), pp. 436-438. The conflict between the old religion and the modern age as a central issue of *The Manor* is discussed by Chametsky.

Hughes, Catherine. "The Two Worlds of Isaac Singer," in *America*. CXVII (November 18, 1967), pp. 611-613. One aspect of Singer's writing is about change while another reaches back to the past. Hughes attempts to reconcile these two sides of Singer's style.

Reviews:

Book World, October 29, 1967, p. 4. 1,450 words.

New Republic. CLVII, November 11, 1967, p. 39. 1,500 words.

New York Review of Books. IX, October 26, 1967, p. 32. 1,750 words.

New York Times Book Review. November 5, 1967, p. 1. 1,350 words.

MAN'S WORLD, WOMAN'S PLACE

Author: Elizabeth Janeway (1913-   )
Publisher: William Morrow and Co., Inc. (New York). 320 pp. $8.95
Type of work: A study in social mythology

A supremely rational, controlled treatment of a highly irrational, diffuse subject— sexual separatism and its effects on our society

This is a book built on an adage and a piece of advice. Elizabeth Janeway takes the adage (it's a man's world— woman's place is in the home) as subject core and takes the advice as a way of examining that core. "Whenever you begin, you will have to begin again twice over," Erik Erikson advises his readers in emphasizing that a therapist deals with a mind, a body, and a creature living in society. Janeway sees in his triple approach a "systematic going around in circles," which is, she says, a mythic symbol "as old and as widespread as any records of the human race we have." The spiral form associated with growth infuses human history. We see it, for example, on the walls of caves, in Indian sand paintings, in ritual dances, in children's street games, and in modern scholarly works. As Janeway examines the "vast superstructure of myth" that has been built by emotion, desire, need and fear around the fact of difference between men and women, the spiraling movement helps the reader tolerate the frustrating, maddening irrationality of numerous examples of mythic thinking in order to see them from enough positions on the spiral to reach some understanding of the need such thinking satisfies. The spiral gives the advantage of fresh viewpoints, and, at the same time, the continuity of a single track to follow.

Janeway buffers the shock at how educated, intelligent people can give voice to what seem, on close examination, to be self-deceptive lies and even wins sympathy for the mythic thinker. Partly she does this by demonstrating that we are all subject to mythic thinking. Myths are produced by profound emotional drives, by a will to believe that what we desire exists—or should exist. ". . . myth has its own, furious, inherent reason-to-be because it is tied to desire. Prove it false a hundred times, and it will still endure because it is true as an expression of feeling." Even when proven false, myths are not distortions of thought similar to neurosis, and one must not arrogantly set out to cure society of its ills by getting rid of this "sickness." Myths endure because "they offer hope, because they justify resentments, but perhaps most of all because they provide a bond of common feeling." There have been good books written recently which disprove traditional myths about woman's role and place but they will overthrow the myths only if they can change the way people feel.

The process of searching out the feelings behind demands that woman stay in a "proper sphere" in man's world begins with a reminder that the facts run counter to the myth in that fewer women are actually keeping to the home. Further groundwork for this study tells us that the home which myth declares to be eternal, has not, in fact, long been the refuge from the world of business it is today. After listening to several voices that insistently proclaim the adage in varying ways, Janeway isolates the mythic principle behind them all by asking why women belong at home. The answer comes from another mythic thinker, giving new form to an old answer—Phyllis McGinley in *Sixpence in Her Shoe:* "By and large . . . the world runs better when men and women keep in their own spheres. . . . And that is, after all, the mysterious honor and obligation of women—to keep this planet in orbit. We are the self-immolators, the sacrificers, the givers, not the eaters-up of life. . . . Few jobs are worth disrupting family life for unless the family profits by it rather than the housewife herself." This takes us a step along the spiral, for the emotional force behind the mythic thought is now obvious. It is part of another basic myth of a golden age in the past which we are constantly trying to recapture—a golden age basic to everyone born into the world with infinite need and a woman to give answer to those needs. So there is an internal, remembered reality—emotion imprinted by the fact that children need care and get it from their mothers. That is a need we can sympathize with, but out of this need "grows the demanding mythic imperative—the assertion that a man does not just need a woman, he has a right to her and that right is a part of the order of the world."

One after another layers of myth are carefully lifted, examined, encircled, and seen again. The myth that woman's place is in the home masks the myth of the golden age; the myth of innate female weakness (incapacity, comparative lack of value) covers the unmentionable myth of female power; and the myth of female power is a para-

dox arising from the primitive and Christian worship of motherhood—not the woman, but the female as mother with her "power" stemming only from the existence of the child.

Extending the study of mythic thinking to how myth specifically affects behavior, Janeway explains the close connection between roles and myth. "We judge people by how they fit into what we expect of them," she says; and like myth, roles have positive aspects. They pattern behavior and help keep society coherent. But an important concern "is to avoid freezing behavior into roles that were appropriate . . . but have now lost so much of their utility. . . ." And this, she contends, is what has happened to woman's role: "the more feminine a woman is, the less can she be part of the major, ongoing trend of life in our society . . ."—those trends that say personal autonomy, individual freedom and responsibility are highly desirable.

Janeway continues to spiral around her subject, constantly contrasting specifics in the conditions of women's lives as demanded by mythic thinking—the major differences between playing the pleasing woman role versus that of the shrew, the loving woman versus the bitch, for instance—and relating these to how "woman's place" is reinforced because of emotional reactions to these roles. Thus, men, who have as children experienced the frightening power of an omnipotent mother, occasionally angry and unloving, may spend some of their time keeping woman in her place just as much out of fear that the no-longer dominated woman may dominate in turn as out of a need for loving service that answers to the emotional pull of the golden age of infancy. The spiraling encompasses women at home, at work, in marriage, in lovemaking, and in divorce.

The final focus on contemporary life with its heightened value on the man-woman relationship, on the basic small social unit of nuclear family in a highly mobile population, defines the main problem as an overinvestment of emotion in sex and in the mother-child relationship. The later chapters touch on the changes possible now that the myths of female weakness and power on which our attitudes are built are being challenged by the increasing possibility of disconnecting sex from childbearing and rearing. And as she puts the women's liberation movement into perspective, she continues to work with spiral contrasts by discussing first the point of view of most women on the challenge to mythic thinking (which will be, for some time at least, fear of the unknown and clinging to the myth by which they have been trained to profit) and then of most men (the fear that women will not stop at equality). She sees the male's "instinctively" fearful reaction as dangerous mythic thinking that disables people from seeing social change as anything constructive:

If there is any hopeful purpose in the writing of this book, it is . . . to suggest that when change confronts us, we refuse to shrink away, overwhelmed by mythic terror and convinced that we are caught in a dilemma of destruction or status quo. If we can think objectively about our myths, we won't be so compelled by them and we will be more able to see change as a chance to try out new approaches to problems.

This is, literally, an "exploration," and the growth of understanding achieved by its author in the process of study is obvious. An early chapter is highly defensive and proclaims perhaps too loudly that this is a book about society, not just women (is it mythic thinking that tells us women are not, by themselves, a worthy subject?). Halfway through the book, the question "can one consider controversy without falling into it?" arises in Janeway's determined struggle to remain objective. By the end, she is clearly committed to some of the most basic ideas of the new feminists—such as the contention that innate psychological differences between the sexes probably do not exist, that those we have are taught (and firmly taught) by cultural pressures. The fulfillment of the "hopeful purpose" of this book, then, is begun with the book itself. Elizabeth Janeway emerges as one who has indeed refused "to shrink away."

Maureen G. Trobec

THE MANSION

Author: William Faulkner (1897-1962)
Publisher: Random House (New York). 436 pp. $4.75
Type of work: Novel
Time: 1908-1946
Locale: Yoknapatawpha County, Mississippi

The concluding novel of the Snopes trilogy, in which a kinsman's gun ends Flem Snopes' cold-blooded pursuit of money, respectability, and power

Principal characters:
 FLEM SNOPES, president of a bank in Jefferson, Mississippi
 LINDA SNOPES KOHL, the daughter of Eula Varner Snopes, now dead
 MINK SNOPES, Flem's cousin, a murderer
 GAVIN STEVENS, the county attorney
 V. K. RATLIFF, a sewing-machine salesman
 CHARLES MALLISON, Stevens' nephew
 J. C. GOODYHAY, a militant rural evangelist

It is within the power of some writers to hit upon the illuminating figure of speech, sentence, or brief passage that echoes through the total body of their work like a meaningful refrain. Offhand, one thinks of Melville's "Call me Ishmael" at the opening of *Moby Dick,* Walt Whitman's declaration, "I was the man, I suffer'd, I was there," and Fitzgerald's penetration deep into the heart of the great middle-class illusion which lights up his legend of the Twenties: "Let me tell you about the very rich. They are different from you and me." A passage of similar import comes at the close of William Faulkner's *Absalom, Absalom!* after Quentin Compson has related to his Canadian roommate at Harvard the long, violent chronicle of Sutpen's innocence and guilt. At the end Shreve McCannon has one more question to ask: "Why do you hate the South?"

"I dont hate it," Quentin said, quickly, at once, immediately; "I dont hate it," he said. *I dont hate it* he thought, panting in the cold air, the iron New England dark; *I dont. I dont! I dont hate it! I dont hate it!*

Quentin's agonized reply betrays something of Faulkner's own ambivalence, the mixed sense of love and guilt in his attitude toward his Mississippi homeland, as well as the ambiguities of character and conduct in his vision of ruin and decay within the Yoknapatawpha scene. Almost everything he has written has been an attempt to define the nature and meaning of his moral history of the human effort and its limitations, and he has the habit of reworking his material, of retelling old stories and presenting familiar characters in a different light, in order to extract fresh meanings and deeper understanding—for himself, it seems, as much as for his readers. In the process, over the years, he has been filling in the details of an elaborate design, one part here, another part there, a new detail somewhere else, with each story adding to the totality of the human situation which will be fully revealed when the Yoknapatawpha saga is complete. *The Mansion,* his latest novel, rounds out one pattern in the complex over-all design, completing a trilogy begun in *The Hamlet* (1940) and continued in *The Town* (1957).

To readers who know the whole body of Faulkner's writing, his habit of going back to or recombining earlier themes and events is not a matter of great importance. Since all his books lead inevitably into one another, the reappearance of old characters, the telling of a new story in a familiar setting, or the conclusion of an episode began in some other novel or short story merely adds to our sense of familiarity with his people and his region. No one should be surprised, then, to find in *The Mansion* a second and more revealing account of Mink Snopes's murder of Jack Houston (first told in *The Hamlet*), to discover at last why Flem Snopes framed Montgomery Ward Snopes, the pornographer, with planted moonshine whiskey and made him an agent in getting Mink's prison term extended another twenty years, or to learn new facts about Gavin Stevens' strange, detached love for Flem's wife Eula, an earthy fertility goddess from a crossroads community, and the even stranger relationship between the middle-aged lawyer and Eula's daughter Linda.

If discrepancies have developed between the earlier novels and *The Mansion*, Faulkner has the answer for their presence. In a brief foreword he informs the reader "that the author has already found more discrepancies and contradictions than he hopes the reader will—contradictions and discrepancies due to the fact that the author has learned, he believes, more about the human heart and its dilemma than he knew thirty-four years

ago; and is sure that, having lived with them that long time, he knows the characters in this chronicle better than he did then."

Members of the grasping Snopes clan came into Faulkner's fiction as early as *Sartoris*, but he did not give them a book of their own until *The Hamlet* appeared in 1940. That novel, rich in folk comedy, grotesque in its horrors, sharp in social criticism, tells how Ab Snopes, ex-bushwhacker, horse trader, and sharecropper won immunity in Frenchman's Bend because of his reputation as a barn burner and how his son Flem became a clerk in Will Varner's store. Before long other members of the family descend like swarming locusts on the village, nibbling away at its social, economic, and moral life until they have picked it as clean as a ham bone at a Sunday School barbecue. Led by Flem, who has set himself up in the world by marrying Eula Varner when she was pregnant with another man's child, they then move on to Jefferson, the county seat.

There, in *The Town*, Flem sets respectability and wealth as his goals, and by following a career of chicanery, conniving, double-dealing, and playing the willing cuckold for years, he ends up as the president of the bank Bayard Sartoris had founded. In the meantime he has cleared his coattails of the more disreputable members of his family— Mink Snopes, the murderer; I. O. Snopes, the bigamist; Montgomery Ward Snopes, a dealer in pornography, and even his wife, who commits suicide as a way of escape from Flem's maneuverings to possess her daughter's inheritance, ruin her lover, and take over the bank.

Presented as a series of episodes narrated by such familiar Faulkner characters as Gavin Stevens, the lawyer; his nephew, Charles Mallison; and V. K. Ratliff, the wry-humored, compassionate, observing sewing-machine salesman, *The Mansion* covers a time span linking Houston's murder with Flem's violent death at the hands of Mink Snopes thirty-eight years later. In this novel, however, much of Flem's trickery and greed for money and power fade into the background and Linda, Eula's daughter, becomes the central figure. After Gavin Stevens has aided her in her escape from Flem at the time of her mother's death, she goes to New York, marries a Jewish sculptor, Barton Kohl, joins the Communist Party to which her husband belongs, and goes with him to Spain during the Spanish Civil War. Kohl and Linda are both casualties of the war. He is killed while flying for the Republicans and she is deafened when the ambulance she is driving detonates a mine, bursting her eardrums in the explosion. Living in a world of silence, unable to hear her own harsh toneless voice, she returns to Jefferson and settles in the old mansion Flem has remodeled.

Gavin Stevens, who had been in love with Eula Snopes, though never her lover, has already transferred his affections to Linda, who is some sixteen years his junior. Their association never passes the bounds of friendship, however, and in the end it is Linda who brings about his marriage to another woman. In the course of this novel Charles Mallison grows up and becomes a participant in rather than an observer of the life of Jefferson. V. K. Ratliff continues to ponder the unpredictable, and generally cussed, ways of man. And Flem goes on his Snopesian way until Mink Snopes, released

from prison through Linda's efforts, commits the second murder for which he has waited almost forty years. The final irony is that an ignorant, vindictive cousin brings Flem to the end he deserves, but there are many in Jefferson—among them Lawyer Stevens and shrewd, humane Ratcliff—who see Flem's death as an act of retribution which the decent people of the town were powerless to administer.

In *The Hamlet* and in the opening sections of *The Town*, Flem Snopes gave every promise of becoming one of Faulkner's great grotesques—a dehumanized, inscrutable, almost sexless, but implacable force of rapacity and greed. As a symbol of the upward climb of predatory Snopeses from mule trading and storekeeping to become the bankers and suspender-snapping politicians of the new South he exhibited those traits of the grotesque and the comic which Faulkner handles with superb ease. But as a respectable member of the social community he is less effective; he remains a background figure, even though we are always conscious that "there aint nothing he will stop at, aint nobody or nothing within his scope and reach that may not anguish and grieve and suffer."

Instead, it is his cousin Mink who dominates this novel. In *The Hamlet* he is a creature of pure malice, sly as a weasel, deadly as a rattlesnake. But in *The Mansion* we learn that the killing of Houston was motivated by more than revenge for failure to get free winter grazing for his cow. The killing, as Faulkner now reveals, was a desperate, violent attempt to retain some measure of human dignity denied him by the moods of nature and the ways of men. It is the same with his hatred for Flem. According to Mink's simple code, a kinsman must stand by his kin.

When Flem fails to appear at the time of Mink's trial, Mink sees the killing of his cousin as a simple act of justice. Flem's use of Montgomery Ward Snopes to maneuver Mink into an attempt to escape and thus double his sentence convinces Mink that it is Old Moster's will that he rid the world of his betrayer. The story of Mink's return from the prison at Parchman, his encounter with J. C. Goodyhay, an ex-Marine sergeant turned evangelist, the buying of the gun, the shooting while Flem sat "chewing faintly again, as though he too were watching the dull point of light on the cock of the hammer when it clicked away"—these scenes show Faulkner at his best.

Unfortunately, not all of the novel is of this quality. *The Mansion* is a discursive, uneven work that is earthily humorous, ironic, violent, and compassionately reflective at times, but rambling and even dull at others. Like most of Faulkner's writing, it has a sound substructure in social morality, and although it lacks much of the dramatic intensity and impassioned rhetoric of this writer at the top of his bent, it is nevertheless, despite its lapses, a richly imagined and somberly moving story. No one has isolated to better advantage the nature of Snopesism, the relentless, dehumanized drive of greed and gain in our materialistic society. These matters stir Faulkner to indignation, and when he is aroused he generates in his fiction a kind of wild, brooding poetry of primitive vision, elemental power, and deep moral insights. Certainly the idea of man's mortality has seldom been presented more simply or beautifully than in the final pages of this novel, as Mink prepares to return his body to the waiting earth.

Sources for Further Study

Criticism:

Beck, Warren. "Faulkner in *The Mansion*," in *Virginia Quarterly Review.* XXXVI (Spring, 1960), pp. 272-292. A general review of Faulkner's philosophy as it comes forth in *The Mansion*. Emphasis on the changes in Faulkner through his other novels, especially the changes in the themes of good and evil. Good character analysis is also helpful for an understanding of the book.

Greene, Theodore M. "The Philosophy of Life Implicit in Faulkner's *The Mansion*," in *Texas Studies in Literature and Language.* II (Winter, 1961), pp. 401-418. Greene delves into Faulkner's rejection of the idea that justice will prevail, but that man can be his own salvation.

Howe, Irving. "Faulkner: End of a Road," in *New Republic.* CXLI (December 7, 1959), pp. 17-21. Howe feels that *The Mansion* is a superb novel, especially in representation of its major theme: that power can have disastrous consequences.

Rossky, William. "Faulkner: The Image of the Child in *The Mansion,*" *Mississippi Quarterly.* XV (Winter, 1961-1962), pp. 17-20. Rossky shows an underlying theme in the novel which develops the child image from traditional innocence to worldliness.

Richardson, Kenneth E. "Force and Faith in the Novels of William Faulkner," in *Studies in American Literature.* VII (1962), pp. 163-171. According to Richardson, many of Faulkner's novels, and especially *The Mansion,* show a test of faith because of the influences of the world.

MARCEL PROUST

Author: Roger Shattuck (1923-   )
Publisher: The Viking Press (New York). 179 pp. $2.95 (paperback)
Type of work: Critical study

A fresh, vital approach to an understanding of one of the most influential novelists of the twentieth century

There are some literary works which, for one reason or another, remain inaccessible to the general reading public. What immediately comes to mind in English literature is such an unwieldly composition as Edmund Spenser's *The Faerie Queene.* That the poem happens to be situated in a historical period far removed from our own gives it a certain kind of "distance." The language of the sixteenth century and its accompanying idioms, the Renaissance philosophy and aesthetic, all have a tendency to separate further the reader from the text. However, once these difficulties have been recognized and provided for, the reader can devote his attention to more specialized problems of analysis and interpretation. There may be complicated passages upon which scholars will stubbornly disagree, but it is still quite possible for the reader to gain a general understanding on a basic or even a relatively sophisticated level.

However, the mere mention of Marcel Proust's *A la recherche du temps perdu* is sufficient to frighten even the most avid literary enthusiast. This monumental *chef-d'oeuvre,* which in French has been defined as a *roman-fleuve,* or extended narrative, moves beyond the boundaries of normal perception. Indeed, the classic image of Proust feverishly composing his novel in the physical atmosphere of a cork-lined room in order to avoid aural contamination from the outside world conjures up for most readers the formidable picture of a fervid yet tortured neurasthenic whose artistic vision was inseparable from life. In the face of such myths and misunderstandings, therefore, Roger Shattuck's fresh, unhackneyed reading of Proust's monumental commentary upon the shifting patterns of French society from the period after the Franco-Prussian War to the post-World War I era is a welcome piece of sound and sensible criticism. The literary historian will at once be aware of the implications of such shifting patterns and such incredible complexity. Shattuck sets the tone of his inquiry by pointedly reminding us that the translation of *A la recherche du temps perdu* is not *Remembrance of Things Past* (as rendered by C. K. Scott-Moncrieff), but *In Search of Lost Time.*

The author's first task is to summarize the major negative judgments which have commonly prevented objective appreciation of Proust's art for many readers. Perhaps the most frequent is the feeling that the artist's work suffers from loose construction and slack or undisciplined style, with the result that the narrative seems boring and interminable. Another obstacle to objectivity is the irritating image of the artist as a "spoiled, sickly, adolescent snob born to wealth on the fringes of . . . high society." More serious objections arise from the impression often generated by *In Search of Lost Time* that Proust's world has been stripped of almost every vestige of human dignity, honesty, and individuality. Many readers perceive the artist's moral universe as one in which human relationships are mere mockeries, and from which decency and generosity, friendship and love have fled. They hear in Proust's tone scorn, snobbery, and self-centeredness, as well as an undermining self-contempt.

After deliberately collecting and displaying these harsh interpretations, Shattuck states that, while most of the charges are seriously overblown and could likely be rebutted, such is not his task. Instead, he seeks "a far more illuminating verdict: *guilty— but not as charged.*" As Shattuck explains:

> Snobbery, megalomania, and unstability of character do indeed loom large in the world Proust creates. The first task of the critic is to prevent the uninitiated reader from reacting against these elements before he understands how they fit together to make a remarkably coherent work of art.

Therefore, Proust's biographer-critic prunes away erroneous interpretations which tend to obscure the healthy artistic organism, and leaves the way clear for unbiased and enlightening analysis.

Although Shattuck addresses himself in Chapter Two—entitled "How to Read a *Roman-fleuve*"—to those "seeking guidance for a first reading of Proust," his intimate knowledge of the elements of Proust's narrative produces insights valuable for even the seasoned student of Proust. The author identifies a tripartite movement in Marcel's experience which governs the narrative. In the first stage, the artist is molded and defined by his immediate family; such definition soon proves too limited, however, especially since his family, although they love him, cannot truly understand him. Marcel, therefore, turns to society—specifically to the aristocratic circles—for the affirmation and support that he craves. Eventually, this source also proves inadequate, and in the third stage the artist turns inward to his own mind.

In Shattuck's words, Proust becomes "a great steady eye":

> . . . he watches, trying never to condemn family or society, but letting us behold the ways in which they fail him. In the end he does not fail us, or himself. For he tells the story in full.

In his final and seminal chapter, entitled "Spinning a Yarn," Shattuck explores the bewilderingly complex issue of the treatment of time and space in Proust's work in such a way that it becomes—perhaps for the first time for many readers—clear, logical, and meaningful. The author identifies two ways of presenting time in fiction: the traditional method is that of temporal order—the reordering of events as they occur in life; the more recent method is that of relating those occasional experiences which take on meaning only as they are filtered through memory. In an interesting diagram called "The Loops of Art," Shattuck summarizes Proust's approach, which combines the two methods: "The pattern central in the *Search* is that of a relationship between a past impression and its resurrection in the present." The author stresses the importance of this pattern as he describes Proust's unique mingling of the two time perspectives:

> . . . The *Search* creates a predominately temporal perspective, scored through deeply at crucial moments by arresting spatial insights. The only synthesis resides in the full dimensions of the work itself.

All too often, the professional critic dismisses the most basic and pertinent observations in the hopes of publishing or advertising his own literary manifestos; Roger Shattuck fortunately avoids this pitfall. Instead, he sets forth insights that are brilliant yet self-effacing, penetrating yet compassionate. He has done his readers as well as Proust an immense service by writing criticism of the most lucid and objective kind.

Pierre Han

MARIANNE THORNTON
A Domestic Biography, 1797–1887

Author: E. M. Forster (1879-1970)
Publisher: Harcourt, Brace and Company (New York). Illustrated. 337 pp. $5.00
Type of work: Biography
Time: 1797-1887
Locale: England

A family picture album in the form of a biography by a distinguished English novelist and essayist who appears briefly in a self-portrait of the artist as a young boy

> Principal personages:
> HENRY THORNTON, M.P., owner of Battersea Rise
> MARIANNE SYKES THORNTON, his wife
> MARIANNE,
> HENRIETTA,
> LUCY,
> LAURA, and
> HENRY, five of their nine children
> THE REV. CHARLES FORSTER, husband of Laura
> EDWARD FORSTER, son of Laura and Charles Forster
> EDWARD MORGAN FORSTER, their son
> WILLIAM WILBERFORCE, English abolitionist
> HANNAH MORE, a "bishop in petticoats"

The oldest of nine children, Marianne Thornton was born in 1797 in Clapham Common, then a pleasant London suburb not to be confused with the noisy, dingy Clapham Junction of a later day. She died there in 1887, in a house not far from the one in which she was born, having lived almost the whole of her ninety years within the environs of greater London. Perhaps the only adventuresome event of her life was a visit to France shortly after the downfall of Napoleon. The scandals and crises which often disrupted dynastic family households of the Victorian Age never touched her directly or disturbed the inner serenity of her nature, although other members of the Thornton family were less fortunate. She never married, and as she grew older she carried on an extensive correspondence with relatives of all ages, her letters characterized by a fluent, vigorous style. When she died she left her favorite great-nephew a legacy of £8,000.

Such an outline, baldly presented, carries with it no suggestion that *Marianne Thornton* is in all probability the most brilliantly conceived and artistically presented biography we are likely to see, not only in 1956, but for a number of publishing seasons to come. Without the legacy, however, the book might never have been written. For the small boy to whom Marianne Thornton left the money was E. M. Forster, and this study of his great-aunt is his graceful acknowledgement of the opportunity she gave him for education, travel, and the leisure to write: "She and no one else made my career as a writer possible, and her love, in a most tangible sense, followed me beyond the grave." Under these circumstances, and in less capable hands, the book might have become a mere sentimentalized memoir. Instead it presents all the facets we have come to recognize in E. M. Forster's subtle and compelling art—the psychological depth combined with easy clarity of style, the skillful manipulation of scene for dramatic effect, character drawing in three-dimensional perspective. Here, too, the use of letters and miscellaneous family papers for documentation creates somewhat the effect of the old-fashioned epistolary novel, a technical device appropriately in keeping with this work which Mr. Forster affectionately labels "A Domestic Biography."

Marianne Thornton is the story of a house, a family, and an era. The house was Battersea Rise, acquired in 1792 by Henry Thornton, M. P., in preparation for marriage and family life. It was a residence intended for a more spacious age than ours, with its thirty-four bedrooms upstairs, downstairs the great oval library designed by William Pitt, and outside the landscaped lawns and gardens. There William Wilberforce once walked after an unhappy interview with Queen Charlotte and exclaimed, "Oh, the beauty of it. Oh, the goodness of God in giving us such alleviations in this hard world. . . . And oh how unlike the Queen's countenance." Young Marianne on another occasion contradicted the same queen on the subject of the Thornton gardens, claiming that those at Battersea Rise were more beautiful than the garden of her Uncle Robert, in which Queen Charlotte was being entertained at the time. Marianne's particular admiration was a lovely tulip tree; one of her childhood nightmares was the fear that Napoleon would invade England and cut down her beloved tree.

The time and the place gave Marianne every opportunity to know the great and the near-great of the early nineteenth century. For the Thorntons belonged to the group known as the Clapham Sect, earnest "low" Anglicans who firmly based their conception of the good life on Christian piety, humanitarian interests, and sound banking principles. Their neighbors included William Wilberforce, the ardent crusader for the abolition of slavery in the British colonies; Zachary Macaulay, father of Thomas Babington Macaulay (at a children's party little Tom, "terrified at electricity, fell asleep over mechanics."); the Trevelyans, related to the Macaulays by marriage, and the "able and alarming Stephen family." Another frequent visitor at Battersea Rise was Hannah More, "that bishop in petticoats," but her reputation as a writer of religious and reform tracts paled beside the fact that her two cats were called Non-resistance and Passive Obedience.

In this prosperous, political, and intellectual atmosphere the young Thorntons grew and flourished. They could hardly have done otherwise, for as Mr. Forster writes of Marianne, "Wherever she walked the child found herself surrounded by assorted saints." He himself treats the Clapham "Saints" with a tolerance not displayed by many who have written about them. He admits that Wilberforce and others fought for reform abroad but ignored the industrial miseries of factories and slums at home, but he concludes:

> . . . I do not share the moral indignation that sometime accompanies [such criticism]. The really bad people, it seems to me, are those who do no good anywhere and help no one either at home or abroad. There are plenty of them about, and, when they are clever as well as selfish, they often manage to slip through their lives unnoticed, and so escape the censure of historians.

Only once was the domestic tranquility and security of the Thorntons vitally disturbed. This was the occasion when Marrianne's younger brother Henry insisted on marrying Emily Dealtry, the sister of his dead wife and a member of the household at Battersea Rise. Such a wedding was then forbidden by English law under the Deceased Wife's Sister Bill and could only be performed abroad. So Henry and Emily were married in France while Clapham seethed with gossip and Battersea Rise stood empty for the first time in more than half a century.

By that time, however, Marianne had passed through her successive stages as big sister and aunt and had finally become the family matriarch to three generations of Thorntons. E. M. Forster knew her first as a firm but kindly old woman who for years had presided over family occasions and memories. Sometimes advice was needed and she gave it. Often she stood like a pillar of strength in times of trouble or bereavement. Again she delighted young nieces and nephews and cousins with her letters and gifts. If she seemed meddlesome and even autocratic at times, this side of her nature can be explained by the fact that the family was her life and her chief interest. Unmarried, she had passed "into spinsterhood without regret," but she was wise enough before her death to find the heir to whom she could pass on her regard for family tradition.

To her, E. M. Forster was always "the Important One," as she called the grandson of her sister Laura and the Rev. Charles Forster. To him, she was "Aunt Monie," and it was in her house, when he was four, that he learned to read for himself. It was a moment from which he "never looked back. . . . No one taught me to read and no one managed to teach me to write." But it was Marianne Thornton who, through her generosity and love, provided the opportunity for both, and this book is his tribute to the woman and a re-creation of the age through which she lived. There are few biographies so clear-cut and detailed in the presentation of character and social scene.

Marianne Thornton illustrates the art Willa Cather had in mind when she said that the test of good writing lies in something sensed between the lines rather than printed on the page. It is this power of evocation, the ability to suggest more than is actually stated, that makes this biography the subtle and entertaining work it is. Alfred Tennyson comes to call and gives the young Thorntons some coins to buy "sugar plumbs." Wilberforce exclaims over an angry queen. Little Tom Macaulay falls asleep at a party. Henry Thornton defies family and public opinion to marry Emily Dealtry. Nurse Hunter quiets a frightened child. Uncle Robert disappears leaving behind him a "disconsolate wife, no children and many debts." Out of domestic details like these E. M. Forster conveys a sense of deeply felt experience throughout his narrative and makes this biography a memorial to a way of life which, like Battersea Rise, has been destroyed by the ruthless processes of time and change.

MARJORIE MORNINGSTAR

Author: Herman Wouk (1915-   )
Publisher: Doubleday and Company (New York). 565 pp. $4.95
Type of work: Novel
Time: 1933-1954
Locale: New York and Paris

A novel depicting the life of a Jewish girl who aspires to the stage

Principal characters:

MARJORIE MORNINGSTAR, née Morgenstern, a stage-struck young
Jewish girl
MARSHA ZELENKO, her best friend
NOEL AIRMAN, born Saul Ehrmann, an aesthete, libertine, and
pseudo-intellectual playwright
WALLY WRONKEN, a young writer and one of Marjorie's suitors
DR. SHAPIRO, another suitor
MIKE EDEN, a worker with the anti-Nazi underground
MILTON SCHWARTZ, a young attorney whom Marjorie eventually
marries
GUY FLAMM, a Broadway producer.

Whether or not Herman Wouk's fourth novel, *Marjorie Morningstar,* deserves the enthusiasm it has received is difficult to conclude. The outstanding popularity and merit of his previous novel, *The Caine Mutiny,* both in its original form and as it appeared on the stage and screen, clouds thinking about the later work, so that a reader may be swayed to feel that it is either better or worse than it really is. Later analyses, objectified by the passage of years, often value a literary work differently from judgments made within a few months of its publication. By concentrating on certain aspects of a work, however, a reasonable evaluation can be approximated at any time.

As novels go generally, and Herman Wouk's particularly, *Marjorie Morningstar* is a long novel. From its bulk alone, one suspects that the author intended it as something of a *magnum opus;* certainly it cannot be interpreted, in terms of bulk or any other respect, as a potboiler. The story itself covers twenty-one years in the life of a beautiful girl who at the age of seventeen decides, almost as groundlessly as young girls usually make such decisions, that she will become a great actress. The novel describes her life and environment from 1933 to 1954, from her seventeenth to her thirty-eighth years. Considering the novel as a fictional biography, the reader finds that it emphasizes the emotional side of the would-be actress' life; more than anything else, biographically speaking, it is the story of Marjorie Morningstar's fruitless love for a male who is not bad enough to be an interesting literary rogue and not good enough to be a real man, but who falls into that limbo reserved for those poor souls who live out their lives in moral and worldly mediocrity. Noel Airman's life is a denial of values, and he turns out to be even emptier than the ephemeral tunes he writes for second-rate musical comedies.

To consider *Marjorie Morningstar* simply as a fictional biography seems insufficient, however. Both Marjorie Morningstar and Noel Airman, the central figures in the novel, begin their adult lives with a denial of the culture and the traditions of the people who produced them, a fact that is important in any sound evaluation of the novel. Both man and woman are New Yorkers, both are of Jewish blood, and both were reared in families conscious and proud of their ancestry and culture. But both young people deny their background, their denial being symbolized in their changing their names, from Ehrmann to Airman and Morgenstern to Morningstar. In the light of the complete novel, especially its emphasis on the life of the Jewish community in New York and the traditions by which it lives, the symbolic and actual denial of their origins by the chief characters is most important. Viewed in this light, the novel takes on considerably more meaning than it might otherwise have.

Much fuss has been made of the novel as the story of the emotional growth of a young girl in love. Much fuss has also been made of the novel as the story of a young girl's struggle to become a success on the stage. Both approaches to the book seem to miss the real purpose for which it was written. Internal evidence indicates that the author has a deep understanding and trust in the traditions of Jewish culture. His characterizations of the people who accept their culture is completely sympathetic. His descriptions of the celebrations of Jewish holidays and ceremonials are honest, straightforward, and full of appreciation for their meanings and the feelings they engender in the people who practice them. The evidence of his earlier novels indicates that Wouk is a skilled craftsman, so conscious of his craft, in fact, that it is absurd to think of the author of *Aurora Dawn* and *The Caine Mutiny* as being satisfied with the triviality and superficiality of fiction more suited to the pages of cheap magazines

than the pages of a reputable novel. If one emphasizes the stage aspirations of Marjorie Morningstar or looks only at her experiences in love, the novel assumes the proportions of such hackneyed fiction. It is unfortunate that the title of the novel and some of the material publicizing it have contributed to such misconceptions.

Every large city is composed of many communities, tightly knit groups of people who exist almost without regard for the rest of the population about them. Such is the Jewish community of New York as it is portrayed by Wouk in the pages of *Marjorie Morningstar*. Part of the final importance of the novel may well rest in the picture of the community presented. Herman Wouk has carefully drawn the great events in the lives of those people—their religious festivities, their marriages, and their deaths. He has also shown them at work, in their homes, and at play. Non-Jewish readers may find here an insight into the lives of people who might otherwise have passed unknown. It is against such a life that Marjorie Morningstar rebels, only to be finally reconciled to it, finding her place within her culture as the wife of Milton Schwartz, a rising young lawyer. In fact, Marjorie was never, perhaps, so very far from reconciliation with her culture and a sober conformity to it. Despite her infatuation for Noel Airman, in spite of her efforts to be advanced and free, she could not break with the mores of her culture, could not break comfortably with such taboos as those which forbade her eating pork and shrimp. She had to learn, however, as almost all adolescents must, that mores change slowly and that those same mores which one rebels against in adolescence, regardless of the segment of culture from which one arises, contain a wisdom that young people are too superficial, too hasty, to see. Only those individuals who persist in denial, only the Noel Airmans who insist on a blind rebellion, fail to find some measure of happiness and contentment in the world. Such seems to be the message implicit in *Marjorie Morningstar*.

Herman Wouk's experience as a playwright seems to have affected his novel writing and to have improved it in some respects. In *Marjorie Morningstar*, as in *The Caine Mutiny*, his writing has precision in depicting action, a precision not found in his earlier novels. His characterizations, too, have improved. The characters in the later novels acquire a depth of personality that is much greater, for example, than those found in *Aurora Dawn*. The relationships between characters in the later novel are more complicated and more convincing. This result may be partly due to the subject matter. It is partly the result of additional emphasis on characterization which is possibly the result of the author's experience as a successful dram-

atist. More than ever Herman Wouk demonstrates his ability to fit the dialogue of his characters to their actions and the situation. Many of the scenes in *Marjorie Morningstar* are dialogues between two people, dialogues with deftly inserted stage directions that might well be used in a stage adaptation of the novel. The scene in Noel Airman's Paris apartment, in which he and Marjorie talk while he prepares dinner, is an excellent example of Wouk's technique in this respect.

These are some of the ways in which *Marjorie Morningstar* seems to excel: it is a splendid documentation of life among the Jewish people of New York and elsewhere; it is the record of the rather senseless, if wholly understandable, struggle against environment by adolescents everywhere; and it is a well-written novel. Most readers will not ask for more. They will read *Marjorie Morningstar* and, for the most part, enjoy doing so. For to provide enjoyable reading, in the best sense of that adjective, is the prime purpose of fiction, a fact that critics and scholars frequently overlook, although readers seldom do.

MARK TWAIN: AN AMERICAN PROPHET

Author: Maxwell Geismar (1909–   )
Publisher: Houghton Mifflin Company (Boston). 564 pp. $10.00
Type of work: Biographical criticism
Time: 1835–1910
Locale: Missouri and the world

A chronological treatment of the works of Twain as a revelation of the author's life and his cultural and social stances

> *Principal personages:*
> SAMUEL LANGHORNE CLEMENS (MARK TWAIN)
> OLIVIA LANGDON CLEMENS, his wife
> SUZY,
> CLARA, and
> JEAN, their daughters
> WILLIAM DEAN HOWELLS, an American novelist
> HENRY HUTTLESTON ROGERS, Twain's financial adviser
> ALBERT BIGELOW PAINE, his friend and biographer

"Most of Mark Twain's work is autobiographical in essence from *Roughing It* and *Life on the Mississippi* to his *Autobiography* in 1924; and the final (semifinal) period of his work was even more directly filled with the personal utterances which are almost always his best statements." So says Professor Maxwell Geismar in a larger than life book about an often larger than life man.

The "factual" matter of Twain's life is summed up in four pages of an introductory chapter. Born of good family in 1835 in Florida, Missouri, and moving four years later to Hannibal, Twain began his lifelong courtship with youth and with seeing through the often simplistic eyes of childhood. From the Mississippi romance to the Nevada and San Francisco experiences, Twain moved to the edenic Hawaii, which was to captivate a part of his future life. Marrying, in 1870, Olivia Langdon, he produced in the next ten years four children and settled in Hartford. The 1880's and 1890's saw Twain's generally admired works and also his bankruptcy through a vari-ety of bad business ventures. With the help of Henry H. Rogers, Twain became solvent again but lost two of his daughters (his son had died in 1872) and his wife. A citizen of the world but in many respects a private writer, his career lasted far beyond his death in 1910.

. . . the central point of the present book is that Samuel Clemens was not a major talent frustrated at midpoint. Not in the least; not at all; not possibly so. And I think that we have more than amply refuted the old and recurrent thesis of Twain's "frustration," his "failure," his final "bitterness." On the contrary we have seen just how Clemens recovered his talent intact from the pit and quagmire of disaster. The whole point is that he surmounted the crisis of mid-life; he survived it and he transcended it.

He entered his mature and later periods of writing quite triumphantly indeed, with all his old powers enhanced, rather than broken or diminished, by his own tragic experience; by his depth realization of life's pain and evil. He retained to the end the central source of his artistic virtue: that untouched spring of pagan, plenary, and edenic innocence, that full sense of joy and pleasure in life, which came to a second and later flowering despite all those civilizational discontents which he, perhaps more than any other American writer, also felt so directly and personally at the center of his being.

Between the four-page "life" and the above-cited summary, Professor Geismar examines Twain's works chronologically as they reveal the political, cultural, social, and religious frame of the author's mind.

Classifying the works of the 1860's and 1870's as those of "A Pagan Puritan," Geismar notes the primitive, violent, and sensual, and regards Tom Sawyer as both orphan and devil. "If *Tom Sawyer* is, on one level, a parody of an adult society of power and manipulation, of property and place, of trading and acquisition—the parody itself is divine, is innocent, is wistful and comic." The works of the 1870's and 1880's are seen as *"a floating through life*, unencumbered by society or civilization, just for the sake of living each moment, hour and day." The "edenic-satanic" theme of the earlier works is to be transposed into the later works in more forceful statement. Thus, Twain becomes more direct in *The Man That Corrupted Hadleyburg* with a proclamation of "the cultural impact of the titans and the trusts; of the new social-economic regime of monopoly capitalism in the United States."

A little more than half way through this appreciative criticism, Twain dies, consequently leaving half the work to be devoted to Twain's posthumous writings which have gone largely ignored by critics. Here it is that Geismar's analysis becomes of greatest importance.

. . . Samuel Clemens had devoutly come to feel that death was indeed the final blessing, the only true refuge from life's pain and suffering and tragedy. He welcomed his own death in this spirit. But destiny would not yet abandon to the blindness and darkness he yearned for, this singular personality. The ironical fact was that Mark Twain would continue to produce "new" books for another fifty years after his own death; that his career would develop and grow to even greater heights after he had so willingly abandoned it; that in the 1960's, above all would appear as if miraculously, some of his very best work: the most pertinent commentary about our own contemporary scene, made resplendent in prose as light as air, as intense as fire, as fresh as the dew.

It is obviously this later section of the work which Geismar's heart is really in and with which critics will most quarrel. Declaring *The Mysterious Stranger* to be "desperate nihilism" and "a comedy of evil," he points out that Twain's "Satan becomes not merely Twain's confidant in these later years, but in Jungian terms, say, the earlier-repressed but now reversed and dominant half of Twain's soul; and in Rankian terms, more accurately, the repressed primitive soul which took rightful power over the 'rational' social soul." The *Autobiography* in Geismar's eyes is a " 'daylight book' ":

Revealing all his nighttime fears only to smile at them, Mark Twain himself emerges, not as a split, divided, tormented figure. But if he still acknowledged and bowed down to all this in a yet rebellious mood of comedy, as a daylight writer of the highest sort who gives us, so many years later, a chronicle full of sweetness, affection, tenderness, and humor *about* the tragic experience of life.

The last three chapters, while continuing to treat Twain's later posthumous works, show not only Geismar's views of the late-late Twain, but more entertainingly his views of Twain critics. "Mr. De Voto is so close to the truth at times, it is depressing to see him always reach the wrong conclusion." "What a medicinal-sounding word ['anecdotic'] Mr. Neider uses instead of the more familiar 'anecdotal.'" "During the Cold War period of the 1950's which conditioned the thinking of both Neider and Kaplan, there was to be very little criticism, in effect none, of a democracy which was considered to be struggling for its very survival against the so-called Russian Frankenstein."

Geismar admires Twain chiefly as a social-cultural-political-religious critic. Hence, the later works (later than *Huckleberry Finn*) weigh more heavily in Geismar's estimate than do those popular works from which one must glean, say, social commentary. Although one may question at times Geismar's conclusions (often new and stimulating and seldom dull), one never loses sight of the clear vision which produced the book. It is a labor of love written by one with no small amount of Mark Twain in himself.

John R. Byers, Jr.

MARKINGS

Author: Dag Hammarskjold (1905-1961)
Translated from the Swedish by Leif Sjoberg and W. H. Auden, with a Foreword by
   W. H. Auden
Publisher: Alfred A. Knopf (New York). 222 pp. $4.95
Type of work: Spiritual Journal
   An epigramatic, spiritual autobiography of the Swedish statesman who was Secretary General of the United Nations from 1953 until his death in 1961

The much-maligned United Nations organization is no place for weaklings, glory seekers, or prophets who expect to move mountains. It is an organization within which men can win immense institutional prestige but almost never equal prestige outside in the world of raw power where national destinies still have priority over the hopes and welfare of the men and women of every nation of the world. It is an organization which cries out for effective power, ought to have power if it is to function effectively, but which has no direct power in its own right whatsoever. The United Nations is the guardian of the world's peace, but has no means to protect itself or the world from the rude assaults of any imperialistic, arrogant power, big or little. The only power the United Nations has is moral power, the power of conscience, the power of ideals steadfastly lived out in the daily lives, in the words and acts, of the men and women who comprise the member delegations.

   In the day of merciless bayonets and cataclysmic bombs, the discovery that the words and meditations of a good man do in fact have power, can make men and nations at least pause before they commit sinister, violent, and Machiavellian acts, is one of profound importance. Dag Hammarskjold was one of the great men whose life and words could move men and nations. He had this power not because he had the authority to order troops into the field or press the buttons of nuclear war, but because he had no authority except that of his word and his faith. Now dead, he still wins our hearts with his posthumously published *Markings*.

   Markings is an artistically fashioned poetic autobiography. It consists of dated entries, the earliest from the years 1925-1930, and the latest dated 24 August 1961, twenty-five days before his death on 18 September of that year. The first and the last entries are poems whose juxtapositions seem wonderfully deliberate. The first is entitled "Thus it was":

> I am being driven forward
> Into an unknown land.
> The pass grows steeper,
> The air colder and sharper.

Doubt and excitement flood his senses. He continues:

> Still the question:
> Shall I ever get there?
> There where life resounds,
> A clear pure note
> In the silence.

The last entry, not titled, is a kind of poetic answer which the achieved life of passionate discipline and controlled longing produced. It could be titled "Thus it is":

> Is it a new country
> In another world of reality
> Than Day's?
> Or did I live there

Before Day was?

The poem concludes with serene faith
and the deep, quiet joy of fulfillment,
the happiness that his faith has justified him:

> The seasons have changed
> And the light and the weather
> And the hour.
> But it is the same land.
> And I begin to know the map
> And to get my bearings.

The tension between the first and the
last poems, the subtle, cumulative
effect of all the various entries of a lifetime of search and struggle, make the
"only true 'profile'" (as he referred to
his book) of the Secretary General
come alive. *Markings* is the often cryptic, epigrammatic, always intense record
in runic paradoxes of Dag Hammarskjold's painful and lonely search to
discipline his mind and heart, to transform his ambitions, to move from
tentative youthful aspirations to tragic
knowledge of human destiny. It is not
easy to know the map of one's soul, or
to discover the bearings of one's destiny. He wrote:

> The longest journey
> Is the journey inwards
> Of him who has chosen his destiny,
> Who has started upon his quest
> For the source of his being . . .

Markings is not a book one can summarize, for the only chronology is that
of bare dates, not events; the only unity
is that of tone, not narrative; the only
theme is that of the lonely quest, not
the solitary journey to the summit won
through hardship and exhaustion from
which both we and the solitary traveler
can ascertain the latitude and longitude, the exact height and depth of the
conquest. There is no planting of the
club flag on the pinnacle of Mt. Ever-
est, no panoramic photograph of the

mighty landscape. The entries consist
of quotations from the Psalms, hymns,
T. S. Eliot, St.-John Perse, Pascal,
Faulkner, Thomas Aquinas, Ibsen, and
others; poems written by Hammarskjold himself, many of them in the
haiku form; paradoxical definitions of
moral qualities and positions; impera-
tives to himself, comments of despair,
hope, and self-contempt; prayers and
comtemplations. One reads *Markings*
not for the argument of a man's life
and convictions, but for *glimpses* of the
private thoughts and feelings of a public man; for *suggestions* of belief; for
surprises. Some of these confessions
are embarrassing because they are intimate and unprotected by disguises.
Others are the usual, the ordinary. We
all know that public men who manage
great human enterprises—a nation, a
church, and expedition—who captain
the ships of state, are lonely men, insistently compelled to sacrifice their
private lives for the common weal.
That Dag Hammarskjold winced and
sang on the age-old anvil of loneliness
and sacrifice should not startle us. It is
the quality, the peculiar individuality
of his pain, the quaintness of his moral
lectures to himself, which engage our
feelings. It is precisely the lack of his-
toricity, the lack of events, narrative,
and particularity which gives *Markings*
its power, and the fallen Secretary General his lasting authority. The chronology of the heart, the unity of anguish
and hope, and the theme of endeavor
through submission and sacrifice give
the book its authenticity.

A persistent utterance of Dag Hammarskjold is, "Not I, but God in me."
Again:

> Lord—Thine the day,
> And I the day's.

Like Marcus Aurelius before him,
Hammarskjold daily schools himself to

be obedient to Nature, to God. Again and again *Markings* suggests comparisons with the *Meditations*. Both are the records of intensely personal inner communions of men who shaped the destinies of the world. Both reveal the grief and anguish of responsibility, as well as the moral, religious, and poetic sensibilities of their writers. But the *Meditations* concludes in the despair of stoic endurance ultimately for the sake of endurance, while *Markings* anticipates the joy and hope of release in the fullness of human acceptance of God's love. Because Dag Hammerskjold could say, "Not I, but God in me," he could bear the galling frustration of possessing the semblance but not the substance of power, the responsibility of power, or acting as if he had the power, while never possessing one shred of the purple robe of the imperial office. The sacrifice he was called to make was not the spectacular one of public martyrdom, but the secret one of denying his instincts to act grandly and positively, to wield the power of the sword. His sacrifice was the private discipline of dying daily to ambition. In his annihilation of self and of ambition, in his submission and obedience, is his strength and the real source of his power, his power itself.

"Thine . . ." A sacrifice—and a liberation—to obey a will for which "I" is in no respect a goal!

"Destined . . ." A reward—or a price —to be committed to a task in comparison with which nothing I could seek for myself is of any value.

One cannot believe that Hammarskjold is indulging himself in the sacrificial pose, the easy ploy for winning sympathy and praise by spinning a nice paradox. Again and again he shatters his own complacency. The truth of

sacrifice is daily tested on his nerves and flesh.

> You told yourself you would accept the decision of fate. But you lost your nerve when you discovered what this would require of you: then you realized how attached you still were to the world which has made you what you were, but which you would now have to leave behind. It felt like an amputation, a "little death," and you even listened to those voices which insinuated that you were deceiving yourself out of ambition. You will have to give up everything. Why, then, weep at this little death? Take it to you—quickly—with a smile die this death, and become free to go further—one with your task, whole in your duty of the moment.

Furthermore he does not assume the specious pose of the stiff-upper-lipped hero, *ad astra* with afterburners glowing. Tears out of weakness and an aching heart are fully human, just as not to give up is truly heroic.

> Weep
> If you can
> Weep,
> But do not complain.
> The way chose you—
> And you must be thankful.

Marcus Aurelius could never really be thankful. Mathew Arnold noted that the saintly stoic was always sad, never possessing the inspiriting joy which alone gives hope. Mathew Arnold himself was sad. "Wandering," as he said, "between two worlds, one dead," and the other, as we now know, stillborn, he could never believe. He was, like Hammarskjold, committed to both Hebraism and Hellenism, loved "Sweetness and Light," yet he could never reveal himself to be thankful. He could never "make a joyful noise unto the Lord." So he lamented elegantly, and let "The unplumbed, salt, estranging sea" divide him from his destiny. Dag Hammarskjold, however, crosses the straits, reaches the "darkling plain . . . where ignorant armies clash by night," and even if he too is "swept with confused alarms of struggle and flight," endures to be thankful. Thus he passes beyond the darkling plain to the mountain country. Because he won the right to say with the Psalmist whom he quotes so often, "Not unto us. O Lord, but unto thy Name give the praise," he can conclude his life and his book with this realization of time and place and self:

> The seasons have changed
> And the light
> And the weather
> And the hour.
> But it is the same land.
> And I begin to know the map
> And to get my bearings.

Gerrit H. Roelofs

MARLBOROUGH'S DUCHESS
A Study in Worldliness

Author: Louis Kronenberger (1904-   )
Publisher: Alfred A. Knopf (New York). Illustrated. 314 pp. $5.75
Type of work: Biography
Time: 1660-1744
Locale: England

A biography of one of England's most striking women in an age of worldliness, bribery, corruption, and brilliance

Principal personages:
SARAH JENNINGS CHURCHILL, Duchess of Marlborough
JOHN CHURCHILL, Duke of Marlborough
JAMES II, the last Stuart king
WILLIAM AND MARY
QUEEN ANNE
SIDNEY, Earl of Godolphin
ROBERT HARLEY, Earl of Oxford
HENRY ST. JOHN, Viscount Bolingbroke
SIR JOHN VANBRUGH
ROBERT WALPOLE
ALEXANDER POPE

Aptly subtitled, Mr. Kronenberger's book, without adding new details to the known life of Sarah Churchill, does add another readable interpretation to the career of that "impossible but incomparable woman." Since existing sources of information bearing directly on the duchess are meager at best, much of *Marlborough's Duchess* consists of extremely good stage-setting, interspersed with vignettes of her life and its influence on many of the leading figures of her age. Most of these vignettes are drawn from letters, and while extremely interesting for the most part, they tend occasionally to detract from the continuity of the narrative. It should be added that the development of Churchill influence corresponded almost exactly with the accumulation of the Churchill wealth. In an age of unabashed greed for money and power, the Churchills employed the necessary means to achieve their desired ends successfully.

Sarah's successes are all the more surprising in view of her modest beginnings. Of an obscure but not entirely unknown Royalist family, Sarah Jennings was introduced to court life at the age of thirteen by her sister, a maid of honor in the service of the Duchess of York. Like her sister, she took service with the duchess. Even at this age, however, certain of her characteristics appear. She had a "falling out" with her mother which eventually resulted in driving her mother out of the court, and a permanent separation of the two women. This is the first known example of Sarah's strong will. Mr. Kronenberger, while discussing her beauty and charm at considerable length, plays down the vixenish side of her nature. When once she entered a contest, however, the issue could be settled only by the complete subjugation of her opponent or by total separation.

At court Sarah met John Churchill, also of an obscure and impoverished Royalist family, and a page to the

Duke of York. Although both John and Sarah apparently agreed on marriage almost from their first meeting, Sarah, from coyness and the desire for some material security, put off the marriage for about two years.

Married in 1677 or 1678, John and Sarah led a precarious existence, financed partly by a five hundred pound annuity purchased with five thousand pounds reportedly received as the result of services John rendered Barbara Villiers, the royal mistress. Despite this annuity, the young Churchills depended largely on the bounty of the Duke of York (the future James II) and the second duchess.

Mr. Kronenberger develops the fact that the accession of James II, with whom John and Sarah had shared exile, presented them with an unenviable problem. In his debt morally and financially, they were attached to the Protestant Succession. Also, being well aware of James's weak position in the country, they had no intention of associating their greater interests with his declining star. Consequently, at the proper moment in the Glorious Revolution, and with considerable personal danger to Sarah, John went over to the side of William of Orange. In this instance it becomes difficult to separate personal, national, and religious loyalties. John was a believer in the Church of England. Therefore, although reasonably tolerant of non-Anglicans, he could hardly have seen benefit to the Church in a Catholic dynasty. At the same time, he tended to equate his interest with those of England. He appears to have felt that whatever improved John Churchill's expectations also benefited England. To his discredit, it must be added that he delayed turning his coat until James's defeat had become all but a certainty.

John and Sarah had betrayed James II, but their betrayal was matched by that of their new patroness. Princess Anne, the future queen, had also betrayed the king, her father. Happily for both Anne and the Churchills, the revolution succeeded and their fortunes prospered. John, who possessed proved military ability, and who had at least ended by supporting the winning side, became an earl and a Gentleman of the Bedchamber. Anne, with James and his son out of the way, became the heiress-presumptive.

Princess Anne, the dull, neglected, colorless daughter of James and the first Duchess of York, found herself virtually hypnotized by the charming and vivacious Sarah, now Countess of Marlborough. Anne, who previously had been close to Sarah, now became her adoring slave. As Mr. Kronenberger points out, the relationship of these two exceptional women remains one of the enigmas of history and personality. Sarah's masculine assertiveness complemented Anne's helplessly feminine loneliness. Sir Winston Churchill described the affections of the pair as "strangely intense," while A. L. Rowse stated that Anne loved Sarah passionately. It appears that Sarah did not reciprocate that emotion and that her motive was a mixture of condescension and opportunism. In Anne's friendless existence, Sarah became her link with bright society. While Anne possessed social station, Sarah, who could chatter wittily in any society, served not only as her spokesman but also as her mentor; and it appears that Anne's great decisions in this period were arrived at by Sarah rather than by Anne.

This period from 1689 to 1710 bears out Mr. Kronenberger's thesis, if such it should be termed, that Sarah was equal to John in political importance. While John led men of ability, Sarah owned the princess and later the queen. Princess Anne heaped what favors she could on the name of Marlborough, but her position of heiress-presumptive gave her little power until the death of Mary and the final illness of William III. In the meantime John engaged in intrigue of a most questionable nature with the exiled James II in France. Princess Anne, faced with the possibility of the loss of her confidante, defended the honor of the Marlboroughs to the extent of exile from court. Once again, Marlborough self-interest was uppermost. Without actually trying to undermine or overthrow William III, Marlborough did not care to bet his neck and fortune all on the front runner. He chose, instead, to bet on both horses in what might conceivably have developed into a close race. Anne, incidentally, regarded the charges against John as an attack on her own position.

Under Queen Anne, who was steadily underestimated by Sarah, England's star rose to its zenith, and the Marlboroughs found adequate occasion to serve her and repair their fortunes. She bestowed offices and honors upon them, and they replied, Sarah through constant attention and even domination, and John through his diplomatic and military services. It is owing to John that there came into existence the incomparable combination of John the soldier; the Earl of Godolphin, the Lord Treasurer, and Robert Harley, leader of the House of Commons. As *Marlborough's Duchess* indicates, it was only with the promise of adequate financing and political support that the Marlborough name was to go down in history as that of one of Britain's great

generals. It was with the help of these great men, and in the name of Queen Anne, that Marlborough won his stunning victories at Blenheim, Ramillies, and Oudenarde.

For his services John received a dukedom, a palace larger than Windsor, and additional honors from the queen. But Sarah's relations with Anne were in the process of decay. Her charming but utterly domineering manner worked well with John, who loved her, and had worked well with Princess Anne, who had been lonely. Now that she was queen, however, Anne began to resent Sarah's domination. She sought out a more congenial companion, and found her in Abigail Hill, later Lady Masham. Sarah replied to this treatment in the only manner possible to her, with even greater demands and outright nagging. Relations between the two women worsened, and in the spring of 1710 they met for the last time at Kensington. Tearfully Sarah pleaded loyalty and attempted to refute lies told about her. Anne adamantly refused to listen and asked for her excuses in writing. Mr. Kronenberger oversimplifies to some extent in implying that Sarah's personality was the major cause of this rupture. John and Sarah had forced expensive Whig policy and expensive Whig politicians on the unwilling Anne. Lady Masham represented both kind and quiet company for Anne, and a liaison with Robert Harley, by this time an opponent of Marlborough's faction. Disgraced and abandoned by the queen, the Great Duchess who had "married a conqueror and ruled a Queen" went into eclipse.

Even though eclipsed, Sarah still had prestige, wealth, and character. Her husband, while he lived, was the greatest military figure of the age. When he died in 1722 she became the richest woman in England. Having failed to control the queen, or a succeeding monarch, Sarah was to spend the greater part of the remainder of her life quarreling. She wrangled with and alienated most of her children and many of her grandchildren. She quarreled with Sir John Vanbrugh, the architect of Blenheim Palace, on such terms that doubt arises as to her motives. She quarreled with Robert Walpole during his rise to political power and raged at her inability to destroy him. *Marlborough's* *Duchess* takes an oddly sympathetic attitude toward her feuds, especially in view of her known incompatibility with most people. Individualism and candor can mitigate but not excuse a lifetime of unnecessary combat. Indeed, in her declining years her unmarred friendship with Alexander Pope stands almost unique. In 1744 she died and was buried in the chapel at Blenheim, beside the body of her husband. Only death could end the career of either one of England's great ladies or a "devilish old shrew," or both.

THE MARQUISE WENT OUT AT FIVE

Author: Claude Mauriac (1914-   )
Translated from the French by Richard Howard
Publisher: George Braziller (New York). 311 pp. $4.95
Type of work: Novel
Time: The present
Locale: Paris

An experimental novel about the sights, sounds, thoughts, impressions and speeches of various people during a one-hour excursion to a newspaper kiosk by a Marquise in Paris

Principal characters:
THE MARQUISE
MARTINE CARNÉJOUX, the wife of a novelist
MONSIEUR DESPREZ, a dealer in historical manuscripts
BERTRAND CARNÉJOUX, a novelist

With *Finnegans Wake* the novel perhaps reached its point of maximum density. What more of experience conveyable by verbal means could prose fiction bear? Yet the novel did not die. During the subsequent quarter of a century the genre has continued to be employed in every conceivable mode and form, and to every degree of difficulty, though in this respect none surpasses Joyce's work. One of Joyce's followers in France, Raymond Queneau, brought, in his *Reflections on Style,* the novelist's pleasure in language to heights of rhetorical hilarity through the pedantic device of one hundred controlled variations on an extremely simple and ephemeral narrative subject. In *Zazie,* Queneau adapted various Joycean elements to produce a very witty comedy of character. Claude Mauriac's new novel, *The Marquise Went Out at Five,* resembles *Finnegans Wake* less in wit and in language than it does in fundamental unreadability, but an unreadability due not to density but to a technique which demands more of a reader than the import of the subject justifies.

Barrès said, "In judging a work of art, the first criterion is its subject matter." This is a quotation forming part of an extensive discussion of the principles of fiction between a novelist and a scenarist who are characters in Mauriac's first novel, *The Dinner Party.* Though Barrès' assertion is countered in the course of the conversation ("A good book can be written on any subject."), a critic of Claude Mauriac's new book may be tempted to invoke it. For all that happens is that a Marquise leaves her Paris apartment exactly on the stroke of five o'clock on a hot summer afternoon and goes down to buy a newspaper at the Carrefour de Buci. She notices a few familiar merchants and other regulars of the neighborhood, as well as a variety of common citizens and chance passersby. Each of these people has in his mind or on his tongue a preoccupation, a brooding thought, on idea, an impression, or a reaction. The articulation of their notions constitutes the text of the novel, which ends at 6 o'clock.

Introductory dots indicate the interior monologues, quotation marks indicate the speeches, but no other identification of thinker or speaker is given. Consequently, it is up to the reader to follow the rapidly changing paragraphs, the sudden shifts of multiple points of view, the abrupt vicissitudes of subject matter. It is theoretically possible to make these identifications on the basis of separated continuities, motifs of subject, or tone, but there is little incentive to do so. The intrinsic interest in what is going on is too slight. The gist of the book is disjointed panorama. In addition to the character representations there are also, in italics, fragments of old lyrics, drinking songs, historical and literary legends—all associated with this corner of Paris and intended to protract the simultaneity of human experience beyond this narrow hour. The pastiche may suggest the universality and eternality in the wriggling forms of a microscopic vision, but the effect of it all is rather confusing, to say nothing of tedious. It is impossible to imagine a skeleton key to *The Marquise Went Out at Five*.

The Dinner Party (1960) is similarly experimental in kind but considerably more coherent and meaningful in terms of the character relationships, which impose a tension and fulfill a form. The most impressive feature of that novel, however, is the perspective drawn upon the novel medium itself. Bertrand Carnéjoux is a novelist who desires to produce a work of fiction even more successful than his last, a new work of artistic integrity which will fuse the thoughts and words of his characters. He discusses literature and his own techniques with a famous screen writer whose strong wish to try the novel form makes him contemplate a book in cinematic terms. Much of what these two are and what they say to each other illuminates the nature of both *The Dinner Party* and *The Marquise Went Out at Five*.

Bertrand refers to the novel he has recently published as "a new experiment in fiction . . . in which, during a dinner such as this one, space and time would be temporarily obliterated." It becomes clear that the novel referred to in *The Dinner Party* is *The Dinner Party* itself. And the projected work he speaks of there at last takes the form of *The Marquise Went Out at Five*.

Bertrand is among the pedestrians around the Carrefour de Buci, as is his wife Martine, who has been visiting Desprez, the manuscript dealer; we find him musing: " 'The Marquise went out at five. All my life I've gone out at five. It's five now. I'm going to go out one last time, not in the street any more, not even out to bed. I'm going to leave life itself. [This is a somewhat different version from the actual opening of *The Marquise*.] Now that could be the beginning of my novel.' " The complexity of an author who is a character in a book talking about a book he has written and a book he means to write, both of which are the books in which he appears as a character, fully asserts itself. If *The Marquise* means anything, it is in the context of this conception. Readers really need to know both books, which in some extraordinarily elaborate sense are sequels.

But then, as if this were not all too complicated already, Claude Mauriac introduces himself into the book. Near the end of *The Marquise*, after some thoughts of Bertrand about his craft, we find this passage: "Thus Bertrand Carnéjoux records in his novel, and I record in the novel in which I have given life and speech to Bertrand Carnéjoux, that impossibility of conceiving what seems so natural in others, what one has spent one's life fearing, knowing oneself ineluctably threatened by it in the beings one loves and in oneself: death. Out of his cousin Agnès, he has made the Mathilde of his book, and I myself know that this dying woman's real name was no more Agnès than it was Mathilde. A triple character, this Bertrand Carnéjoux, since he's supposed to write the books in which he himself plays a hero's part. A novelist animated by a novelist whom I (myself a novelist) have put into a novel in which, however, nothing was invented, a labyrinth of mirrors capturing some of life's sensations, feelings and thoughts. . . ."

There is, of course, an explanation of all this from Mauriac: "Thus the novel has in its penultimate pages gradually faded away, and disappeared, without masks or make-believe, giving way to the novelist who, if he has put himself directly into his book, has at the end purified it of its last traces of fiction by granting it a truth in which literal exactitude was preferred to literature. The Marquise did not go out at five . . ." And that is the end of the novel.

It is possible to appreciate this highly skilled unfolding of a theory and a plan. In fact, it is possible to appreciate the idea of the book more than the book itself.

One last note on the title: In explaining his reticence to write a novel, the great Valéry said he could not bear to write down the words, "The Marquise went out at five." Certainly, at least the conventionality of the medium implied by Valéry's mocking words was averted by Mauriac in this acceptance of the literary challenge.

MARRIAGES AND INFIDELITIES

Author: Joyce Carol Oates (1938-   )
Publisher: The Vanguard Press (New York). 497 pp. $7.95
Type of work: Short stories
Time: The late 1960's and early 1970's
Locale: Detroit, upstate New York, and suburbs of various American cities

A collection of stories in which marriage and adultery are treated as both symptoms and causes of a moral, psychological, and physiological sickness that afflicts middle-class America

In "Problems of Adjustment in Survivors of Natural/Unnatural Disasters," one of the twenty-four stories in this new collection by the prolific Joyce Carol Oates, Sylvia, the mother of a mentally-ill child, quotes for her ex-husband a passage from the diaries of Franz Kafka: " 'What an effort to keep alive! Erecting a monument does not require the expenditure of so much strength.' " The anguished cry echoes throughout this volume. For the majority of Oates's characters, the mere process of living is an ordeal; they suffer from many of the familiar modern ailments —alienation, isolation, loss of identity—and their agony is intensified rather than mitigated by the discovery of love.

Joyce Carol Oates, at thirty-five the author of twelve books and winner of numerous awards, including the National Book Award in 1970 for her novel, *them,* approaches the pessimism of Kafka in her vision of modern life. The largely middle-class world which she depicts becomes a kind of Penal Colony in which characters are offered a choice of tortures: *marriage,* and the sterility and fearful symmetries of suburban life; or *infidelity,* and the often terrifying and ultimately corrosive effects of passion.

For Ann Cassity, the housewife in "Extraordinary Popular Delusions," the choice, initially, seems simple. Having come to despise her domestic routine and to feel alienated from her husband and children, she feels "redeemed" by an extramarital affair. But this relationship has its poisonous effect also. Almost from the outset, it carries connotations of death: "His last name was Stanford; it floated to her like pollen, light and deadly." Her passion, as it gets out of control, becomes physically and psychologically destructive: she discovers that she has "another body, made nervous and lean by sensuality, tendons laid bare, limbs slick with perspiration, eyes burning in their sockets . . . ." As she broods over their relationship, she discovers that her love for Stanford has been associated with death from their first meeting, when they shared a morbid thrill over Stanford's story of his dead student. She recalls feeling that "he was seducing her with this story." In the end, her adultery becomes as much a form of spiritual death to her as her marriage.

A similar situation is developed in the story "Love and Death." Marshall Hughes, successful and comfortably married, flies to Boston to visit his father and encounters Cynthia, a woman with whom he had once had an affair and who is now a prostitute. Marshall's passion is rekindled, and as the nature of their earlier relationship is gradually revealed, we find that it too involved a close association of passion and death. Morbidly curious about the death of Cynthia's mother, Marshall had pressed her for details, finally insisting that they make love in the actual deathbed. For Marshall, love in marriage is passionless and innocuous, while in infidelity it is passionate—and hateful:

> The more his wife chatted about her friends and her bridge circle, the more he felt that he loved her and could forget about her. . . . She could never disturb him. Their affection was the affection of friends or companions, there was nothing passionate or brutal about it. He loved her. He hated that woman who was blackmailing him, and his body stirred at the thought of her, excited and furious at the same time.

When Cynthia finally vanishes, Marshall reacts with a mixture of frustration and relief. He never returns to Boston, not even for his father's funeral, taking refuge in marriage for emotions which he cannot master.

None of Oates's characters, in fact, ever quite masters his emotions. Like so many of the gray protagonists of modern fiction, they are a singularly weak, vulnerable aggregation, struggling unsuccessfully with conflicting impulses and ambivalent attitudes and desires. In "The Lady with the Pet Dog," for example, Anna's attitudes toward her lover vacillate between murderous jealousy on the one hand, and hatred and fear on the other ("Why," she wonders, "why did he love her, why did he pursue her? Why did he want her to die?")

Similarly, the adulterous wife in "Scenes of Passion and Despair," as she struggles through the mud to reach her lover's cabin, realizes that "she hates the man she is running from . . . and she hates the man she is running toward." Behind this seemingly hopeless ambivalence is the dual attraction-repulsion principle that Oates regards as inevitable in any powerful physical passion, for she does not overlook the moral influences on her characters' feelings.

Unlike Flannery O'Connor, with whom she has sometimes been compared, Joyce Carol Oates does not write openly "from the standpoint of Christian orthodoxy." She does not drag her characters before the bar of Divine Justice. Instead, she is content, in her literary coroner's report, to list the moral sense as simply being among the causes of death. In "Scenes of Passion and Despair," referred to above, the symbolic significance of the deep mud through which the woman struggles is made obvious, and an air of filth and disorder clings to the descriptions of the lovemaking. Though she hates her husband, the protagonist feels that if " . . . he killed himself she would abandon her lover and wear black. Years of mourning. Guilt. Sin." She persists in believing that she has found a true and permanent "marriage" with her lover, but in the end their lovemaking remains painful, even repellent, and she imagines it being performed before a movie camera and an avid audience.

For Oates's characters, therefore, love is ultimately just another delusion—like drugs, a temporary anodyne against a destructive self-awareness. The most passionate love affair produces only a temporary "high," which soon wears off and becomes progressively harder to achieve. Ruth, the protagonist in "Loving, Losing, Loving a Man," allows herself to be seduced by Federico Soldati shortly after leaving the hospital room of her terminally ill lover, Harry. She rationalizes her action by conceiving love as being, in even a physical sense, a means of thwarting fate and achieving "immortality":

> Her love was immortal. It passed through her, it grew in her, the gift of Harry's body. In her, so deeply embedded, in that most secret part of her body, it might now radiate out through her veins and bones into Federico's body, transforming him.

In the total context of the story, however, Ruth's rationale appears as merely self-deception. Has she ever been seriously ill, Harry asks her? Has she ever had to face the reality he now faces? Her negative reply strikes him as "a sign of her desperate innocence." The fact of approaching death has given him a vision of the individual's existential fate, a fate that even love cannot alleviate. "What," he asks her, "do people have to do with each other, anyway?" The question is repeated often in these stories.

Morally, psychologically, even physiologically, the America of Joyce Carol Oates's fiction is riddled with disease. At least half of the stories in this volume, for example, deal with some form of serious mental illness, and some of these are narrated from the inside with a chilling intensity that recalls Poe. In "Stalking," Gretchen, an alienated, frustrated adolescent, pursues an imaginary "Adversary" (the embodiment, apparently, of all her frustrations) through a shopping center, committing senseless acts of vandalism and gloating when the "Adversary" is finally struck by a car. In "Where I Lived, and What I Lived For," an unnamed narrator dramatizes his bitter inner conflict in the form of a desperate and grisly pursuit—his tormented ego the victim, and his savage and relentless self-hatred the pursuer. And equally nightmarish is the story "29 Inventions," in which a "nurse"-narrator creates an imaginary rival for the love of an imaginary psychiatrist, has her murdered by her husband, then "erases" everything, including herself. Though Oates may intend these stories to represent symbolically what she regards as the generally diseased condition of American life, some of them are little more than morbid case histories, reflecting the kind of clinical fascination with the macabre that is characteristic of so much of her work.

"Sickness" is clearly symbolic, however, in one of the stories in which physical deterioration is the subject. The sudden collapse and rapid decline of the successful auto salesman, Matthew Brown, which the author describes in graphic detail in "The Metamorphosis," may suggest the precariousness of the entire middle-class, commercial way of life. Like Willy Loman, Brown is held together by his absorbing self-conceit as crack salesman and perfect family man. Price quotations, customer files, sales records are the tendons and ganglia that hold him together and keep him running. Then, one afternoon as he sits contemplating a crack in his desk and the failures of others in the auto business, waiting all the while for a customer who never comes, Matthew Brown becomes ill. The artificial ties that have held him together dissolve; at home, in bed, he becomes aware of a new reality, a physical being over which he has no control. As he rapidly drifts into delirium, the specter of the missing customer hovers about his bed. The symbolism is clear, but the physical decay itself fascinates Oates. She insists on noting, from the point of view of both Matthew and his family, each grim stage of his gradual dissolution, like Maryliz Tone in "Happy Onion," who, after the death from cancer of her rock singer fiancé, insists on being present at his au-topsy, witnessing every grisly, grotesque detail.

Joyce Carol Oates's stories, indeed, are often more like autopsies than analyses. Her capacity for minutely detailed character dissection is impressive, but it is sometimes responsible for one of the major defects of her fiction: the fact that, at times, her characters, through this very minute analysis, are refined out of the vivid, objective dramatic existence requisite for the characters of great fiction. At her worst, she is merely a pathologist with a high verbal aptitude; at her best, she is a penetrating, symbolic artist, a seer seeking in the tangled viscera of her characters an augury of human fate.

Denis Lape

MARTEREAU

Author: Nathalie Sarraute (1902-   )
Translated from the French by Maria Jolas
Publisher: George Braziller (New York). 250 pp. $3.75
Type of work: Novel
Time: The present
Locale: France

A relentless search, chiefly by means of the narrator's stream of consciousness, into hidden meanings behind the characters' actions and conversation

> Principal characters:
> THE NARRATOR, a tubercular young man
> HIS UNCLE, a wealthy self-made man
> HIS AUNT
> MARTEREAU, the uncle's friend
> MADAME MARTEREAU

Martereau is a novel which disregards both plot and characterization to probe the motives lying behind the pretenses that form a part of all human relationships. This is not to say that the characters are unconvincing or that the story line is dull, but that both are subordinate to a study of the inmost reality of the self.

The story can be outlined in a few sentences. A rich Parisian buys a suburban house. In order to evade income tax the house is bought in the name of a relatively poor and unsuccessful friend, Martereau. The money is conveyed to Martereau by the rich man's daughter and nephew, who do not ask for a receipt. Martereau and his wife move into the house under the pretext of supervising repairs and seem well established there, so that they react with injured pride and resentment to all demands for statements which could be used as proof that the house is really the rich man's. Eventually they do move out, however, turning the property over to him. Throughout, Martereau has been having a furtive love affair with the wife of the wealthy man.

Simple as the story is, the relationships of the characters to one another are so complex that they cannot be summarized at all, but only suggested. The reader, in fact, never feels that he has come to grips with the characters, for they change constantly, like real-life people, still retaining the basic characteristics which make them individuals. There are innumerable insights into the motives which govern the most commonplace events, but the total effect is to give the reader a sense of one person's basic inability to understand either himself or another.

Nathalie Sarraute has chosen the ideal narrator for such a novel. A tubercular young man living in the household of a wealthy uncle, his enforced idleness gives him opportunity to concentrate on his fascinated preoccupation with motive, while his illness makes him more sensitive to the subconscious cruelties he observes everywhere. He is not an appealing character, but he is an effective narrator. Hypersensitive, deceitful in masking his reactions lest he put the objects of his dissection on their guard, ruled as much as anyone by his own ego, his weakness forces him to take this method of retribution in dealing with a competitive world for which he is physically unfit.

The young man's uncle is on the surface a relatively simple character. Underneath, he too is seething with unacknowledged frustrations and antagonisms, but they are more easy to define because he is basically an aggressive, unintellectual man who is not given to the self-justifications and rationalizations of a more introspective nature. He is a self-made man, successful and rich, both contemptuous and envious of qualities of taste and sensitivity which he lacks. A shrewd and able businessman who tends to dominate all his relationships, he is no match for his wife in the struggles that go on between them—chiefly because her coöperation and approval are necessary to him, while she is wholly indifferent to his feelings for her.

Silence is the weapon she uses most effectively against him; that and her lack of enthusiasm for whatever he is excited about at the moment always bring her husband to heel. Though the latter method is more immediately crushing, silence has more long-lasting effects. The narrator's aunt is probably the most repellent character in the book. Married without love, idle, disappointed in her daughter's looks and interests, she is a woman of intellectual and artistic pretensions without any kind of dedication. A patroness of the arts early in her marriage, she had at one point left her husband to take up painting. But her only success, like her only real influence, lies in the fact that she is married to a rich and powerful man. This circumstance makes her resent him as she does. It is partly this resentment of her husband and partly physical attraction which have prompted her to take Martereau as a lover—for here again there is no sug-

gestion of real devoted love in her feelings. She enjoys bullying Martereau also, and she finds a source of much amusement in his awkwardness and unfamiliarity with the sophisticated places to which she takes him.

Martereau, handsome, warm-hearted, spontaneous, and friendly, seems on the surface very much the "natural man." But he too has frustrations and resentments, and although their source is very simple, they have affected him in extremely complex ways. Apparently happily married, honorable, and a devoted and admiring friend of the narrator's uncle, his actions and motivations are so complicated as to be left completely in doubt at the end of the novel. A relatively poor man who has tried unsuccessfully a variety of jobs, he is aware of the implied insults in the uncle's unconsciously patronizing manner to him. (The uncle advises him that success in business comes from "hammering on the same nail.") He resents, also, the aunt's subtle ridicule, even though he is attracted by her sophistication and fashionable handsomeness, qualities wholly lacking in his hopelessly bourgeoise wife. It is Martereau who finds the house which the uncle later buys. The question arises as to whether this is really an act of friendship, or a means of retribution on both the uncle and the aunt. The house is practical but ugly —just what the aunt loathes but which her husband is sure to buy. Does Martereau have a secret pact with the owner of the house, so that he will gain from the sale, thus beating the businessman-uncle in a shady deal? Also, once Martereau has the clear legal title to the house, without the uncle's having any written proof of his purchase, does Martereau intend to keep it? When the Martereaus finally vacate, is it because of their still unsoiled integrity, or are they governed by fear?

These are only a few of the problems of motivation which confront one in reading *Martereau*. It is a fascinating book, and one which gives the reader fresh insights into familiar relationships. It is also, however, an intellectual's book, and most readers will feel that it lacks the warmth and human sympathy which should give life to great fiction. Perhaps its chief importance lies in the fact that it illustrates the novel form sometimes designated as the anti-novel, product of the trend called the New Realist movement in France.

THE MARTYRED

Author: Richard E. Kim (1932-   )
Publisher: George Braziller (New York). 316 pp. $4.50
Type of work: Novel
Time: Winter, 1950
Locale: Pyongyang, North Korea

A stirring account of the conflict in the souls of Christians during periods of great stress and of the evanescent nature of truth

Principal personages:
> CAPTAIN LEE, an officer in a South Korean Army Intelligence unit
> COLONEL CHANG, Chief of Army Political Intelligence
> CAPTAIN INDOE PARK, the friend of Captain Lee and son of one of the murdered ministers
> MR. SHIN and
> MR. HANN, ministers who had been captured by Communists but not murdered

Seven days before the North Korean Army crossed the border in its invasion of South Korea, fourteen Christian ministers in the North Korean capitol of Pyongyang were imprisoned by the Communists. On the day the invasion began, two of the fourteen were sent to another prison; meanwhile the fate of the remaining twelve remained in doubt. When the ROK and U.N. forces occupied Pyongyang some five months later, the two ministers, Mr. Shin and Mr. Hann, were released from prison.

A South Korean Army Political Intelligence unit moved into Pyongyang and undertook an investigation of the matter of the Christian ministers. This was an extremely sensitive area for several reasons. The intelligence unit was interested in finding out why Shin and Hann had escaped the fate of the other ministers. (Had they "cooperated" with the Reds?) But extreme care had to be taken so as not to antagonize the Christian world by seeming to persecute the two ministers. The prevailing attitude is expressed in the words of Colonel Chang, head of Army Political Intelligence:

". . . I don't want to create the impression that I am handling Christians roughly. Christians in this country are quite influential these days. . . . Everyone seems to be Christian nowadays; it seems fashionable to be one. From the President to cabinet members, generals, colonels, all the way down to privates. Why even the Army has to have Christian chaplains just to please the American advisors."

Further, Colonel Chang wanted to use the twelve ministers as propaganda material against the Communists: "A grave case of religious persecution by the Communists. Of international significance, if I may add, sir, particularly in America."

Captain Lee, a young university instructor in history transferred from infantry duty to intelligence, was assigned the thankless task of undertaking the investigation of the ministers. Lee's position was complicated by his own questioning attitude toward Christianity and the fact that one of his best friends was the son of one of the missing ministers. This son, Captain Indoe Park, had been disavowed by his father because of religious differences.

Shortly after Lee's arrival in Pyongyang, it became obvious that the twelve ministers had been executed by the Reds. Lee asked Mr. Shin to explain how he and Mr. Hann had escaped the fate of the others. Shin's answer was, "It was through divine intervention." This obviously inadequate—if not untrue—statement was greeted with great laughter by Colonel Chang, who instructed Captain Lee to continue the investigation. In subsequent conversations with Mr. Shin, Captain Lee raised the question which is the crux of this novel. This question, which could well be asked all Christians, stemmed from a rather harsh scene of human suffering witnessed by the young officer. "Your god," he said to Mr. Shin, "is he aware of the suffering of his people?" Mr. Shin refuses to answer the question; instead, he walks away.

These, then, are the intertwining plots. Did the two ministers who escaped death betray their fellow ministers and were they released because of this act of treachery? Did the twelve who died leave this world bravely, shouting the praises of God, and could they, therefore, serve excellent propaganda purposes as martyrs? Or were they cowards whose faith left them at their moment of truth? Finally, how can Christianity explain the vast amount of suffering, death, and pain permitted by God?

From a variety of sources, including a captured North Korean intelligence officer who was in charge of the ministers, the true story of the interrogation and execution emerges. In the words of the Red intelligence officer, Mr. Hann had been saved because "he went crazy . . . like a mad dog. . . . I don't shoot mad men." Mr. Shin, on the other hand, "was the only one who put up a fight. I like a good fight. He had guts. He was the only one to have the guts to spit in my face. I admire anyone who can spit in my face. That's why I didn't shoot him."

But what of the other twelve ministers? "It gives me great pleasure to tell you that your great heroes and martyrs died like dogs. Like dogs, whimpering, whining, wailing. It pleased me to hear them beg for mercy, to hear them denounce their god and one another." In the face of this rather shocking statement, how could the ministers be treated like martyrs when, in truth, they had shown themselves to be men of little faith? The answer to this problem came in an act of great heorism on the part of Mr. Shin. Speaking from the pulpit of his church, he "confesses" that he had betrayed the ministers, that because of this betrayal they had all been executed, but that they had died bravely with full faith in the rewards which would be theirs in God's Kingdom. For his own weakness Mr. Shin asked forgiveness, but he told his congregation that Christians everywhere could be proud of the Korean martyrs. This false statement by Mr. Shin provokes a mob scene that would have resulted in the death of the minister had not Captain Lee intervened.

In a dramatic confrontation between Lee and Shin, the former charges that Shin's god has no interest in the suffering of people, that "he doesn't want to have anything to do with miseries, murders, starving people, wars, and all the horrors!" Shin, obviously suffering mightily, then makes what must be the most difficult of all statements for a minister to utter: "All my life I have searched for God, Captain, but I found only man with all his suffering . . . and death, inexorable death!" Then, when asked about his belief in the life after death, the minister whispers, "Nothing, nothing."

Why, then, did he confess to a lie? Why try to sell his people a faith that he feels is false? Why give his people the illusion of hope when he feels none himself? "Because they are men. Despair is the disease of those weary of life, life here and now full of meaningless sufferings . . . [we must] not let the sickness of despair corrupt the life of man and reduce him to a mere scarecrow."

The story closes quickly after this confession by Mr. Shin. A great memorial service is held for the "martyrs." The Allies are forced back out of Pyongyang, and Mr. Shin is once more arrested by the Communists and this time he is executed. The story of his confession, however, has had the effect of giving to the people new hope and new faith in the God that Mr. Shin had never been able to find.

The novel closes with Captain Lee visiting a small church in a refugee camp in South Korea. As he listens to the beginning of the service, Lee wonders:

How long will the people listen to the voices whispering to them, one from within history (their nation?), the other from far beyond history (the church?), each promising them salvation and justice, each asking them to pledge themselves to its promise?

As for Lee—and, one supposes, for Kim—he leaves the church and joins a group of refugees "gathered under the starry dome of the night sky, humming in unison a song of homage to their homeland."

This is not an anti-church novel. It does, however, raise some very basic questions that Christians must face if their faith is to spread among those outside the Western world. It further raises the question of the proper relationship between church and state, and it brings into stark relief the brutal facts of life: times when the truth is not enough and even times when truth must be set aside in the interests of the greater good for the greater number.

Kim is not yet a finished writer. Some of his characters lack depth, and he attempts too many plots and subplots. But he does have a talent for irritating his reader, the *sine qua non* of all good novelists, and in his role of the artist as gadfly he appeals to the consciences of his readers because at its best his writing generates considerable psychological and moral force.

Frank K. Gibson

MARY

Author: Vladimir Nabokov (1899–   )
Translated from the Russian by Michael Glenny in collaboration with the author
Publisher: McGraw-Hill Book Company (New York). 114 pp. $6.95
Type of work: Novel
Time: 1924
Locale: Berlin

The first novel by the author of Lolita and Ada, translated from the Russian for the first time

Principal characters:

LEV GLEVOVICH GANIN, a twenty-six-year-old, impoverished, upper-class Russian refugee

LYDIA NIKOLAEVA DORN, the widowed landlady of the pension in which all the characters live

ALEKSEY ALFYOROV, separated from his wife Mary for four years,

ANTON SERGEYEVICH PODTYAGIN, an old, well known Russian poet,

KLARA, the friend of Lyudmila and in love with Ganin,

LYUDMILA, Ganin's girl friend,

KOLIN and

GORNOTSVETIV, two homosexual ballet dancers, all Russian refugees and Ganin's fellow boarders

MARY, Ganin's first and early love, now the wife of Alfyorov; her arrival is anticipated by Alfyorov and Ganin throughout the week covered by the novel

Vladimir Nabokov's first novel, *Mary*, could be more accurately titled *A Portrait of the Artist as a Young Refugee*, for it is the story of Ganin, a young Russian refugee with the imagination of an artist. The story focuses on the drab life he leads in exile, but his everyday tedium is balanced by the vivid life of his creative imagination and memory, which are able to conjure up an existence more beautiful than real life could ever be.

The novel opens with Alfyorov and Ganin trapped in a darkened, stalled elevator in Berlin. Alfyorov finds their confinement "symbolic" of their condition as refugees: "stopped, motionless, in this darkness . . . this perpetual waiting." When the elevator suddenly revives for no apparent reason, Alfyorov exclaims, ". . . a miracle. Up we came and yet there's no one here.

That's symbolic too." Alfyorov is, of course, a boor. His room is sloppy and so is his mind. His gushing sentimentality about his wife; his condemnation of the "new Russia"; his getting drunk the night before his wife arrives; his hypersensitive guilt about a one-night affair with a prostitute during his four-year separation from his wife—his every attitude and action testifies to his third-rate intelligence. Yet that one time in the elevator he was right in his assessment of their situation. The scene is a microcosm of the whole novel.

As the characters are introduced, the reader becomes aware that each is "motionless," "waiting" to resume living again. They are all frozen in time and place, sketched with an economy of detail that indicates the later Nabokov genius. Alfyorov waits for the arrival of his wife, Mary, to give him life again. Kolin and Gornotsvetiv, the homosexual ballet dancers "giggly as women," are waiting for the anticipated job which will allow them to dance together again. Klara, who spends her dead days dressed in black before a typewriter, wonders on her twenty-sixth birthday if life will continue to lack all meaning. She hopes for love; more specifically, she hopes for the love of Ganin. Her friend Lyudmila—of the blue-red lips, yellow hair, coal-black lashes and sharp nails —is Ganin's girl friend of the moment. Lyudmila is also waiting for love, but her vividly detailed portrait exposes her incredible shallowness. She is shown to be incapable of living a real life. Ganin is repulsed by "the falsity which she trailed around everywhere like her scent, the falsity of her babytalk, of her exquisite senses, of her passion for some imaginary orchids, as well as for Poe and Baudelaire, whom she had never read." Balancing these young refugees, who live in a suspended state, is the old poet, Podtyagin, who is suffering from heart attacks and realizes that his life is at an end. He hopes only to "escape," to leave Berlin where the literary magazine he founded has failed and where life has become for him mountains of paper and red tape. His dream is to escape to Paris where he has a niece. He dreams of cheap wine and a climate that is free.

Like those who surround him, Ganin too hopes to escape the dreary existence in which he finds himself immersed. He dreams of breaking off his affair with Lyudmila and leaving Berlin with Mary, but Ganin seems unable to exercise either his will or his body to make the break. Of all the characters, however, he is the most aware of the inertia which has them all trapped in their metaphorical elevator; he sees clearly how none of them is alive any more. Even his physical prowess is deserting him: his body has become flabby in exile; he can no longer walk on his hands; at times he cannot even force himself to move from his chair. He has acquired a stoop and suffers from insomnia. Ganin describes his internal state as "dispersion of the will," a "dull sense of unease" in which he can neither make decisions nor force himself to act. His inability to act he attributes to an absence of the desire to change his present conditions, conditions which he describes at various times as like those of a ghost, a shade, a shadow.

Besides the elevator incident there are two other analogies which give emotional emphasis to the emigrees' situation in Berlin. First there is the lengthy description of Frau Dorn's furniture in the pension which, like the refugees, is dispersed and lifeless. Frau Dorn has divided her ownings to furnish the various rooms: "Separated, the pieces of furniture at once faded, took on the inept, dejected look of a dismembered skeleton's bones." The condition of her furniture is a mirror image of the condition of her boarders who live with the furniture; they are all separated, lifeless, and fading.

Nabokov found his most effective analogy, however, in the Berlin film industry which in 1924 was making its now famous "street films." Nabokov draws upon this phenomenon when he writes that "the whole of life seemed like a piece of film-making where heedless extras knew nothing of the picture in which they were taking part." When Ganin takes Lyudmila and Klara to a movie he discovers that he has appeared as just such a heedless extra. Seeing himself on the screen, he is struck with a sense of shame. He cannot escape the "fleeting evanescence of human life." Finally he thinks, "We know not what we do." Repulsed, Ganin is unable to watch the movie any longer.

This view of life in which men have no control over their destinies is a reflection of the political forces which exiled these people in Berlin. This kind of uncontrollable destiny is seen most clearly in the failure of Podtyagin's hopes of escaping from Berlin. For six months he has tried unsuccessfully to obtain a visa. Having finally completed all the requirements, he loses the passport before he can use it. In disgust, he gives up: "I'm doomed not to leave here. It was preordained." This last failure leaves him depressed. He is convinced that his poetry has been worthless. The successive blows bring on his final heart attack, and he dies, sucked into "the abyss" with the realization that "his whole life had been stupid and fruitless, and that he didn't know why he had lived, or why he was dying."

Thus it would seem that Alfyorov is correct in his analysis of the refugees' condition: motionless, in the dark. The stalled elevator is the proper metaphor for their plight. However, the second part of the elevator incident is equally important to the tone and theme of the novel. When the elevator mysteriously revives, Alfyorov observes: "Up we came and yet there's no one here." Ganin, the central character of the novel, does "come up," although he is the only character to manage the feat. When the interplay of coincidences reveals that Alfyorov's awaited wife, Mary, is Ganin's own lost first love, Ganin's fond memory of their earlier

relationship is the outside force which motivates his will. Ganin breaks off his relationship with Lyudmila and spends the next three days on a sentimental journey, reliving in memory the details of his relationship with Mary. Ganin's imaginatively re-created past contrasts starkly with his present conditions: his gray life with Lyudmila in Berlin is juxtaposed against the warm glow of his young love with Mary in rural Russia. Somewhat ironically, Mary is not so much the focus of his revery as is his love for her; Ganin is more concerned with his own feelings than with Mary as a distinct person. Of all the characters in the book, Mary is the vaguest; only her dark hair, her black bow, and her dark Tartar eyes are clearly visualized. What is distinct is the tender mood of reminiscence evoked by Ganin's memory.

As Ganin plans to recapture this early love by running away with Mary from the death-in-life trap of Berlin, his imagination reasserts itself in other areas of his life. Podtyagin's death, for example, reaffirms the uses of the imagination. Although his death seems to represent the passing of the Russia of the romantic past, it also indicates the triumph of the creative imagination. While Ganin's romance of the past is doomed to die, Ganin is still able to find two of Podtyagin's verses endowed with "warm, undying love." Ganin's imagination transforms the death of this failed, old poet into a vision of life itself: "For a moment he saw life in all the thrilling beauty of its despair and happiness, and everything became exalted and deeply mysterious."

The final emphasis of the novel is not on the character, Mary, nor even on young love; the novel focuses, rather, on the revivifying powers of the memory and the imagination. These powers, carried within each person, are presented as the true source of life. Nabokov's technique and theme have been suggested before. A romantic from another age could have been describing this novel when he described poetry as "a spontaneous overflow of emotion recollected in tranquility" by "a man, who, possessed by more than usual organic sensibility, had also thought long and deeply." Coleridge, in turn, suggested that the imagination was "the living power and prime agent of all human perception," "a repetition in the finite mind of the eternal act of creation."

Students of Nabokov may be interested in comparing Ganin and Mary with Nabokov and Tamara from his autobiography, *Speak, Memory,* and also with Van Veen and Ada in the novel *Ada.* But the reader should beware of such comparisons, for Nabokov, himself, has said in the Preface to *Mary:* "The best part of a writer's biography is not the record of his adventures but the story of his style. Only in that light can one properly assess the relationship, if any, between my first heroine and Ada." He adds: "I can as well say there is none."

The reader needs no such comparisons to enjoy *Mary,* for the glories of youth, first love, and rural life have a nostaglic appeal to all readers over twenty. It is this tone of glowing, tender reminiscence pervading the story that informs the reader's reaction to all that occurs. The suspension of the critical senses which occurs in revery carries over even to matters of style. Sentences which are awkward, passages which lose control under the burden of too many exhilarating words —all are part of that very youth and love which is the heart of the novel. Critical judgment is left unexercised; the style is unimportant; the tender, glowing mood is all.

Ann E. Reynolds

MARY QUEEN OF SCOTS

Author: Lady Antonia Fraser (1932–   )
Publisher: Delacorte Press (New York). Illustrated. 613 pp. $10.00
Type of work: Biography
Time: 1542–1587
Locale: France, Scotland, England

A detailed and scholarly biography of the Queen who became a romantic legend in her own lifetime

Principal personages:
MARY, Queen of Scots
FRANCIS II, King of France, her first husband
HENRY STEWART, Lord Darnley, her second husband
JAMES HEPBURN, Earl of Bothwell, her third husband
JAMES STEWART, Earl of Moray, her bastard half brother
JAMES VI and I, her son
ELIZABETH I, Queen of England

The author of this monumental biography is the daughter of the Countess of Longford who, in 1965, produced the equally monumental *Queen Victoria*; thus it might be said that a talent for biography runs in the family. Both works are based upon vast research and meticulous scholarship, the present volume having a bibliography that fills nine large pages, so that the reader can be assured that all authorities available have been consulted. If the final solution to such mysteries as that of the "Casket Letters" is not given here, the answer is that the mystery is incapable of solution by the author or by anybody else.

As in the case of *Queen Victoria,* one might well ask: Why another book on Mary of Scotland, that romantic figure who has held so many spellbound for four hundred years? Is it possible to say anything new, to find any new facts after the diggings of so many historians? To the second half of the question the answer is: probably not. But though a biographer may not be able to produce any hitherto-unknown data, he can state familiar facts from a new angle and interpret the character of his subject in a different way. Such has been this author's purpose. She is frankly partisan, a Marian to the heart. So she gives us an immensely sympathetic portrait of a tragic woman who seemed endlessly pursued by ill-fortune; fated, almost always, to make the wrong decision; who, indeed, belonged to a doomed family. And since there has been no full-length study of Queen Mary since 1905, it is time for a new biography.

Most readers will doubtless be familiar with at least outstanding events of Mary's life in Scotland and of her long imprisonment in England. Not so familiar is the period covered by the first hundred pages of the book: her life in France until her nineteenth year. These were the halcyon days, spent in the sunshine of the cultivated French court as it moved on its endless perigrinations from chateau to chateau in the soft air of the Loire country. Mary was half French, or rather half Lorraine, her mother being Mary of Guise, that ambitious and able cadet branch of the sovereign House of Lorraine. It was this Mary of Guise, widow of James V of Scotland, who acted as regent of that kingdom during her daughter's youth. The younger Mary absorbed all of the new culture of the Renaissance that bloomed so splendidly in France. It was during this idyllic period that she contracted her first marriage, to the pathetic Dauphin, later King Francis II, the eldest of three childless brothers who in turn inherited the French throne and brought to an end the Valois dynasty. The King died at sixteen of an infection of the ear, and there is some question as to whether he was even able to consummate the marriage.

Perhaps Mary's tragic destiny was inherent in her unique dynastic position. She was simultaneously Queen Dowager of France, hereditary Queen of Scotland, and heir presumptive to the throne of England. She and Elizabeth I were what, in modern terms, would be called first cousins once removed, Elizabeth being the granddaughter and Mary the great-granddaughter of Henry VII of England. Thus Mary was an important piece in the infinitely complicated chess game of dynastic politics. And then there was the question of religion to complicate the game still further. This was the period of the bitter struggles brought on by the Reformation, and nowhere was the hatred between Protestants and Catholics greater than in Scotland, where the bigoted John Knox was thundering his sermons. In England, Elizabeth was trying to stamp out the Roman faith and establish the Anglican Church; across the northern border was Catholic Mary, with the Pope and the Kings of France and Spain on her side. As the tragic years passed, this question of religion played an increasingly important role.

The modern reader, on being introduced to the kingdom of Scotland at the time when Mary came there to begin her personal rule, will probably feel that only a sovereign compounded of Machiavelli and Ivan the Terrible could have succeeded in the task of ruling. Scotland was still in the Middle Ages. The great nobles were unmanageable; they were rapacious, cruel, and treacherous. The idea of nationalism, which was blossoming in England, had yet to take root in Scotland. Each noble thought only of the aggrandizement of his family; the well-being of Scotland as a nation meant little to him. There were innumerable family feuds going back for generations; family alliances that were made, only to be dissolved. The "state of the realm" was not unlike that of England during the Wars of the Roses. So it was into this spider web of Scottish politics that Mary stepped, an inexperienced girl reared in the far more civilized climate of France. For all her unquestioned courage and her sense of sovereignty, she was simply not strong enough to master the situation. The author also makes the telling point that Mary always lacked good and faithful advisers. Her cousin Elizabeth had Cecil, who, in spite of his unpleasant character and dubious methods, was a real statesman. For a while Mary could lean on her half brother, Moray, but he in the end betrayed her and became her most implacable enemy.

The young Queen was by no means deficient in the qualities that make a good ruler. On her first arrival in Scotland she quickly gained the love of her subjects—except for such sour reformers as Knox—by her beauty and charm that had fascinated the French court. She had great courage. And she had, for the age in which she lived, a remarkable sense of religious toleration. She was a devout Catholic all of her life, yet she had no desire, as her cousin Mary Tudor had had, to attempt to turn back the hands of the clock to the days before Luther. All she asked was that she be allowed to practice her own religion and let others do likewise, Catholic or Protestant, as the case might be. The attitude was humane and, one might think, reasonable —but not in the sixteenth century when religious toleration was a meaningless phrase to almost all people, high and low.

But Mary's beauty, her charm, her courage, and her high intelligence were all over-balanced by her fatal propensity for making bad decisions at crucial moments. Worst of all were her choices of husbands. It was essential that she marry and have an heir to the throne of Scotland and perhaps that of England. But whom to marry—a foreign prince or one of the Scottish magnates? The final selection of Lord Darnley was, at least on the surface, an appropriate one. He was her half first cousin and next in line to the throne. His portrait at the age of seventeen, reproduced in this book, shows a long-legged youth, with a vacuous but not unpleasant face. The marriage was an utter disaster. There was, to be sure, a son, the future James VI and I, from whom all of the subsequent monarchs of England are descended. Darnley, however, had nothing to him. He was brainless, jealous, and proud. He was dissipated and dissatisfied with his position as King in name only. His arrogance finally drove a group of the nobles into the plot that culminated in the bizarre murder at Kirk o' Field, where the house in which he was lodging was blown into rubble, and he, having somehow escaped the explosion, was found strangled in the garden. The episode, fantastic even in an age

of fantastic assassinations, provided the first of the mysteries in Mary's life. How much did she know; how deeply was she implicated? Scholars differ, but she was later accused of instigating the murder.

If the marriage to Darnley were a disaster, there are no words by which to describe the indecently hasty marriage to Bothwell. Another mystery at once arises: was Mary forced into this union or did she gladly consent to it? But the combination of the murder (in which Bothwell was involved) and the marriage to him was too much even for Mary to carry off; the great nobles revolted, and she was imprisoned in Lochleven Castle and forced to abdicate.

After her romantic escape from the supposedly escape-proof Lochleven; Mary made her ultimate bad decision: to take refuge in England rather than in France which she might well have succeeded in reaching. Again, why? But after all, Elizabeth was her cousin, nine years her senior and unmarried; the crown of England seemed not too remote. She hoped for English help in regaining the Scottish throne, since her abdication had been forced from her and was not legal. Elizabeth would surely realize that revolt against one monarch was a threat to all monarchs. And, above all, she trusted Elizabeth. This trust was the worst mistake of all. She was promptly imprisoned and remained so for the rest of her life.

The story of this long imprisonment is involved and infinitely sad. She was moved from castle to castle; her possessions were sequestered or actually stolen; her papers were taken from her. There was held in London an investigation of the Darnley murder at which the Scottish lords appeared, headed by Moray. It was here that the most famous of all the mysteries was unveiled: the celebrated "Casket Letters," which have been a riddle to historians for generations. Brought by Moray and purporting to prove Mary's part in the murder, they appeared out of nowhere, were taken back to Scotland, and, in 1584, vanished into nowhere. The originals have never been seen since; only copies survive. The investigation, by modern standards of jurisprudence, was a farce; Mary was not allowed to appear in her own defense; hence, Moray was able to get his charges heard without having to prove them. Lady Antonia, by the way, regards the "Casket Letters" to be, for the most part, forgeries.

In few modern books has Queen Elizabeth I—the "Good Queen Bess" of legend—appeared in a worse light than in this one. She played a cat-and-mouse game with her prisoner, gradually tightening the confinement as the weary years passed. But in justice to Elizabeth it should be made clear that she had the proverbial tiger by the tail and could not let go. Once she had allowed Mary to enter her kingdom and had then clapped her in prison, all sorts of problems arose. There were diplomatic maneuvers with Scotland and with other nations. Since Mary was rapidly becoming a Catholic martyr, she was bound to be the rallying-point for Catholic plots against the Protestant throne of England. And the Pope added fuel to these flames by launching a bull of excommunication against Elizabeth which released her many still Catholic subjects from their allegiance to the Queen. By so doing, the Pope quite literally drove another nail into Mary's coffin. Nevertheless, Elizabeth did play the part of a capricious tyrant; she would never meet Mary face to face to hear her side of the story, never give her a fair trial. Indeed, all the actions against Mary were, in every sense of the word, illegal. She was a sovereign Queen, not answerable to the English courts. Even had she been answerable, the laws of England held it as fundamental that a man could be tried only by a jury of his peers. Mary had no peer in England save Elizabeth herself.

However, the cunning Cecil and his agent Walsingham were determined to bring Mary's life to an end. First, a compliant Parliament passed the astonishing Act of Association in 1585, by which statute anyone in whose favor a plot to dethrone Elizabeth was formed was liable to execution, whether that person was aware of the conspiracy or not. In other words, should a conspirator plot to murder Elizabeth and put Mary in her place, Mary was guilty even though she might be in complete ignorance of the scheme. Once this statute was on the books, the ingenious Walsingham had only to concoct the "Babington conspiracy," and Mary's death warrant was sealed.

And so the Queen of Scots was tried and, of course, found guilty. The trial was a travesty; Mary was allowed no counsel and was denied access to all of her papers. She had to depend only on her wits. She defended herself bravely to the end, but the verdict was a foregone conclusion, as she well knew.

It was during the three-month interval between the signing of the death-warrant and the execution that Mary rose to her greatest heights as woman and Queen. She was perfectly serene, perfectly sure that she was dying a martyr to the One True Faith. Her amazing courage was her great legacy to her grandson, Charles I of England.

The execution in the great hall of Fotheringhay Castle is, naturally, the high point of the book; and the reader who is familiar with Froude's description of the same scene, written in 1870 and one of the famous "set pieces" of Victorian prose, will be eager to compare the two accounts. It can be said that Lady Antonia is easily equal to the standard of the great historian. Her account is almost unbearable in its pathos, and the reader will have to admit that, whatever her errors as a Queen, Mary was heroic as a woman.

Then follows the strange anticlimax: Elizabeth's pretended rage at the execution which led her to throw into the Tower the unfortunate Davison who had carried the warrant to Fotheringhay, on the pretext that she had intended the warrant to be kept but not used. And all this when she had privately suggested to Sir Amyas Paulet, Mary's jailer, that he murder his prisoner secretly, a suggestion that even that grim Puritan refused to listen to. And then came the solemn burial in the Cathedral at Peterborough, for Elizabeth refused even Mary's last wish—to be buried in France, the country where she had been happy as a girl and of which she was still the Dowager Queen.

This is a story with many villains and few heroes. The heroes, aside from Mary herself, are mostly humble people—the servants who stood by her to the end, enduring with her the long years of imprisonment. All the great people betrayed her or turned against her, and it is with some satisfaction that the reader learns that justice was meted out to some of them: Moray was assassinated and Morton executed. Mary had a sinister power of bringing death to those whose lives were involved with hers: Châtelard, Riccio, Darnley, Moray, Morton, Norfolk. Even Bothwell died horribly in Denmark. Her son James escaped. but he cuts a sorry figure in her story. Granted that he had not seen his mother since his infancy and that he had been taught to regard her as the murderess of his father, nevertheless he never lifted a finger to save her. Obviously the throne of Scotland and the future throne of England were more important to him than his country's honor and his mother's life.

Mary's complex nature and the equally complex causes of her tragedy are hard to sum up. Perhaps two lines of a song that John Drinkwater used in his play *Mary Stuart* may give the answer. The Queen says of her enemies:

> Though brighter wits had I than these,
> Their cunning brought me down. . . .

She possessed intelligence of a high order, but she lacked the cunning of her opponents. Or is the answer to be found in the favorite word of her mother-in-law, Catherine de Medicis: "Fatality"?

This is a very long and detailed biography—as it must be, for it deals with a very involved story that includes a multitude of characters. But the "general reader" need not be scared away from the book by these facts. *Mary Queen of Scots* is not written only for the specialist in sixteenth century history. It is colorful, exciting, and eminently readable. It unquestionably deserves commendation as one of the best biographies of recent years.

Tench Francis Tilghman

Sources for Further Study

Reviews:

Book World. November 16, 1969, p. 1. 2,350 words.

Economist. CCXXXI, June 21, 1969, p. 52. 800 words.

New York Review of Books. XIII, November 6, 1969, p. 40. 3,000 words.

Time. XCIV, October 17, 1969, p. 110. 1,550 words.

Times Literary Supplement. July 3, 1969, p. 729. 2,450 words.

MARY WOLLSTONECRAFT: A BIOGRAPHY

Author: Eleanor Flexner (1908-   )
Publisher: Coward, McCann & Geoghegan (New York). Illustrated. 307 pp. $8.95
Type of work: Biography
Time: 1759-1797
Locale: England, Wales, Ireland, France, Scandinavia

A study of the development of a poor but intelligent girl into a leading English radical and intellectual, a champion of woman's rights and education, and an individualist of great courage and passion

Principal personages:
MARY WOLLSTONECRAFT,
EVERINA WOLLSTONECRAFT, and
ELIZA WOLLSTONECRAFT BISHOP, her younger sisters
FANNY BLOOD, a girlhood friend
JOSEPH JOHNSON, a radical London publisher
HENRY FUSELI, an artist
GILBERT IMLAY, an American adventurer, Mary's lover
FANNY IMLAY, their infant daughter
WILLIAM GODWIN, English philosopher, Mary's lover, later her
husband
MARY WOLLSTONECRAFT GODWIN, their infant daughter, born
shortly before Mary's death

The mother of Mary Shelley and the author of *A Vindication of the Rights of Woman,* Mary Wollstonecraft is remembered chiefly for these two accomplishments. Eleanor Flexner's biography focuses on experiences crucial to that important book, yet also reveals the patterns of behavior which brought this independent woman to a contented marriage with philosopher William Godwin and death in childbirth at the age of thirty-eight.

Daughter of a London weaver, young Mary knew how few were the rights of women in her class. Her father, aspiring to move upward, turned to farming and failed with a series of small, isolated farms. Worse than poverty was his addiction to drink and his violent temper. Mary, born in 1759, the eldest daughter and second of six children, always despised him. Obsessed with responsibility, she often stood between her mother and her father's brutality. But the mother, hardened by years of misery, displayed little affection or sympathy, providing only an example of submissive resignation which Mary both hated and admired. The younger children developed a demanding dependence upon their sister, which she both fostered and resisted. Without encouragement, often with opposition, she struggled to educate herself. Thus, the Wollstonecraft family itself —exemplifying for Mary the bitterest cases of deprivation, of the unjust tyranny of an incompetent father, and of the ineffectuality of a spiritless mother—laid the groundwork for *A Vindication of the Rights of Woman.* However, Mary Wollstonecraft was not a violent young rebel. Flexner stresses the importance of her religion as a stabilizing force. Her personal faith, theologically vague, was similar to the Unitarianism of her radical London friends. Her doctrines concerning the rights of man, her concept of virtue and social responsibility—above all, her fortitude and moral courage—she credited to a benevolent God. Sustained by faith, she could "look on misfortunes as blessings." Only in her tumultuous last five years did this faith waver, and the biographer rightly makes a point of its influence in the formative and productive years.

If Mary's sense of injustice was sharpened by personal circumstances and kept in check by faith, another trait often disturbed her emotional balance. This was a recklessness in her personal relationships arising from a "need for a 'particular affection' which recurs like a leitmotif all through her life." In commenting on the disastrous affair with Gilbert Imlay, Flexner remarks that if Mary "had not needed love and security so deeply, her love for Imlay might have been less total and unquestioning." The biographer details four serious relationships—with a girlhood friend Fanny Blood, with the artist Henry Fuseli, with Gilbert Imlay, and with Godwin—the last three occurring after Mary had secured prestige as the author of the *A Vindication of the Rights of Woman* and was certain of public scrutiny and censure. However, when she loved, she was driven to extremes of conduct shocking not only by the conventions of the day, but also by her own principles of independence and responsibility. Thus she deserted her

school in Newington Green, as well as her poor sisters, to hurry to Fanny Blood, dying in Portugal. Better known is the case of Mary's infatuation with Fuseli, her absurd proposal to Mrs. Fuseli that she become a member of their household, and the humiliating rebuff which sent her rushing off to Revolutionary Paris alone.

The affair with the American adventurer Imlay, however, most painfully reveals the extent of Mary's capacity for sacrifice in love. Alone in Paris in 1793, unhapppy over the futility of her love for Fuseli, at thirty-four still a virgin, she was quite vulnerable when she met the dashing Imlay. Once more the "experience of loving and being loved blotted out every other consideration—her family, her anguish over Fuseli, even immediate preoccupation with politics or the future." Imlay's love was brief, his subsequent treatment of Mary unforgivable. Nonetheless, having borne their daughter Fanny (named for the dead Fanny Blood whom she had also loved "better than life itself"), Mary felt herself bound to him with a passion beyond reason. But the affair wore itself out in anguish through her recriminations, pleadings, and an assortment of frenzied actions, including attempted suicide.

The romance with Godwin, begun when Mary was recovering from the Imlay affair, was conducted more discreetly, but once under way, it too was all in all. When she found herself pregnant, they decided to marry immediately, to the astonishment of all London. Fortunately, this time Mary's rashness was wisdom; the "tie between them was never ruptured but grew steadily stronger," even after marriage in March, 1797, until her death in September, 1797.

This pattern of behavior, as well as Mary's chronic spells of depression, headaches, and digestive complaints, the author interprets in modern terms as symptomatic of "deeply repressed anger." However, the biographer stresses Mary's more usual capacity for dealing successfully with life. Ordinarily, she applied her energetic intelligence, stubborn courage, and optimistic faith to making opportunities out of obstacles. Her youthful bitterness was given new dimensions through frustrations and humiliations she suffered as companion to a rich old woman (1778) and as governess to the children of the wealthy Kingsborough family in Ireland (1787). Observing, as she believed, results of affluence and mis-education in the triviality of wealthy women, she not only found evidence of her later theory that proper education is the most powerful means of restoring women to their natural human dignity, but also generated within herself sufficient moral outrage to drive her onward. Her brief success as schoolmistress (1783-1786) and the publication of her first book, *Thoughts on the Education of Daughters,* issued by the radical publisher Joseph Johnson in 1786, confirmed the value of her efforts to educate herself.

Late in 1787 she went to London to begin a career then extraordinary for a single woman—not to flout convention, but simply to support herself and help her feckless family without having to endure the servitude of a governess' life. Writing for the benevolent Johnson, she earned her own way and maintained her own house. Intellectually she blossomed, both through her work and through her reception into Johnson's circle, which included prominent radicals—both English and American—other gifted women such as Mrs. Inchbald the playwright, and artists and writers —Blake, for example, who illustrated one of her books, or Godwin, who was not then ready to look with favor upon a woman so forward as Miss Wollstonecraft. Speaking of Mary's decisive progress during this period, the author says: "What actually happened . . . was that the twenty-eight-year-old 'girl' . . . took a long stride toward becoming a woman." Thus it was with confidence well-warranted that she dared to publish one of the first rebuttals of Edmund Burke's reactionary *Reflections on the Revolution in France.*

A Vindication of the Rights of Woman in 1792 brought lasting fame. Flexner notes that this book was "not the outgrowth of previous social or philosophical thought, except insofar as it arose within the wide movement for social change in Western Europe and the United States." Experience had convinced Mary that the "grand source of female folly and vice has ever appeared to arise from narrowness of mind." Mary's position, Flexner states, is this:

> To deny woman the power of reason is to deny her what Christian faith has promised her. Reason cannot, therefore, be the property of one sex alone, and by its very nature it cannot be different in one sex from another.

She was attacking roles that society,

not God, had imposed upon all women, the rich as well as the poor. As Flexner asserts quite validly, despite its obvious flaws in style and sometimes in logic, *A Vindication of the Rights of Woman* is a great human document. Moreover, it gains significance through this distinguished biography of its author.

A Vindication of the Rights of Woman was not Wollstonecraft's last work, for she continued writing until just before her death five years later. However, those years were marked by the turmoil of unfettered emotions rather than by the discipline of intellect and pen. Even so, she published two more books, and when Godwin fell in love with her, she was again a working writer for Johnson.

Eleanor Flexner's *Mary Wollstonecraft: A Biography* is a scholarly and well-documented work, equipped with useful notes, a number of illustrations (including two charming portraits of Mary by John Opie and three of Blake's illustrations for her *Original Stories from Real Life*), and appendices providing material fascinating in itself, though not central to the biography.

The triumph of this biography is the impression it builds of the living Mary Wollstonecraft, complexly human, a woman developing slowly, exasperating both in her strength and in her weakness, downright priggish at times, gloriously untrammeled at others, dedicated to truth, yet flagrantly dishonest with herself and others, childish, yet enormously adult —in all, a living person. Flexner's closing sentence applies to Mary Wollstonecraft's concept of woman's "right to self-development" as a religious and moral responsibility, and to the life which, "except for the few occasions when she strayed to the verge of aberration, exemplified that belief." But it is also a sentence which might well be applied to this excellent biography: "It is surely not irrelevant today."

Catherine E. Moore

A MASS FOR THE DEAD

Author: William Gibson (1914–   )
Publisher: Atheneum Publishers (New York). 431 pp. $7.95
Type of work: Autobiography
Time: From the 1880's to 1964
Locale: New York City

A successful writer re-creates his life with his parents to atone for failing to express his love when they were alive, to prepare for his own old age as a father, and to pass on to his children what he has learned

> *Principal personages:*
> WILLIAM GIBSON, novelist, playwright, poet
> GEORGE GIBSON, his father, a postal clerk in a large bank
> "POP" GIBSON, George's father, a cratemaker
> JIM GIBSON, George's brother, an egg candler, killed in World War II
> ADA GIBSON, George's sister, a missionary to Africa
> WILL GIBSON, George's brother, a carpenter
> FLORENCE GIBSON, William's mother
> MARY DORE, Florence's mother
> BEN DORE, Florence's brother, a salesman
> GEORGE DORE, Florence's wealthy brother
> WILLIAM'S WIFE and
> TWO BOYS (unnamed)
> WILLIAM'S SISTER (unnamed)

After twenty years of bitter struggle to become a writer, William Gibson is now well known as the author of a novel, *The Cobweb,* three plays, *The Miracle Worker, Dinny and the Witches,* and *Two for the See-Saw,* and an account of his disillusionments with the Broadway theater, *The See-Saw Log;* as a poet, he is less well known, but his poems appear frequently in literary publications, and twenty of them are scattered as lyrical, elegiac counterpoints throughout *A Mass for the Dead.* But this is not the autobiography of a famous writer; it is the autobiography of a son, and thus Gibson's biography of his parents.

Gibson depicts his own life almost entirely as influenced by his parents— his abject dependence upon them as a child and his cruel rejection of them as a young man. As a "fearful child" of fifty, Gibson strives to achieve a spirit-ual love of parents he could not love in the flesh; he exhumes a profound love that even steadfast devotion might have concealed. Gibson draws his readers into this intensely private experience on the assumption that the desire of children to atone to parents is universal. The empathetic reader will emerge with Gibson from the long ordeal of expiation in a celebration of love and life. Had the author failed to achieve this affirmation, he would have written one of the most obscene books of the century, a hideous, pathological desecration of the dead, and have gone down in literary history as the most possessed necrophiliac since Poe.

Gibson's father and mother represented everything for which American intellectuals have always had a virulent hatred and contempt. Having expended most of their youthful energy throwing off the tendrils of their parents' teachings, they spent most of their middle age trying to retrieve the life they lost through perverted love disguised as continued attack in satire and camp art or through conscious celebration in deliberate salvage. One thinks of James Agee's autobiographical novel, *A Death in the Family;* Gibson's imaginative nonfiction is in some ways a better book.

Gibson is haunted by a persistent image of his father: "It is night, and my father is up. . . . At one window a cigarette glows, where a wordless silhouette, the figure who will overhang my life, sits in the dark with his thoughts." Escaping his father's "vision" of him, Gibson found a substitute father in his writing teacher, a Jew, who welcomed him to "an act of communion" and "confirmed" his life. The man died, and Gibson "left forever unsaid that in him I had come upon my true father, with whom I had all in common. Except, of course, that he did not love me." During his father's long dying of cancer, Gibson gave him morphine and a poem. But, as with his substitute father, ignorant of what was in his heart, he "never said that he was my true love," and he could never forgive his mother that she was forever between them. Dying unloved, his father "lived again, and died, too, over and over" in Gibson's dreams.

Gibson says of his mother: "Everything in her character for years scoured me the wrong way, even after I saw it as a soulcleansing." She had a "lifelong" "apprehension of doing the wrong thing," and plagued him with "What will people think?" Living with her Protestant in-laws, his Catholic mother "tutored herself to the marrow in happy decorum," and amid "subterranean tensions" developed an ulcer. "I had been to school with her in the rig-

ors of control, and her rule book of self-help bred me to exactions of myself as harsh as hers," says Gibson, who also developed an ulcer. "All my life the notch below infallibility was humiliation." In his rebellious adolescence, she was to Gibson the "flagbearer of the enemy." But living on the "outskirts" of her life, during "the long coda of yea" that was her widowhood, Gibson learned to tolerate his mother's differences and feel affection. When she came to help out during his sons' illnesses, his wife summed up his mother's character by announcing, "The marines have landed," and the doctor said of the dying woman that "she's like a pioneer."

A Mass for the Dead reeks of the sweet odor of rotting flesh. The prolonged sickness of his father and the briefer sickness of his "cheerful demon" mother are recounted in exhaustive detail, though not to satisfy a morbid curiosity; but Gibson's hunger is so embracive that he draws nourishment for his evolving love from every detail, even from putrefaction. When he had to give her a shot of morphine, his mother said, "Oh, Billy, you have to see everything." "My glimpse of the lean groin wherein I was conceived was not innocent of a flicker of the erotic." After she was dead of cancer, the "great haggard doll of evil in the bed, unclean and sickening" was not his mother, "but matter stopped, my mother was its motion. . . . No mystery is in her matter now, it is plain as a chair, the sitter gone, and soul is a word which, derided in my teens, I have found the sense of again."

But Gibson constantly balances his father's and his mother's wastings with their tenacious hold on life through work and selflessness. She was a woman who "took a dim view of rest," and "her usual therapy was housework, a triumph of conscience over the flesh," which young Gibson thought was only "for the neighbor's opinion." She saw goodness even in her sickness, realizing that her daughter loved her (Gibson's sister is a dim figure in the book, eclipsed by young Gibson's sullen egocentricity.). "I think I must be dying," she said, expressing life's saddest paradox, "everyone is so good to me." A woman who "believed in nothing more firmly than that tomorrow was a better day, but to be earned," she felt that she was an insignificant woman whose "only significance was in helping other people."

Gibson succeeds in showing his parents as "the nation's lower-middle class coming out of its cocoon," for theirs was a "wedding of everyman and everywoman" and marriage and the rearing of two children were "their chief business in life." If Gibson failed to return their love while they lived, their lives were full of people they loved and who loved them, "laughing, boisterous" friends, "joined for life." And a "rule of their marriage" was "never to go to sleep angry, lest 'something happen' in the night." It is in that endless night that Gibson now tries to find his way.

In his youth, Gibson took no interest in his ancestors: "my own twigdom was all, but now that I have more past than future I turn toward them." Ironically, his researches reveal more about his family than even his parents knew. "Nowhere in the city am I out of our soilbed." The book is a re-creation of the saga of his Irish clan in New York City—"a willful, clannish, hard-drinking, fornicating, blasphemous tribe." It is rich in characters and incidents—not always sad and calamitous, for a rather brittle humor buoys up the narrative. We get a full sense of the class, religion, life style, and manner of death of each member of Gibson's family. The death in World War I of his father's brother, Jim, haunted Gibson's childhood. Thirty-five years later he learned that the all-American hero loved to kill, and thus "my uncle's shadow falls upon my boys." His Aunt Ada's life-style had an insidious but even stronger effect on his vision of life. Somehow young Gibson saw his aunt's life as a missionary in the African jungles as "the height of conformity. . . . What I did not understand was that individuals like water seek their own levels of conformity, and I had not yet settled to mine." Most of his kin suffered sad declines. Uncle Will, a carpenter, died insane of inherited syphilis; Grandfather Gibson died of cancer of the rectum on Ward's Island, among madmen, "our last workingman." His mother's brother, Ben, "the son who never left" home, known as "Gentleman Ben" for his dress and manners, languished in an "endless twilight," and died, at seventy-four, in the senile ward, suspected to have been killed by an inmate.

Gibson's maternal grandmother, Mary Dore, had a mangy flat in the middle of Harlem. "In the flow of my childhood that flat . . . was the ancestral rock, and in it I imagined all the family tales." Mary Dore, who had danced with General Grant, and who had her nineteenth child when she was fifty-three, liked her beer, made off-color remarks, and was "fond of playing the horses," but all agreed that she had dignity. Her family was in show business, playing classy music on the banjo. Music was the medium in which all their hearts beat high and grieved; Gibson's father and Gibson himself made their living for a while playing and teaching piano. Gibson's rich, haughty Uncle George came "to personify the moral that success, like crime, did not pay; something had gone amiss" with the American Dream. "The charm of my Catholics was their alacrity to forgive themselves every sin," but his father's Protestant clan across the Hudson was "wholesome as honeysuckle," "as undissonant as hymns." Young Gibson judged all his elders liars, but his mother's family's "lies were more like vaudeville."

The family moved frequently before Gibson entered college; he has revisited those houses and seems haunted by them all. The center of the most memorable neighborhood—"a skein of friendships" tied "school, church, street games, holidays, into one knot of living"—was a hill. His family often tried moving back, but "we never found the hill again." It was to live only in Gibson the artist, "a green haven I could never find my way home to, until . . . checking the beds of my unwitting boys I perceived I was back in the garden" of that hill. But the comfortable, middle-class home of his late adolescence he loved also, though bitterly. "To me the house was a crystallization not only of the family, but of a class . . . in any of our rooms I was in a heartland of the country, enemy territory, whose name was my parents' happiness." He never escaped that "colossal lie."

Gibson depicts the gray emotional squalor of adolescence. Though on the surface, his youth was the cliché of the sports- and girl- shy kid who retreats into books and daydreams, it emerges as the fascinating portrait of the artist as a sullen young prisoner suffering ennui in surburban home, public school, and a variety of stultifying jobs. Taller than his schoolmates, he had no friends and

his life was a "parenthesis" in the life of his family. "I took their love, gifts, homage, for granted." But each difference from his parents was "willy nilly a mimicry," and his "victories over them, were theirs." Feeling at his "throat the hand of love like a strangler," he told his father they had nothing in common. As their friends and relatives were dying around them, Gibson's growing up was "another kind of death" to his parents. He sees now that "children are poor in love," and that it was intolerance of himself, self-contempt for his cowardice, and his masturbation that made him so insensitive. "I could love no one until I had earned my self-love."

Gibson's mole-like existence ended when a young man introduced him to music "masterworks, radicals, and girls." Graduated from high school during the Depression, Gibson "can remember no year in which I did not feel endangered by my country." In religion he was a "Sermon on the Mount atheist," and "for a lungful of self I was bidden to disown kin, class, country." As a free-style Communist, he "saw poverty too as a homecoming, and was equating it, not foolishly, with liberty." Throughout the book Gibson evokes what Camus called the "nostalgia of poverty." Even his mother spoke of the days when they lived in a primitive, infested tenement flat as "the old days in Highbridge, where we were all so happy." "I was no worse than most, survivor, ingrate, renegade, self-server, failure, adulterer." In the fifteen years between the burial of his father and the birth of his first son, the mourning of his father and his "stillbirths as a writer" seem interrelated, and through his writing ran the theme of resurrection. But as soon as he had a child to support, Gibson found that he was able to make a living as a writer.

Sitting beside his mother's deathbed almost a decade ago, reading her Book of Common Prayer, Gibson was struck by this phrase: "Write, blessed are the dead." In his story he works off a "ghostly collection of broken faiths like debts." His "long meditation" became a "running sore" that he wearily kept open, trying to re-create in words what nature had undone in the flesh, to enrich willfully now his own spirit, impoverished by ill-will in the past. Saying his belated mass, he becomes an agnostic priest to his Protestant father and Catholic mother, buried together in unconsecrated ground. Browning called poets God's spies. *A Mass for the Dead* is the spy's agonized attempt to find common cause deeper than flesh with those upon whom he spied and whom he judged. We watch a man struggling with the dead hand of the past that has him by the throat until we too feel the pressure. Gibson relates the scenes he re-creates to earlier and later scenes, sustaining a time and event continuum that keeps the reader oriented to his major task, which is not simply to recount but to understand the pattern.

We experience with Gibson the insights he achieves, cumulatively, as the book progresses. "Every writer in the twig of himself is working back into branch, trunk, heartwood, into a confluence of souls in the word." Out of death Gibson makes something of "use, shapeliness, joy," and learns that "to *see* is a work of love." His own travail shows that for those to whom it comes slowly love is strained through hatred, contempt, ill-will, intolerance, the shock of death, the membrane of a shroud. Visiting the cemetery recently, he perceived that each headstone "stands as a massive last page in a fam-

ily tale identical with mine." He declares that none of his people "begged to be delivered out of this vale of tears. I think our history is worth the telling because it is so ordinary, and it contains no suicide." His fifty-year-old father banged on the wall with his last strength: "I'm too young to die!" And his mother disregarded death as she cleaned house and looked after others in her own illness—; her last words were "I thank you, God, for everything," and she meant all the good and bad that went with "the gift of life." Gibson thinks his "wreath of words is as real" as a headstone, "but poor, and itself a hallucination: what more have I told of her" than the brass faucets she shined just before she died?

Once, Gibsons credo was expressed in negatives: "I believe in no god, and in no country, not ours, not theirs, and in no cause." But in living he learned that all his "disbeliefs were afterthoughts, skin deep." Now he believes in "my parents, therefore in myself, therefore, in my children . . . and in life everlasting." He hopes for a future in which the supreme commandment is "thou shalt not die" and life is a "comedy whose text is blessed are the living," and "consciousness is all."

Gazing upon his own growing children "running naked and beautiful" under the apple trees as he writes, Gibson, "on the wrong side of fifty," passes on, with his Aunt Ada's missionary zeal, what he has learned. His book is dedicated to his son's grandchildren, exhorting them to "Take heed to thyself," and often he speaks directly to his children and thus to those of the reader. His own present as husband and father, an igniter of life through love, is the reiterated vantage point from which he reflects upon the long past, interprets the transient present, and prepares himself for his own brief future.

With the birth of his son, Gibson was "back in the human family . . . so long deferred a joy that for several years I was drunk on fatherhood." He sees now that with "every birth the tale, not yet finished, begins anew," and in living and writing it he works to achieve salvation, "a state which is neither simple nor enchanted, but conditional, and paid for by the day in the commonest coin of domesticity." He perceives the truth, having lived it, of what Grandfather Gibson once said: "What we owe our parents, we pay to our children." Each of his sons must "separate our hand and his throat." "When in my boys the sap of green wisdom is cruel, let me think twice that they relive me, as I relive my parents, and every twig is the tale of the tree." The joy he felt at his mother's deathbed, knowing he loved her, makes him "less afraid of his own death." Immortality through one's children is a "poor immortality, always in change and dark to itself, but indestructible as the buds" of the cemetery trees. In the history of his family, Gibson feels the relativity of time, for his own was less than a blink; in childhood innocence "now is forever"; still, in his "boy's loins is a billion years yet to come."

With his "joyous and mournful time as the family bookkeeper" done, Gibson ends with an invocation: "Into Paradise may the angels in whom I do not believe lead thee." At the end of summer, sitting with his family in Cape Cod by the ocean, he offers a benediction: "This landscape and the cottage are new ground; none of my dead ever set foot in this place. . . . Behold, I make all things new." This is true of his family's future and of the Mass he has finished.

This record of American life in the first half of our century may seem at moments to become submerged in an orgy of nostalgia. Rich in Americana, the early pages of *A Mass for the Dead* are like thumbing through some remembered record of the past. Irish eloquence seems fated never to be free of Irish sentimentality, especially when Irishmen write of death and of attendant guilt and love. If sentimentality in phrasing permeates the book, Gibson avoids it when dealing with stereotypic occasions for it. His people are, of course, predictably sentimental, but his book is a kind of saga of the decay of a lower-middle-class family and of its sentimentality.

The Elizabethan language of the Missal is carried over occasionally into Gibson's own style, but its use is as ironical as it is literary. Sometimes the rhetoric, always Irish, is too literary-Irish. Gibson's wit, usually more of language than thought, is sometimes forced and condescending, but hits more often than it misses, even though it seldom profoundly illuminates. This is a terrifying book, and the author's wit, now as when he was a young man, is a defense against the sources of that terror and against the sentimentality that his parents cultivated as *their* defense.

Latin phrases from the Mass alternate with secular titles for sections and chapters that are as lyrical and evocative as the poetic interludes. Conceptually, the interludes are fitting, but they are all so abstract as to seem too similar and interchangeable, and the poetic flow of the prose itself contrasts in style with the rather mediocre poetry. Still, the use of poetic interludes does succeed in loosening up autobiography as a form, suggesting new possibilities.

An imaginative groping for new ways to tell about one's life, a breakdown of chronological and conventional procedures is evident in some brilliant autobiographies of recent years. Rich in content, *A Mass for the Dead* is an impressive and lasting achievement, superior in feeling, style, and conception. It has the virtues of honesty and artistic innovation that distinguish some recent autobiographies, but its aesthetic conception would be lifeless without the controlled obsession that motivates the book. Gibson seldom reveals himself as a professional writer calculating effects in language, incident, and structure (as such, he plays masterfully behind the veil); rather, he is persistently the driven, anguished, haunted man convulsively trying to throw off guilt and to triumph over time and death. And that is what makes this book rare. He has thrown himself into a Promethean and dangerous task. Out of his inspired egoism and humility, Gibson takes such massive risks against prudence and propriety with his passion and his art that the responses of his readers can only be extreme. The man who exhumes his parents' bones and pokes about in the dust, even with words, runs the risk that the bones will speak differently to strangers. As Emerson said, "Words are acts" and thus have a life of their own. After reading *A Mass for the Dead,* one believes, in a special way, in ghosts.

David Madden

MASSACRE AT MONTSÉGUR

Author: Zoë Oldenbourg (1916-   )
Translated from the French by Peter Green
Publisher: Pantheon Books (New York). 420 pp. $6.95
Type of work: History
Time: 1208-1244
Locale: The South of France

A history of the Albigensian Crusade that gives a sympathetic account of the suffering of both the Catharist heretics and their orthodox fellow countrymen

In a mountain fortress south of Toulouse one hundred men-at-arms held out from May of 1243 until the following March against a besieging force of nearly ten thousand crusaders from the North of France. When they were finally forced to capitulate, the defending soldiers were spared, but half of the four hundred men and women who had endured the siege within the fortress of Montségur were led by the French crusaders down the steep hill from the fortress into a large palisade piled high with faggots. There they were burned alive. Thus ended the Albigensian Crusade.

The two hundred Catharist heretics burned at Montségur, many of whom were old and infirm, were not the leaders of the Catharist Church, nor did their martyrdom mean that the heresy had been forever extirpated from Languedoc, as Pope Innocent III had hoped it would be when he initiated the Crusade in 1208. The massacre at Montségur was, however, the climax of a thirty-five-year struggle during which the people of the South of France fought to preserve their political and cultural independence from the North and during which the Catharist Church—a minority and heretical sect with its strongest roots in Languedoc, but not at Albi as the name Albigensian would suggest—was a serious rival of the Papacy.

Zoë Oldenbourg's first nonfiction historical narrative is the story of that struggle.

Languedoc had during the twelfth century enjoyed the flowering of a prosperous and vital civilization. Its permanent contribution to Western culture was the Provençal lyric of the troubadours, from which we have derived, through the French trouvères, the German Minnesinger, and the Italian predecessors of Dante and Petrarch, not only our conception of the lyric poem but also an idealization of physical love which for eight centuries has dominated Western notions of the proper relationship between the sexes. Whether this brilliant aristocratic civilization would have flickered into extinction if left in peace we cannot ever know. We do know, however, that it ended forever with the warfare, military occupation, Inquisition, and mass executions of pious citizens that were the Albigensian Crusade. At the beginning of the thirteenth century, Raymond VI, Count of Toulouse and ruler of Languedoc, was one of the most powerful princes in Christendom. Two forces worked toward the destruction of his country as an independent cultural and political unit. Very crudely, these forces can be labeled the King of France and the Pope.

To the modern intelligence, Raymond VI is an attractive figure as Madame Oldenbourg presents him. His private morality may have been far from exemplary, but he identified himself so thoroughly with his people that his public actions were symbolic of his country's values and of what its citizens believed to be their best interests. Above all, he respected the religious tolerance that had become a part of their civilization. Raymond himself was a Catholic, but he steadfastly refused to persecute or aid significantly in the persecution of the Catharist heretics who every year were growing in number and influence in Languedoc. When the Papal Legate, Peter of Castelnau, who had been sent to Toulouse by Innocent III to combat the Catharist heresy, was murdered by one of Raymond's officers in January of 1208, the Pope responded by in effect declaring war. He called for a Christian crusade against a Christian country, and there were brave and restless knights in the North to answer the call.

After a preliminary chapter on the background of the Crusade, Madame Oldenbourg describes in Chapter II the Catharist Church and its beliefs. Relating the religion of the Cathars (or "pure ones") to earlier heresies, particularly Gnosticism and Manicheism, she explains the process by which the doctrine of Bogomilism was brought into Europe from Asia by the Bulgars, and from the Balkans disseminated to northern Italy and southern France as Catharism. The Cathars were dualists, believing in the reality of cosmic Evil as well as cosmic Good. Whereas orthodox Christians believe that evil is simply the absence of good and that it therefore has no existence or creator, the Catharists believed in a continual

warfare between the two forces. Evil they identified with the visible world, physical nature, the flesh, and Satan, their creator; good with the spirit and its creator, God. Like the primitive Christians who often put off baptism until just before death for fear they might commit sin and thus fall away from purity, the Cathars initiated only a small fraction of their believers, or *credenti,* into the sanctity of the Church. With the rite known as the *consolamentum* the *credenti* became *perfecti,* assuming the black robe and leading the life of extreme asceticism that symbolized their pure state. Since all flesh was evil, it was wrong to propagate flesh through sexual union, to eat food that resulted from sexual reproduction (as the process was then understood this did not include fish or vegetables), or to kill an animal or human being, in whom the spirit might be striving to escape the flesh. Those souls who had not become purified at death returned in various forms for subsequent lives and trials. In contrast to the working clergy of the Catholic Church, the Catharist *perfecti* must have appeared models of piety and self-denial. And they preached most convincingly the truth of their way as against the falseness of the Romish Babylon.

In Chapter III, on the pre-heretical Church, the writer traces the papal reaction to Catharism during the late twelfth century. Toward the end of this period even the bishops in Languedoc had to be relieved of their offices because of their sympathy with their countrymen and their resentment of harsh papal policy directed against a heresy which clearly endangered neither the state nor public morality. The extermination of the *perfecti* was the mission, first of papal legates, and then of the Crusade. Mere *credenti* often coöperated sufficiently with their examiners to earn acquittal. In terms of Catharist doctrine they had little to lose by swearing false oaths. It was unthinkable, however, for a *perfectus* to do so. Chapters IV through VI describe the initial campaigns of the Crusade in 1209 and the career of Simon de Montfort, who led the Crusade until his violent death in battle at the siege of Toulouse in 1218. Simon was a principal actor in the Crusade and was rewarded for his extraordinary skill and energy with seignory over all Languedoc. In 1215, Raymond VI abdicated as Count of Toulouse in favor of his adolescent son, Raymond VII. Pope Innocent III died in 1216, to be succeeded by Honorius III. Thus the first generation of the Crusade was replaced by a second. Simon de Montfort's replacement, as the leader of the Crusade but not as seigneur of Languedoc, which was again in the hands of Raymond VII, was Prince Louis, later King Louis VIII of France. The second stage of the Crusade, described in Chapters VII and VIII, was concluded when, in 1229, after the death of Louis, Raymond VII agreed to the terms of the Treaty of Meaux, by which Languedoc was united to France through the betrothal of Raymond's nine-year-old daughter to a nine-year-old brother of the King of France. The third stage is told in the next three chapters, where we learn of the establishment in 1233 of a permanent Inquisition with officials whose sole duty was the extirpation of heresy, the activities of the Inquisition in Languedoc, and the Cathar resistance to systematic exter-

mination. The final chapter describes the siege and massacre at Montségur. Nineteen illustrations and a collection of relevant documents in the appendices add to the vividness of Madame Oldenbourg's fascinating narrative.

If we allow our modern abhorrence of military aggression and religious intolerance to govern our feelings about the Albigensian Crusade, it is easy to make villains of the forces which destroyed the independence of Languedoc in the name of Christian unity. And this is what Madame Oldenbourg does. The thesis of *Massacre at Montségur* is that with the excesses of the Albigensian Crusade in particular and of the Inquisition in general, the Church of Rome forfeited her right to the epithet "Catholic" and submitted to a degeneration of morality from which the Christian world has not recovered to this day. This is, of course, very deep water, and although her thesis may ultimately raise questions more important than what happened in thirteenth century Languedoc, there is also the danger that it may interfere with our ascertaining even these facts. The sustained comparison of the best of Catharism with the worst of Catholicism is suspect. How the Cathars would have behaved publicly and in a position of power is impossible to say from the testimony of religious ritual and statements of doctrine. Many aspects of the Albigensian Crusade resemble the tragic complexity of the American Civil War, a complexity best viewed from a position of neutrality. Many passages in *Massacre at Montségur* suggest to us that we are getting a version of history distinctly Southern in its sympathies.

THE MASTER OF GO

Author: Yasunari Kawabata (1899-1972)
Translated from the Japanese by Edward G. Seidensticker
Publisher: Alfred A. Knopf (New York). 182 pp. $5.95
Type of work: Novel
Time: 1938-1940
Locale: Japan

An elegant and elegiac "chronicle-novel," part fiction and part reportage, based upon an actual 1938 Go match

Principal characters:
SHUSAI THE MASTER, the aging protagonist and title bearer
OTAKE, his challenger
URAGAMI, a reporter covering the match

The Master of Go is the fourth novel to be published in English by the late Nobel Prize recipient, Yasunari Kawabata. Although completed and available to the Japanese public in 1954, it has taken until 1972, the same year as the author's suicide, to reach the Western reader. Its arrival through Edward G. Seidensticker's excellent translation justifies the recognition Kawabata received for his two famous earlier novels, *Snow Country* (1956) and *Thousand Cranes* (1959), and the international renown he gained when awarded the Nobel Prize in 1968. For those already familiar with the author whom the Japanese acknowledge as their dean of fiction, the appearance in English of *The Master of Go* is a welcome addition, and should be a great help in estimating the value of his contribution to world literature.

There are two minor obstacles, however, which the initiate into Kawabata's world must overcome, if this book is to act as an introduction. The action in the book centers around the ancient Oriental game of Go, a game which may loosely be equated with chess in terms of its demands for mental concentration and combative spirit. With the help of the notes, charts, and explanatory introduction that Seidensticker provides, and a little discipline on the reader's part, however, the rudiments of the game can be mastered sufficiently for even a nonplayer to feel the drama and daring of certain key moves.

The second problem that must be faced by those making a preliminary approach to Kawabata through *The Master of Go* is that it is not pure fiction. As the translator warns in his introduction, "Mr. Kawabata has described *The Master of Go* as 'a faithful chronicle-novel,' " and he goes on to explain that the Japanese term for this genre is *shosetsu,* a word that connotes a looser, more generous form than "novel." In this respect it bears a strong resemblance to what has been called the New Journalism in the United States, and those who are undecided about whether to classify this hybrid as art or merely personalized reporting may do well to examine this Oriental version of it.

It would be unfair to Kawabata, however, to relegate him to this group on the basis of this one book.

The eroticism and cosmopolitanism in *Thousand Cranes* and *Snow Country* that helped assure the popularity of his fiction in the West may be missed by some in *The Master of Go,* but the haiku-like delicacy of prose and the keen eye for detail are still present. The mixed form is also perfectly suited to Kawabata's subject matter, for in describing the match between the old Master and the young Challenger, the author/reporter is aware that more is at stake than a mere title; there is a conflict also between generations, of modern rational Japan and the older, more ceremonial and aristocratic order.

Kawabata covered the actual Go match, which took place over a period of six months in 1938, for twin Osaka and Tokyo newspapers. The present book is an elegiac recollection and meditation upon that match, colored and intensified by fiction. The author appears in this account under the fictional name of Uragami, and demonstrates a clear bias in favor of the old Master, although his respect for the Challenger, Otaké, is also evident. As is typical in Kawabata's novels, however, the main creative energies are devoted to character portrayal, often at the expense of plot. The shape of the book also gives evidence that an artistic hand is ordering and controlling the events recorded, thereby elevating the account out of the realm of journalism. The outcome of the match and the death of the Master are made known at the beginning; and yet Kawabata manages to maintain interest and suspense, primarily through time shifts, changes of locale that offer him opportunities to display his poetic descriptive abilities, and the careful construction of characters, especially where minor conflicts reveal them to be symbols of opposing ways of life.

Shusai the Master, the example, is a transitional figure between pre-Westernized and modern Japan, a kind of living, feudal relic, and last surviving master "revered in the tradition of Go as a way of life and art." During this, his last match (one that is, incidentally, sponsored by a newspaper to increase its circulation) he is plagued with a heart condition, and yet despite his need to take frequent rests at St. Luke's Hospital and the necessity of being under a doctor's supervision, he refuses to forfeit the match. He has something of a Zen Buddhist's devotion to his game; he peers off into space while his enemy considers moves, and his expressionless face at times makes it appear as if he were "face to face with a void," as if he had "lost all consciousness of his own identity." The Master's ability to conceal all emotions while at the game board often has disquieting effects upon his opponents, and his perfect self-control has allowed him to chalk up more than one victory to the virtue of patience.

This cold, almost inhuman "vagueness" and total absorption in his own game, however, has its negative side too, for it makes the Master totally indifferent to his opponent's character and insensitive to the feelings of others. Kawabata makes this point clear in a passage that also demonstrates his remarkable power of eliciting a mood from a scene depicted in a few well-chosen words:

It was one of those warm late-autumn days when the island of Oshima lies in a mist. Kites skimmed and dipped over the warm, calm sea. At the far edge of the lawn was a row of pines, framing the sea in green. Several pairs of newlyweds were standing along the line between the grass and the sea. Perhaps because of the brightness and expansiveness of the scene, they seemed unusually self-possessed for newlyweds. From afar, against the pines and the sea, the kimonos seemed fresher and brighter, I thought, than they would have from near at hand. People who came to Kawana belonged to the affluent classes.

"Newlyweds, all of them, I suppose," I said to the Master, feeling an envy that approached resentment.

The Master's response to the newlyweds and the beauty of his surroundings, however, is muttered in four words, "They must be bored." He is so disciplined in his art that he has lost the better part of reality, but because of this total and lifelong dedication, his character assumes a tragic nature.

The Challenger, Otaké, who is modeled after the real-life figure of Kitani Minoru, brings a more exuberant and modern spirit to the game board. Whereas the Master exudes a quiet atmosphere, the young adversary enlivens the room with his bold maneuvers and jocular manner. Addicted to drinking tea, he suffers from enuresis. The result of this is a humorously high frequency of departures from the room, and although it is a natural handicap, it seems a trifle irreverent when contrasted to the Master's almost religious discipline and devotion to the art of Go.

During a rain storm, for instance, he jokingly comments that the sky has a kidney condition, a remark recorded by the reporter Uragami, but also, and more importantly, one used by the novelist Kawabata to emphasize the close similarity in temperament between Otaké and a squall. His style at the game board is aggressive and strong, characterized by a nervous agitation, an unfaltering will to win, and a strict adherence to even the most minor of the rules. In this respect he differs from the Master, whose desire to win is conditioned by his sense of Go as an art. When Otaké moves his massive wall of black stones into a direct attack upon the Master's more subtly placed white ones, Kawabata aptly describes the ensuing battle with the word "storm," for the word indicates not only the ferocity of Otaké's style, but also that the source of the challenger's power is external, whereas the Master is motivated by an inner sense of harmony, almost a kind of inspiration.

The decisive move of the match is made by Otaké in what seems to be a shocking retreat from the heat of battle. It is so unprecedented a maneuver that the judge must take some few minutes locating its position among the three hundred and sixty-one coordinates of the board; and although once it is found, the Master responds by placing his stone within two minutes, a few plays later he makes a move that ensures his own defeat. Otaké's move is not so much brilliant as it is diabolically insensitive to the natural flow of the masterpiece Shusai has created in his game. It leaves the old Master heartbroken and shatters his resolve to win: " 'The match is over,' " he remarks during the next recess. " 'Mr. Otaké ruined it with that sealed play. It was like smearing ink over the picture we had painted.' " Within a year of this defeat, Shusai, the old Master, dies.

The book ends where the reader knew all along it would, with the death of Shusai. Despite its lack of a clear linear movement to that point, however, the tragic nature of that loss is more keenly felt in the final, elegiac chapter than when stated plainly in the opening one. Although Kawabata has concentrated upon a unique and real-life individual, Shusai, the created character emerges as a symbol for a disappearing way of life. In using the game of Go as a metaphor for the meeting of two different ages and attitudes, Kawabata appears at times almost too blunt in exposing his meaning. Uragami, for instance, at one point explicitly tells Otaké that he is a representative of the new era and that he has a responsibility to carry on the heritage of the Go title, despite the alterations wrought upon it by modern times. This passage marks the one speech of any considerable length made by Uragami and would perhaps be inexcusably blatant in a work of pure fiction, but is pardonable because of the *shosetsu* form of the book. Such a stark statement may be justified by the fact that while Uragami is acting as a mediator between the two opponents in this scene, Kawabata is operating on another level to reconcile the opposing forces of journalism and fiction.

It is indeed the tension between these two elements, between reportage in newspaper style of an esoteric game, and the fictional substances of delicately described scenery, season, and character, that produces the greater part of the pleasure derived from reading *The Master of Go*. By occasionally letting his novelist's eye wander from the game board and focus upon the diminutive frame and large head, or the single long hair growing upon the eyebrow of the Master, or by letting his eyes fix themselves briefly upon a wilting arrangement of dahlias, Kawabata can masterfully create an elegiac tone. Likewise, he can give an accurate play-by-play account of the contest. Taken into conjunction, however, and arranged so as to give the reader alternate sensations of mental concentration and aesthetic relief, these kinds of passages succeed in giving even the nonplayer an intense impression of the famous 1938 Go match and of the forces and personalities behind it. It is this synthesizing power that makes *The Master of Go* a splendid demonstration of the possibilities of elevating journalism into art.

John Hollwedel

Sources for Further Study

Reviews:

Atlantic. CCXXX, October, 1972, p. 126. 800 words.

Christian Science Monitor. October 11, 1972, p. 11. 800 words.

Nation. CCXV, November 6, 1972, p. 4. 900 words.

New York Times Book Review. October 22, 1972, p. 4. 900 words.

Time. C, October 9, 1972, p. 87. 700 words.

MASTERS OF DECEIT

Author: J. Edgar Hoover (1895-1972)
Publisher: Henry Holt and Company (New York). 374 pp. $5.00
Type of work: Political commentary
Time: 1848-1948
Locale: United States

The story of communism in the United States, and how to fight it, by the head of the F.B.I.

Principal personages:
KARL MARX
FRIEDRICH ENGELS
VLADIMIR I. LENIN
JOSEPH STALIN
NIKITA KHRUSHCHEV
WILLIAM Z. FOSTER
EARL BROWDER

"Every citizen has a duty to learn more about the menace that threatens his future, his home, his children, and the peace of the world," declares the Director of the Federal Bureau of Investigation, "and that is why I have written the book." The result is a volume that could be read with profit by everybody. It has already been proposed as required reading for courses in Civics and American Government in the schools and colleges of the nation.

The author calls it a primer. Certainly it puts facts clearly, for, after all, communism has nothing mysterious about it. The leaders have definitely stated what they intend to do, and their beliefs have often been revealed. The famous F.B.I. head once more sets down what communism is, how it works, what it hopes to accomplish, and, above all, how we can overcome it and put an end to the waste of millions of dollars spent in ever-increasing quantities in defense against it since the end of World War II.

Communism is no recent interest of J. Edgar Hoover. As Special Assistant to the Attorney General of the United States, he was assigned in 1919 the task of preparing a legal brief on what was then a new political party in the United States. After studying the documents of American communism, as well as the writings of Marx, Engels, and Lenin, he issued his first warning, which he now repeats and makes more emphatic forty years later. In the meantime he has seen communism grow from a small disorganized group of fanatics to a "conspiratorial group operating under modern conditions as an arm of revolution." To his fellow citizens, Hoover declares that their country is now the prime target of international communism.

The book begins with a consideration of "Who is your enemy?" Every party member is pledged to make the United States a Communistic nation; the collective accomplishment has been to win twenty-five percent of the world's surface and forty percent of its population within four decades. Though figures show a drop in communist membership in the United States, from a top of 80,000 in 1944 to a quarter of that number at present, "it has been estimated by the Communist leaders themselves that for every Party member ten others are ready, willing, and able to do the Party's work." Against them, Hoover has the optimistic vision of millions of Americans informing themselves and working together to keep the country free.

Part II is historical, tracing the idea of communism from primitive tribes who lived in common and shared property, food, and housing. Hoover dates modern communism, the "science of Marxism-Leninism," from the meeting of Marx and Engels in 1842, and from the Communist Manifesto of 1848. The two advocated a class struggle, a revolution against capitalism. It was Lenin, however, who took their theory and translated it into organization and action. His followers seized power in Russia, and while for a time he was eclipsed, he has been restored, by the "downgrading" of his successor Stalin, to his pedestal as the ideal Communist leader. Hoover cites Lenin's frequent use of the word "ruthlessness" as the clue to his purposes. Khrushchev later declared: "We will do the same, but with more emphasis."

In the United States, the Communist Party was born through a split in the Socialist Party in Chicago in 1919, at a time when the leftwingers had been thrilled by the October Revolution in Russia. The ashes of Charles Ruthenberg, who led the revolt, now rest in the Kremlin. Under control from Russia, the various American branches were unified in 1921, with the Workers Party of America as the legal outlet for the underground Communist Party. Party members who concealed their affiliations and fellow travelers who supported the program, though without joining the Party, were also part of its strength. Hoover provides anecdotes of the activities of

Communists of all shades.

"The Claims of the Communists," and "The Subversive Organizations," provide additional admonitions. "Liberal," "progressive," "social reformers," "democratic," and "American," says Hoover, are all fake labels the Communists give themselves to attract dupes into their organization.

In one chapter he asks: "Why do people become Communists?" This is, perhaps, one of the weakest sections because it ignores the psychological motivations in our culture that sweep young people into an underground movement. The few examples given represent only a few of those who did join. The succeeding chapter, "Why People Break with Communism," is also somewhat unsubtle. But, after all, most of the readers of this volume will never be tempted to join and will not need to understand why, once in, they do not remain Communists forever.

Part IV, "Life in the Party," is more essential. The methods of operation and the demands on the time of the members are revealed by descriptions of actual meetings on which the F.B.I. eavesdropped. Some of the demands may seem to readers better reasons for leaving the Party than those given in the chapter under that title. Discipline is strict. "The Party is a vast workshop where the member is polished and shined, his impurities melted out, his loyalties to communism strengthened. He is made into a *Communist man.*" In another chapter Hoover shows by illustrative anecdotes how this result is achieved. He must not think. He must accept the Party line, even if each day it contradicts the assertions of the previous day. He must be fanatical in agreeing to sacrifice everything for the Party. Everything is slanted toward the purposes of the Party. For instance, Lenin taught that art is a weapon of class struggle. Summarizing, Hoover declares that communism aims to promote an alien way of life in America.

One of the weapons employed is Communist discipline. Anyone who rebels is stigmatized, "villified, blackened, and made to appear the scum of the earth." The higher his position in the Party, the greater the effort to defame him, and examples prove the author's assertion. Having prepared its members, the Communist Party then uses them in attacking the noncommunist society of the United States, as is shown in Part V, "The Communist Trojan Horse in Action." To the Party leader, each day is a dress rehearsal for the big day of social revolution. He sees it in terms of warfare, with victory to be achieved by force and violence. Lacking numbers to win by direct attack, he uses the strategic retreat as battle tactics. The author shows how the battle plans are changed according to the particular person or class being approached. Back of it all is agitation: Keep the people, and through them the government, upset and off balance. As William Z. Foster boasted, "Capitalism will die, sword in hand, fighting in vain to beat back the oncoming revolutionary proletariat."

Hitting more directly at the situation, not unknown but unbelieved and unadmitted by most Americans, come Chapters 16 and 17, about the organizations which, not generally recognized as communistic, purvey communistic propaganda. Hoover shows how infiltration is likely to take place and what the average American can do about it. The special interest of the Communist is Labor, and much of Chapter 16 is a revelation of the tricks to get control of locals. Tests for identification of subversive organizations are also furnished. The attitude of the Party toward the Negro fills many pages and its selfish interest in other minority groups is also laid bare.

The history of the Party is concluded with a treatise on the underground. In his Foreword the author warns that he does not intend to disclose knowledge possessed exclusively by the F.B.I., but he provides undramatic and depersonalized data, material drawn largely from the accumulations of the F.B.I. As long as the Party has legal status, it will work above ground, though always keeping some of its members concealed. There is little romance and adventure in the underground, as Hoover reveals it. It is drudgery, involving absence from home for months and even years, and living under assumed names. Sabotage and espionage are generally involved. Thus the free government can be weakened. Originally the American Communists coöperated under orders from Russia, but now, according to Hoover, the Soviet does its own spying, for fear of leaks from American associates.

Hoover feels that following the steps he has set forth will help defend the nation from the Communists he has been describing. But measures obeyed too enthusiastically or without the responsibility, he argues, can bring another round of McCarthyism; nothing must be allowed to discourage intelligent differences of opinion on the basic issues of today. Readers who use with discretion the final section of *Masters of Deceit* will benefit from this book, which reveals both the "major menace of our times" and the personality of the F.B.I. chief who has served his country so well. Perhaps he has imbued the reader with some of his own faith.

The appendix provides short biographies of outstanding Communist authors and summaries of their works, dates in the history of both the Russian and the American Communist Parties, and a complete index to the material covered in the volume.

MAURICE

Author: E. M. Forster (1879-1970)
Publisher: W. W. Norton and Company (New York). 256 pp. $6.95
Type of work: Novel
Time: Early twentieth century
Locale: England

Into the greenwood with the Love That Dare Not Speak Its Name

Principal characters:
MAURICE HALL, a middle class young man
MRS. HALL, his mother
ADA and KITTY, his sisters
DR. BARRY, a family friend
CECIL DURHAM, a Cambridge contemporary
RISLEY, another Cambridge undergraduate
LASKER JONES, a doctor practising hypnotism
ALEC SCUDDER, gamekeeper on Durham's estate

Written in 1913 and 1914, in the period between Forster's first visit to India and his longer official sojourn in Alexandria during World War I, *Maurice* remained unpublished throughout the author's lifetime. The first quarter of the century was witnessing the beginnings of the sexual revolution which has since made it possible, among other things, for serious writers to treat physiological matters honestly and explicitly, but Forster realized, at the time of the novel's composition, that it was still probably too early for fictional presentation by a major writer of an acknowledged homosexual relationship to be generally acceptable. André Gide's *L'Immoraliste,* in 1904, had only hinted at the hero's physical and psychological problems, while Radclyffe Hall's *Well of Loneliness,* dealing with female homosexuality, was not published until 1928. At the time that Forster wrote *Maurice,* Marcel Proust was only beginning to think of introducing homosexuality as a major subject in *À la recherche du temps perdu,* where it is presented extensively but with total authorial condemnation, as in the mas-

terful portrait of M. de Charlus, the homosexual as comic victim and villain.

More important to Forster than the possibility of the public's refusing to accept the fact of homosexuality in a novel by him was his own refusal to fit his characters into the still-prevailing Victorian stereotype of the sexual transgressors who must ultimately receive some kind of engineered and obligatory punishment. The principal point made by the author in his own comments on the book is that, from the first, he had decided to provide a happy ending.

> I shouldn't have bothered to write otherwise. I was determined that in fiction anyway two men should fall in love and remain in it for the ever and ever that fiction allows. . . . If it ended unhappily, with a lad dangling from a noose or with a suicide pact, all would be well, for there is no pornography or seduction of minors. But the lovers get away unpunished and consequently recommend crime.

Only during the last years of Forster's life did homosexual contact, between consenting adults, cease to be a crime in Great Britain; but by that time, ironically enough, he appears to have decided that the novel could only have "period interest" for contemporary readers. In any case, it was only at length published in the year following Forster's death by the Trustees of his Estate. Now, some sixty years after its composition, *Maurice* can be fitted into the chronology of his fiction between *Howards End* (1910) and *A Passage to India* (1924).

Essentially a *bildungsroman*, the novel traces the development of its eponymous hero from early adolescence to a maturity which is characterized by self-knowledge and self-acceptance. The serio-comic opening scene suggests, in abbreviated and highlighted form, the progression that is to follow. About to leave his primary school, thirteen-year-old Maurice Hall, presented as a perfectly ordinary middle-class youth, is taken for a seashore walk by one of his masters. Mr. Ducie, "soaked in evolution" and convinced that he is doing "what is right," proceeds to deliver a lecture on the mystery of sex, illustrated with anatomical diagrams in the sand, only to be horrified by the possibility that two approaching ladies will see his drawings. Sensing the uselessness of such an approach, Maurice despises his master and thinks, "Liar, coward, he's told me nothing." What Maurice comes to know about sex will have to be learned in his own way, and Forster indicates that the dawn of such knowledge will be slow and painful for the boy.

At Sunnington, Maurice is only "a mediocre member of a mediocre school," and these years are passed over rapidly. His home, in a comfortable London suburb, is fatherless, and his mother appears as the presiding genius of an essentially emasculating environment. Maurice is loved and catered to by his mother and sisters, but the atmosphere of home stifles and restricts. Only in a recurring dream are other possibilities suggested.

He scarcely saw a face, scarcely heard a voice say, "That is your friend," and then it was over, having filled him with beauty and taught him tenderness. He could die for such a friend, he would allow such a friend to die for him; they would make any sacrifice for each other, and count the world nothing, neither death nor distance nor crossness could part them, because "this is my friend."

Maurice's significant development begins during his second year at Cambridge, more particularly when he meets Clive Durham, the son of a prominent county family, to whom he is attracted, although feeling that he must proceed cautiously in this friendship since their backgrounds have been so different. Professing unorthodoxy and an admiration for the ideas of Plato's *Symposium*, Clive is the first to move towards intimacy, when he tells Maurice that he loves him. Maurice's reaction is conditioned by his class and his education.

"Durham, you're an Englishman. I'm another. Don't talk nonsense. . . . It's the only subject absolutely beyond the limit as you know, it's the worst crime in the calendar, and you must never mention it again."

Later, however, after an agonized struggle toward some sense of what Forster significantly calls the "I" he had been trained to obscure, Maurice realizes that he too is in love and now has "the highest gift to offer." Going to Trinity College at night, he hears his name spoken from Clive's room, and he enters by the window. "His friends had called him . . . out of dreams."

The relationship thus initiated, as the author makes perfectly clear, is wholly non-sexual, since Clive is incapable of trusting the body, and it also belongs very much to the specialized world of Cambridge. When Maurice is sent down for a minor infraction of college rules, he finds himself in an anomalous position at home and in that very worst of Forsterian conditions, a muddle. During the next few years, while Clive finishes his education and Maurice goes into the stock brokerage business, the two friends try to maintain the kind of closeness they had had at the university, but on a visit to Penge, the Durham estate, Maurice is aware of impending difficulties. Clive's mother is obviously wife-hunting, and Clive himself is now thinking of the need for an heir to the property. In London, on the eve of a trip to Greece, Clive tells Maurice, "Would that we had never been lovers!", and later from Athens he writes his friend, "Against my will I have become normal. I cannot help it." The author's comment is interesting.

> The body is deeper than the soul and its secrets inscrutable. There had been no warning—just a blind alteration of the life spirit, just an announcement, "You who loved men, will henceforward love women. Understand or not, it's the same to me."

Back in London, after an ugly confrontation during which Maurice accuses Clive of flirting with his sister Ada, Clive escapes from his former lover.

"He too suffered, and exclaimed, 'What an ending!' but he was promised a dawn."

The following period is Maurice's dark night of estrangement and despair. Feeling that he no longer possesses a "light within," he entertains thoughts of suicide and is horrified in particular by two incidents: in the one, he finds himself physically attracted to the adolescent nephew of a neighbor; in the other, he is solicited by a repellently obvious invert on the train. Pushed almost beyond endurance, Maurice finally confesses to the family doctor that he is an "unspeakable of the Oscar Wilde sort," only to be told that the whole thing is just "Rubbish!"

> Dr. Barry had given the best advice he could. He had read no scientific works on Maurice's subject. . . . Averse to it by temperament, he endorsed the verdict of society gladly; that is to say, his verdict was theological. He held that only the most depraved could glance at Sodom, and so, when a man of good antecedents and physique confessed the tendency, "Rubbish, rubbish!" was his natural reply.

Even a hypnotist whom the young man consults can do nothing for him but can suggest, somewhat more practically, that Maurice consider living on the Continent where his "tendency" is at least not a crime. Despite the fact that he looks and acts like a solid young citizen, Nature has pitted Maurice "against the extraordinary, which only saints can subdue unaided, and he began to lose ground."

The climax comes during another visit to Penge where Clive, now married, jocularly dismisses all their past closeness by observing, "We were young idiots, weren't we?" Feeling out of place in the conventional and limited county society with which Clive now surrounds himself, Maurice's only solace is the sense of well-being that comes from the beauty of the natural world. He also notices a brown-eyed young gamekeeper whose occasional presence in the middle distance seems to be a part of that feeling. At night, Maurice senses that "there was something better in life than this rubbish, if only he could get to it." In a somnambulistic state he goes to the window of his bedroom and calls out, "Come." In response, the gamekeeper, Scudder, climbs a ladder to the window and asks gently, "Sir, was you calling out for me?"

The concluding chapters of the novel show how Maurice and Scudder come to accept the relationship so abruptly begun. Wondering how he can so far have forgotten himself as to step outside his own class, Maurice leaves immediately for London, assuming that problems which can't be faced can be avoided. Scudder writes, asking for another meeting in the boathouse at Penge, but Maurice does not answer him. In a second letter, Scudder almost threatens Maurice; he has his own pride and is, just as much as Maurice, "embedded in class." Choosing the neutral ground of the British Museum, Maurice finally assents to a meeting which begins antagonistically on both sides but ends with the two men spending the night in a hotel together. Although he has known for some time that Scudder plans to emigrate to South America with his brother, Maurice, now in love, hopes that he will stay on in England, but common sense tells him that Alec is "not a hero or a god," and will do what his family has planned for him. A few days later,

Maurice despondently goes to Southampton to see Alec off, only to discover that his friend is not on the ship —he is in the boathouse at Penge waiting for Maurice. In a final scene, which brings the book full circle by confronting theoretician and actualist, Maurice tells a shocked Clive, "I have shared with Alec . . . all I have. Which includes my body." Outrage and expostulation are greeted with forthright admission and cheerful laughter. Then, without Clive's being aware of the precise moment, Maurice disappears into the shrubbery, "leaving no trace of his presence except a little pile of the petals of the evening primrose, which mourned from the ground like an expiring fire." The outlaw lovers have gone into the greenwood.

A typical Forster protagonist, Maurice Hall sets out on that long journey which may or may not lead to self-fulfillment, usually presented in terms of a significantly realized relationship with another person. (Lucy Honeychurch, in *A Room with a View*, is last seen on her honeymoon with George Emerson, the railway clerk, under the warm and permissive skies of Italy; in *The Longest Journey*, Rickie Elliott dies under the wheels of a train, having failed to come to terms either with his overly-conventional wife or his free-spirited illegitimate brother.) Again, personal fulfillment is associated with behavior that goes against the norms established by the English middle class, whose highest desire is for shelter against whatever may threaten the sense of its own moral and societal superiority. The physical settings of the novel provide a characteristic triad: London, where Maurice lives and works, represents "the incalculable influence of the family" and the demands of what Forster names elsewhere "the life we miscall real"; Cambridge is the very precious, but circumscribed, world of youthful enthusiasm and aspiration, much as it was in *The Longest Journey;* and Penge provides, ironically, the background both for a reformed, conventionalized Cecil and for a natural, spontaneous Alec. Overall, there is a sense of oppositions (pagan and Christian, individual and group, middle and lower class) between which the author, as always, desires to establish a life-saving connection. "Only connect the passion and the prose," as Margaret Schlegel would have it in *Howards End.* To show ways of connecting the prose of a viable life in the modern world with the passion of an individual's idealistic striving toward perfect love and knowledge was Forster's objective in all of his works. The accomplishment of *Maurice* may appear a lesser one, in comparison with the other novels, only because here Forster deliberately limited himself to one specific area of human experience.

The structure and balance are what one has come to expect in a Forster novel. Maurice's intense, but essentially ordered and cerebral, relationship with Cecil in the first part of the novel is played against his equally intense, but now spontaneous and physical, relationship with Alec in the latter part. In both cases, a window is climbed to and a call for love acknowledged, but in the former the love is incomplete and the outcome tragic, or potentially so, while in the latter the love is total and the outcome comic. Comic, that is, in the sense that Maurice and Alec abstract themselves from the "real" world of Cecil Durhams and Dr. Barrys into the ideal world of the greenwood. They

go to join the mythic company of Sherwood Forest, where non-conformists who were once considered outlaws and criminals can now be seen, at a romantic remove, as free spirits, almost folk heroes. In this respect, the end of the novel is perhaps closer to the wish-fulfillment fantasy of some of Forster's short stories where, for example, a regimented suburban boy is finally allowed to cross the rainbow bridge and mingle with great authors and their creations on an equal footing, or where a nature-oriented young lady engaged to a stuffy provincial with a strong sense of property can re-enact the fate of Daphne and literally become a part of the forest. *Maurice,* after all, is dedicated to "a Happier Year," and in 1914 that year could only be a mythic one.

In another context, Forster admitted that, "in no book have I got down more than the people I like, the person I think I am, and the people who irritate me," and this perhaps suggests where the principal weaknesses of *Maurice* lie. In order to avoid a narrowingly and misleadingly autobiographic reading of the book, Forster tells us that "in Maurice I tried to create a character who was completely unlike myself, or what I supposed myself to be," and one is more aware of the effort than the accomplishment.

> Maurice was not intellectual nor religious, nor had he that strange solace of self-pity that is granted to some. Except on one point his temperament was normal . . .

By stressing an overall normalcy and ordinariness in his protagonist, Forster runs the risk of losing the reader's interest in, if not his sympathy for, Maurice's difficulties. In fiction this problem is frequently there when a more developed sensibility limits itself to the perceptions of a lesser one, although Forster preserves the option of authorial comment. Thematically Maurice is the necessary center of the novel, but assuming that he is to be what the author himself called a "round character," he is not always fully realized. Similarly, Alec Scudder fails to convince, despite Forster's efforts in rewriting to fill out his background and give him a more believable motivation. He remains too much the dream lover, acquiescent and physically gratifying, too much the symbol and too little the human presence. Of the three major characters it is, ironically, Cecil, toward whom the author admits an unconcealable aversion, who comes across most completely. Although he is a perfect example of Forster's conception of the "underdeveloped heart," he is undeniably convincing as a character. He clearly belongs to the group of people who "irritate" Forster, but there are quite possibly unadmitted affinities which might explain the strength and conviction of his characterization.

Imperfect as the novel is on several counts, and unfitted as it may be to rank with *The Longest Journey, Howards End,* and *A Passage to India, Maurice* is still a necessary volume in the Forster canon. Like the other novels, and like the man himself, it is courageous, tolerant, fair-minded and ultimately truth-seeking.

> It is not that the Englishman can't feel —it is that he is afraid to feel. He has been taught at his public school that feeling is bad form. . . . He must bottle up his emotions, or let them out only on very special occasions.

Forster was all for the un-bottling of emotions, if they are valuable ones for the individual, and this is what happens, joyously if unconventionally, at the end of *Maurice*.

James H. Durbin, Jr.

Sources for Further Study

Criticism:

Bolling, Douglass. "The Distanced Heart: Artistry in E. M. Forster's *Maurice,*" in *Modern Fiction Studies.* XX (1974), pp. 157-167. A scholarly analysis of the stylistic merits of Forster's novel.

Rising, C. "E. M. Forster's *Maurice*: A Summing Up," in *Texas Quarterly.* XVII (1974), pp. 84-96. Rising sees the character Maurice as the most powerful of all of Forster's heroes. He also analyzes the role of homosexuality in the novel and Forster's underlying plea for tolerance and compassion by society.

Reviews:

Atlantic. CCXXVIII, November 1, 1971, p. 140. 2,550 words.

Nation. CCXIII, November 29, 1971, p. 565. 2,450 words.

New Yorker. XLVII, October 9, 1971, p. 158. 2,400 words.

Saturday Review. LIV, October 16, 1971, p. 39. 1,050 words.

Times Literary Supplement. October 8, 1971, p. 1,215. 1,150 words.

MAX

Author: Lord David Cecil (1902-   )
Publisher: Houghton Mifflin Company (Boston). Illustrated. 507 pp. $6.95
Type of work: Biography
Time: 1872-1956
Locale: England, mainly London; Italy, mainly Rapallo

A carefully detailed biography which primarily portrays Max Beerbohm and his mind during each phase of his lengthy, interesting life

> Principal personages:
> MAX BEERBOHM
> JULIUS EWALD BEERBOHM, his father
> ELIZA DRAPER BEERBOHM, his mother
> HERBERT BEERBOHM, his half brother
> DORA, his favorite sister
> OSCAR WILDE
> AUBREY BEARDSLEY
> REGINALD TURNER
> WILLIAM ROTHENSTEIN
> GRACE CONOVER, and
> CONSTANCE COLLIER, actresses to whom Max was briefly engaged
> FLORENCE KAHN, the American actress whom he married
> ELISABETH JUNGMAN, the friend whom Max married on his deathbed

When Lord David Cecil was approached by the widow of Max Beerbohm and was told that Sir Max had wanted him to write his autobiography, Lord David was both complimented and enthusiastic. But he was also aware that he faced a difficult task. Max Beerbohm's life, although a lengthy one, was relatively uneventful, especially after he left London social life and went to Italy to live in semiseclusion with his wife. Moreover, Max himself was a person who wore an impenetrable mask, and Cecil realized that it would be his task, if not to see beneath this mask, at least to offer the most accurate glimpse of the true Max attainable.

Because of the first of these difficulties, Lord David proposes not so much to relate the story of Max's life as to offer a portrait of the man and his mind throughout his lifetime. Furthermore, the work was intended as straight biography, rather than a critical study; so the author warns the reader not to look for extensive criticism of either Max's artistic or literary works. In actuality, however, the book is a story of Max's life as well as a character portrayal. For Lord David has used the straightforward chronological approach in painting his portrait of Max and thus could not avoid reconstructing his life. Moreover, there is more critical opinion of Max's works than one might expect after reading the author's prefatory remarks. Such criticism is valuable, especially for its insights into the development of Max's art and literature from his first attempts to his mature accomplishments.

The biography is divided into four parts, the first dealing with Max's childhood and schooling at Charterhouse, his years at Oxford University, and his association with *The Yellow Book*. The youngest of a large family,

Henry Maximilian (he abhorred the pretentiousness of his middle name) was a happy boy who even in his childhood had the capacity to see life humorously. He was imaginative and pictured himself growing up to become a dandy. Even at this young age, he was conscious of the figure he would cut in life.

As a student at Charterhouse, he disliked the Spartan training (Max was never athletically inclined) and despised some of his academic subjects; but he enjoyed the fellowship with other students and learned much about getting along with people, something he always considered of primary importance. Throughout his boyhood years Max worshipped his actor half brother, Herbert Beerbohm Tree, was envious of the circle in which the sophisticate Tree moved, and aspired to hobnob with the same company. He also developed a close relationship with Dora, his favorite sister. Perhaps more than anyone, Dora saw through the mask worn by Max, a mask which even in his youth was rarely lifted.

Next to the congenial, intimate family life Max enjoyed, Oxford University was the chief formative influence on his development. Here he was influenced by the aesthetic movement of the 1890's, an approach to life and art which had a lasting influence on his own theory of art. Also at Oxford he assumed the histrionic strain, the dramatizing of himself, that was to be an integral part of his personality for years to come.

Because of his interest in the aesthetic movement and his close friendship with Reginald Turner, a member of Oscar Wilde's circle, Max became associated in the 1890's with Wilde and his group and also with Aubrey Beardsley and the publishers of *The Yellow Book*. Though too independent ever to give himself completely to groups, Max nevertheless cherished his friendships with Wilde's circle (though he had no leanings toward the homoeroticism of the group) and admired Wilde's literary style. He always remained Oscar's friend, even when scandal caused Wilde to be imprisoned. As in his art, Max adopted an amoral attitude toward his friend's actions and stood by him in time of trouble, unconcerned about the unfavorable reputation such a friendship might cause.

His acquaintanceship with the Decadents in the years following 1893 led to the essays he wrote for *The Yellow Book*, a quarterly devoted to literary and artistic interests. Although these efforts were ephemeral and not characteristic of the more mature style and subject matter of his work, they earned Max public recognition, and he became as well known as Aubrey Beardsley himself.

Part II begins with 1895, the year that marked the end of Max's formative phase; it treats his first major works, his role as a dramatic critic, and his love and marriage. During these years Max outgrew his association with *The Yellow Book*, which had been a part of his life as an undergraduate, and he likewise lost his flair for showing off. Turning his attention to more serious matters, he produced in 1896 *Caricatures of Twenty-Five Gentlemen*, contributed critical essays, meditations, and fanciful trivia to journals of the day, and in the same year published two books which were to inaugurate his literary career and establish his reputation: *The Works of Max Beerbohm*, a collection of essays, and *The Happy Hypocrite*, a deceptively simple story which deals with a very real concern of Max's—masks.

Max's literary success led to his being asked to succeed George Bernard Shaw as dramatic critic for the *Saturday Review* in 1898. Max did not want the job; he was tired of the stage, his appetite for the theater having been satiated by his close association with his brother's dramatic circle; and he was wary of being saddled with the rigors of supplying weekly reviews. Nevertheless, he accepted the position, primarily because of the financial straits of his family. Max was not a natural drama critic. He lacked an overwhelming love of the theater and could never enter a playwright's feelings adequately. His best reviews were really essays in which he strayed from the play and indulged in meditations about art. In drama, as in all the arts, Max called for beauty. His standards for judging a play were beauty, reality, and intelligence. Seldom did he find all three.

As in his social contacts, Max always remained independent in his critical expression. He had intellectual courage as a reviewer. If he found a particular play or aspect of a play laudable, he was quick to praise it, even if it happened to appeal also to philistine taste. Never did Max merely parrot the critical opinions of the sophisticated intellectuals of the day.

Max had always been fascinated by women, except for those of the blue stocking variety, and for several years was engaged to Grace Conover, or Kilseen, an actress, and still later to another actress, Constance Collier. In 1904 he met the woman he would marry. Florence Kahn was a shy, somewhat provincial American actress who was in London trying to establish herself on the stage. Attracted to her at once, Max courted her (often indiffer-

ently) for several years before proposing marriage in 1908. Weary of his weekly grind on the *Saturday Review* and of his life in high society with its exacting demands, he was ready to move to Italy and settle down with a wife. Florence, with her anti-social attitude and her desire to devote her entire attention to him, was the companion he needed. Thus he resigned his position as drama critic in 1910, married Florence, and moved to Italy.

Max's life between 1910 and 1947 is covered in Part III. Marriage proved to be the turning point in his life. No longer did he struggle with a dual personality, one side of him attuned to social life, the other reserved for his private, contemplative moments. The former vanished as, in bowing out of London life at the age of thirty-eight, he no longer cared about cutting a figure. Comfortably settled at the Villino Chiaro, near Rapallo, Max was to enjoy this quiet, relaxed environment for the rest of his life. Only during the two world wars did he and Florence return to London for extensive sojourns.

From this time on, Max's life was relatively uneventful. He attended exhibitions of his caricatures and cartoons in London, continued to write, entertained noted literati at his home, and inaugurated a successful radio career in 1935 by giving lectures for the B.B.C. But his life was without the quick pace and excitement of the years prior to 1910. He did publish in 1910 his most ambitious literary work, *Zuleika Dobson,* a fantasy based on his Oxford days. And in 1919 he published *Seven Men,* an important group of satires in which his writing reaches what Cecil calls its "final and most fully matured expression." His last and most important volume of essays. *And Even Now,* appeared in 1921. These pieces are more serious, more varied, and tell us more of Max than his former writings.

But after 1922 he wrote very little. His artistic inspiration was leaving him. Though he always remained young in spirit and loved humor, he aged faster than most men physically and nervously. His caricatures likewise lost their poignant quality. For as Max aged, he became more good natured and more concerned about not hurting people's feelings. As Lord David Cecil points out, "Caricature and good nature go ill together."

Max's latter days, from 1947 to 1956, are the subject of Part IV. They were unproductive, yet mellow years. He did a few radio programs from Italy, and he continued to cultivate friendships. When Florence died in 1951, his long-time friend Elisabeth Jungmann became Max's constant companion. He married her on his deathbed in 1956 to insure her inheriting his estate. It was an act typical of the man, for he was always concerned with the well-being of others.

Lord David Cecil, then, presents a careful reconstruction of Max Beerbohm the man. Among its strong points, the book is attractively illustrated with some thirty photographs of Max and his acquaintances and with reproductions of caricatures by Max. At times Cecil is overly attentive to detail, quoting unduly from Max's letters, journals, and books. And he is sometimes repetitious when, in keeping with the chronological approach, he discusses an artistic or literary work at the time of its inception and again at the time of its appearance.

This very successful biography is quite worthy of its subject. It is a revealing study of a man who strove in his art to blend the beautiful with the comic, to laugh at what he loved, and love what he laughed at; a man who never had great ambitions but only the desire to put to good use what talent he had.

David B. Kesterson

MAX JAMISON

Author: Wilfrid Sheed (1930-   )
Publisher: Farrar, Straus and Giroux (New York). 260 pp. $6.50
Type of work: Novel
Time: 1969
Locale: New York City

A famous Broadway critic, under criticism by his wife, friends, and self, passes successfully through a personal crisis by employing his own professional skills

Principal characters:
MAX JAMISON, an influential drama critic
HELEN JAMISON, his wife
JUSTIN and
CHARLIE, their sons
EVE SAMPLE, a divorcee and student
SUSAN CRAM, a bohemian with whom Jamison has a casual affair
GENE MUNGO, a painter
FLASHMAN and
BRUFFIN, critics

Wilfrid Sheed's sixth book details, in four witty parts and an epilogue, a personal crisis in the life of critic Maximilian P. Jamison, cured by the very qualities which caused it. Sheed's irony wheels through the story and turns back upon itself; this is both the novel's strength and weakness. The effect resembles a snake savoring his own tail as a tasty tidbit in lieu of a full banquet.

Max Jamison, dean of America's drama critics, reviews Broadway plays and films for two magazines with significant titles: *Rearview* (highbrow, literary) and *Now* (popular, newsweekly). His standards are high, his judgments harsh. He is over six feet tall, looks like an English police sergeant, and is living through a period of severe self-judgment which tries his objectivity. As chief narrator, Jamison gives the author license to devise and discard metaphors, to state opinions and repudiate them, to hold wildcat debates with himself. Rarely has a self-critic carried the professional credentials of a Max Jamison, and his caustic interior monologues are the best parts of the novel. Subjects include: cinema buffs, his past and future, parenthood, the role of the critic, today's youth, academe, and possible ways to change his life.

Helen, Jamison's second wife, came from a family which wouldn t have criticized Mickey Mouse. (You haven't heard *his* side.) A former student, she remained the pupil in their marriage until she learned Max's techniques of criticism too well and found that—by Max's own standards—Max was mediocre. She accused him of making criticism an end in itself, and of failure to grow and change. As the novel opens, Max and Helen are separated and Max pays painful Sunday visits to his two sons, Justin and Charlie. Their broken marriage (his second) has damaged the self-confidence which is Max's stock in trade. He is also troubled about his two jobs, the effort to mix serious and popular criticism: has he sold out? Perhaps Helen is right, too, that he has followed one non-creative career to an arid dead end and simply feeds like a parasite on the work of those who at least attempt works of art.

A night spent with Susan Cram brings Max all the pleasure of a workout in a gymnasium and, while he does not value her praise, he is stung by her disapproval of his recent reviews for *Now*. In the Guggenheim Museum he meets Eve Sample, a divorcee and another student, and begins a more serious affair. Part Two interweaves chapters about his professional and private life: Eve, a lecture, Helen, a panel at which Bruffin, a fellow critic, insults him, Eve, a college speech with a young man crying from the audience, "You ruin art by verbalizing about it." Worst of all is Helen's announcement that she will take his two sons to the country and spend her summer with artist Gene Mungo who, Max feels, "can't even draw an apple."

Deciding he must change his life while there is still something left to change, Max tries omitting his famed irony from reviews, since irony has "killed all ideas." Angry and desperate, he duels in words with Bruffin at the Critics Circle, then strikes him, drives to Windemere but cannot bring himself to burst into Helen's new household. When Eve admits she would rather not be a mother to his sons, he walks out of her apartment for the last time.

Part Four switches briefly to Helen's viewpoint. Living with her lazy but virile artist, she sums up all that was wrong with being Mrs. Max Jamison. Max, she says, brought his standards of a good performance even into the bedroom. She talks about him constantly: his arrogant opinions, the jokes which could raise blisters on their friends. "Max taught me to be critical," she explains to Gene—judging Max, gradually judging Gene as well. Mean-

while Max, in what he describes as his "breakdown," is mailing vicious letters to her, to Eve, even to his first wife, Georgette. This explosion of written bile proves therapeutic. Eventually the letters deal with why they are being written; they criticize themselves, and art creeps back into his work. Gene, seeing Helen's preoccupation with Max, moves out and the Jamisons arrive at a truce.

Max has changed, calmed, become even bland and tame. For a time he joins the faculty of Winslow University, but as he continues to regain his mental health he regains his natural critical gifts as well. Soon the drama department is outraged and young actresses are in tears. In the end he returns to New York, to his serious articles for *Rearview*, while Helen enjoys book club success with her work on gardening.

Plot summaries do novels no justice, but in *Max Jamison* the wit is a line-by-line adornment which cannot be reproduced here, and the theme is small: *Mr. Sammler's Planet*, greatly reduced.

One imagines that Wilfrid Sheed began with the idea of turning the tables, and in casting about for a main character considered a critic who succumbed to criticism and—*Aha!* Once there was a criticized critic who became his own worst critic and. . . .

The best quality of the novel is neither story line nor theme, but Mr. Sheed's sharp eye, which looks out of Max Jamison's head at his contemporaries and bores relentlessly in upon himself. The observations are sometimes merely clever, but often intelligent and always entertaining. If *Max Jamison* is a novel to be serialized in *Now* rather than *Rearview*, it is still the product of a mind which fully un-

derstands that difference and which
has already explored this very dilemma

in a narrative which manages to have
its cake and eat it too.

Doris Betts

MAY WE BORROW YOUR HUSBAND?
And Other Comedies of the Sexual Life

Author: Graham Greene (1904–   )
Publisher: The Viking Press (New York). 183 pp. $4.50
Type of work: Short stories
   Twelve stories of human frailty, written by a leading novelist and master craftsman

Graham Greene is primarily a novelist; however, the twelve stories which appear in this collection indicate that he is very much at home in the shorter medium. There is evident delight in technical mastery and in the perfection of his style, a style in which there are no wasted words and the maximum of communication is combined with great economy of means. The present examples have appeared in various periodicals during the past decade; they vary greatly in length and significance, but all reflect his preoccupation with human behavior and all exhibit his uncanny skill in terms of presentation.

The subtitle of this collection may be misleading to some readers. These "comedies" are such, for the most part, in a purely literary sense—that is, they depict people in absurdly human situations which are not necessarily funny. If laughter is evoked, it is often the kind of laughter that comes as a last resort and is in a sense unwelcome. The theme of sexuality is also somewhat misleading in that sex is merely incidental to some of the tales, and in certain others is present only by virtue of the fact that the characters do belong to one sex or the other. In no case does the "sexual life" presented furnish gonadal stimulation for the reader; in this sense it may be misleading too. He who expects gay ribaldry will find little of it here.

However, those who take the subtitle with a grain of salt will find much variety, some food for speculation, and a large measure of entertainment.

There is a sort of wizardry in Greene's ability to intimate, depict, and express all things save unqualified happiness—yet he never fails to do so impeccably and sparsely. And he is a master in regard to the revealing snapshot. Consider the following portrait of a woman who enters a man's room in his absence and sees a letter: ". . . with the simple unscrupulousness of an intellectual she began to read it with her ears cocked for any sound in the passage." Further, the reader almost inevitably becomes involved in the story, whether he wills it or no; and it can be said that one does not enter the world of Graham Greene and emerge from it entirely unmarked or unmoved. It is a world in which pleasure is seldom if ever unalloyed with pain; its inhabitants are helplessly caught in absurd but inescapable situations, and their chief emotions are disillusionment, regret, or despair. In it, even on sunny days, there is a cold and melancholy rain falling upon the spirit. These qualities of Greene are especially notable in his prewar "entertainments," *This Gun for Hire, The Confidential Agent,* and *The Ministry of Fear.* They are echoed in the present volume, which resembles them more in mood and intent than do his more serious novels. The latter are melancholy, and their purpose is not necessarily to entertain.

The most powerful story in this collection is "Cheap in August." In it the thirty-nine-year-old English wife of an American college professor vacations in

Jamaica while her husband does research in Europe. She is determined to have an affair like those her friends boast of before she grows too old to feel adventurous; and she wishes her husband were guilty of infidelity, thus furnishing some justification other than boredom. Her stay is an endless monotony of bitter sunlight, repellent tourists, enervating heat, and loneliness. She meets an American who becomes interested in her; he is past seventy, gross and unattractive, but there is something inevitable about their relationship. Eventually, when she learns that he is afraid of dying alone in the dark, she spends a night with him: thus her anticipated "holiday affair" turns out to be a fleeting sexual contact with a broken and frightened old man. He is left to face the next lonely night and she returns, no happier than before, to an unsuspecting husband. No lasting bond has been established: both figures are lonely and desperate; both are here because the expense is less in August. The sexual culmination of their relationship is almost automatic, devoid of enjoyment or moral considerations, and their mutual reward is a momentary relief from anguish.

At this point the perceptive reader is made aware of another aspect of Greene's genius. Why did Mary Watson give herself to the old man? Greene does not say. Some critics will make much of her noble and overmastering pity; others will assert that her action was the result of boredom or a form of indifference, or perhaps self-pity. This is a highly sophisticated variation of "The Lady or the Tiger," and any sentiments ascribed to Mary Watson—or to Greene, for that matter—are almost certainly those of the reader.

The title story is equally powerful in its way. It is a little less dismal, a little more absurd, and the inevitability is not quite as obvious. "Cheap in August" derives much of its power through mood, while that of "May We Borrow Your Husband?" is derived through action and more complex human relationships. It is a long anecdote employing the "detached observer" framework and in many ways resembles certain works of Maugham; its reminiscent style carries the ring of personal experience. The narrator, a middle-aged writer, is staying at a hotel in southern France. The tourist season is over when two additional guests arrive; they are male homosexuals and distinctly unpleasant. Presently two more guests appear, this time a pair of honeymooners. The two homosexuals instinctively recognize one of their own kind in the groom and begin an elaborate—and ultimately successful—campaign of seduction. The narrator feels a deep sympathy for the naïve and unsuspecting bride but cannot bring himself to tell her what is really going on; in addition, he is too old to consider seriously any attempt to win her for himself. The more aggressive homosexual captures the groom and discards his former companion; the bride is overjoyed by her husband's new-found virility and happiness. The final irony is that the narrator, for all his experience and worldly wisdom, feels that he could have saved the marriage had he been able to make himself interfere. It is long since obvious to the reader, however, that the groom has had prior homosexual contacts and has already committed himself to the way of life he finally adopts. Greene's narrators are so skilfully plausible that we sometimes fail to realize they are characters too and not the voice of the author. Nor are they always the detached observers one expects them to be: they are guilty of normal inconsistencies and sometimes become deeply involved.

Another homosexual tale, also utilizing a narrator and the Antibes setting, takes place in a café. Again seduction is accomplished: a middle-aged lesbian sympathizes with a pretty young widow, gets her drunk, and makes off with her.

The remaining stories in the volume exhibit considerable variety, with several examples of humor ranging from the agreeable joke to the grotesque or the macabre. Among the more light-hearted of these is the mildly Rabelaisian anecdote about a men's drinking club in the Germany of sixty years ago, a group forced to meet in secret in order to avoid a fanatical busybody its members could not otherwise exclude. Still more amusing is the brief sketch of an earnest old doctor who created a mild furor during the same era by stoutly maintaining that sex causes cancer. Another story in this vein is that of the young man whose father was killed in Italy by a falling pig, and who cannot obtain a properly sympathetic response when he tells about it. "Mortmain" describes the sweetly fiendish way in which a discarded mistress accomplishes her revenge. There is also the sketch of an aggressive and domineering girl whose first novel is being published. She tells her fiancé over and over about the keen powers of observation her publisher has admired in her, yet fails to notice the eight Japanese gentlemen dining incongruously at the next table. "Beauty" is the vignette of a doting middle-aged woman who worships her Pekingese and considers it superior to all other creatures; the dog proves his canine identity, however, when he rummages in the garbage and makes off with a length of rotting animal gut.

Although there are chilling touches here and there, there is only one genuine horror story in the collection. "The Overnight Bag" is a grotesque tale grimly underplayed, in which an apparently sexless little man returns from Europe to his mother. The overnight bag in his hand contains a dead baby; he assures his fellow passenger on the plane, a large woman who reads love letters from girl friends, that it is not his but his wife's. Later he and a cab-driver have a similar conversation, with some discussion of the merits of refrigeration as a preservative. When the little man arrives at his mother's house, we learn that he loves the strange paintings of Hieronymus Bosch and likes to describe the toe he found in his marmalade.

"Two Gentle People" returns us to the essential Greene and to the mood of "Cheap in August." A middle-aged man and woman meet by chance in a park and share the same bench; the man kills a pigeon injured by teenagers. They discuss the act of mercy quietly together and he invites her to dinner at a nearby restaurant. The event is a species of idyl for both. They enjoy this companionship but do not reveal their private lives: thus neither knows it is a brief oasis of peace for the other. After the meal they part forever —he returns to his wife, a querulous, jealous invalid; she rejoins her husband, a homosexual whose delight it is to entertain his lovers in the adjoining room.

Many readers, critical or otherwise, credit Greene with great compassion, warm sympathy, and a deep and abiding pity. Others find in his work a cold and melancholy austerity. Both, perhaps, are there. Certainly he understands his characters, and they are cast in intensely human mold; their flawed and often hopeless progress through his world is entirely credible. However, the author's real skill in this context is that the compassion and pity evoked by his music—or the repellently fascinating melancholy and disgust that are their opposites—are actually supplied by the reader. Greene provides, with marvelous finesse, the framework and the actors; his audience willingly credits him with much that he may not feel and never actually expresses. Greene, rather than his narrator, is the real detached observer: he displays no emotion, makes no judgments, gives no editorial comment on his characters during their brief lives. All reactions to them are those of the reader, whose involvement makes him one of the characters too—trapped in the story by, quite possibly, his own self-pity.

John W. Evans

THE MAZE

Author: Eileen Simpson
Publisher: Simon and Schuster (New York). 250 pp. $7.95
Type of work: Novel
Time: The 1950's
Locale: Italy, England, and Massachusetts

A double exploration into the nature of genius and the qualities that compose a marriage, and into the demands which both make upon the individual personality

Principal characters:
> BENJAMIN BOLD, an American poet
> ROXANA (ROSY), his wife
> RODNEY MUNSON, Benjamin's old friend
> MARGARET MUNSON, his wife
> THEO ADDIS, a writer and lecturer, Rosy's possible lover
> TULLIO FANCELLI, a friend of Benjamin and well-known Italian novelist
> ANDREW MALLORY, Benjamin's friend and fellow poet

The Maze is a novel about survival, about the struggle of the individual to survive in the face of psychological and moral disasters, and about the equally fierce struggle of talent, or genius, to survive in a world that refuses to yield to its demands. The clash between these forces creates much of the drama in this vivid and subtle portrayal of a disintegrating marriage. Benjamin Bold is forty, an American poet who has waited twenty years for fame. Having at last completed the long poem that he expects will make his reputation, Bold seeks to recuperate from the creative effort by traveling to Italy with his wife. In Rome, they encounter other Americans, mostly academics and writers, who tend to grate upon one another's egos. It soon becomes obvious that Bold is a suicidal drunk who cannot resist any opportunity to make scenes or to offend those who might help him. The presence of his wife makes him behave even worse. Gradually, she tries to make her way through the maze that Bold has imposed upon her life. Much of the story deals with her efforts to survive as a person while attempting to hold together her marriage. Finally, realizing that he wants to be rid of her, she leaves him, only to find that he expects her to return. Bold is unchanged at the end of the novel, and one feels that he will never change, but his wife, the long-suffering Rosy, has learned to recognize just what kind of people they are, and courageously has taken the first steps toward an independent and viable life.

The Maze takes place almost entirely inside Rosy's consciousness. The character of Bold is fascinating, with his collection of contradictions and eccentricities, but he is also exasperating. There is nothing sympathetic about him. One believes in his genius, but cannot respect his behavior. The author has achieved the difficult feat of creating a person who is both real and unpleasant, dynamic and self-alienating. Benjamin Bold is as selfish as he is talented, and would willingly sacrifice every other human being in the world to his poetry. It is a measure of Eileen Simpson's skill that the reader does not become too disgusted with Bold's antics, as seen from his wife's point of view, to continue the book. Actually, Bold provides much of the life in the book, for Rosy is as weak as he is strong. She clearly cannot define herself except in terms of a man, but we do not know why she is this way. As the central consciousness in the novel, Rosy might have been probed more deeply. The reader craves to understand better *why* she endured her husband as long as she did.

Although at times the book seems rather like a case history, and is filled with unnecessary and empty chattering by crowds of minor characters, the author has a sharp eye for the complexity of people's emotional lives. This, perhaps, is the real strength of the book. Simpson is the former wife of the late poet John Berryman; she knows of what she writes and never oversimplifies. A clinical psychiatrist, Simpson made a study of creativity in poets, a study which served as her thesis for a graduate degree in psychology at New York University. The reader feels this authority on every page. The immediacy of some of the scenes is almost unbearable. Yet, she avoids "big" scenes or melodramatic situations, preferring to rely upon the telling gesture and precise dialogue.

Creativity always has fascinated both writers and readers. How do genuine talents function? How are the towering works of music and art and literature created? What are the torments that drive these great artistic geniuses? The author has addressed

herself to these questions and has succeeded in producing a vivid and compelling portrait of such a genius. Perhaps one could make too much of the similarities between Benjamin Bold and John Berryman, yet one cannot forget the fact that Simpson's portrait inevitably owes much to her intimate knowledge of that poet. Berryman and Bold were both of the generation that matured in the Depression and began to produce during the World War II years. Both were educated first at American universities, after which Berryman studied at Oxford, Bold at Cambridge. Both taught at various American universities and won many awards and fellowships. And both wrote experimental poetry, poetry which strove to make clear, direct statements with sharply-honed imagery. As Berryman said of his own poetry, Bold believed that poetry should have "guts." And both men were poets of integrity, poets who stood by their work and dared to let their work stand against the best poetry of the past. By the end of the book, the reader has glimpsed, as if by flashes of lightning, the creative process and the inevitable pains that follow such intense efforts. It is a hazardous existence, for both the poet and those close to him. One is both grateful that anyone is willing to endure such an existence in order to create the art that illuminates life for the rest of humanity, and alarmed by the torments endured by the poet and those around him.

Subsidiary characters represent other types of creative artists, from the most successful to the not-so-successful. Tullio Fancelli, a friend of Bold and a well-known Italian novelist, typifies the "successful" writer who has achieved both critical recognition and economic rewards. But he has sacrificed something for his success, or, perhaps, merely lost something as he gained it, for the other characters all feel that he was more "interesting" when he was young and struggling. The author explores with sensitivity the dangers of success versus the agony of failure. Andrew Mallory and Theo Addis are different kinds of writers, satisfied with limited success and recognition, neither struggling with the terrible pressures of genius. Both are willing to compromise, to settle for the "good life" and a reasonable portion of happiness. But, whatever else Benjamin Bold is capable of, he cannot compromise with his poetry. It is his religion.

A minor theme, gradually developed in the novel, is that of the human need for some kind of religion. Rosy is a lapsed Catholic. She finds, as she tears herself away from Benjamin, that she needs the consolation of her Church. But Bold's religion is art, creation, his own genius. The symbolism of the novel, from Hadrian's Villa and the temples of ancient Rome to the medieval and Renaissance churches, suggests that man's needs for art and religion are one. Without either, we have hopelessness and death. It is significant that the novel begins with Bold waking up from a nightmare, part of the suffering that he experiences after the completion of his great poem. He cannot find peace except in creation. The process itself is hellish, yet to *not* be creating is worse agony.

Another metaphor developed for the process of artistic creation is that of giving birth to a child. Bold never wanted an actual child. Perhaps he was afraid of a rival for his wife's affection, but more than that he saw his works of art as his children. He felt that the creation of a poem was the same as the growth in the womb and the birth of an actual baby. He even believed that he suffered a postpartum depression such as mothers sometimes experience. He is both the child and the parent, demanding that Rosy both mother him and help him to give birth to his poetry. At the same time, he insists that she worship at the altar of his genius and worship *him,* as the creator, and his poetry, the "holy" child to which he has given birth. The symbols and metaphors in the book are richly and cunningly developed; they are both psychologically and morally compelling.

But it is the maze which is the ultimate and central metaphor in the novel. Rosy sees her life as a maze such as those found in Italian gardens, a maze full of false clues, cul-de-sacs, and mislabeled paths. She tries to plan her escape, to outsmart her jailer, but, as panic engulfs her, she finds herself frantically racing up and down the endless paths. The maze is Benjamin Bold, his genius, his erratic life style, his temperament, his selfishness, and his love. Finally, the maze is their marriage together, the bloody scenes of their life, and the false starts that they continue to make together. The only way to escape the maze is to escape Benjamin, the one decision most painful for her to make.

The maze metaphor is subtly developed as Rosy travels around Italy and Europe. She flees from an outraged, drunken Benjamin and becomes lost in Rome; wandering

4848   *The Maze*/SIMPSON

through the dangerous, dark streets of the Eternal City, she confronts her essential problem, and realizes that she has let herself be led into this emotional and physical trap which is her marriage. And on the ancient island of Ponza, a place which for centuries served as a prison, she also ponders her life and the future of her marriage. Other men offer her options, but she rejects them as false escapes. If she does find the way out it must be alone, for nobody can save her but herself. The individual must stand, finally, separate from everyone else. Benjamin Bold, as a poet and a man, must function in self-imposed isolation, and Rosy, as a woman, as a human being, must find her own unique salvation. No one, Simpson implies, can save anyone else, but, perhaps, we can win a little time for ourselves.

Bruce D. Reeves

THE MAZE MAKER

Author: Michael Aytron (1921-1975)
Publisher: Holt, Rinehart and Winston (New York). 320 pp. $6.95
Type of work: Novel
Time: The second millennium, B.C.
Locale: Greece, Crete, Italy, and Sicily

An absorbing re-creation of the myths surrounding Daedalus and the course of his life

Principal characters:
    DAEDALUS, the "maze maker"
    METION, his father
    IPHINOË, his mother
    PERDIX, his sister
    TALOS, her son
    LYCUS, the ruler of Euboea
    DACTYLOS, a myterious craftsman and teacher of Daedalus
    AEGEUS, the ruler of Athens
    LAERCES and
    ENDOIOS, assistants to Daedalus and Talos
    PALLAS, the ruler of Sounion
    NAUCRATE, Daedalus' wife, a princess of Crete
    ICARUS, their son
    MINOS, the king of Crete
    PASIPHAË, the queen
    ARIADNE, their daughter
    TAUROS, the queen's bodyguard and the king's general
    THE GREEK SPEAKER, the leader of the small people in Gaia, the "Mother"
    AUSONIAS, one of the makers of winds
    AEOLUS, the ruler of Aeolia and a maker of winds
    COCALUS, the ruler of Sicily
    IOLAÜS, the nephew of Heracles

Thomas Mann once wrote that "life in the myth, life, so to speak, in quotation, is a kind of celebration, in that is a making present of the past. . . ." It is with this statement in mind that one can read Michael Aytron's *The Maze Maker,* following somewhat in the footsteps of Mary Renault and William Golding. Mary Renault's *The Last of the Wine, The King Must Die,* and *The Bull From the Sea* are all attempts at making mythology a reasonable or acceptable account of what actually could have happened and how the myths were created and became the distorted views we have today. She im-

plants the human element into the tragic characters of her books. William Golding, in *The Inheritors,* brought to life characters of the Paleolithic period. We have no real knowledge of all their actions, beliefs, fears, or modes of living, but from the little that has been learned Mr. Golding created a situation which is acceptable and seemingly real. Now Mr. Aytron has written the "autobiography" of Daedalus, *The Maze Maker.*

Daedalus introduces himself immediately and explains to us that he is speaking across the barriers of time:

Time is part of the problem. What I mean by time as I write of it, is the liquid in which legend is suspended. What I write her you will read as though it concerns matters sunk many thousand years into the past, yet clearly I am writing it today. I address you man to man.

He tells us of his childhood and corrects the story that Eupalamos was his father. If this account had been true, then Metion, his earth father, would certainly have mentioned it, and Iphinoë, his mother, would have bragged about it, but neither had discussed this possibility. When Daedalus was thirteen his cousin Aegeus captured Athens, sending Daedalus and his mother fleeing for their lives to Euboea; there Lycus kept a watchful eye over them. While Daedalus was in Euboea he received his training in art and craftsmanship under a strange barbarian smith who called himself Dactylos. The craftsman told Daedalus, "The sole dishonor is to die with a work unfinished. . . ."

After two years, Daedalus and his mother returned to Athens at the request of Aegeus. There, for three years, Daedalus worked with his sister's son, Talos. The two boys were lovers in the Greek sense. It was an honorable and respected situation and was never made sordid. But Perdix, Talos' mother, was jealous of the relationship and set about to destroy it. Talos and Laerces, Daedalus' assistant, fought one evening in the sacred garden and the battle ended in Laerces' death. Talos left the country at night in fear of being executed for fighting in the sacred garden and it was reported that Daedalus had killed Talos. Perdix had Endoios, Talos' assistant, testify that the tale was true and so Daedalus, unable to prove his innocence, was forced into exile.

His next place of residence was Sounion in Attica, where his cousin Pallas ruled. Pallas kept Daedalus busy making intricate toys for him, including a serving table which rolled to him when he called. While the young craftsman was in Sounion he met Naucrate, a princess of the court in Crete. It was she who was eventually to lead him to Knossos to build the great maze which is still in evidence today. Naucrate was fifteen when she gave birth to their son, Icarus. When they sailed for Crete, Daedalus received from one of the rowers the ominous signs of his son's tragic future.

In Knossos, Daedalus was received by the court with bland courtesy. His wife and son were separated from him by his devotion to his craft. He studied the Cretan methods of creating their fine craft and found that their figures lacked any feeling of strength; in fact, they were effeminate and comely. Daedalus had been in Crete several months before he met Minos and it was during their second meeting that the king requested the building of the great maze, "The task took fifteen years and in all that time I kept the pattern of the maze in my mind. No one knew its plan except Minos and myself." When the maze was almost completed, Pasiphaë, the queen, sent for the craftsman in secret. Tauros, the queen's bodyguard and the king's general, explained to him what was desired of him. He was to build a cow—one in which the queen could be placed so as to be mated with the white bull. "The white bull contains the god himself in his epiphany. Zeus inhabits him." Daedalus performed his task well and Pasiphaë was mated to the white bull, but trouble arose when people learned of the deed. When it became known that the queen was pregnant, the stories surrounding the mating grew and hate for Daedalus became open. The master craftsman discounts the myths that became distorted about this incident, leaving the actual event almost plausible.

Daedalus again had to run, but he remained on Crete with his assistant's mother. He stayed with her for a year and during this time he studied the flight of birds. At the end of the year Endoios appeared to warn him that Talos was on the island, half crazed and wanting to kill his former lover. Talos now appeared everywhere in bronze, under the belief that Daedalus had killed him and he had been remade in bronze. Also, Endoios told him of the birth of the queen's son. The child was not in the complete shape of a human. Daedalus set out for Knossos and on his way he met Talos, whom he overcame. It was discovered that the seeming giant had used stilts of different lengths to make himself taller and more fearful to those beholding him as he limped toward them.

Upon his return to Knossos, Daedalus discounts the myths surrounding the creation and use of the great maze. He discusses the Minotaur and the stories that related to his birth and care. He explains the reasons for going into the labyrinth with his son Icarus. The wings which he constructed are described and a detailed description of how they were made follows. Minos' character is given some light as is that of Ariadne, his daughter. Daedalus laughs at the idea that he killed Minos and continues by stating his belief that Minos probably fathered a son by his daughter before her encounter with Theseus or her marriage to Dionysus. Knossos was in turmoil when Daedalus and Icarus prepared to make their

famous flight. The earth grumbled and "the air whined and grew hot." The flight is described as though Daedalus were a navigator. Their flight becomes reality, acceptable because it is not made to seem unnatural. It appears simple, successful on the first try. Icarus' death came not because he flew so close to the sun that the heat melted the wax, but because he wanted and did manage to mate with the god. Apollo cindered Icarus for his actions and Daedalus could never find his son's body.

Daedalus landed near the rock of Cumae. Apollo's temple stood at the top. While the master craftsman watched, Apollo burned down the temple and forced the craftsman underground with the orders to build a new temple. It took some time for Daedalus to communicate with the leader of the underground dwellers. They were a people who did not know the outside world—did not know what the heat or light of Apollo could be like. They had always lived in Gaia, "the Mother," and cared for her; in return she provided them with the necessities of life. The apparent leader of these people was called, by Daedalus, the Greek Speaker, for he was the only one of the small people who ever communicated with him. The leader explained to the craftsman that before they would help him with his task he must make a golden honeycomb to be offered to Gaia. If it were accepted, then Daedalus would have all the laborers he needed. The honeycomb was truly a work of art and was readily accepted, and so the temple was constructed.

Apollo allowed Daedalus to leave "the Mother" and again journey alone and unsure of anything. He spent the winter in a fishing village and then continued on toward Sicily, stopping on the island of Aeolia to thank Aeolus for the winds that allowed him to make his flight possible. Daedalus made an elaborate series of tunnels through which Aeolus could send his winds and create music to keep himself amused.

Sicily was due south of Aeolia and Daedalus reached the island in two days, thanks to Ausonias, the captain who had brought him to Aeolia and now whistled him a good wind. Cocalus ruled Sicily somewhat but not really as an actual king. While Daedalus was in Sicily he made a golden honeycomb for Cocalus, but it was made as an offering for the security he had been given by the ruler. The job which awaited the craftsman here was the building of an external maze. The purpose of the maze was to keep an invading force of Cretans from overpowering a small number of protectors. Ausonias from Aeolia came to the aid of Cocalus, as did Iolaüs on his way to Sardinia with the fifty grandsons of Thespius. The maze enclosed a palace with hot and cold running water and natural steam heat. The enemy fleet arrived and Daedalus' maze proved its worth when the Cretan leader, Tauros, pretending to be Minos, was killed in the steam baths. Talo led the army against the fortress, but after he had killed Ausonias, the wind-maker, Talos and the troops turned and fled from sheer terror of their deed.

Daedalus ends his story by stating that

> Today I shall end this writing, not because my life is ended, and not because I know exactly what will happen next, but rather, that I am so sure of the eventual outcome. I do not think there will be time to write more. I have agreed to sail with Iolaüs and to-

day they launched their new-built ships. When the wind is right we shall begin our voyage and if it is not, for we no longer have Ausonias to make it so, then those sons of Heracles can doubtless row. . . . I have called myself Maze Maker with a certain irony because although I believe myself preeminent in many crafts, I have been, as Minos described me, first and last a maker of labyrinths. . . . I shall build one more and that will be my last. It will be in Sardinia and there I shall dig a twisting path back into Gaia so that the sun will no longer persecute me, for he will have no further cause.

Michael Aytron has written an interesting fictional autobiography. It is apparent that the work was obsessive in its origins. The writer says of Daedalus: "So powerful has been this obsession that I have struggled to free myself of him even to the extent of writing his life." There is much to be said for this book: Mr. Aytron's knowledge of the different methods used in making sculpture or casting are quite apparent. There are descriptive passages which show this knowledge and are well written. Some of the most effective are the accounts of building of the moving table, the internal and external mazes, the cow for Pasiphaë, the wings for the famous flight, the honeycomb for Gaia, and the statue of Apollo for the temple on Cumae.

The creation of the character of Daedalus shows that Mr. Aytron seems to have had a strong connection with the past. This craftsman, this man of so many talents is almost made real. His pride, bitterness, love, and desires are all brought forth. Daedalus was constantly fleeing some tragedy, a tragedy he usually brought upon himself by his own great works. His dreams, his recollections, the meetings with the different gods and goddesses are vivid.

The manner in which Mr. Aytron has Daedalus discount many of the myths is interesting. He tells of the many feats of Daedalus, but he also manages to make the whole business seem logical and acceptable. *The Maze Maker* is a refreshing work of art casting new light on an ancient story as retold by a writer who is himself a distinguished artist.

Lee Petrie Ruddle

MEASURE MY LOVE

Author: Helga Sandburg (1918-   )
Publisher: McDowell, Obolensky (New York). 180 pp. $3.50
Type of work: Novel
Time: The present
Locale: Rural Michigan

A story of a flawed marriage and the testing of human character, acted out in the presence of nature poetically evoked in all weathers and seasons

Principal characters:
FAITH SUMMERS BAIN, a young farm wife
BUDDY BAIN, her younger, easy-going husband
JOB SUMMERS, her father
DOLLY, his wife
FLOSS,
LACY,
IRENE, and
THANKFUL, other Summers children
GRANNY, Mrs. Summers' mother
MRS. BAIN, Buddy's mother
CHOICE BAIN, her older son
WYOMA, Mrs. Bain's sister
PETER and
DAVID, the young sons of Faith and Buddy Bain

When Helga Sandburg published her first novel, *The Wheel of Earth,* in 1958, criticism gave the book the well-wishing and respectful attention it deserved. Almost every reviewer, however, including this one, called attention to the fact that she is Carl Sandburg's daughter. Some even made the association of their names sound like an act of grace, the laying on of hands in a literary succession. Apparently it occurred to no one to say in print that Miss Sandburg might be a highly promising talent in her own right.

The time has come to correct that omission. Helga Sandburg has now published her second novel, and in many ways *Measure My Love* is a better work than *The Wheel of Earth.* The news will be reassuring to those who hold that the second novel is likely to be the deciding one, for better or worse, in a writer's career. Every-

one, it is said, has at least one good story to tell. The test is whether the young novelist possesses resources enough for a second, a third, a fourth. For this reason the second novel is likely to be a signpost of sorts indicating the direction in which its author is heading. It is also a commitment to a shaping vision of the world and to the discipline which imposes order on the chaos of life. These matters testify to the scope and soundness of the novelist's materials, just as his craftsmanship in the handling of structure, symbol, and language provides the clues to the nature of his sensibility and the order of his moral insight.

The Wheel of Earth was impressive in its whole-hearted, abundant earthiness and poetic imagery. *Measure My Love* is more restrained in theme, breadth, and style. Like its predecessor, it is simple in outline, quite different in technique and effect from what we have learned to look for in the modern novel. In fact, Miss Sandburg seems at times a rather old-fashioned writer. The term is not used in any derogatory sense. But she presents no anguished vision of good and evil, dredges no portentous symbols from mystic depths, creates no specialized milieu charged with ambiguity or fantasy, evokes no private moods of guilt, despair, or doom, makes no assaults on technique or language. In her fiction it is very much as if nothing has happened in the development of the novel since the time of Thomas Hardy.

The name of Hardy is not idly suggested, for his example serves to bring certain qualities of Helga Sandburg's writing into sharper focus. There is in her novels much that is comparable, though not in any imitative manner, with the work of the nineteenth century English novelist—not the cosmic pessimist and the inquirer into the ways of the irrational universe, but the author of *Under the Greenwood Tree* and *Far from the Madding Crowd*, the poet of landscape and man's simple earthiness, the chronicler of a way of life that moved in rhythm with nature and the seasons, the compassionate observer of human folly and the inscrutable ironies and inevitable justices of life. Like Hardy, too, Miss Sandburg tells stories as stark and traditional as any ballad. In her work, as in old ballads and folk songs, her people and the circumstances of their everyday lives exist in a world illuminated by the glow and mystery of poetry, but without loss of that sense of reality which the novelist must convey if his writing is to re-create in art the familiar in life. Her people we know more by their passions than by the social facts of their surroundings

and actions. It is this recognition of the poetic in everyday experience that sets Miss Sandburg apart from the novelists of her generation.

Measure My Love is ballad-like in its shaping theme of love, passion, and betrayal. Faith Summers was twenty-seven when she married Buddy Bain, five years her junior. Of the four daughters in Job Summers' household, she had always been the self-reliant one and his favorite, taking the place of the son he had never had until Dolly, his wife, bore a sickly boy, Thankful. No one in the family ever expected Faith, spinsterish in looks and speech, to marry, but when Choice and Buddy Bain, sons of a prosperous widow, came courting, Faith bloomed briefly. She might have had older, steadier Choice, who was awkwardly in love with her, but she preferred handsome, full-blooded, irresponsible Buddy.

Settled on the rented Toombes farm, the young couple work hard to reclaim the neglected land. During the first summer of their marriage the passion they share is as intense and warming as the sun that renews and exhausts them at their labors in the fields. Misunderstandings arise, as when Buddy uses to buy a quail and cuckoo clock the money Faith has saved to purchase some geese, but these are soon forgotten. Then, about the time their son Peter is born, Buddy reverts to his old ways. It is Irene, the foolish youngest Summers daughter, who blurts out the news that Buddy is pursuing frivolous, pretty Lacy Summers. Faith is again pregnant when her husband shamefacedly breaks the news that Lacy claims she is carrying his child. The news is not true, and for a time there is greater understanding, if not trust, between Faith and Buddy. But it is not in Faith's nature to compromise; their relationship must be lived on her terms, she feels, or not at all. The irony of the situation lies in the fact that she drives Buddy to the act of violence which brings a great tree crashing down on him, causing his death.

But *Measure My Love* is more than the account of a marriage that failed because a wife was too strong, her husband too weak. Many people are involved in this story set against a background of rural Michigan. The true relationship of the two women of the Toombes household, Mrs. Toombes and her sister Wyoma, and of Buddy's dead father comes slowly to light. Floss, Faith's sister and the mother of a slovenly brood, is unhappily married to Clyde Barefoot. Irene is raped by one hired man on the Summers farm, married to another. It is revealed that Lacy is not Job's daughter; her father was a traveling peddler whom Dolly had used to revenge herself on her husband. Choice, who has loved Faith, turns to Lacy and Faith loses him forever. In the end, however, she has her two small sons and the Toombes farm as her own; the turmoil of her short married life has been replaced by her love for Buddy's sons and her passion for the land. Her life submerged in the timeless cycle of nature, Faith sees her world with new understanding:

There had been a new force about Buddy at the last. Suppose he had been trying to change himself as he had stated. Supposing he had prized her after all, and had resolved to stop hiding his acts from her. . . . But the straight of it was that Buddy had ever humored his wants. And she demanded too much, insisted he conform to her mold, the traditional husband. So he had strained and chafed. Their natures built the flaw.

Here another of life's little ironies is disclosed, the point of revelation toward which the whole course of the novel has been tending. Helga Sandburg is convinced of the necessities of her people and of their actions, whether they love wisely or foolishly or not at all, as a part of the shifts and changes and casual cruelties in human relationships.

One of the great virtues of this novel is its strong sense of place. "Location," as Eudora Welty has observed, "is the crossroads of circumstance." This achieved world of appearance is more than a setting. It is the background of community experience and belief, the measure of man's ties with his environment. Helga Sandburg's landscapes are real, not because she describes them in concrete detail and with appropriate imagery but because her men and women inhabit them and both possess and are possessed by them. Her people share in the ancient, instinctive kinship of man and nature. Here is a picture of Faith as she faces the emptiness of her widowhood:

Still holding David to her, she went out on the stoop. Stars were locked upon the expanse past the tree branches. The child put his warm plump arm about her, murmuring, nuzzling his face against her neck. She walked by the geese that hissed up to her in greeting, then settled back where they nestled. She went down to the fence that circled the pasture. It was hers now! Job would give her all the young trees she needed for a fruit farm. It would go to her sons some day if they wanted it. The moist heated smell of the spring night was coming on. House voices sifted unreal; Granny's rebuke and a young inquiring voice. The moon was budding red and glowing. In time it flowered whitely among the stars, the strengthless reflective light streaming over the slow plodding beasts that grazed on the hillside, silent. The south hill's crest had changed in outline, the line of trees now cropped. She was turning back with the sleeping David, toward the small light of the house.

Here is more than a capture of emo-

tion or mood. The passage conveys also a sense of the abiding earth, more mysterious in its turnings and rhythms than the tensions of love and hate or the moral concerns of man. In this novel these aspects of the particular and the universal are held in delicate balance by the sustaining forces of the novelist's observation, sensibility, and intelligent reading of the lessons of human personality and conduct.

THE MEASURE OF MAN

Author: Joseph Wood Krutch (1893–1970)
Publisher: The Bobbs-Merrill Company (Indianapolis). 261 pp. $3.50
Type of work: Social philosophy
   A sociological and historical study that attempts to take the measurements of twentienth century man and his institutions in a work that may be read as a sequel to this writer's The Modern Temper

Joseph Wood Krutch's learned, levelheaded arguments against the tendency in modern culture to accept a widely prevalent deterministic orthodoxy constitute, in effect, an invitation to modern man to take one more long, hard look at himself before submitting to a programmed, conditioned, mechanistic existence in which looking at oneself would no longer be an activity.

Man, in Krutch's view, has not been measuring himself very successfully. Though certain intellectual giants like Freud and B. F. Skinner have offered various views of man, their views have been as confusing as useful. Most men do not know what, if any, values they have or should have. Increasingly, modern man is quietly acquiescing to the inevitability of living in worlds like those described in Aldous Huxley's *Brave New World* and Skinner's *Walden II.* Krutch's arguments against such over-controlled worlds make *The Measure of Man* a profoundly unavoidable book (just as Krutch's previous book, *The Modern Temper,* was discussed for over a quarter of a century).

Krutch argues convincingly, by combining great common sense with an almost immeasurable depth of reading, that if we, as human beings, are anything more than "products" in a huge, imperfectly perceived but entirely predetermined universe, we probably don't have much time left in which to prove it. The "highest" (most recent) insects are the group to which the ant belongs. Ants are "successfully" achieving a flourishing and prolonged survival because "they have solved their social problem so perfectly that they do not even need to practice the techniques of 'conditioning.' They are born properly conditioned, and they would no doubt argue, if they were capable of arguing, that a reflex which has become fixed by heredity is 'higher' than one which must be impressed upon each new individual."

The point is that if men are attracted to a society such as that established through conditioning in Skinner's *Walden II,* they should look forward, at best, to a life of tedium such as that of the ants, with the corresponding loss of individual value, freedom, and choice. Of course, it is possible, as Krutch concedes, that there really is no freedom, no choice, and that man, by believing in his own autonomy, has simply been holding up his own evolution. If, therefore, man's delusion of being more than a machine is finally eliminated (as it may well be), the character of his conditioning will change and accelerate him toward a life more closely resembling that of the ant. As Krutch summarizes it: ". . . gradually he [man] will be conditioned to accept the fact that he is nothing in himself, and even the epiphenomena associated with consciousness and the delusions regarding choice and value will disappear."

Krutch believes that much of man's humane discourse is weak, and has been overly concerned with trying to account for all the phenomena which exist in both the universe and in the consciousness. Krutch is amazed by man's apparent inability to admit that there is a great deal he cannot know or hope to know; it is time to start placing limitations on the human understanding, and also time to cease trying to "reduce ultimate reality to a comprehensible unity from which everything paradoxical has been removed." More often than not, working principles are hardened into dogmas, even though those dogmas may eventually prove to be inadequate.

Thomas Henry Huxley once explained that "if some great power would agree to make me always think what is true and do what is right, on condition of being turned into a sort of clock and wound up every morning before I got out of bed, I should instantly close with the offer." This attitude, Krutch explains, is at the heart of Skinner's *Walden II* society—a society which Krutch, at great length, analyzes and attacks, even while recognizing that man's scientific ability to create with precision such a controlled society has been growing rapidly and will continue to do so.

Krutch also criticizes man's tendency to equate "success" with prolonged existence. The cockroach has flourished and has not changed appreciably from his fossilized ancestors who flourished 250 million years ago; however, is the cockroach therefore automatically more "successful" than man? "Are there no reasons," Krutch asks, "why it is 'better' to be a man than an insect?" Most so-called Utopians must not really think so.

Clearly, as Krutch's title suggests, man cannot be measured by the same yardsticks as the cockroach. If you study man, furthermore, by a method suited to chemistry, or even with reference to what you have learned about rats and dogs, you will, in effect, be discovering what chemistry and what animal behavior have to teach; but by such methods you will not discover anything else.

Krutch argues that man cannot really be "measured" at all. There is no reason, however, therefore to treat him in ways similar to those by which one treats other phenomena. There is no reason, either, to embrace the notion that man is basically a machine capable of conditioned behavior. And even, Krutch argues, those who reject mechanistic and deterministic theories and instead opt for some kind of formal religious creed are not really improving the situation. What, then, is the alternative? Those who reject determinism are losing ground all the time, partly because of the nature of the discourse man has long been involved in. Those who would seize the machinery of conditioning and try to make things come out differently would be betraying their own cause, for "one can hardly use the methods of the enemy without accepting more of his premises than we can afford to accept."

The only answer is to try to assume that everything is not fixed and inevitable since the dawn of creation, and that if this is so, then it must be either because of a random element in the universe or because "an effective freedom to choose exists somewhere." And, taking the latter line, where it exists, for Krutch, is in man himself. What man must choose is some point safely outside the physically and mentally determined world on which to rest his lever; "that fulcrum cannot be anything except 'values' deliberately chosen." By operating *that* lever, who knows what force the free man may yet exert? This, to Krutch, seems vastly preferable to gambling that a mechanically evolving universe will move man to an existence which he, by his present standards, could never consider desirable.

Christopher R. Reaske

THE MEDIEVAL FOUNDATION OF ENGLAND
A Social History of England from the Beginnings to the Fifteenth Century

Author: Sir Arthur Bryant (1899–   )
Publisher: Doubleday and Company (Garden City, New York), 270 pp. $4.95
Type of work: History
Time: The Bronze Age to the fifteenth century
Locale: England

A brief but engaging history of England and English institutions from the period of the earliest settlers to the time of Wyclif

This is a curious book. Its author, Sir Arthur Bryant, who has published widely on English history, set himself a very difficult task, one that was nearly impossible to fulfill: to write a brief history on so large a subject as the medieval foundation of England, and to write it in such a way as to justify saying little that is new in a book of this size. The reader will have to judge Sir Arthur's success for himself.

The task facing the author was indeed enormous. Many good histories of England during the Middle Ages have already been written: by Bennett, by Coulton, by Trevelyan, even one by G. O. Sayles with a similar title, *The Medieval Foundations of England.* Sir Arthur's volume adds almost nothing to what those men have said; by its very size the writer found it necessary to ignore and simplify most of what they were able to include.

To say this is not to give the impression that this book is a popularization or that it is childish; not at all. Sir Arthur knows his English history well and writes about it competently, but one wishes that there were more. The early chapters especially suffer from brevity: the prologue on "Freedom's Island," "Rude Settlers," and "The Cross and the Sword." The Anglo-Saxon invasions and settlements simply cannot be described in twenty-two pages. And the attempt leads the author, it is felt, to vagueness, occasionally to a flabbiness of style, and consequently to dullness.

These first chapters are almost without anecdote and incident. They have little life and little sense of either time or place. As the language becomes abstract it becomes nebulous and, unless one loves England as does Sir Arthur, it is a bit sentimental. The Celts are "fierce red-haired;" the Anglo-Saxons "simple forest folk"; the industry of the former combined with the "honesty" of the latter to form the motherland. "It is this perhaps that has accounted for the intermixture in the British blood of the matter-of-fact with the poetic; of love of home with the itch to adventure; of business aptitude with fantasy, speculation with idealism."

Above all, this is a book about "our" England. The American will be somewhat alien between its covers. The first chapters, as has already been intimated, are full of pride of nation. Sir Arthur's love of his country comes across clearly on every page. But the American reader may not know how to react to lists of English place names, may not even know where they are, and may not even have heard of them: "Puttock's End, Cow Common, Crab's Green, Woolard's Ash, Doodle Oak," and the like may be as meaningless to us as a Whitman catalogue of American rivers may be to a European.

In the interests of economy the author has limited the number of footnotes; one does not get caught up in the annoying habit of reading two books at once. And the eye is not continually glancing at the bottom of the page. But often enough one would like to see an authority cited or a passage identified. Many quotations of poetry and of historian's prose are given without reference. There is no doubt about the author's honesty or competence, but the footnote can be a valuable guide to further study on a particular subject. And so, on balance, one misses them.

The heart of the book, its strongest chapters, concern the emerging English legal system—appropriately so, as the dedication is to the former Lord Chief Justice of England. But here, in Chapters Five and Six, one finds the first real meat. The remarkable system of law to which all—including the king—were subject gets fuller treatment. We see the great "theoretical" documents of medieval England as practical compromises of the moment. The Magna Carta, for instance, was called "great" because of its length and not because of its lofty principles. It made King John responsible at least in part to his barons for the conduct of the state. The Charter consisted of more than sixty clauses, all of them addressed to specific problems. Most of these dealt with the relationship of the king to his subjects. But perhaps most importantly, it provided the means for resolving conflicts within the bounds of the existing state. A breach of the social contract would not mean a dissolution of the nation. And thus the principle which was not spoken was that the state was an entity of itself which would survive human personality and internal conflict. The Charter led, of course, to the first Parliament.

The legal and governmental system which evolved in England is of great importance to all the countries of the West—and now even to many African and Asian countries which were formerly British colonies—and is really the foundation of this book. The early pages, roughly sketched in, point toward the "legal" chapters. There is little social history; little political in the international aspect, little about medieval commerce, and too little, one feels, about the Church. But the discussions of English law prepare the way for those of "village" and "travelers," and, after a curious section on "Gothic Glory," we see the Church in its decline.

But from the settling of petty squabbles in the village, the protection of pilgrims on the road, even the failure of the Church to unite the English, we see the law emerging as the hero of this history and, perhaps, as the saviour of the English people. That is the bent of this book and the most impressive point it has to make.

Bruce A. Rosenberg

THE MEDITERRANEAN
and the Mediterranean World in the Age of Philip II

Author: Fernand Braudel (1902-   )
Translated from the French by Siân Reynolds
Publisher: Harper & Row Publishers (New York). Illustrated. 2 vols. 1,375 pp.
$35.00
Type of work: History
Time: Second half of the sixteenth century
Locale: Mediterranean Sea and the countries surrounding it

An encyclopedic panorama of the Mediterranean world, its people, its problems, and its civilizations

Principal personages:
PHILIP II OF HABSBURG, King of Spain, 1556-1598
DON JOHN OF AUSTRIA, illegitimate half-brother of Philip II and commander of the fleet of the Holy League in the Battle of Lepanto

Fernand Braudel, the distinguished French historian, brought out the first edition of *The Mediterranean and the Mediterranean World in the Age of Philip II* in 1949. The second revised edition of his massive, erudite study appeared in 1966 and formed the basis, with further revisions, of the excellent English translation which was published in 1972-1973. The revisions in both subsequent editions were mainly designed to take into account fresh knowledge and new approaches to historical problems and thereby strengthen the objective of this enormous monograph, namely that of presenting a complete, dynamic description of the entire Mediterranean world in the age of Philip II of Spain. Braudel, however, as the title of his book might otherwise suggest, does not confine himself solely to the period of Philip II; on the contrary, to attain his objective of understanding the Mediterranean world in depth, he investigates the historical antecedents of his subject back to ancient times. In pursuing his

objective, Braudel divides his study into three parts, each virtually a book unto itself. First, he undertakes an investigation of the impact of the environment and geography of the Mediterranean world on the human condition in the sixteenth century; then he examines social structures of the time, including the nature of societies, civilizations, economic systems, empires, and forms of war. Finally, he provides a traditional political history of Mediterranean Europe during the epoch of Philip II. Braudel states that the book's three parts constitute a dissection of history into various planes—the division of historical time into geographical time, social time, and individual time.

In analyzing the geographical and social foundations of Mediterranean man, Braudel is attempting, in his own words, "to encompass the history of the Mediterranean in its complex totality." He accomplishes this enormous task of writing total history through exhaustive research in numerous archives and by drawing upon the writings of specialists in disciplines related to history, including, among others, anthropology, geography, botany, and geology. The resulting synthesis in Parts I and II is by far the most valuable contribution of the book, as it provides the reader with a veritable mine of information on a wide range of diverse, yet related, topics. By the very vastness of its scope, Braudel's synthesis fulfills his conception of history as one involving all facets of man's environment and development, not just the political and diplomatic events of his past.

Braudel seeks in Part I, "The Role of the Environment," to define the interrelationship between the physical and human geography during that "brief moment of Mediterranean life, between 1550 and 1600." In discussing the mountains, plateaus, and plains that make up the peninsulas of the Mediterranean world, or in describing its islands, coastal areas, and climate, Braudel makes geography come alive by showing how, over the centuries, these various elements of the environment have influenced the tone and level of civilization. He uses the comparative method, drawing analogies between the same types of geographic entities in various parts of the Mediterranean basin, and demonstrating how similar developments are discernible in each. The result is the emergence of a historical pattern.

For example, in his discourse on the nature of the mountains which encircle the area, the author observes that civilization in the mountainous regions is never very stable. This instability is particularly evident in the shallow attitudes which the mountaineers have held in the past toward

the established religion of the neighboring plain. He demonstrates that because the relatively isolated Christian mountaineers in such diverse places as the Caucasus, the Balkans, and Crete were only slightly influenced by Christianity, they converted *en masse* to the advancing tide, in various centuries, of Islam. Because of their location and their method of conversion, these mountain people were no more confirmed in their new faith than they had been in their old one. Hence, according to Braudel, a separate religious geography seems to emerge for the mountain world, which constantly had to be conquered and reconquered. Numerous minor facts, he observes, which are encountered in traditional history take on new meaning in this light. Seminal ideas such as this (subject, to be sure, to argument and controversy among historians) characterize the entire book.

Braudel concludes his analysis of the Mediterranean environment with a chapter on cities and the communications between them. Here he devotes his attention exclusively to human geography and demonstrates that it was only through human ingenuity, and the land and sea routes thereby developed, that the unity of the Mediterranean was created. This unity was not a political one, but more significantly, a permanent unified human construction slowly imposed on geographical space by cities and their various forms of communications. The main intention of the author throughout Part I is to explore, using the concept of geographical space, the nature of the permanent, slow-moving or recurrent features of Mediterranean life.

In Part II, "Collective Destinies and General Trends," Braudel deals with social history and is obliged, he observes, to meet two contradictory purposes. First, he has to be concerned with social structures, including economic systems, states, societies, civilizations, and forms of war; that is, those mechanisms which more or less withstand the march of time. Secondly, but simultaneously, he must address himself to the development of these structures. In order to discover the collective destiny of the sixteenth century Mediterranean, therefore, Braudel must combine what he refers to as structure and conjuncture, the permanent and ephemeral sides of an institution—in his words, "the slow-moving and the fast." True to his twofold purpose, Braudel analyzes, for example, the origin and nature of the Spanish and Turkish empires and the process of their respective declines by 1600. He also discusses the character of the traditional classes of society, the nobility, the bourgeoisie, and the poor, and observes that between 1550 and 1600 a gradual polarization of rich and poor took place which resulted in crisis in the next century.

In analyzing the economic systems, Braudel acknowledges the great impact which the New World had on Europe. He devotes considerable space to the question of the impact which gold and silver from the Spanish Indies had on the inflationary crises of the period. Citing leading authorities on both sides of the argument, he explains that prices had begun to rise in Europe before Columbus sailed to America, in part because of the devaluations of money in various countries.

The concluding section of the book, "Events, Politics and People," is traditional history, in which the author evaluates major political currents and events and describes the deeds and exploits of individual men. Despite his conviction that he must include in his book a traditional history of his subject, the author confesses that he is by temperament a "structuralist" little tempted by historical events, and is convinced that what freedom the individual in history possesses is limited by a destiny which he has had little hand in shaping.

The central individual in Braudel's survey of the later sixteenth century is Philip II, King of Spain from 1556 to 1598. Major attention is focused on the problems of the Spanish and Turkish empires and on the great clash between the two in the Battle of Lepanto in 1571. Braudel offers a vivid description of the role in this naval engagement of the commander of the fleet of the Holy League (Spain Venice, and the Papacy), Don John of Austria, the illegitimate half-brother of Philip II. Most historians have dismissed the significance of the Christian victory at Lepanto because the allied fleet did not pursue the Turks, who managed by the following year to rebuild completely their shattered navy. Braudel, however, regards the victory as the end of a period of genuine inferiority complex on the part of Christendom and as a halt to further Turkish advances. At the close of Part III, the author reflects on the death of Philip II, a man of narrow vision, Braudel avers, who probably never had a clear concept of the Mediterranean and its significance; geography had not been part of his education. These are all sufficient reasons, according to the author, why Philip's death was not a crucial event in the history of the region. True to his concept of history, Braudel asserts that the life and death of Philip II offer good reasons for reflecting upon the distance separating biographical history from the history of structure, and especially from the history of geographical areas.

Fernand Braudel's brilliant study of the Mediterranean world is towering in its scope and sweep. It provides an excellent example of the effort of one historian to write what he calls "total history," a construct based on the interdisciplinary and comparative methods. The end product is a monumental synthesis in which the author, by harmonizing the three levels of human geography, social groups, and individual exploits, conveys to his readers a philosophy of history which emphasizes the importance of structure. Although at times Braudel's explanations of the mechanics of his philosophy of history are less than lucid, his study offers a rich harvest of ideas for all readers, whether specialist or nonspecialist. Numerous charts and illustrations, and a massive critical bibliography of more than sixty pages, are admirable additions to this authoritative and distinguished work.

Edward P. Keleher

MEET ME IN THE GREEN GLEN

Author: Robert Penn Warren (1905-   )
Publisher: Random House (New York). 376 pp. $7.95
Type of work: Novel
Time: Mid-twentieth century
Locale: Rural Tennessee

> Principal characters:
>
> CASSIE SPOTTWOOD, an aging and frustrated recluse
> SUNDER SPOTTWOOD, her invalid husband
> ANGELO PASSETTO, her Sicilian lover
> CY GRINDER, the sweetheart of Cassie's youth
> MURRAY GUILFORT, friend and benefactor of the Spottwoods

Meet Me in the Green Glen, Robert Penn Warren's ninth novel, is yet another account of what the author calls "the truth of the human condition." Like each of its predecessors, this new novel is laced with poetic elements that add considerable depth and complexity to its portrayal of man's situation. As one familiar with Warren's other fiction might expect, the subject here is sin and salvation—the prevalence of corruption and the possibility of hope. Here, as before, "sin" is depicted as separation from the human community; its hallmark is lust and its product is guilt. "Salvation," on the other hand, is shown to be union with the community (or, at least, with one of its representatives) through love. In his subtle working out of the tensions between the two, Warren proves once again that he, like his fellow Southerner William Faulkner, is a storyteller of compelling power.

Set in rural Tennessee at mid-century, *Meet Me in the Green Glen* is the deceptively simple tale of Cassie Spottwood, a rapidly aging and sexually frustrated woman whose craving for love eventually leads to the violent deaths of three of the four men in her sad life. The immediate source of her frustration is her twelve-year entomb-ment in a remote, ramshackle house with her invalid husband Sunder, a one-time sexual animal now turned vegetable by a stroke. Sunder's incomprehensible moans and murmurings constantly toll Cassie's living death knell. All this is changed, however, by the mysterious coming of Angelo Passetto, an exotic young Sicilian in flight from the Mafia. Seeming to Cassie a kind of angel of mercy sent at the eleventh hour to restore her to life and to love, he is a potential source of her rebirth, an apparently impossible realization of a long forgotten dream.

Yet it is not to be. The hot-blooded Angelo, his passion unfulfilled by the willing but faded recluse, runs off with a beautiful black girl-woman named Charlene, and his defection sets in motion a spiral of violence that sucks in each of the novel's major characters. The angel of mercy becomes, indirectly, an angel of death. The bedridden Sunder is murdered, and Angelo is summarily arrested, tried, and convicted of the crime. Despite Cassie's last-minute confession that it was actually she who had killed her husband, all appeals fail. The Sicilian lover, despised as a foreigner by the small-town Southern community, is sent off to be executed. In a moment of high melodrama that is typical of Warren's fiction, Cassie follows him and at the instant of his death lies "huddled against the stonework of the (prison) wall . . . at the base of one of the towers."

Thus in death, as in life, the tie that binds Cassie and Angelo is primarily sexual; in an obviously symbolic scene, she hugs the phallic tower while the electricity surges through him. Yet in the end there is a major difference that is saving for some characters, damning for others. Unexpectedly, Angelo emerges as one of the redeemed. In contrast with his early liaison with Cassie which is, for his part, largely a matter of lust, he goes to his grave a genuine lover, his lust having been converted to love by the overpowering impact of Cassie's selfless courtroom confession. In the long run, then, it is Cassie, and not Angelo, who is the angel of mercy.

Murray Guilfort, friend and benefactor of the hapless Spottwoods, is not as fortunate as the "dago" he hates. A voyeur with pathetic delusions of grandeur—salvation to him is a seat on the state supreme court—Murray is beyond redemption. He is a familiar Warren "type," a man whose inability to face up to "the truth of the human condition" condemns him to a meaningless existence in isolation from the community around him. Motivated entirely by self-interest (his kindness to Cassie and Sunder is a sham), Guilfort is a user and abuser of others, a man who thinks and acts solely in terms of status, money, and lust. Though his grasping manipulations do eventually get him to the supreme court, he finds his life as empty there as elsewhere. With no higher place to go, he finally wakes up to discover himself utterly alone in the void he has created. That

discovery, which is brought into focus by the love of Cassie and Angelo, is fittingly sealed with sleeping pills.

Of the major characters in *Meet Me in the Green Glen,* only Murray is a thoroughly condemned sinner. Despite the murder of one man, the execution of another, and the suicide of a third, the novel is ultimately a testament to life, and to the author's faith in the sustaining power of love. Knowing full well that the triumph of compassion is neither easy nor guaranteed, Warren has filled this book (like most of his others) with violence and corruption in order to underscore the value of love's difficult victory, a victory which is never totally won. So difficult, in fact, is that victory that even Cassie, the ministering angel, fails to emerge from the struggle unscarred. She is, in the end, judged insane and institutionalized by a community unable to comprehend the nature of her love for Angelo. Consequently, the final triumph is secured not by Cassie, but by the fourth man in her life—Cy Grinder.

As a youth Grinder had hoped to marry Cassie, but because of the poverty and minimal social status of his family ("pore white trash," according to Cassie's stuffy mother) those hopes were effectively dashed. Purely out of spite, he had instead married the homely Gladys Peegrum. During the long, stoically endured years of marriage, the thought of actually loving Gladys had clearly never entered Cy's head. As *Meet Me in the Green Glen* closes, however, the example of Cassie's abiding love for Angelo has started a painful awakening in him. For the first time, "he began to wonder what she thought, what she felt; and his wondering was mysterious to him. He wondered what she had ever thought, what she had ever felt. He realized, slowly, that never, in all the years, had he wondered that before." With this realization, Cy Grinder is on his way to the sort of genuine communion with another human being that is denied each of the other major characters in the novel. To be sure, this is a muted triumph for love, but triumph it is. Cy still has far to go in order to re-kindle and redirect his long-dormant powers of compassion and affection, but Warren leaves little doubt that victory is in sight. The book ends on an affirmatively symbolic note: "When the time came, he (Cy) stepped out of the shadow of the tree. He looked up. There was the moon, with the sky, and the whole world, in its light."

The language of this quietly power-ful closing passage is typical of *Meet Me in the Green Glen*, and, indeed, of all of Warren's fiction. Like many other Southern writers with whom he is often compared, Warren is a master of rhetorical splendor and linguistic bra-vado. At times his rhetorical talent gets carried away, allowing such phrases as "deliquescent torpor" to grate upon the reader with irritating frequency. But these lapses are forgivable because they are outnumbered by breathtaking ex-amples of the author's ability to evoke a mood by the sheer power of lan-guage: "Far off, up yonder, the mist and the drizzle of rain made the road and the woods, and the sky too, what you could see of it above the heave of the bluff, all one splotchy, sliding-down grayness, as though everything, the sky and the world, was being washed away with old dishwater."

This striking passage both sets the tone for the early pages of *Meet Me in the Green Glen* and serves as an effec-tive balance for the symbolic bright moonlight that brings the book to a close. As a romantic and philosophical writer, Warren is not afraid either to convert the prosaic into the poetic—he is, after all, a superb poet, too—or to construct orderly plots that seem somewhat out-of-date to many critics. Indeed, in an old-fashioned way, *Meet Me in the Green Glen* does wear its heart on its sleeve. Its traditional structure lends it a certain inevitability of character and plot that appears to be out of step with our unpredictable time. Rather like a classic tragedy, it contains few real surprises. The remote-ness of its setting, the disembodied na-ture of some of its people, and the lush-ness of its language combine to give the novel a romantic, dream-like qual-ity. Even the title suggests a Never-Never Land away off yonder some-where.

Of course, all this is intentional. Like most Southern novelists, Warren is a romantic yarn-spinner, a story-teller whose tales revolve around ele-mental, heroic, and timeless themes—life and death, cowardice and bravery, honor and dishonor, charity and re-venge, and so on. *Meet Me in the Green Glen* is no exception. It is a story of love, sex, violent death, and insanity. It also has a moral—the sav-ing power of love—that serves to re-solve most of the tension and mop up most of the bloody rancor at the end. Few questions are left unanswered. As a novel with a definite message, *Meet Me in the Green Glen* may not appeal to readers who are more interested in fashion than in substance. Still, the novel is a good one. Its message, though hardly revolutionary, is important. It deserves to be heard.

Robert H. Chambers

MEETING AT POTSDAM

Author: Charles L. Mee, Jr. (1938-   )
Publisher: M. Evans & Company (New York). Illustrated. 370 pp. $10.95
Type of work: History
Time: July and August, 1945
Locale: Potsdam, Germany

A study of the Potsdam Conference and of the personalities and national aims of the Big Three leaders

> Principal personages:
> HARRY TRUMAN, thirty-third President of the United States, 1945-1952
> JOSEPH STALIN, Soviet Dictator, 1924-1953
> SIR WINSTON CHURCHILL, Prime Minister of Great Britain, 1940-1945; 1951-1955

In his book *Meeting at Potsdam,* Charles L. Mee, Jr., for many years the editor of *Horizon* Magazine, presents a readable—if highly debatable—account of the last major conference of the Big Three Allies held during World War II. Mee's thesis is that the Big Three leaders, Harry Truman, Joseph Stalin, and Winston Churchill, each used the Potsdam Conference to increase the power of their countries and of themselves. Perceiving that they could enhance their quest for power more certainly in a world of discord than in one of peace, Mee contends that they deliberately set out to quarrel. The result of their quarrel was, by the end of the conference, not the dawning of peace but rather the outbreak of the Cold War. In part, Mee arrives at these conclusions by relying heavily and selectively on anecdotal material contained, as he observes in his Prologue, "in the notes of the informal chats, in the recollections of dinner parties, in the jokes and the laughter" of the Big Three leaders. This approach, combined with the absence of any substantial reflections on the

Yalta Conference held in February, 1945, leaves the reader with a book on the Potsdam Conference which is a pleasure to read but which fails to establish a proper historical context in which to understand the attitudes of the Big Three leaders prior to their last wartime meeting.

The first three chapters of *Meeting at Potsdam* are devoted respectively to Truman, Churchill, and Stalin and their careers and aspirations, with brief portrayals of the advisers and statesmen who surrounded them. Writing in a breezy style, Mee sorts through a wide collection of anecdotes in an effort to find some sinister purpose in the minds of the two Western leaders. Truman thus comes off as a poker-playing politician, a product of the Pendergast machine, who confidently arrived in Potsdam intent on building the "American Century" based on the recent American victory in Europe and the possession of the atomic bomb. Citing the date of July 12, the author dramatically observes that while the bomb's plutonium core was being transported to the testing grounds of

Alamogordo, New Mexico, high spirits prevailed among Truman and his party as they sailed for Europe; this mood contrasted sharply with the gloom in Tokyo where, on the same day, Emperor Hirohito expressed his anxious desire to end the war as soon as possible.

In contrast to his description of Truman as a vigorous and confident leader of a powerful nation, Mee depicts Churchill as being just as exhausted as the country he represented. Both he and Great Britain had passed their zenith, Mee remarks, though neither yet realized it. In a subsequent passage, however, the author contradicts this point by attributing to Churchill a strategy at Potsdam that was necessarily based on a clear realization of his country's exhausted condition. Churchill's strategy, according to Mee, consisted of exaggerating the Russian threat and exacerbating the difference between Russia and America so that he could grab the leadership over a Western European bloc. The author attempts to strengthen his criticism of Churchill and his grand design by offering a few random quotations from Machiavelli, comparing the Prime Minister with the Prince, and by expressing shock over Churchill's willingness to use captured German troops to help block any further advance of the Red Army. He ignores the fact that the Western Allies made similar use of German troops against the Bolsheviks for some months after World War I. The historical evidence simply does not support Mee's view that Churchill deliberately sought to disrupt relations between the United States and the Soviet Union.

Mee has little image-breaking to do where Stalin is concerned; relying heavily on Adam Ulam's recent massive biography on the Soviet dictator, he flatly regards him as "one of the supremely evil men of history." The author, therefore, devotes more attention to what he regards as Stalin's solid grasp of military and political realities and to his skill as a negotiator. When analyzing Stalin's conduct of Soviet foreign policy, however, both at this point and throughout the book, Mee strangely failed to consult Ulam's equally important study, *Expansion and Coexistence*. Nevertheless, he presents a much better portrait of Stalin than of Truman and Churchill. The Soviet dictator is shown testing the Americans before and during the Potsdam Conference to see whether on such questions as Russia's demand for a friendly Polish government, they were naïve, determined ideological crusaders for freedom, or possessed of some ulterior motives. In order to understand America's true position on the fate of Eastern Europe, Stalin saw fit to raise the desirability of encouraging the Spanish people to overthrow Franco's fascist dictatorship. Furthermore, as Mee points out, Stalin deliberately made demands for any number of things which were of no real interest to him. By dropping these sham demands, he hoped to gain concessions from his Western counterparts on those subjects which involved Russia's security in Eastern Europe and in East Asia.

With these estimations of the Big Three leaders in hand, the author devotes most of the remaining chapters of his book to day-by-day summaries of the Potsdam Conference, which ran from July 17 to August 2, 1945. He also discusses one of the more interesting subjects relating to the Potsdam Conference and the days immediately following its conclusion: President Truman's decision to drop the atomic bomb on Japan. On July 21, Truman received a full report from Washington that the atomic bomb test at Alamogordo had been a complete success. Mee observes that an earlier plan among the President and his advisers about using the bomb to intimidate the Russians in Europe could now be tested, since Truman possessed the atomic power to back up his word. Hence, during the next several days of the Potsdam Conference, Truman attempted to negotiate forcefully with Stalin on such issues as Poland's frontiers and German reparations. Stalin, who as yet knew nothing about the bomb, did not allow himself to be pinned down by Truman on any of these questions. When at the close of the conference session of July 24, Truman finally informed Stalin of America's possession of the atomic bomb, the Soviet leader showed no special interest. Hence, according to Mee, Truman was unable to intimidate Stalin, whether he knew of the bomb's existence or not, short of actually dropping it on the Russians.

Mee's assessment of the failure of the atomic bomb to intimidate the Russians is correct up to this point, but he then proceeds to the theory that President Truman, still persisting in his efforts to intimidate the Russians while obviously not willing to drop the bomb on them, decided instead to drop it on Japan. Mee contends that the dropping of the bomb was not a military necessity, as Japan would have surrendered any-

way. Stalin, in Mee's view, held to this position in August, 1945, and hence was most impressed when the United States used its new weapon to obliterate Hiroshima and Nagasaki. Although ultimately the dropping of the bomb on Japan may not have been necessary, Truman's primary motive in using it was to end the war as soon as possible—not, as Mee states, to impress or intimidate Stalin. In fact, Stalin, during the initial Cold War period, 1945-1947, as surveyed by Mee in the epilogue to his book, did not allow America's fleeting monopoly of atomic weapons to intimidate him, as he proceeded to violate the Potsdam accord and tighten his grip on Eastern Europe. *Meeting at Potsdam* is an absorbing excursion into popular history which provides the reader with a view of the Potsdam Conference that is better described as solid entertainment, in the best sense of that word, than as solid historical analysis and interpretation. Many of Mee's assertions on such matters as the postwar policies of the Big Three leaders and America's aims in dropping the atomic bomb on Japan can be subjected to considerable criticism, as can his statement that the Big Three deliberately used the Potsdam Conference to launch the Cold War. He fails to realize that the Big Three needed one another less in July, 1945, than at the time of the Yalta Conference, when they were still fighting against Germany. As so often happens in history, the worst thing that can happen to a wartime alliance is the final defeat of its common foe. The collapse of Hitler's Reich produced immediate misunderstandings between Russia and the Western powers as to how the Big Three were to manage postwar Europe. These misunderstandings are the proper point of departure for an examination of what happened in the Potsdam Conference.

Despite these serious shortcomings, the student of history who wants to savor the atmosphere of a major wartime conference can profit from this book. Its value is further enhanced by two sections of photographs and two appendices that provide the texts of the Potsdam Proclamation, in which the United States, Great Britain, and the Republic of China called upon Japan to surrender unconditionally; and the Potsdam Declaration, in which the decisions reached by the Big Three powers at the conference were set forth. Finally, the book contains a useful bibliography, although one wishes that the author had also consulted both Adam Ulam's aforementioned study, *Expansion and Coexistence,* and Diane Clemen's *Yalta,* for the sake of providing a more judicious treatment of the background of the Potsdam Conference.

Edward P. Keleher

MELBOURNE

Author: Lord David Cecil (1902-   )
Publisher: Bobbs-Merrill Company (Indianapolis and New York). 450 pp. $5.00
Type of work: Biography
Time: 1778-1847
Locale: England

The definitive biography of William Lamb, Lord Melbourne, adviser to Queen Victoria

Principal personages:
WILLIAM LAMB, Lord Melbourne
SIR PENISTON LAMB, his father
ELIZABETH MILBANKE, his mother
LORD EGREMONT, Lady Melbourne's lover
CAROLINE PONSONBY, William's wife
GEORGE IV, Prince Regent and King

In 1939, Lord David Cecil published *The Young Melbourne*, a work covering Melbourne's life up to his years in office as Prime Minister of England. He had intended to cover the whole life in one volume, but circumstances prevented this. He thought it better to print what was ready and hope he would some day be able to complete the biography. The original volume was praised as one of the most fascinating accounts of a historical figure in recent years because the subject was treated as a person and not a figurehead. The book was as warm and glowing as the people in it.

By 1954 the author had prepared the remainder of the biography, that which is Part III of the present volume and called "The Years of Influence," showing Melbourne as a man of importance in his country and to his Queen. Since that part seemed to be without foundation without constant reference to the earlier book, the writer finally reprinted the earlier volume as Parts I and II of this one and called them "The Formative Period" and "The Finished Product." With this arrangement he finally carried out his original intention. Happily, he has been able to carry on with the same style he used in 1939, so that there is no break between the sections composed fifteen years apart. His is still the clear, smooth, and sprightly style found earlier.

The casual reader of history may be inclined to assume, because Melbourne was Queen Victoria's adviser, that he was characterized by the narrow stiffness later to be known as Victorianism. Such an assumption is far from the truth. Melbourne was the last great Whig, a kind of political figure that the mid-nineteenth century killed.

As a Whig, Melbourne was typical of his background and his upbringing. The Whigs were for years the backbone of British politics. They were wealthy landowners with an intense interest in their country's welfare. They lived the life of the ordinary Englishman, but on a large scale. They added a flourish of elegance and culture, and they felt the security of long-established power.

As a landed group, they had an appealing naturalness and charm. They had, too, an earthy exuberance that embraced everything. They expended a terrific amount of energy in the pursuit of practical accomplishments and happiness. They were not noted for their self-control. They were kings of their domain, and they appreciated their power. But, as a ruling group, they were doomed by the Industrial Revolution.

When businessmen grew powerful along with their machines, they soon became politically conscious and began to demand a voice in the government. When they did, only Melbourne was left to show them that power need not preclude charm.

William Lamb was the second son of Elizabeth Milbanke, Lady Melbourne. It was current opinion that he was not the son of Sir Peniston Lamb, Lord Melbourne, an ineffectual man with a large fortune, but rather the son of Lady Melbourne's lover, Lord Egremont, a distinguished, wealthy, fashionable eccentric. Lady Melbourne was beautiful and ambitious. Another of her boys was said to be the son of the Prince Regent, later George IV. She had a large family which she kept united by her interests and plans despite their varied lineage. Theirs was a typical family of the Whig dynasty, full of good humor and intellectual vigor. All the children were vital, sensual, and clever. They assumed a freedom of manners and morals. Of all the children William seemed to his mother to be destined for higher things and she concentrated on preparing him for whatever would come. When he finished at Cambridge, she persuaded him to study law, giving him also a taste of frugal Scottish scholarship.

When he was ready for life he was an agreeable, genial, and sensible fellow with his mother's good looks and her zest for life. Yet he was apt to be questioning. He could always see more than one side to a question and seldom tried to determine which was the more

important. Nothing ever seemed quite worth the trouble. He never set his heart on any office; those he received fell into his lap.

Perhaps his greatest weakness was his need for a companionable woman. His mother filled this need in his childhood and set the pattern for others to follow. Thereafter he wanted only companions who were as strong, easygoing, and brilliant as she. When he was twenty-one he fell in love with the fourteen-year-old Caroline Ponsonby, known later for her devil-may-care devotion to Lord Byron. At fourteen Caroline was an elfin creature, slight and willful and already play-acting her way through life. Her beauty and dynamic personality complemented William Lamb's geniality. Without a fortune of his own, he could not declare his love until his older brother died, making him Lord Melbourne's heir.

His marriage to Caroline began badly when she threw a hysterical fit during the wedding ceremony and tore her dress to ribbons. It was never a peaceful marriage, but William stuck by her to the end, despite her tantrums, the hostility of former friends, and her eventual insanity.

His entrance into politics came in 1827 when he was made Chief Secretary for Ireland. He was already forty-six years old. He made a favorable impression on the Irish because he was informal and unbiased, unlike the usual Englishman sent to that troubled state. It was the time of the demand for Catholic emancipation. This was one reform that Melbourne could approve because he believed in religious tolerance, though ordinarily he feared reforms because they upset society as he knew it. But Catholic emancipation was not yet ripe. He was content to wait for a more decisive time. All his life he put off decisions as long as he could. From that time on he was in and out of the government.

Twice before he was Victoria's Prime Minister he was taken to court by husbands who tried to prove he had compromised their wives. Both times he was exonerated, but at his death he left annuities to both women, noting in only one instance that his friendship had been entirely innocent.

When Victoria became Queen suddenly in 1837, Melbourne had been Prime Minister for nearly three years. Ordinarily a secretary would have been found to be the kind of adviser the new Queen needed. Melbourne took no chances of allowing someone to lead the Queen away from the Whig party. He began to enjoy his daily visits with her. She wrote of him daily in her diary as "Dear Lord M." And they found it necessary to write to each other two or three times a day. Victoria became the center of his life.

In only one respect could Victoria have reminded him of his wife; that was in her dynamic and restless actions. At seventeen Victoria was extravagantly interested in everything as Caroline had been thirty-two years before. With Victoria, Melbourne found the most perfect personal relationship he had known since the early days of his marriage. The other women in his life had filled the gap between Caroline and Victoria in different ways, but these two meant most to him.

Lord David Cecil records carefully the effects upon each other of a great aristocrat and a great queen. Victoria depended on Melbourne, though she did not always agree with him, until her marriage to Albert. As Albert's sun rose, Melbourne's set. With the loss of his office in 1841, Melbourne's life hung suspended until his death seven years later.

The irony of it was that his death created no more than a ripple in the bustling, mid-century world he had helped to mold. "The proper formalities were observed. Palmerston wrote announcing the sad news to the Queen; the Queen sent her condolences to Lady Palmerston; and a lengthy, if unenthusiastic, estimate of his character and achievements appeared in the *Times*. But, in fact, Melbourne's death made little stir. The world was changing fast in the nineteenth century. And, though he was only sixty-nine when he died, he had outlived his time." The age that Lytton Strachey satirized in *Eminent Victorians* and *Queen Victoria* had already begun.

MEMED, MY HAWK

Author: Yashar Kemal (1922-   )
Translated from the Turkish by Edouard Roditi
Publisher: Pantheon Books (New York). 371 pp. $4.95
Type of work: Novel
Time: The recent past
Locale: Turkey

A novel dealing with the romantic, event-packed career of a young Turkish brigand

Principal characters:
INCE MEMED, a Turkish brigand
HATCHE, Memed's beloved
DEUNEH, Memed's mother, a poor peasant widow
ABDI AGHA, Memed's landlord and mortal enemy
JABBAR, one of Memed's henchmen
SERGEANT REJEB, another of Memed's henchmen
SERGEANT ASIM, a policeman sent to hunt Memed

A Turkish novel is still something of a novelty in the world of letters, for the novel does not flourish in a land where the people are still, for the most part, illiterate. *Memed, My Hawk* has, however, been successful in Turkey and has, in translation, been welcomed abroad. The author, Yashar Kemal, is still a young man, although renowned as a literary light in his own country. He was born in southern Anatolia, a Turkish province, in 1922. He was orphaned at an early age and was forced to work in order to earn enough money to finish a secondary-school education. After a series of varied jobs, which included picking cotton, harvesting rice, and writing letters for the illiterate, he became a newspaper reporter. He was quickly successful as a journalist, winning both reputation and prizes for his work. He is known in Turkey as an influential writer on land reform and other problems of Turkish life. He has even been credited with inspiring the reform group that overthrew the Menderes regime.

Yashar Kemal's novel is a highly romantic account of a Turkish Robin Hood, a young brigand named Memed who, working entirely outside the law, tries to rescue Turkish villages from grasping, cruel landlords who literally steal the bread from the peasants' mouths and so starve them to death. Memed becomes a kind of folk hero, the kind of hero found in the narrative poetry of cultures from every corner of the earth. He escapes time and time again from the police; he disdains to kill his enemies for revenge only; he suffers untold hardships; he is wisdom personified; and he suffers Prometheus-like for his people high in the Taurus Mountains of Turkey. Like so many folk heroes, Memed begins his life in poverty. Like his author, he is orphaned at an early age when his father is murdered. Memed and his mother live in the poor village of Deyirmenoluk. Their lives are bitterly hard, and their landlord, Abdi Agha, is a cruel master. While still a lad of ten, Memed, tortured by overwork and severe beatings, flees his native village to find a haven over the mountain. Instead, he is found and brought home again. He is not beaten this time. Rather, he and his mother are subjected to prolonged cruelty, their landlord starving them almost to death by taking most of their crops.

But the story of Memed is not that of a child. It is the story of a young man. Memed grows up and, manlike, falls in love. Abdi Agha has other plans for the beautiful Hatche, Memed's beloved; he intends that the girl shall marry his own nephew. The lovers outwit Abdi Agha and elope, only to be tracked down in the forest. Defending his love, Memed kills the would-be bridegroom and wounds Abdi Agha. Only one road is left for him to travel then; he must flee to the mountains to join an outlaw band. Thus begins his life of crime and violence. But while he lurks in the Taurus Mountains, Hatche languishes in prison, framed by Abdi Agha's suborned witnesses. These events, of course, and the background against which they are laid, do more than recount a romantic tale. Better than any government's report, better than any set of statistics, the story tells of the harsh, bleak life of the Turkish peasantry who, at least till recently, were victims of a system which made officials uninterested in their plight or, at best, hopelessly inefficient to deal with the problems of the Turkish people, leaving them to be robbed, beaten, and starved by landlords who cruelly abused the wretches over whom they exercised almost absolute power. Obviously Yashar Kemal has more than literary intent in his book. The novel is also a fine propaganda tool, informing the world of a situation almost unbelievable in the modern world.

Ince Memed's career as a brigand is the career of an essentially good man forced outside the law. He breaks with his fellow brigands, who are cruel to everyone, to form his own band, which robs the rich and helps the poor. Evading ambush after ambush, Memed and his men seek to help the nomads, the villagers, the farmers. On

their side, the people helped by Memed aid him, furnish him with food, money, ammunition, and information. In the eyes of the scattered mountains people Memed becomes a hero. His exploits are told and sung and his proportions become heroic, much to the chagrin of his enemies, the police and the landlords. Driven to a large town for safety, Abdi Agha still fears the young man he has wronged. The fear has sound basis, for Memed, having sworn vengeance, seeks several times to kill his former landlord. In the Agha's absence, too, Memed institutes agricultural reforms, returns land to the peasants, and sees to it that they keep the crops they have grown, the crops that stand between them and utter starvation.

Memed's most daring exploit is his rescue of Hatche from prison. With her and an older woman he returns to the mountains, living among the snowy peaks, hunted by the angry authorities, who even enlist the help of rival brigands in an effort to bring Memed to his death or to prison. Through a long mountain winter the three fugitives hide, sustained by supplies from friendly villagers and nomads, high in the mountain fastnesses where eagles nest. There Memed's son is born, and there his beloved Hatche dies, struck down by a policeman's bullet. Irony is present. Hatche's death occurs just a short time before a general amnesty from the Turkish government is to go into effect. When the amnesty is granted, Abdi Agha is still unpunished. Memed rides down from the mountains, only to face a defeat if he accepts pardon. If he chooses freedom and peace, Abdi Agha may continue to live and actually undo the land reforms Memed has worked so hard to bring into effect. Faced by an almost unbearable situation, Memed makes his choice. His final deed is the murder of Abdi Agha, whose death saves the people from his rapacity and achieves Memed's revenge. But the murder also places Memed outside the law for all time. He flees once more.

Woven into this tale is some splendid narrative, especially the portions telling of Memed's fights with the police and with his fellow brigands. Equally well done are many descriptive passages. Noteworthy are the descriptions of the homes and the way of life of the peasants and nomads. Description of the countryside is comparatively sparse after the initial passages of the book, which outline the general setting, the region near the Taurus Mountains. The emphasis of the novel is on action; the lack of description for its own sake is reminiscent of a folk ballad. Sometimes the reader feels out of touch with the contemporary world, as though what he reads is from another age, as well as from another country. It is as though one were reading of medieval, rather than modern, times. Yet this very quality of distance is fascinating for the reader because it is so vividly and sharply drawn. Kemal's wild characters and wild setting may overwhelm the social message of the book, no great fault in a novel in which so much is memorably conveyed with dramatic and emotional effect.

MEMOIRS, Volume I
Year of Decisions

Author: Harry S. Truman (1884-1972)
Publisher: Doubleday and Company (New York). Illustrated. 596 pp. $5.00
Type of work: Autobiography and history
Time: 1945-1946
Locale: The United States

The first volume of ex-President Harry S. Truman's memoirs

Principal personages:
  PRESIDENT HARRY S. TRUMAN
  MRS. TRUMAN
  MARGARET TRUMAN
  MRS. MARTHA TRUMAN, the President's mother
  HENRY L. STIMSON, Secretary of War
  EDWARD R. STETTINIUS, JR., Secretary of State, succeeded by
  JAMES F. BYRNES
  JAMES V. FORRESTAL, Secretary of the Navy
  GENERAL GEORGE C. MARSHALL, Army Chief of Staff, succeeded
    by
  DWIGHT D. EISENHOWER
  ADMIRAL WILLIAM D. LEAHY, Chief of Staff to the President
  VANNEVAR BUSH, head of the Office of Scientific Research and De-
    velopment
  THOMAS J. PENDERGAST, Truman's political mentor
  WINSTON CHURCHILL, English Prime Minister, succeeded by
  CLEMENT ATTLEE
  ANTHONY EDEN, British Foreign Minister, succeeded by
  ERNEST BEVIN
  GENERALISSIMO JOSEPH STALIN
  V. M. MOLOTOV, Russian Foreign Minister

Mr. Truman, a genuine if rather erratic student of history in his own right, feels that much history has been lost because so few Presidents of the United States have written their own stories, personal accounts of their years in high office which would have been helpful to succeeding generations by informing posterity what thoughts holders of the Presidency had and what forces brought about their actions while they filled that high office. Because of his belief in the importance of such records, Mr. Truman has begun publication of his own memoirs. In the preface to the first volume he writes:

"I should like to record, before it is too late, as much of the story of my occupancy of the White House as I am able to tell. The events, as I saw them and as I put them down here, I hope may prove helpful in informing some people and in setting others straight on the facts." He also points out that for reasons of national security and out of consideration for people still alive it is impossible to write a complete record; that it may be many years, even many generations, before some materials can be released to the general public.

Year of Decisions is primarily the

record of the first twelve months of the Truman administration, which began, of course, within a few hours of the death of President Franklin D. Roosevelt in April, 1945. Only a little more than three months of President Roosevelt's fourth term in office had passed. The first word of Roosevelt's death, the event that was to change Harry S. Truman's whole later life, came to the Vice-President from his predecessor's widow, who said simply, "Harry, the President is dead." The shock of those few words was a great one to Harry Truman; he thought he had come to the White House to see the President, only to find upon his arrival that he himself was the President of the United States.

The entire account of his first year in office is told by him as simply, as directly, and at times as effectively as his account of receiving word of Franklin D. Roosevelt's death and being sworn in as the new Chief Executive by Chief Justice Stone. *Year of Decisions* includes the story of many events fateful to the people of the United States, fateful, indeed, to people all over the world. In the book are recorded the President's difficulties with Stalin and other representatives of the Russian government, as much as can be told of the preparation and use of the first atomic weapons, the President's thoughts and activities in connection with the United Nations organization in the formative stage of its existence, and the many problems Mr. Truman faced as the country, victorious over its enemies in Europe and the Pacific, turned from mobilization for all-out war to the manifold activities of peacetime living. In addition, there is the recurrent thread of the personal life of Harry Truman: the difficulties

of moving his family from a modest Washington apartment to the goldfish-in-a-bowl existence of the occupants of the White House, including the bother of an ever-present guard of Secret Service agents, the complexities of such a simple action as walking the few hundred yards from Blair House to the White House, and preparations for guests of the Truman family in the White House. An important insight into the private life and character of President Truman is gained from his inclusion of the texts of many of the letters he wrote regularly to his mother and sister while he was in office. A third, but also important, aspect of *Year of Decisions* is the account it gives of Truman's life before he became President. Two chapters recite the events and influences of his childhood, his service as an artillery officer in World War I, and his early civilian life, including his ill-fated excursion into the business world and the beginning of his career as a politician and public servant. Further chapters also relate the work Mr. Truman did as a senator from Missouri, including his chairmanship of the important and effective Senate Committee to Investigate the National Defense Program.

Although he faced many difficult decisions during his years as the leader of American government, particularly during the first twelve months in office, probably no decision will weigh as heavily, because of its implications, on Mr. Truman's mind as the decision he had to make regarding the use of the first atomic bombs against Japan. It is true that the decision involved willing loss of life and infliction of pain upon many thousands of men, women, and children, but the first use of the atomic bomb was even more significant in the precedent it set for the use of weapons which by their very nature cannot discriminate between the guilty and the innocent or between military objectives and those which are of no strategic value. In our time the very annihilation of whole peoples in a cataclysmic holocaust has become a part of possible history. On that score Mr. Truman has written, "The thought that frightens me is the possibility of the deliberate annihilation of whole peoples as a political-military objective. There were indications of such madness in the Nazi leadership group, and it could happen elsewhere. Terms of surrender have no meaning here. The only thing that does have meaning, and in all my thinking I have found no alternative, is organized international effort. I know of no other way to meet this terrible menace."

Even before he knew of its existence, much less the nature and magnitude of the atomic bomb's destruction, President Truman placed great hope in the United Nations organization. His first official act as President was to reaffirm the conference on the United Nations which before Roosevelt's death had been scheduled for a date late in April, 1945.

Throughout his first months in office, President Truman had problems within his official family. He inherited a ready-made executive organization with the office, but it was an organization set up by Franklin D. Roosevelt and manned by people he had appointed. It was inevitable that President Truman should want to keep many of these people, even the Cabinet, during the first period of his administration. This action would have been true of any Vice-President who succeeded so suddenly to the Presidency. It was

even truer of the successor to Franklin D. Roosevelt, who had gathered great executive powers during his twelve years in office, had run the executive branch in a very personal fashion, and had not coached the Vice-President on what would have to be done to fill the office of President. Roosevelt had been friendly to Truman, but they had not been close. If it was inevitable that he should keep the executive organization intact at first, it was also inevitable that Mr. Truman should wish to change the membership, particularly among those who were his close advisers, as he began to understand more completely the role he was compelled to fill in the White House. Mr. Truman has recorded in his book his feelings on both counts. He had decided notions on what were the responsibilities on his shoulders as President, and he did not choose to fail in carrying out those responsibilities. He intended to make his own decisions and not be ruled by members of the Cabinet or their staffs, particularly in matters of foreign affairs. That President Truman would brook no interference in foreign policy by those not qualified to take responsibility, because of the need for a clear-cut foreign policy in trying times, was made very evident on occasion. Both James Byrnes, as Secretary of State, and Henry Wallace, as Secretary of Agriculture, presumed on presidential prerogatives in foreign affairs and placed the President in an embarrassing position. As is recorded in *Year of Decisions*, one was given a strong reprimand and the other was asked to resign.

Many charges have been made that the Truman administration was ineffective. No President of the United States can please everyone in the country. Harry S. Truman seemed to incur the displeasure of many persons, people who were quite vocal about their feelings. *Year of Decisions* does not attempt to justify or rationalize the antagonisms that were aroused. Rather, it presents the facts as President Truman sees them. It is a patently sincere document setting forth what the President's evaluations were, why he acted the way he did, and what objectives he hoped to achieve by his actions. That he had a temper that can be and was sometimes ruffled is not denied, but it would appear that there were occasions when a tinge of irascibility served good ends; it was a reaction on the President's part that was plain enough for people to understand, even such persons as Premier Stalin and John L. Lewis, both of whom received the barb of Truman's wrath upon occasion.

There can be no doubt in the mind of one who reads his memoirs that Harry S. Truman is a fighter, if that point needs to be made. There can also be no doubt that he has done his best to present his career in high office, a career in which he sought to serve America with his best, as carefully as he could. Anyone who has written and served in such fashion can review his labors contentedly, knowing that honor is still intact. Without doubt, many books will be written in the future about the Truman administration. Having greater time and distance between themselves and the events than Mr. Truman has, the authors of later books will have a greater objectivity. But whether or not they agree with what Mr. Truman has written, the authors of later books will have to take his account into consideration.

MEMOIRS, Volume II
Years of Trial and Hope

Author: Harry S. Truman (1884-1972)
Publisher: Doubleday and Company (New York). 594 pp. $5.00
Type of work: Autobiography and history
Time: 1946-1952
Locale: The United States

The richly documented second volume of the former President's reminiscences, reflecting his "Give 'em hell" attitude

Principal personages:
PRESIDENT HARRY S. TRUMAN
DEAN ACHESON, Secretary of State
GENERAL GEORGE C. MARSHALL, Army Chief of Staff
CLEMENT ATLEE, English Prime Minister
GENERAL DOUGLAS MACARTHUR, United Nations Commander in Korea

Mr. Truman's writing will probably never be used to exemplify effective literary style, but his book will unquestionably be read and studied for many years as a source book by students of history, government, and political science. Perhaps the writing would leave a different impression were the tartness of the author's voice not so vivid in the reader's mind. Colored or not by this recollection, Mr. Truman's depiction of events is the record of a man determined "to be right." While we wait for the final opinion of both posterity and history, it is perhaps enough to say that Mr. Truman in his second volume completes his full-length portrait of the Chief Executive and in these pages gives view of what a President should be.

The ex-President's self-confidence, as mentioned, permeates this account of his term in office. The canvas is broader here than it was in *Year of Decisions,* and many topics must be covered pertaining to those crucial years. But whether he is dealing with the Fair Deal doctrine, domestic strikes, the MacArthur crisis, or political opposition to the atomic energy program, nowhere is his forthrightness more forcibly shown than in his memorandum, written April 16, 1950, and then locked away, expressing his decision not to be a candidate for re-election in 1952. After noting his thirty years in office, Mr. Truman wrote critically of Grant, Theodore Roosevelt, and F. D. Roosevelt, those Presidents who had attempted to break the two-term precedent. "I know I could be elected again," he wrote, "and continue to break the old precedent as it was broken by F. D. R."

His irascibility is equally apparent. If he invited, requested, or suggested, it seemed beyond his comprehension that anyone would decline or resist. When he did not get acceptance, the Truman temper rose. A case in point is his reaction to a telegram from General Eisenhower. Since his announcement that he was not a candidate in 1952, Mr. Truman had given considerable thought to the problem of an orderly turnover of the government to his successor. Even before the election, Mr. Truman was making gestures to Eisenhower toward this end, and on August 13, 1952, the Chief Executive invited the Republican candidate to a Cabinet luncheon to discuss the foreign situation.

In a lengthy telegram, General Eisenhower declined the invitation with appropriate gratitude, pointing out that at that time the people were deciding the country's leadership for the next four years. The decision, the General went on, rested between the Republican and Democratic nominees. Under these circumstances Eisenhower concluded that his and the President's "communications should be only those which are known to all the American people."

The President's reaction was "Eisenhower's telegram angered me. It was apparent that the politicians had already begun to mishandle him." In Truman's long-hand personal answer, he mentioned his regret "that you have allowed a bunch of screwballs to come between us."

Truman pictures a definite coldness when Eisenhower did come as President-elect for a conference toward "orderly turn-over" on November 18: "Eisenhower was unsmiling. I thought he looked tense. I wanted him to be at his ease." The President talked to his guest about the paintings hanging in his office, and then about a large globe Eisenhower had used in World War II and had given to Truman in Frankfurt, during the Potsdam Conference. "I offered to leave this globe for him in the White House. He accepted. He remained unsmiling. I then got down to business."

It is only to be expected that Mr. Truman would devote considerable space to the "MacArthur incident." There is justification for this, of course. The Korean war was the matrix for MacArthur's activities immediately preceding his release from "all his com-

mands" on April 10, 1951.

The full treatment of events and attitudes leading up to the President's action, one which raised international questions and violently stirred national emotions, is illuminating but tedious. In the extenuating causes for such a decision, the reader gets a sharp look at Congressmen, cabinet members, and foreign diplomats.

As with so many of his points, Mr. Truman reiterates the reason for MacArthur's failure: he was out of touch with the thinking of the American people, having been in the Orient for eighteen years. Repeated efforts to get the U.N. Commander to Washington for conference failing, Truman went to Wake Island for the historic session with MacArthur. The conference was "very friendly—I might say much more so than I had expected."

MacArthur's reversal of opinion on using Chinese Nationalists in the Korean effort, issuance of arms for Korean youth, and vacillation on U.N. successes at the 38th parallel seemed to be disturbing to the Commander-in-Chief. The main bone of contention was MacArthur's repeated violation of an order calling for Washington clearance of any public statement regarding the war.

MacArthur's military leadership, as such, was splendid, as in previous wars. His difficulty lay in his not accepting "civilian control of the military," a principle which Truman calls "one of the strongest foundations of our system of free government."

Truman philosophizes that the chief difference between the conduct of civil and military leaders lies in the lack of opportunity for the latter to learn the humility necessary for good public service. The civil, or elected, official succeeds by "a mixture of principles steadfastly maintained and adjustments made at the proper time and place—adjustments to conditions, not adjustment of principles." The words "command" and "obedience" dominate the thinking of the military officer.

In connection with the seizure by the government of the steel mills on April 7, 1952, Mr. Truman turns sociologist to discuss the value of unions to the worker. In our machine age, in which the individual has little chance to feel that what he is doing is important, the union, according to Mr. Truman, gives him the sense of joining with others to do something worth while, and a sense of human dignity.

Too, Truman considered the profits of the steel companies. If the industry were allowed to hike steel prices, the government price-stabilization program would be invalidated, and prices of everyday necessities "would start jumping all around us." Another consideration of profits had to do with the soldier. If some Americans were serving the country on the battlefield, it was not just that industries should be reaping great profits, much of which would be at government expense, because the defense program depended so widely on steel.

Obviously stated, the Chief Executive's main concern over curtailment of steel production was the crippling effect on the United States' contribution to the war effort in Korea.

The constitutional power vested in him to seize an industry is interpreted as "the greatest trust that can be placed in any man by the American people." In one of his many historical references, Mr. Truman mentions Alexander, Caesar, and Napoleon as men "who have liked power and the glamour that goes with it. . . . I never did."

A minute but telling detail lies in Truman's selection of words in the Truman Doctrine, the declaration of foreign policy given before a joint session of the Congress on March 12, 1947. The key sentence, as written by the State Department, began: "I believe that it should be the policy of the United States . . ." Here, as in several places in the document, the President penciled out words, changing "should" to "must." He did not like "half-hearted" measures.

In requesting that the original statement of the declaration be rewritten, Mr. Truman showed one of his interests, implied and pointed up throughout the book. His first concern was the people, their being informed and protected. He felt that the original draft of the doctrine, full of background data and statistical figures, sounded like "an investment prospectus" and would be understood by very few.

So the six-year period of trials and hopes is described. The problems involved in the national health program, the Berlin blockade, affairs of Palestine, Russian access to atomic secrets, the Nationalist debacle in China, Truman's selection of a presidential nominee in 1952—all of these, in the author's opinion, presented trials for the people through their government.

There is a suggestion of One-Worldism in the recurring point regarding our relationships with other countries, the insistence that our way of life has become so internationalized that we cannot ignore the connection between our domestic life and our foreign policy. This aspect of world affairs, in Truman's view, makes it imperative that the President of the United States be a positive individual. Our Federal system cannot stand another inactive or negative President. In running the government, "you do not operate some-where in a theoretical heaven but with a tough set of tough situations that have to be met—and met without hesitation. It takes practical men to run a government."

These matters are—or recently were —of domestic or global import, and certainly the very title of Mr. Truman's book affords him the right to include minutiae of events and personalities to get his case on the record. Yet his book would probably be more valuable and undoubtedly more readable had he taken time to write a shorter one.

MEMOIRS AND OPINIONS: 1926-1974

Author: Allen Tate (1899-   )
Publisher: The Swallow Press (Chicago). 225 pp. $8.95
Type of work: Essays, speeches, memoirs
Time: Mid-twentieth century
Locale: The American South, Paris

A collection of essays, speeches, and memoirs which are equally divided between recollections of life with good friends and opinions of the state of literature in America

Allen Tate is a man of letters, an elder statesman of American literature, a link with controversies of the past, and a commentator on the contemporary literary scene who can speak from a perspective of long experience that few can match. In a long and distinguished career as a poet and critic, he has received most of the honors which America can bestow on its men of literature. Whatever he says or writes is therefore always of great importance; he commands our attention and respect as only those who have lived so long and have participated in so much have a right to expect. In recent years, Tate has acknowledged his position at the end of his career, at least implicitly, by engaging in projects of summing up, projects which bring together his past achievements and indicate those things which he wishes to be remembered for. The most notable of these is his recent *Essays of Four Decades* (1968), a compilation of those works of literary criticism which he feels are worthy of preservation. If the present work is a more relaxed volume, a collection of more occasional and informal pieces, it too has its rightful place in the summation of a career. In it, we get a glimpse of Tate in a reflective, remembering mood, commenting on Ernest Hemingway, Gertrude Stein,

Robert Frost, John Crowe Ransom, T. S. Eliot, and other founders, with Tate, of a distinctively modern American literature. We are asked to recall the early and exciting years of this century—the people and the events which made American literature not just the writing of a new, isolated, and provincial nation but a major literature of the world. We are also asked to remember the literature of the American past which made that mature literature possible, and to reflect on the outcome of all the hopes and dreams of that time, as they have been realized or shattered in the intervening years. To read this volume is to spend a relaxed and pleasant evening in the presence of a rare creature in our age—a great writer who is also a gentleman. If these essays do not always challenge us, if occasionally some of the controversies reviewed seem dated, they serve always to remind us of the heritage of contemporary American literary life in all its richness and diversity. For that we must be grateful to Allen Tate.

Tate's involvement in modern American literature has always been from the perspective of his Southern past. A member of the Fugitive group at Vanderbilt University from its earliest days, and later a participant in the agrarian movement and contributor to its manifesto *I'll Take My Stand,* Tate shows in this volume that the concerns of those days are still living issues for him. He reprints here his memoirs of the Fugitives ("*The Fugitive,* 1922-1925: A Personal Recollection Twenty Years After"), his tribute to John Crowe Ransom, and his essay attacking the humanism of Irving Babbitt, Norman Foerster, and Paul Elmer More ("Humanism and Naturalism"). Present in all these is a deep sense of regret at the urbanization and industrialization of the South, its remaking in the image of the conquering North, and its acceptance of the values and ways of thinking which support the abandonment of an agrarian society. Tate has opposed all these things with remarkable consistency; one can only imagine the profound regret he must feel that those processes he opposed so long ago have gone so much further than even he and his fellow agrarians could have understood or predicted in the 1920's and 1930's. Yet his more recent writing is remarkably without bitterness; the only trace of it in these pages is in his hint of annoyance with William Faulkner that Faulkner never joined with other Southern writers in a united front. An admirer of Faulkner, Tate complains that he pretended to be a farmer, and this "was not a friend of anybody who conceivably could have been his peer" ("William Faulkner: 1897-1962").

A number of the essays in this volume are reminiscences of Tate's days in Paris during the late 1920's, the time of the "Lost Generation" expatriates, when Gertrude Stein's salon was the center of life for Americans in Paris. In the light of recent celebration of the importance of the circle of Americans around Stein in the formation of modern American literature, Tate's perspective is strikingly refreshing. If Hemingway learned to write there, if American modernism was born there, Tate seems strangely untouched by it all. He remembers that he never got any of Alice B. Toklas' American cake, "not even much education"; although he admits his provinciality by wondering how Miss Stein could be a great lady without being a lady first, and is perhaps more revealing than he might intend in his confession that he spent most of his time in Paris writing a biography of Jefferson Davis, the President of the Confederacy. Tate's response to the other Americans in Paris implies a set of values which are distinctively Southern; it suggests strongly the role of the South in the United States as a unique subculture, a distinct province, as Tate describes it at one point, with its own sense of the nature of ladies and gentlemen, its own deeply ingrained view of the order of things. If the Southerner in his native clime is comfortable in his values because the culture of the region supports him in holding them, when he confronts the realities of modern life outside the South he appears as a man apart, able, as Tate does here, to see things in ways different from most of those involved.

The response of Tate and many of his fellow agrarians to the coming of industrialism in the South was to create a world of value in art, especially in poetry. In this way, if not politically, Tate and other agrarians such as John Crowe Ransom, Robert Penn Warren, and Cleanth Brooks have reshaped American thought in significant ways. What they created was a way of thinking and talking about literature, especially about poetry, which has come to be called the New Criticism. Based on a close reading of the diction, images, and ambiguities of poetic language, the New Criticism has enriched our experience of poetry in a radical way. All contemporary criticism of literature is either modeled on its approach or is a reaction against it. Tate's essays in criticism in this volume remind us once again that the New Criticism is best practiced, and best understood, by those who founded it. Essential to this approach to poetry is a sensitivity to language, to all its nuances and shadings of meaning, which Tate masterfully displays here in his readings of Robert Frost ("Robert Frost as Metaphysical Poet") and Edgar Allan Poe ("The Poetry of Edgar Allan Poe"). Also significant in this regard are Tate's memories of other founders of the New Criticism, especially John Crowe Ransom, and of that contributor to the movement, T. S. Eliot ("Homage to T. S. Eliot"). Tate, the Southerner, and Eliot, the expatriot Midwesterner, shared a sense of unease with the mainstream of twentieth century American life; both men sought in tradition and in authoritarian society and religion a sense of order and stability to serve as an antidote for the rootlessness and restlessness of much of American society. Tate's tribute to Eliot is one of the most moving pieces in this volume. His sensitivity to the private Eliot, his sense of the gulf between the public figure and the essential man, attest to the two men's deep sympathy for each other. Tate's sense of "Tom" Eliot

the man, as distinct from T. S. Eliot the public poet, anticipates, as well, recent trends in the discussion of Eliot's work.

The essays which begin and end *Memoirs and Opinions* take us from Tate's boyhood in Kentucky and Virginia to his old age, as poet laureate of the South, a resident of Sewanee, Tennessee. The first essay, entitled "A Lost Traveler's Dream," is an affectionate reminiscence of childhood and young adulthood. Largely anecdotal, it surveys Tate's discovery of his birthplace in Kentucky, years after his mother told him he was born in Virginia. Such an incident is typical; Tate's family was restless and traveled widely in search of a place in which his mother would feel comfortable—they never lived in one place more than three years. This search for a place becomes for Tate a search for identity; when he is taken to visit an ancient former slave who tells him he resembles his grandpa, he gets clues to that identity in a sense of a past. The past becomes, first, a Southern past; later it is to become a literary past. This second sense of the past, and with it, a sense of identity, is fully in the foreground of the concluding essay, "A Sequence of Stanzas Compiled and Read to a Group of Friends on My Seventy-Fifth Birthday." Tate's text in this piece is a quotation from Walter Savage Landor, in which the older poet on *his* seventy-fifth birthday proclaims his readiness for death in an appeal to nature and to art. Tate says that since 1850 man has done violence to nature; therefore, nature is not open to appeal. All that is left is art; in this mood Tate quotes from a few of his own poems before turning to ones by Edwin Muir and George Seferis. Muir makes the claim that Tate would affirm; "Love gathers all." Seferis sets the tone for what is to come; "And it is now time for us to say the few words/ we have to say/ Because tomorrow our soul sets sail." Secure in his poetic voice, secure in the faith that poetry speaks the words which can be heard and believed, Tate accepts the life that has been his and the life that is yet to be his. With this, he accepts his identity as poet, as one who says the few words that can be believed. No one can deny him his success in that role.

John N. Wall, Jr.

MEMOIRS: 1925–1950

Author: George F. Kennan (1904–   )
Publisher: Atlantic-Little, Brown and Company (Boston). 583 pp. $10.00
Type of work: Autobiography and essays on foreign policy
Time: 1925–1950
Locale: Moscow, Washington, Berlin, Prague, Tokyo, Tallinn, Riga

What may prove, perhaps, the most important political autobiography of the mid-century, America's most distinguished expert on the U.S.S.R. presents a personal overview of twenty-five years of diplomatic history with appended documents relating his contemporary suggestions for the course the U.S.A. should have taken in crises

Principal personages:
GEORGE F. KENNAN
FRANKLIN D. ROOSEVELT
HARRY S TRUMAN
JOSEPH STALIN
EDWARD R. STETTINIUS, JR., Undersecretary and Secretary of State (1944–1945)
GEORGE C. MARSHALL, Secretary of State (1947–1949)
DEAN G. ACHESON, Undersecretary of, Advisor to, and Secretary of State (1945–1953)
JOHN FOSTER DULLES, delegate to U.N. (1945–1950), Consultant to Secretary of State (1950), Presidential Envoy to Japan (1951), Secretary of State (1953–1959)
WILLIAM C. BULLITT, Ambassador to Russia (1933–1936)
JOSEPH E. DAVIES, Ambassador to Russia (1936–1938)
W. AVERELL HARRIMAN, Ambassador to Russia (1941, 1943–1946), later Ambassador to Great Britain and Ambassador-at-large
HARRY HOPKINS, assistant to President Roosevelt (1943–1945) and envoy to Moscow (1945)
HENRY L. STIMSON, Secretary of War (1940–1945)
WILLIAM D. LEAHY, Admiral, U.S.N., and Presidential Chief of Staff (1942–1949)
CHARLES EUSTIS BOHLEN, friend, Foreign Service officer, Consul at Moscow (1934, 1938), Secretary at Moscow (1934, 1942–1944), Ambassador to Russia, and to France, Counselor of Embassy at Moscow (1938)
HELMUTH VON MOLTKE, Civilian legal aide to the German General Staff and an anti-Nazi
GOTTFRIED VON BISMARCK, Governor of Brandenburg and an anti-Nazi
JOHN G. WINANT, Ambassador to Great Britain and American Member of Allied European Advisory Commission (1941–1946)
JAMES WEBB, Under Secretary of State (1949–1952)
DOUGLAS MACARTHUR, General U.S.A., Allied Commander of Occupation Forces in Japan (1945–1951)
DEAN RUSK, State Department Official (1946–1949), Assistant Secretary of State (1949–1951)
JOHN PATTON DAVIES, Secretary of the Moscow Embassy (1945–1947) and Member Policy Planning Staff of Department of State (1947–1952)

SIR WILLIAM STRANG, British Undersecretary of State and member of the Allied European Advisory Committee (1943–1945)

His youth in Milwaukee and student years at Princeton gave no cause to predict that George F. Kennan would become America's most noted authority on the U.S.S.R. and on world diplomacy at mid-century. Earlier, Princeton gave him a love for English literature important to one who declares that his career has been largely literary—writing diplomatic reports no one in Washington ever read. More than for his historical works, Kennan probably will be remembered for his *Memoirs,* which in some respects stand to America at mid-century as *The Education of Henry Adams* did to America of the early 1900's.

His acceptance in 1925 into the new U. S. Foreign Service Corps came as a surprise shared by readers of his *Memoirs.* His subsequent education in the arts of diplomacy relating especially to Russia makes a strong case for the old-fashioned study of a country's history, language, literature, and long-run cultural attitudes, rather than for present-minded emphasis on its short-run socio-economic system. Apprenticeship in U.S. diplomatic and consular posts and graduate study at the University of Berlin, perfected him as a Russian specialist. He chose this area of concentration both because he admired his namesake and distant cousin, George Kennan the nineteenth century author of *Siberia and the Exile System,* and because he anticipated favorable opportunities in that field, as the U.S.A. had had no official relations with Russia since 1918.

While at student at Berlin, Kennan married a Norwegian girl, Annelise Soerensen. Despite the title *Memoirs,* there is in this book little about the happy family life of the Kennans and their two daughters.

Kennan was ready to enter upon his career at the time when the U.S.A. and the U.S.S.R. renewed diplomatic relations in 1933. Desirous of such a dialogue, he scoffed at extravagant advantages which some foresaw for America. He denied that such recognition would restrain the Nazis and Japanese militarists. Never has he considered the Soviet Union a fit ally or associate of the U.S.A. Critical of President Roosevelt for giving the appearance that "things were being taken care of," rather than facing issues, he unsuccessfully warned Washington against American naïvete in trusting such written assurances as treaty clauses protecting U.S. citizens in Russia. According to Kennan, President Roosevelt was typical of Americans of the twentieth century in bending diplomacy to serve U.S. public opinion and in using too pretentious language for the achievement of a mature foreign policy.

In 1933, Ambassador William C. Bullitt took Kennan to Moscow as Secretary of Legation to establish the new embassy. The younger man admired and respected Bullitt's charm and ability to hold his own intellectually with such Old Bolsheviks as Radek and Bukharin. He saw Bullitt's optimism change to impatience as President Roosevelt ignored the ambassador's advocacy of a "hard line" towards Moscow. He was aghast that Bullitt's successor, Joseph E. Davies, relied more on newspapermen than on his own expert staff; and he alleges that Davies placed "considerable credence" in the "fantastic charges" against the Old Bolsheviks during the Moscow Purge Trials of 1937. He believes that pro-Soviet influence high in the U.S. government simultaneously caused the dismantlement of an independent Russian Division in the Department of State.

Kennan was posted to the Russian desk at Washington after it was subordinated to general European interests, succeeding his friend and fellow Russian expert Charles Eustis Bohlen. Because Kennan's views on Russia were "badly out of accord" with those of Davies and the Roosevelt Administration in 1938, all soon were relieved by Kennan's appointment as Secretary of Legation at Prague.

On the day of the Munich Conference, Kennan arrived at the Czechoslovak capital, where he reported upon the sad and haphazard partition of the country. Later, he termed the seizure of the rump of the Czech state one of Hitler's "greatest mistakes" because it destroyed his credibility and forced the British to promise to fight any further expansion by the Nazis. Upon the outbreak of war in the fall of 1939, Kennan was ordered to Berlin, where the able Alexander Kirk was *chargé d'affaires* until October of 1940. Kennan closed U.S. consular offices and interceded on behalf of Jews, first in Germany and then throughout the new German imperium. These tasks multiplied, as neutral America assumed responsibility for the interests of other nations.

In relating events, Kennan quotes his contemporary views; subsequently he states his changes of opinion; and he provides in appendices his full diplomatic reports from which he quoted. As a writer, he achieves a magisterial effect by use of what is almost the "fog of war" technique in dealing step by step with the German problem which

he believes to have been and to be the crux of world diplomacy in his time.

In 1940, he recommended to the U.S. State Department that Germany be dismembered after the war in order to insure peace. That he then fancifully suggested re-establishing the old small kingdoms was, he admits in 1968, sheer nostalgia. He doggedly asserts his admiration for many German aristocrats and for the laborers of Berlin and Hamburg because they disliked the Nazis and the war even during victory parades. For more than a year he had clandestine conversations with the civilian legal aide to the German General Staff, the anti-Nazi Count Helmuth von Moltke, who was implicated in plots against Hitler's life and executed in 1945. Convinced that the future of a democratic Germany really depended on such idealistic aristocrats as Moltke and Gottfried von Bismarck, Kennan was shocked to learn in conversation with President Roosevelt that the latter believed such Junkers to be Hitler's mainstay.

As early as June of 1940, Kennan concluded that Germany's military victories never would solve her administrative, ideological, and political dilemmas. Prolonged military occupation of Europe he deemed almost impossible; for the conquerors long to accommodate their pretensions with even puppet régimes was to him no less possible. By mid-1945, Kennan realized that the same argument held true against the U.S.S.R. in its relation with its East European satellites; nationalism had become the dominant force, even in the Communist world.

In the spring of 1941 Kennan alerted Washington to the imminence of Hitler's invasion of Russia, but U.S. warnings to Moscow were ignored. To Kennan, war on the eastern front posed a critical problem for the U.S.A., even though this country was still officially neutral; and his proposed course of action, though not devoid of *realpolitik,* emphasized the moral factor. Regretting Churchill's welcome of Stalin as an ally, he declared that the U.S.A. must withhold "moral support" of the U.S.S.R., whose policies at home and whose earlier encouragement of Hitler's western ambitions entitled her to no sympathy. He advocated American material aid to Russia, however, on condition that it be kept free of Stalin's ideological or territorial aims. When, by 1944, Russia had rewon her ·historic borders, he advocated that America cease aid which would only facilitate conquest of non-Russian lands. At the time of the Potsdam Conference in 1945, he was bitterly ashamed that his country condoned Russia's absorption of the Baltic States and of most of East Prussia.

Kennan's *Memoirs* suffer from an almost unmitigated series of Cassandra-like admonitions. It is rare that hindsight has proved Kennan wrong. Were he less modest, the work might seem arrogant. A rare instance of his approval of a decision made in Washington was ending Lend-Lease aid to Russia, which he really desired to terminate sooner. Such views placed Kennan in disagreement with the government until 1946.

Following his internment for several months after Pearl Harbor, Kennan in the fall of 1942 was posted to Lisbon, first as Counselor of Legation and then as *chargé d'affaires.* Perceiving the strategic importance of the Azores at the same time that the British did, but before anyone in Washington thought of it, he urged negotiations for their use by the U.S.A. The imbroglio that ensued shows U.S. policy- and decision-making at its worst. He excuses Secretary of State Edward R. Stettinius, Jr., as a victim both of President Roosevelt's delight in parallel lines of communication between which he was the only link and of the wartime subservience of officialdom to Secretary of War Henry L. Stimson. That Harry Hopkins and Admiral Leahy secured for Kennan direct access to the President and that the Azores situation was resolved satisfactorily provides a happy, but disturbing conclusion: the ostensible hero, President Roosevelt, appears to have been the hidden cause of all difficulties.

Kennan's assignment in 1943 to London was to help the overworked Ambassador John G. Winant on the Big Three's European Advisory Commission, of which Britain's Sir William Strang and the Soviet Ambassador at London were the other members. Only the British were "adequately represented," says Kennan. Not only had President Roosevelt been "reluctant" to agree to the commission's establishment, but the U.S. War Department resisted its work "to the point of insubordination." Kennan's effort to draw a more easterly boundary for the proposed Russian zone of occupation in Germany was so long blocked by lack of communication with Washington— despite Kennan's flying to Washington for a personal interview with the President—that the British agreed to back the Russian boundary demand. For Kennan, this fiasco of decision-making repeated that concerning the Azores, but with no happy ending.

With the help of Charles Bohlen, Kennan in 1944 returned to Moscow as minister-counselor under Ambassador Averell Harriamn. He greatly respected Harriman's executive leadership and scrupulous execution of instructions whose wisdom he suspected the Ambassador doubted. During Harriman's absence, Kennan and his colleague, John Patton Davies, the East-Asian expert, concurred that the visiting Patrick J. Hurley, Ambassador to China, was excessively optimistic in reporting Stalin's intentions concerning postwar China. Their counter-report, endorsed by Harriman, caused Davies to be harassed during the Joseph McCarthy Red scare of the 1950's. Kennan flatly declares that Davies did not have "an ounce of pro-Communist sympathies."

Because he believed it fruitless to dissuade the Soviets, Kennan desired that the U.S.A. publicly stand aside from their reorganization of eastern Europe. Similarly, he disapproved of U.S. participation in the war crimes trials of Axis leaders, because Soviet judges represented a government equally guilty of genocide at home and abroad. Although admiring the genial Russian people, Kennan concluded before 1946 that, because the U.S.A. cannot help the people of a Communist-dominated country without helping their tyrannical rulers, it is better to leave such people alone. He admits that Marxist *theory* includes some ingredients which someday may prove useful for U.S. adoption, but he despises the Communist *system* as practiced in Russia. Amusingly, he describes the Communist Party in Russia as being a "collective Walter Mitty," fabricating dreamlike official versions of true occurrences and capable of talking in terms of either. His judgment of Stalin is not based on personal encounters, although they met several times. This "old battle-scarred tiger" with yellow eyes, he deems to have been great "primarily in his iniquity," which was boundless.

Not involved in plans for the United Nations, Kennan holds it and "world opinion" in low esteem. For him, the decision-taking of diplomacy is the province of the technocrats of *realpolitik*.

That the U.S.S.R. would not join the World Bank to aid world economic recovery after World War II came as a surprise to Washington, but not to Kennan. When, for a change, Washington asked his opinion, the diplomat replied in an 8,000-word telegram—his first report to gain wide official audience and concurrence. Secretary of the Navy Forrestal was so impressed that he facilitated Kennan's assignment in the spring of 1946 to the National War College at Washington.

During the next three years, Kennan formulated so brilliant a conception of America's role in world affairs that it has become the yardstick against which Presidents and their Secretaries of State of this period are measured. The diplomat often reiterates that one of the greatest U.S. errors of judgment after World War II was in assessing the U.S.S.R. on the basis of its capability rather than its intentions. He worked out what might be called two laws of thermo-nuclear dynamics. Because the nineteenth century war aim of total destruction of an enemy "would no longer work," he concluded first that "we would have to revert to the concepts of limited warfare" prevalent during the eighteenth century and second that only a politico-economic revival would contain an expression of the Communist imperium by means of coups or wars of national liberation.

When in early 1947 Great Britain ended her aid to Greece, Kennan helped frame for Secretary of State George C. Marshall the proposal that America avert an economic collapse and Communist coup there. This became the Truman Doctrine, which to Kennan's sorrow was expanded to include Turkey and was dressed up in "grandiose and more sweeping" terms. The promise to aid "free peoples" threatened with subjugation by "outside pressures" or "by armed minorities" seemed too all-inclusive, and he and Under-secretary of Sate Dean Acheson vainly tried to emphasize that aid depended on the merits of each individual case.

In May of 1947, Secretary Marshall named Kennan to head the new Policy Planning Staff of the State Department, whose first task was to recommend a long-term program of U.S. aid in averting the collapse of the West European economies. Quick to credit Marshall and President Truman as authors of the Marshall Plan, he is proud of his staff's role in stipulating that formal requests for aid come from Europe, that German recovery was essential to that of Europe as a whole, that the Europeans work out the details, and that the American offer include Russia and its satellites. Kennan says that he "loved" Marshall for his courteousness, conscientiousness, integrity, and modesty; but he thinks that Marshall "never fully understood the rationale" behind the plan that bears his name. Success of the Marshall Plan exceeded Kennan's hopes, but he had predicted that it would stimulate the Russians to consolidate their control of Czechoslovakia. That they did so and also blockaded Berlin, he found insufficient cause for America's resulting war scare and augmentation of military forces. Before the Russians achieved naval and air strength, Kennan advocated chief reliance on smallish units of the U.S. Marine Corps.

In June of 1947, publication of his article on Russia's policies in the *Foreign Affairs Quarterly* under the signature of "X" caused a furor. His proposal that Russia's political expansion be contained by political means was misinterpreted both generally and officially to mean military containment of military power. Discounting both Russian intentions and capabilities for military aggression, he deplored NATO because it needlessly threatened Russia, prejudiced the creation of a neutralized Germany, and thwarted France's efforts to organize a self-reliant European hegemony. Kennan played little part in planning for NATO. He opposed it within the State Department and lists unfortunate subsequent events—such as the De Gaulle squabble of the 1960's—which probably were reactions to NATO.

When Dean Acheson succeeded Marshall as Secretary of state, Kennan remained head of the Policy Planning Staff, but he soon realized that the staff no longer was to participate in decision-taking and that he himself was a kind of "court jester, expected to enliven discussion . . . but not to be taken fully seriously." Although Kennan the courteous diplomat professes admiration for Acheson and outrage at the scurrilous attacks upon him, he resented the latter's valuing his Foreign Service experience too little to act on his counsel. Creation of the West German government separated them. Acheson cared less, and Kennan more, about Europe east of the Elbe than the symbols of Atlantic political unity. Kennan manfully admits twenty years later that he was too pessimistic about West German economic recovery and about the speed of transferring power from "politically illiterate" American military occupation officials to the

West Germans. But he perseveres in opposing measures which by dividing Europe he says imperils peace. Instead, he calls for a unified and demilitarized Germany, on whose periphery the great powers should quarter troops in enclaves.

Although Kennan never considered himself a Far Eastern specialist, he contributed greatly to American policy by persuading General Douglas Mac-Arthur to stop punitive measures against the Japanese, and in helping to effect a swifter transfer of power to them. While granting the moral fervor of such State Department men as Dean Rusk in their opposition to Red China, Kennan devastatingly reveals that the China Lobby of the later 1940's and early 1950's was at root the expression of an inferiority complex by the Pacific states and their educational institutions which, he says, compelled them to insist that the eastern establishment accord to the Orient importance equal to Europe. He denies that there is sufficient American self-interest or U.S.-Asian mutuality for U.S. intervention there. Instead, he advocates, as a last alternative, Marine Corps operations from insular or peninsular enclaves. As early as 1944 he concluded that the U.S.A. ought not to attempt to aid underdeveloped countries because the vagaries of foreign policy under the U.S. democratic system militate against consistency and the long-run approach needed; similar problems of erosion of land and people remain unsolved at home; and America is incapable of assuming the awesome responsibilities flowing from probable misbehavior of such recipients of American aid. These are among the most prophetic of Kannan's Cassandra-like observations, which may be applied to Vietnam subsequent to 1950.

He urges that the U.S.A. abstain from even worthy "crusades" because the childlike American people abandon them.

Dimunition of the Policy Planning Staff brought Kennan's resignation from the State Department. Its recommendations no longer went directly to the Secretary for consideration as a policy position, but now passed through bureaucratic channels to Undersecretary Webb, who would meld them with proposals of the military, old State and War Department hands, and public relations men. At Acheson's request, however, Kennan postponed his departure because of the Korean War.

Kennan shows U.S. failure to stop at the thirty-eighth parallel to have been a disastrous error, in that the Soviets saw our advance to the Yalu and towards Vladivostok as a very real threat to themselves and felt compelled to prolong the conflict through their Korean and Chinese intermediaries. Kennan advocated that the U.S.A. accept India's offer to mediate the war on condition that Red China be seated in the U.S. Security Council, because he believed that at worst two vetoes were no stronger than one and that at best a public division of Sino-Russian solidarity would ensue. In the interest of political bipartisanship at home, John Foster Dulles took part in this decision to sidestep India's mediation—unfortunately, says Kennan, because of Dulles' subservience to a public opinion frightened by China lobby. It was with relief, therefore, that in August of 1950 Kennan resigned to enter the Institute for Advanced Study at Princeton, hopeful that he could contribute more to his country as a historian who might be read than as a planner of foreign policy who was not listened to.

Besides the provocative details of U.S. foreign policy between 1933 and 1950, Kennan's *Memoirs* offers much more for thoughtful men of the second half of this century. Dismayed by the suicidal weapons of the age and by the weight of rudderless public opinion, he reminds himself and his readers that, although the state of man is innately tragic, the ameliorating benefits of enlightenment and of Christianity are worthy of preservation.

George Green Shackelford

MEMOIRS: 1950-1963

Author: George F. Kennan (1904-   )
Publisher: Little, Brown and Company (Boston). 368 pp. $12.50
Type of work: Autobiography and essays on foreign policy
Time: 1950-1963
Locale: Washington, Moscow, Princeton, Chicago, London, Oxford, Belgrade, Brioni

The second volume of a classic autobiography whose wisdom and literary style greatly enhances interest in the men and problems of American domestic and foreign policy during the Cold War

> *Principal personages:*
> GEORGE F. KENNAN
> HARRY S TRUMAN
> DWIGHT D. EISENHOWER
> JOHN F. KENNEDY
> DEAN G. ACHESON, Secretary of State (1949-1953)
> JOHN FOSTER DULLES, Secretary of State (1953-1959)
> D. DEAN RUSK, Assistant Secretary (1950-1953) and Secretary of State (1961-1969)
> CHARLES E. BOHLEN, friend, Ambassador to Russia (1953-1957), to the Philippines (1957-1959) and to France (1962-1968)
> GEORGE C. MARSHALL, General of the Army, Secretary of State (1947-1949), Secretary of Defense (1950-1951)
> DOUGLAS MACARTHUR, General of the Army, Commander of U.S. Occupation Forces in Japan (1945-1951) and of U.N. Forces in South Korea (1950-1951)
> JOSEPH R. MCCARTHY, Senator from Wisconsin (1947-1957)
> ALGER HISS, State Department official (1936-1947) and President of Carnegie Endowment for International Peace (1947-1950)
> ALLEN W. DULLES, friend, Deputy (1951) and Director (1953-1961) of U.S. Central Intelligence Agency
> JOHN PATTON DAVIES and
> JOHN STEWART SERVICE, U.S. Foreign Service Officers in China during World War II who served under Kennan in postwar Washington
> PHILLIP C. JESSUP, authority on international law, U.S. Delegate to U.N. (1948-1953)
> J. ROBERT OPPENHEIMER, atomic physicist, Chairman of Advisory Committee of U.S. Atomic Energy Commission (1946-1952)
> WILBUR D. MILLS, Representative from Arkansas (1941-   ), Chairman of House Appropriations Committee
> WILLIAM PROXMIRE, Senator from Wisconsin (1957-   )
> JACOB MALIK, Russian Delegate to U.N. (1948-1952, 1960-1968)
> JOSIP BROZ TITO, ruler of Yugoslavia since 1945 and dissident from Russian-style Communism

The first volume of these memoirs received both the Pulitzer Prize and the National Book Award for 1967. Both volumes have dealt with the evolution of a philosophy of public affairs in general and of foreign affairs in particular. That they were not more exclusively diplomatic was the result of the author's adoption of a career as a scholar and publicist during more than half of the thirteen years between 1950 and 1963.

Special and diverse gifts made Kennan both a great scholar-teacher-historian and a diplomat. Twice in the 1950's he forsook the active world of diplomacy for the Institute of Advanced Study at Princeton. There he enjoyed friendship with, among others, J. Robert Oppenheimer, the atomic physicist. He was grateful to Princeton University, his *alma mater* of which he became a trustee, for affording him generous facilities when he published his great historical work: his two-volume account of *Soviet-American Relations, 1917-1920,* whose first volume won the Pulitzer Prize, the National Book Award, and other honors; his small volume *American Diplomacy, 1900-1950*; and his *Russia and the West Under Lenin and Stalin.* The popularity of his academic lectures at Chicago, Oxford, Princeton, and elsewhere was matched by demands on him as a popular speaker on the Reith radio lectures in Great Britain (and rebroadcast elsewhere) and at commencement exercises and conventions. Sacrificing time and effort from more private scholarship, he shouldered the burden of being America's greatest living Kremlinologist and attempted to make a broadly educational contribution to the extra-mural people of the Western world.

But Kennan was never really free from the calls of diplomacy. He advised with Secretary of State Acheson and Secretary of Defense Marshall concerning the Korean War. Skeptical of our having rooted the Japanese out of Formosa, Korea, and Okinawa, he was willing that we shoulder any burdens in the first two of those former Japanese possessions only as an alternative to their domination by Russia or China. He condemned General MacArthur's reckless march north of the 38th Parallel as unduly provocative of the U.S.S.R. and sure at least to lead to China's intervention. In the face of the consequent disaster, he, Acheson, and Marshall agreed that a beachhead must be held, even though MacArthur despaired of doing so without massive reinforcements that were not to be had. At Acheson's request, Kennan conducted quiet, private talks with the Russian delegate to the U.N., Jacob Malik, whose ensuing explanations to Moscow Kennan believed helped reduce the Korean crisis from instant big-power confrontation to protracted haggling over the details of settling a brush war between South and North Korea.

Kennan also was unequivocal in urging that the French quit Indo-China and in counseling America against the East Asian adventures. He was contemptuous of China's pretensions as a great power, and he urged the United States to avoid closer relationship with the ruthless, pitiless, arrogant Chinese, whom he alleged have always sought and gotten foolish hostages from the Occident in the form of missionaries, merchants, and diplomats.

In 1952 President Truman appointed Kennan Ambassador to Russia. This should have been, but was not, the glittering apex of his career. He was disheartened that neither Truman nor Acheson gave him any goals to accomplish, but instead desired Russo-American affairs to be quiescent while they at Washington settled major international problems. Professing deep admiration and friendship for Acheson, George Kennan has never cloaked strong disagreement with him over perpetuating the division of Germany (Kennan urged unification and withdrawal of all foreign forces), NATO (Kennan opposed its creation and West Germany's inclusion; he prophesied that in-depth paramilitary forces to combat subversion was more needed than World War II-style military units), nuclear arms (Kennan advocated a disarmament pact before others than the U.S.A., Great Britain, and the U.S.S.R. developed them), a separate peace treaty with Japan (why hurry?), and transforming Japan into an American ally (surely antagonistic to Russia).

Kennan found Moscow very different from the city he had known in 1933 and 1944; suspicion and fear hung like a cloud over the city in 1952, the last year of Stalin's life. He never saw the aging dictator, who was suspected of being so ill that a dummy took his place in the May Day parade. Kennan had few encounters with Soviet officials and none with ordinary Russian citizens, from whom he was insulated by police guards. At Berlin en route to a conference, he indiscreetly remarked to the press on the similarity between his restricted life at Moscow and his internment by the Nazis at the beginning of World War II. Promptly the U.S.S.R. declared him *persona non grata* and

would not even permit him to return to Moscow in order to escort his wife and small son from the country.

As a Foreign Service Officer, Kennan believed that he was outside politics. He was hurt and surprised that the Eisenhower administration did not utilize his talents for more than an occasional briefing at the behest of the President rather than of the Secretary of State. Before the 1953 inauguration, he made a public address (cleared in advance with the State Department) in which he derided the proposal that the United States should and could aid "captive nations" of Eastern Europe in recovering their "freedom." Some Republicans had used this as a campaign issue, and soon Secretary of State John Foster Dulles endorsed it in principle. After several months of explanations, given, received, and accepted, Kennan resigned. This experience caused him to make an important appraisal of Dulles and Eisenhower.

Despite Dulles's advantages of background, education, and experience, Kennan wrote him off as a colossal failure as a man: inhuman, impersonal, insensitive, and impious. Despite differences in rhetoric which were not to Dulles's advantage, Kennan considered that there was little difference between his and Acheson's diplomacy on such matters as Germany, Japan, Russia, and nuclear arms. He castigated Dulles for "shameful and indefensible" neglect of Anglo-American relations which at the time of the Suez crisis of 1956 brought American diplomacy to its "low point" since 1945. In Kennan's opnion, Dulles's greatest flaw was his failure to defend innocent persons in the State Department from Senator Joseph McCarthy's purge of suspected Communists.

Admitting at the outset that Eisenhower was "one of the most enigmatic figures in American life," Kennan saw him as a man of "keen political intelligence, particularly in foreign affairs" who was a "pathetic" victim of the Army game—homeless in his own country, with few real friends and conditioned to pretend an interest restricted to superficialities. More like a circumscribed European head of state than a powerful American President, Eisenhower left Kennan with the sad belief that "he could have done a great deal more than he did."

Kennan's analysis of the United States Red Scare of 1948-1954 resembles in its distinction between cause and effect his magisterial dispatches concerning the conditions in countries to which he was accredited. Aware of and concerned about Communist penetration of United States officialdom since the 1930's, he concluded before 1948 that it was no longer more dangerous or extensive than could be expected under the circumstances of big-power rivalry. There were two reasons for his decision: fellow-travelers had become disenchanted with the U.S.S.R. as they learned details in the late 1940's of Russian subjugation of East European liberties; and the Truman administration (and especially the Department of State) had evolved as adequate security and screening measures as could be expected outside a police state. Kennan does not say more of the Alger Hiss case and of the investigations after President Kennedy's assassination than to de-

clare that we either lack or have not used the proper means to bring out all the facts necessary for a verdict on the real question, and consequently do not pose the real question. He does remark that he did not think Hiss qualified to be a senior adviser at the Yalta Conference of 1945 and that he does not think that Hiss could have influenced its results.

Between 1950 and 1954, Senator Joseph McCarthy made persistent charges that there were "card-carrying Communists" in the State Department. Kennan was not so accused. When President Eisenhower nominated Charles E. Bohlen to succeed Kennan as Ambassador to Russia, Kennan was able to dispell the doubts of several conservative senators in Bohlen's favor.

Philip C. Jessup, John Stewart Service, and John Patton Davies were not so fortunate as to avoid having their careers blighted by unproven charges of having been pro-Communist. Although a distinguished international lawyer whose governmental service began in the days of Elihu Root and was marked by recent successes in the U.N. Security Council, Jessup was smeared and defeated in subcommittee when nominated for a second term in the U.N. Assembly. Service had been a Foreign Service Officer in China, 1943-1944, whose reports on the prospects of the nationalists and Communists warned against the latter's success. In the climate of the Red Scare, these reports were twisted into advocacy of the Communists and made the cause of the successive investigations which hounded him out of the government's employ. Within the State Department, Kennan protested Jessup's and Service's ability, innocence, and previous commendation. But it was to Davies' defense that Kennan came most strongly.

Kennan had more reason to feel responsible for John Patton Davies. The latter had survived harassment by the China Lobby during the late 1940's on alleged grounds (which Kennan vehemently denied) that as a Foreign Service Officer in China, 1942-1944, he had favored the Communists over the nationalists. Davies served under Kennan both at Moscow 1944-1946, and at Washington on the State Department's Policy Planning Staff, 1949-1950. Because the Central Intelligence Agency then was deficient as a spy agency, Kennan and his friend Allen Dulles, who had headed the wartime Office of Strategic Services and was John Foster Dulles's brother, organized "what came later to be referred to as 'a department of dirty tricks.'" To do so needed the Defense Department's agreement, a task which Kennan delegated to Davies. In the process Davies developed hypothetical cases which subsequently were leaked and made to appear as serious proposals. Bound to secrecy, Davies was unable to explain them and Secretary of State John Foster Dulles was willing to sacrifice him to satisfy the anti-Communist crusade.

Kennan welcomed John F. Kennedy's election as President in 1961. The latter several times had written to him in complimentary terms without endorsing his controversial views concerning Germany, disengagement, and nuclear arms. Recognizing that because of these views Acheson, Rusk, or others of the State Department's "establishment" would not ac-cept him as a Presidential adviser on major problems of the cold war, Kennan was gratified to be named Ambassador to Yugoslavia, where he served from 1961 to 1963. The chief issue which arose between the two countries during these years sprang from Americans' confusion of trade with aid and of nonaligned countries with Communist-bloc countries. Suffering hangover from the McCarthy Red Scare, Senator William Proxmire and Representative Wilbur D. Mills amended foreign trade legislation so as to withdraw from "red" Yugoslavia the most favored-nation status which she had enjoyed ever since her grandparent Serbia secured it in 1881. Few in Washington knew or cared that, although Yugoslavia previously had received aid, she had requested its cessation and had paid cash for both food and military supplies for several years. When Kennan was unable to avert this undeserved and also unnecessary blow, he resigned his post and returned to Princeton. He did so with good memories of the Yugoslavs, while fully conscious that as a good Communist, Tito desired Moscow's approval more than Washington's.

Besides illuminating the great problems of the Cold War, Kennan's *Memoirs: 1950-1963* reveal an American who, as a result of being somewhat out of touch with his country, can appraise it more clearly. He laments the hallmarks of our urbanized national life in which he observes such alarming decivilization: the demolition of the well-built houses and manors of 1900-1914, which are most comfortable for him whether in a friend's *dacha* outside Moscow, his Pennsylvania farm, his house on a shady street in Princeton, or in Yugoslavia. Though he is careful to avoid the clever condescension of Aldous Huxley concerning the follies of California, which are, after all, the work of humans too, he fears California as both the fulfillment of McCarthy's prophetic Red Scare and the portent of a twenty-first century "latinized" America—a people of attenuated childhood who will require a stern parental dictator to provide them with romantic heroics in place of a rational political dialogue.

Kennan's *Memoirs: 1950-1963* is to America at mid-century what the *Education of Henry Adams* was to America of 1900-1920. The comparison does not make the future seem inviting.

George Green Shackelford

THE MEMOIRS OF A SURVIVOR

Author: Doris Lessing (1919-   )
Publisher: Alfred A. Knopf (New York). 213 pp. $6.95
Type of work: Novel
Time: The future
Locale: A large city

A dark, futuristic fantasy-fable about three people's struggles to survive in the nightmarish setting of an urban center which has reverted to anarchy and barbarism

Principal characters:

THE NARRATOR, an elderly, genteel woman
EMILY, the child mysteriously left to her guardianship
HUGO, Emily's devoted beast
GERALD, Emily's lover and leader of a commune of children

Memoirs of a Survivor is about the last gasp of a failed civilization. The narrator, an elderly woman, describes the scene from her window; what happens there on the pavement, in her block of flats and around the neighborhood, shows in microcosm a worldwide reversion to barbarism. The narrator herself is genteel, well off, and solitary. Her tone is calm, expository, as she describes the events of "the protracted period of unease and tension before the end." The state of things was such, she says, that normalcy was abnormal; which inversion lends plausibility to the two axes of the story: her guardianship of the girl Emily, and her adventures "beyond the wall."

Emily's arrival is unexpected and unexplained; the little girl appears in her flat, accompanied by a man who says simply, "She's your responsibility," and departs. She brings with her only her clothes and her strange animal Hugo. A pretty, healthy twelve-year-old, she foils the narrator's attempts at friendliness with a bright protective shell of cleverness and politeness. At first she is content to stay indoors with her beast and to view the increasingly anarchic life of the street from the safety of a window. But her body, forced into hothouse bloom by the exigencies of the times, propels her out to mingle with the tribes of young people forming up to migrate into the still-unravished northwest. Her protectress fears that she will depart with one of these bands, but she chooses to stay with her animal, who must remain hidden to keep from being eaten.

Emily attaches herself to the young chieftain Gerald, leader of a band of children. She and Gerald set up housekeeping in an abandoned building and organize the children into a commune, employing considerable ingenuity in gathering and growing food, procuring clean water and other essentials, and defending their encampment. Though spending most of her time looking after her household, Emily still remains true to Hugo and her guardian, spending some hours at the flat each day.

The emergence of the "kids from the Underground" ends this idyl. A gang of very young children emerges from the subway tunnels, where they have been living on rats, and terrorize the district. Gerald persuades his group to take them in, but the kids, utterly wild, cannot grasp the idea of communal responsibility; they snatch food from the mouths of others, spread filth everywhere, tread down the garden, and generally bite the hands that feed them. The commune disbands, Emily returns home, and Gerald, obsessed by a sense of responsibility, stays with the kids from the Underground in hopes of taming and saving them.

By this time the neighborhood is virtually deserted; migrating tribes no longer form up in the vacant lots, the street markets and peddlers have vanished, the air becomes daily more foul. Emily and her protectress live alone with Hugo, waiting for the end. In the flat above lives Gerald, a prisoner of his terrible little charges. One night the kids murder a passerby, haul him upstairs, and eat him; Gerald, unstrung, wanders out into the snow and is rescued by Emily. After that, the four of them huddle together in the dark and cold, waiting.

This outward reality has its correlative "beyond the wall." Just before Emily's arrival, the narrator finds her living room wall becoming transparent, permeable; one day she actually walks through it to find herself in a set of rooms, long unused, which someone, possibly herself, is about to refurbish. She senses "a promise, which did not leave me, no matter how difficult things later became, both in my own life and in these hidden rooms." The rooms behind the wall seem to her to be her true home; the advent of Emily brings her reluctantly back to the actual world. Soon afterward she realizes

that there is a connection between the scenes behind the wall and her life with Emily; further, that these scenes are of two kinds: "personal" and "impersonal." The "personal" experiences have a characteristic atmosphere of tension, of imprisonment and constraint; in them the narrator recognizes Emily as an infant and child, her mother and father, her nurse, her younger brother. In the "impersonal" realm, a feeling of lightness and possibility prevails; though she seldom sees the same rooms twice, and though there are always problems to be solved and work to be done, she feels the near presence and approbation, and later the counsel and guidance, of a mysterious female personage.

The personal scenes reveal the tenor of Emily's childhood. The disliked and disparaged first child of an energetic and self-confident woman, she was made to bear the brunt of her mother's rebellion against maternity. Her infancy had been ruled by the clock, by custom, and by the iron strictures of her parents' characters, her mother's vivid self-absorption backed by her father's guilty neutrality. Her efforts to claim her parents' love time after time met with rebuff, so that the need to prove herself lovable and useful had grown into a passion. Thus the uncritical love of the beast Hugo and the need of Gerald and the commune children touch the deep springs of her character. And not only of Emily's character: in one episode in which a little girl is found playing with her own feces and given a tongue-lashing and a scalding bath, the narrator comes to realize that the child, whose miserable, abandoned weeping penetrates the wall, is both Emily and the hearty, self-sufficient woman who is her mother.

The impersonal realm is small at first, consisting of a finite set of rooms, but gradually expands into a kind of dream-labyrinth. The narrator sees rooms in all stages of disrepair and neglect, sumptuous rooms in which all the furnishings are slightly shopworn, empty rooms ready for repainting, rooms with broken walls and grass growing through the floor; the state of things behind the wall becomes more ruinous as real life outside the flat deteriorates. In each room she notes what needs to be done, sometimes overwhelmed by the work before her, sometimes actually accomplishing it, but always accepting without question her responsibility to cope, and always with a sense of the invisible female presence. "Very strong was the feeling that I did as I was bid and as I must; that I was being taken, was being led, was being shown, was held always in the hollow of a great hand which enclosed my life." Above all, even when things are at their most disordered in the rooms behind the wall, she feels that choice is possible, that one might repair some, or all, or throw everything out and start again. In the personal rooms, on the contrary, the smallest things, the ticks of the clock, have been elevated into law.

As time passes, the wall seems to thin, so that the narrator feels moods and urgencies from beyond it streaming through into real life. She senses a ripening, a coming to terms. Denned up with the two young people and the faithful beast, in the cold and dark at the end of the world, she waits, calm. One morning the wall opens, the hungered-for Presence beckons, and the four walk through, transfigured, into the future.

A key to this dreamlike and enigmatic climax is the set of virtues clustered under the heading of responsibility. Characters and groups stand or fall by whether or not they possess a sense of responsibility: the narrator puts aside her explorations behind the wall to accept guardianship of Emily; Gerald and Emily hold the commune together by accepting responsibility for the well-being of all. Conversely, the tribes of youths seem to have relinquished individual responsibility; the kids from the Underground seem never to have learned it. It is her sense of responsibility for the upkeep of the rooms, her desire to comfort and nurture the neglected child, that the narrator feels is most approved by the Presence behind the wall. Emily stays with Hugo because "she could not leave him without harm to herself." About the kids from the Underground, Gerald feels that "to give them up was to abandon . . . the best part of himself." Responsibility, in short, is the saving virtue, the key to the future.

But what is the future? To what place of peace and rest is this history related? Two powerful images suggest an answer. The first occurs as a scene behind the wall: a room in which a dozen people stand gazing down at a patterned carpet. The pattern is empty of color, without force; from time to time, someone applies a bit of cloth to it which fits exactly, causing that part of the carpet to come alive, at which the other people express relief and quiet pleasure. The narrator enters the room; she too extracts a piece from a jumble of rags, fits it into place, and then moves on. Unable to find this room later, she nonetheless retains a sense that the activity there continues, that its importance is enormous, not only to those engaged in it but to everyone. The second image occurs twice, and is frequently referred to: the egg as a metaphor for potential, hatching as a breaking down of constraints and imprisoning certainties. When the narrator first becomes aware of sounds from beyond the wall she puts her hand on it and feels it pulsing like an egg about to hatch. A wall that she scrubs down and paints finely reminds her of "a cleaned-out eggshell." At one point she sees Emily and her parents admiring a gigantic egg on a wide green lawn; at the end she sees the egg, blackened and pitted, suddenly open to reveal the life-metaphor, the room of the unfinished carpet. Then that too fades, leaving only the sought-for She, the apotheosis of love and care, leading onward "as the last walls dissolved."

Jan Kennedy Foster

MEMOIRS OF AN EX-PROM QUEEN

Author: Alix Kates Shulman (1932-   )
Publisher: Alfred A. Knopf (New York). 274 pp. $6.95
Type of work: Novel
Time: The present
Locale: Ohio, Germany, Spain, Italy, New York

A bitter, amusing, and unforgettable indictment of the role the American female is required to play

Principal characters:
SASHA DAVIS, the protagonist, an American woman
FRANKLIN RAYBEL, history professor and her first husband
DONALD ALPORT, her philosophy instructor and first encounter with "love"
ROXANNE DU BOIS, her best friend and fellow sufferer
WILLIAM BURKE, her second husband, a businessman, and father of her children

Tormented heroines unhappy with the female lot have long been a staple of literature, but perhaps the 1970's will be cited as the decade when that torment became respectable and indeed almost mandatory. In the past, a woman was expected to be satisfied with the role in which nature and society had cast her; those who refused contentment were advised to pray, to have a baby, and/or "to get hold of themselves." Although literary ladies might toy with ideas of liberation and express tentative resentment or rebellion, those who did not repent and return to standard paths were certain to find disaster, usually in the form of suicide. But books such as Alix Kates Shulman's *Memoirs of an Ex-Prom Queen,* its sardonic title revealing the brilliant insight it contains, put us on notice that today's female, insistently and often unpleasantly screaming for recognition of the injustice she feels envelops her, declines to admit she is mistaken.

The author, whose first published work was a section of this novel appearing in the feminist journal *Aphra* in 1969, is herself married and the mother of two. Attractive and young, she has also published three books for children and a biography and collected speeches of Emma Goldman, the Russian-born American anarchist who died in 1940.

Sasha Davis, the "queen," is also somewhat of an anarchist although as yet unannounced. Irritating, selfish, amusingly bitter, rationally irrational, as a human being she is very much a failure. Yet, the author asks, what chance do women really have to be human beings? Fate has spoken, and they can be slaves or saboteurs. Any intermediate course is impossible. We might judge harshly a male embodying Sasha's embellishments, but Sasha is not simply A Character but rather Woman, faced with inescapable and monstrous paradoxes. Murder on the battlefield is not viewed the same as murder on the streets.

A need to be told, to be retold, to be constantly told that she is beautiful is the focus of Sasha's agony. "My mother wanting happiness for me, gave me braces and dancing lessons. My father, valuing learning and success, gave me his library of Little Leather Books." Poor father. Straight teeth and a smooth dance step are much more meaningful in Sasha's society of sororities and sex. Beauty, she soon learns, is a woman's only valuable asset, and it is a fleeting one at that.

At the age of fifteen, Sasha enjoys her only perfect moment of happiness, a brief meshing of glory and total assurance of her beauty. Laugh if you will, but her coronation as Prom Queen provides that perfection. But alas, fifteen turns to sixteen, and sixteen to twenty-five. "Make me Queen and I'll never ask for anything more," she had prayed. Someone kept His side of the bargain. Her life, if one defines the term to mean a time of freedom, lasted one shiny evening aswirl with net and perfume and corsages. Unfortunately, the corpse lived on.

"The evidence suggests that nature is probably unbalanced, that ten is no truer than four, that reason does not prevail. Accordingly, doubt is my motto," Sasha tells us. The Hit Parade, *Seventeen* magazine, and "Questions Girls Ask" prepare her for their version of love. ("Remember it's just as easy to love a rich man as a poor one.") She knows that the only way to control her future is through the right man, that she must exert all her efforts to remain in the marriage market, to make herself available and desirable. She is an expert in the game, but not at handling the Doubt, which may be summarized in the phrase of a popular song: "Is this all there is?"

She marries twice, has a serious affair, and a total of twenty-five lovers by her birthday of the same number, yet the Doubt remains. Her first husband admires her because she is lovely and smart; she can aid him in his career. Her own studies in philosophy are an arty sideline he permits her to have, myopically missing the furious competition in which she views them as engaged. He cannot imagine that she loathes him; in order to effect a split she must take a lover and taunt him with the fact, thus giving *him* a reason to leave *her*. Her simple hatred he cannot perceive. He expects that his slave will not only endure but indeed revel in her bondage.

All the men in the book are equally dense versions of the master. Her father, teasing her about a pimple and laughing at her fury; her professor, easily seduced by a student who hungrily yearns to understand Truth, Justice, Beauty; her second husband, lying and shouting to escape the Babyland they have built together— none is a monster, yet all do monstrous damage to Sasha. Each betrays the offering she makes by ignoring her cries for an answer to the Doubt.

Many readers will feel that the book is hardly serious. They will see Sasha as a ridiculous and bitchy creature who deserves much of her pain, who seemingly has all that any woman should seek, who, to be polite about it, ought to shut up and sit down. Yet the author, by choosing as her spokesman a woman who is not ugly or old or in need of objective, external changes, forcefully illuminates the basic plight of the female.

She seems to assert: If a woman who has everything has nothing, just what do the rest of us have?

The book's conclusion poignantly pictures how deadly womanhood really is. Hating herself, Sasha is suddenly and frantically committed to Dr. Spock and baby food and potties. "But see what the tiniest baby will do to the woman. Stretching her belly and waist into the ghastliest shapes before it even emerges from the womb. . . . Producing spots at the hairline, dark hairs down her midline, bleeding gums, stretch marks

. . . and that's only the beginning. In time comes the ugly crease in the brow between the eyes hewn by incessant anxiety and sporadic rage, the rasp in the voice, the knot in the gut, the regret." Her gentle, once-loving husband, angered by her frame of mind, sours. She enters a land he has helped to create yet cannot or will not inhabit, a land she cannot escape. Once again the Doubt is foremost, and at the end, despite Sasha's apparent determination to seek an answer, we know that for her the future, as the past, is bleak.

Judith Bolch

THE MEMOIRS OF FIELD-MARSHAL
THE VISCOUNT MONTGOMERY OF ALAMEIN, K.G.

Author: Bernard Law, Viscount Montgomery of Alamein (1887-1976)
Publisher: The World Publishing Company (Cleveland and New York). Illustrated.
  508 pp. $6.00
Type of work: Autobiography
Time: 1887-1958
Locale: England, France, Palestine, Africa

An account of his life and career written by Great Britain's outstanding general officer during World War II and its postwar Chief of the Imperial General Staff

Principal personages:
> FIELD MARSHAL THE VISCOUNT MONTGOMERY, hero of El Alamein
> SIR WINSTON CHURCHILL, wartime Prime Minister of England
> GENERAL DWIGHT D. EISENHOWER, Supreme Allied Commander in Europe
> GENERAL OMAR BRADLEY, USA
> CLEMENT ATLEE, Prime Minister of England after World War II

Since the end of World War II many generals have written books about their participation in that conflict and have reviewed the events of that war as they saw and experienced them. Field Marshal Montgomery's *Memoirs* proves to be one of the most interesting and outspoken books, just as the man himself was one of the most interesting and outspoken, if flamboyant and controversial, figures of World War II.

Quite obviously Montgomery believes his service during and after the great war the important part of his life. Of thirty-three chapters in his book, only three deal with his life prior to the outbreak of war in 1939: his London childhood in "an average Victorian family," St. Paul's School, Sandhurst, service in France during World War I, duty in India, Palestine, and Egypt between wars. While this fact may be disappointing to a reader who would know more about the experiences which created the great military leader, it is understandable that Montgomery should emphasize his later career. His *Memoirs* show him to be a man of the moment, a man who looks at the present and future rather than to the past, and it is undoubtedly this attitude which helped him become a great military commander. A sure historical perspective and a backward orientation are fine attributes in a scholar and historian, but they are not the qualities which produce great fighting generals. As Montgomery himself says, it was the backward look which caused Great Britain's military leaders to prepare during the 1930's to fight the same kind of war they had fought in 1914-1918. The greatness of Montgomery may well be rooted in the fact that he, a student of current warfare and a confident leader, was able to view the strategic pattern of war as it was being fought in the 1940's and to do battle with the Germans in terms of the strategy, tactics, organization, and paraphernalia of the times.

As he portrays himself, Montgomery is a thoroughgoing professional soldier, one who devotes his life to his profession and his country, studying always to keep abreast of military and political events with which he may have to deal, and contributing his best thinking and leadership to his command and country whenever and wherever he can. In the concluding chapters of his book Montgomery devotes himself to the world situation as he sees it today, and readers will probably agree that what he writes is both timely and worth consideration, not the outdated mutterings of a retired and senile old man, even though Montgomery has passed his seventieth year.

Montgomery sees the future of the world to be still in the hands of the people of Western Europe, if they can grow in unity. The great block to unity, as he sees it, is the tendency for the national groups to want self-sufficiency in defense, instead of being willing to participate in an international alliance for mutual aid and protection. A second deterrent to unity, according to Montgomery, is that the nations of Europe want peace above all. The author's own answer to this attitude is that the real need is for freedom within the law and that peace is a by-product: "A nation which worked for these things, and was prepared [in the 1940's and 1950's] to risk war to defend the Western way of life would have peace. What was the use of peace if you lost your soul to Communism?" In addition, Montgomery believes that the general officers of the nations of continental Europe, having spent the years of World War II in London or in German prison camps, are unprepared to produce the kind of forces suitable for modern warfare. Not having known from personal experience in leadership the demands of modern war, they cannot understand the complexity of world conflict in our time; such is Montgomery's conclusion.

Of vast interest coming from so successful a general as Montgomery is his doctrine of command, which is set forth in a chapter of its own, as well as the comment in pertinent passages dealing with the conduct of his operations in Northern Africa, Italy, and Western Europe, during the period between 1942 and 1946. As one might expect from a man of the field marshal's temperament, he believes firmly in the need for a single military leader who creates a plan and makes decisions. As he puts it, "The matter of 'decision' is vital. The modern tendency is to avoid making decisions and to procrastinate in the hope that things will come out all right in the wash. The only policy for the military leader is decision in action and calmness in the crisis: no bad doctrine for the political leader either. I hold the view that the leader must know what he himself wants. He must see his objective clearly and then strive to attain it; he must let everyone else know what he wants and what are the basic fundamentals of his policy. He must, in fact, give firm guidance and a clear lead. It is necessary for him to create what I would call 'atmosphere,' and in that atmosphere his subordinate commanders will live and work."

Being a magnetic and strong personality himself, Montgomery advocates, both openly and implicitly, the personal touch in leadership, whether for civilians or the military. His wearing such an unusual piece of headgear as his famous beret with two emblems during World War II he accounts for as being part of his conscious effort to let his troops know who he was and to acquire a distinct personality for them to recognize. Another way in which he let his troops know him was to walk down the ranks during parade while the men stood at ease, free to look at him as he looked at them. Prior to the Normandy invasion of 1944 he had walked the ranks before hundreds of thousands of men. He also frequently sent messages to his troops. He sums up his interest in his men as follows:

> The raw material with which the general has to deal is men. The same is true in civil life. Managers of large industrial concerns have not always seemed to me to have understood this point; they think of their raw material as iron ore, or cotton, or rubber—not men but commodities. In conversation with them I have disagreed and insisted that their basic raw material is *men*. Many generals have also not fully grasped this vital matter, nor understood its full implications, and that is one reason why some have failed.

In considering men, Montgomery deals with generals as well as private soldiers. He speaks clearly in these matters, and some famous military leaders must be uneasy, even embarrassed, as they read his evaluations. Not that Montgomery offers his evaluations carelessly; he has obviously given what he says careful thought over many years. Even the men he most admires and reveres as his friends —President Dwight D. Eisenhower and Sir Winston Churchill—have their activities reviewed critically.

Somewhat more difficult to accept are Montgomery's conclusions on the conduct of the war to defeat the Nazis. He maintains that the European phase of the war could have been finished by Christmas, 1944, and should have been, if the overall Allied strategy had been to follow plans he suggested to the Supreme Commander at various times. The essential point in Montgomery's case is that a single thrust, his own strategic doctrine, would have done the task more effectively than the "several-front" strategy which actually was followed. Such an event as the Battle of the Bulge, in which Montgomery acquitted himself admirably, he claims need never have taken place if the Allies had kept the Germans off balance and had themselves selected the Nazis' weak point for a single attack. One can only say, of course, that the empirical evidence will never be available for Montgomery's case, since his plan was not used. The analogy he draws between the Western Front and the war as he fought it in the African desert is obviously too insufficient to be regarded as proof.

The epigraph to Montgomery's *Memoirs* is taken from the Book of Job: "Yet man is born unto trouble, as the sparks fly upward." By this quotation the author admits that his comments, his actions, and his very personality have often been controversial; however, he makes no apology. He offers in explanation the view that, if he has been controversial and a source of irritation to others, the reason is that his conduct has been based on his inward convictions, his duty, and his conscience; that he has not sought in his life, professional or private, to win the approval of others or to regard the opinions of mankind as a sufficient criterion for conduct. Of his book he says, "I have not attempted to answer my critics but rather to tell the story of my long and enjoyable military life as I see it, and as simply as possible. Some of my comrades-in-arms of the Second World War have told their story about those days; this is mine."

MEMOIRS OF HECATE COUNTY

Author: Edmund Wilson (1895-1972)
Publisher: L. C. Page and Company (Boston). 447 pp. $6.00
Type of work: Short stories
Time: Mid-1920's-early 1940's
Locale: Hecate County, in American Suburbia

Six short stories of varying lengths present a sociological and philosophic picture of American life within a moral limbo that is both fantastic and real

> *Principal characters:*
> THE NARRATOR, a critic and art historian
> ASA M. STRYKER, a manufacturer of turtle soup
> CLARENCE LATOUCHE, an advertising copywriter
> ELLEN TERHUNE, a psychoneurotic musician
> WILBUR FLICK, a wealthy fellow traveler
> IMOGENE LOOMIS, a married woman loved by the Narrator
> ANNA LENIHAN, a dance-hall hostess
> JO GATES, the Narrator's mistress
> WARREN MILHOLLAND, a book-club executive
> JIM MILHOLLAND, his brother, an editor
> SPIKE MILHOLLAND, a literary opportunist and broadcaster
> MR. BLACKBURN, a man of mysterious background
> KATE BLACKBURN, his wife
> SI BANKS, the Narrator's friend

Censorship has been having a hard time of it lately. First there was *Lolita*, by Vladimir Nabokov, which raised almost as great a storm without the use of four-letter words as *Lady Chatterley's Lover* did with them. No sooner had the sound and fury over D. H. Lawrence's novel begun to subside than Edmund Wilson's *Memoirs of Hecate County* reappeared, and the tumult of praise and protest seemed about to begin all over again. But by that time frustration or inertia may have set in. At any rate the book has been allowed to make its way without legal hindrance in every part of the country except New York state, where it is still banned under the decision handed down in 1946 by the Court of Special Sessions of New York.

The history of *Memoirs of Hecate County* is surely one of the most complicated in the records of American publishing. The book first appeared in March, 1946, was well reviewed, and sold about sixty thousand copies. Because it contained several frankly clinical scenes of sexual relations between men and women, the New York Society for the Suppression of Vice brought action against the publisher, Doubleday and Company. Late in 1946 the Court of Special Sessions, by a 2-1 decision, found the book obscene and fined the publisher $1,000. Appeals from this conviction finally brought the case to the Supreme Court, which in 1948 left the lower court decision standing by a 4-4 split. (Justice Felix Frankfurter had disqualified himself because he had previously discussed the book with Mr. Wilson.) With the book banned in New York, Doubleday decided to withdraw it completely, and the plates were destroyed.

The book was then out of print until 1950, when it was published in England and booksellers, including those in New York, began to import copies from abroad. Now it has been reissued and is legally for sale in the country at large. The situation, however, is this: It has been published in Boston, where books were once banned at the drop of an asterisk, by a company which is a subsidiary of Farrar, Straus, and Cudahy, a New York publishing house. To add to the confusion, the book was printed in Pennsylvania and is being distributed from New Jersey. Literary merit aside, the circumstances surrounding its withdrawal and reappearance are in themselves enough to create interest in Edmund Wilson's picture of suburbia by the sea.

Works of fiction which achieve their initial success in an atmosphere of notoriety have a rather unfortunate habit of taking on a cold and mortuary air by the time they emerge once more in a reprint edition. (Witness *Lady Chatterley's Lover*, sections of which now read like a period piece stuffed with ideas and attitudes of the 1920's.) The fact that on second reading *Memoirs of Hecate County* seems neither dulled by the literary license of the past decade nor staled by time is due entirely to qualities which lift this cycle of stories above the books that titillate or shock: the intelligently observant point of view that functions throughout and the substratum of moral seriousness revealed by the manner in which the tales face up to the problems of evil in our time.

In this new edition a brief prefatory note by the author calls attention to the revised text. The changes are minor, however, more of manner than of substance. An altered phrase here, a more explicit word in context, or the reshaping of the turn of a sentence has in a number of instances given greater clarity and firmness to Mr. Wilson's prose. In larger outline, however, the six stories—the effect is somewhat that of a novel arranged in episodes—remain what they were in the beginning, an altogether unsparing examination of suburban America's manners and morals.

Like William Faulkner's Yoknapatawpha setting, Hecate County has its recognizable counterparts in time and space. Located an hour or two outside New York, it apparently combines parts of Westchester and Fairfield counties with some features of several Long Island Sound communities thrown in for good measure. On Mr. Wilson's map of a moral universe, however, it is the suburban limbo of professional middle-class Americans who talk brightly, read widely, often drink to excess, usually love unwisely, and make money or don't, all without realizing that they are characters in a drama of conflict between good and evil as stylized as any medieval morality play. Two of the stories incorporate the Manichean belief in the physical presence of evil, and in one the devil himself, or a man who is assumed to be the devil, delivers a twelve-page harangue, in archaic French, on his difficulties in the modern world. If Mr. Wilson has borrowed traits from real personalities, a book club, a radio network, or a publishing house, he has done so with imagination and subtlety, and adapted them skillfully to his purposes.

The stories are related in that all are told through the "I" of a single narrator who suffers the isolation of the intellectual in a world of breezy opportunism and lapsed standards of private and public morality. In the course of these tales he follows a course of deterioration in his own life; the realization of what is happening around him lends significance to his own ineffectuality and makes him a shrewd observer of the social strivings, moral laxity, and economic strategies of his neighbors.

"The Man Who Shot Snapping Turtles," the opening story, creates the moral atmosphere for a great deal that follows in this book. Asa M. Stryker, a well-to-do man of uncertain antecedents, hates the snapping turtles that destroy the young of wild ducks nesting near a pond on his estate. "If God has created the mallard," he declares, "a thing of beauty and grace, how can He allow these filthy mud-turtles to prey upon his handiwork and destroy it? . . . But if the Evil triumphs there it may triumph everywhere, and we must fight it with every weapon in our power." His concern for the innocent birds finally leads him to drive them away. Instead, he allows the turtles to breed, acquires more, and eventually makes a small fortune selling canned Deep South Snapper Soup. In the end, convinced that Mr. Stryker himself has become the embodiment of malevolence and evil, an advertising writer shoots him. We have been reading a Manichean fable.

"Ellen Terhune" is a ghost story told with Jamesian overtones. This story carries the writer backward in time through the life of a woman musician and composer who seems to be going insane. Eventually he encounters Ellen's mother as an unmarried girl, but their conversation is broken in on as Ellen, in the next room, plays the sonata on which she has been working. But when he tries to find Ellen, to tell her how good her composition is, the music room is empty; the woman, as he learns later, had died suddenly that same afternoon in a New York hotel. "Glimpses of Wilbur Flick," which deals with a wealthy tool of Communist exploitation, appears in some ways a more meaningful story today than it did when it first appeared. The claim cannot be made for "The Princess with the Golden Hair," the longest story in the book. The account of the narrator's frustrating love affair with one woman, his sensual encounters with another, and his tenuous relations with a third, this story is still good as a story of passion metamorphosed into mere sensation, and it makes its point neatly. But to a public insulated by the frankness of much modern writing, it now appears rather old-fashioned and drably clinical in its dissection of the anatomy of man's emotions and physical desires. "The Milhollands and Their Damned Soul" is satire verging on burlesque in its picture of life on publishers' row and among the literary racketeers. "Mr. and Mrs. Blackburn at Home" presents the devil in his latest incarnation. His grievance is that personal sin has been replaced by the impersonal cruelty of modern society; his hope is to get a revival movement started in order to snare some truly damned souls. The story is somewhat reminiscent of *The Screwtape Letters*, by C. S. Lewis. From that confrontation of evil the narrator goes off to the Southwest with his mistress:

> So still we turned West, as our fathers had done, for the new life we could still hope to find—so we sought to regain the new world which seemed

still to be just at hand, with its wild forest trails and fresh waters, but from which we now found ourselves divided by a pane of invisible glass. It was not really new country any more; it was the old country: we had passed it in history; and the loves and achievements of our youth had all taken place somewhere else. . . . We were to find the fears and suffocations, the drugged energies of Hecate County; I had packed my bad nights with my baggage. . . .

Memoirs of Hecate County is fiction, but its author is also a literary critic, a social historian, and an analyst of manners and morals. For this reason the book is of a piece with the rest of his writing, detached yet keenly observant, reflective in its awareness of effects and causes. "Civilized writing" is a rare term to apply to contemporary fiction, but in this case it comprehensively describes Mr. Wilson's tales of a mythical county where the devil gives cocktail parties for suburbanites and over whose landscape presides Hecate, the goddess of witchcraft and of Circe-like women who bewitch men.

Sources for Further Study

Criticism:

Mizener, Arthur. "Edmund Wilson's New Republic," in *New Republic.* May 9, 1970, pp. 28-30. A discussion of Wilson's thought which illustrates his view of the intellectual as prophet in *Memoirs of Hecate County.*

Reviews:

Nation. CLXII, March 30, 1946, p. 379. 1,550 words.

New York Times. March 31, 1946, p. 7. 1,300 words.

Saturday Review of Literature. XXIX, March 23, 1946, p. 22. 1,100 words.

Time. XLVII, March 25, 1946, p. 102. 1,050 words.

Weekly Book Review. March 10, 1946, p. 3. 1,200 words.

and agony of rejection of a young man:

> If I could go to her and prove by putting my hand into the fire till I had burned it badly, would not that make her understand that devotion like mine should [not] be lightly thrown away? Often as I went to see her I had that thought in mind, and I do not think it was fear of pain that prevented me, but fear of being mad. I wondered at moments if I was not really mad.

The sense of exultation he feels at sharing reveries and dreams with Maud is eroded as she becomes more heavily involved with local politics, like amnesty for Irish political prisoners, a monument for Wolfe Tone in Dublin, and the Jubilee Riots. His pride in her ability to move a crowd wars with his jealousy at having to share her. Her reason, and a very strange reason it is, for the widening gulf between the two is revealed in the very last episode of the "Autobiography." The woman whom Yeats has idealized reveals her past: At nineteen, she became the mistress of Millevoye, editor of *La Patrie,* by whom she had an illegitimate child. When this child died, Maud, who believed sexual love was only justified by children, returned to Millevoye to conceive another child. Although Yeats still offers her marriage after this confession, she replied "I have a horror and terror of physical love." When Yeats is urged by his friends to continue his pursuit, he can only reply: "No, I am too exhausted; I can do no more." The irony, and the touch of pathos, is deliberate. For Yeats will try again and the inscrutable Maud will marry another.

Another thread in the first draft, and perhaps the least accessible and understandable to the contemporary reader, is Yeats's spiritualism. "I sought passion, religious passion above all, as the greatest good of life, and I always cherished the secret hope of some mysterious initiation." Yeats and his company of friends rely heavily upon the symbolism of dreams and emanations through which the other world reveals its existence to the sensitively attuned. Lengthy descriptions of these trances and visions abound, and each occurrence is accompanied by a corresponding interpretation, in so far as this is possible. Yeats is helped considerably in these instances by hindsight, and the reader feels here more strongly than elsewhere the mature mind working with the material of youth.

The final locus is literature, and Yeats believed that "the greatest kind of literature is passion." His disappointment with the political realm, his sadness over Maud Gonne, and the symbolic evocations of spiritualism are all united in this one, which is the greatest passion. He speaks of the difficulty in surviving physically as a writer, of the need for making money editing, of the triviality of the concerns of the middle class, and of the impact of such people as Walter Pater, Arthur Symons, and John Synge on his literary development. One can trace faintly the formulation of certain literary ideals as he, Synge, and Lady Gregory struggle to establish an Irish Literary Theatre and as he founds the Rhymers Club. This first draft of the "Autobiography," then, reveals those aspects of Yeats's early life which interweave with each other to make the man and the mask more complicated.

The "Journal" has no such series of unifying threads. In fact, Yeats's expressed desire is:

> To keep these notes natural and useful to me in my life I must keep one note from leading on to another. To do that is to surrender oneself to literature. Every note must first have come as a casual thought, then it will be my life.

These daily jottings primarily cover the years from 1908-1910, although there are sporadic entries as late as 1930. Segments from this work were published separately as "Estrangement" and "The Death of Synge," although the remaining entries have not been published previously. While the "Autobiography" concentrates on a sweep of personalities, the "Journal" details the private anguish of a man in crisis, searching for his own essence. One of the testing episodes is a wryly comic one, a departure in a book which has little humor. Edmund Gosse attempts to secure a Civil List pension for Yeats, through the mediation of Lady Gregory. After Gosse wrote her an apparently unmotivated insulting letter, Yeats countered, breaking off relations, although he badly needed the money. The shrewd Lady Gregory did not post Yeats's letter, and so he received the pension, although he quarreled with his conscience about it.

The various entries adumbrate further how the poet's mind works as he presents poetic and philosophic theories, ideas for poems, and revisions of the poems. One motif is his preoccupation with grasping and defining the essence of the mask and

relating it to literary definitions of tragedy and comedy. This becomes one of his primary poetic devices and it eventually is part of his complex work, *A Vision*.

Here Yeats discusses quite explicitly the disappointment in things Irish, which is only an implicit undercurrent in the "Autobiography." The *Playboy* riots, the heavy censorship of the Catholic Church, and the repression of the creative arts lead Yeats to conclude with more than a touch of bitterness:

> In our age it is impossible to create, as I had dreamed, an heroic and passionate conception of life worthy of the study of men elsewhere and at other times, and to make that conception the special dream of the Irish people . . . Instead, [they] cry out for stones and vapour, pedantry and hysteria, rhetoric and sentiment.

This disappointment with the "ill breeding" of the Irish leads Yeats towards increasingly aristocratic notions of class, refinement, elegance, and beauty. He sees himself and John Synge as caught in the middle of this discovery. As founders of the Abbey Theatre, they had hoped to educate and to inculcate appreciation in all levels of society. The illness and death of Synge, which occurred in the midst of these outbreaks, only further alienated Yeats.

The most personal *leitmotif* consists of the terse entries dealing with Yeats's physical problems; the bouts of nervousness resulting in breakdowns, the fits of depression, the incapacitating headaches, and the enervating periods of apathy all signify a certain physical and psychological frailty beneath the externally very busy, creative, and productive writer. "I cry out continually against my life!" encapsulates the feeling of these entries.

Memoirs, then, brings the reader nearer to William Butler Yeats, stripped of the poses and gestures which characterize his later, more public writings. The book will hardly alter anyone's conception of Yeats, but it does add details which broaden and elaborate the portrait of the man and of his associates. The intimate conversations with Maud Gonne, which reveal the complexity of the woman, his relationship with Mrs. Shakespear, an account of his sexual passions, details on the Jubilee Riots of 1897, the Wolfe Tone asociation, and the Rhymers Club are all new pieces of information. Although there is something rather curiously modern about our desire to know the intimate details of a great man's life, we can conclude, with Yeats, that "truths are necessary."

Lori Hall Burghardt

Sources for Further Study

Reviews:

Christian Science Monitor. May 9, 1973, p. 13. 800 words.

New Statesman. LXXXV, January 12, 1973, p. 54. 2,000 words.

New York Review of Books. XX, December 13, 1973, p. 43. 300 words.

New York Times Book Review. April 29, 1973, p. 2. 2,550 words.

Times Literary Supplement. January 19, 1973, p. 53. 1,150 words.

MEMORIES OF A CATHOLIC GIRLHOOD

Author: Mary McCarthy (1912–   )
Publisher: Harcourt, Brace and Company (New York). 245 pp. $3.95
Type of work: Autobiographical sketches
Time: 1912–1930
Locale: Seattle and Minneapolis

A series of candid reminiscences of childhood and girlhood by one of the least
sentimental writers of our time

Principal characters:
MARY McCARTHY, the author
UNCLE MYERS, her brutal guardian
AUNT MARGARET, her great aunt, Uncle Myers' wife
LIZZIE SHERIDAN McCARTHY, her Catholic grandmother
HAROLD PRESTON, her Protestant grandfather
AUGUSTA MORGANSTERN PRESTON, her Jewish grandmother
MISS GOWRIE, a Latin teacher

Memories of a Catholic Girlhood is a beautifully written book. The author's style is precise, witty, and literate, and the sentences seem to have been finished, almost perfected, with the greatest care and skill. Mary McCarthy is primarily interested in character, however. Her attitude is one of detachment; she observes people carefully and presents them as she sees them, honestly, without sentimentality, and usually without sympathy. Her fiction has been condemned for its heartlessness. In *Memories of a Catholic Girlhood* there are portraits of people she obviously loved and admired greatly, her mother's parents, her rigidly uncompromising Latin teacher. But even in this book it is obvious that she can much more easily discern the faults in people she loved than the virtues in people she hated.

Of the nine chapters in *Memories of a Catholic Girlhood,* six appeared originally in *The New Yorker* and one in *Harper's Bazaar.* The arrangement is chronological and each chapter but the last is followed by a few pages of explanation in which the author states

exactly how much she is certain really happened as described, how much may have been distorted, and how much she has discovered later to have been false.

The first chapter is primarily an introduction. The author begins by explaining that her memoirs are as accurate as her memory. No character or incident is purely invented, though certain details—those of conversations, for example—are of necessity fictional. She describes, rather briefly, her family background and the happy life she and her three brothers led with their carefree, handsome parents who died during the flu epidemic of 1918.

The two chapters which follow are perhaps the most arresting in the book, probably because evil is more fascinating than mere human normality. When the four children were orphaned, Mary, the eldest, was only six. Their father's rich parents allotted a generous sum of money for their support and placed them under the care of a great-aunt and her husband. Uncle Myers, who apparently embezzled the money intended for the children, was as inhuman a character as can be imagined; his wife, Aunt Margaret, was completely subservient to him. The children were beaten regularly, often without reason. On one occasion, for example, Uncle Myers beat Mary severely for winning an essay contest, to prevent her becoming "stuck-up." Playmates were forbidden, as was almost all reading. The food was wretched. "Aunt Margaret managed to approximate, on a small scale, the conditions prevailing in the orphan asylums we four children were always dreaming of being let into." On Saturdays and Sundays they were forced to stay outside three hours in the morning and three in the afternoon; in temperatures of twenty-four below zero they could only stand beating on the windows, vainly begging to be let in. The beautiful toys sent by their mother's parents were "too good for them" and were put away to be brought out only when representatives of the Preston family came to call.

Mary McCarthy is as harsh in her condemnation of her grandmother McCarthy. This "cold, grudging, disputatious old woman," having arranged that Margaret and Myers take the children, never paid them a visit. She shut her eyes to their sufferings and shared in the general opinion that "it was a generous impulse that kept us in the family at all." The children, regarding wealth as equivalent to bounty, reserved their hatred for their guardians and looked on their grandmother with the gratitude she expected.

The children were finally rescued by the intervention of their Protestant grandfather from Seattle. He took charge of Mary, and her brothers were placed in the care of younger and more agreeable members of the McCarthy family. Mary, now her grandfather Preston's legal ward, attended school at the Convent of the Sacred Heart. Immediately she fell victim to a group of unattractive, unwanted girls; she seemed doomed to be one of them. Determined to be recognized by the popular girls, she hit on the attention-getting scheme of losing her faith. Very ostentatiously, she set about it. The entire convent was aroused. The Mother Superior arranged conferences wtih two Jesuit priests. Mary knew she would have to have atheistic arguments, but since she could not gain access to such literature in the convent, she was forced to think up arguments of her own. She presented them to the priests, in turn, expecting proof in contradiction. The answers, besides repetition of arguments she had found unsatisfactory already, were always the same: she was too young to understand such matters; she must have faith. Her pride offended, she argued with new feeling, and gradually her doubts became real. Before the end of the first interview she knew that she doubted the existence of God.

Her original plan had worked; the whole convent was concerned; one of the most popular girls had invited her home. Mary tried hard to regain her faith, if only as a public duty, but found it impossible. The only thing left for her to do was to simulate a conversion.

From that time on, Mary's life in the convent became a mass of pretenses. She persuaded her grandparents to transfer her to the public high school, where she spent a year following sports events and making bad grades. Finally her grandparents determined to send her to a private boarding school. There she fell in love with Caesar and was instrumental in reviving the Latin Club play, partly because of her affection for the rigid and much-disliked Miss Gowrie, a Latin teacher brilliantly characterized.

Though Mary was not allowed to have dates until her college years, she was permitted to visit two school friends in Montana. Expecting a prosperous resort town, gay dances, and college boys as dates, she found an ugly, dusty town and only one unmarried boy, claimed by one of her hostesses. The wife of Mary's date was away. They drank enormously and stayed out almost all night. Mary was continually passing out; only her youth—she was fifteen—saved her virginity. She went home, considerably wiser and almost glad that she still had, officially, three more years of childhood to serve.

The book concludes with a long and excellent study of Mary's Jewish grandmother, Augusta Morganstern Preston, a beautiful, rather prosaic, and very enigmatic lady. The characterization is perhaps best illustrated by a quotation:

> She was lonely. That was the thing that made her seem so garish and caused people to turn their heads when she went by. Loneliness is a garish quality, and my grandmother's wardrobe and elaborate toilette appeared flamboyant because they emphasized her isolation. An old woman trying to look young is a common enough sight, but my grandmother was something stranger and sadder—a hermit all dressed up for a gala, a recluse on stubborn parade. Tagging along, even as a little girl, I was half conscious of the bizarre figure my grandmother cut, and if I had not known her, my imagination might have woven some story around her for a school composition—the holocaust, at the very least, of all her nearest and dearest, her husband gone to prison, her children branded as traitors. . . .

MEN DIE

Author: H. L. Humes (1926-   )
Publisher: Random House (New York). 184 pp. $3.50
Type of work: Novel
Time: 1941
Locale: An island in the Caribbean; Washington, D.C. and its environs

A taut novel dealing with the explosion of a naval ammunition depot and the consequences of this event in the lives of a man and a woman

> *Principal characters:*
> LIEUTENANT (J.G.) TURNER SULGRAVE, USNR
> LIEUTENANT BENJAMIN DOLFUS, his friend
> COMMANDER BONUSO SEVERN HAKE, their superior officer
> VANESSA HAKE, the commander's wife

Men Die is a terse little title for a book that is correspondingly compact. The author's second novel, it contrasts sharply with his first, which was long (over seven hundred pages) and leisurely of pace, centering about an American who had been involved with the French Resistance during World War II. This first novel by Humes, titled *The Underground City*, called forth critical comparison with the first efforts of James Jones and Norman Mailer—an effect not altogether strange, since all three writers had begun their careers with ambitious, full-bodied narratives which dealt with war or the military life. Nevertheless, such a comparison had to be a superficial one. Even in his first novel, Humes exhibited a higher boiling point than Jones and Mailer and a less noticeable affinity for bawdiness. His indictments of war and a war-torn world were also less high-pitched though they did not lack in seriousness and intensity.

Men Die quickly reveals that its author is not a one-shot novelist; it also reveals a literary change of pace almost startling in its abruptness. Less than two hundred pages in length, the book uses a style which is swift and incisive and a focus which covers only a few characters. One shocking occurrence provides the fulcrum upon which the story turns, an event so moving and dramatic that the author has, perhaps, little choice but to handle it in an unconventional and striking way.

This event is a tragic, murderous explosion. It rips apart Manacle Shoal Rock, a barren, lonesome spot in the Caribbean, ordinarily shunned by men as unfit for human habitation. This time, however, the men are there, for the rock island is being tunneled to serve as an ammunition supply base, and they die—all but seven of them—practically pulverized by the force of the blast. The survivors, six black prisoners and their white warder, gather up the head and shoulders of their dead Navy commander, along with a trunk and assorted arms and legs, and put them in a box to be sent stateside for burial.

From this beginning, the story takes its seesaw course, rocking backward and forward, with a deliberate alternation between past and present time which sets the author's pattern of narration. A central point from which to view the action is provided by the one white survivor of the explosion, Lieutenant (j.g.) Everett Turner Sulgrave, USNR. For the twenty-three-year-old lieutenant, nothing will ever be quite the same again after the calamity which has wiped the earth clean of men with whom he has been so closely connected. Two of these are especially important to him: his friend, Lieutenant Benjamin Dolfus, and his moody, erratic superior officer, Commander Hake, USN. What went before the catastrophe and what succeeds it are shown in short narrative flashes which attain a speed and color almost kaleidoscopic in intensity.

By a quirk of fate, Turner Sulgrave and six Negro enlisted men are in an impregnable underground bunker when the blast comes. They realize, instantly, what it means. "No, God, no!" cries the lieutenant; and one of the blacks, with a brother above ground, sags limply onto an empty ammunition chest. While their shelter shudders and sways to the wild music of exploding ammunition, they know that, outside, everything is gone, the ammunition ship, piers and buildings, all their navy mates. Blown sky-high are all the stores of powder and shell stuffed into the caves and tunnels of Manacle Rock, making it an unsinkable ammunition ship of the U. S. Navy.

Destiny is not finished with Lieutenant Sulgrave. In the confused aftermath of the accident, he is driven by a strange compulsion to learn more of his demon-ridden commander and of the puzzling link which has existed between the latter and Lieutenant Dolfus. In the grip of this feeling, he permits himself to read the contents of the dead commander's letter box. The curiosity thus whetted finds partial satisfaction after he is ordered to Annapolis to be Vanessa Hake's escort at her husband's military funeral.

Turner Sulgrave's experience has hardly prepared him for a woman like Vanessa Hake. Thirty-eight and still beautiful, she is almost swamped in the sea of her own perplexities. Panic-stricken and rudderless, she finds in the young lieutenant a source of forgetfulness; and she encourages the escort to become the lover almost before Commander Hake is settled in his grave. In the hotel-room idyl which follows, Vanessa convinces herself that, for the first time in her life, she is sure of what she wants. Even this belief is denied her, however, when the impact of another explosion—this time from Pearl Harbor—tears her and her lover apart.

Thus enigmatically does Humes end the story which began out of chaos at Manacle Rock and closes in the chaos of Pearl Harbor. In the complex dance of its narrative movement, it is now Hake, again Dolfus, and still more often Vanessa who is allowed to occupy the center of the stage. Their common mirror is Sulgrave, the callow youth in whose consciousness they gradually assume form, vitality, and importance. During this process, Sulgrave himself acquires a certain degree of maturity; he becomes more wary, less vulnerable, even though his natural unsophistication never quite disappears.

The guilt complex which rides Vanessa Hake finds partial relief in her confessions to Sulgrave, after she has managed to seduce him. At other times her inward writhings are revealed in stream-of-consciousness interludes: her sudden widowhood, her vanishing youth, and her cheerless memories of the past combine to prod her with lances of pain and remorse. The almost complete limitation of this technique to Vanessa Hake sets her somewhat apart from the other characters and emphasizes the author's interest in her as a complex and intriguing figure. The reader will share this interest up to a point, though he may find it hard to account for her undisciplined aimless-

ness as well as the girlish ignorance—
as she herself recalls it—of where babies come from.

The author's constant juggling of
time and scene is handled with extreme
dexterity; consequently, the unorthodox structure of the novel seems natural enough after the first few pages.
Less fortunate, however, is his straining
for the unusual in language effects.
The price of attention comes high in
such phrases as "watch the sun squat
into the purple sea" or "naked as a hat
rack." Happily, however, these traces of
bush-league Hemingway are rare. More
noteworthy by far is the fierce concentration of *Men Die* and the burning
frustration of its characters. These aspects lift it out of the ordinary and
demonstrate another side of its author's
already established talents.

MEN TO MATCH MY MOUNTAINS
The Opening of the Far West, 1840-1900

Author: Irving Stone (1903-   )
Publisher: Doubleday and Company (New York). 459 pp. $5.95
Type of work: History
Time: 1840 to 1900
Locale: California, Utah, Nevada, Colorado

A full, easy-to-read account, most recent volume in the Mainstream of America Series, of the opening of the Far West, with emphasis on the people rather than on events

Principal personages:
JOHN SUTTER, founder of Sutter's Fort
MARIANO VALLEJO, commander of the Mexican forces in the North
JOHN C. FRÉMONT, officer in the U.S. Topographical Corps; later U.S. Senator from California
BRIGHAM YOUNG, leader of the Mormons
HENRY COMSTOCK, gold prospector
KIT CARSON, mountain guide and scout
MARK HOPKINS, merchant and railroad tycoon
LELAND STANFORD, merchant, politician, railroad tycoon
COLLIS HUNTINGTON, railroad tycoon
CHARLES CROCKER, railroad builder
HUBERT HOWE BANCROFT, historian of the Far West

Assemble a cast of characters that would make a Cecil B. de Mille production look like a kindergarten play. Put the cast on a revolving stage the size of the four-state region of California, Utah, Nevada, and Colorado. Set all this in a sixty-year span. In these facets of dramaturgy you have, as Mr. Stone titles his first chapter, "The Time, the Place, the Cast," for "one of the most colorful, dramatic, tumultuous and heroic sagas of man's movement across the face of the earth."

Although there are myriad crises among the characters, the chief protagonist and antagonist of this production are men and mountains, as indicated in Mr. Stone's title, which is borrowed from Sam Walter Foss's poem, "The Coming American":

Bring me men to match my mountains,
Bring me men to match my plains,

Men with empires in their purpose
And new eras in their brains.

Mr. Stone reminds his reader of the theme of his story when the men do not match the mountains, as well as when they do. The mountains were formidable adversaries, but the first victory was John Charles Frémont's. In 1842, this lieutenant in the U.S. Topographical Corps, with Kit Carson as his guide, made the first "indention" in the Rockies as the beginning of new routes along which thousands of Americans would travel to settle the Far West. Further progress came two years later when Frémont and Carson led their party across the Sierra Nevada into the Sacramento Valley.

In this production, as in most plays and always in life, a large supporting cast sustains the action of the principals. Although Frémont and Carson are stock characters in an account of this period, there are other names important in the achievements these men are remembered for. Mr. Stone gives recognition to the Broken Hand Fitzpatricks, the Joseph Chileses, and the Joseph Walkers for their contributions to the successes of the stars.

It is this fuller picture that makes Mr. Stone's writing enjoyable and personal, despite the tendency here and there toward minutiae in the introduction of so many individuals. This feature makes for a peopled backdrop to his stupendous story of political, commercial, and religious activities. But there are times when it seems as if Mr. Stone overwrites the parts played by some of his characters to give them roles disproportionate to the significance of their contributions.

The second phase of the struggle between men and mountains centered around the gold industry. Beginning on the western side of the Sierra Nevada in 1848 with the circumstantial discovery of gold by James Marshall, the action spread to the eastern slope of the mountain, then to Colorado. Each change of scene was marked by phenomenal successes and failures for individuals and groups from all over the earth.

Applicable to this lust for riches and the wishful thinking of the thousands of Germans, Irish, Chileans, Australians, and Americans who crowded into the mining areas is another of Foss's poetic thoughts: "There are purple grapes in the Land of Git-Thare." "Purple grapes" or yellow gold—the West was truly "the Land of Git-Thare."

The first year of gold-mining was characterized by honesty, for a man's pick or shovel on the spot was enough to make his claim legal. There was no social life, few camps having even one woman; friendship was the men's greatest pleasure. This congenial quietude was soon to end. With $20,000,000 worth of gold taken from the mountains in 1849, the inevitable greed, abuse, and rascality gave rise to the conduct so often reflected in the melodramatic depiction of this period. The Fifty-Niners of Colorado were a match for California's Forty-Niners in excitement and color. Lavish living accompanied the gold activity, with wines and liqueurs, tins of oysters and caviar not uncommon fare for the miners.

All this is told with full, fresh flavor in Mr. Stone's description of the domination of the Californios by the Americans, the uprisings of Indians, the death-dealing hardships of the emigrating parties to the West, and the overnight reverses that so often changed the tenor of the scene from luxury and ease to virtual desolation. Such was the Nevada situation in 1860. Wide-open mining laws, widespread stock speculation made possible by the telegraph lines, and the worst storm in six years, with floods destroying houses, hay and grain, and filling mine shafts, wiped out most of the $37,000,000 capital stock working nineteen major mines.

Concurrent with and contributary to the expansion of the gold industry was the development of transportation. This aspect of the West's growth is another act in Mr. Stone's drama between men and mountains. From the "jackass express"—a solitary rider over the mountains, carrying mail at $4.00 per letter and bullion at five per cent of assayed value—to multi-million dollar railroads like the Southern Pacific and the Santa Fe, the story of gold is repeated. The few—Mark Hopkins, Leland Stanford, Collis Huntington, Charles Crocker—reaped the monetary rewards from the sweat, industry, and suffering of the many. In the Sierra Nevada thousands of Chinese laborers chipped away at the mountainside for roadbed, making only eight inches a day.

The railroads had more than an economic significance in the expansion of the West. Whereas vast wealth had come from gold, giving rise to personal fortunes, employment for thousands, and the beginning and growth of urban centers, the railroads, in addition to facilitating these developments, served politically to join California, Utah, Nevada, and Colorado, and to make the Far West a part of the greater United States.

The commercial and social center of all this sprawling, violent activity was San Francisco. In the midst of the honorable behavior of good citizens, other elements, like lawless, undisciplined adolescents, were rampant. The first semblance of municipal law enforcement was the vigilante committee, an organization (not without its own internal corruptions) used for the establishment of order in this and other fast-rising, fast-growing towns.

According to the author, the West developed as the result of two institutions: gold and Mormonism. The religious milieu of Utah, the fourth portion of "The New Land," was the antithesis of the industrial growth that preceded statehood for California, Nevada, and Colorado. Although religious freedom, the Mormon's motivation for settling a new country, was a far cry from the impelling force of the prospector, his part in this drama was just

as troubled and suspenseful as that of his brothers in the mines and on the roadbeds. The cleavage in the roles played by these two institutions was accentuated when Brigham Young forbade participation in the gold trade among his followers, their enterprises to be agriculture and merchandising.

Mr. Stone presents his picture of Mormonism with fine objectivity. He pictures the good and the bad in this culture, so deplored by many historians and sociologists. He records the accomplishments of the Mormons as they improved the land, built cities, maintained order. He also gives account of the evils of polygamy, which he calls "the twin relic of barbarism"—the other relic was slavery.

From the outset of his story with the description of Californio—the original territory comprising the four-state area —"a pretty girl, everybody wants her," to his tribute to Hubert Howe Bancroft for creating "the greatest of all source histories of the West," Mr. Stone's book is highly readable. His narrative style and his comprehensive research reflected in the multi-faceted treatment of the episodes and character studies give a front-row, center view of men and women as they "plunge into unmapped land, break trail over mountains and across white salt deserts."

Although Mr. Stone never wanders, in the strict sense of the word, occasionally one wishes he did not change backdrops so often as he shifts from California to Utah to Colorado and back again. But perhaps this change is unavoidable in such a mammoth panorama, both temporal and geographical.

MERCIER AND CAMIER

Author: Samuel Beckett (1906-   )
Translated from the original French by the author
Publisher: Grove Press (New York). 123 pp. $6.95
Type of work: Novel
Time: The present
Locale: A vaguely Irish city, village, and countryside

A novel about the pain, meaninglessness, and absurdity of life

Principal characters:
MERCIER, a man who leaves his wife and children behind
CAMIER, a man who leaves his job as private investigator behind

Mercier and Camier is a rarity in the field of publishing: a book that the author did *not* want published. In 1947, Samuel Beckett withdrew it from his Parisian publisher, and for twenty-four years has refused to permit its publication, claiming that it was only a working draft, an experiment in new fictional technique. In 1970, his French publishers finally convinced Beckett that he should publish an authoritative version; three years later, the author's own English translation was finally completed. The slender volume is an important and valuable addition to the Beckett canon for two reasons: it marks the shift in Beckett's writing from English to French, and it introduces the vagabond vaudevillian couple, a device which became extremely successful in later prose and dramatic work. In addition, Beckett scholars will find recurrent themes and techniques in this novel that are found in all of his major works: *Malloy, Malone Dies, The Unnamable, Waiting for Godot,* and *Endgame.* It is, however, important to remember that Beckett has never considered this novel a finished, polished literary work.

The essence of the work defies reduction and over-simplification in either plot or theme, but its basic vision of the human condition is constant. Life is presented as a journey or as waiting. The narrator of *Mercier and Camier* makes it clear in the first paragraph that this journey will not be the heroic and successful Grail Quest of a medieval knight, nor even the journey of an adventurer such as Gulliver or Robinson Crusoe; he details all the dangers and sufferings that the two protagonists will *not* have to meet. In addition, their goal is obscure: the Grail has vanished, is no longer remembered; rituals as well as heroes have been reduced to insignificance. Only the traditional wasteland of the quest remains, in the form of labyrinths and mazes of cities, empty fields, bogs, and ruins. Man as heroic Knight Errant, as adventurer-explorer, has here given way to man as nonheroic, unpretentious tramp-wanderer, stripped not only of glory, but of most of his humanity. Mercier and Camier, like other Beckett "heroes," stumble along as pathetic, almost transparent nonbeings; their journey is predestined to failure. The reader realizes that they will not progress, but will instead pursue their certain circular path until it is interrupted finally by insanity, suicide, or anguishing despair and *ennui.* This disintegrated condition of man

and of his quest underlies the majority of Beckett's major work.

As Mercier and Camier proceed
on their intermittent, often delayed
journey toward their unknown goal,
the reader encounters more of the
familiar Beckett themes. The two
main characters find themselves progressively alienated from society,
God, nature, and even from the
basic necessities of life—possessions,
clothes, food, sex—and finally from
each other. Their alienation from society is evident as Mercier abandons
his wife and family, blaming himself
for participating in his children's conception, and Camier destroys all that
connects him with his job in society.
Most dramatically, they seal their
separation from society by brutally
beating a policeman to death. Their
alienation from God and nature is
equally clear. Early in the novel,
Mercier curses God; nature itself is
hostile to them, as the almost continual rain, wind, and darkness dis-
heartens them, making their journey
more difficult. When they do leave
the city for the countryside, they
find only fields and hedges that all
seem the same, or the desolation of
bogs and ruins, landscapes with nothing to offer man except a place to
die.

Typically, Beckett reduces the
necessities of his heroes to the bare
minimum. Mercier and Camier have
only a few essentials: a rucksack, an
umbrella, a bicycle, and a raincoat;
before leaving the city, they lose all
but the latter, which they abandon as
useless. Later, in a vague hope that
their lost possessions might be important, they return to the city only to
discover them useless or irrevocably
lost. Functions such as eating and

sex are also stripped to the minimum:
food becomes an occasional snack,
while sex is reduced to the level of
the mechanical copulation of the dogs
in the first scene.

In the midst of this alienation,
Mercier and Camier still have the
consolation of each other's friendship, although, like Didi and Gogo,
it is a blend of love and recoil. Because of a failure of communication
at first, they almost never get together. When they separate for an
afternoon, Camier realizes that he
basically dreads Mercier's return and
the burden of friendship. As they
leave on their last journey, their isolation from each other is emphasized as
each one walks on the far side of the
road from the other. Only when
physical and mental strength vanish
and touching is necessary for survival
do they go arm in arm. But a final
breakdown in communication occurs
the next morning, and, without speaking, with Chaplinesque courtesy,
each bids farewell to the other, as
they go their way in total alienation.
Their quest to escape loneliness,
meaninglessness, and darkness, has
been in vain.

The total meaninglessness and pain
and absurdity of life is stated many
times. "One does what one can, but
one can do nothing. Only squirm and
wriggle, to end up in the evening
where you were in the morning."
Suicide seems, at first, a desirable
solution; accidental death, even more
appealing. However, Mercier later
states that they might as well accept
"this preposterous penalty and placid-
ly await the executioner." Beckett's
nonheroes face the existentialist position, but they refuse to impose meaning on it, realizing that to do so

would only be to impose a known fiction upon chaos.

Technically, *Mercier and Camier* is an interesting experiment. Beckett here works out the dialogue form which is used so successfully in *Waiting for Godot,* using puns, rhythm, *non sequiturs,* and vaudeville routines between the heroes to create warmth, humor, and humanity. Traditional elements of the novel— character, setting, clock time, causal plot—all disintegrate as this story moves on. Beckett also establishes the device of resurrecting "heroes" from other works, as in the case of the appearance of Watt in the concluding scenes. Experimentally most interesting is Beckett's use of the narrator to underscore themes of the journey. The narrator fluctuates between an objective yet sympathetic view of his main characters, and a stance of ironic detachment. Likewise, Beckett's use of plot structure and setting follows a similar course. Structurally, the interspersing of short summaries of the action after every two chapters serves to mock that "action," while the many fragmented references only serve to emphasize the triviality of what has occurred. Just as time in the heroes' lives is wasted, so repetitious and irrelevant incidents in the plot accumulate.

In addition, Beckett creates a sense of fragmentation by having the narrator alienate the reader from characters such as the policeman, and even Mercier and Camier, and dropping constant reminders that the heroes' world is artificial rather than real. This occurs most forcefully in the conversation between Mercier and Camier in which they declare that it would take two fat volumes apiece to recount their lives. Beckett's narrator thus ironically undercuts his own tale, which recounts *both* their adventures in a padded 123 pages. Neither characters nor narrator know where they are headed; Beckett refuses to control or guide them as an omniscient author, to consider them as real human beings. Their predicament is thus parallel to the situation, as the author sees it, of man in this world: that of a lost creature deprived of his belief in an all-knowing God who orders and makes meaningful his life and universe.

Ann E. Reynolds

MERCIFUL DISGUISES

Author: Mona Van Duyn (1921-   )
Publisher: Atheneum Publishers (New York), 245 pp. $10.00
Type of work: Poetry
  The collected poems of a versatile, urbane, and mature poet

Mona Van Duyn is difficult to categorize. Reviewers such as Josephine Jacobsen and James Dickey have lauded her as a fine woman poet; Kenneth Rexroth points to her metaphysical wittiness, Howard Nemerov to her passion, and others to her craftsmanship; and to some degree these are all perceptive remarks about a diversified but dedicated poet. *Merciful Disguises: Published and Unpublished Poems,* essentially the collected works of Mona Van Duyn, reveals a fine, sometimes brilliant mind. Although the poems seem nearly Victorian in their long lines and complex imagery, the insights and feelings they evoke have no time reference. Poetry, writes Van Duyn in "Three Valentines to the Wide World," the first poem in the volume, "is simultaneous/discovery and reminiscence." The poet creates and remembers, but the processes feed each other to build new insights. Throughout *Merciful Disguises,* this simultaneous experience pervades, of looking back, understanding and encountering and thereby being able to write a poem which assimilates this perspective into a new view. The consistent *persona* is a mature person, having learned through living, communicating this double process poetically.

Merciful Disguises consists of five sections. The first four are the nearly complete volumes published previously: *Valentines to the Wide World,*

1959; *A Time of Bees,* 1964; *To See, To Take,* 1970; and *Bedtime Stories,* 1972. The final section is a group of hitherto unpublished poems written between 1965 and 1973. *To See, To Take* received the National Book Award in 1971 and is the most memorable book in terms of the poet's agility and perception. That, along with her first book, *Valentines to the Wide World,* best represents the range of ideas and scope of craftsmanship which Mona Van Duyn has so far produced.

Although the subjects of the poems vary widely, the *persona* remains fairly consistent. Behind the apparent movement in the poems is the poet, wise and somewhat removed. "Paratrooper," an early poem, reflects the course of this growth through the rather complex metaphor of falling through the air and being born into maturity: "From the dark side, feet first, breech birth, the fighter falls" and as he moves through space, he finds that his journey is lonely and perilous. The world is large and ill-defined and he battles beween crying out for security and fiercely willing his independence. In his fall, which is simultaneously his growth, he experiences love, hate, good fortune and bad, the gamut of human emotion and failure, but he survives "and he breaks through the membrane of history and sees the trees." He has arrived at a stopping place after encountering the challenges that life flings at him: "And now he bends his knees and the delicate bones of his feet/strike earth, his short-haired, hell and heaven hard, maturity."

Van Duyn is a fighter and her maturity is not a static condition; it is an encounter and an embrace. "Towards a Definition of Marriage" illustrates this attitude quite precisely *because* the poet never defines her subject, merely approaches it from several different directions. To Van Duyn, marriage is "closest to picaresque, but essentially artless"; in addition, it is a "duel of amateurs," a circus, and a pure vision held by a blind man. In other words, it is a myriad of maneuvers, motivated by imperfect understanding, misconceptions, and illusions. If a marriage and therefore the people in it attain some measure of stability and harmony, it may even be by accident, for the essential formula for a viable marriage is by definition always lacking. The poet speaks in analogies to approach the concrete, and the title "Towards a definition . . ." reminds us that marriage, self-knowledge, maturity (or other such words and states) is always imperfectly achieved. The *persona,* confident, urbane, linguistically lively, records uncertainty and tentativeness. Marriage, "the perfect idea" of a perfect union, can fall apart in real life and become finally a series of accommodations and compromises, "the politics of love."

These struggles seem to be most persistently explored in *To See, To Take,* which concentrates on the sensibility of the poet as a woman, artist, and wife. Not surprisingly, the opening poem "Outlandish Agon" speaks about a struggle with "that baby-faced boy." Cupid? Traditional Love

with its implication of surrender and sacrifice for the woman? Yes and no. The boy or the feelings that the boy represents are both external to and within the speaker. "This was a fight for my life," the speaker claims, the desire to write, to "make a name for myself sooner or later" and the less admirable, but persistent need for softness, domesticity, motherhood. The fight continues; she, large and seemingly powerful, using her last bit of strength against a boy "half [her] height." ("I don't quite know how I managed to hang on.") The result is a double victory: being true to her primary desire while acknowledging the power and strength of other qualities implied by love: "I believe in his power, beyond the power of words,/ beyond himself even, flexed in my own belief." She has her career but she also recognizes the very real demands that her personal needs and dependencies can make on her.

The contrast and the struggle between living and writing poetry continues in a later poem "Creation." This poem, ostensibly written in response to a friend's death, wrestles with the problem of trying to redeem and reclaim artistically what life provides—in this case, the joyful pleasures of a loving friendship. The poet tries to create anew the face of the dead friend by recounting the incidents that were shared and the events which seemed best to typify their friendship, but the fact of her death remains, and this event cannot be shared, even by a close friend. "Your death was your own," the poet states, acknowledging a fact and an abiding problem in art—the final impossibility of converting these facts into artifacts. The poet's real love for this person eclipses her ability to convey it artistically, and in fact even the poet sees her poem as an attempt "to rob [her friend] with words." Art, with all the power it offers the poet, is limited, finally, by life. Van Duyn the artist bows to Van Duyn the woman. The battle and the victory described in "Outlandish Agon" assume more profound implications here as the poet struggles against the limitations of her own art. In a later poem, "A Day in Late October," the poet slips into prose to try to express the irresolvable conflict between a fact such as death and its expression in art:

> I want to say no bright or seasonal thing, only that there is too much the incorruptible poem refuses to swallow. At the end of each line, a clench of teeth and something falling away — tasteless memory, irreducible hunk of love, unbelievably bitter repetition, rancid failure at feeling and naming. And the poem's revulsions become a lost world, which also contains what cannot be imagined: your death, my death.

It is perhaps the continued clash of "the dream of possibility" which sustains the poetry of Van Duyn. In "What I Want to Say," the poet describes the poetic process and its collision with reality in terms of a negative sensibility: "and not because it is there, because it is not yet there,/ and who knows if it is complex, or simple." The "it" remains without reference. It is an abstraction with which the mind plays, converting the data of life to the language of art. The mind is intrigued by the *possibility* of creation, not its actuality. Definitions, of love, of marriage, of

death, fill in that space, limit the poet, but "that music neither of us can hear,/not transformations but changes,/will move us yet."

What we do not know but long for impels all of us towards some higher state. Faced with our own limitations, we simultaneously accept and challenge them. The poet looks at birth and death as indices of her own mortality but also uses these events as creative opportunities. In this context, it is interesting to compare two poems "Leda" and "Leda Reconsidered" and to watch the change in posture and possibility which Van Duyn makes.

The quotation which forms the subtitle of "Leda" is the last two lines of Yeats's poem "Leda and the Swan": "Did she put on his knowledge with his power/Before the indifferent beak could let her drop?" Both poems are in some measure responses to the question of how to handle not only a rape, but an assault on one's total sensibility. Yeats wonders finally whether Leda learned from her encounter with overwhelming power, and in her first response to this question Van Duyn writes: "Not even for a moment." Leda is taken unawares because she is insensitive and dull, a pawn of events in life which can overwhelm. "Later, with the children in school, she opened her eyes" but she really cannot come to terms with the events (sex, marriage, birth) which have radically altered her life. "She tried for a while to understand what it was/ that had happened, and then decided to let it drop."

The tone of this poem, witty, removed, somewhat disdainful, sharply changes in "Leda Reconsidered." It is almost as if Van Duyn discovered that she had fallen into the same power game as Zeus, by taking an easy victory and claiming mastery. Leda's weakness diminishes Zeus's prowess; Van Duyn's glibness reduces her own poetic impact. The Leda of the second poem is an experienced and sober woman. She understands "more than he knew" the phenomenon of powerlessness, and she has learned to examine critically, carefully, the forces which attempt to reduce her. Here, she imagines what the swan sees as he looks at her and thereby assesses her own posture at this moment in her life. In striking contrast to the earlier poem, this Leda can handle events; she possesses "something—a heaviness,/ as if she could bear things." But more than that, she is wondering how she can convert the experience of rape into an opportunity for growth. Gazing at the bird, she sees the god and, implicitly, her own limitations. Godliness, however, she now understands means "risk of the whole self . . . [in order] to love with the whole imagination." It is never a retreat but rather a continual confrontation and commitment. This risk, taken with the knowledge that, in one sense, she will always lose because she is a finite creature, is articulated and experienced at the end of this poem:

> She waited for him so quietly that
> he came on her quietly,
> almost with tenderness,
> not treading her.
> Her hand moved into the dense
>   plumes
> on his breast to touch
> the utter stranger.

The events which we fear the most can be converted imaginatively into possibilities for beauty and insight, and it is the enlarging of these possibilities that Mona Van Duyn, at her best, creates in her poetry.

Faith Gabelnick

THE MERCY OF GOD

Author: Jean Cau (1925-   )
Translated from the French by Richard Howard
Publisher: Atheneum Publishers (New York). 310 pp. $5.00
Type of work: Novel
Time: The present
Locale: A prison in France

*An existentialist novel which, despite its technical brilliance, reworks the familiar
ground of the absurd world of Malraux and Sartre*

Principal characters:
THE DOCTOR, a madman and murderer
EUGENE, a crane operator, drunk, and murderer
ALEX, a boxer, brute, and murderer
MATCH, a gambler and murderer

That Jean Cau was for a time Jean-Paul Sartre's secretary and that his first novel, *The Mercy of God,* won the Prix Goncourt are, perhaps, reasons enough for a serious consideration of the novel, and they are, at the same time, indications that this is a conservative novel, one more closely akin to the existentialist fiction of .the forties and fifties than with the French *nouveau roman* or the American and European renascence of imaginative and fantastic fiction. Although Cau's novel exhibits some entirely successful technical innovations, his characters and themes belong to the existentialist tradition of Malraux, Sartre, and Camus. Cau's characters are also trapped in a world with "no exit," and they, too, are deeply concerned with problems made unanswerable by the silence of God, who either does not exist or does not choose to answer the cries of men.

The four central characters of this novel share a cell in a prison the location of which they do not know, and they are all murderers. They describe themselves as a madman, a drunk, a brute, and a gambler, and they are all totally involved in a double task: to create an imaginary external world in which to believe and to re-create their own past lives to discover the nature of

themselves, guilt, sin, love, and, ultimately, of God. Throughout the novel and in a variety of ways, they attempt to establish an order to transcend the mutable and absurd world, a world giving rise to answerless questions which result only in despair:

Why, O Lord, why must earthly happiness be more fragile than the gut of a fish line, for perch, shaken by a swordfish? Why does the furious cyclone fall upon the happy isles, tearing away the palm fronds and strewing the yellow beaches with black coconuts? Why is the gentle poodle suddenly seized with madness? Why does the flower lose its perfume and the mother her child? Why does the satyr rape the innocent virgin who then, red with blood and shame, hurls herself from the top of the cliff?

The narrative technique of the novel is a reflection of the only answer the prisoners can find, aside from despair, for those questions—the establishment of a unity and order among themselves in which, to some degree, each prisoner becomes each of his cellmates. The novel is narrated in the first person, but the narrator is not one of the prisoners; he is, rather, all of them, a constantly shifting perspective which, because of the nature of the prisoners' relationships remains constant. Just as they have created an outside world (a world gone mad with war, death, and injustice) by means of imaginary newscasts by one of their number, so they have created their own cell world where one must answer all questions (but the truth of one's answer may vary from day to day) and where, as their mutual identity begins to blur and disintegrate their specific identities, "Everything we think happens."

However, unlike the hero of Jack Richardson's *The Prison Life of Harris Filmore*, who finds a perfectly orderly and happy life in a prison world, the prisoners in Cau's existentialist prison are forced by circumstance and their quest for the nature of God beyond the peace and joy of a selfless, group identity to an even more artificial and absurd order, one which seems to contain Cau's vision of man's position in a world faced with Pascal's frightening "silence of these infinite spaces." When a fifth prisoner is to be added to their cell, the prisoners fall into despair, fearing that their artificial order will become foolish in the eyes of a stranger, a man from an outside world about which they wish to know nothing beyond what they have decided for themselves. The Doctor, who is at once the smartest and the maddest of the prisoners, saves their world by suggesting correctly that the new prisoner can be driven to suicide by their silence and their staring gaze.

In their elation over the success of their plan and the restoration of their orderly life, the prisoners lose all identity and become, for a winter, a new entity of four interchangeable parts: "Like God, plus one more . . . gentle, good, virtuous, transparent." But, with the coming of spring, their elation fades and, with it, their new communal God, and they continue their

quest for the answers. They define themselves simply as criminals, and a criminal "is a man who realizes that love is impossible." Who, then, is God and of what will his mercy consist?

God Himself doesn't know what mercy will inspire him on Judgment Day. "Is *that* what my humanity was? Is that what you are, my human beings? Poor wretches!"

The Doctor finally, after deciding that the universe is solipsistic and that he is the dreamer of it all, declares himself God. The others, out of fear or because being dreamed suits them, agree with the Doctor's decision, although they do not decide to worship him. They become, then, a new entity, the drunk, the brute, the gambler and the madman, a surrogate man, composed of murder and recognizing as God only its own damaged, dreaming brain. If the mercy of God and God Himself are unintelligible, then a human and therefore artificial God is, according to the Doctor, "logical, quite logical. He said it had to end this way."

Jean Cau has constructed, in this novel, another artifact of the existentialist mind like those of his former employer, Sartre, before him. Unlike so many of his American and European contemporaries, he places faith in neither the creative imagination nor the creative will, and, unlike his French contemporaries involved in the *nouveau roman*, he remains in the familiar precincts of a world absurd and beyond hope or despair. *The Mercy of God* is the novel of an artist. Like too many French novels, however, it is a work which grows out of no faith in art and, thus, of no faith in that part of men's nature, imperfect as it may be, which makes art possible and necessary.

R. H. W. Dillard

MERIWETHER LEWIS: A BIOGRAPHY

Author: Richard Dillon (1924-   )
Publisher: Coward-McCann (New York). Illustrated. 364 pp. $6.95
Type of work: Biography
Time: 1774-1809
Locale: The United States, Washington, D. C., to Oregon

The story of the leader of the Lewis and Clark expedition to the Pacific in a biography that tells how he prepared himself for leadership and how he made the march

Principal personages:
> MERIWETHER LEWIS
> WILLIAM CLARK, his ostensible equal, yet subordinate
> PERNIA, the servant of Meriwether Lewis
> PRESIDENT THOMAS JEFFERSON
> HENRY DEARBORN, the Secretary of War
> WILLIAM EUSTIS, the pinch-penny Secretary of State
> TOUSSAINT CHARBONNEAU, interpreter for the expedition
> SACAJAWEA, his squaw
> GEORGE DROUILLARD, chief scout and hunter of the expedition
> MAJOR JAMES NEELLY, the Chickasaw Indian Agent
> CHARLES WILLSON PEALE, American artist
> MRS. ROBERT GRINDER, a settler near Nashville

The invisible leader of the exploratory expedition that opened the Far West, in the opinion of Richard Dillon, head of the Sutro Library in San Francisco and author of a quartet of studies of the Pacific coast, was a red-haired gentleman who never left the President's desk in Washington: "Jefferson, the father of our American West." This biography is the story of the man he selected to take his place, how he trained him, and how that man carried out his duties. The work is an attempt by Richard Dillon to provide surgery on a two-headed exploratory freak called Lewisandclark and to separate into two rugged individualists the men who are frequently regarded as the Siamese twins of the Western trails. After all, the two explorers were inseparable only during the years on the march, from 1804 to 1806. Mr. Dillon warns clearly in his introduction that he is telling the story of Meriwether Lewis and keeping William Clark "as a background figure to await his biographical turn." So if Clark is here a shadowy figure, as some critics of this biography complain, the biographer planned it so. For those who want them considered on equal terms, there is John Bakeless' book, *Lewis and Clark, Partners in Discovery*, published in 1947.

Almost with the discovery of the New World began the search for the Northwest Passage, a mythical waterway to the Pacific Ocean. Thomas Jefferson was one of many who encouraged explorers to go looking for it. After the failure of Major Robert Rogers, he tried to persuade George Rogers Clark to undertake the venture, with the plea that he do it before the British could complete their plans for a similar expedition. Finally, after several failures, he found the ideal leader, Meriwether Lewis.

Lewis was born on August 18, 1774, in Jefferson's own county of Virginia.

Having lost his father during the Revolutionary War, and his stepfather at the age of sixteen, Meriwether assumed responsibility for his mother and her four other children until the Whiskey Rebellion of 1794 interrupted his career as a gentleman farmer and made him a soldier. He was in the army of Mad Anthony Wayne when he first met his future partner, William Clark. Later he was promoted to regimental paymaster of troops in the Ohio Valley.

The newly-elected President Jefferson freed him from routine army life by a letter in February, 1801, asking him, because of his knowledge of army routine and of the "Western Country," to come to Washington as his private secretary. Lewis was not an amanuensis, the biographer explains, but looked after guests, made contacts with Congress, and was a sort of shadow, lightening the President's burdens. At the same time, he was learning social graces and diplomacy.

The President, however, had something else in mind for the young man; and they often discussed it in Jefferson's map-lined work room: an exploratory expedition to the Far West. Some have questioned whether commerce or conquest might have been the principal motive, but the biographer quotes later letters making completely clear the President's objective.

With world conditions as they were, he could not openly reveal his purpose; instead, he asked Congress for funds to continue the trading posts already established and to purchase more Indian lands. In the final paragraph of his secret message to Congress of January 18, 1803, he asked for $2,500 to permit an intelligent officer with a dozen men to explore from the Missouri River to the Western Ocean. Congress, anxious to break the British fur monopoly, voted that sum.

Mr. Dillon's account of outfitting the expedition proves how minutely he conducted his research. Besides describing a boat Lewis had designed, a craft whose iron frame weighed 1,770 pounds, he tells of such items as "a pair of pocket pistols with secret triggers," and eighty dollars' worth of ammunition. Actually Lewis acquired several thousand dollars' worth of arms by requisitions from the Schuykill Arsenal. Much of the cash was for presents for the Indians, catalogued at length, even to "130 pigtails of tobacco."

Finally, prepared and with minute instructions from Jefferson, the twenty-nine-year-old leader left Pittsburgh on August 31, 1803. Dillon makes it clear that Captain Meriwether Lewis was in complete charge. It was he who chose his former army friend, Lieutenant William Clark, as his second officer, and it was he who gave Clark an unofficial advance to the rank of captain when the War Department refused the promotion.

In a record seventeen days after leaving Pittsburgh, the "Corps of Discovery" reached the Mississippi, and on December 12 they saw St. Louis and the Missouri River. En route, and during his stay there, Lewis sought information from everyone. He had prepared for his errand through briefings in Washington by leading botanists, zoologists, mineralogists, and Indian historians. He had learned to determine latitude and longitude. He had been provided with British and French passports, though unfortunately, as he learned later, not with Spanish documents. He was already collecting information that he sent back to Washington. During his wait in St. Louis he served as the President's representative on March 9 and 10, 1804, when the territory of the Louisiana Purchase was turned over to its new owners in simple ceremonies described by the historian.

On May 14 the expedition started from St. Louis up "The Big Muddy." Ten days later they passed La Charrette, the last outpost of civilization on the Missouri. Much of the time Clark, the better navigator, steered the twenty-two-oared keelboat, while many members of the expedition toughened themselves by following on foot along the shore.

The first eight-volume *Original Journals of the Lewis and Clark Expedition, 1804-1806*, edited by Reuben Gold Thwaites, was condensed by Bernard de Voto into a single volume. It is further abridged here, but with ample details to give the readers a sense of participation. Many unessential but interesting episodes are included, such as Lewis' first Indian pow-wow near Council Bluffs, and his introduction to beavers and watermelons. There are also accounts of the first buffaloes and prairie dogs seen and the discovery of a forty-five-foot fossil skeleton of what was probably some Cretaceous reptile. The historian also discusses Lewis' problems. No company of fifty independent, semi-literate frontiersmen could be turned by magic into obedient, cheerful explorers, and some had to be punished by lashes for sleeping on guard, for stealing liquor, for trying to desert.

Now they met Sioux Indians, whose name means "Enemy" and who were even more treacherous than floating logs and rapids. But they went ahead, until, warned by the first flurries of snow late in October, the expedition established winter quarters among the Mandan Indians on the upper Missouri. Here Lewis hired the interpreter Toussaint Charbonneau and on November 11 first met his squaw, Sacajawea, whose enormous contributions to the success of the expedition are recognized by Dillon.

On April 7, 1805, they divided forces. Some returned downstream with specimens and reports for Washington. The others, thirty-one in all, including Sacajawea and her infant son, in six small canoes and two large pirogues, headed for the Western Sea, two thousand miles away. Sacajawea was the housekeeper, Shoshone style, for the entire detachment, but she was also responsible later for the decision on which fork of the Missouri to follow at a critical moment.

The author describes the crossing of the Continental Divide by the expedition in September and the arrival of the explorers on the shores of the Columbia River after the snows of October had began to fall. Delayed by falls and rapids of the Columbia, they did not see the Pacific until November 8, 1805. By Christmas they had completed Fort Clatsop on the south shore of the Columbia, near its mouth, and there they remained until the time came to begin their return journey eastward the next March. Before departing, Lewis fastened a document to the fort which, as the historian says, "staked U.S. claims on the Oregon Country that the Astorian and Oregon trail overlanders would consolidate."

Several chapters cover the story of the return trip. On September 23, 1806, the expedition arrived at St. Louis. On December 28, Lewis reached Washington. He was received at the White House on the thirtieth. Clark, stopping to arrange for his marriage, was delayed for several weeks.

According to War Department Accountant Simmons, the exploration cost the United States $38,722.25. In addition, each of the two leaders received sixteen hundred acres of land west of the Mississippi. All the other members of the expedition were given 320 acres each and back pay of $10 a month. William Clark was made Agent for Indian Affairs and Lewis became Governor of Upper Louisiana.

The three years left of life to Lewis were not, according to his biographer, happy ones. He could not control a great geographical region as he had controlled his expedition. Personal and national rivalries hampered him, and with the inauguration of a new President and the appointment of new officials in Washington, he was constantly in trouble. The refusal of Secretary of State Eustis to repay some of his expenditures forced him to give up his land as security for debts.

The manner of his death has always been a mystery. Did he commit suicide or was he murdered? Traveling to Washington in an attempt to untangle his affairs, he was accompanied by his servant, Pernia, Indian Agent Major Neelly, and several Indians. To explain his situation, he had already dispatched a letter to President Madison, a document whose many erasures led some to believe the writer was suffering from neurosis.

Lewis was still shaky from an attack of fever when they crossed the Tennessee River on October 8, 1809. The next night several of their horses strayed, and Neelly and his servants delayed to look for them while Lewis and Pernia went ahead, with arrangements to wait at the first white settlement they found. This was a small cluster of crude log cabins called Grinder's Stand, in territory known as the Natchez Trace.

According to one of several versions told later by Mrs. Grinder, Lewis appeared alone and asked for lodgings for the night, explaining that his companions would soon be along. Pernia, according to this account, arrived after supper. Following a conversation with his servant, Lewis began muttering wildly. This agitation continued after the servant had gone to sleep in the hayloft and Mrs. Grinder had made her bed in the kitchen. About three o'clock in the morning, she testified, she heard a gunshot and the thud of a body in Lewis' cabin. He called for help and through the logs she saw him crawling, but this pioneer woman, though accustomed to violence, did nothing until daybreak. Then she sent one of the children to rouse Lewis' servant. One of her stories was that she had seen him with a gaping head wound, and that he begged her to take a gun and finish killing him.

Major Neelly wrote Jefferson from Nashville, with confirmation by Pernia, that Lewis had killed himself. Believing Lewis' traveling companions and making no attempt to confirm the account, Jefferson spread the story in the foreword he wrote for the Journal. But there were many others who were not convinced because they believed suicide out of character for the explorer. Besides, he had just agreed to go into the fur business with his brother Reuben and his old partner Clark. Also, only a few days before, he had talked confidently about finishing a book. Dillon devotes twenty-five pages to evidence, then gives his verdict that Lewis was not guilty of suicide. Instead, he points to a half dozen possible murderers.

The illustrations, taken largely from the first printed account of the expedition, are excellent. The account of the westward journey is exciting in itself and for many readers unacquainted with the details might have been made more so. However, this is biography at

its best. From the book emerges an adventurous, honorable man worthy of the tribute by Jefferson that appeared on the monument at the out-of-the-way location of Meriwether Lewis' death when, in 1848, people got around to honoring the man who had contributed so much to the winning of the West:

"Of courage undaunted, possessing a firmness and perseverance of purpose which nothing but impossibilities could divert from its direction."

Willis Knapp Jones

THE MERMAID MADONNA

Author: Stratis Myrivilis (Stratēs Myribēlēs, 1892-   )
Translated from the Greek by Abbott Rick
Publisher: The Thomas Y. Crowell Company (New York). 310 pp. $4.50
Type of work: Novel
Time: 1922-1939
Locale: The Greek island of Mytilene

A novel of life in a Greek refugee fishing village and of the passionate virginity of a strange and beautiful girl drawn from the sea

Principal characters:
SMARAGTHI, a girl found abandoned in a fishing boat
VAROUHOS, her foster father, a refugee from Anatolia
NERANDJI, his wife
FORTIS, the keeper of a coffee house, Smaragthi's godfather
LAMBIS, his son
AVGUSTIS, a fanatic schoolmaster
LATHIOS, an honest fisherman
AUNT PERMAHOULA, an aged visionary
GADJALIS, a dishonest tavern keeper and smuggler

Since the death of Nikos Kazantzakis in 1957, the foremost literary figure in Greece has been Stratis Myrivilis, a sun-bronzed, sixty-eight-year-old veteran of several wars and the author of many novels, short stories, and poems. He has received almost every honor his country could possibly give him, capped in 1958 by his election to the National Academy of Greece. Although he has been widely translated and praised throughout Europe, *The Mermaid Madonna* marks his first appearance on the American literary scene.

Myrivilis is a shrewd old literary *naïf* who writes as if no fundamental changes have taken place in the art of storytelling since the days of Homer. In spite of the fact that the events of *The Mermaid Madonna* are catapulted into motion by an incident of modern history, the flight of Greek refugees from Turkish persecution in Anatolia in 1922, the essential plot could have taken place at any time since the Greeks became Christians. Simple fishermen have struggled with the sea and loved and hated one another in just this fashion almost everywhere in all ages, and Myrivilis captures their talk and their passions in a simple prose style of almost legendary quality. In this connection recognition and praise should also go to Abbott Rick, whose excellent translation echoes the poetry and primitive spirit of the original.

The first two short chapters of the novel constitute a kind of prologue telling how a chapel came to be built and a mural of the mermaid madonna was painted to adorn it. A group of stonemasons aboard a ship caught in a violent squall began to pray, "Save us, Holy Virgin, and we will build you a chapel!" The storm immediately subsided and the masons hastily erected on a rocky promontory of Mytilene a solid, foursquare, ugly chapel. Years later a strange sea captain, nicknamed *dedes* (the hermit), came to repair the chapel and to stay on as its attendant. On the day he disappeared as mysteriously as he had arrived the villagers found on one wall the portrait of a strange madonna—a dark-complexioned, green-eyed figure metamorphosed into a blue-scaled fish from the waist down. In one hand she held a ship and in the other the trident of Poseidon; she was

> a new Greek divinity who in a miraculous manner united all the epochs and all the meanings of the race—a race that struggles with the elements and tempests of the world, half on land and half on sea, with the plowshare and the keel, always subject to a war-like divinity, female and virgin.

This legendary goddess, part pagan, part Christian, but mostly fishermen's fancy, hovers and broods over the events of the novel and makes the characters appear at times like actors in some fate-determined drama.

The story proper begins when the refugees from Anatolia begin to arrive in Mytilene, one with his eyes gouged out, another clutching a dead child, still others with swollen, stinking limbs. Inflamed by the patriotic speeches of the fanatic schoolmaster, Avgustis, they at first refuse to settle down in Skala, the village built for them by the Greek government, an act which they consider tantamount to giving up all hope of returning to their own homes seized by the Turks in Anatolia. But the bishop on the mainland, acting through his fisherman kinsman, Varouhos, finally succeeds in reconciling the refugees to their lot, and Avgustis declines into drunkenness.

On this scene golden-haired, green-eyed Smaragthi appears mysteriously. When Varouhos, returning from seeing the bishop, finds the baby abandoned in his boat, he and his wife welcome her as a child sent by the mermaid madonna to take the place of their own dead daughter. As the girl grows up, her story becomes a part of the villagers' tales of their exile and their new life on Mytilene. Strangely resembling the mermaid madonna, Smaragthi is loved by all and feels happy and secure until the day Markos, an old watchdog, leaps on her and rips her dress. The terror-stricken girl can never forget the memory of his hairy muzzle on her face and the touch of his shaggy pelt. Later she recalls that experience with even greater terror when, some months after Nerandji's death, Varouhos returns from watching a provocative dancer at Gadjalis' tavern and tries to assault the sleeping girl. Only the intervention of Fortis keeps the villagers from tearing the drink-sodden old man limb from limb, and he leaves Skala, never to return and never to be mentioned again.

Fortis tries to comfort the girl with an adage he had learned from a consumptive Greek poet, Telemachos Stefanides, in America: "In the soul of every evildoer a saint is imprisoned, weeping and waiting for his release." After Varouhos' departure Smaragthi finds a second home with Lathios, a fisherman, and his family, and she spends much of her time with Aunt Permahoula, a century-old woman wise with fables, secrets of the sea, and mystic lore, who impresses on the girl's mind that her mother was a mermaid. Smaragthi goes fishing regularly with Lathios and his sons, and when she is able to handle a boat, the nets, and the javelin as well as any *pallikari* her godfather buys her a boat of her own which they name *Nerandji*. One day, shortly before her death, Aunt Permahoula passes her hand over the girl's swelling breasts and flanks and says, "The fruit is ripe. May the harvester not be slow in coming. Choose a *pallikari*."

Although Smaragthi shrinks from the thought of any man's touch, eligible men of all ages, villagers and strangers alike, try to attract her attention—sometimes with comic and sometimes with tragic results. Nothing that ever happened in the village was more hilarious or longer remembered than the sight of Kokos Achtarides, the dandified new tax collector, running sopping wet and howling through the streets with Smaragthi's darning needle deep in his buttocks. A more tragic incident follows when Lambis, the only son of Fortis, begins to spy on her secretly and to follow her wherever she goes. One night he saves her from drowning while she is swimming in the moonlit sea. On another the Gadjalis family finds him hiding in a fig tree and assumes that he is spying on Yana, the daughter of the house. After they beat him horribly, Lambis, unable to bear the humiliation, leaps from the cliff of the madonna into the sea. Finally people begin to whisper that Smaragthi has brought bad luck to those who loved her most. But other would-be lovers continue to court her in spite of her prayers to the madonna asking that men leave her in peace. In the end she decides to give up her fishing boat in order to keep house for lonely old Fortis and to look after the chapel of the mermaid madonna.

Plainly Smaragthi is intended to be a symbol of the earthy mysticism and deep folk feeling which pervade the novel. The world which Stratis Myrivilis evokes suggests much that is archaic and timeless. For this reason his book may be compared with a work by one of his contemporaries, Ilias Venezis' *Beyond the Aegean,* published in this country in 1956. In both writers the reader may sense the appeal of the pastoral and the primitive; both belong to the spirit of that eternal Greece, the ancient, beloved homeland for which the anguished schoolmaster speaks with such patriotic feeling and sense of more than personal loss when he declares: "In all I left behind two thousand years of Greece and civilization."

The Mermaid Madonna contains no moral; all that it attempts to say is that this is the way life can be in an Aegean fishing village—harsh, foolish, strange. The story is leisurely told, with no attempt to resist tantalizing digressions, and some of the finest passages in the book are brief inserted narratives or the remarks of the old and the wise that sum up the knowledge of people who have lived a long time in one place. Even though these people have been uprooted, that wisdom is their consolation and their strength. Stratis Myrivilis' sense of humanity makes this a remarkable and rewarding novel. No doubt it will be followed by translations of other novels he has written.

THE MERMAIDS

Author: Eva Boros (1911-   )
Publisher: Farrar, Straus, and Cudahy (New York). 216 pp. $3.50
Type of work: Novel
Time: 1936
Locale: Budapest, Hungary

The story of a young man who falls in love with a girl whose illness makes her something of a doll and something of a mermaid

Principal characters:
ALADAR BRANKOVICH, director of a flour mill export office
LALLA PIROLA, a patient in a tuberculosis sanatorium
FRANCISKA and
KATI, friends of Lalla, out-patients
COUNT PALOCZY, an out-patient

Not since Thomas Mann's *The Magic Mountain* has the peculiar world of the tuberculosis sanatorium been so effectively expressed or presented with attention to the same aspects: to time and its perverted perspectives, to patients and their eccentric personalities, and to the hard line of division between the well and the unwell.

The Mermaids is primarily a mood novel. The patients, as Miss Boros puts it, are "eternal patients" and the visitors to the sanatorium "eternal visitors." Their status can never change, and the progression in the novel can only be a progression of discovery; each side must come to see that the two can never meet.

The effective moods of this book are not only the moods of persons; the confined, alien world of the patients has its own moods which the patients reflect. In turn, their attitudes condition the character of the place:

Hospitals, like prisons, create their own time. Weeks pass unnoticed, while minutes seem to last for hours and days. You are aware of this change in the rhythm of time as soon as you enter the place. It affects you unpleas-antly, like the smell of disinfectants and drugs. It feels like anxiety. You glance at your watch, for instinctively you know that there is something wrong with the time. . . . You are already counting in minutes and in seconds; the afternoon is never going to end. . . . But while you were walking down the corridor hours have passed in a flash. . . .

Aladar Brankovich, director of the Brankovich mills export office in Budapest, is drawn into the mysterious sanatorium world by Lalla Pirola, a girl he comes across on the walk beside the Danube. She confuses him with her conversation until he decides that her tales of being a dancer and of touring Europe are all expressions of dreams she can never realize. She is, as he discovers, a victim of tuberculosis; and she has decided that consequently she can never marry, never have children. Later on in their friendship, when Aladar suggests that she is well enough to live outside the hospital, she answers that no hotel would ever take her, "What with my sputum-mug and all that."

From the start of their relationship it is clear to the reader that Aladar and

Lalla are worlds apart: hers is the time-confused, artificial life of the sanatorium; his is the life of a business man who cannot see the impossibility of bringing her back to health and out of her different world. The gulf between them is not just a matter of health; it is a matter of temperament emphasized by the fact of illness. One supposes that if tuberculosis had not given Lalla her excuse for separation from normal life, she would have found another. Indeed, the author suggests that, at least in her case, the disease is not so much a cause of her isolation as an effect of her personality.

The patients, then, are like mermaids—young, withdrawn, content, coming to the surface and along the shore for a moment of contact with human beings, only to retreat beneath the surface when some actual demand is made upon them, some demand that mermaids can never satisfy without leaving the sea. This image occurs several times in the novel, and it fits the characters. Lalla, for example, dresses in green and is never at ease outside the sanatorium. One time a patient in one of the hospitals she was in let down a parcel on a string, dangling it before her as she sat on the balcony below. She opened the parcel and found a boiled sweet. Lalla, reporting the patient's comment to Aladar, tells him: "He said that as long as he lived he would always remember that spring. How he was fishing in Austria, fishing in the blue sky. And how he caught a mermaid with a boiled sweet."

But Lalla is not only a mermaid; she is also a doll. Although her hair is naturally golden, she bleaches it in order to make it a startling, artificial white. She covers her face with a great deal of makeup, so as to give it the wide-eyed, empty appearance of a doll's face. When Aladar buys flowers for her he buys little roses, Baba roses, "roses for dolls." She has blue eyes; she is "tanned like a baby"; she has "little frosted-pink ear-lobes"; and when Aladar first hears her voice he wonders: "Her voice; or was it her smile that reminded him of children's parties and birthday cakes; of dolled up little girls, all ready for admiration?"

Aladar visits Lalla in the sanatorium and falls in love with her, although he never feels sure that his love is returned. He pays her bills at the hospital and does not let her know. Gradually he realizes that if Lalla never leaves the place, she will never be enough of a woman to love him. Confined to her little room, she is nothing more than a doll, a creature of her own imagination, artificial, unresponsive. When her friend Kati is taken away and later dies, Lalla is disturbed; she asks Aladar whether he wants her to be *always* happy" as if she realizes the possibility of an existence which is not just painted on like a doll's face. But it is only the recognition of death that forces this human response from her. Immediately she begins to build up a dream defense again, and she is happy to be returned to the sanatorium after a shopping trip to the village.

The other characters of the story emphasize the difference between the patients and the outsiders. Even the tuberculosis-infected persons who live in the village are bound in many ways to the sanatorium, and none of them seems able to have grown past the moment of first being touched by the disease. When photographs of former times are passed around, the pictures seem false, for the life they knew is not merely past: it is entirely disconnected. Franciska, a friend of Lalla, goes away to live with some of her family for a time, but when she discovers that her silverware is marked with elastic bands and that her glass is labeled, she knows that she can never believe that she belongs with them. It is as if a mermaid tried to live on shore and failed. Count Paloczy, another friend, is an elderly man who has spent decades in the village. He sometimes hopes that he is the best-liked man in town, but he knows that no one has ever whole-heartedly accepted him. The only life possible for him, then, is a life with the little dolls, the mermaids, of the sanatorium.

Throughout the novel Aladar is something of a spectator and something of a participant. Because, as a spectator, he comes to see the artificial character of the sanatorium life, he realizes, as a participant, that he has been, not a benefactor, but a "fugitive from his own useless, barren existence." Although Lalla had resigned herself to life as an invalid, she had believed that Aladar had faith in the possibility of her return to normal life. When his act of providing a house for her in the village shows that he, too, has come to see her as the "eternal patient," she leaves the sanatorium and him. Aladar knows that somewhere else she will be at ease again in the sea of patients, but his yearning for her continues and he thinks that he will try to find her.

As a carefully sustained mood-portrait of a world apart. *The Mermaids* is a first novel worth attending to. Perhaps there are other worlds for Miss Boros to conquer.

MERRY MONARCH

The Life and Likeness of Charles II

Author: Hesketh Pearson (1887-1964)
Publisher: Harper and Brothers (New York). Illustrated. 274 pp. $5.00
Type of work: Biography
Time: 1630-1685
Locale: England, Scotland, and the Continent

A life of the English king of whom it was claimed that "he never said a foolish thing and never did a wise one"

> Principal personages:
> CHARLES I, King of England
> HENRIETTA MARIA, his wife
> CHARLES II,
> JAMES, Duke of York, afterwards King James II, and
> HENRY, Duke of Gloucester, their sons
> MARY, Princess of Orange, and
> HENRIETTE ANNE, Duchess of Orleans, their daughters
> CATHERINE OF BRAGANZA, wife of Charles II
> LUCY WALTER,
> BARBARA, Duchess of Cleveland,
> NELL GWYNN, and
> LOUISE DE KEROUALLE, Duchess of Portsmouth, Charles' mistresses
> JAMES, Duke of Monmouth, Charles' illegitimate son by Lucy Walter
> EDWARD HYDE, first Earl of Clarendon, Lord Chancellor of England
> GEORGE VILLIERS, second Duke of Buckingham, and
> JOHN WILMOT, second Earl of Rochester, Charles' favorites

Hesketh Pearson has been a most prolific writer of popular biographies, usually of literary figures; and he has produced lives of such dissimilar writers as Dickens and Wilde, Scott and Shaw. But of his score of volumes this is the first to tackle a royal personage. He is a "popular biographer" in that he does not attempt to burrow deeply after information, but rather to give a portrait of his subject, to see the man from a fresh point of view, and, above all, to be entertaining.

Such is his life of Charles II of England. It would be almost impossible to unearth any hitherto unknown facts about Charles because the history of the period is well documented and has been thoroughly covered by historical specialists. Pearson's aim, therefore, is to give a new interpretation of Charles' character and to display him in a much more favorable light than has been the custom. His method thus allows him to pass quickly over certain events in the life of his subject that might detain a political, economic, or military historian and to dwell at length upon episodes that, while perhaps less important in the history of England, illustrate a certain aspect of Charles' complex character. For example, the author gives but a few pages to the Battle of Worcester and a very long chapter to the six weeks after the battle, during which Charles wandered in disguise about England in a finally successful effort to get a ship that would take him to France.

The author begins his story "in medias res" and introduces us to Charles when the prince, at the age of sixteen, had to flee from England as the Civil War was nearing its end. Of Charles I, we get but a glimpse; the author dismisses that "fair and fatal King" as a solemn man with no imagination and no common sense, doggedly bent upon bringing about his own ruin. A fuller portrait is given of Henrietta Maria, daughter of the great Henry of Navarre, beloved of all Marylanders for bestowing her name upon their state, and considered by many historians as a contributing cause of her husband's downfall. She and her eldest son were thoroughly uncongenial; she worried him with her Roman Catholicism almost as much as the Scots with their Presbyterianism, for Charles had a very human dislike of being annoyed with doctrinal arguments. After the collapse of the Royalist cause, the queen was received in France with all the deference due a daughter of Henry IV, and immediately set to work at promoting a match between Charles and the Duchesse de Montpensier. It would have been an excellent marriage for a penniless exile, since the duchesse was the richest woman in Europe and more than eager for a crown; but Charles mysteriously lost his command of the French language when in her company, and the project came to nothing.

The story of Charles' life is familiar enough even to unscholarly readers, so that Pearson needs only to touch upon the salient points. After the death of Charles I in 1649, there were eleven years of wandering about the Continent from country to country, eleven years of waiting for a turn of the tide in England. It was a maddening experience for Charles; he was always in want for money, so poor, indeed, that he sometimes lacked the clothes suitable even for a private gentleman. His shadow court—a "government in exile," as we would say today—was beset by all the confusions and jealousies that commonly afflict such groups: advisers pulling in different directions and intriguing for power that did not exist. And since Cromwell had the most efficient secret service in Europe, all of the uncrowned king's plans were known in London. Further, so great was the fear inspired by Cromwell, that Charles found himself an unwelcome guest at most of the European courts. But the years of adversity had their effect on Charles by teaching him a great deal about human nature.

In 1651 he undertook his abortive invasion of England by way of Scotland. There he found many of the natives as faithless to him as they had been to his father, whom they had sold to the English Parliament for hard cash with which to pay their army. The invasion ended with the Battle of Worcester in which Charles fought hand-to-hand with exemplary bravery. But Cromwell—whom the author describes as a brilliant general, for all his fanaticism and heartless cruelty—was too much for Charles, and the battle was lost. The story of Charles' escape from England is pure romance, straight out of Dumas. That he was never betrayed reflects great credit on the innate loyalty of the British people, for the price put upon his head would have made many a man rich. The author, however, is probably correct in his theory that the last thing that Cromwell's government wanted was Charles' capture:

they had the blood of one Stuart king on their hands, and that was enough.

Cromwell was one of the few dictators in history to die in his bed, but his son lacked the ability and the desire to succeed him. Largely through the influence of General George Monk— a turncoat in an age of such—the relics of the Commonwealth were swept away, and in 1660 the Restoration was accomplished. The king had come into his own again.

We have all read, usually in Pepys' diary, of the almost delirious joy that burst out in England at the end of the Commonwealth and the return of Charles. Years of Puritanical gloom and Cromwellian oppression had been too much; military government, with the country divided into districts, each ruled by a major general, gave the English a hearty dislike for militarism that has lasted until today. And the Restoration—given the customs of the age— was not marked by bloody vengeance. Some regicides were executed, and the bodies of Cromwell and his closest adherents were exhumed and hanged— but this latter act, as Pearson says, "did no one any harm and the enthusiastic onlookers a lot of good." Charles was not a cruel man; all he wanted was rest after his long exile.

The twenty-five years of his reign were not, however, tranquil. There were endless wrangles with Parliament over money, and there were the anti-Catholic troubles fomented by the loathsome Titus Oates. There were the great plague and the great fire of London and wars with the Dutch. And, towards the end of the reign, there were the difficulties caused by the Duke of York's Catholicism that threatened the Protestant succession, for James was heir to the throne. Nor

were matters helped by the behavior of the empty-headed Duke of Monmouth, Charles' oldest and favorite bastard, who set himself up as the champion of Protestantism. This pretension was later to cost the scatter-brained duke his head. But Charles, who had long ago learned how to bend with the wind, lived through it all and died peacefully in 1685.

To nineteenth century historians, nurtured in the Whig tradition, Charles II was second only to his brother James as the greatest villain in modern English history. He was cynical and immoral; his court was licentious; he sold England to Louis XIV of France in return for a pension. Pearson endeavors in this biography to redress the balance and to give a more favorable picture of Charles. It cannot be denied that he was licentious even by the standards of a very loose age. His "amorous propensities," as Dr. Johnson would have called them, were enormous; as one courtier observed, he was quite literally the father of many of his subjects. But Pearson denies that he was ever really influenced by his mistresses in any of his important political decisions; though he gave them money and titles, he went his own way in statecraft. As for his supposed subservience to France, Pearson maintains that Charles was actually the shrewdest politician in Europe and got money from Louis without giving anything significant in return. It was Louis, not he, who was duped. Charles played the French against the Dutch, shifting the balance of power until England had gobbled up the Dutch trade that was to insure her future commercial prosperity and had consolidated her American colonial empire at the expense of Holland. As for France, Charles, by the same process, insured the defeat of Louis in the reign of Queen Anne. In domestic political affairs, Pearson gives Charles only one black mark: the serious error of trying to force episcopacy upon the Scots.

In his heredity, Charles was a curious mixture: his father was half Scotch and half Danish, his mother, half French and half Italian. The ancestor whom he most closely resembled was his maternal grandfather, Henry of Navarre, who had declared that Paris was worth a Mass. From Henry, Charles inherited the tremendous physical vigor of the Bourbons as well as his grandfather's easy camaraderie that enabled him to get along with anyone. It should also be remembered that Henry had been famous as a lover. Charles had the typical English love of sports and the charm that marked all of the Stuarts, even the gloomy James II. And perhaps from his Medici ancestors came his astute political sense that kept him on his throne.

But the quality that, according to Pearson, marked Charles as a man ahead of his age was his tolerance. The seventeenth century was an era of unparalleled religious fanaticism; the phrase "religious toleration" would have been meaningless to most people. And Charles had seen this intolerance at its worst. There was his bigoted Roman Catholic mother pulling him in that direction. Scotland was full of grim and fanatical Covenanters who wanted to force their beliefs on him and on everyone else, and England was full of equally grim and fanatical Puritans with exactly the same end in view. Pearson dismisses most of these people as "religious lunatics," and indeed there seems to be small choice among them. Charles was a tolerant man in an intolerant age. When reading of this era, we can better understand Arnold Toynbee's thesis that it was the religious fanaticism of the sixteenth and seventeenth centuries that turned Western civilization away from its Christian heritage and towards the worship of the technology that began to emerge during Charles' reign. In an atmosphere of science, men felt, there would be no room for fanaticism; reason alone would rule. Charles himself was much interested in natural science, and his reign saw the founding of the Royal Academy.

Pearson gives his final summary of Charles as "the sanest, most human and civilized of monarchs," a judgment that must be causing Macaulay to revolve in his grave. But the reader of this biography will feel that the author has made good his case.

THE MESSAGE IN THE BOTTLE

Author: Walker Percy (1916-   )
Publisher: Farrar, Straus and Giroux (New York). 352 pp. $8.95
Type of work: Essays
   "An attempt to sketch the beginnings of a theory of man for a new age"
based on his language-making capacities

Walker Percy, author of three fine and important novels (*The Moviegoer,* 1961; *The Last Gentleman,* 1966; *Love in the Ruins,* 1971), has compiled a deeply serious collection of personal essays with an apparently flip title: *The Message in the Bottle: How Queer Man Is, How Queer Language Is, and What One Has to Do with the Other.* But the title contains the substance of the book.

Percy begins by talking about the "queerness" of man, especially modern man, and the fact that, despite the mass of data available, there is no coherent theory to explain that queerness. The first five pages of the book are devoted to a series of provocative questions which culminates with this query:

> What does a man do when he finds himself living after an age has ended and he can no longer understand himself because the theories of man of the former age no longer work and the theories of the new age are not yet known, for not even the name of the new age is known, and so everything is upside down, people feeling bad when they should feel good, good when they should feel bad?

Although hardly a modest collection, Percy does not claim to answer all these questions. He does, however, posit a theory which he likens to "the sort of crude guess a visitor from Mars might make if he landed on earth and spent a year observing man and the beasts." His theory has surprising unity and coherence considering that the book is actually a gathering of essays written over a twenty-year span and previously printed in such wide-ranging publications as the *Sewanee Review, Psychiatry, The New Scholasticism,* and *Philosophy and Phenomenological Research.* Ideally, *The Message in the Bottle* should be reviewed by a committee made up of a literary critic, existentialist philosopher, M.D., ethnologist, behaviorist, Jungian analyst, semiologist, psycholinguist, and theologian, so diverse are the points of view of its essays.

Actually, it is appropriate that the book be reviewed by an amateur, since Percy emphatically claims that label for himself without apology or irony. Taking Webster's first definition of an amateur as "a person who does something for the pleasure of it," the label fits. Percy's self-designation also implies an assumption about "experts" that runs through all of the essays: "language is too important to be left to the linguisticians," the mind to the psychiatrists, religion to the theologians, and so on. All such "professionals" are partisans, advocates of parochial views with built-in prejudices, inconsistencies, and blind spots. Morevoer, one of the reasons for contemporary man's dilemma is that he has conceded these vital areas to the professionals and accepted their dogmatic judgments on faith.

The "amateur" has the fresh view and disinterested posture that is necessary if a new synthesis is to be found; that is the rationale behind Percy's identification of himself as a "Martian." "One must be a Martian or a survivor poking among the ruins to see how extremely odd the people were who lived there."

But lest the title of the book and use of terms like "amateur" and "Martian" suggest a casualness or superficiality in these essays, let the reader be warned: *The Message in the Bottle* is an extremely difficult, sometimes abstract, sometimes technical, frequently abstruse set of essays that get more difficult as the book goes along. Amateur or not, Percy has read deeply, widely, and thoroughly in the literature of all the disciplines he treats, and he spares the reader not at all. He meets the experts in their own territories with their own weapons and battles them at least even; the dilettante will be lost a good deal of the time. Percy himself has no illusions about the general appeal of his rhetoric:

> Most readers will not want to read all chapters. It is hard, for example, to imagine anyone at all at the present time who would want to read the last. Only after writing it did it occur to me that it had, for the moment at least, no readership whatever.

So why bother? Because Percy has asked the most fundamental questions, asserted himself against the most important dogmas of his time, and suggested approaches to these problems in most of his essays that can be pondered to great benefit by any sensitive, intelligent person willing to make the effort. The more technical and foreboding essays need not put off the willing reader, since Percy's message is stated with precision and density in the first two-thirds of the book.

In the first essay, "The Delta Factor," Percy singles out language as the distinctive human trait upon which to build his theory—but not language as it is usually thought of and studied. Of all human activities, Percy believes, the use of language is the least understood and most misrepresented, despite all the volumes written on the subject. To the author, language is neither a static, objective entity to be described (the linguistic theorists) nor a psycho-physiological process to be tested (the behaviorists); it is a distinctively human act and its importance lies in that fact. "So the book is not about language but about the creatures who use it and what happens when they do."

Since Percy's fascination with language as act leads him to a new philosophical vision, he proposes this approach to the reader: "Instead of starting out with such large vexed subjects as soul, mind, ideas, consciousness, why not begin with language, which no one denies, and see how far it takes us toward the rest?" Where it ultimately takes us is to a theory of language which does not actually *explain* the phenomenon, but which suggests that it is an attribute which confirms man's identity as a unique creature in a God-centered universe. To understand the development of this view it is necessary to look at Percy's philosophical and religious underpinnings.

Two unusual facets of Percy's personality—unusual for a contemporary American novelist, at least—have shaped his thinking: he is a believing Catholic and a trained scientist (an M.D.). It greatly oversimplifies Percy's view of language to say that he considers it a divine gift, although that implication is central to the essays. His scientific training has given him, on the one hand, a hard-headed empiricism, but on the other, a solid awareness of the limits of science; he sees inflated claims for science as a central factor in man's present confusion and loss of meaning. As a scientist he wants an objective, empirically valid explanation for the phenomenon of language; as a Christian he expects that theory to confirm the uniqueness of man and his divine connections.

His theory provides such a confirmation by resolving the intellectual paradoxes evident in man's current view of himself and the bizarre contradictions between his beliefs and his actions. In "The Delta Factor" Percy points out the incompatability between the scientific notion of man as "an organism in an environment . . . endowed genetically like other organisms with needs and drives, who through evolution has developed strategies for learning and surviving," and the religious view that he is "somehow endowed with certain other unique properties which he does not share with other organisms—with certain inalienable rights, reason, freedom, and an intrinsic dignity." The result of this the author describes with the popular catch-all phrase "alienation," although he gives the term a very personal definition in the course of his essays. "A theory of man must account for the alienation

of man," he concludes. "A theory of organisms in environments cannot account for it, for in fact organisms in environments are not alienated."

Percy's answer, which he labels the "Delta Factor" in this essay, came to him almost like a religious revelation. He recounts the time when, reading about Helen Keller's first symbolic use of language, he realized suddenly that her experience was a microcosm of the dawning of human intelligence. One morning in 1887, as Miss Sullivan poured water into one of Helen's hands and wrote the word on the other, the girl suddenly made the connection between the two, and began to name everything in her environment.

. . . . Eight-year-old Helen made her breakthrough from the good responding animal which behaviorists study so successfully to the strange name-giving and sentence-uttering creature who begins by naming shoes and ships and sealing wax, and later tells jokes, curses, reads the paper, writes *La sua volontade e nostra pace,* or becomes a Hegel and composes an entire system of philosophy.

This naming process, man's capacity to symbolize, this mysterious ability to make connections, Percy insists cannot be explained behavioristically or linguistically or in any other way: the "Delta Factor" is a unique, spontaneous capacity that accounts both for man's special place in the world and for his feelings of alienation from it.

In "The Loss of the Creature," Percy shows how modern society, particularly through education, has contributed to this alienation by telling the individual what a thing ought to be like and what his proper response to it should be, thus depriving him of the authentic experience ("the thing is lost through its packaging"). Scientific theory then disposes of the object by turning it into a "specimen" rather than an autonomous, particular thing. He describes various literary approaches to alienation in "The Man on the Train," but ultimately suggests that the problem is not aesthetic, scientific, or cultural; it is religious. And in the Christian view of man, the condition of alienation is the essential human situation.

But orthodox religious belief has dissipated, he concedes; its "vocabulary is worn out," he laments in "Notes for a Novel About the End of the World" (written three years prior to *Love in the Ruins*). The vague possibility of a rejuvenation through language is sketched brilliantly in "The Message in the Bottle," the title essay; and in "The Mystery of Language," a deceptively short and mild introduction to the dense, technical discussion of language that makes up the latter part of the book, Percy returns to his central theme.

These last essays, bearing such foreboding titles as "Culture: The Antinomy of the Scientific Method" and "Symbol as Hermeneutic in Existentialism," are actually extended technical footnotes which define and elaborate on the assumptions and analyses of the central essays. Readers with the interest and expertise will find them fascinating and/or irritating. But the substance of Percy's message—with all of its religious connotations—is found in the first essay, "The Delta Factor," and expanded in "The Message in the Bottle." In the last essays Percy is the psychologist-semiologist-existentialist-linguist gadfly challenging the experts; in the earlier essays he brings to bear all of his formidable skills both as a thinker and also as a novelist in order to present a most compelling and provocative discussion of modern man's condition.

Keith Neilson

MF

Author: Anthony Burgess (1917-   )
Publisher: Alfred A. Knopf (New York). 242 pp. $5.95
Type of work: Novel
Time: Between the beginning and the end
Locale: The "isle of Castita"

A novel presenting serious aesthetic and metaphysical questions masquerading as scatalogical events

> Principal characters:
> MILES FABER, a young student in search of riddles to be answered
> CATHERINE, his unattractive sister
> SIB LEGERU, incest incarnate; the deceased poet of our deepest fears

If James Joyce had restricted *Ulysses* to a study of how Stephen Dedalus "proved by algebra that Hamlet's grandson is Shakespeare's grandfather and that he himself is the ghost of his own father," he might have given us a novel as delightful, and as forgettable, as *MF,* Anthony Burgess' latest novel.

This is not to say that *MF* is not an important work of art, for it is. However, its appeal will undoubtedly be so esoteric that any reputation that it might enjoy will be far overshadowed by Burgess's more generally appealing works such as *A Clockwork Orange, Enderby,* and *The Novel Now.* For an author whose stated purpose for writing is primarily the desire for monetary gain, Burgess qualifies with *MF* by the title alone; the pages inside the covers will, however, sorely disappoint the browsing pornophile. Perhaps Burgess has baked a literary cake which he intends to keep and eat at the same time.

The influence of James Joyce on this novel is obvious. Not only is the narrator, *MF,* or Miles Faber, a solver of riddles, but he is also on a quest or "pilgrimage," and the novel as a whole is based on the myths of Greek tragedy, specifically the fate of the house of Atreus. A fourth similarity between *Ulysses* and *MF* is that Burgess utilizes verbal pyrotechnics in an admirable, yet perverse, attempt to free himself from the artificial boundaries of his craft in its present state of evolution.

Miles Faber is involved in a quest that evolves into something greater than originally bargained for. As a young, brilliant, and rebellious student, he is compelled, against the will of his deceased father, to go to the isle of Castita to study the forgotten works of Sib Legeru ("legging or ligging or lying with one's own sib, it means incest.") His quest is hindered by agents of Faber's dead father who are instructed to get Miles's sister, Catherine, off the island in order to prevent any incestuous relationship, a taboo which has been previously broken by the father with his own sister. Inevitably, incidents begin to occur which ultimately result in the marriage of Miles to Catherine.

An example of Burgess' verbal techniques as well as Faber's masterful penchant for solving intellectual riddles is displayed early in *MF:*

> —A difficult clue. Listen.
> He read out, or seemed to:
> —Up, I am a rolling river;
> Down, a scent-and-color-giver.
> The answer was obvious: flower. But

the throb told me not to give Loewe the answer. Why not? I'd been quick enough with that answer to Keteki. Then I knew why not. Loewe was being, for some reason, deceitful. The *up* and *down* of his clue referred to the respective tongue-positions that started the dipthongs of *flow* and *flower*. No crossword, except in a linguistics journal, would have so learned a clue, and linguistics journals did not go in for crosswords. Loewe smiled saccholacti-cally.

Obviously the charge could be made that *MF* not only fails to mirror the everyday experience, but also fails to do justice to the emotions which are eternally involved in our common lot. True. *MF* only pretends to do so, but the masquerade is not wholly illegiti-mate. Once the real flesh behind the mask is discovered, *MF* is revealed as a novel equal in visceral exposure and painful examination of vital conditions to any subject explored by the contem-porary artist; in this instance, the con-cern is with the artist's very reason for being.

It is in the last twenty pages of the novel that Burgess begins to unravel the true riddle of *MF*. "A man with a clubfoot had once answered the unan-swerable and moved on to sleep with his mother. Riddles are there for a good purpose—not to be answered." How-ever, Faber is promised that all will end well, and it is at this point that one be-gins to understand that Faber is not only all of us but Burgess in particular. "You are good at word games. You should also be good at palindromes," which is perhaps an explanation for the novel's being structured as a mem-oir.

I did not understand for a moment

what he said. I was thinking that his glee was the inhuman one of some fic-tional intellectual higher policeman who sees suffering as the expulsable pipesmoke that fills a room devoted to the pleasures of jigsaws or battleplans. The whole of history has been taken up with pretense after pretense that the void between the two voids can be filled with something other than play. Yet if nature does all the serious work, what is there left for man?

The answer to this question of man's meaningless role in the world of nature is conventional, yet is given a unique twist by Burgess which creates the core of his novel:

Those works of Sib Legeru exhibit the nastiest aspects of incest—and I use the term in its widest sense to signify the breakdown of order, the collapse of communication, the irresponsible cul-tivation of chaos. . . . It is man's job to impose manifest order on the uni-verse, not to yearn for Chapter Zero of the Book of Genesis.

The first step in the solution of this paradox is our condemnation of "incest because it's the negation of social com-munication. It's like writing a book in which every sentence is a tautology." The second crucial piece to be fitted into the jigsaw of *MF* is the name Miles Faber. Miles—thousands of paces; Faber—the maker. Man makes thousands of paces between the genetic and apocalyptic voids ("Tomorrow, and tomorrow, and tomorrow, creeps in this petty pace from day to day, to the last syllable of recorded time";). Burgess fully acknowledges the total futility of his craft, as well as the ultimate tragic result (e.g. Oedipus') of trying to solve this riddle of man's place or meaning in the natural scheme of things.

Through Faber, Burgess underlines *MF*'s cynical historical view with an objective statement on the purposes of the artist: "Art takes the raw material of the world about us and attempts to shape it into signification. Antiart takes the same material and seeks insignification." Burgess has realized that the novelist's craft is verbal incest and the greater his attempt to break free from its demands for clarity, order, and general communication, the greater the degree of his incestuous relationship with words as words, and not as universal symbols.

Miles Faber has understood the total absurdity of his incestuous quest from the beginning. "Words and colors totally free because totally meaningless. That's what I expect to find in the works of Sib Legeru." These words of young Faber resolve themselves into a concentrated epigram which contains the entire equation of incest, communication, chaos, and curse: "Such as that mania for total liberty is really a mania for prison, and you'll get there by way of incest."

Burgess, as the true "father" of Miles Faber, "chose a freedom that not many would choose. Or should I say he was compelled into that freedom, turning it into a bondage. He committed incest." A large graffito noticed by Faber early in the novel, "SCREW MAILER," completes the meaningless compulsion of man, the maker. Norman Mailer has repeatedly advertised the act of writing as battling a Bitch whom he is desperately trying to overcome; his art has a sexual basis. He, like Burgess, is energetically involved in an incestuous relationship with his own creations. As the struggle or ardor of the battle increases, the greater the freedom sought, the more incestuous the relationship.

The incomprehensibility of *Finnegans Wake* would thus be a result of Joyce's incestuous or philological fantasies. *MF*, as a title, is a beautiful pun that belies, of course, the fact that Burgess is actually giving us a dramatized key to such works as Joyce's *Finnegans Wake*, Rimbaud's *A Season in Hell*, or Pound's *Cantos*, rather than "a sort of morality cartoon you could stick a shocking label on."

J. J. Johnson

MIDCENTURY

Author: John Dos Passos (1896-1970)
Publisher: Houghton Mifflin Company (Boston). 496 pp. $5.95
Type of work: Novel
Time: c. 1900-1960
Locale: The United States

A historical and fictional survey of the sociopolitical scene in the United States since World War II

Principal characters:
> TERRY BRYANT, an officer in the local union at a Raritan rubber company plant
> BLACKIE BOWMAN, an old-time philosophical anarchist
> FRANK WORTHINGTON, President of the National Union
> JASPER MILLIRON, Vice-President in charge of the Eastern Division of Abington Mills
> WILL JENKS, Jasper's son-in-law, owner of a taxicab company

Principal personages:
> GENERAL DOUGLAS MACARTHUR
> SAM GOLDWYN
> HARRY BRIDGES
> ELEANOR ROOSEVELT
> SENATOR JOHN MCCLELLAN
> ROBERT R. YOUNG
> ROBERT OPPENHEIMER
> BOB LA FOLLETTE, JR.
> GENERAL WILLIAM F. DEAN
> JAMES DEAN

Midcentury adds another chapter to Dos Passos' compendious history of twentieth century America, begun over thirty years ago. To *The 42nd Parallel* (1930) Dos Passos added *Nineteen-Nineteen* and *The Big Money* to make up the triology *U.S.A.* (1936), a vast chronicle covering the first three decades of the century. Another triology, *District of Columbia* (1952) brought the story up to the closing years of the Roosevelt administration, and *Midcentury* brings it up to date by surveying the uneasy years between the end of World War II and the present.

In conception and technique *Midcentury* is very much like *The 42nd Parallel*. Once more Dos Passos uses the devices which made him famous in the thirties—the Profiles, vivid biographical sketches of actual people who played some significant role in the nation's history or who epitomize its moods and values; the Newsreels, a montage of newspaper headlines, slogans from advertising, paragraphs from popular magazines, snatches of popular songs, and the like; and the Camera Eye, brief lyrical interludes expressing the author's subjective reactions to the passing parade. Against this brilliantly impressionistic background of contemporary history, Dos Passos sets his loosely related fictional narratives, each of which dramatizes the impact on representative people of some particular aspect of American society. In his sweeping view of the scene in *Midcentury*, the author demonstrates once again his passionate conviction, not essentially changed since *U.S.A.,* that America is an epic failure.

Society, Dos Passos' thesis runs, is on the verge of total moral dissolution. Unprincipled vested interests, wielding vast social and economic powers, create an atmosphere of terror and hatred. Gangster-infested labor unions enslave and exploit millions; big business freezes individual initiative and promotes the morality of the herd; big government plays the sinister game of power politics; and the opinion makers and publicists addle the critical judgment and pervert the tastes of the public at large. Honest men are doomed to humiliation and defeat; and though the hatred of the people for the "tin-pot pharaohs" who hold the power in our massive social organizations will eventually defeat them, it will also corrupt the haters themselves. "The hate remains," Dos Passos writes in the dirge which closes the book, "to strangle the still small private voice that is God's spark in man. Man drowns in his own scum."

The nation's leaders and heroes of the past fifteen years, the author shows in the biographical profiles, are power seekers, misguided do-gooders, servants of sinister interests. General MacArthur, sealed off from the world by the "hymenopterous punctilio of military stratification" wields enormous powers "without knowing whether it's raining or sunshine until he's briefed by his staff." Harry Bridges, much admired in the "proletariat's Promised Land where every man owns everything except his own life," rules thousands of American lives. The penniless immigrant Samuel Goldwyn for whom the promise of America, Old Style, was

most wonderfully fulfilled is honored for hundreds of movies celebrating the tender sentimentalities of the Horatio Alger dream. Senator McClellan, the would-be scourge of union gangsters, is frustrated by lobbies and timid politicians, and can only advise honest workers to stand up courageously to the wrath of organized crime. Mrs. Roosevelt is the ineffectual liberal do-gooder devoted earnestly but injudiciously to worthy causes. Walter Reuther is the freedom fighter turned strong man, and Young Bob La Follette, a rare voice crying in the moral wilderness, falls into the despair of hopeless defeat and ends his life as a suicide.

In this gloomy context Dos Passos sets his fictional exampla. "The Beginning of Home" is the story of Terry Bryant, ex-sergeant in the marines who comes home from the beaches of the South Pacific on the verge of nervous collapse. Restored to health by a therapeutic love affair, he marries and takes up his old job in a rubber plant. But his wages are inadequate to support his family and he leads a movement to establish a local union. The company, recognizing the inevitability of a union shop, offers no opposition.

As an officer in the local Terry is responsible for enforcing newly adopted safety policies, but when he tries to do so he learns that his union superiors are actually company agents working against union interests. When he refuses to coöperate, he is fired from his job and dismissed from the union. He writes a report of the situation and addresses it personally to the national president, Frank Worthington, whose efforts to run an honest union are frustrated by his political-minded colleagues in the head office. Frank orders an investigation, but no real action is taken. Terry is still jobless months later. An attempt to bring the case before a government arbitration official is smothered in a flurry of devious legalities.

Barred from his vocation, he moves west to Duquesne and takes a job as a driver for the Swiftcab Company. Swiftcab is nearly bankrupt because a rival, the Redtop Company, owned by local politicians seeking a transportation monopoly in the city, has employed gangsters to intimidate Swiftcab drivers and sabotage their cars. A young businessman from the East buys the floundering company and through courage and persistence wins, with Terry's assistance, his fight against the gangsters. But on the eve of victory Terry is ambushed by thugs and beaten to death when he resists their attempts to burn his cab.

The hero of "Blackie Bowman Speaking" is an old-time wobblie who tells the story of his life from his death bed in a hospital. Blackie ran away to sea in his early teens, jumped ship in New Orleans, and took to the open road he was to follow for more than forty years. He met in a boxcar in Louisiana a hobo named Earl Gates, a radical socialist steeped in Marx and Henry George. Educated by Earl, Blackie chased the rainbow of the worker's revolution through the skid rows, hobo jungles, and bohemias all over America.

But Blackie never really believed in systems and organizations. He believed in the freedom and camaraderie of the open road and vaguely in the brotherhood of man; his forty-year sojourn among revolutionaries, bohemians, and radical idealists taught him only that the Promised Land of the Proletariat is a mirage which systems and dogmas can never realize. "It's mass organization," he reflects, "that turns man into a louse. We wobblies used to think every man ought to think his own right word up for himself." But, he reflects once, "There's no place left in this world for a philosophical anarchist. If I weren't in this here hospital I'd be a hermit in a shack in the mountains. And I never did learn to cook, lazy as a hound about housework." The thought sums up Blackie Bowman: he is the last of the incorrigible dreamers, those incorruptible but futile visionaries whose shiftless irresponsibility makes them insufficient even to their own needs.

"The Big Office" traces the career of Frank Worthington, the Indiana farm boy whose administrative genius and unflagging dedication to the cause of the working man carry him to the top in the National Labor Union. Frank's principle is the Golden Rule. He does not believe in political favors, payoffs, or patronage; and though his honesty is often a source of embarrassment to other high officials in the union, they find his popularity with the rank and file and his organizational talents indispensable. Grant Graham is the union stage manager who fixes things with the "boys" on the sly. When Frank receives Terry's letter about his troubles with thugs in the rubber factory local, the notorious Slansky brothers, Graham reminds Frank that the Slanskys control a sizable block of union votes. Frank demands an investigation anyway. "And don't forget to report to me on it," he orders as Graham walks out with Terry's report. A minute later he is deeply absorbed in a mountainous pile of paper work, frowning over the wearying complexities of his tangled bureaucracy. No action is taken on Terry's complaint.

"Prime Mover" deals with another kind of bureaucracy. Jasper Milliron is Executive Vice-President of the Eastern Division of Abington Mills, protégé of ailing old Mr. Allardyce, founder of the corporation. Just before he dies Mr. Allardyce appoints Jasper to head Easttern and sets in motion the machinery for a multi-million-dollar plant modernization. But the timid, reactionary board is bitterly opposed to these decisions, partly because the members are jealous of Jasper's promotion and partly because they resent Allardyce's progressive business policies. As soon as Jasper leaves town, they cancel the modernization project. Jasper rescinds the order and assumes personal responsibility for the construction, depending upon the financier Alphonse Lewin to buy up the holding company controlling Abington Mills and restore the plans old Allardyce had made for the company's future.

But Jasper, meanwhile, has been carrying on an affair with Suzy Standish, who with phenomenal success represents Abington products on television to millions of housewives. When Lewin learns that the board spitefully plans to expose the affair in order to discredit Jasper, he withdraws his support, fearing that the move may severely damage the popularity of Abington products. Defeated, Jasper resigns, obtains a divorce from his unsympathetic wife, and marries Suzy. Months later we learn from his cynical teen-age nephew that Jasper has become a heavy drinker and has earned the boy's contempt for being an "immature old clod" who "stuck his neck out and got all messed up trying to tangle with one of the biggest milling concerns in the country over some kind of screwy new machinery."

Jasper's son-in-law is Will Jenks, the young ex-marine captain who buys the Swiftcab Company in Duquesne and successfully fights off the politicians and gangsters in "The Great Taxicab War." Visiting back East, the victorious Will meets Lewin at a dinner party at Jasper's home and learns that he controls the rival Redtop Company. Will is outraged by Lewin's philosophy of life: "My science," the tycoon explains, "is that special little section of arithmetic known as finance. . . . When I assume control of a corporation through the use of my own private skills, I have to consider it a problem in pure finance. I can't be bothered with what it makes or what it sells. I can't be distracted by worrying about administration, who gets fired from what job, all the grubby little lives involved. . . ." But Will, warned beforehand "to be careful," makes no comment. Later Lewin suggests a merger of the hard-won Swiftcab with Redtop, pointing out that the national administration of his company could use "youthful energies" like Will's. Alone in their own room after the party, Will tries to explain his sense of the moral dilemma to his wife, Maddie: "It's hard to know how to do right." To which Maddie yawns, "Let's sleep on it."

Most readers will probably feel that this caustic indictment of American society suffers the same weaknesses Edmund Wilson pointed out in a discussion of Dos Passos' novels and plays as long ago as 1929. At bottom, Dos Passos is a melodramatist whose keen observation and genuine insights are vitiated by sentimentality and hysteria. In his novels there are basically two kinds of people, those on the right side of the social question and those on the wrong, and both are defeated, the good men by the evil violence of the bad and the bad men by their own lusts and moral perversions. The same strictures are applicable to *Midcentury*. The author's outrage and sense of futility seem more bitter and intense than ever before, and

despite eloquent, keen-sighted, and relentlessly defiant writing, the reader feels a basic imbalance of judgment in it. One wonders how, if these nights are as dark as *Midcentury* shows them to be, the author found enough light to write it by.

Sources for Further Study

Criticism:

Brantley, J. D. *The Fiction of John Dos Passos*. The Hague: Mouton, 1968, pp. 122-126. Brantley tries to establish the position of this novel among the later works of the author, and to compare this group with his earlier, more powerful novels.

Davis, Robert G. *John Dos Passos*. Minneapolis: University of Minneapolis Press, 1962, pp. 39-44. Davis deals with the themes and philosophy implicit in *Midcentury* and relates them to other novels in the Dos Passos canon.

Dos Passos, John. *Talks with Authors*. Edited by C. F. Madden. Carbondale and Edwardsville: Southern Illinois University Press, 1968, pp. 3-11. In his own words, Dos Passos tries to explain his point of view in *Midcentury*.

Reviews:

New York Times Book Review. February 26, 1961, p. 1. 1,550 words.

Saturday Review. XLIV, February 25, 1961, p. 25. 1,200 words.

Time. LXXVII, March 3, 1961, p. 94. 950 words.